Praise for *Software Test Engineering with IBM Rational Functional Tester*

"Finally, a manual for the Software Test Engineer! Many manuals on the market today are geared toward developers, and none exist for Rational Functional Tester. This is one of the first manuals geared toward the Automated Test Engineer acknowledging the depth of knowledge required for a very complex job. The manual will assist all levels of test engineering with very specific steps and hands-on advice. This manual is a reference book that no Automated Test Engineer using RFT should be without!"

—**Penny Bowser**, CTFL, CHE, QA Manager

"The authors succeed in walking a line between sharing a wealth of technical knowledge and providing enough context to ensure the readers understand what they need to do and why. Novices and skilled practitioners alike should find the work a good read and a solid reference. Automating functional testing tends to receive less investment than it should, to the detriment of organizations everywhere. If the reader is seeking to improve his knowledge of Rational Functional Tester and make an impact using that knowledge, there is no better reference than this excellent distillation of years of field-proven experience."

—**David J. Trent**, Market Manager of Process and Best Practices Segment for Rational Software, IBM

"As a former manager of the group that tested IBM's Rational Functional Tester, like a few others, I see clearly how this book can help teams multiply the benefits they derive from this product."

—**Ted Rivera**, Senior Agile Transformation Architect, IBM Software Group

"This book is a wonderful, in-depth resource for novice and expert users alike."

—**Brian McCall**, former IBM IT Specialist

"This collection of Rational Functional Tester information is a 'must have' for anyone using this solution. Everyone from beginners to advanced users will find this book very helpful."

—**Lew Cote**, IBM Technical Solution Architect

"This much needed book describes effectively the value of Rational Functional Tester for functional testing needs. The book is well organized, thought through, and has all the latest information. The authors are no doubt subject matter experts."

—**Kamala Parvathanathan**, Senior Manager, IBM Rational

D1568425

Related Books of Interest

Outside-in Software Development

Kessler, Sweitzer

ISBN: 0-13-157551-1

Implementing the IBM Rational Unified Process and Solutions

Barnes

ISBN: 0-321-36945-9

Requirements Management Using IBM Rational RequisitePro

Zielczynski

ISBN: 0-321-38300-1

IBM Rational Unified Process Reference and Certification Guide

Shuja, Krebs

ISBN: 0-13-156292-4

IBM Rational ClearCase, Ant, and CruiseControl

Lee

ISBN: 0-321-35699-3

Implementing IBM Rational ClearQuest

Buckley, Pulsipher, Scott

ISBN: 0-321-33486-8

Visual Modeling with IBM Rational Software Architect and UML

Quatrani, Palistrant

ISBN: 0-321-23808-7

Project Management with the IBM Rational Unified Process

Gibbs

ISBN: 0-321-33639-9

Software Configuration Management Strategies and IBM Rational ClearCase

Bellagio, Milligan

ISBN: 0-321-20019-5

Developing Quality Technical Information

Hargis, Carey, Hernandez, Hughes, Longo, Rouiller, Wilde

ISBN: 0-13-147749-8

Service-Oriented Architecture (SOA) Compass

Bieberstein, Bose, Fiammante, Jones, Shah

ISBN: 0-13-187002-5

Software Test Engineering with IBM Rational Functional Tester

The Definitive Resource

Chip Davis, Daniel Chirillo, Daniel Gouveia, Fariz Saracevic,

Jeffrey R. Bocarsly, Larry Quesada, Lee B. Thomas, and Marc van Lint

IBM Press
Pearson plc
Upper Saddle River, NJ • Boston • Indianapolis • San Francisco
New York • Toronto • Montreal • London • Munich • Paris • Madrid
Cape Town • Sydney • Tokyo • Singapore • Mexico City

Ibmpressbooks.com

The authors and publisher have taken care in the preparation of this book, but make no expressed or implied warranty of any kind and assume no responsibility for errors or omissions. No liability is assumed for incidental or consequential damages in connection with or arising out of the use of the information or programs contained herein.

IBM Press Program Managers: Steven M. Stansel, Ellice Uffer
Cover design: IBM Corporation

Associate Publisher: Greg Wiegand
Marketing Manager: Kourtnaye Sturgeon
Publicist: Heather Fox
Acquisitions Editor: Chris Guzikowski
Development Editor: Sheri Cain
Managing Editor: Kristy Hart
Designer: Alan Clements
Project Editor: Anne Goebel
Copy Editor: Deadline Driven Publishing
Indexer: Brad Herriman
Compositor: Jake McFarland
Proofreader: Leslie Joseph
Manufacturing Buyer: Dan Uhrig

Published by Pearson plc
Publishing as IBM Press

IBM Press offers excellent discounts on this book when ordered in quantity for bulk purchases or special sales, which may include electronic versions and/or custom covers and content particular to your business, training goals, marketing focus, and branding interests. For more information, please contact:

U.S. Corporate and Government Sales
1-800-382-3419
corpsales@pearsontechgroup.com

For sales outside the U.S., please contact:

International Sales
international@pearsoned.com

Library of Congress Cataloging-in-Publication Data
Software test engineering with IBM Rational functional tester : the definitive resource / Chip Davis ... [et al.].
  p. cm.
 Includes index.
 ISBN 978-0-13-700066-1 (pbk. : alk. paper) 1. IBM Rational functional tester. 2. Computer software—Testing. 3. Object-oriented methods (Computer science) 4. Software engineering. I. Davis, Chip, 1969-
 QA76.76.T48S635 2009
 005.1—dc22

                                2009030295

ISBN-13: 978-0-13-700066-1
ISBN-10: 0-13-700066-9

Text printed in the United States on recycled paper at R.R. Donnelley in Crawfordsville, Indiana.
First printing October 2009

I dedicate this book to my kids Liam and Katie who were very patient the whole time their Dad was busy writing on his laptop.
—Chip Davis

To Sinisá and Stefanie
—Daniel Chirillo

This book is dedicated to my beautiful wife Megan and wonderful children Julia and Lily who spent many tireless hours having fun without me.
—Daniel Gouveia

To my wife Nermina and our two precious ones, Alen and Omar
—Fariz Saracevic

To Danya, Mati, Rafi, and Shai
—Jeffrey R. Bocarsley

To Hang, Justin, and Jason
—Larry Quesada

To my wife Vicki and my children Brandon, Brittany, and Brenna—may God bless you still more
—Lee Thomas

I dedicate this book to Mirjam, Ruben, Menno, and Inge. Thanks for your support to accomplish this.
—Marc van Lint

Contents

Foreword

The American novelist and historian Edward Eggleston once wrote that "persistent people begin their success where others end in failure." The tremendous accomplishment of writing this book is a perfect reflection of Eggleston's perspective.

As a long-time practitioner in the automated tools landscape, it is my opinion that the competency and technical capabilities of the authors and the information they provide are *undisputed* in many ways. Having had the privilege of working closely with these individuals (and even on occasion serving as a mentor), I am wholly impressed with the talent they have demonstrated.

Perhaps more impressive, however, is their successful collaborative efforts over the course of many long months, notwithstanding the fact that each was heavily engaged with time-consuming corporate- or customer-facing projects. Having followed the group in their journey from a distance, there were times when the idea of publication seemed a distant goal. In addition to being a technical contributor, it must be said that Daniel Gouveia's undying determination serviced the project in many exceptional ways; for that, we are most grateful.

This book serves as a unique and useful tool for quality practitioners of all levels who wish to learn, reference, build upon, and implement technical best-in-class automation techniques for functional tests. The real power of this book is the fact that much of the content originates from the needs of real users and real customer situations, where introductory and advanced concepts are defined, constructed, and implemented.

The advancements in automated testing have dramatically changed the landscape in terms of traditional tester roles of the past. Rational Functional Tester has updated, matured, and changed in ways that now attract a wide range of technical and nontechnical testers. In particular, this change presents tremendous opportunity for users who are in traditional business roles to now diversify and pursue the more challenging aspects of test automation. We welcome and embrace this technical and cultural shift in the hopes that other technical disciplines will eventually follow suit.

To the authors, I salute your persistence and determination and congratulate you in a job well done on a book well worth reading.

With much gratitude,
    Patrick L. Mancini,
    IBM WW Quality Management Practice Lead

Preface

Rational Functional Tester (RFT) is a tool for automated testing of software applications. It mimics the actions and assessments of a human tester. To understand the value of Rational Functional Tester, it is best to know some of the history of software testing.

Brief History of Software Testing

In the earliest days of computing, programs and their results were rigorously tested by hand. Computing resources were so expensive and scarce that there was no margin for error on the part of a programmer. Confirming that a program was correct required a great deal of manual effort.

As computing power became more readily available, the number of programs written and the complexity of programs increased rapidly. The result was that manual testing could no longer keep pace.

Furthermore, testing an application once is an interesting exercise, but testing that same application repeatedly through multiple bug fix cycles is boring and error-prone. Plus, the time to test applications in the early waterfall-style development lifecycle was limited (and was often cut further when the development phase could not deliver on time), adding pressure on the tester, which increased errors.

The only way to avoid these problems was to automate the testing effort. However, most user interfaces were not created with an automation-friendly interface as a requirement. The earliest UI automation testing tools were able to perform an action only at a coordinate-based location, and derive text for verification from a coordinate-based rectangle, leading to highly fragile automation code. This meant that applications could be tested automatically, but only if the application's UI did not change significantly. Unfortunately, application maintenance frequently required *both* business logic changes *and* UI changes. This meant recreating many if not all tests every time the application's UI changed.

With the rise of object-oriented programming, user interfaces began to be constructed from libraries of UI objects. These objects could accept actions in the form of method invocations, and they could return properties including text, font, color, and so on. Automated testing tools followed the development technologies, and were refashioned to operate on an object-recognition basis instead of a screen-coordinate basis. Tool assets (known in Rational Functional Tester as test scripts because they are similar to scripts given to actors in a stage play) could be reused from one build to the next, even when objects were moved within the UI.

However, several problems still remained. A developer might change an object so that the testing tool could no longer recognize it (for example, by changing the value of one of the object's critical properties), causing the script to fail. Or, a programmer might move an object to a different part of the UI hierarchy, where the testing tool might be unable to find it. Many applications were developed using custom objects (such as those for Enterprise Resource Planning [ERP] applications), and not those provided to developers by the operating system. In addition, more complex verification of text was required, particularly in the case where an application displayed data retrieved from or generated by a server. Also, assets such as test scripts were increasingly recognized as programs (in spite of recording capabilities and wizards that reduced the need to create or modify assets by programming), and were worthy of sophisticated editing tools available to developers. Increasingly, developers involved in test automation insisted that coding a test be as straightforward and simple as coding any other asset. Finally, testers began to develop and share open source code, which required the testing tool and its programming language be compatible with sharing.

IBM Rational Functional Tester

Rational Functional Tester was developed specifically to address these latest concerns of testers and developers. Rational Functional Tester is available in two flavors: one built on the popular open source Eclipse framework and the other built on the Microsoft Visual Studio framework, putting testers and developers in the same Integrated Development Environment. Rational Functional Tester uses either the Java programming language or VB.NET, providing access to a large body of code made available on the Internet, giving testers a choice of industry-standard languages, and allowing developers to code in a language that is already familiar to them.

Rational Functional Tester uses advanced, patented technology to find objects, and it provides controls to the tester to permit flexible recognition and control over what happens when an object is not found or only partially recognized. Rational Functional Tester includes advanced object recognition and advanced verification features based on a pattern-matching mechanism.

The combination of modern Integrated Development Environments (IDEs) and programming languages means that Rational Functional Tester is easily extended to support automation of not only ERP environments, but other environments, too. In many cases, these extensions can be performed by the tester directly.

With all of these capabilities, Rational Functional Tester makes test automation an activity that delivers significant return on its investment. Large regression test suites can be created with the assurance that they will provide high value via limited maintenance, common tooling, low barrier to adoption, and adaptability for the future.

Total Quality Solution

By itself, Rational Functional Tester is a powerful tool. It enables test teams to automate large portions of their test suites, enabling them to expedite their test cycles and expand on the amount of testing that is done. However, it is just one arrow in a team's quiver. It lacks the capability to pull metrics beyond what passed and failed. Plugging it into a quality management and defect tracking solution enables them to take advantage of the benefits of automation while capturing valuable test metrics (density, trending, and so on), tracing test results back to requirements, and so on.

IBM Rational Quality Manager is a total quality management solution built on the Jazz platform. It is completely web-based, providing rich reports, dashboards, and useful web 2.0 capabilities (such as RSS feeds). Rational Quality Manager (RQM) allows teams to create robust test plans, tracing their test cases back to requirements. Rational Functional Tester is one of the tools that can be used to automate test cases in RQM. The end result is a complete testing solution that provides end-to-end traceability—requirements to test cases to any defects that might be uncovered—using Rational Functional Tester's rich automation for unattended testing on a selected subset of test cases.

Introductions to Eclipse and to Visual Studio

If you are new to the Rational Functional Tester flavor that you are about to start using, you might benefit from a general introduction to your Rational Functional Tester IDE. Because Eclipse and Visual Studio are so prominent in the computing world, there is a wealth of resources of all different types at all different levels. The following list includes a few introductory-level articles and books, but this list is far from comprehensive. The following suggestions are just to get you started; you are encouraged to pursue the vast range of information that is available.

Eclipse

What is Eclipse, and how do I use it?
www.ibm.com/developerworks/opensource/library/os-eclipse.html

Getting started with the Eclipse Platform.
www.ibm.com/developerworks/opensource/library/os-ecov/?Open&ca=daw-ec-dr

An introduction to Eclipse for Visual Studio users.
www.ibm.com/developerworks/opensource/library/os-eclipse-visualstudio/
?ca=dgr-lnxw01Eclipse-VS

Eclipse: Step by Step. Joe Pluta. Lewisville, TX: MC Press Online (2003).

Eclipse IDE Pocket Guide. Ed Burnette. Sebastopol, CA: O'Reilly (2005).

Visual Studio .NET

Introduction to Visual Studio .NET.
http://msdn.microsoft.com/en-us/library/ms973867.aspx

Quick Tour of the Integrated Development Environment.
http://msdn.microsoft.com/en-us/library/ms165088(VS.80).aspx

Visual Basic 2005 in a Nutshell, **Third Edition.** Tim Patrick, Steven Roman, Ron Petrusha, Paul Lomax. Sebastopol, CA: O'Reilly (2006).

Beginning VB 2008: From Novice to Professional. Christian Gross. Berkeley, CA: Apress (2008).

How to Use This Book

This book is a reference for both novice and advanced users. The initial chapters focus on the basics of using Rational Functional Tester, whereas the latter chapters become more advanced. Ideally, you will find that as your automation abilities mature, you will get more value from the specialized content found deeper in the book.

Although you might find value in reading this book cover to cover, it was conceived for use on a topic-by-topic basis. Many chapters are standalone; however, some are related and build on each other. In addition, the initial chapters were crafted specifically for the novice Rational Functional Tester user, whereas the latter chapters were written with the experienced user or power user in mind. The following chapter list "calls out" these relationships.

Chapter 1, Overview of Rational Functional Tester—An introductory chapter for the novice user that gives a broad overview of Rational Functional Tester and its basic features.

Chapter 2, Storyboard Testing—A description of the RFT Simple Scripting Visual Editor, introduced in RFT 8.1, to open up RFT scripting to the nontechnical user and to the novice user.

Chapter 3, General Script Enhancements—This chapter provides a grab-bag of highly useful techniques ranging from basic data capture to script synchronization, to an introduction to `TestObjects`. It is for the intermediate level user.

Chapter 4, XML and Rational Functional Tester—A tour of basic XML programming in Rational Functional Tester to familiarize the reader with the XML libraries in Rational Functional Tester for testing with XML and for dealing with Rational Functional Tester's own XML infrastructure. It is for the intermediate or advanced user.

Chapter 5, Managing Script Data—An in-depth chapter discussing Rational Functional Tester Datapools, database access from Rational Functional Tester, and the use of properties files, XML files, and flat files with Rational Functional Tester. It is for the intermediate level user or the advanced level user.

Chapter 6, Debugging Scripts—Eclipse and Visual Studio have powerful, integrated debuggers. As you build your scripts, the IDE debuggers can provide valuable information for pinpointing the root cause of script problems. This chapter surveys the debugging tools most useful for RFT script development. It is for the intermediate level user or the advanced level user.

Chapter 7, Managing Script Execution—This chapter covers the different aspects of controlling the execution flow in scripts. Topics include manipulating playback settings, using conditional and looping logic to optimize script flow, handling errors that scripts encounter, regression scripts, and executing outside of the Rational Functional Tester environment. It is for the intermediate level user.

Chapter 8, Handling Unsupported Domain Objects—A discussion of the Rational Functional Tester API for dealing with domains that are not supported by Rational Functional Tester. It is for the advanced user.

Chapter 9, Advanced Rational Functional Tester Object Map Topics—A detailed examination of the Rational Functional Tester Object Map features and underpinnings for the advanced user. This chapter pairs with Chapter 10 to supply the background for how `TestObjects` are handled by Rational Functional Tester.

Chapter 10, Advanced Scripting with Rational Functional Tester TestObjects—A discussion of `TestObjects`, how they are used by the Object Map, how they can be used without the Object Map, and how they can be used to manipulate unsupported controls. It is for the advanced user.

Chapter 11, Testing Specialized Applications—An examination of specialized environments, where Rational Functional Tester requires special setup or produces scripts with notable characteristics. It covers scripting for terminal-based (mainframe) applications, SAP, Siebel, and Adobe Flex. It is for the intermediate or advanced user.

Chapter 12, Extend Rational Functional Tester with External Libraries—This chapter shows how to call a range of external libraries from Rational Functional Tester, including log4j and log4net (to create custom logging solutions), JAWIN and Microsoft Interop libraries (to create an Excel reporting utility), and PDFBox and IKVM.Net (to test PDF files). It is for the advanced user.

Chapter 13, Building Support for New Objects with the Proxy SDK—A step-by-step discussion of how to develop Rational Functional Tester support for third-party Java or .NET controls with the Rational Functional Tester Proxy SDK. Chapter 10 provides useful background. It is for the advanced user.

Chapter 14, Developing Scripts in the VB.NET Environment—Rational Functional Tester historically is a creature of Eclipse and Java. More recently, it has entered the world of Visual Studio and VB.NET. This chapter offers tips and tricks for using Rational Functional Tester in the Visual Studio environment. It is for the intermediate to advanced user.

Chapter 15, Using Rational Functional Tester in a Linux Environment—This chapter describes the major similarities and differences between a Rational Functional Tester

Linux environment and the Rational Functional Tester Windows environment. A basic installation procedure is discussed in addition to the creation of a basic script. It is for the novice user.

Chapter 16, Internationalized Testing with Rational Functional Tester—A discussion of how to set up internationalized testing in the Rational Functional Tester framework. Rational Functional Tester has all the core functionality to handle testing of internationalized applications; this chapter shows one way to use basic Rational Functional Tester features to create an internationalized testing framework. Chapters 9 and 10 offer the background for this discussion. It is for the advanced user.

Appendix A, Advanced Logging Techniques—A tour of using advanced logging packages and methods in Rational Functional Tester scripting, including emailing results, XSL transformation of the RFT XML log, and custom logging. It is for the advanced user.

Appendix B, Regular Expressions in Rational Functional Tester—A detailed discussion of the use of regular expressions in Rational Functional Tester scripting. It is for the advanced user.

Finally, as an additional aide, all code listings for the book are available via download as Rational Functional Tester project exports. Readers can access these code samples at http://www.ibm.com/developerworks/rational/library/09/testengineeringrft/index.html.

Acknowledgments

We collectively want to thank the organizations and individuals whose support made this project come to fruition. First, we'd like to thank our publishers IBM Press and Pearson Education's Addison-Wesley for considering this project. We especially want to thank Raina Chrobak and Sheri Cain at Addison-Wesley for moving us along the path to a publishable manuscript. We'd also like to acknowledge the efforts of our reviewers Penny Bowser, Brian McCall, David Trent, and Kamala Parvathanathan; their thoughtful suggestions improved our text significantly. Their time investments reading and evaluating the manuscript are deeply appreciated. Finally, we'd like to thank our employers for supporting this effort by providing hardware, software, meeting time, and flexibility to make this project work for multiple busy schedules.

Daniel Gouveia: First, I want to point out that this was a team effort, and therefore, I would like to thank the fine authors who participated in this endeavor (Chip, Dan, Fariz, Jeff, Larry, Lee, and Marc). Secondly, I would like to thank Nitin Sharma. I truly appreciate your SDK lessons and kind offer to review my chapter from a developer's point-of-view. I would also like to thank the fearless leaders of the Quality Management Community of Practice, Lew and Pat. This idea wouldn't have gotten off the ground without you. Lastly, I would like to thank the many others who participated in this book whether as a reviewer, someone to bounce ideas off of, or as a friendly person who listened and advised.

Fariz Saracevic: I want to thank Christina Carlson, the test automation lead at IBM Software Group, Strategy, for helping with validating sample codes.

Jeffrey R. Bocarsly: I'd like to thank the coauthors for pitching in and pulling this project together while maintaining their full-time jobs and full-time lives. I'd especially like to acknowledge

Dan Gouveia's role as unofficial ring leader of our authoring team; the success of our group collaboration is due to his efforts in no small measure. Finally, I'd like to thank all the fine people at RTTS with whom I've worked, especially our leaders Bill Hayduk and Ron Axelrod, who have, over many years, had the foresight to build and nurture a strong relationship with IBM Rational and a strong practice in software quality with the IBM Rational product line.

Lee Thomas: In no particular order, I'd like to thank Al Wagner, Alex Linkov, Barry Graham, Bill Tobin, Bob Kennedy, Brian Bryson, Brian Massey, Chip Davis, Dan Gouveia, Davyd Norris, Dennis Elenburg, Dennis Moya, Dennis Schultz, Don Nguyen, Fariz Saracevic, Geoff Bessin, Jeff Schuster, Joshua Burton, Kamala Parvathanathan, Kurt Shymanski, Larry Quesada, Lew Cote, Lydia Woodson, Mark Cesario, Mark Victory, Marty Swafford, Nayna Malavia, Paul Murray, Robert Quinn, Sandy Wilkey, Saurabh Malhotra, Susann Ulrich, and many others. "The right word at the right time is like a custom-made piece of jewelry, and a wise friend's timely reprimand is like a gold ring slipped on your finger."

Marc van Lint: I want to thank Dan and the other coauthors of the book. Because of your support, it was possible for this Dutch guy to blend in so well. Thank you.

About the Authors

Chip Davis is a member of the IBM Rational Brand Services organization. In this role, he leads the development of service assets, offerings, and other intellectual capital that accelerate customers' business results and successes achieved via their uses of IBM tools, methods, and solutions. He has worked for Rational Software, and then IBM, since 1999 deploying solutions for various clients across North America. Chip can be reached at chip.davis@us.ibm.com.

Daniel Chirillo is a Senior Consulting IT Specialist with the IBM Rational Brand Services organization. In his current role, he helps customers deploy and become successful with Rational tools, with a focus on Rational's testing and change-management tools. Before computing, he worked as a translator and interpreter, resettlement counselor, and instructor for English as a second language. He holds a bachelor of arts degree in Russian Language and Literature from Rutgers University. Daniel can be reached at chirillo@us.ibm.com.

Daniel Gouveia is a Certified Consulting IT Specialist with the IBM Rational Technical Sales organization. He works with customers to implement Rational's functional- and performance-testing tools in the most effective manner. Dan has a particular interest in addressing challenging problems that require out-of-the-box thinking. He has led initiatives to develop custom solutions for and with the Rational testing tools using Java, Visual Basic, and VB .NET. Dan has worked with Rational since 2000 as a customer services consultant and technical seller. Dan can be reached at dgouveia@us.ibm.com.

Fariz Saracevic is a member of the Automated Software Quality Product Management team. In this role, he is focused on advancing capabilities and defining customer inputs into requirements for Rational Functional Tester. He has worked for IBM Rational Brand Services organization since 2004 and he has worked in the IT field since 1995. He holds a master's degree in Information Technology from Virginia Tech and a bachelor of science degree from George Mason University. Fariz can be reached at fariz@us.ibm.com.

Jeffrey R. Bocarsly is Vice President and Division Manager for Functional Testing Services at Real-Time Technology Solutions, Inc. (RTTS). His team at RTTS implements automated software-testing projects across a broad range of industries, including financial services, ISVs, media, utilities, pharmaceutical, insurance, and reinsurance. The Functional Testing group at RTTS specializes in implementing test automation solutions and custom tool integration and methodology solutions. Jeff holds a bachelor of science from UCLA and master of science and doctorate degrees (chemistry) from Columbia University.

Larry Quesada has worked in the software industry since 1992. He became an expert in software development through extensive experience in the full software-development lifecycle. Larry has been successful in driving technical sales and delivering consulting services to help customers adopt IBM Rational technologies. Currently, Larry is a sales representative for Amazon Web Services. He holds a bachelor of science degree in computer science from the University of Michigan and a master of science degree in computer science from Johns Hopkins University Whiting School of Engineering.

Lee Thomas is an Open Group Master Certified IT Specialist at IBM Rational Brand Services organization. He is a senior software-testing subject matter expert for all phases, from unit tests to user acceptance tests. He has helped clients to advance the state of their testing practices in industries as varied as insurance, telephony, network appliances, automotives, medical devices, and retail. Lee is a recognized leader in testing of real-time systems, in management of testing efforts, and manual and automated testing for functional and performance requirements. Lee has been a consultant at IBM Rational Brand Services organization since 2000. Lee can be reached at leethomas@us.ibm.com.

Marc van Lint started at IBM as a technical professional for CAD, CAM, and CAE systems. In this role, he helps customers adopt new technologies in their mechanical design offices. In 2005, Marc accepted the role of technical professional in the IBM Rational Brand Services organization. His focus is on the product and processes that obtain quality in the software-delivery process. Marc has a bachelor of science degree in computer science. He can be reached at marc_van_lint@nl.ibm.com.

Overview of Rational Functional Tester

Chip Davis, Daniel Gouveia, Fariz Saracevic, Lee B. Thomas, Marc van Lint

*This chapter provides an overview of the basic concepts and the primary usages of Rational®
Functional Tester. The goal is not to duplicate what is documented in the product's Help,
although some of this information can be found there. This chapter does not attempt to go into
great detail about any particular topic; subsequent chapters fulfill that purpose. By the end of this
chapter, you should have a general understanding of what Rational Functional Tester is and how
to use its key capabilities.*

Architecture of Rational Functional Tester

This section introduces the general architecture of Rational Functional Tester, which is described
in detail throughout the rest of the book. You can think of Rational Functional Tester as having
three different modes of operation: normal edit mode, recording mode, and playback mode. Most
of the time, you will work in edit mode. Recording and playback modes are significant because
they are not passive about what you do with the keyboard and mouse of your computer. This is
explained in the sections "How Tests Are Recorded" and "How Tests Are Executed."

How Test Assets Are Stored

Rational Functional Tester is a desktop file-based tool and does not have a server component. All
Rational Functional Tester information is stored in files, primarily Java™ and XML, which users
typically access from shared folders. You can use a configuration management tool such as Rational
Team Concert, IBM® Rational ClearCase®, or simpler tools such as PVS to version control individual test assets. There is no database component, although it is possible to get test data

directly from a database table. This is less common, however, and you will typically keep test data in files along with the other test assets.

If you use Rational Functional Tester Java scripting, your Functional Test project is a special kind of Java project in Eclipse™. If you use Rational Functional Tester Visual Basic®.NET scripting, your Functional Test project is a special kind of Visual Basic project in Microsoft® Visual Studio®. Both kinds of projects are created through Rational Functional Tester.

You can become highly proficient with Rational Functional Tester, even an expert user, without needing to concern yourself with most of the underlying files created by the tool. All of the test assets that you work with are created, edited, and maintained through the Rational Functional Tester interfaces. Most of the test assets, such as a test script, consist of different underlying files on the file system. The exact file structure for the Java scripting and Visual Basic .NET scripting versions are almost exactly the same with only minor differences.

How Test Results are Stored

Test results are stored in test logs, which can be stored in several different formats of your choice. You can choose how to save test logs based on the nature of the particular testing effort and what you use for test management. For example, a small informal testing effort might simply save all test results into HTML files. Another larger testing effort might send the test results to a test management tool, such as IBM Rational Quality Manager. Following are the options for storing test logs in Rational Functional Tester:

- HTML
- Text
- Test and Performance Tools Platform (TPTP)
- XML
- Rational Quality Manager

NOTE   Note that IBM Rational Quality Manager is not required for test logging or for any other functions or uses described in this book. This is presented only as an optional tool for test management, which is often employed in testing efforts.

How Tests Are Recorded

You are likely to use the recorder in Rational Functional Tester to create new test scripts. The reason for this is that the recorder is usually the fastest and easiest way to generate lines of test script, even if that script is extensively modified later. Whether you capture long linear test procedures, developing a keyword-driven test framework, or do something in between, the recording mode is the same. When Rational Functional Tester goes into recording mode, it captures all keyboard and mouse input that goes to all enabled applications and environments. Every time you press a key or perform anything with a mouse, other than simply moving the pointer, it gets captured into the test recording. The exceptions to this are: Rational Functional Tester does not record itself and it does not record applications that are not enabled. You must be careful when you are recording and be sure that you do not click or type anything that you do not want to be part of your test.

Rational Functional Tester creates the test script as it is recording; there are no intermediate files or steps to generate the test script, and you can view the steps as you record. Some information about the test is stored in files that are different from the test script; this includes test objects, verification points, and test data. These files are hidden, and you see abstractions of them only as test assets in the test script.

The test scripts are either Java or Visual Basic .NET files, which must be executed through Rational Functional Tester. These are not just any Java or Visual Basic .NET files, however. They are extensions of the `com.rational.test.ft.script` package and include several other packages for functional testing, which is what makes them automated tests. Using the recorder or creating a new blank test from within Rational Functional Tester automatically sets up the required packages so you do not have to manually do this.

Although there are many techniques for recording tests, you always capture steps that interact with an application or system interface. Unlike many unit testing or developer testing tools, there is nothing that automatically generates tests by "pointing" to a class, interface, or package.

How Tests Are Executed

When you run a test in Rational Functional Tester, the machine goes into playback mode. In playback mode, Rational Functional Tester sends all of the mouse and keyboard actions that you recorded to the application under test. While Rational Functional Tester is "driving" the computer, it does not lock the user out from also using the mouse and keyboard. In general, you should not touch the keyboard or mouse when Rational Functional Tester is in playback mode. However, at times you can run tests in interactive mode to manipulate potential playback issues.

A test script is comprised largely of statements that interact, including performing tests, with various objects in the application under test. When you execute a test script, Rational Functional Tester first has to identify and find each object by matching recognition properties in the script's saved test object map against the actual objects that are present at runtime. If Rational Functional Tester cannot find a close enough match, it logs an error and either attempts to continue or aborts. If Rational Functional Tester does find a matching object, it performs the action on the object. These actions might be user interactions, such as clicking, selections, or other operations such as getting or setting values. Finally, the actions performed on the object might be a test (a verification point), in which case Rational Functional Tester compares some saved expected value or range with an actual runtime result. Although every statement (line of code) in the script produces a result, you normally see only verification points (the tests) and other key results in the test log that are created for every test run.

You can either play a test back on the same machine or on any other machine running a Rational Agent, which gets installed by default with Rational Functional Tester. You can also run multiple tests on multiple remote machines for distributed functional testing. This makes it possible to complete much more testing in a shorter period of time. A given machine can run only one test at a time, or many sequentially, but you cannot run multiple tests in parallel on the same machine. Although it is not required, you can also execute Rational Functional Tester tests on remote machines using test management tools, such as Rational Quality Manager.

Integrations with Other Applications

Rational Functional Tester is a stand alone product that does not require other tools or applications. Integration with other tools or applications is optional and based on your particular needs. Following are some of the common types of applications that you can integrate with Rational Functional Tester:

- Test management or quality management, such as IBM Rational Quality Manager
- Defect tracking or change request management, such as IBM Rational ClearQuest
- Configuration management or version control, such as IBM Rational Team Concert and IBM Rational ClearCase
- Unit or developer testing tools, such as JUnit
- Automated testing tools, such as IBM Rational Performance Tester
- Development tools, such as IBM Rational Application Developer

Most of the applications listed previously, especially those developed by IBM, require little or no work to set up the integration. Many applications and tools, such as JUnit, Rational Service Tester, Rational Software Architect, or WebSphere® Integration Developer (to name a few) run in the Eclipse shell and can share the same interface as Rational Functional Tester. With these tools, you can switch between Rational Functional Tester and the other tools simply by switching perspectives (tabs).

In addition to these applications, you can also integrate Rational Functional Tester with many other kinds of applications. This requires varying amounts of work to implement the integration, although you can find existing examples on IBM developerWorks® (www.ibm.com\developerworks\rational\). These include:

- Custom-built test harnesses (extending the test execution)
- Spreadsheets (for logging or simple test management)
- Email notifications

Installation and Licensing

You learn about product installation and licensing in the subsequent sections.

Product Installation

It is important to properly install Rational Functional Tester. The installation process has been streamlined with the Rational Functional Tester v8.0, and Installation Manager is used for its installation.

If you do not have Installation Manager, you are installing a Rational product using Installation Manager for the first time. In that case, you install Rational Functional Tester v8.0 either by clicking on launchpad.exe or install.exe, located under ..\disk1\InstallerImage_win32\. In this scenario, Installation Manager and Rational Functional Tester are installed at the same time.

This installation is based on the Rational Functional Tester installation via the existing Installation Manager. You can start Installation Manager if you select **Start > Programs > IBM Installation Manager > IBM Installation Manager**. Click **File > Preferences** to select **Repository used for Rational Functional Tester installation** as shown in Figure 1.1.

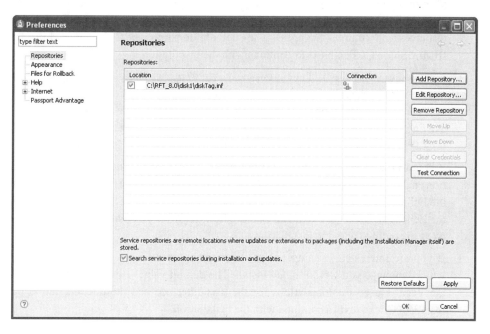

Figure 1.1   Installation Manager preferences

When you select Repository, be sure that you use the letter drive for the installation path (for example, C:\RFT_8.0\disk1\diskTag.inf). Using the Universal Naming Convention (UNC) path is known to cause issues.

After Repository is selected, click the **Install** button in the main window of the Installation Manager. You might be prompted to install the updated version of the Installation Manager. If that is the case, a new version of the Installation Manager is installed first and Installation Manager restarts. You need to click the **Install** button again, and the Rational Functional Tester installation process starts:

- Install Packages window provides details about the installation package. You can click the Check for Other Versions and Extensions button. This provides details about other available versions for installation. If you do not select the Show all versions checkbox, only the latest version is displayed. Select the desired version of the Rational Functional Tester to proceed with the installation.

- On the next window, you are prompted to read and accept the terms in the license agreement. You need to accept the terms, so that the Rational Functional Tester installation can continue.

- Upon acceptance of the terms of the license agreement, you are prompted to specify the location of the shared resources directory. For the best results, you should select the drive with the most available space because it must have adequate space for the shared resources of future packages. The default location is C:\Program Files\IBM\ IBMIMShared. Click **Next** to continue with the installation.

- You need to select the package group next. A *package group* is a location that contains one or more packages. If this is the first IBM Rational installation, you need to create a new package group. If there is an existing package group, you can select to reuse the existing package group. You need to specify the installation directory. The default value is C:\Program Files\IBM\SDP. Click **Next** to continue with the installation.

- If you want to extend an existing version of Eclipse, Rational Functional Tester installation enables you to select Eclipse IDE and JVM. Be sure to have a compatible version of the Eclipse IDE on your system. If you are not sure if you have a compatible version of the Eclipse IDE, do not extend an existing Eclipse. After you make your selection, click **Next** to continue with the installation.

- If you are interested in using one of the ten supported languages, you need to select which language you would like to install. The default value is English. Selection of the language is used for translations for the user interface and the documentation being installed. Click **Next** to continue with the installation.

- You need to select features that you want to install. The default feature value is Java Scripting. You might select to install .NET 2003 or 2005 scripting instead. To see the dependency relationships between features, click **Show Dependencies**. Rational Functional Tester 8.1 has an option for Rational Team Concert.

- On the subsequent window, you are prompted to review summary information that contains information about packages, features, environment, and the repository selected. After you verify summary information, the installation can start.

- Installation Manager provides a status at the end of the installation. If successful, you should get a success message with the listing of the installed package as shown in Figure 1.2.

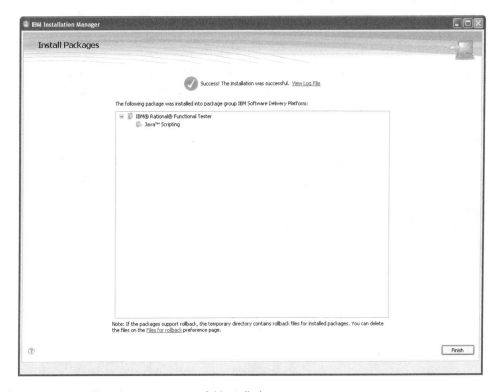

Figure 1.2 Install packages—successful installation message

Product Licensing

The market is shifting away from charging for individual GUI control sets for functional testing. Therefore, starting with Rational Functional Tester v8.0, all GUI control set extensions are included in the base installation.

The Rational Functional Tester v8.0 license is configured using Installation Manager. There are two supported license mechanisms. One uses a product activation kit and the other uses a floating license. The product activation kit is stored in a *.jar file. Configuring with the activation kit is considered as a permanent license key.

If you use a floating license enforcement, you can enable floating licenses for Rational Functional Tester with a permanent license key. You need to obtain the license server connection information from your Rational administration. You then configure a connection to a license

server in the Installation Manager to obtain access to floating license keys installed on a license
server.

Enabling the Environment for Testing

Before you start creating test scripts against your application, you need to enable the environment
for testing. Enabling the environment for testing ensures that controls used within environments
are accessible by Rational Functional Tester.

Clicking **Configure > Enable Environments for Testing** from the Rational Functional
Tester menu opens a dialog box where you can add web browsers, Java environments, and the
Eclipse or SAP GUI platform to the list, and then enable them for testing.

Enabling Web Browsers

The Web Browsers enabler must be run before you can use Rational Functional Tester to test an
HTML application. Depending on the platform where Rational Functional Tester is installed,
enabler behaves differently. On Windows® systems, the enablers look in the registry to discover
any installed browser, and on UNIX®, the enabler scans hard drive(s) for any installed browsers.

Rational Functional Tester automatically enables Internet Explorer if it is present on the
system. If you have different browsers such as Mozilla or Netscape 6 or 7, you must add and
enable them manually via the Enable Environments Wizard shown in Figure 1.3.

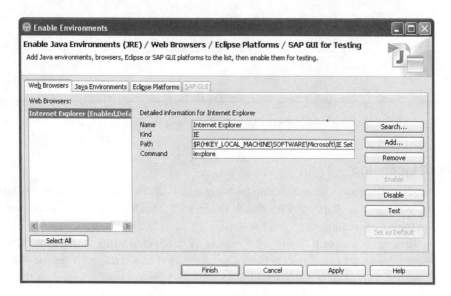

Figure 1.3   Enabling Web Browsers

You should use Test button to validate if the web browser was properly enabled. Clicking
the **Test** button invokes the Brower Enablement Diagnostic Tool. You need to run a diagnostic test

to validate proper enablement of the web browser. If the web browser-enablement test result displays a success status, you have properly enabled web browser. If there are issues, the web browser-enablement test result shows a state failure with an explanation of the failure. Click the **Problem and Solution** tab for instructions about how to fix the problem.

Also, note that the first time you run Rational Functional Tester, it automatically enables the JVM of your browser's Java plug-in so that HTML recording works properly. If you install a different JVM, you must rerun the enabler to enable it.

Enabling Java Environments

The Java Environment tab is used to enable Java environments and to add or configure Java environments, as shown in Figure 1.4. Java enabler must be run before you can use Rational Functional Tester to test Java applications. The enabler scans hard drive(s) looking for Java environments. It enables the Rational Functional Tester to "see" your Java environments by adding files to the directory where your Java Runtime Environments (JRE) are located.

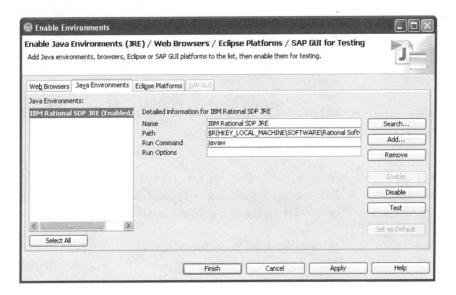

Figure 1.4   Enabling Java environments

You should always perform a test when you add a new Java environment. Click the **Test** button, which invokes the JRE Tester. If the test runs successfully, JRE Tester displays the JRE version, vendor, and a message that JRE successfully enabled. If there is an issue, you need to rectify the issue before recording a test.

Rational Functional Tester is shipped with a JRE that is automatically enabled during installation. It is called IBM Rational SDP JRE. After the name of the Java environments, the enabler indicates in parentheses whether that environment is currently enabled.

Enabling Eclipse Platforms

The Eclipse Platforms tab is used to enable Eclipse or WebSphere WorkBench based platforms. Rational Functional Tester supports testing applications based on Eclipse 2.0 and 3.0, as shown in Figure 1.5.

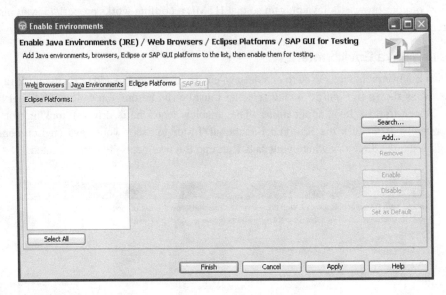

Figure 1.5   Enabling Eclipse platforms

The Eclipse enabler must be run before you can use Rational Functional Tester to test Eclipse or WebSphere WorkBench based platforms, or applications hosted in one of these platforms. The enabler scans your hard drive(s) looking for any installed versions of Eclipse or WebSphere WorkBench.

If your Eclipse shell is not enabled, the Recording Monitor is blank when you try to record against it. For this reason, leave the Recording Monitor in view while recording. If you see this symptom, you need to run the enabler.

Enabling SAP GUI

To use Rational Functional Tester to test SAP applications, you need to enable the SAP GUI client. You can enable the SAP GUI client in the SAP GUI tab only for the Windows operating system. The SAP GUI tab is not present in Linux®. Also, you need to ensure that you have administrator privileges so that you can use the SAP GUI enabler.

If you do not have the supported version of SAP GUI client in the Windows operating system, the SAP GUI tab is disabled.

Configuring Applications for Testing

Rational Functional Tester enables you to configure your applications for testing, so you can start an application under a test within Rational Functional Tester. This method is simple to configure and does not require knowledge of the scripting language used in Rational Functional Tester. This is the best practice because it makes playing back the tests more reliable.

You configure the application for testing by opening the Application Configuration Tool. This is performed either from Rational Functional Tester by clicking **Configure > Configure Applications for Testing**, or by clicking the **Edit** button in the Start Application dialog box.

When the Application Configuration Tool is opened, as shown in Figure 1.6, click the **Add** button. The Add Application dialog box opens. Here, you add the application configuration, so when you start recording against your application under a test, Rational Functional Tester can open the application during recording.

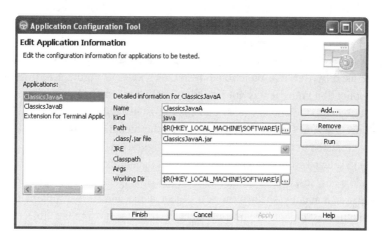

Figure 1.6   The Application Configuration Tool

There are four different types of applications that can be added, as shown in Figure 1.7:

Figure 1.7   Add an application

- Java Application—You need to browse to a .class or .jar file type.

- HTML Application—You need to browse to either Local or URL. If it is Local, you need to browse to an .html or .htm file. If it is URL, you need to specify a URL address.

- Executable or Batch File—You need to browse to any executable or batch file.

- SAP Application—You need to select SAP executable from the drop-down list. You can also browse to the SAP shortcut file with the .sal or .sap extension. You must have SAPGUI installed in your computer to be able to select SAP Application.

Configuring Object Recognition Properties

Rational Functional Tester v8.0 introduces a new feature that enables you to configure object recognition properties. This feature uses the Object Properties Configuration Tool to configure the object recognition properties in the customized object library. While recording test scripts, the customized object library file is used as a reference for setting object recognition properties and the property weights in the object map.

The Object Properties Configuration Tool lists the default objects and the customized objects that are used by Rational Functional Tester, as shown in Figure 1.8. If the required test object of the application under test is not listed in the Object Properties Configuration Tool, you can add the test object to the object library and customize its recognition properties and weights.

You can use the Add Object dialog box to add the recognition properties for the existing test objects that are listed in the Object Properties Configuration Tool.

You need to select Test domain from the list, and then click **Add Object**. This opens a new dialog box to add a new test object for the selected domain. There are two options for adding the test object: you can manually specify the test object name and have it inherit the recognition properties from other test objects or you can select the test object using the Object Finder tool, as shown in Figure 1.9.

Recording a First Script

Rational Functional Tester is a flexible tool that enables various ways of working. This section describes the process of a basic recording. Some enhancements are added using wizards. At various points in the scenario, options or additions can be clarified. This is done in a limited way to keep the scenario simple.

Before Recording

Before you start recording, you need to take care of several things:

- Be sure the application under test is available including the correct setup of its environment. Doing this results in an expected behavior.

- The application under test must be configured for testing. See the "Configuring Applications for Testing" section for more information.

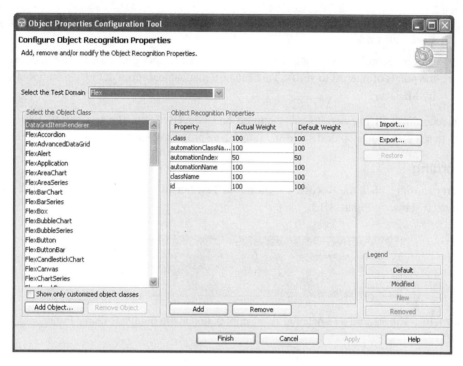

Figure 1.8 Object Properties Configuration Tool

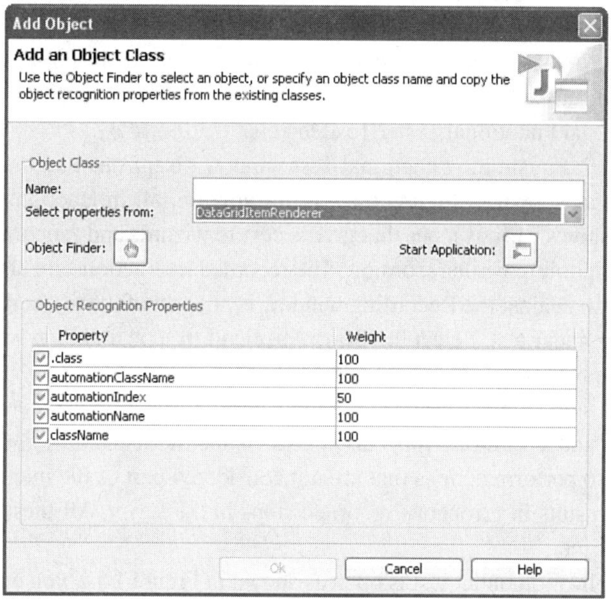

Figure 1.9 Add Object

- A Rational Functional Test project is created and available. This is the area where you store your work.

- Before recording, you should already have a test script describing the interactions and the points of interest to verify. This can be a manual test script defined in Rational Quality Manager.

When recording, all interactions are captured and converted into the test script. Experience proves that it is wise to stop or disable any interfering programs, such as messaging programs.

Recording

To start recording, click the **Record a Functional Test Script** button in the Functional Test perspective, as shown in Figure 1.10.

Figure 1.10   The Record a Functional Test Script button in the default Rational Functional Tester workbench

A new window opens, as shown in Figure 1.11. You need to enter the test script name and the project where it is stored. With the exception of the dollar sign ($) and the underscore (_) spaces and special characters are not allowed for test script names.

When you click **Next**, a second screen opens where some advanced settings can be defined. These settings are discussed in Chapter 5, "Managing Script Data," and Chapter 10, "Advanced Scripting with Rational Functional Tester TestObjects."

When you click Finish, the Functional Test window disappears and the recording window becomes available, as shown in Figure 1.12. From now on, all interactions are recorded! The recording window shows various icons that give access to wizards and functions, such as verification points and data pooling while recording. The recorded interactions are also displayed.

Any interaction against the Recording window is not part of the test script. You first have to start the application under test. Select the **Start Application** icon and then select the application from the drop-down list, as shown in Figure 1.13.

Selecting OK starts the application. Remember that this action is recorded and it results in an action statement added to the script. This is also visible in the recording window. It is normal for first-time users to perform actions that are not considered part of the intended test script, and as a consequence, results in erroneous recorded steps in the script. All these user errors can be corrected at a later time.

When the application under test is open as shown in Figure 1.14, you can perform required test steps. First select composer **Bach**, and then specify the CD selection. Click the **Place Order** button and log in as the default user.

Figure 1.11 Record a functional test script window where you define the project to store the script and define its name.

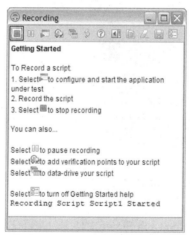

Figure 1.12 The recording window.

To validate expected execution of the application under test, the test script must be enhanced with check points called verification points. A *verification point* is a check that the current execution corresponds with your expectations, which is called the *baseline*. A difference between actual and baseline results in a fail status in the execution log. Differences in the consecutive application builds that are not checked with a verification point are not captured and do not result in failures. It is best practice to verify only what makes sense because verification points act as your eyes.

Figure 1.13   The Start Application window where you can select the application under text. This starts the application and generates the steps in the script.

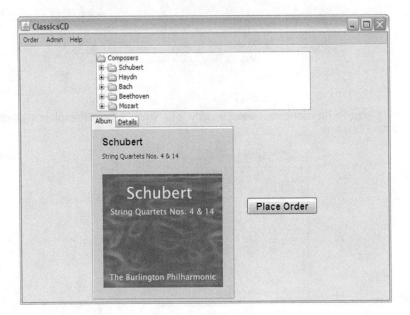

Figure 1.14   The ClassicsCD application

The Verification Point icon shown in Figure 1.15 enables access to Verification Point. Let us say that we need to verify that the total price is $15.99. While recording, select the **Verification Point** icon on the recording window.

Figure 1.15   The Verification Point icon gives access to the verification points.

The Verification Point and Action Wizard is displayed as shown in Figure 1.16.

Figure 1.16   The Verification Point and Action Wizard gives you the options to identify the object to be verified.

Drag the hand icon over the $15.99 value. As a preselection, a red square is drawn around the object, as shown in Figure 1.17. When you release the cursor, this object is selected.

Figure 1.17   When you drag the hand icon to objects, Rational Functional Tester provides a preselection for easy identification.

When you release the cursor, the properties of the object selected become visible at the bottom of the wizard. You can validate that you have selected the correct object. Click the **Next** button to advance to the next window. In this window, you define what kind of verification point has to be created; following are the available options:

- Data Verification—Use this for validating the actual data in an object.
- Properties Verification—Use this for validating one or more properties of an object (for example, if it is selected or it is color).
- Get a Specific Property Value—Use this to get a specific property value into a Java variable.
- Wait for Selected Test Object—Rational Functional Tester waits until this object becomes available. Use this as an intelligent mechanism to synchronize with the application under test.
- Perform Image Verification Point—A graphical verification point.

This scenario uses the Data Verification Point. Click **Next**. In the next screen, you can give an appropriate name and influence the default wait for settings. Click **Next**. You can see data here and make modifications if necessary. Click **Finish**. The Data Verification Point is created and inserted as code in the program. You can continue recording the interactions. While recording, you can add various verification points.

After closing the application under test, you have to stop recording by clicking the **Stop Recording** button in the Recorder window. When it is selected, Rational Functional Tester's main screen displays and test script is created.

After Recording

After recording, you can improve the recording by:

- Adding comments where possible. Any tester should be able to read test script and understand the logic.
- Correcting the user's mistakes, which were recorded and converted into statements.
- Correcting the actions by removing the recorded errors and backspaces.

NOTE   Data-driven testing is not covered in this simple recording. It is covered in more detail in Chapter 5.

Validating Execution

A first validation of correctness must be done by executing the test script against the environment where it was recorded. Keep in mind that not only the application is under test, but so is the test environment, which should be reset to its original state. For example, a double creation of the same customer probably results in an execution error.

Timing Issues

It is common for an application to be slower than the Rational Functional Tester expects. For example, an interaction with a web page might be hindered by slow network traffic. This results in a problematic execution. In this case, you have to slow down the execution. Several options are available:

- Get an overall slowdown using the Rational Functional Test parameter shown in Figure 1.18.

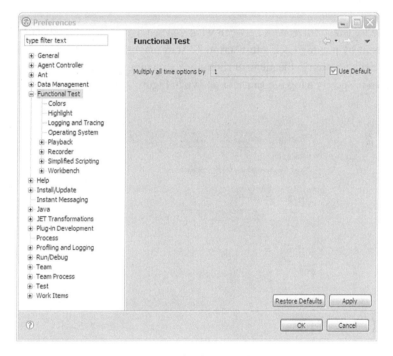

Figure 1.18   The overall slowdown parameter for Rational Functional Tester; 30 is roughly 1 interaction per second. Reset it again when running in production.

- Add hard `sleep` statements:

  ```
  sleep(2.0);
  ```

- Add `wait-for-existence`:

  ```
  ObjectInApplication().waitForExistence();
  ```

- Lengthen the `wait-for` parameters in `waitForExistence` or `VerificationPoints`:

  ```
  ObjectInApplication().performTest(ObjectSubmit_textVP(), 2.0, 40.0);
  ```

It is normal to have these kinds of troubles. The default settings will typically work, but which application is normal?

Playing Back a Script and Viewing Results

You learn about playing back a test script and viewing test results in subsequent sections. This section provides basic playback and behavior information based on normal settings. Only an overview is provided here.

Playback

It is possible to detect differences between what you see in the current application build and the expected result by playing back a test script. To start playback of a script, click the **Run Functional Test Script** button in the menu or right-click a specific test script, and then select **Run**. You are prompted to specify a log file name, as shown in Figure 1.19.

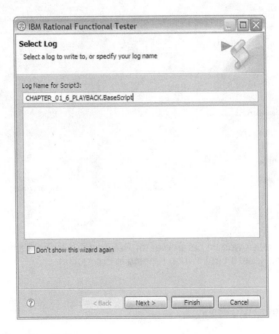

Figure 1.19   The define log window

You can define the name of a test log in the Select Log window. After selecting Finish, the execution begins. Because Rational Functional Tester uses a mouse and keyboard, it is impossible to do work in parallel during execution, or lock the computer.

The progress of the playback can be followed on a screen, and anomalies can be noted. In the playback monitor, you can see which statement Rational Functional Tester executes. Normally, Rational Functional Tester waits for objects to display or to become active.

When the execution ends, Rational Functional Tester returns to its normal state and shows a log file. If the HTML log type is selected, the web browser displays the execution log file. Again, assume that you have default settings active for Rational Functional Tester.

View Results

This section discusses the analysis of the log file in the HTML variant, which is the default setting. After execution of a test script, the browser shows a log file. You can also double-click a log file in Rational Functional Tester to view it. HTML log file shows you three types of information:

- Failures
- Warnings
- Verification Points

You can select any of these options to quickly show you more detail in the main window, as shown in Figure 1.20.

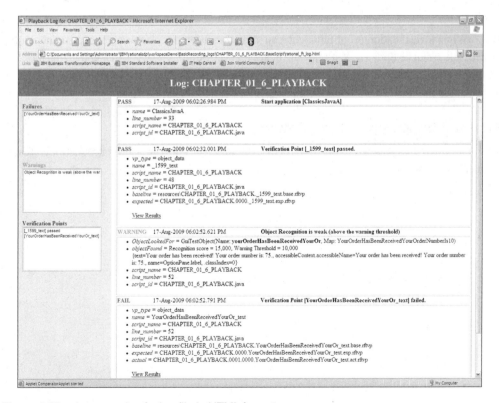

Figure 1.20   An example of a log file in HTML format

In the case of a failing verification point, you can view the difference between the expected and actual by activating the Verification Point Comparator as shown in Figure 1.21, and by selecting View Results of each verification point.

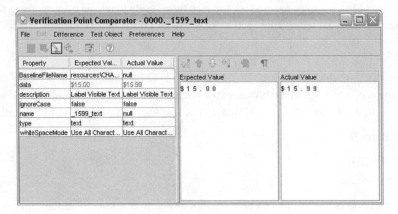

Figure 1.21   Verification Point Comparator

When a verification point fails, you can view the differences between expected and actual. The baseline can be updated. With the Verification Point Comparator, you can update the baseline with the Replace Baseline with actual result option. It is also possible to start the Verification Point Comparator directly from the logs in Rational Functional Tester.

Script Editing and Augmentation

There are many reasons why you should edit and augment a test in Rational Functional Tester. You edit a test to:

- Correct an error or unintended behavior in the test
- Update tests to work with newer application builds
- Separate longer tests into smaller modular tests
- Integrate tests with other automated tests
- Verify functionality or other system requirements
- Associate test data with a test
- Modify or manipulate playback timing
- Modify or control test flow
- Add logging and reporting of test results
- Improve test readability and reuse

How to Correct or Update a Test Script

The most frequent type of editing you will probably perform to a test script is fixing or updating. After you finish reading this book and start employing the best test script development practices, these corrections and updates should be short and simple. The two general steps in this activity are removing unwanted test script lines and adding new lines. This section does not go into the details of debugging, but it does describe the general editing steps for doing this.

Removing Lines from a Test Script

You can remove unwanted lines of a test script by deleting the lines or by commenting them out (making them into comments). You should begin with the latter because there is always a chance that you might need to restore the original lines. You can comment out multiple lines of a test script as follows:

1. Select the multiple lines of script. This assumes that you know which lines of the test you want to disable.

2. Comment the lines: For Java in Eclipse, choose the menu **Script > Toggle Comment** or press Ctrl+/. For Visual Studio, choose the menu **Edit > Advanced > Comment Selection** or press Ctrl+K, and then press Ctrl+C.

Adding Lines to a Test Script

You can add new lines to a test script by inserting a recording into an existing script or by manually adding lines. Refer to the section, "How to Manually Add Script Code," for an explanation of manually adding code to a test script.

It is typically easier to add lines with the recorder. This is easy to do, although you have to ensure that the newly recorded steps flow correctly with the existing recorded steps. You can record new lines into an existing script as follows:

1. Get the application under test to the initial state for the new recording. You can play back the test script in debug mode, breaking (pausing) at the spot where you want to add or rerecord steps.

2. Carefully position the cursor on a blank line in the test script where you want to add new steps.

3. Select **Script > Insert Recording** from the menu, or click the **Insert Recording into Active Functional Test Script** button from a toolbar. You immediately go into recording mode.

4. Click the **Stop** button to finish the recording.

Just as you must ensure the starting point of the new recording is carefully set, you must also ensure that the point that you stop recording flows correctly into the next steps of the test script.

How to Use Test Object Maps

The next most frequent type of editing you are likely do to on a test is update and modify test object maps. A test object map is normally created when you record a new test script, as shown in Figure 1.22. You can also create an object map independently from script recording. Every test script has a test object map to use, and every test object map needs a test script to have a purpose.

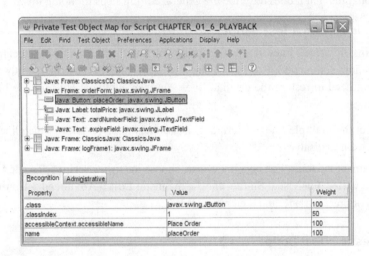

Figure 1.22   Editing the test object map

Each test script also contains a list of test objects, visible in the script explorer. This is only a subset of all test objects, as shown in Figure 1.23. The list contains only the objects required for this particular test script.

Figure 1.23   Script explorer test objects

The most common kind of editing that you perform on a test object map is:

- Adding new objects
- Updating objects for a newer version of the application under test
- Modifying object recognition properties

Test objects are explained in greater detail in Chapter 3, "General Script Enhancements," and Chapter 9, "Advanced Rational Functional Tester Object Map Topics"; this section explains only the basics of editing test object maps.

Test object maps have a separate window where you can view, edit, and manage the objects used by test script. The test script itself contains a reference of an object and the action that is performed on it. The following is an example of a line of test script in Java that references a test object named placeOrder.

```
placeOrder().click();
```

If you want to learn more about this test object, you can open it from the Script Explorer, which opens the test object map and highlights the object as shown in Figure 1.24.

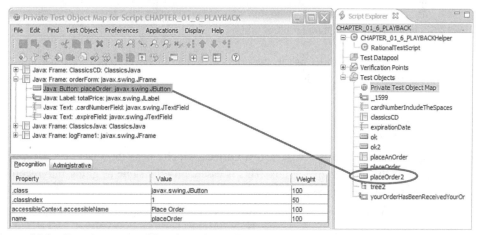

Figure 1.24   Opening a test object from the script

Private Versus Shared

There are two types of test object maps: private and shared. The only difference between the two is that a private map is associated exclusively to one test script, whereas a shared object map can be used by many test scripts. You can open a private test object map from the Script Explorer. You can open a shared test object map from the Project Explorer or from the Script Explorer. The test object map editor and almost all editing capabilities are the same for both private and shared test object maps.

You can create a shared test object map from a private map, and then associate the original test script with the new shared map, changing the private map into a shared one. You can also merge objects from one shared map into another, combining and reducing the number of shared maps. You cannot revert a shared object map back into a private map, but you can merge objects from a shared map into an existing private map.

Ultimately, you need to have primarily shared test object maps instead of private object maps. As a general rule, you should reduce the overall number of different maps.

Adding, Modifying, and Deleting Test Objects

Over time, the objects in the application under test that your test scripts interact with will change. You therefore need to add, modify, and delete test objects in Rational Functional Tester. These changes occur at two levels: in the map containing the test objects and in the test scripts that reference the test objects. The test object map is the primary storage location for a test object. This is where you ultimately maintain the test objects and their current recognition properties.

Adding Test Objects

You can add a new test object to a test script, as shown in Figure 1.25, which adds it to the associated test object map as follows:

Figure 1.25   Insert New Test Object toolbar button

1. Get the application under test to the point with the object (graphical or other interface object) that you need to add to the test.

2. Position the cursor to a blank line in the test script where you want to add the reference to the new object. This is typically an action on the object, such as clicking or selecting from the object.

3. Select the menu **Script > Insert Test Object**, which opens the **Insert a GUI Object into the Object Map** dialog box. This is essentially the same as going into recording mode, except that you do not see the recorder monitor.

4. Use the Object Finder to select the object you want to add, and then click **Finish**.

SELECTING AN OBJECT

Alternately, you could use the Test Object Browser to select the object you want to add. Refer to the product Help documentation for more information on using the Test Object Browser.

As a consequence, this adds the object to the test object map and to the list of test objects for the script, and it will add a reference to the object in the test script where you positioned your cursor.

The initial object reference in the script will not be complete since it will not contain any operation (for example, a click action). You can either manually add the desired operation, assuming that it works with the test procedure recorded in the script, or you can simply comment or delete the line and add some actions for the object at a later time.

Modifying Test Objects

You can modify a test object by double-clicking on an object in the script explorer, which will open the test object map and highlight the object. If you want to modify an object that is not in the list of test objects in the script explorer, then you can open the test object map and either browse or search to find the object. There are a number of reasons you might modify a test object, most of which are described in Chapter 9.

One kind of modification that you can make to a test object that does not require opening the test object map is renaming. You can rename an object directly from the script explorer, as explained in this chapter. Note that you can rename objects from the test object map as well.

Deleting Test Objects

There are two reasons why you might want to delete a test object. First, you may want to remove an object from a test script but leave it in the test object map. You might do this if the object map is shared and the object is used by other test scripts, or you might simply want to leave the object in the map in case you need to add it back into the script at a later time. The second reason you would delete a test object is when you really know that it is no longer needed by any script and you want to delete it from the test object map.

For the first case, when you simply want to remove an object from a script, you can delete an object from the list of test objects in the script explorer. This will not affect the test object map or any other scripts that may use the same map. This also will not remove the reference to the object in the script; you will have to delete or comment the line of code referencing the deleted object yourself. Rational Functional Tester will automatically indicate an error which makes it easier to clean up the script. If you comment out the lines then it will be easier to add it back again later, if needed.

For the second case, when you want to completely delete the object from a test object map, you can open the map and delete the test object. When you do this, Rational Functional Tester will run a short wizard to help ensure you are not deleting something that you need. The first step simply shows the name and recognition properties of the object. The second step, as shown in Figure 1.26, shows all of the test scripts that will be affected by the deletion.

If you realize that you do not want to delete the object you can cancel. Otherwise clicking on **Finish** will delete the object from the map and all references to the object. Similar to deleting an object from the script explorer, this will *not* delete the line of code in the script that references the object but it will be reflected in object map as shown in Figure 1.27.

Figure 1.26   Deleting a test object from the map

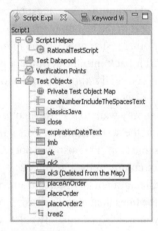

Figure 1.27   Object in script deleted from the map

How to Add Verification Points to a Test Script

Verification points are what make test script a test as they are primarily what provide the pass or fail results. You will find that it is generally easier to add verification points when you first record a script. However, you might want to first record the user scenarios and steps and then add verification points later. You might also realize additional or more effective verification points after recording the script. In these cases, you can add verification points as shown in Figure 1.28 using following steps:

1.   Get the application under test to the appropriate point for what you want to check. You might want to play back the test script in debug mode, breaking (pausing) at the spot where you want to add your verification.

Figure 1.28   Insert New Verification toolbar button

2. Position the cursor on a blank line in the test script where you want to add the verification point.

3. Select the menu **Script > Insert Verification Point**, which will open the Verification Point wizard. This is essentially the same as going into recording mode except that you will not see the recorder monitor.

4. Complete the wizard to create your verification point. You can find more about the verification point wizard in the online Help.

5. Click on **Finish** to return to the test script.

CHOOSING A VERIFICATION POINT

Your choice of verification points should not be arbitrary or chosen on the fly. You should always determine the best way to validate the test case or requirement that the test is implementing. You also need to consider the possibility of errors in proper verification across all test environments and conditions.

Datapools

You often record tests using specific values, for input and expected values, which become hard-coded (literals) into the script. Even if you choose certain test data to be variable using the data driven test wizard, you may not realize other hard-coded values that will later need to be changed. You can change static test data in a script into dynamic values by adding datapool variables. You can use datapools for both test input and for expected values (verification points). Datapools are explained in greater detail in Chapter 5 but we explain the basics of editing tests to include datapools.

You can add a data driven code (commands that input test data from a datapool) using the Insert Data Driven Actions wizard as follows:

1. Get the application under test to the appropriate point where the test data should be added. You might want to play back the test script in debug mode, breaking (pausing) at the data input form or dialog.

2. Position the cursor on a blank line in the test script where you want to add the data driven commands.

3. Select the menu **Script > Insert Data Driven Commands**, which will open the Data Driven Commands wizard as shown in Figure 1.29. This is essentially the same as going into recording mode except that you will not see the recorder monitor.

4. Complete the wizard to select the data input objects. You can find more about the Data Driven Commands wizard in the online Help.

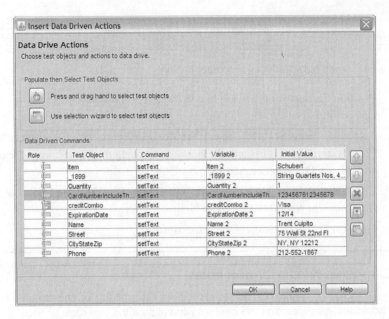

Figure 1.29   Insert data driven actions wizard

If you had not already created or added a datapool for the test script, then a new one will be created. Note that this wizard will add new lines of code to set (input) datapool values to the test object selected in the wizard. If you had already recorded typing or selecting values then the script will set the values twice. In this case, you can either delete the redundant script lines, or you can replace the literal test input values as described in the following paragraphs.

If you already have a shared datapool then you can add it to your test script as follows:

1. Right-click on the Test Datapool folder in the Script Explorer and select **Associate with Datapool.**

2. Select one datapool, and then click **OK**. You can then see the datapool listed in the Script Explorer. You can associate only one datapool with a test script.

At this point, you have associated only the datapool with the test script. You need to replace the literal strings (hard-coded values) with values from the datapool. You do this as follows:

1. Select the menu **Script > Find Literals and Replace with Datapool Reference**. Script menu selection Find Literals and Replace with Datapool will be enabled if you have a script open that already has a datapool associated with it. Otherwise, this menu line is disabled.

2. In the Datapool Literal Substitution window, as shown in Figure 1.30, select the variable (column) you want to use from the Datapool Variable drop-down list.

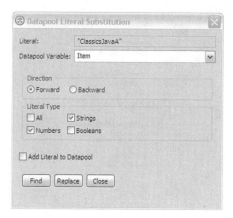

Figure 1.30 Replacing literals with datapool values

3. Click **Find** repeatedly until the correct value is highlighted in the script and then click the **Replace** button.

4. Repeat step 2 until you have replaced all occurrences in the script.

5. You can select another Datapool variable from the drop-down list and repeat steps 2 through 3 for other values.

6. Click **Close** when you have finished replacing values.

You might already have a datapool with some substitutions for script values, but realize you need to replace additional literal values. You can repeat steps 3 through 6 to add more datapool substitutions to your test script at any time.

How to Manually Add Script Code

So far, we have discussed different ways to add recorded lines and test objects, verification points, and datapool commands to a test script using wizards and other recording or capture techniques. If you are familiar with the test script syntax, then you might find it useful to manually add these things directly to the script.

Adding Test Steps

If you have already captured test objects in a map, you can add them to your script along with actions for the test to perform as shown in Figure 1.31, or with verification points to check. You do this as follows:

1. Position the cursor on a blank line in the script where you want to add the new test step.

2. Right-click either a verification point or a test object in the Script Explorer and select **Insert at Cursor**.

Figure 1.31   Adding an existing test element to the script

You now have an incomplete reference to either a test object or a verification point in the script. If you add an object, you need to then select an operation (test action) to perform. If you add a verification point, you need an object and not just any object but one capable of returning the expected value. Complete the test script statement for either a test object or verification point:

- For a test object, select an operation from the drop-down list of methods. For example, select click() to make the script click on the test object during test playback. This action is added *after* the object reference.

- For a verification point, you must add a test object reference. You can either type or copy the object name, or you can add it from the Script Explorer using **Insert at Cursor**. This object must be added *before* the performTest operation.

With both Java and Visual Basic .NET scripting, if you position your cursor at the end of a test object call (class), just after the parenthesis, and type a period, you will see the list of methods available for that class. If you add the object from the Script Explorer, you might have to press Backspace over the period and retype it. If you then select the method from the list, the editor adds the operation to your script. Figures 1.32 and 1.33 show this for both Eclipse and Visual Studio.

For Java, you also have to type the ending semi-colon yourself.

Adding Programming Code to Your Tests

Rational Functional Tester scripts are implemented in either Java or Visual Basic .NET and are in fact just programs with specific testing functions. Therefore, in addition to adding test steps as described in the previous section, you can also add virtually any programming devices or functions

Figure 1.32   Selecting an operation for a test object in Java

Figure 1.33   Selecting an operation for a test object in Visual Basic .NET

that you would develop for any other Java or Visual Basic program. This includes not only simple looping or conditional constructs, but also calls to more elaborate programming classes. The constraints to this are that the test script must be an extension of `com.rational.test.ft.` `script.RationalTestScript` and they must be executed from Rational Functional Tester execution mechanisms.

If you add more programming to your test scripts, you should take advantage of the many development features of the test script editor being used, either Eclipse for Java or Visual Studio for Visual Basic .NET. Chapter 12, "Extending Rational Functional Tester with External Libraries," provides Java examples of open-source solutions.

Other Script Enhancements

So far, we have discussed several ways to edit test scripts to modify, complete, enhance, or extend their capabilities. Another purpose of editing tests is to improve their readability and potential reuse. This is done by adding comments and descriptions, naming or renaming test elements, and possibly restructuring test scripts into smaller modular tests.

Comments and Descriptions

In a given testing effort, you create many tests, object maps, datapools, and other test elements. There are most likely be other people who have to use or reference these same test artifacts.

Comments and descriptions should be added to test artifacts and elements to explain their purposes, usages, and any other relevant information. This makes it much easier for someone else other than the test's creator to understand. This also increases the value of the tests as software development artifacts.

You add comments directly into the test scripts. You can add as many as you like without affecting the execution, and in general, the more, the better. You can add comments during recording using the Script Support Functions, or at any time after recording. Here are examples of comments in each scripting language:

```
// This is a comment in Java
' This is a comment in Visual Basic
```

If you are using Rational Functional Tester with Java scripting, then you can also use Javadoc documentation in your test scripts. Some of this is generated automatically at the beginning of each test script in Java, and you can add more text or tags if you need. More information on Javadoc can be found in the Rational Functional Tester Help.

```
/**
 * Description : This is Javadoc content
 * @author You
 */
```

You can add *descriptions* for certain test elements including test scripts, test objects, and verification points. Descriptions for test scripts are simply Javadoc comments. You can add a description for test objects by opening the object map, selecting an object, and then selecting **Test Object > Description Property** from the menu, as shown in Figure 1.34.

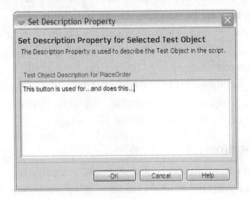

Figure 1.34   Adding a description for a test object

You can add a description for a verification point by opening the verification point and editing the description property, as shown in Figure 1.35.

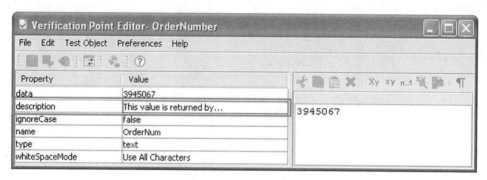

Figure 1.35   Adding a description for a verification point

Naming and Reuse

In addition to adding comments and descriptions, you can improve the readability of a test by renaming test elements to more accurately reflect their meaning or purpose. This is perhaps most important for verification points because you interpret test results largely from these. You have a much harder time understanding a test log or report that has a failure on _1695Text than one with a failure on OrderTotal. You might also consider renaming test objects, datapool variables (columns), and test scripts.

NAMES FOR YOUR TEST ELEMENTS

Although this discussion is about renaming things, the best time to name your test elements, especially verification points, is when you first record or develop your test.

Renaming Objects and Verification Points

You can rename test objects and verification points by right-clicking the item in the Script Explorer and selecting **Rename**, as shown in Figure 1.36. This automatically renames the reference to the object or verification point in the test script.

Renaming Datapool Variables

You may need to rename datapool variables, especially if they are generated by the test data wizard, which copies the test object names. The variables (columns names) are used to reference the values in the script, and the name should reflect the real value or purpose. You can rename a datapool variable by opening the datapool (or the script for a private datapool), clicking on the variable name (column header), and entering a new name for the variable as shown in Figure 1.37. This automatically renames the reference to the datapool variable in the test scripts.

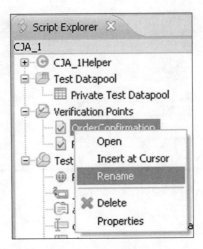

Figure 1.36   Renaming script elements in the Script Explorer

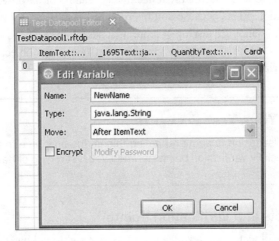

Figure 1.37   Renaming datapool columns

If you rename a variable in a shared datapool, the Rational Functional Tester automatically lets you know which scripts are updated with the new name as shown in Figure 1.38.

Renaming Scripts

You might want to rename a test script to better reflect its function or purpose or to comply with project naming conventions. You can do this by right-clicking the item in the Project Explorer and selecting **Rename**. This will automatically rename all the hidden files associated with the test script, such as the helper and verification point files.

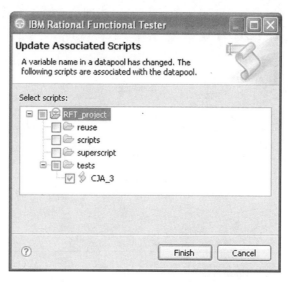

Figure 1.38   Updating all scripts with a new datapool variable name

ScriptAssure

This section describes the integrated technique called ScriptAssure®, which is the recognition algorithm.

Property Value Weights

The success of an automated test is highly dependent on the robustness of the test script. Small changes often force development to adapt test scripts before running successfully. This reduces productivity because maintenance must be applied to the test scripts for a successful run.

For example, the old record and playback tools recorded based on recording graphical interaction. The actual x, y coordinates of a selection were stored in the script. When a button was moved or a different screen layout was applied to the application, the script became useless. It resulted in a lot of rework and crash maintenance to get scripts running.

Rational Functional Tester recognizes objects in the application under test. This means that objects can be moved around or changed graphically. Recognition is done based on all the properties of the object. Not only the visible label (the OK), but object properties are recorded. When one or more properties changes, Rational Functional Tester keeps running!

Sample 1: Login

An example is the button GO in a login screen, as shown in Figure 1.39.

The base GO button has the following properties:

- ID = "GO"
- TYPE = "submit"

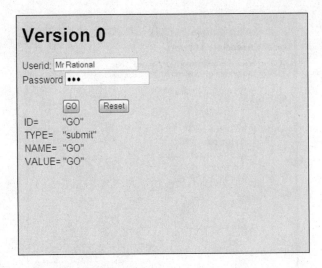

Figure 1.39   The login screen and GO button

- NAME = "GO"
- VALUE = "GO"

One can easily find these values in the HTML source of the button (this is true of any programming environment):

```
<INPUT ID="GO" TYPE="submit" NAME="GO" VALUE="GO"
ONCLICK="logincheck(username.value,password.value);">
```

When recording a script, the script contains the following line:

```
button_g0submit().click();
```

The `button_g0submit` is the object in the Script Explorer view, as shown in Figure 1.40. A click is the action to be performed on that object.

Double-clicking the object in the tree opens the object map; here, you can interrogate the properties of the object, as shown in Figure 1.41.

When the script is run to validate the script, it finds the object with all properties matching. The recognition algorithm is as easy as it is powerful; every mismatch results in 100 times the weight. The object with the minimum penalty points is selected.

One Property Change

Suppose the visible property GO is changed to Login, as shown in Figure 1.42. An automatic test tool that recognizes only object visible labels fails, resulting in the test process stopping and an urgent need for maintenance.

Figure 1.40   Script, Explorer view

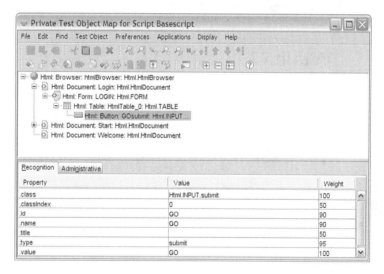

Figure 1.41   Test Object Map browser

Rational Functional Tester uses the same object or the one with minimal difference. In this case, Rational Functional Tester selects the Login, despite the difference in label, position, and format. The Reset button is not selected because there is a difference in all properties.

Two Properties Changed

Now with version 2, there are two properties changed, as shown in Figure 1.43. Does Rational Functional Tester find the button?

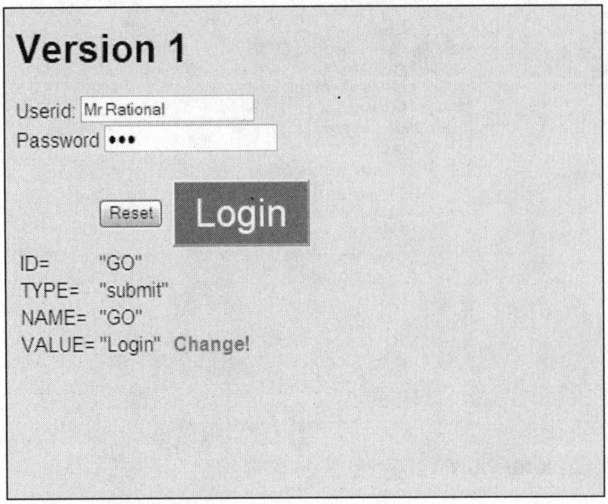

Figure 1.42   Changing one visible property

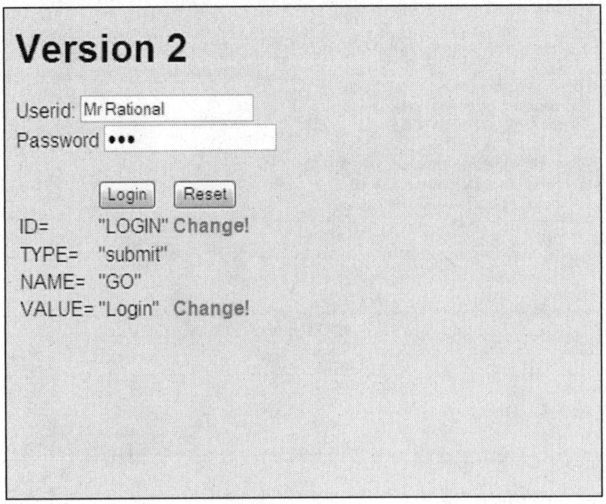

Figure 1.43   Changing two visible properties

With the default settings, Rational Functional Tester stores a message in the test log, as shown in Figure 1.44. The `Object Recognition is weak` message indicates that Rational Functional Tester has found one object that is comparable. Rational Functional Tester uses this object to continue execution. Additionally, there is a recognition score (failing score) visible that is 19.000. The calculation can be derived by the rule that every mismatch results in 100 times the weight. This example shows a miss at ID (weight 90) and Value (weight 100), resulting in a 19.000. When no differences are found, this recognition score is 0.

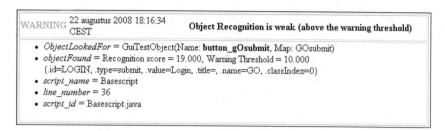

WARNING | 22 augustus 2008 18:16:34 CEST | Object Recognition is weak (above the warning threshold)

- *ObjectLookedFor* = GuiTestObject(Name: **button_gOsubmit**, Map: GOsubmit)
- *objectFound* = Recognition score = 19.000, Warning Threshold = 10.000
  (.id=LOGIN, .type=submit, .value=Login, .title=, .name=GO, .classIndex=0)
- *script_name* = Basescript
- *line_number* = 36
- *script_id* = Basescript.java

Figure 1.44   Viewing the message in the test log

Three Properties Changed

In the next version of the application, there are three properties changed, as shown in Figure 1.45.

Now the object to be found and the object available in the application differ too much. A window opens to ask the user for advice, as shown in Figure 1.46.

Version 3

Userid: Mr Rational
Password ●●●

[Login] [Reset]

ID=   "LOGIN" Change!
TYPE=   "submit"
NAME= "LOGIN" Change!
VALUE= "Login" Change!

Figure 1.45   Changing three visible properties

With the object browser, one can update the properties of the object to be found. The Playback Options become available just after starting a script. The previous interactive menu can be suppressed by deselecting the option Perform playback in interactive mode in the second screen of the Playback Options, as shown in Figure 1.47.

If you update the properties of the object, you get a similar error message as shown in Figure 1.48.

Rational Functional Tester does find an object candidate, but it has a failing score of 28500, as described in the log. This is above the value Last chance recognition score, which is set by

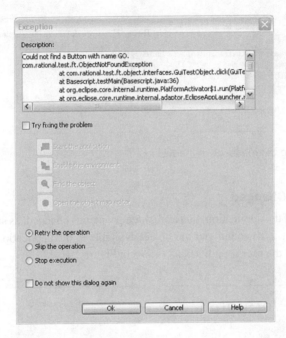

Figure 1.46   Exception window

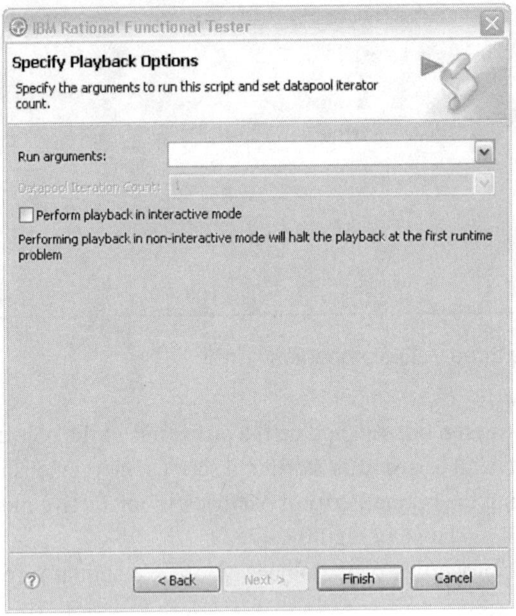

Figure 1.47   Specify Playback Options

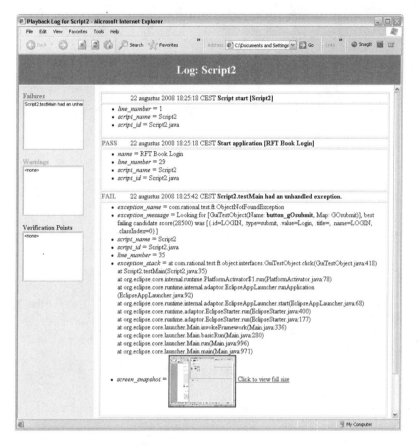

Figure 1.48   Test log with error message

default to 20000. If you increase this value to 50000, the script does find the Login button and provides a warning, as shown in Figure 1.49.

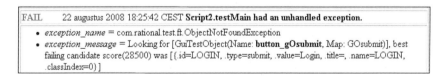

Figure 1.49   Test log with warning message

Sample 2: Two Buttons

The previous examples clarify the behavior of ScriptAssure. The following example is somewhat more complex while we have two buttons, which are similar as shown in Figure 1.50.

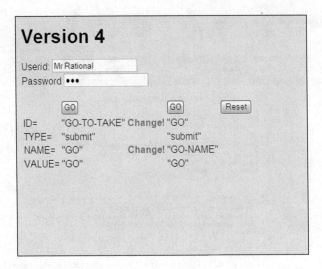

Figure 1.50   Sample 2: two buttons

When the script is run, which of the buttons is selected, the "GO" (left) or the "GO" (right) button? Both have one change in a property. A part of the source of this menu is:

```
<INPUT ID="GO-TO-TAKE" TYPE="submit" NAME="GO" VALUE="GO"
ONCLICK="...action...">
<INPUT ID="GO" TYPE="submit" NAME="GO-NAME" VALUE="GO"
ONCLICK="...action...">
```

The object to be searched for is defined in the object map, as shown in Figure 1.51.

Property	Value	Weight
.class	Html.INPUT.submit	100
.classIndex	0	0
.id	GO	90
.name	GO	95
.title		50
.type	submit	95
.value	GO	100

Figure 1.51   Searched object in the object map

Calculate the penalty points of the "Login" and the "GO" button, as shown in Table 1.1 and Table 1.2.

Table 1.1 Table for the First Go Button

Label	Property	Weight	Found	Result
.id	GO-TO-TAKE	90	No	9000
.name	GO	95	Yes	0
.type	Submit	95	Yes	0
.value	GO	100	Yes	0
Total				9000

Table 1.2 Table for a Second Go Button

Label	Property	Weight	Found	Result
.id	GO	90	Yes	0
.name	GO-NAME	95	No	9500
.type	Submit	95	Yes	0
.value	GO	100	Yes	0
Total				9500

If you replay with default ScriptAssure settings, you get the message `AmbiguousRecognitionException`, as shown in Figure 1.52. This is because the two GOs are much the same.

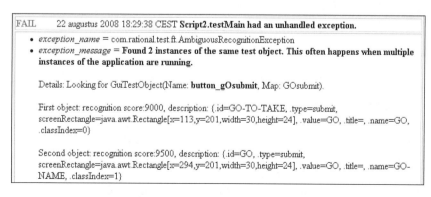

Figure 1.52 Log file with two instances of the same test object

When we decrease the Ambiguous recognition scores difference threshold to 200, for example, the script continues. So, the action attached to the GO-TO-TAKE button is used. If you are interested in verifying the properties of the object, the following is created in the object map, as shown in Figure 1.53.

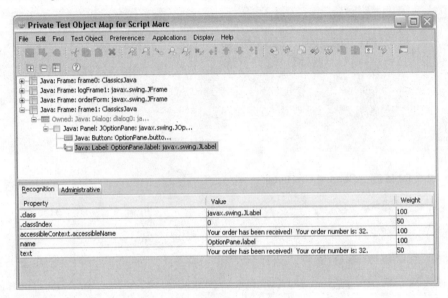

Figure 1.53   Created object in the object map

When you execute test script next time, the order number will not be 25. This results in penalty points, as shown in Figure 1.54.

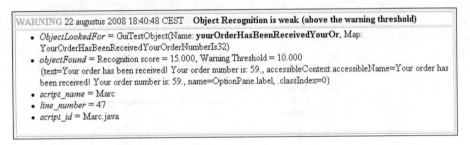

Figure 1.54   Log file displays a weak object recognition

By setting the weight of `accessibleContext.accessibleName` and text to 0, there is a full match, but the recognition power is weaker. A better approach is to apply a regular expression as a value. This can be created via the contextual menu on the value. In this case, use a decimal definition \d+ as shown in Figure 1.55. The point is preceded by a backslash because the point is also a special character. For additional information about regular expressions, refer to Appendix B, "Regular Expressions in Rational Functional Tester."

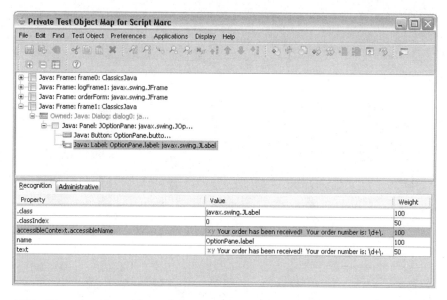

Figure 1.55 Property value with regular expression set

This sample is about the object to be searched for. For the changing value in the verification point, you can use a regular expression in the verification point.

ScriptAssure Playback Settings

The recognition and the warning levels can be influenced with settings at **Window > Preferences > Functional Test > Playback > ScriptAssure**.

The standard visualization gives two sliders to move in either direction, as shown in Figure 1.56. In line with the error messages and the calculation described previously, you can use the advanced visualization.

If you click the Advance button, you get what's shown in Figure 1.57.

The ScriptAssure Advanced page has the following controls:

- **Maximum acceptable recognition score**—Indicates the maximum score an object can have to be recognized as a candidate. Objects with higher recognition scores are not considered as matches until the time specified in Maximum time to attempt to find Test Object has elapsed.

- **Last chance recognition score**—Indicates the maximum acceptable score an object must have to be recognized as a candidate, if Functional Tester does not find a suitable match after the time specified in Maximum time to attempt to find Test Object has elapsed. Objects with higher recognition scores are not considered.

- **Ambiguous recognition scores difference threshold**—Writes an `Ambiguous-RecognitionException` to the log if the scores of top candidates differ by less than

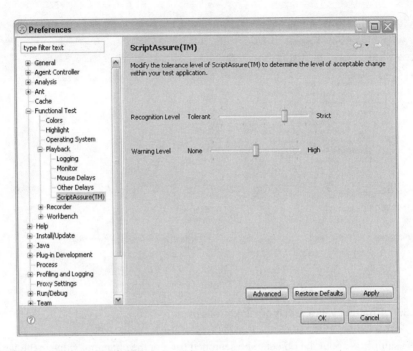

Figure 1.56   ScriptAssure preferences

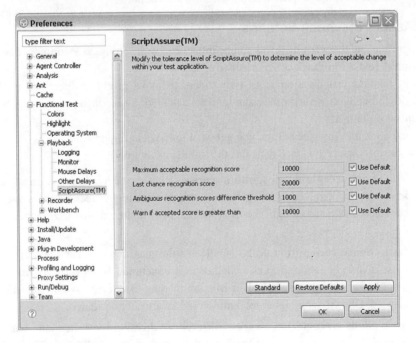

Figure 1.57   Advance ScriptAssure preferences

the value specified in this field. If Rational Functional Tester sees two objects as the same, the difference between their scores must be at least this value to prefer one object. You can override the exception by using an event handler in the script.

- **Warn if accepted score is greater than**—Writes a warning to the log if Rational Functional Tester accepts a candidate whose score is greater than or equal to the value in this field.

The Maximum time to attempt to find Test Object is defined in the general playback of Rational Functional Tester.

What are interesting settings? Defaults to start with because they work well. If you are in more of a dynamic user interface, you can increase the various values to acceptable levels. If you are doing acceptance testing, you can tighten the values and set the warn if option to 1. You always get a warning when something changes, but Rational Functional Tester continues to run.

Playback Settings

Rational Functional Tester provides a myriad of playback settings, available through its user interface. These settings enable you to control the behavior of how Rational Functional Tester handles such things as delays, logging, and object recognition. You can access the playback settings by selecting **Window > Preferences > Functional Test > Playback**. This launches a window similar to the one in Figure 1.58.

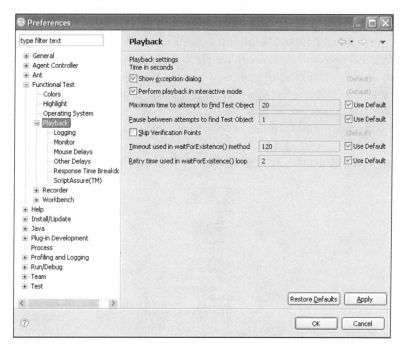

Figure 1.58   Primary playback settings for Eclipse

If you are using Rational Functional Tester VB.NET, you can access the playback settings by selecting **Tools > Options > Functional Test > Playback**. Figure 1.59 shows what the resulting Options window should look like when displaying the Playback settings.

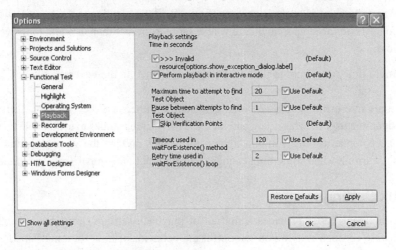

Figure 1.59   Primary playback settings for .NET Studio

You usually turn to the primary playback settings displayed in Figure 1.58 (Figure 1.59 for VB.NET) when you need to override Rational Functional Tester's default synchronization with the application under test (for example, its capability to wait long enough for the necessary GUI objects to render). When Rational Functional Tester isn't waiting long enough for your application to render a GUI object, you can access the playback settings and increase the Maximum time to attempt to find Test Object setting to more than 20 seconds. This tells Rational Functional Tester to wait longer for the object to render. This is useful when your application tends to have slow days.

When you further drill down into the playback settings, as shown in Figure 1.60, you can control mouse delays, keyboard delays, and Rational Functional Tester's Script Assure technology. Typically, you should focus mainly on adjusting your logging and Script Assure settings.

Figure 1.60   Playback settings: subsettings

Selecting the Logging option enables you to choose the type of log to write (for example, text, HTML, none, XML, and so on), and it enables you to specify the level of information to log, outside of what is captured by default. These options are displayed in Figure 1.61.

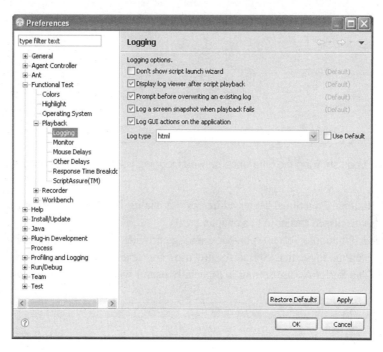

Figure 1.61   Playback settings: logging

There might be instances where you have to increase your level of logging to include GUI actions performed by your script. This is useful when trying to debug playback issues. You can see the actions that were performed up to the point where your script failed. To accomplish this, simply select the **Log GUI actions on the application** check box. Figure 1.62 shows a comparison between two RFT logs. The one on the left shows the default information that gets logged. The one on the right displays the default information along with the added GUI actions, enabling you to see the sequence of events your script performed.

The first log shows the default level of logging. It captures the major events of playback. These are things such as Script start, Start Application, and so on. The second log shows the major events plus it shows the GUI actions that were performed by IBM Rational Functional Tester. These are delineated by phrases such as, "click on the tree," "click on the button," and so on. You should choose to add the GUI actions into your log when runtime errors occur in your script. The extra logging helps narrow down where the problem is occurring.

The key to success for any automated test tool is the capability to find GUI objects (for example, buttons, checkboxes, combo boxes, and so on). This must occur *every* time a script

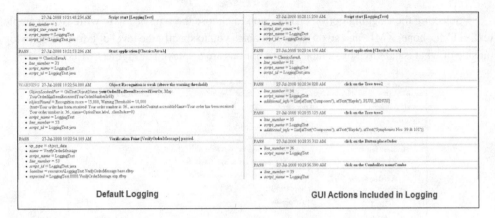

Default Logging   GUI Actions included in Logging

Figure 1.62   Logs showing the difference between logging your script's GUI actions and not logging them

plays back. Rational Functional Tester addresses this via its Test Object Map and Script Assure technology, as discussed earlier in this chapter.

Rational Functional Tester's playback settings provide you with the capability to control the fuzzy matching logic that Script Assure uses for object recognition. This is shown in Figure 1.63. The Script Assure setting is especially useful when you begin automating early in

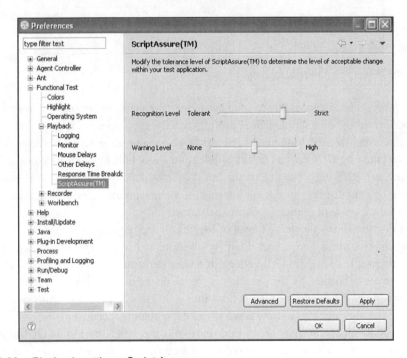

Figure 1.63   Playback settings: Script Assure

the GUI development lifecycle. GUI objects and their properties are unstable at this stage. Their internal values can, and often do, change multiple times. You can use the Script Assure playback settings to adjust IBM Rational Functional Tester's object recognition capabilities to handle this. Sliding the Recognition Level to the left (Tolerant) enables IBM Rational Functional Tester the freedom to find GUI objects, even when a couple of object recognition properties change. Clicking the **Advanced** button enables you to fine tune the fuzzy matching. You also come here to adjust the level of information to display in the test log when GUI object recognition values change. This is helpful for identifying where you need to make updates in your test object map. Warning messages are placed in your log file, citing which objects had recognition values that changed.

This section covered the more widely used playback settings. You might explore some of the other settings found here. Some reasons for doing so include:

- Tweaking a drag-and-drop action and using the mouse up and mouse down options found in the Mouse Delays subsetting.
- Turning the monitor display off during playback and using the Show monitor during playback option found in the Monitor subsetting.
- Turning off the log to test script playback and using the Log type option found in the Logging subsetting.

Summary

This chapter provided an overview of major IBM Rational Functional Tester functionalities. It started with a brief introduction to IBM Rational Functional Tester and how it can be installed. It then discussed its preference capabilities, followed by the simple record/playback against application under test. This chapter also explored how IBM Rational Functional Tester finds particular objects and the value of ScriptAssure. This chapter is a great place to learn the basics.

Storyboard Testing

Fariz Saracevic, Lee B. Thomas

This chapter explains the Storyboard Testing feature introduced in the 8.1 version of Rational Functional Tester. Storyboard Testing provides all the capabilities of Rational Functional Tester, but displays them in a manner that is easier to adopt and more productive for nontechnical users. The term Simplified Scripting is used interchangeably with Storyboard Testing to identify this new Rational Functional Tester capability. We use the term Storyboard Testing throughout the book to make it simpler for readers.

To enable you to easily compare Storyboard Testing to the traditional perspective, this chapter reuses the example from Chapter 1, "Overview of Rational Functional Tester." By the end of this chapter, you should understand how to record, play back, and edit scripts with Storyboard Testing, and you should know what options are available.

Overview of Storyboard Testing

This section provides an overview of the Storyboard Testing feature. Storyboard Testing is a new feature introduced in Rational Functional Tester version 8.1. Its purpose is to enable automated test creation by testers who might have significant subject matter expertise with application under test but might not have programming skills.

A Look Back at Test Automation

Originally, all test automation was done by programming. To use those early tools, testers had to learn a programming language and become proficient at it. This was a barrier for testers who might have had expertise in the subject matter of the business, but who had no training in programming.

Record-and-playback technology enabled nonprogrammers to create automated test scripts and execute them. However, if the application being tested was changed (as one would expect it would be in the course of maintaining it), then the test scripts often needed to be recorded again. Unless the automated script was executed frequently, the savings of a tester's time through test automation would decrease because maintenance of test automation required almost as much time as executing the tests manually.

The use of wizards simplified some tasks that would otherwise have required rerecording or programming, but for other tasks, the only recourse was to learn the programming language or assign the task to someone who did know the language. Again, the nontechnical user was shut out.

Whether the script was programmed or recorded, the fact that the script was represented as a program required the tester to visualize what the application looked like at each statement of the script, rather than by seeing the interface itself. This also tended to favor those with programming backgrounds because this kind of visualization is an essential part of a programmer's training.

Overall, test automation required too much skill in programming. Subject matter experts needed an easier way to create test automation, one that would not require them to become coders.

Rational Functional Tester provides this easier way. Storyboard Testing enables nontechnical users to see their scripts in a human language instead of in a programming language.

Similarities and Differences to Chapter 1

This section shows which sections of Chapter 1 are unchanged when you use Storyboard Testing and which sections of Chapter 1 do not apply without modification. Although Storyboard Testing gives nontechnical users great power to easily automate tests, when you use it you are creating, editing, and executing the same assets as in the traditional perspective. None of the underlying components of RFT are different; Storyboard Testing is just a new set of views of those components. You can refer to most of Chapter 1 whether you use Storyboard Testing or you don't. The following sections explain this.

Sections That Are Unchanged from Chapter 1

These sections at the beginning of Chapter 1 are unchanged for both the traditional Functional Test Perspective set of views and the new Storyboard Testing views:

- Architecture of Rational Functional Tester
- Installation and Licensing
- Enabling the Environment for Testing
- Configuring Applications for Testing
- Configuring Object Recognition Properties

Similarly, these sections at the end of Chapter 1 are unchanged for both perspectives:

- ScriptAssure
- Playback Settings

This means that you can install and configure the Rational Functional Tester in the same way, whether you use the Storyboard Testing feature or not. In fact, your Functional Test Project can contain scripts created with the feature and scripts created without the feature. You can edit both types of scripts in the same instance of Rational Functional Tester; there is no need to exit from Rational Functional Tester and restart it. All the integrations with other tools work identically for both types of Rational Functional Tester scripts.

Storyboard Testing works with all the environments you can enable and supports all the applications you can configure for testing. ScriptAssure and the playback settings work identically for both script types.

If you are administering Rational Functional Tester, you can deploy it to all your users in the same way, provided you or your nontechnical users enable the Storyboard Testing preference that is shown in the section "How to Enable Storyboard Testing" later in this chapter. If you are a nontechnical user, you do not need any special setup or configuration to use Storyboard Testing. Plus, your Storyboard Testing scripts can use all the features of Rational Functional Tester and can include any extensions created by a Java programmer. Your scripts are executed by Rational Functional Tester just like scripts created with the traditional perspective.

Sections That Differ from Chapter 1

Using Storyboard Testing is different from using the traditional Functional Test perspective set of views for these sections of Chapter 1:

- Recording a First Script
- Playing Back a Script and Viewing Results
- Script Editing and Augmentation

This means that you can install and configure the Rational Functional Tester in the same way whether you use the Storyboard Testing feature or not. In fact, your Functional Test Project can contain scripts created with the feature and scripts without the feature. You can edit both types of scripts within the same instance of Rational Functional Tester; there is no need to exit from Rational Functional Tester and restart it. All the integrations with other tools work identically for both types of Rational Functional Tester scripts.

Storyboard Testing works with all the environments you can enable and supports all the applications you can configure for testing. ScriptAssure and the playback settings work identically for both script types.

Enabling Storyboard Testing

Storyboard Testing is enabled by default in Rational Functional Tester; you do not need to do anything to be able to use it unless it has been disabled in your installed copy of Rational Functional Tester. The next section shows you how to disable and re-enable this feature. The section "Considerations for Enabling Storyboard Testing" explains how Rational Functional Tester operates when Storyboard Testing is enabled and disabled.

How to Enable Storyboard Testing

To enable Storyboard Testing, first open the Preferences dialog box by clicking **Window > Preferences**. In the dialog box, expand **Functional Test** in the left navigation pane, and then click **Simplified Scripting,** as shown in Figure 2.1. Finally, click the **Apply** button to save this preference. If you have no other preferences to change at this time, you can click the **OK** button to close the dialog box.

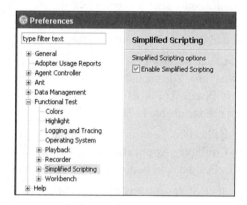

Figure 2.1   The option in Functional Test preferences to enable Storyboard Testing

Considerations for Enabling Storyboard Testing

When you check this preference, from that time forward, all new scripts you create (whether by recording or by editing an empty script) use Storyboard Testing. To return to the traditional perspective, uncheck this preference and all new scripts are recorded and edited in the traditional manner until you change this preference again.

This preference has no effect on scripts that already exist; Rational Functional Tester stores the type of script (Storyboard Testing or traditional) with the script, and opens the appropriate views in the Functional Test Perspective. You can edit Storyboard Testing scripts alongside traditional scripts within the same running instance of Rational Functional Tester and as you switch between the different script types. As you select a different type of script, the Functional Test Perspective changes the views to match the type of script being edited.

The Storyboard Testing feature includes additional preferences you can modify. Those preferences are explained later in this chapter. First, we cover how Storyboard Testing affects recording, playback, editing, and augmentation of scripts.

Recording a First Script

Storyboard Testing does not directly affect the recording process. The following sections are identical to the sections in Chapter 1, except explanations have been added to areas where you might notice a difference.

Before Recording

Prior to recording, you must have already created a Functional Test Project, enabled your application's environment within Rational Functional Tester, configured your application for testing, and ensured that the test environment has been configured correctly.

- To create a Functional Test Project, click the menu item **File > New > Project**, expand **Functional Test**, and then click **Functional Test Project**. Follow the steps of the wizard.

- To enable your application's environment, click the menu item **Configure > Enable Environments for Testing**, and then ensure that your application's environment is already enabled or add your environment with the help of the dialog.

- When Rational Functional Tester is installed, it enables the environments installed on your computer at that time. You should need to enable only environments that you have added after RFT is installed. For example, if you download Mozilla Firefox after installing RFT, you need to enable Firefox.

- To configure your application for testing by Rational Functional Tester, click the menu item **Configure > Configure Applications for Testing**, and if your application is not already configured, click the **Add** button and follow the steps in the wizard.

- To configure the test environment, ensure that your application has been installed correctly and can be executed outside of Rational Functional Tester (as if you were testing manually). Also, ensure that any data, files, or other items that your application uses have been set to the correct state for the test you are recording.

NOTE   It is advisable to disable instant messages, email programs, and any other applications in your computer's work environment that might interfere with your recording.

In the following sections, you use the ClassicsJavaA application that is provided with Rational Functional Tester as a sample. ClassicsJavaA does not require you to provide or reset any data or add or delete files to your file system, even if you execute it many times.

When the application under test is open, you can perform the steps as required by your test. You perform the test with these steps:

- Start the application.
- Choose a CD.
- Log in as the default user.
- Enter the required data into the form.
- Verify that the price of the CD is correct. (For this exercise, simply assume that the price is correct. You learn how to capture data. In actual testing, presumably you would have a reference that would enable you to verify the correctness of the displayed data.)

- Place the order.
- Exit the application.

It is normal for first-time users to perform actions that are unintentional and result in erroneous recorded steps in the script. Any user errors can be corrected later, so there is no need to stop recording and start over if you make a mistake.

Recording

To start recording, follow these steps:

1. Click the **Record a Functional Test Script** button, as shown in Figure 2.2.

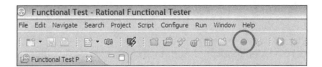

Figure 2.2 The Record a Functional Test Script button in the default Rational Functional Tester workbench

2. A new window opens up, as shown in Figure 2.3. Enter the test script name and select the project where it will be stored. The test script name must not contain any spaces or any special characters except **$** and _ (the underscore character). For this exercise, you can select any Functional Test Project, and you can use the name of the script as it was created by Rational Functional Tester.

3. Click **Finish.** The Rational Functional Tester window minimizes, and the Recording Monitor becomes available, as shown in Figure 2.4.

   You can interact with the Recording Monitor, and those interactions do not generate statements in the script unless you explicitly press a button in a dialog that is intended to create a statement. By default, the Recording Monitor displays a small row of buttons. You can expand it to display a list of reminders for common recording actions and to display a log of actions you perform.

4. Click the **Display Monitor** icon to open the Recording Monitor, as shown in Figure 2.5.

   You use another button on the Recording Monitor to start your application. This causes Rational Functional Tester to start your application every time the script is executed, which eliminates the need for you to open the application yourself. When you record the starting of the application in your script, you should remember to close your application at

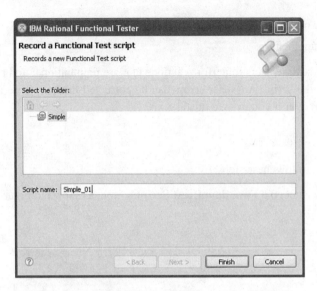

Figure 2.3   The Record a Functional Test Script window, where you select the project to store the script and define the name of the script

Figure 2.4   The Recording Monitor. The recorded interactions are shown here. The various icons give access to wizards accessing functions such as verification points.

the end of recording. In addition, prior to executing your script, you must remember to close all copies of your application that you might have open, so that Rational Functional Tester does not need to choose between multiple open copies, including the one started by the script.

5.   You now start the application under test. Click the **Start Application** icon and then click the application on the drop-down list, as shown in Figure 2.6. For this exercise, click **ClassicsJavaA**.

6.   Click **OK** to start the application. This causes Rational Functional Tester to add a statement to the script to start your application. You can see the statement that is in your script by looking at the Recording Monitor; see Figure 2.7.

In the Recording Monitor, you can see the difference between recording in the traditional perspective and recording with Storyboard Testing. Instead of a line from a programming language for starting the application, there is a line in English natural language.

7.   Click the + to the left of Bach to expand the tree, exposing two CD selections for that composer. Next, click **Violin Concertos** to select it. The ClassicsJavaA application and the Recording Monitor should now look like Figure 2.8.

8.   Click the **Place Order** button. The Member login dialog box should display; see Figure 2.9.

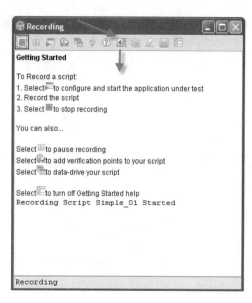

Figure 2.5 The Start Application window where you can select the application under text. This starts the application and generates an action in your script to start the application.

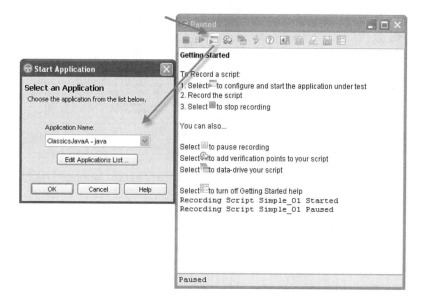

Figure 2.6 The Start Application window where you can select the application under text. This starts the application and generates an action in your script to start the application.

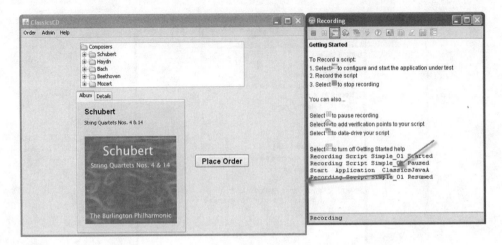

Figure 2.7   The Recording Monitor dialog where you can see an entry for the action to start the application under test

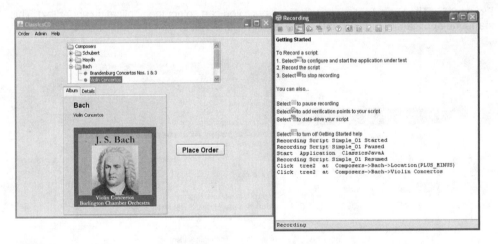

Figure 2.8   The ClassicsJavaA application with the Bach Violin Concerto selected

9. Log in with the default user by clicking the **OK** button. The Place an Order dialog box should display, as shown in Figure 2.10.

10. Fill in the Card Number field with data such as 4444 4444 4444 4444.

11. Click the **Expiration Date** field and enter data such as 02/2012. See Figure 2.11.

To prove that the application under test produces the same answers when you run the test script as when you recorded it, your test script must be enhanced with verification points.

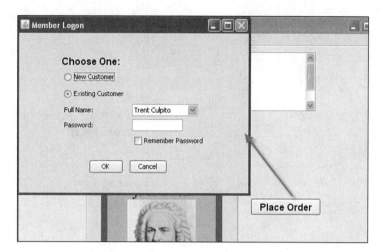

Figure 2.9 The Member Login dialog box

Figure 2.10 The Place an Order dialog box

Figure 2.11   The completed Place an Order dialog box

A *verification point* is a check that the actual data and its properties shown in the currently executing application match your expectations for the data and properties. Our expectations are called the baseline. A difference between actual and baseline causes Rational Functional Tester to write a fail status for the verification point into the execution log. Verification points are important because they are the only means in Rational Functional Tester to confirm that the application under test gives correct information to its users.

12. As part of your testing of ClassicsJavaA, you need to verify that the total price displayed is $15.99. Click the **Verification Point and Action Wizard** icon in the Recording Monitor, as shown in Figure 2.12. The Verification Point and Action Wizard displays, as shown in Figure 2.13.

13. Click the **hand** icon, but hold down the mouse button. Drag the **hand** icon to the $15.99 value. To indicate your selection, a red rectangle is drawn around the text of the total, as shown in Figure 2.14. Release the mouse button to select this text for verification.

When you release the cursor, the properties of the object selected become visible at the

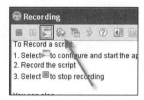

Figure 2.12   Clicking the Verification Point and Action Wizard icon causes the Recording Monitor window to disappear and the Wizard to display.

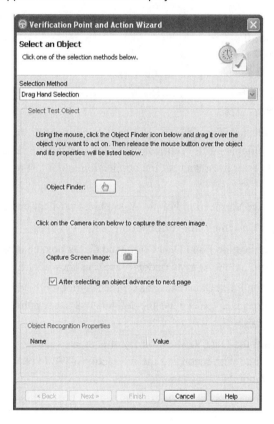

Figure 2.13   The Verification Point and Action Wizard gives you the options to identify the object to be verified.

bottom of the wizard. You can use those properties to confirm that you have selected the correct object.

In this window, you can define what kind of verification point has to be created. These are the available options:

• Data Verification—Use to validate the displayed text of an object.

Figure 2.14   When you drag the hand icon over an object in the application, Functional Tester displays a red rectangle that enables you to confirm that you have selected the correct object.

- Properties Verification—Use to validate one or more properties of an object, including its text (if any), font, color, or any combination of properties (for example, if it is both selected and has a particular color).

- Get a Specific Property Value—Use to get a specific property value so it can be tested in your script.

- Wait for Selected Test Object—Rational Functional Tester waits until this object becomes available. This verification point is used in situations where Rational Functional Tester must wait for the application under test to create a window or dialog box.

- Perform Image Verification Point—A graphical verification point.

14. For this exercise, use the Data Verification Point. Click **Next**.

15. In the Insert Verification Point Data Command dialog box, change the name of the verification point from _1599_text to Order_Total, as shown in Figure 2.15. Click **Next**.

16. In the Verification Point Data dialog box, you can modify the data or affect how it is verified. For this exercise, you can use the defaults that are supplied by Rational Functional Tester. Click **Finish**.

    At this moment, the Data Verification Point is created and inserted as code in the program. We continue with recording the interactions. While recording, you can add various verification points.

17. In the ClassicsJavaA Place an Order window, click the **Place Order** button. A dialog box should display, showing that your order has been received; see Figure 2.16. Click the **OK** button, and this dialog box should disappear.

18. Close ClassicsJavaA by clicking on the **X** in the upper right-hand corner of the ClassicsJavaA window; see Figure 2.17. All ClassicsJavaA windows (there should be only one at this point) should disappear.

19. Click the **Stop Recording** button in the Recording Monitor window, as shown in Figure 2.18. The Rational Functional Tester main screen automatically reappears, displaying your test script (see Figure 2.19).

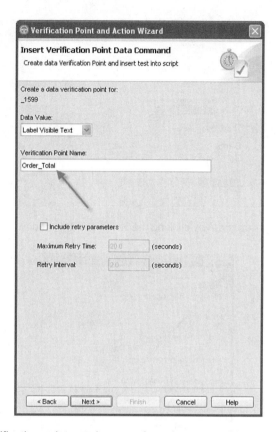

Figure 2.15 The verification point gets its name from the name of the object you select, but you can use a more meaningful name instead.

Figure 2.16 Your order has been received, and the dialog shows your order number.

Your Recorded Script

After recording, you can view your test script in a test view. This view is also an editor, so you can make changes at this time. Editing is discussed in the "Script Editing and Augmentation" section.

Test View, Script Tab

The most noticeable change from the traditional views is the scripting language. For Storyboard Testing, the test script is represented in English statements. During recording, Rational

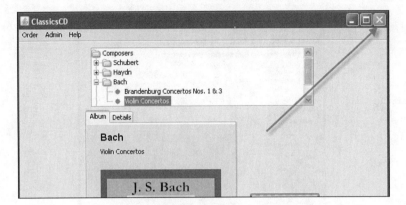

Figure 2.17   Close ClassicsJavaA by clicking the X to close the window.

Figure 2.18   The Stop Recording button stops recording, causing the Rational Functional Tester main window to reappear.

Functional Tester inserts statements into the script corresponding to the actions you performed in recording the test. See Figure 2.20.

Each time a new window or dialog box displays in the application under test, Rational Functional Tester creates a new group. The name of the group is the same as the caption for the window or dialog box. All the actions taken in that window or dialog box are indented under that group. You can rename a group by clicking on the name of the group and typing a new name.

Each statement begins with an icon indicating the type of object acted upon by the statement. A statement clicking in a tree has a tree icon, a statement clicking on a button has a button icon, and so on.

The action, such as click or type, is followed by the name of the object being acted upon. In some cases, this is followed by where in the object the action should occur, as with clicking on the portion of the tree that contains the Bach Violin Concertos CD being represented as **Composers > Bach > ViolinConcertos**.

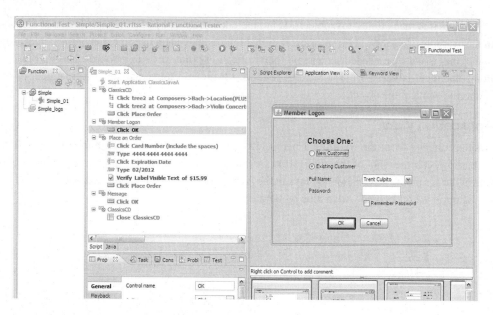

Figure 2.19　The appearance of Rational Functional Tester after recording a script with Storyboard Testing enabled.

Figure 2.20　A Storyboard Testing script, showing statements in groups. Nontechnical users find that these scripts are easier to read than the equivalent programming language.

Verification points begin with an icon for a checkmark on a page, followed by the word Verify. This is followed by the verifying action that you selected: Verify Data in the object, Verify Properties of the object, Get Property of the object and which property to get, Delay Execution for the existence of the object, and Verify Image of the object.

Note that many times, text objects do not include a proper object name; this is true of the total in the example of $15.99. In these cases, Rational Functional Tester uses the text of the object as its name; this is why we needed to rename the verification point to `Order_Total`. The Verification Point statement is Verify Data in $15.99, reflecting Rational Functional Tester's treatment of the text as the name of the object.

Application View

Another change from the traditional perspective is the presence of the Application view. This view shows a screenshot of the application for each action in the script. If you click a particular line in the script, the screenshot displays in the Application view, and the particular object you are acting upon is highlighted with a blue rectangle. See Figure 2.21.

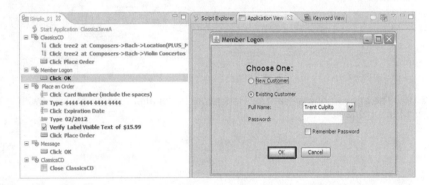

Figure 2.21   A Storyboard Testing script, showing the screenshot in the Application view. You have just clicked the line Click Place Order in the script, and the Place Order button is highlighted in the screenshot.

If you hover your mouse cursor over an object in the screenshot in the Application view, the object is outlined in red. This enables you to see the various "user interface controls"—the objects you can act on or verify—that are used in the application.

You can change the colors used for highlight and for hover by clicking the View menu at the upper left of the Application view; see Figure 2.22. Selecting one of the items brings up a color palette that permits you to change the color to one you prefer.

If you click successive lines of your script, you can use the Application view to visualize how you drove the application during recording. This is useful if someone other than you created the recording; you can see what they did by reading the script or by looking at the screenshots of the application.

In addition, the bottom of the Application view shows all the screenshots from the application under test, in small thumbnail form. See Figure 2.23. If you hover your mouse over one of

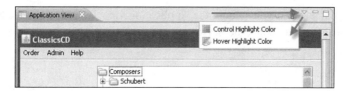

Figure 2.22   The View Menu for the Application View enables you to change the color used for highlighting the object (or control) that you acted upon when you were recording and change the color used when you hover your mouse cursor over an object.

these screenshots, it automatically enlarges into a new dialog so you can see it clearly. To close one of these enlarged views, click anywhere in the Rational Functional Tester main window. You can also add comments to these thumbnail screenshots to give a reminder to yourself or someone else about a particular screen or object.

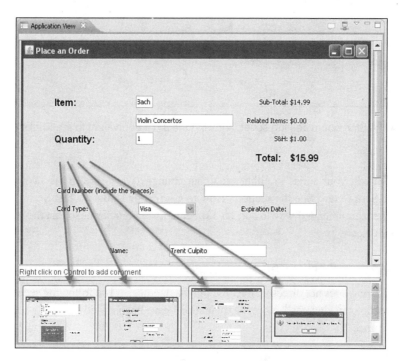

Figure 2.23   The bottom of the Application view contains thumbnail views of all the screens you visited when you created your recording. Any screens you did not visit are not shown.

Storyboard Testing View, Java Tab

Click the **Java** tab at the bottom of the Script view; it is the tab to the right of the Script tab. You can click these two tabs to switch between the English statements and the Java statements. See

Figure 2.24. Note that when you switch, the Application view is hidden and the Script Explorer view becomes visible. If you click the **Script** tab, the Application view reappears.

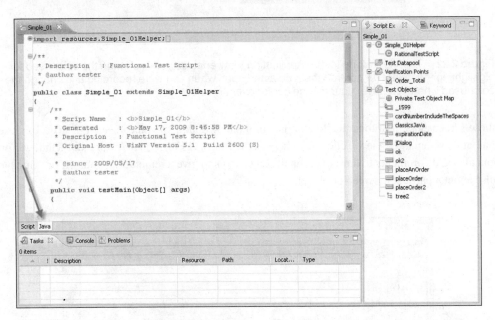

Figure 2.24   A Storyboard Testing script, showing the Java equivalent to the English language statements

You can edit your script in either view, but changes you make in the Java view are not shown in the Script view. See the section "How to Correct or Update a Test Script" later in this chapter for the recommended way to add Java statements to your script so that the statements are visible in both views.

Playing Back a Script and Viewing Results

Storyboard Testing does not directly affect the playback process. The following sections are identical to the sections in Chapter 1, except explanations have been added to areas where you might notice a difference.

Resetting the Test Environment Prior to Playback

To play back successfully, you must reset your application to its original state. For the example, the ClassicsJavaA application was closed. If you create a recording that begins with your application open and display a particular screen, you should reset the application to that screen prior to playing back the script. You should ensure that no other windows or dialogs from your application are open. You should also close any other applications or browser windows that are open; your desktop should look the same as it did when you recorded your script.

In addition, you should reset the test environment to the same condition it was in when you created the recording. This might require that you delete data you created during the recording process. For example, your application might not allow you to create two records by entering the same data. To play back your script, you should first delete the record.

ClassicsJavaA does not require you to provide or reset any data or add or delete files to your file system, even if you execute it many times. For this exercise, you can proceed directly to playing back the script. However, when you are testing your own application, you should ensure that you have correctly reset your test environment.

Playing Back the Script

It is possible to detect differences between what you see in the current application build and excepted result by playing back a test script.

NOTE   When you use Rational Quality Manager as your test management solution, executing a test case causes the test script to be executed. Execution is started from the web interface of Rational Quality Manager.

---

1. Click the **Run Functional Test Script** button in the menu (you can also right-click a specific test script and click **Run** on the pop-up menu). You are prompted to specify log file name as shown in Figure 2.25.

Figure 2.25   The Select Log window

2. Define the name of the test log in the **Select Log** window. For this example, you can select the default, which is the same as the name of your script but uses a different file extension.

3. Click the **Finish** button. Test execution begins. Because Rational Functional Tester requires exclusive access to the mouse and keyboard, it is not possible for you to use other applications, lock the computer, or allow the screensaver to become active while the test is executing. If you move the mouse during execution, Rational Functional Tester may click on the wrong object. If you make a window active during execution, Rational Functional Tester will direct all its input to that window. Either of these actions can cause your script to fail.

4. Watch the progress of the playback. Note any behavior in your application that does not match the behavior it exhibited when you recorded the script.

In the Playback Monitor, you can see which statement Rational Functional Tester is executing. Rational Functional Tester spends the bulk of the time during playback waiting for objects to appear or to become active. When the test execution ends, the Rational Functional Tester editing window reappears.

View Results

If you selected the HTML log type or left the log file preference set at the default, a browser appears to display the execution log file. You can also double-click a log file in Rational Functional Tester to view it. The HTML log file contains three sections that enable you to navigate quickly through the display:

- Failures
- Warnings
- Verification Points

You can click any of these entries in these sections, and the browser scrolls to display that entry in detail, as shown in Figure 2.26.

In the case of a failing verification point, you can view the difference between expected and actual by clicking the **View Results** hyperlink. This activates the Verification Point Comparator, as shown in Figure 2.27. You should not have a failing verification point; the figure has been captured from a different script.

With the Verification Point Comparator, you can update the baseline with the Replace Baseline with actual result option. It is also possible to start the Verification Point Comparator directly from the logs in Rational Functional Tester.

Timing Issues

It might be that playback failed with a timeout error. This occurs because Rational Functional Tester attempts to play back your script as fast as possible, and sometimes your application runs slower than usual. For example, excessive network traffic might slow your application's capability

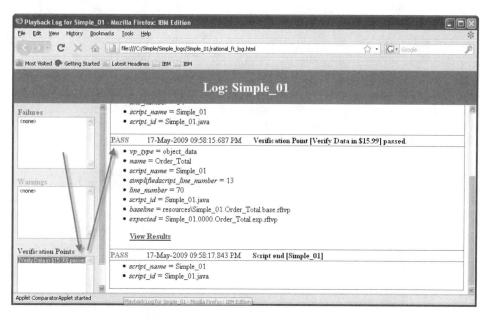

Figure 2.26   An example log file in HTML format

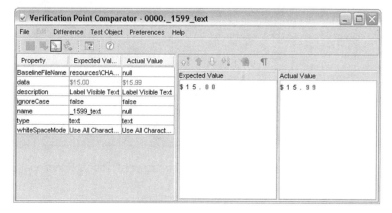

Figure 2.27   When a verification point fails, you can view the differences between expected and actual. The baseline can be updated.

to retrieve data from a server. One way to correct for this and enable your script to execute is to slow down the script execution. Several options are available:

- Slow down by modifying the Rational Functional Tester "Multiply all time operations by" preference, as shown in Figure 2.28. If you change this value to a 2, your script takes roughly twice as long to execute. Setting the value to 3 makes your script run 3 times as long. For example, a script that would run in 5 minutes if the value was 1, would take about 15 minutes for a value of 3, and so on for other values. However, changing this value to 3 also makes Rational Functional Tester wait 3 times as long for responses from your application, which is exactly the desired effect when the application is responding 3 times slower than usual. You should remember to reset this parameter because otherwise all test scripts you execute run slower.

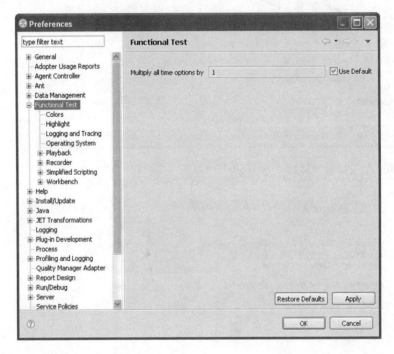

Figure 2.28   The Multiply all time operations by preference for Rational Functional Tester. Reset when running in production.

- Adding a sleep statement. This statement causes Rational Functional Tester to wait for a specified number of seconds. Note that Rational Functional Tester always waits for this number of seconds, even if your application happens to be running fast. You can add a sleep statement by finding a line of your script that is before where the timeout occurs; the sleep statement is added after the line you select. You then click the **Insert Recording into Active Functional Test Script** icon on the Rational Functional Tester toolbar. When the Recording Monitor displays, click the **Insert Script Support Commands** icon. In the Script Support Functions dialog box, click the **Sleep** tab. Enter the number of seconds you would like Rational Functional Tester to wait, then click the **Insert Code** button. Next, click the **Close** button. Finally, click the **Stop Recording** icon.

- Adding a `waitForExistence` verification point. If your script fails with a timeout error because a window, dialog box, or some other object does not display quickly enough, you can insert a `waitForExistence` verification point. As with adding a sleep statement, you find the point in your script where the dialog should display. Typically, this is the first statement in a group where the group contains the name of the new window or dialog. Click the **Insert Recording into Active Functional Test Script** icon on the Rational Functional Tester toolbar. When the Recording Monitor displays, click the **Verification Point and Action Wizard** icon. Drag the hand onto the window or dialog or other object, and then release the mouse button. In the Verification Point and Action Wizard dialog box, click **Wait for Selected Test Object**. Click **Next**. The default is for Rational Functional Tester to test to see if the object exists, and if it does, proceed with the remainder of the test script. If the object does not exist, Rational Functional Tester waits for the Check Interval, which is by default 2 seconds, and then test again to see if the object exists. This test-and-wait cycle continues until either the object finally exists, or else the Maximum Wait Time is reached. The default Maximum Wait Time is 120 seconds, or 2 minutes.

- If a `waitForExistence` verification point fails with a timeout error, you can change the Maximum Wait Time to a larger value. You can add the retry parameters to the other verification points (except for Get a Specific Property Value), either during recording or while editing.

Script Editing and Augmentation

Storyboard Testing makes several major changes to the editing and augmentation process. The following sections are similar to the sections in Chapter 1, but the major simplifications that Storyboard Testing permits are described here.

There are many reasons why you should edit and augment a test in Rational Functional Tester. You edit a test to:

- Correct an error or unintended behavior in the test
- Update tests to work with newer application builds
- Separate longer tests into smaller modular tests
- Integrate tests with other automated tests
- Verify functionality or other system requirements
- Associate test data with a test
- Modify or manipulate playback timing

- Modify or control test flow
- Add logging and reporting of test results
- Improve test readability and reuse

How to Correct or Update a Test Script

The most frequent type of editing you probably perform to a test script is fixing or updating. After you finish reading this book and start employing the best test script development practices, these corrections and updates should be short and simple. The two general steps in this activity are removing unwanted test script lines and adding new lines. This section does not go into details of debugging here, but describes the general editing steps to do this.

Removing Lines from a Test Script

You can remove unwanted lines of a Storyboard Testing test script in two ways: by deleting the lines or by disabling them. You always want to begin with the latter because you might need to restore the original lines. You can disable multiple lines of a test script as follows:

1. Select multiple lines of the script by clicking the first line to disable, holding down the Shift key, clicking on the last line to disable, and releasing the Shift key. All the lines should have a dark blue background indicating they are selected. See Figure 2.29.

Figure 2.29   Highlighting multiple lines in a script

2. With your mouse cursor over the highlighted lines, right-click to bring up the popup menu, and click **Enable/Disable Action**. (The word Action refers to the action Rational

Functional Tester takes against the application under test, not your action of enabling or disabling.) See Figure 2.30.

Figure 2.30 The popup menu that displays when you right-click with one or more lines highlighted

3. Click another line in the script to see that the selected lines are disabled. See Figure 2.31.

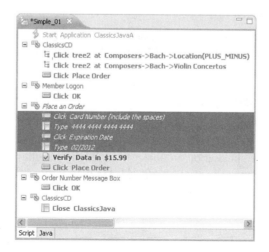

Figure 2.31 The lines are disabled because they appear in a light, italic font.

Adding Lines to a Test Script

You can add new lines to a test script by inserting a recording into an existing script or by manually adding lines. Refer to the section "How to Use the Application View" later in this chapter for an explanation of manually adding code to a test script.

It is typically easier to add lines with the recorder. This is easy to do, although you have to ensure that the newly recorded steps flow correctly with the existing recorded steps. You can record new lines in an existing script as follows:

1. Execute the application under test, driving it to the point where you want to add steps to your script. You can start your application, if necessary, either as you normally do outside of Rational Functional Tester or by starting it from the menu item **Configure > Configure Applications for Testing**, where the dialog has a Run button.

2. Click the line in the test script where you want to add new steps. The steps are added after the line you select.

3. Click **Script > Insert Recording** from the menu, or click the **toolbar** button. You immediately go into recording mode.

4. Perform the actions you want to add to your script.

5. Click the **Stop** button to finish the recording.

Just as you must ensure that you choose the correct starting point for your new steps, you must also ensure that the step immediately after your new steps is able to execute. For example, if you finish recording without closing a dialog box, the next step in your script attempts to act on that dialog box. If it should act on a window instead, you should be certain to close the dialog box before stopping your recording.

Moving Lines in a Test Script

You can move a line in your test script by clicking on it to highlight it, then dragging it to the new location and releasing the mouse button. An I-cursor displays the location where the line moves when you release the mouse button.

How to Use the Application View

The next most frequent type of editing you likely do to a test is update your script by selecting an object in the Application view and adding an action against it to your script.

You can do this by clicking on an object to highlight it, right-clicking, and selecting an action from the pop-up menu. The statement is added to your script.

The specific actions you are able to perform depend on the type of object you have selected, but in general, you are able to insert a command, insert a comment, insert a verification point, or update the visual.

For this example, you add selecting a credit card type to the script, after entering the card number and expiration date. You can also drag any object from the Application view and drop it into your script. This inserts an action on the object, which is typically to click it. After the statement is inserted, you can go to the Properties view to change the type of action; see Figure 2.32.

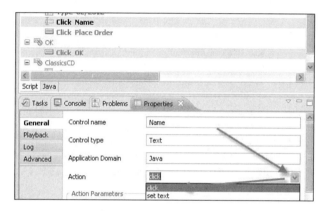

Figure 2.32   Changing the action on an object via the Properties view

NOTE   The default actions can be modified by editing the file C:\Program Files\IBM\SDP\FunctionalTester\bin\simplifiedScriptAction.rftssa.

Finally, you can select a Group statement in the Script view, and then in the Application view, you can add verification points for all the objects on a screen from the right-click menu.

Properties View

The Properties view enables you to see and edit properties for the line you have selected in your script. The properties are grouped into General, Playback, Log, and Advanced tabs. Each tab contains specific properties that depend on the particular line you have selected. See Figure 2.33.

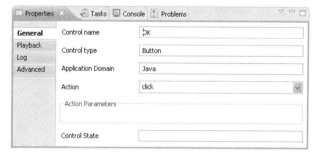

Figure 2.33   The Properties tab enables you to change properties of any statement in your script.

Datapools

While you are recording, you can insert data drive commands in the same way as described in the "Datapools" section of Chapter 1. The command that is inserted for Storyboard Testing is shown in Figure 2.34.

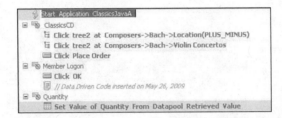

Figure 2.34   In Storyboard Testing, a data drive command appears as Set Value...From Datapool Retrieved.

In addition, you can insert a data drive command from the Application view. Find the location in your script where you would like to drive an object using datapool data. In the Application view, right-click the object, and click **Insert Data Driven Commands**, as shown in Figure 2.35.

Figure 2.35   Inserting a data drive command from the Application view

Adding Programming Code to Your Tests

You can insert (or have someone insert for you) Java code into your script. This can be done either by right-clicking in the **Script** view and selecting **Insert Java code snippet**, or **Insert Java method**. When you select one of these options, template Java code with TODO comment will be inserted under **Java** tab in the Test View. Your Java code should be placed instead of TODO comment. All changes made with either right-click option are visible in the Script view as a single line indicating additions in Java.

Other Script Enhancements

So far, you have seen several ways to edit test scripts to modify, complete, enhance, or extend their capabilities. Another purpose of editing tests is to improve their readability and potential reuse. This is done by adding comments and descriptions, naming or renaming test elements, and possibly restructuring test scripts into smaller modular tests.

Comments and Descriptions

In a given testing effort, you create many tests, object maps, datapools, and other test elements. Most likely, other people have to use or reference these same test artifacts. Comments and descriptions should be added to test artifacts and elements to explain their purposes, usages, and any other relevant information. This makes it much easier for people other than the test's creator to understand. This also increases the value of the tests as software development artifacts.

You add comments directly into the test scripts. You can add as many as you like without affecting the execution, and in general, the more, the better. You can add comments during recording using the Script Support Functions, or at any time after recording. To add a comment, right-click a statement in the Script view and click **Insert Comment**. Your comment is added after the statement you selected.

Setting Preferences for Storyboard Testing

The Storyboard Testing feature includes additional preferences you can modify. This section describes each preference and gives an example of how that preference affects your script when the preference is checked and when it is not checked.

Preferences for Application Visuals

The Storyboard Testing preference can be expanded in the left-hand navigation area of the Preference dialog box. Expanding it shows a selection that enables you to change preferences for Application Visuals, as shown in Figure 2.36.

If this preference is unchecked, the other preferences are not available.

Enable Capturing of Application Visuals

By default, Rational Functional Tester captures application visuals while you are recording. If you click the check box to deselect this preference, application visuals are not recorded for any script you subsequently record. You need to rerecord the script to add application visuals to it. Deselecting this preference also causes the other preferences for Application Visuals to be grayed out.

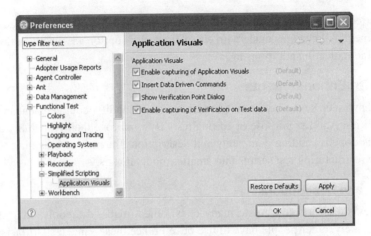

Figure 2.36   The options within Storyboard Testing for Application Visuals

Insert Data-Driven Commands

If you select to insert data-driven commands, a datapool is associated with your script during recording. As you interact with objects during recording, you can add the objects to the datapool as columns, and the statements include actions to retrieve the data from the datapool instead of using the data you type.

Show Verification Point Dialog

If you select to show Verification Point dialog, the Verification Point wizard dialog box will be presented when you are selecting the Data Verification Points using the Application View.

Enable Capturing of Verification on Test Data

Select the check box to enable the option to capture verification on test data, and during recording, Rational Functional Tester will capture and persist all the verification point data associated with the object available on an application under test page. This will allow you to insert Data Verification Points using the application visuals displayed in the Application View.

Summary

This chapter provided an overview of the Storyboard Testing feature of Rational Functional Tester. The chapter started with similarities to the traditional perspective of Rational Functional Tester and showed that installation, configuration, and major options work unchanged in either perspective. Then the chapter duplicated the example of Chapter 1 in recording and playing back against an application under test. You should now be able to create, modify, and execute scripts in a natural manner.

General Script Enhancements

Chip Davis, Daniel Chirillo, Daniel Gouveia

Record and playback can be a successful technique when automating your test cases. It provides a quick and simple means to create the minute programs that verify pieces of your application. Of course, the degree of success for this technique depends upon the complexity of the application you are testing. The more complex your application becomes (for example, using third-party controls, multiple tiers of communication, and so on), the less successful a record-and-playback approach becomes.

This chapter is meant to serve as a next step to simply recording and playing back scripts. It serves as a basis for you to build core test automation skills. Subsequent chapters expound on some of the topics found in this chapter. However, before you run (for example, debugging your custom scripting, handling custom controls, building your own proxies, and so on), you must learn to walk. Here you learn to take steps toward running with any automation effort. These steps include: learning how to synchronize your scripts with any latency found in your application, manipulating data, using the Clipboard object (think, "cut, copy, and paste"), working with the data found in a test object, creating your own custom verification points, and developing your own custom methods that reuse one or more of these techniques.

Test Script Synchronization

It is critical for script playback to stay synchronized with the application it tests. In Chapter 1, "Overview of Rational Functional Tester," you saw that Rational Functional Tester had playback settings that enabled you to increase the amount of time it would wait for a GUI object to render. The playback settings affect all scripts, not just the ones with which you are experiencing issues.

Further, they are specific to each installation of Rational Functional Tester. You need to be cognizant of this when your team members want to run your scripts from their installations.

This section focuses on building synchronization right into your scripts. You learn how to free yourself from the dependencies of installation-specific, global playback settings. Topics covered include:

- Creating general delays in your scripts using the `sleep()` methods
- Introducing intelligent delays into your scripts using the `waitForExistence()` methods
- Writing delays that are triggered by object properties
- Using timers to understand how long a piece of your script takes to execute

The aim of this section is to help you become familiar with enhancing Rational Functional Tester's default synchronization without being dependent upon global settings. If you build the necessary delays into your scripts, you can take advantage of them from any installation of Rational Functional Tester without the need to adjust playback settings.

Placing a Generic Delay in Your Script

Enhancing Rational Functional Tester's default synchronization can be as simple as adding a generic delay to your script. You can use the `sleep()` method (`Sleep()` function in the .NET version). This is available to you while recording or via coding.

When you are recording and notice that your application is slow to respond, you can turn to the Script Support Functions button on your toolbar. This is shown in Figure 3.1.

Figure 3.1   The Script Support Functions button on the Recording toolbar

Engaging this button provides you with the option to place a `sleep()` method into your script. Please refer to Figure 3.2 for a visual reference.

To use this function, you specify the number of seconds that you think your script will need to handle any latency issues with your application. You then click the **Insert** button. If you were using the Eclipse version of Rational Functional Tester, you would see a line in your script that looks like the following:

```
sleep(2.0);
```

Otherwise, using the .NET Studio version of Rational Functional Tester, you would see:

```
Sleep(2.0)
```

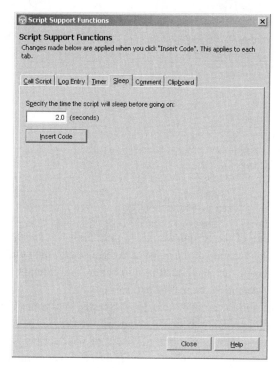

Figure 3.2 Script Support Functions Sleep tab

Listing 3.1 shows what these lines look like in the context of a test script:

Listing 3.1 Using `sleep()` / `Sleep()` in a script

Java

```
public void testMain(Object[] args)
{
        startApp("ClassicsJavaA");

        // PAUSE EXECUTION, USING sleep() METHOD, FOR 2 SECONDS
        sleep(2.0);

        // Frame: ClassicsCD
        tree2().performTest(VerifyComposerListVP());
        classicsJava(ANY,MAY_EXIT).close();
}
```

VB.NET
```
Public Function TestMain(ByVal args() As Object) As Object
      StartApp("ClassicsJavaA")


      ' PAUSE EXECUTION, USING sleep() METHOD, FOR 2 SECONDS
      Sleep(2.0)


      ' Frame: ClassicsCD
      Tree2().PerformTest(VerifyComposerListVP())
      ClassicsJava(ANY,MAY_EXIT).Close()
      Return Nothing
End Function
```

If you execute either of the scripts displayed in Listing 3.1, execution pauses when it hits the `sleep()` method. The duration of the pause is determined by the number of seconds that was specified in the argument to the method (the number in the parentheses). In the case of the examples in Listing 3.1, execution pauses for two seconds.

You also have the ability to code these lines directly into your scripts. For instance, you might not have recorded these delays because you didn't experience poor performance with your application while recording. However, upon playback of your scripts, you see periodic latency issues that surpass the default synchronization built into Rational Functional Tester. Using, the playback logs, you can find out what object was unable to be found on playback. This enables you to go into your script and code in the necessary `sleep()` lines. Please remember that you need to provide, as an argument to the method, the number of seconds to pause. This should be a floating number (for example, 2.0, 3.5, and so on).

The benefit of using the `sleep()` method is that you can now place extended synchronization capabilities right within your scripts, freeing you from the dependency of global playback settings. The downside of using the `sleep()` method is you are dealing with a static period of time. In other words, your script has to pause for the specified period of time regardless of whether or not the application responds faster than anticipated.

Waiting for Test Objects to Come into Existence

When GUI objects aren't rendered in a timely manner, you simply want your script to wait until they appear. Chapter 1 discussed the pros and cons of using global delay settings (for example, using Rational Functional Tester's playback settings). You also just learned about using the `sleep()` method in the previous section. This is helpful because the delay is specific to a script, releasing your dependencies on the global tool settings. However, it is a static delay. It waits until a specified number of seconds elapse, regardless of whether the GUI object appears sooner or not. This section discusses a happy medium between the global delay settings and the `sleep()` method.

The Rational Functional Java API provides a useful `waitForExistence()` method or `WaitForExistence()` function if you're using VB.NET. In either case, it comes in two variants. One is dependent upon global playback settings. The other is script-specific.

To use this method, you need to call it from a test object. Simply put, you need to tell your script which object to wait for. You can either type the name of the object, followed by opening and closing parentheses, directly into your code and hit the period key, or you can simply place your cursor in the script where you wish the command to go, right-click the test object in the Test Objects folder (within the Script Explorer view), and click **Insert at Cursor** from the displayed menu. Either of these two options displays an IntelliSense drop-down window (some people refer to this as "code complete"). This window provides you with a list of methods and functions that you can call. Typing the word wait shows you the methods and functions that begin with wait. The `waitForExistence()` method is among them. Figures 3.3 and 3.4 show how to call the `waitForExistence()` method, using the Eclipse and .NET Studio environments, respectively.

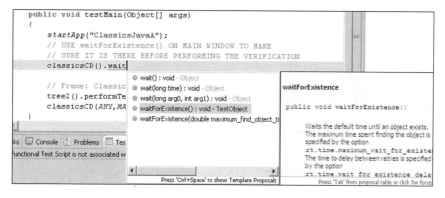

Figure 3.3 Calling the `waitForExistence()` method—Java language

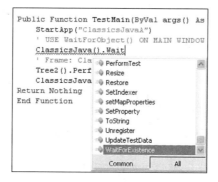

Figure 3.4 Calling the `WaitForExistence()` function—VB.NET language

If you use the Java language, you need to append a semicolon at the end of the line. If you use the VB.NET language, you are set and there is nothing further to do. Listing 3.2 shows you how the command looks in the same Rational Functional Tester script, using Java and VB.NET, respectively.

Listing 3.2 Using `waitForExistence()` / `WaitForExistence()` in a script

Java
```
public void testMain(Object[] args)
{
        startApp("ClassicsJavaA");

    // USE waitForExistence() ON MAIN WINDOW TO MAKE
    // SURE IT IS THERE BEFORE PERFORMING VERIFICATION
    classicsJava().waitForExistence();

    // Frame: ClassicsCD
    tree2().performTest(VerifyComposerListVP());
    classicsJava(ANY,MAY_EXIT).close();
}
```

VB.NET
```
Public Function TestMain(ByVal args() As Object) As Object
    StartApp("ClassicsJavaA")

    ' USE WaitForExistence() ON MAIN WINDOW TO MAKE
    ' SURE IT IS THERE BEFORE PERFORMING VERIFICATION
    ClassicsJava().WaitForExistence()

    ' Frame: ClassicsCD
    Tree2().PerformTest(VerifyComposerListVP())
    ClassicsJava(ANY,MAY_EXIT).Close()
    Return Nothing
End Function
```

In Listing 3.2, `ClassicsJava()` is a test object, representing the main window of the application. You call this test object's `waitForExistence()` method to tell your script that it needs to wait until this object appears, prior to executing the next line. The value of this method is that it immediately continues execution of the script after the test object renders on the screen (versus waiting a static period of time). However, this particular variant of the method is dependent upon global delay settings accessed from Rational Functional Tester's primary playback settings. Figures 3.5 and 3.6 show these options for Java and VB.NET.

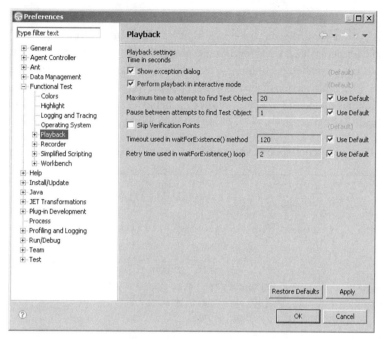

Figure 3.5   Primary playback settings—`waitForExistence()` options in Java

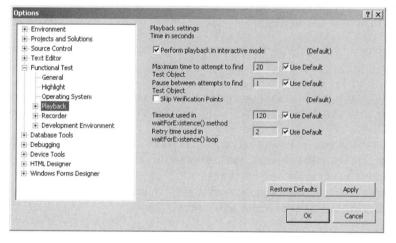

Figure 3.6   Primary playback settings—`WaitForExistence()` options in VB.NET

The last two settings are specific to the `waitForExistence()`/`WaitForExistence()` method. If you want to change how long it waits or how often it checks for a test object's existence, you simply override the defaults and supply your own values. You should note that using this variant of the method keeps you dependent upon Rational Functional Tester's global settings.

To become script-specific, you would use the second variant of this method—waitForExistence(double arg0, double arg1). This enables you to provide the maximum amount of time script playback waits for the object to render (that is arg0). You also enter the amount of time it waits between attempts to find the test object (that is arg1). You specify these two values using seconds. Using this version of the method keeps your scripts independent from the values in the global delay settings for the waitForExistence() method. Listing 3.3 shows how this would look in both Java and VB.NET.

Listing 3.3   Using the script-specific version of waitForExistence()/WaitForExistence() in a script

Java
```
public void testMain(Object[] args)
{
      startApp("ClassicsJavaA");

      // USE waitForExistence() ON MAIN WINDOW TO MAKE
      // SURE IT IS THERE BEFORE PERFORMING VERIFICATION
      // WAIT A MAXIMUM OF 180 SECONDS/3 MINUTES
      // CHECK FOR THE MAIN WINDOW EVERY 2 SECONDS
      classicsJava().waitForExistence(180.0, 2.0);

      // Frame: ClassicsCD
      tree2().performTest(VerifyComposerListVP());
      classicsJava(ANY,MAY_EXIT).close();
}
```

VB.NET
```
Public Function TestMain(ByVal args() As Object) As Object
      StartApp("ClassicsJavaA")

      ' USE WaitForExistence() ON MAIN WINDOW TO MAKE
      ' SURE IT IS THERE BEFORE PERFORMING VERIFICATION
      ' WAIT A MAXIMUM OF 180 SECONDS/3 MINUTES
      ' CHECK FOR THE MAIN WINDOW EVERY 2 SECONDS
      ClassicsJava().WaitForExistence(180.0, 2.0)

      ' Frame: ClassicsCD
      Tree2().PerformTest(VerifyComposerListVP())
      ClassicsJava(ANY,MAY_EXIT).Close()
      Return Nothing
End Function
```

You can see that your script now waits for the main window (for example, `classicsJava`) of the application for a maximum of 180 seconds, searching for it every two seconds.

Of the three synchronization topics that you have seen thus far, this is the most desirable. It provides you with the ability to have your scripts wait until a test object appears versus waiting for a static amount of time to elapse. Further, it enables you to become script-specific, allowing any tester on your team to run it without having to adjust global playback delay settings.

Timing How Long Something Takes to Execute in a Script

Rational Functional Tester provides timers that give an indication of the amount of time that elapsed during script playback. You can use these to estimate how long your scripts take to complete. You can also use these for capturing how long a specific section of your script takes to play back.

The first option that Rational Functional Tester provides is the built-in timer. You can use this option while recording. You can also add it to your scripts later, using two simple lines of code.

While recording, you can define a timer from the GUI recording options, resulting in the appropriate piece of code being written into your script. This option is available from the Script Support Functions button on your Recording toolbar. Figure 3.7 shows this option.

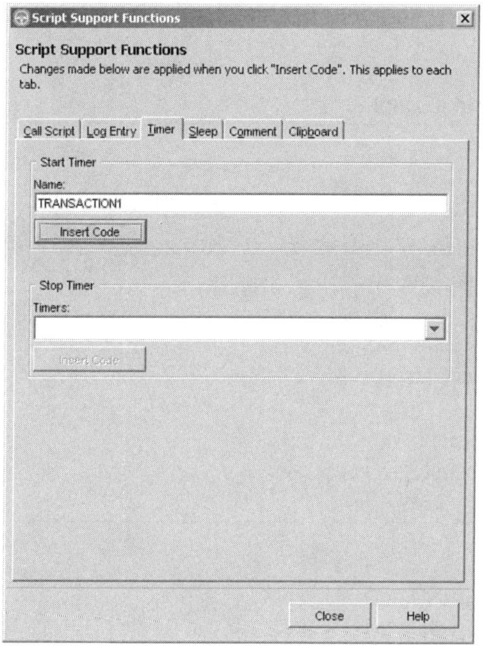

Figure 3.7   Script Support Functions—Timer tab

You need to enter only a name for your timer, and then click the **Insert Code** button. This creates the following line in your script:

```
timerStart("TRANSACTION1");
```

If you use Rational Functional Tester .NET, you see the following line instead:

```
TimerStart("TRANSACTION1")
```

You need to create the corresponding command to stop your timer. To do this, you simply perform the following steps:

1. Access your Script Support Functions.
2. Choose the **Timer** tab.
3. Click the name of timer (you would like to stop) from within the **Timers:** combobox.
4. Click the **Insert Code** button.

This will insert either a `timerStop("TRANSACTION1");` line or a `TimerStop ("TRANSACTION1")` line into your script, depending on which version of Rational Functional Tester you are using, Java or .NET, respectively.

These can be added manually, too. You simply type in the necessary `timerStart()` and `timerStop()` methods. For instance, Listing 3.4 shows how to use the `timerStart()` and `timerStop()` methods for timing how long it takes for the main window of the application to render.

Listing 3.4 Using timers in a script

Java
```
public void testMain(Object[] args)
{
      // TIME HOW LONG MAIN WINDOW TAKES TO RENDER
      // AFTER STARTING THE APP
      timerStart("TRANSACTION1");
      startApp("ClassicsJavaA");
      timerStop("TRANSACTION1");

      // Frame: ClassicsCD
      classicsJava(ANY,MAY_EXIT).close();
}
```

VB.NET
```
Public Function TestMain(ByVal args() As Object) As Object
' TIME HOW LONG MAIN WINDOW TAKES TO RENDER
' AFTER STARTING THE APP
```

```
TimerStart("TRANSACTION1")
StartApp("ClassicsJavaA")
TimerStop("TRANSACTION1")

' Frame: ClassicsCD
ClassicsJava(ANY,MAY_EXIT).Close()

Return Nothing
End Function
```

The prior two scripts result in a couple of events being written into the test log. The first is the timer getting started by the script. The second is the timer stopping. The stop event also displays the amount of time that elapsed. Figure 3.8 shows what these events look like in the HTML log.

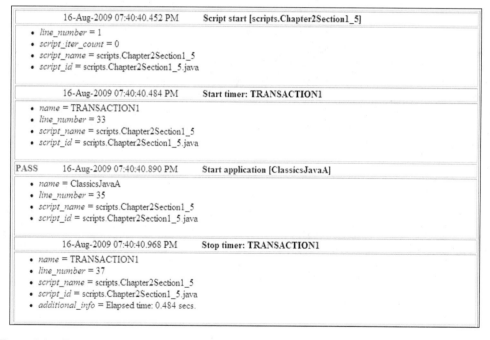

Figure 3.8 Timer events in the HTML log

Note that Rational Functional Tester's Script Assure technology can influence timers. If a test object's property values change and it is wrapped in between timer commands, you can, and often do, see excessive elapsed times in your log files. This is because the time it takes to find a test object gets captured and added into the timer.

One downside of Rational Functional Tester's timers is that they don't return a value for external consumption. For instance, you might want to write the elapsed time out to an external file (for example, if you have a test harness that has its own logging mechanism). This is where you can turn to the native scripting language, Java, or VB.NET.

Java's System class provides the `currentTimeMillis()` method for capturing transaction times. It returns a long data type. It is a native method that directly calls out to the operating system. Therefore, its resolution can vary when you run your tests on different machines running different operating systems. Listing 3.5 revisits the `waitForExistence(double arg0, double arg1)` method. This time the `System.currentTimeMillis()` method is used to capture how long the `waitForExistence()` method actually had to wait.

Listing 3.5   Capturing elapsed times using native Java capabilities

```
public void testMain(Object[] args)
{
      startApp("ClassicsJavaA");

      // START TIMER - first call to System.currentTimeMillis()
      long startTime = System.currentTimeMillis();

      // USE waitForObject() ON MAIN WINDOW TO MAKE
      // SURE IT IS THERE BEFORE PERFORMING VERIFICATION
      classicsJava().waitForExistence(180.0, 2.0);

      // END TIMER - second call to System.currentTimeMillis()
      long stopTime = System.currentTimeMillis();

      // CALCULATE HOW LONG THE waitForExistence METHOD TOOK
      long intervalTime = stopTime - startTime;

      // WRITE INTERVAL TO LOG
      logInfo("Playback needed to wait " + intervalTime + " ms for
application to launch");

      // AND CONSOLE
      System.out.println("Playback needed to wait " + intervalTime + "
ms for application to launch");

      // AND EXTERNAL FILE (TO BE IMPLEMENTED)
      // TODO - ADD CODE TO WRITE TO FILE

      // Frame: ClassicsCD
      tree2().performTest(VerifyComposerListVP());
      classicsJava(ANY,MAY_EXIT).close();

}
```

VB.NET's `System` namespace offers the `DateTime` and `TimeSpan` structures for acquiring elapsed times. To use these, you first obtain the value contained in `DateTime`'s `Now` property to capture the start time. You capture `Now`'s value again when you want to get the stop time. To gather the total elapsed time, you use the `TimeSpan` structure and initialize it with the difference between your stop and start times. Depending upon how you want to view the elapsed time, `TimeSpan` lets you display it in hours, minutes, seconds, milliseconds, and so on. Listing 3.6 shows how this comes together. This builds off of an earlier script that used the `WaitForExistence()` function.

Listing 3.6   Capturing elapsed times using native VB.NET capabilities

```
Public Function TestMain(ByVal args() As Object) As Object
     StartApp("ClassicsJavaA")

' START TIMER - first call to System.DateTime.Now
Dim startTime As System.DateTime = System.DateTime.Now

' USE WaitForObject() ON MAIN WINDOW TO MAKE SURE IT IS THERE BEFORE
PERFORMING VERIFICATION
ClassicsJava().WaitForExistence(180.0, 2.0)

' END TIMER - second call to System.DateTime.Now
Dim stopTime As System.DateTime = System.DateTime.Now

' CALCULATE HOW LONG THE waitForExistence METHOD TOOK
Dim intervalTime As System.TimeSpan = stopTime - startTime

' WRITE INTERVAL TO LOG
LogInfo("Playback needed to wait " & intervalTime.TotalMilliseconds & "
ms for application to launch")
' AND MsgBox
MsgBox("Playback needed to wait " & intervalTime.TotalMilliseconds & "
ms for application to launch")

' AND EXTERNAL FILE (TO BE IMPLEMENTED)
' TODO - ADD CODE TO WRITE TO FILE

' Frame: ClassicsCD
     Tree2().PerformTest(VerifyComposerListVP())
     ClassicsJava(ANY,MAY_EXIT).Close()
     Return Nothing
End Function
```

Synchronization and timing are two critical tools in an automation engineer's toolbox. They help you determine how long a piece of your script takes to execute and, perhaps more importantly, they help you keep your scripts—or pieces of them—in synch with your application's playback.

This section covered the appropriate timing and synchronization methods provided by Rational Functional Tester. You saw how you can use delays to wait a specified number of seconds. You also saw how you can tell your scripts to wait until a desired test object appears. Lastly, you learned how to use timers to capture how long a piece of your script takes to execute.

You should now be able to apply the appropriate techniques and script code to deal with any latency issues that appear in the application you test. You can use timers to determine the duration of the latencies. You can then select the appropriate method for dealing with them.

Working with Test Objects

Chapter 1 discussed the use of test object maps at a high level. It also provided an overview on test objects including adding, modifying, and deleting them. Rational Functional Tester records and uses these objects to interact with an application's user interface. You begin to unleash the power of Rational Functional Tester when you choose to manipulate these objects.

Test objects offer more than what you see when you are done recording. Typically, a recorded script shows you actions against test objects. You see things such as clicks, double-clicks, text-entry commands, and so on. When you dig deeper into these, you find that you can access interesting information. You can programmatically access properties that describe the object and the data that it contains. You also have access to an object's methods that can be invoked from your script. Chapter 10, "Advanced Scripting with Rational Functional Tester TestObjects," covers this topic. For the purposes of this chapter, you examine the basics of accessing test object properties and data using the scripting language.

After you have the basics of programmatically accessing test object data, you get a look at how you can start encapsulating your custom scripting to develop your own methods and functions. This is a great means for other members of your team to take advantage of the work you did, avoiding any redundant custom scripting.

Working with the Clipboard Object

Rational Functional Tester gives you a type of verification point that works with textual data on the Windows Clipboard. You might ask, "Why would I want to use the Windows Clipboard with Rational Functional Tester?" You want to do this for several reasons, but in most cases, it comes down to an easy way to get around object recognition difficulties. Often you need a test script to do something, such as checking a value, and if the normal way to do this (in this example, using a verification point) doesn't immediately work, using the Clipboard might be the fastest way to make it work.

Getting a test script to work reliably with the application interface you are testing often comes down to robust object recognition. Dealing with object recognition is covered in more detail in Chapter 8, "Handling Unsupported Domain Objects," and in Chapter 9, "Advanced Rational Functional Tester Object Map Topics." In some cases, you want to follow that information to fully implement Rational Functional Tester's recognition and interface with the test objects. The reason that you might not follow that approach, but instead use the Clipboard, usually has to do with how quickly you need to get something to work. Do not think of the Clipboard approach as a work-around or interim solution, though, as it is often the most effective and efficient way to automate a test procedure.

You use the Clipboard for handling object recognition with Rational Functional Tester, which specifically means getting, setting, or otherwise using values from the application under test or associated applications. You might do this for any of the following reasons:

- Verifying some functionality or output from the application
- Controlling the timing of your test scripts
- Manipulating the flow of the test procedures
- Logging additional information into the test results

When you use this technique, you record steps to copy and/or paste data to the Clipboard, and then use it as a kind of data source. The Clipboard can be used as an intermediate place to hold data from the application under test, and Rational Functional Tester can get data from the Clipboard or send data to it. You can also test anything that gets onto the Clipboard with a verification point.

There are three general approaches to using the Clipboard with automated testing:

1. Verifying some value from the application
2. Getting some value from the application to use in the test
3. Sending some value from the test to the application

For each of these tactics, you usually record some steps to select and copy data from some GUI, and then add some Clipboard actions into the test script. This chapter describes several examples, with specific steps, for each of the three approaches.

You do not have to manually code the methods previously described; you can simply use the Recorder toolbar to generate the Clipboard code. You add these Clipboard actions much like you would other kinds of verification points or script actions. The wizards for adding Clipboard actions into a test are found in the Script Support Functions on the Recorder toolbar.

Figure 3.9 illustrates how to access the Clipboard actions from the Rational Functional Tester Recorder toolbar.

Like all of Rational Functional Tester's script support functions, you need to click **Insert code** to add the commands to your test script.

The first consideration you have when using the Clipboard is determining exactly how you can select and copy, or perhaps paste, data to and from the Clipboard. In some cases, you might select text using a mouse click and drag, followed by a Ctrl+C keyboard shortcut. In other cases, you might have a menu option in the application under test to copy information to the Clipboard. You might have to use a combination of interactions with the application under test, the operating system, various keyboard inputs, and right-clicking or other menu selections.

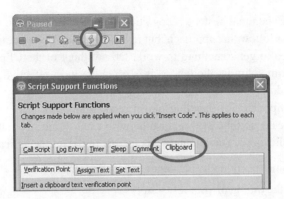

Figure 3.9   Recorder toolbar—the Clipboard

The exact method used to get data to and from the Clipboard is of critical importance to the resilience of the automated test script. Some of the steps that you record, such as clicking and dragging, rely on coordinates within an object. These methods are therefore more susceptible to playback failure. You should always strive to record actions that are most likely to replay in the maximum (and reasonable) test environments and playback conditions.

The following looks at several related examples of creating test scripts that use the Clipboard and starts with one possible scenario of creating automated test scripts leveraging the Clipboard. This is not intended to be the most realistic scenario possible, but it illustrates different ways of using the Clipboard with Rational Functional Tester.

In this scenario, you have to test a system that includes an older reporting component. Rational Functional Tester can recognize only parts of this component's interface and doesn't seem to automatically capture a particular value: the current job number. This alphanumeric string has to be checked against expected values and it is used as an input value to another test. Finally, because this is a lower priority test case, you cannot spend too much time developing the test script.

You can figure out how to get Rational Functional Tester to recognize the objects and properties to access the job number value, but that might take time. You realize that the job number field can be easily selected and copied to the Clipboard, so you use the Clipboard to quickly get a working automated test script.

First, you create a Clipboard verification point for the job number value. This differs from other verification points in that you do not directly access the object or properties to get the value. You can record a test script to do this as follows:

1. Record the initial steps of the test script, getting to the point where the job number (the value we want to verify) is displayed.

2. Select the job number text and copy it to the Clipboard. A robust method for doing this could be tabbing to the field if the application GUI is not likely to change.

3. Open the **Script Support Functions** from the Recorder toolbar, and click **Clipboard > Verification Point Tab** (see Figure 3.10). You will see the value that was copied in the verification value field.

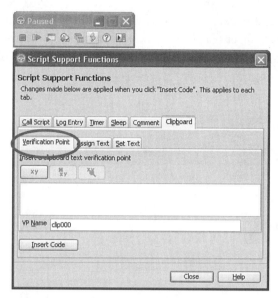

Figure 3.10   Clipboard verification point

NOTE   You have the option of creating a regular expression from the Clipboard value. This works the same way as other verification points.

CLEARING THE CLIPBOARD

Any time you are using the Clipboard as part of a procedure, it is a good practice to clear the Clipboard as an initial step. Copying to the Clipboard normally replaces any prior data, but clearing it first ensures that you are not inadvertently including unwanted data. The exact steps to do this depend on the operating system and version and the applications you use.

---

4.   Enter a descriptive name for the verification point in the VP Name field.

5.   Click **Insert Code,** and then click **Close** to exit the Script Support Functions and return to recording mode.

At this point, the script contains the code for a Clipboard verification point, as shown here:

```
getSystemClipboard().performTest(JobNumberVP());
```

You now get the job number value and store it in a local variable within the test script. You can record a test script to do this as follows:

1.   Record any initial steps of the test script or continue the previous example, getting to the point where the job number (the value we want to capture) is displayed.

2. Select the job number text and copy it to the Clipboard. If you combine this with the previous verification point example, you can skip directly to the next step.

3. Open the **Script Support Functions**, and click **Clipboard > Assign Text Tab** (see Figure 3.11).

Figure 3.11   Getting a value from the Clipboard

NOTE   You do *not* see the value that was copied to the Clipboard here. If you want to check that the right value was copied, you can switch to the Verification Point tab where you will see it, and then switch back to the Assign Text tab.

4. Enter a descriptive name for the script variable in the Variable Name field, and then select **Precede variable assignment with type declaration**.

5. Click **Insert Code**, then click **Close** to exit the Script Support Functions and return to recording mode.

At this point, the script contains the code for a new string variable to hold whatever was copied to the Clipboard, as shown here:

```
String JobNum = getSystemClipboard().getText();
```

This variable can now be used for any number of reasons within the test.

You also have the ability to send data to the Clipboard. You might want to do this if you need to test your application's paste function. If you set the data in the Clipboard immediately before performing a paste function, you can ensure that you know what should be pasted into your application. Another reason you might do this is for continuity. For example, if one piece of your application provides a record number, you might wish to store it in a variable (for example, JobNum in the preceding line of script). You can then use this variable to paste into the piece of your application that does a record lookup. In any case, setting the Clipboard is easy. You simply use the following line of code in your script:

```
getSystemClipboard().setText(JobNum);
```

Returning to the scenario, you now need to enter a new job number, different from the current one, into the application. You want to paste this value from the Clipboard into the application GUI field. You therefore need to set the value contained in the Clipboard. You might calculate or look up the particular value in several ways, but for this example, you simply show a static string. You can record a test script to do this as follows:

1. Record any initial steps of the test script or continue the previous example, getting to the point where you enter the new value.

2. Open the **Script Support Functions**, and then click **Clipboard > Set Text Tab**. The value field on this tab is empty (shown in Figure 3.12).

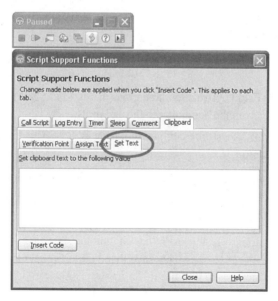

Figure 3.12   Sending a value to the Clipboard

3. Enter the value that you want to send to the Clipboard. You might simply enter a placeholder value when you are recording and then replace it in the script to some calculated or retrieved variable (for example, JobNum).

4. Click **Insert Code**, then click **Close** to exit the Script Support Functions and return to recording mode.

At this point, the script now contains the code to set the value of the Clipboard, as shown here:

```
getSystemClipboard().setText("SomeValue");
```

As mentioned in step 3, you might want to replace the hard-coded value entered during recording mode (`IncrementedJobNumber`) with some variable or other value. An incomplete example of this is shown in following code snippet.

```
// retrieve JobNum from the getText() method
String JobNum = getSystemClipboard().getText();
...
//replace recorded setText() value to JobNum variable
getSystemClipboard().setText(JobNum);
```

Instead of using the recorder, you might want to manually add the code for Clipboard interactions. This is easy to do because you would have to add only one line of code for each type of Clipboard action, not counting the lines of script to select, copy, or paste the data. An example of a line to capture something to the Clipboard is:

```
someTextField().inputKeys("{ExtHome}+{ExtEnd}^c");
```

The preceding line of code performs the following steps:

1. Press the **Home** key (that is `{ExtHome}`)—This places the cursor at the beginning of the field.

2. Perform a **Shift+End** keystroke combination (that is `+{ExtEnd}`)—This selects everything in the field (from the beginning to the end of it).

3. Perform the **Ctrl+C** keystroke combination (that is `^c`)—This executes the copy function of the application.

After this, you can manually add the following line to your script for a Clipboard verification point:

```
getSystemClipboard().performTest(myClipVP());
```

The Rational Functional Tester API has a public interface `IClipboard` in the `com.rational.test.ft.script` package that defines the set of methods exposed for a Clipboard. The three methods in this are:

- `getText`—Returns a copy of the text from this Clipboard.
- `setText`—Copies the supplied text value to this Clipboard.
- `performTest`:—Captures, compares, and logs active Clipboard text against the supplied baseline data.

NOTE There are four variations of the `performTest` method for various verification point settings such as retry and timeout values. Refer to the Rational Functional Tester API reference in the online Help for more information.

There are several things to consider when using the Clipboard with Rational Functional Tester:

- The Clipboard is often used to verify, get, and set data without mapping and directly accessing objects and properties. This can make script maintenance more difficult because you do not have an object map of the objects containing the values.

- The steps used to capture data to the Clipboard or paste data from it might be less resilient and more susceptible to playback problems. This can be a risk if you have to resort to click and drag or other actions using coordinates.

- There is a risk with the system Clipboard that scripts might not play back the same way in different test environments. Although this should ideally work the same way on Windows and Linux operating systems, it can also fail on the same operating system due to different conditions in the test environment.

Viewing an Object's Properties

Rational Functional Tester has a useful (and often overlooked) utility called the Test Object Inspector that you can use to examine a wealth of information about test objects (including properties). No coding is required to use the Inspector. It is a design-time tool that can often be used to gather information you need to write your own code. It's powerful because it shows you *almost* everything that you can manipulate in the test object through Rational Functional Tester.

To launch the Inspector, click **Run > Test Object Inspector** (in Eclipse) or **Tools > Test Object Inspector** (in Visual Studio). After the Inspector displays, by default it remains on top of all windows on your Desktop. As you move your mouse over objects, the Inspector captures information and displays it in the Inspector window. To inspect any object on your desktop, simply hover over the object and press the Pause key on your keyboard. This tells the Inspector to freeze with the information currently captured, and enables you to move your mouse and not lose the information currently displayed in the Inspector window.

After you pause it, you can view information about the test object. The Inspector can show five broad categories of information: Parent Hierarchy, Inheritance Hierarchy, Properties, Non-Value Properties, and Method information.

To select what you want the Inspector to display, press the corresponding button on the toolbar or make your selection under the Inspector's Show menu. In addition to these broad

categories, there are options that you can turn on and off under the Options menu. The following examines five examples:

- **Parent Hierarchy**—Shows the hierarchical path from the test object to the top-level
  window. For example, if you inspected the Google Search button on www.google.com
  (http://www.google.com), the Inspector shows what is displayed in Figure 3.13.

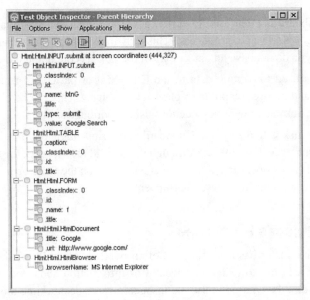

Figure 3.13   Test Object Inspector—Parent Hierarchy for Google application

The Inspector displays the same recognition information (hierarchy and recognition
property names and current values) that the object map would store for the button,
except that the tree is upside down (the browser window is the bottom, not at the top, as
in the object map) and the hierarchy is flattened (there are no indentations).

You might turn on this option when viewing a test object's parent hierarchy that does a full
disclosure of sorts. This option expands what's displayed in the Parent Hierarchy to
include *nonmappable* objects. To turn this option on, toggle **Hide not Mappable** under
the Options menu. Nonmappable objects are objects that RFT does not think are interesting and does not, therefore, add to the object map (RFT doesn't record any actions against
nonmappable objects). However, sometimes you want to know about nonmappable
objects. In such situations, turning on this option is useful. Figure 3.14 shows the Parent
Hierarchy for the Google Search button.

Without displaying nonmappable objects, the parent of the button is the HTML table;
when you include nonmappable objects, you see that the parent (the real parent in a

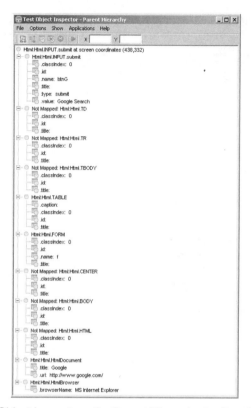

Figure 3.14 Test Object Inspector—the Parent Hierarchy for Google application, nonmappable objects

sense) is the TD HTML element. To differentiate between these two views of test object parentage, you say that the table is the button's *mappable parent* and the TD is its *nonmappable* parent. The RFT API differentiates between mappable and nonmappable parents and children.

- **Inheritance Hierarchy**—Shows class inheritance hierarchy of the test object's class. This option does not apply the HTML test objects. Figure 3.15 shows the inheritance hierarchy for the Place Order button in Classics.

  Here, the Inspector shows that the (Java) class of the button is `javax.swing.JButton`, which inherits from `AbstractButton`, which inherits from `JComponent`, and so on up to `Object`, the root class of all classes in Java.

- **Properties**—Shows all the test object's value properties (property names and values). Figure 3.16 shows what you get when you examine the properties of the Place Order button in Classics.

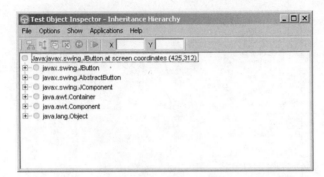

Figure 3.15   Test Object Inspector—Inheritance Hierarchy

Figure 3.16   Test Object Inspector—properties

- **NonValueProperties**—Shows all the test object's nonvalue property names and each nonvalue property's data type. Using the Place Order button, the Inspector shows the following nonvalue properties (displayed in Figure 3.17).

- **Method Information**—Shows all the methods that can be invoked directly on the test object via RFT's `invoke()` method (which we cover in Chapter 10). The methods are grouped by the test object class' inheritance chain. An example of this is shown in Figure 3.18.

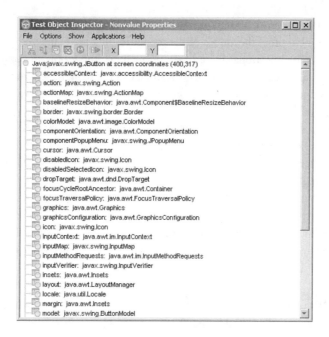

Figure 3.17 Test Object Inspector—nonvalue properties

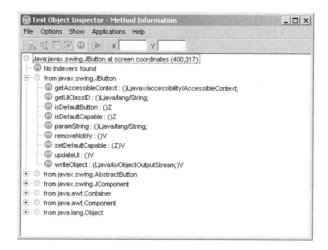

Figure 3.18 Test Object Inspector—Method Information

To the right of each method name, the Inspector shows the method's JNI signature (argument list and return type).

What is the difference between a value property and a nonvalue property? A *value property* is a property whose value Rational Functional Tester can reconstruct in its own JVM and store and compare it to other values in another context. There is a practical application of this: When you perform a Properties verification point, for example, Rational Functional Tester captures and must then store (as a baseline) the values of the properties that are being verified. When the verification point is executed, Rational Functional Tester must know how to compare the baseline values with the actual values. The properties Rational Functional Tester can manipulate in this manner are referred to collectively as *value properties*. Properties whose values Rational Functional Tester does not know how to store and compare are called *nonvalue properties*.

If you look at the list of value properties, you can see that the value of each property is either a `String` (actionCommand), `boolean` (enabled), `numeric` (alignment), or a Java class that consists of numeric fields (`Rectangle` and `Color`). These values can easily be restructured, stored, and compared in another context (RFT's JVM or a baseline VP file).

The nonvalue properties, on the other hand, are different in nature. In the nonvalue property list, you see properties such as `graphicsConfiguration`, icon, and cursor. It's not difficult to appreciate that it is difficult (at best) for RFT to store the value of a `Cursor` object or any of the other nonvalue properties. Both value and nonvalue property values are available to you through coding.

Retrieving All Properties of a Test Object

The two sets of properties discussed in the "Viewing an Object's Properties" section—value and nonvalue properties—can be retrieved from a test object in a script by invoking `getProperties()` and `getNonValueProperties()`, respectively. Each of these methods returns a Hashtable of property names and values. For nonvalue properties, the values are references to the actual objects in the target application (remote JVM). Listing 3.7 shows three methods: one that retrieves value properties, one that retrieves nonvalue properties, and one that calls both methods.

Listing 3.7 Methods for retrieving all properties of a test object

```java
Java
public void printValueProperties(TestObject testObject) {

    Hashtable valueProperties = testObject.getProperties();
    Enumeration valuePropNames = valueProperties.keys();
    Enumeration valuePropValues = valueProperties.elements();
    while (valuePropNames.hasMoreElements()) {
        System.out.println(valuePropNames.nextElement() + ":"
        + valuePropValues.nextElement());
    }
}


public void printNonValueProperties(TestObject testObject) {

    Hashtable nonValueProperties = testObject.getNonValueProperties();
```

```
        Enumeration nonValuePropNames = nonValueProperties.keys();
        Enumeration nonValuePropValues = nonValueProperties.elements();
        while (nonValuePropNames.hasMoreElements()) {
              System.out.println(nonValuePropNames.nextElement() + ":"
              + nonValuePropValues.nextElement());
        }
}


public void printAllProperties(TestObject testObject) {

      printValueProperties(testObject);
      printNonValueProperties(testObject);
}
```

VB.NET

```
Public Sub printAllProperties(ByVal testObject As TestObject)
   printValueProperties(testObject)
   printNonValueProperties(testObject)
End Sub

Public Sub printValueProperties(ByVal testobject As TestObject)
   Dim valueProperties As Hashtable = testobject.GetProperties
   Dim valuePropNames As ICollection = valueProperties.Keys
   Dim valuePropValues As ICollection = valueProperties.Values

   Dim enumPropNames As IEnumerator = valuePropNames.GetEnumerator()
   Dim enumPropVals As IEnumerator = valuePropValues.GetEnumerator()

   Do While enumPropNames.MoveNext And enumPropVals.MoveNext
      Dim currentProp As String = enumPropNames.Current
      Dim currentPropVal As Object = enumPropVals.Current
         If TypeOf currentPropVal Is Object Then
            If Not (TypeOf currentPropVal Is String) Then
               currentPropVal = currentPropVal.ToString
            End If
         End If
         Console.WriteLine(currentProp + ":" + currentPropVal)
   Loop
End Sub


Public Sub printNonValueProperties(ByVal testobject As TestObject)
```

```
Dim valueProperties As Hashtable = testobject.GetNonValueProperties
Dim valuePropNames As ICollection = valueProperties.Keys
Dim valuePropValues As ICollection = valueProperties.Values

Dim enumPropNames As IEnumerator = valuePropNames.GetEnumerator()
Dim enumPropVals As IEnumerator = valuePropValues.GetEnumerator()

Do While enumPropNames.MoveNext And enumPropVals.MoveNext
   Console.WriteLine(enumPropNames.Current + ": " +
         enumPropVals.Current)
Loop
End Sub
```

Retrieving the Value of a Single Property

To retrieve the value of a single property, use the `getProperty()` method in the `TestObject` class. You can use `getProperty()` with both value and nonvalue properties. In this section, the discussion is limited to value properties. The signature of `getProperty()` for Java is:

```
Object getProperty( String propertyName )
```

The signature of `getProperty()` for VB.NET is:

```
Function GetProperty( propertyName as String) as Object
```

The argument is the name of the property whose value you want to retrieve. Because `getProperty` can be used with any value or nonvalue property, the return type is generic `Object`. You typically want to cast to a specific type (for example, `String`).

For value properties, you can even use Rational Functional Tester to generate the code for you.

1. Place your cursor at the line in your script where you want the code to generate.

2. Insert recording.

3. Launch the Verification Point and Action Wizard.

4. Click the desired test object.

5. In the Select an Action window, click **Get a Specific Property Value**.

6. The wizard will then display all the test object's value property names and values. Click the property you want, and then click **Next**.

7. In the Variable Name window, enter a variable name to hold the returned value (RFT generates a variable name for you but you will typically always want to change the variable name), and click **Finish**.

If you selected the label property, Rational Functional Tester generates the following code.

In VB.NET:

```
Dim buttonLabel As String = PlaceOrder().GetProperty( "label" )
```

In Java:

```
String buttonLabel = (String)placeOrder().getProperty( "label" );
```

In Java, you need to explicitly cast to the correct type. For example, if you retrieve a non-String property value, such as the Background property, you see:

```
java.awt.Color buttonBackground =
(java.awt.Color)placeOrder().getProperty( "background" );
```

If you pass a property name that does not exist in the object, Rational Functional Tester throws a PropertyNotFoundException.

As you become more comfortable with Rational Functional Tester, you can rely less on the wizard to generate code for you.

Programmatically Retrieving Data from an Object in My Application

Retrieving data from objects in your application is a critical and fundamental task. You might need to get the data so that you can use it at a later point in your test; you might get it because you're creating your own verification point. No matter what your motivation is for pulling data from an object, the RFT API makes extracting data easy.

For the purposes of this chapter, the world of test objects is divided into two broad categories: those in which the RFT Verification Point Wizard sees data and those in which the RFT Verification Point Wizard doesn't see data. The TestObject techniques discussed in this chapter (with the exception of the "Working with the Clipboard Object" section) are limited to the former category of test objects, which is covered in other chapters.

You use one of two methods to get data from a test object: getProperty() or getTestData(). getProperty() is appropriate if the data is available as a property of the test object and the format of the data as a property value suites your needs. For example, if you want to get the visual text on a button (such as the Place Order button in Classics or the Search button at www.google.com), getProperty() would work fine. If you examine these objects using the Test Object Inspector (see the "Viewing an Object's Properties" section), you can see that in Classics, you need to get the value of the label property; the Google button would require that you get the value property.

Things become more interesting when the data you're interested in is available as a property, but not in the desired format. For example, on the Rational Support home page, there is a list of products (see Figure 3.19).

Imagine you wanted to get the list values. Examining the list under the Test Object Inspector microscope reveals a .text property whose value is the contents of the list. There's a problem, though: It's one big string—you don't know where the breaks between items are. Sometimes it is not a critical issue. For instance, you might just want to know if "Functional Tester" appears

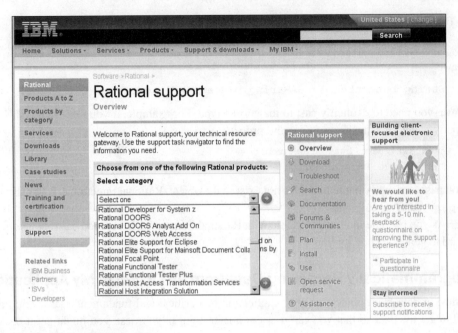

Figure 3.19   Rational Support site

anywhere in the list. If that is the case, you can simply use getProperty() to capture the .text property and be done with it. However, what if you want to know how many items are in the list? To achieve this, getProperty() does not suit your needs. In this instance, the usage of getTestData() would aid your efforts.

If you run Rational Functional Tester's Verification Point and Action Wizard and click **Data Verification Point**, you see that Rational Functional Tester is able to identify each list item discretely. Because Rational Functional Tester's Data Verification Point Wizard is able to capture the data, you can capture the data in code. In fact, any data that the Rational Functional Tester Data Verification Point Wizard is able to capture can be retrieved programmatically in a script.

Your script can retrieve any data from a test object that is accessible to the Data Verification Point Wizard by invoking the getTestData() method on the test object. Here is the method signature:

```
ITestData getTestData( String testDataType )
```

getTestData() does precisely what its name suggests: It gets and returns data from a test object. That's it. It does not verify anything. It requires a String argument—the *test data type*—to capture from the test object. The notion of a test data type requires some explanation.

Test Data Types

Recall that when you use Rational Functional Tester's Verification Point Wizard, you have to indicate to the wizard which test data to verify. For example, if you've selected a list object (as in the case of the Rational Support site example), you have to express if you want Rational Functional Tester to verify all the values in the list or just the selected elements. You can see this in Figure 3.20.

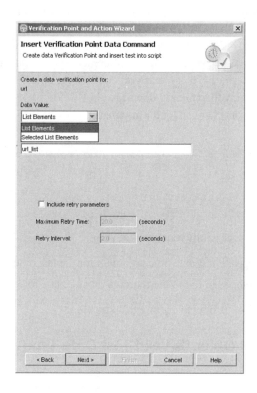

Figure 3.20   *Verification Point and Action Wizard*

The argument passed to `getTestData()` indicates to `getTestData()` that same detail that you express to the Verification Point Wizard when you select a value in the Data Value list. In the case of a recorded verification point, it tells Rational Functional Tester which data to retrieve and verify; in the case of `getTestData()`, it indicates which data to retrieve and return to the caller of `getTestData()`.

ITestData

`getTestData()` returns the data as a Java interface type: `ITestData`. The `ITestData` interface is inherited by several subinterfaces, each of which has methods to store and manipulate specific types of data, for example, `ItestDataList` (for data in lists), `ITestDataTable` (for data in tables), and `ITestDataTree` (for data in trees). Each of these interfaces has methods to query and extract data in the manner appropriate for that data structure. For example, if you retrieved the data in a table, you might want to know how many columns and rows of data there are. You might also want to get all the values in row 3 or column 2. `ITestDataTable` has methods that make this possible in an intuitive fashion. When working with lists, you might want to know how many items are in the list and get all the values. `ITestDataList` has methods to do this.

Even though the signature of the return type of `getTestData()` is `ITestData` (the base interface type), what will actually be returned is a reference to a subinterface of `ITestData`, for example, `ITestDataTable`. Even though you can always treat any of the returned data as base `ITestData` (that is you can upcast the returned reference), you almost always assign to a variable of the specific subinterface type so that you can call the specific methods available in the subtype. In the case of Java, you explicitly downcast; in VB.NET, you can use an implicit downcast. For example (don't worry here about the argument to `getTestData()`; the focus here is on the downcasting), Java:

```
ITestDataTable iData = (ITestDataTable)someTable().getTestData(
"contents" );
```

In VB. Net:

```
Dim iData As ITestDataTable = someTable.GetTestData( "contents" )
```

Using `getTestData()` successfully requires that you:

- Know the appropriate test data type argument for the test object in question.
- Know which methods to use in the returned `ITestData` to access the data elements.

In the next sections, we look at how to acquire this knowledge.

Determining a Test Object's Valid Test Data Type Arguments to getTestData()

You can use two techniques to determine a test object's valid data type arguments:

1. Call `getTestDataTypes()` on the test object you need to get data from. `getTestDataTypes()` is a method in the TestObject class that returns a `Hashtable`, which holds the same information that the Rational Functional Tester Verification Point Wizard displays (and then some).

2. Right-click the test object in the Script Explorer, and click **Interface Summary**. This displays a page in the Rational Functional Tester documentation that summarizes how it works with the selected test object, including the valid data types it can use.

For example, if you invoke `getTestDataTypes()` on the Orders table in the Classics sample application (**Admin > Orders**) and print the returned hashtable to the console (Output window in Visual Studio), you have the following:

In Java:

```
System.out.println( orderTable().getTestDataTypes() );
```

In VB.NET:

```
Console.WriteLine(someTable.GetTestDataTypes)
```

You see something similar to what is displayed in Figure 3.21.

Figure 3.21   Console output of `orderTable().getTestDataTypes()`

The keys in the hashtable (contents, visible contents, selected, and selected and visible selected) are the valid test data type arguments to `getTestData()` for the test object in question; the value of each hashtable key is a description (for you, not Rational Functional Tester) of the test data type. Based on that output, the following are all valid calls to make on the Orders table:

```
orderTable().getTestData( "contents" );
orderTable().getTestData( "selected" );
orderTable().getTestData( "visible contents" );
orderTable().getTestData( "visible selected" );
```

Using getTestData to Extract Data from a Text Field

The first example of using `getTestData()` is one that might not initially seem interesting. You can use `getTestData()` to retrieve data from text fields. To do so, pass `getTestData()` an argument of "text;" it returns the text as `ITestDataText`, which is the simplest subinterface in the `ITestData` family to work with. It's simple because you need to know only one method to get the data into a usable string: `getText()`. As an example, look at these two text fields:

- The Search field at www.google.com <http://www.google.com> (HTML domain)
- The Name field on Classics' Place an Order window (Java domain)

If you fire up and point the Inspector (see the "Viewing an Object's Properties" section in this chapter) at each of these objects, you can see that in the case of the HTML text field, you need to get the `value` property. In the case of the Java Swing field, you need to get the `text` property. If you use `getTestData()`, in both cases, you pass an argument of text. This is useful if you want to create a generic method that retrieves text (expressed as a single string) from any type of test object. Listing 3.8 shows both a Java and VB.NET example of using `getTestData()`.

Listing 3.8   Getting data from a text field

Java
```
ITestDataText iData = (ITestDataText)textField().getTestData( "text" );
String value = iData.getText();
```

VB.NET
```
Dim iData as ItestDataText  = textField().getTestData( "text" )
dim value as String = iData.getText()
```

Notice that in Java, you must explicitly cast to `ITestDataText`.

Using getTestData to Extract Data from a List

Lists are relatively easy objects to start with, though there are two twists that follow. The first issue is the test data types:

First twist: If you retrieve the selected element from a Swing `JList`, the data is returned as `ITestDataText` (in this case, you then call `getText()` and you're done); for any other type of list, the data is returned as `ITestDataList`.

Second twist (relates only to `ITestDataList`): Getting the individual data values out of the `ITestDataList` requires a little more work than you might like. You work with three interface types: `ITestDataList`, `ITestDataElementList`, and `ITestDataElement`.

Tables 3.1 and 3.2 show the most commonly used methods in each of these interfaces.

Table 3.1   List Object Data Types

Data Type	Return Type	Comments
List	`ITestDataList`	Retrieves all list elements.
Selected	`ITestDataList` `ITestDataText`	Retrieves the selected items. The selected elements in HTML and .Net lists are returned as `ITestDataList`; selected data in Swing lists (`javx.swing.JList`) is returned as `ITest DataText`.

Table 3.2   List Object Interface Methods

Interface	Methods
`ITestDataList`	`int getElementCount() ITestDataElementList getElements()`
`ITestDataElementList`	`ITestDataElement getElement( int )`
`ItestDataElement`	`Object getElement()`

At a high level, this is the algorithm to get list data:

1. Call `getTestData()` on your list test object. The data will be returned as `ITestDataList`.

2. On the returned `ITestDataList`, call `getElementCount()` on the returned `ITestDataList` to find out how many elements are in the `ITestDataList`.

3. Call `getElements()` on the returned `ITestDataList`. This returns another interface: `ITestDataElementList`.

4. From the returned `ITestDataElementList`, you can now get any individual element by calling `getElement(int)`. The integer argument passed to `getElement()` is the index of the element you want (you start counting at zero). `getElement()` returns yet another interface type: `ITestDataElement`.

5. After you have an individual list item as an `ITestDataElement`, you can call `getElement()` to get actual data value. `getElement()` returns the data as an `Object`, so if you're working in Java, you need an explicit cast to a `String`.

Listing 3.9 offers two examples: one that retrieves all elements and one that retrieves selected elements. In both examples, the data is returned as an array of `Strings`.

Listing 3.9 Getting all elements from a list

Java
```java
public String[] getAllListElements(TestObject testObject) {
    String[] all = null;
    ITestDataList iList = (ITestDataList)
                        testObject.getTestData("list");
    int count = iList.getElementCount();
    all = new String[count];
    ITestDataElementList iElementList = iList.getElements();
    for (int i = 0; i < count; i++) {
        ITestDataElement iElement = iElementList.getElement(i);
        String value = iElement.getElement().toString();
        all[i] = value;
    }
    return all;
}
```

VB.NET

```
Public Function getAllListElements(ByVal testObject As TestObject) _
  As String()
    Dim iData As ITestDataList = testObject.GetTestData("list")
    Dim count As Integer = iData.GetElementCount()
    Dim all(count - 1) As String
    Dim iElementList As ITestDataElementList = iData.GetElements()

    For i As Integer = 0 To count - 1
      Dim iElement As ITestDataElement = iElementList.GetElement(i)
      Dim value As String = iElement.GetElement().ToString()
      all(i) = value
    Next

    Return all
End Function
```

Getting selected elements from a list

Java

```
public String[] getSelectedElements(TestObject testObject) {
      String[] selected = null;
      ITestData iData = testObject.getTestData("selected");
      if (iData instanceof ITestDataList) {
        ITestDataList iList = (ITestDataList) iData;
        int count = iList.getElementCount();
        selected = new String[count];
        ITestDataElementList iElementList = iList.getElements();
        for (int i = 0; i < count; i++) {
          ITestDataElement iElement = iElementList.getElement(i);
          String value = iElement.getElement().toString();
          selected[i] = value;
        }
      } else if (iData instanceof ITestDataText) {
          ITestDataText iText = (ITestDataText) iData;
          selected = new String[0];
          selected[0] = iText.getText();
      }
return selected;
}
```

VB.NET

```
Public Function getSelectedElements(ByVal TestObject As TestObject) As String()
   Dim selected() As String = Nothing
   Dim iData As ITestData = TestObject.GetTestData("selected")

   If (TypeOf iData Is ITestDataList) Then
     Dim iList As ITestDataList = iData
     Dim count As Integer = iList.GetElementCount()
     ReDim selected(count - 1)
     Dim iElementList As ITestDataElementList = iList.GetElements()
     For i As Integer = 0 To count - 1
       Dim iElement As ITestDataElement = iElementList.GetElement(i)
       Dim value As String = iElement.GetElement()
       selected(i) = value
     Next

   ElseIf (TypeOf iData Is ITestDataText) Then
     Dim iText As ITestDataText = iData
     ReDim selected(1)
     Dim value As String = iText.GetText
     selected(0) = value
   End If

   getSelectedElements = selected
End Function
```

The last two script examples in Listing 3.9 illustrate a technique for handling the special case of getTestData() returning ITestDataText and not ITestDataList.

Using getTestData() to Read Data in a Table

As opposed to lists, which require several method calls (and three interfaces) to get list values, tabular table is straightforward; you use only one interface. The initial learning challenge is the test data type arguments. There are quite a few; some are test object domain-specific. (See Tables 3.3, 3.4, and 3.5.)

Table 3.3   HTML Tables

Test Data Type	Return Type	Comments	Provides Access to Column and Row Header Data?
Contents	`ITestData Table`	Returns all table data, including hidden rows/columns.	Yes
Grid	`ITestData Table`	Returns all table data, including hidden rows/columns.	No
visiblecontents	`ITestData Table`	Returns all data displayed in the table.	Yes
visiblegrid	`ITestData Table`	Returns all data displayed in the table.	No
Text	`ItestData Text`	Returns the entire contents of the tables as a single string.	No

Table 3.4   Swing Tables

Test Data Type	Return Type	Comments	Provides Access to Colum and Row Header Data?
contents	`ITestData Table`	Returns all data, including hidden rows/columns.	Yes
visible contents	`ITestData Table`	Returns all data displayed in the table.	Yes
selected	`ITestData Table`	Returns all selected data, including hidden rows/columns.	Yes
visible selected	`ITestData Table`	Returns all displayed selected data.	Yes

Table 3.6 lists the most commonly used methods in `ITestDataTable`.

Table 3.5   Microsoft .NET Grids

Test Data	Return Type	Comments	Provides Access to Colum and Row Header Data?
viewcontents	`ITestData Table`	Returns all data displayed in the table.	Yes
Sourcecontents	`ITestData Table`	Returns all data in the table source, i.e., includes rows/columns not displayed in the table.	Yes
Viewselectedrow	`ITestData Table`	Returns all data displayed in the selected row(s).	Yes
Sourceselectedrow	`ITestData Table`	Returns all data in table source, i.e., includes rows/columns not displayed in the table.	Yes
Viewcurrentrow	`ITestData Table`	Returns all data displayed in the currently active row. i.e., the row with focus.	Yes
Sourcecurrentrow	`ITestData Table`	Returns all data in the source of the currently active row.	Yes

Table 3.6   Most Commonly Used `ITestDataTable` Methods

Method	Comments
`int getRowCount()`	Returns the number of rows in the data returned.
`int getColumnCount()`	Returns the number of columns in the data returned.
`Object getColumnHeader(int)`	Returns the value of the column title at the specific index. Because the data is returned as Object, you typically cast to a String.
`Object getRowHeader(int)`	Returns the value of the row header at the specific index. Because the data is returned as Object, you typically cast to a String.
`Object getCell (int, int)`	Returns the data in the row, column pair passed. Because the data is returned as Object, you typically cast to a String.

Listing 3.10 provides two examples that print to the console (Output window in Visual Studio) all the test data types available in the (table) test object passed. This method (function in VB.NET) can be used at design time to compare what is returned in each case and to help you determine the appropriate test data type argument for a table you are coding against.

Listing 3.10   Printing all of a table's test data types

Java
```java
public void printTableData(TestObject table) {

    Enumeration<String> testDataTypes = table.getTestDataTypes()
                                                        .keys();

    while (testDataTypes.hasMoreElements()) {
        String testDataType = testDataTypes.nextElement();
        System.out.println(testDataType);
        ITestData iData = table.getTestData(testDataType);
        if (iData instanceof ITestDataTable) {
            ITestDataTable iTableData = (ITestDataTable) table
                                    .getTestData(testDataType);
            int rows = iTableData.getRowCount();
            int cols = iTableData.getColumnCount();
            for (int col = 0; col < cols; col++) {
                System.out.print(iTableData.getColumnHeader(col));
                System.out.print("\t\t");
            }
            System.out.print("\n");
            for (int row = 0; row < rows; row++) {
                for (int col = 0; col < cols; col++) {
                    System.out.print(iTableData.getCell(row, col));
                    System.out.print("\t\t");
                }
                System.out.print("\n\n");
            }
            System.out.print("\n");
        } else if ( iData instanceof ITestDataText ) {
            ITestDataText iText = (ITestDataText) iData;
            String text = iText.getText();
        System.out.println(text + "\n\n" );
    }
        }
    }
```

VB.NET

```
Public Sub printTableData(ByVal table As TestObject)
    Dim testDataTypes As System.Collections.ICollection = _
                                    table.GetTestDataTypes.Keys
    For Each testDataType As String In testDataTypes
        Dim iData As ITestData = table.GetTestData(testDataType)
        Console.WriteLine(testDataType)
        If TypeOf iData Is ITestDataTable Then
            Dim iTableData As ITestDataTable = CType(iData, ITestDataTable)
            Dim rows As Integer = iTableData.GetRowCount()
            Dim cols As Integer = iTableData.GetColumnCount()

            ' First print column headers if available
            Try
                For col As Integer = 0 To cols
                    Console.Write(iTableData.GetColumnHeader(col))
                    Console.Write(Chr(9) + Chr(9))
                Next
                Console.Write(Chr(13))
            Catch ex As Exception
                Console.WriteLine("COLUMN HEADERS NOT AVAILABLE")
            End Try
            For row As Integer = 0 To rows
                For col As Integer = 0 To cols
                    Console.Write(iTableData.GetCell(row, col))
                    Console.Write(Chr(9) + Chr(9))
                Next
                Console.Write(Chr(13))
            Next
            Console.Write(Chr(13))
        ElseIf (TypeOf iData Is ITestDataText) Then
            Dim iText As ITestDataText = CType(iData, ITestDataText)
            Dim text As String = iText.GetText()
            Console.WriteLine( text + chr(13) + chr(13) )
        End If
    Next
End Sub
```

Referring to the previous code samples, note the following. First, you want to note that the target (control) of the code is a Swing table. To get all test data types applicable to the table, you call getTestDataTypes. The ITestDataTable object (returned by the call to getTestData()) can be used to determine the number of rows and columns in the table by calling getRowCount() and getColumnCount(). If column headers are not available, an exception can be thrown; you therefore use a try block to prevent the script from failing. To retrieve the value in any particular cell, call `getCell(row, col)`, passing in the row and column index of the cell you're interested in (start counting at 0). `getCell()` returns the value as an object, which you almost always downcast to a string. In Swing tables, the column and row headers are separate Swing objects from the table object. The data in these headers, however, can be retrieved via methods in the `ITestDataTable` object returned by calling `getTestData()` on the table. In other words, your scripts do not need to worry about having (or getting) separate column or row header `TestObjects`. After you have the `ITestDataTable` in the table, call `getColumnHeader()` and `getRowHeader()` methods, respectively.

Using getTestData() to Extract Data from a Tree

From a test data type perspective, trees are simple. There are only two test data types: tree and selected.

Table 3.7   Tree Object Data Types

Data Type	Return Type	Comments
Tree	ItestDataTree	Retrieves the entire tree hierarchy.
selected	ItestDataTree	Retrieves the selected tree nodes.

Tree Talk

There's a special vocabulary used with trees with which you might not be familiar. A tree consists of elements referred to as *nodes*. Each node can have a parent, siblings, and children. A node that has no parent is called a *root node*. A tree can have one root node (the Classics music tree) or multiple root nodes (the tree in the Rational Functional Tester Preferences dialog box). A node that has no children is called a *leaf* or *terminal node*.

In the Classics music tree, Composers is the root node. Composers has no siblings. Its children are Schubert, Haydn, Bach, Beethoven, and Mozart. Mozart has three children. Symphony No. 34 has no children and is therefore a leaf node.

Before continuing, you need to clarify what is returned with respect to *selected* tree nodes. If you click Bach's Violin Concertos in Classics, it is the selected node. You might think that in this scenario if you get selected data from the tree, just Violin Concertos will be returned. This is not the case. To see what `getTestData()` returns, insert a Data verification point on the tree with Bach's Violin Concertos selected and select **Selected tree hierarchy**. You see something similar to what is displayed in Figure 3.22.

Notice that Rational Functional Tester captures the selected element along with its ancestor nodes all the way up to the root node. If multiple nodes are selected (hold down the Ctrl key and

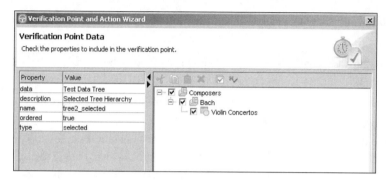

Figure 3.22   Data verification point—Selected tree hierarchy (single node selected)

select Symphony No. 9 and Mozart's Symphony in C, No. 41: Jupiter), the selected tree hierarchy would look like Figure 3.23.

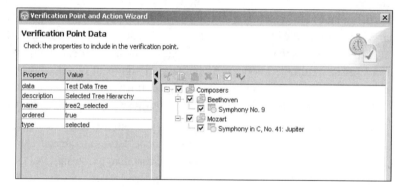

Figure 3.23   Data verification point—Selected tree hierarchy (multiple nodes selected)

Table 3.8 lists the interfaces for accessing tree data and the commonly used methods in each interface.

Table 3.8   Interfaces and Their Methods Used for Accessing Trees

Interface	Methods
ITestDataTree	ITestDataTreeNodes getTreeNodes()
ITestDataTree Nodes	int getNodeCount() int getRootNodeCount() ITestDataTree Node[] getRootNodes()
ITestDataTree Node	int getChildCount() ItestDataTreeNode[] getChildren() ItestDataTreeNode getParent() Object getNode()

The following steps can be used as a generic template for acquiring the root nodes of a tree control.

1. Call the tree control's `getTestData()` method. The data will be returned as an `ITestDataTree` interface.

2. On the `ITestDataTree` reference, call `getTreeNodes()`. This returns the data as an `ITestDataTreeNodes` interface.

    Note that if you want to get to the selected leaf nodes in the tree, you need to start at the top of the tree and traverse down to them (such as using some sort of loop). To get to the top of a tree, call `getRootNodes()`, which returns an array of individual `ITestDataTreeNodes`. It returns an array because depending on the tree, there can be more than one root node.

    Also note that after you have the data contained in an `ITestDataTreeNodes` interface, you can find out how many nodes are in the data returned by calling `getNodeCount()`. It's important to note that `getNodeCount()` doesn't necessarily return the number of nodes in the test object; it returns the number of nodes in the data returned by the initial call to `getTestData()`. If you pass `getTestData()` an argument of tree, it returns the total number of nodes in the tree (for example, the Composer tree in Classics returns 20 nodes). If you pass an argument of selected, it returns the number of nodes in the selected tree hierarchy. If Bach Violin Concertos is selected, it returns three (because the nodes returned are **Composers > Bach > Violin Concertos**).

3. As listed in Table 3.8, there are three key methods you can invoke on an `ITestDataTreeNode`. `getNode()` returns the node data as an Object. Thus, if you call `getNode()` on the first (and only) root node and cast that to a string, you can print it out (or more likely store it in a variable for further processing).

Listing 3.11 provides two examples—one Java and one VB.NET—that exemplify the previous template steps.

Listing 3.11   Printing a tree's root nodes

Java

```java
public void printRootNodes( TestObject tree ) {
    String selectedNode = null;

    ITestDataTree iTreeData =
(ITestDataTree)tree.getTestData("selected");
    ITestDataTreeNodes iNodes = iTreeData.getTreeNodes();
    ITestDataTreeNode[] rootNodes = iNodes.getRootNodes();
    for(int i = 0; i < rootNodes.length; i++) {
```

```
      String nodeData = rootNodes[i].getNode().toString();
      System.out.println( nodeData );
   }
}
```

VB.NET

```
Public Sub printRootNodes(ByVal tree As TestObject)
   Dim selectedNode As String = Nothing
   Dim iTreeData As ITestDataTree = tree.GetTestData("tree")
   Dim iNodes As ITestDataTreeNodes = iTreeData.GetTreeNodes()

   Dim rootNodes As ITestDataTreeNode() = iNodes.GetRootNodes()
   For i As Integer = 0 To rootNodes.length - 1
      Dim nodeData As String = rootNodes(i).GetNode.ToString
      Console.WriteLine( nodeData )
   Next
End Sub
```

The next code sample in Listing 3.12 builds off the prior steps. In particular, after you acquire the root node as an ITestDataTreeNode, you can start traversing it. To descend one level, call getChildren(). This returns the ITestDataTreeNode's children (in the returned data, not the test object) as an array of ITestDataTreeNodes. Note that the data type of the root nodes is the same as any other node in a tree, namely ITestDataTreeNode. After you have the array of child ITestDataTreeNodes, you can acquire their data, using the getNode() method and casting it to a string—similar to what was accomplished in Listing 3.11.

Listing 3.12 Get the text of the selected node in a tree

Java

```
public String getSelectedTreeNode( TestObject tree ) {
   String selectedNode = null;

   ITestDataTree iTreeData =
(ITestDataTree)tree.getTestData("selected");
   ITestDataTreeNodes iNodes = iTreeData.getTreeNodes();
   int nodeCount = iNodes.getNodeCount();
   System.out.println("node count = " + nodeCount);
   if( nodeCount != 0) {
      ITestDataTreeNode[] node = iNodes.getRootNodes();
      for(int i = 0; i < nodeCount - 1; i++) {
```

```
        ITestDataTreeNode[] children = node[0].getChildren();
        node = children;
    }
    selectedNode = node[0].getNode().toString();
}
return selectedNode;
}
```

VB.NET
```
Public Function getSelectedTreeNode(ByVal tree As TestObject) As String
    Dim selectedNode As String = Nothing
    Dim iTreeData As ITestDataTree = tree.GetTestData("selected")
    Dim iNodes As ITestDataTreeNodes = iTreeData.GetTreeNodes()
    Dim nodeCount As Integer = iNodes.GetNodeCount()

    Console.WriteLine("Nodecount = " + nodeCount.ToString)
    If (nodeCount <> 0) Then
        Dim node As ITestDataTreeNode() = iNodes.GetRootNodes()
        For i As Integer = 1 To nodeCount - 1
            Dim children As ITestDataTreeNode() = node(0).GetChildren()
            node = children
        Next
        selectedNode = node(0).GetNode().ToString()
    End If

    Return selectedNode
End Function
```

Obtaining Data from a Test Object That the Rational Functional Tester Verification Point Wizard Does Not Capture

This large topic is discussed here and explored in more detail in other sections. Several techniques are used to deal with this challenge, the simplest of which from a coding perspective is to try to get the data into the Clipboard. If this can *reliably* be done, you can get the data into a script variable (though this technique might not be your first choice).

As discussed in the "Working with the Clipboard Object" section in this chapter, Rational Functional Tester gives you access to the system Clipboard. This provides access to the two methods used for manipulating the Clipboard: setText() and getText(). These enable you to work with test objects that Rational Functional Tester has difficulty extracting data from.

The following reference example is an open document in Microsoft Word. If you point the Rational Functional Tester Verification Point Wizard at a Microsoft Word document, it does not see the contents of the document. You can, however, get the data into a variable in your script by using the keyboard and a little code.

First, you click the document to place keyboard focus on it. Then you use the keyboard to put the data into the Clipboard (versus trying to manipulate the Word menu). The Rational Functional Tester API has two methods to work with the keyboard: `inputChars()` and `inputKeys()`. Both take string arguments, but there's a key difference between them: `inputChars()` treats every character it has passed literally, and `inputKeys()` assigns special meaning to certain characters, as shown in Table 3.9.

Table 3.9   Characters with Special Meanings in Scripts

^	Apply Ctrl to the next character.
%	Apply Alt to the next character.
+	Apply Shift to the next character.
~	Enter key.

Passing `inputKeys` ^a^c causes Rational Functional Tester to press Ctrl+A (select all) and then Ctrl+C (copy), copying the contents of the entire document to the Clipboard. After the data is copied to the Clipboard, you are home free. To get the data in the Clipboard, you call `getSystemClipboard().getText()`. This is detailed in Listing 3.13.

Listing 3.13   Using the Clipboard to get data from a test object

Java
```
microsoftWordDocumentwindow().click();
((TopLevelSubitemTestObject) microsoftWordDocumentwindow()
                    .getTopMappableParent()).inputKeys("^a^c");

String text = getSystemClipboard().getText();
System.out.println(text);
```

Creating a Custom Verification Point

In addition to the flexibility of being able to use datapool references in verification points created with the Rational Functional Tester Verification Point Wizard, you can create your own dynamic verification points in code. `RationalTestScript` (the root of all script classes) has a method, `vpManual()`, which you can use to create verification points.

`vpManual()` is used when you want your script to do all the work of verifying data. That work consists of capturing expected data, capturing actual data, comparing actual data with expected data, and logging the results of the comparison. Think of *manual* as referring to manual coding.

This discussion begins with the first signature (which you will likely use most often). In vpManual's three-argument version, you supply a name for your verification point along with the baseline and actual data associated with the verification point. vpManual() then creates and returns a reference to an object; specifically, one that implements Rational Functional Tester's IFtVerificationPoint interface. The verification point metadata (name, expected, and actual data) are stored in the returned IFtVerificationPoint.

```
IFtVerificationPoint myVP = vpManual( "FirstName", "Sasha", "Pasha");
Dim myVP as IFtVerificationPoint = vpManual( "FirstName", "Sasha", "Pasha" )
```

There are a couple of items to note about using vpManual():

- **vpName**—The verification point name must be a script-unique valid Java (or .net) method name and be less than 30 (.net) or 75 (Java) characters.

- **Baseline and Actual data**—The compiler accepts a reference to anything that inherits from Object (which means that in .NET, any argument you pass is acceptable; Java allows anything other than primitives, such as int, bool, and so on); however, you need to satisfy more than the compiler. To automate the comparison of baseline with actual data, you need to pass data types that Rational Functional Tester knows how to compare (you don't want to have to build your own compare method). This limits you to passing value classes. Some examples of legal value classes are: any data returned by getTestData(), strings, primitives, wrapper classes (Integer, Boolean, and so on), common classes that consist of value class fields (for example, Background, Color, Bounds, ITestData, meaning, anything returned by getTestData()), and arrays (one and two-dimensional), vectors, and hashtables that contain value class elements.

What do you do with the IFtVerificationPoint that vpManual() returns? In the simplest case, you call performTest() and get on with things. performTest() compares the baseline with the actual and logs the results (boolean) of the comparison. See Listing 3.14.

Listing 3.14   A simple comparison

Java
```
IFtVerificationPoint myVP = vpManual( "FirstName", "Sasha", "Pasha");
boolean passed = myVP.performTest();
```

VB.NET
```
Dim myVP As IFtVerificationPoint = VpManual("FirstName", "Sasha", _ "Pasha")
Dim passed As Boolean = myVP.PerformTest
```

In two lines of code, you have done quite a bit. You created a verification point and compared and logged the results of comparing the baseline to the actual data. It's common to combine these two statements into one:

```
vpManual( "FirstName", "Minsk", "Pinsk").performTest();
```

You use this style when the only method you need to invoke on the IFtVerificationPoint returned by vpManual() is performTest().

It's important to note that the three-argument version of vpManual() does not persist baseline data to the file system for future runs. It's also important to stress the importance of the uniqueness of the name in the script.

To illustrate how Rational Functional Tester behaves when a verification point is not unique, consider the simple example where vpManual is called in a loop (demonstrated in Listing 3.15). The loop in each code sample simply compares two numbers. To introduce some variety, you force the actual value to equal the baseline value only when the baseline value is even.

Listing 3.15   Consequences of a nonunique verification point name

Java
```
for(int baseline = 1; baseline <= 10; baseline++ ) {
    int actual = baseline % 2 == 0 ? baseline : baseline + 1;
    vpManual("CompareNumbers", baseline, actual).performTest();
}
```

VB.NET
```
For baseline As Integer = 1 To 10
    Dim actual As Integer
    If (baseline Mod 2 = 0) Then
        actual = actual
    Else
        actual = baseline + 1
    End If
    VpManual("CompareNumbers", baseline, actual).PerformTest()
Next
```

If you execute this code, you see two interesting results in the log:

- The pass/fail status for each verification point is what's expected (half pass, half fail).
- The comparator shows the correct actual values for each verification point, but a baseline value of 1 for every verification point. The reason for this is that after an IFtVerificationPoint has been created, the baseline cannot be updated.

The common technique to deal with this issue (in a looping context) is to append a counter to the verification point name, guaranteeing a unique name per iteration. This is shown in Listing 3.16.

Listing 3.16   Guaranteeing a unique verification point name

Java
```java
for(int baseline = 1; baseline <= 10; baseline++ ) {
    int actual = baseline % 2 == 0 ? baseline : baseline + 1;
    vpManual("CompareNumbers_" + baseline, baseline,
                                        actual).performTest();
}
```

VB.NET
```vbnet
For baseline As Integer = 1 To 10
    Dim actual As Integer
    If (baseline Mod 2 = 0) Then
        actual = actual
    Else
        actual = baseline + 1
    End If
    VpManual("CompareNumbers_" & baseline, _
                        baseline, actual).PerformTest()

Next
```

Persisting Baseline Data

In addition to the three-argument version of vpManual(), there is a two-argument version of vpManual():

```java
IFtVerificationPoint vpManual( String vpName, Object data )
```

The two-argument version is used when you want to persist the baseline data to the Rational Functional Tester project. Here's how it works. The first time performTest() is called on an IFtVerificationPoint with a given name (the name passed to vpManual()), no comparison is done. The baseline data is written to the RFT project and a verification point displays in the Script Explorer (and an informational message is written to the log). With each *subsequent* execution of performTest() on an IFtVerificationPoint with the same name, the data argument passed to vpManual() is treated as actual data, and performTest() executes the comparison, logging the result.

Changing the Value of a Test Object's Property

Properties cannot only be read using `getProperty()`, but they can be changed using `setProperty()`:

```
public void setProperty( String propertyName, Object propertyValue )
```

Although you most likely will not use `setProperty()` nearly as often as you use `getProperty()`, it is a method worth knowing about. `SetProperty()` takes two arguments: the property to change and the value to change the property to.

The reference example is one that involves setting data field values in test objects (for example, text fields). In general, you should use `inputKeys()` or `inputChars()` to enter data into the SUT. With some cases, however, this becomes challenging. One such context is internationalization testing. `inputKeys()` and `inputChars()` can enter characters only in the current keyboard's character set. If the current keyboard is set to English, for example, RFT throws a `StringNotInCodePageException` if your script attempts to enter any nonEnglish characters.

One potentially viable solution is to use `setProperty()` instead of `inputKeys()` to set the field value. The first step is to determine the property you need to set. Manually set a value, and then examine the test object using either the Inspector or the Verification Point and Action Wizard. Search for a property whose value is the data value you entered. If you enter a search term of Pasta Norma in a Google search field and examine the field with the Inspector, you see two properties whose values are Pasta Norma: `value` and `.value`. This is not uncommon: It's possible that the data value is represented by more than one property. It's a good idea to note all these property names because some might be read-only. If you try to set a property value that's read-only, Rational Functional Tester throws an exception.

If you had a datapool with different search strings in different character sets, you can manipulate the scripts to perform multiple searches, as shown in Listing 3.17.

Listing 3.17   Using `SetProperty()` to set data in a test object

Java
```
while (!dpDone()) {
    text_q().setProperty(".value", dpString("SearchItem"));
    // Do what we need to do
    dpNext();
}
```

VB.NET
```
Do until(dpDone())
    text_q.SetProperty(".value", dpString("SearchItem"))
    ' Do what we need to do
    dpNext()
loop
```

Why Is InputKeys() Preferred?

To illustrate why `inputKeys()` is the preferred method to enter data into objects, test what happens if you set the quantity of CDs to buy in the Classics sample application:

```
quantityText().setProperty("Text", "4");
```

You see something odd happen (or, *not happen* in this case): The total amount is not updated to reflect the new value. The reason for this is that the total amount is updated when the `inputKeys` event is fired. `setProperty()` does not cause this event to fire and is therefore not a possible technique to set the quantity field.

Evolving Custom Scripting into Reusable Methods

Up to this point, you have learned how to make different types of enhancements to your scripts, making them more robust. You saw how to add delays, introduce timers, work with the Windows Clipboard, manipulate different objects you recorded (such as test objects and verification points), and so on. Rational Functional Tester enables you to expand these techniques by turning them into generic, reusable methods.

Methods that are reusable and, ideally generic, enable you to apply them to more than one object or script. You can often use them across your entire test project. This enables you to create methods that benefit everybody on your team, saving time on your overall test automation effort.

The first thing that is involved with creating custom methods is setting up the signature. Basically, you specify the type of data your method needs to receive and the type of data it needs to send back when it's done executing. You can work with the typical data types and objects that the Java and VB.NET languages work with. For example, you might have an add method with a signature that looks like the following:

```
public int add(int i, int j)
```

The VB.NET equivalent is:

```
Public Function add(ByVal i As Integer, ByVal j As Integer) As Integer
```

In both instances, you are merely passing two integers into the method (function in VB.NET), returning the sum of them as an integer.

Rational Functional Tester enables you to pass and return test objects. This gives you the ability to create custom methods for the objects that you capture in your test object map. A simple instance of this might be a method to test if an object is enabled or not. The method signature would like the following Java example:

```
public Boolean isEnabled(TestObject myGuiObject)
```

In VB.NET, you see:

```
Public Function isEnabled(ByVal myGuiObject As TestObject) As Boolean
```

If you use a signature, such as the preceding examples, you can pass any test object that contains enabled property to your custom method. You can test if a button is enabled before you click it, a tree is enabled before you navigate it, a text box is enabled before typing in it, and so on.

After you have the signature defined for your method, it is a matter of providing the code that accomplishes your desired task. You might write reusable methods that wait for test object properties to change, that acquire data from test objects, and set properties for test objects. Regardless of the methods that you create, you can organize and package them into *Helper Superclasses*, calling them from your scripts.

Helper Superclasses (also called Helper Base Classes in the VB.NET version of the tool) are an excellent way for you to create a simple, project-wide means for storing your reusable methods. You can easily create a Helper Superclass in Rational Functional Tester by performing the following steps:

1. Click **File > New > Helper Superclass** (this launches the Create Script Helper Superclass Wizard).

2. Select the location to store your Helper Superclass.

3. Provide a name for your Helper Superclass.

4. Click the **Finish** button.

If you are using the VB.NET version, the steps are:

1. Click **File > New > Add Helper Base Class** (this will launch the Add New Item Wizard, preselecting the Script Helper Base Class template).

2. Provide a name for your Helper Base Class.

3. Provide a location for your Helper Base Class.

4. Click the **Add** button.

In either case, you end up with an empty class, prebuilt to extend the default capabilities of Rational Functional Tester's **RationalTestScript** class. This is where you start constructing your custom, reusable methods. The following code samples, contained in Listing 3.18, show a Java and a .NET helper class. These contain the following sample methods from prior sections:

- `printValueProperties()`—"Retrieving All Properties of a Test Object" section
- `getAllListElements()`—"Using getTestData to Extract Data from a List" section
- `printRootNodes()`—"Using getTestData to Extract Data from a Tree" section

Listing 3.18   Helper Classes

Java
```java
package HelperSuperclasses;

import java.util.Enumeration;
import java.util.Hashtable;

import com.rational.test.ft.object.interfaces.TestObject;
import com.rational.test.ft.script.RationalTestScript;
import com.rational.test.ft.vp.ITestDataElement;
import com.rational.test.ft.vp.ITestDataElementList;
import com.rational.test.ft.vp.ITestDataList;
import com.rational.test.ft.vp.ITestDataTree;
import com.rational.test.ft.vp.ITestDataTreeNode;
import com.rational.test.ft.vp.ITestDataTreeNodes;

public abstract class MyHelperSuperclass extends RationalTestScript
{
      public void printValueProperties(TestObject testObject) {

            Hashtable valueProperties = testObject.getProperties();
            Enumeration valuePropNames = valueProperties.keys();
            Enumeration valuePropValues = valueProperties.elements();
            while (valuePropNames.hasMoreElements()) {
                  System.out.println(valuePropNames.nextElement() + ":"
                              + valuePropValues.nextElement());
            }
      }

      public String[] getAllListElements(TestObject testObject) {
            String[] all = null;
            ITestDataList iList = (ITestDataList)
            testObject.getTestData("list");
            int count = iList.getElementCount();
            all = new String[count];
            ITestDataElementList iElementList = iList.getElements();
            for (int i = 0; i < count; i++) {
                  ITestDataElement iElement = iElementList.getElement(i);
                  String value = iElement.getElement().toString();
                  all[i] = value;
            }
            return all;
```

```java
        }


    public void printRootNodes( TestObject tree ) {
            String selectedNode = null;

            ITestDataTree iTreeData =
                    (ITestDataTree)tree.getTestData("selected");
            ITestDataTreeNodes iNodes = iTreeData.getTreeNodes();
            ITestDataTreeNode[] rootNodes = iNodes.getRootNodes();
            for(int i = 0; i < rootNodes.length; i++) {
                    String nodeData = rootNodes[i].getNode().toString();
                    System.out.println( nodeData );
            }
    }
}
```

VB.NET

```vbnet
Imports Rational.Test.Ft.Script
Imports Rational.Test.Ft.Vp
Imports System
Imports System.Collections
Imports Rational.Test.Ft.Object.Interfaces

Namespace ScriptHelperBaseClasses

    Public MustInherit Class MyScriptHelperBaseClass
        Inherits RationalTestScript

        Public Sub printValueProperties(ByVal testobject As TestObject)
            Dim valueProperties As Hashtable = testobject.GetProperties
            Dim valuePropNames As ICollection = valueProperties.Keys
            Dim valuePropValues As ICollection = valueProperties.Values

            Dim enumPropNames As IEnumerator = valuePropNames.GetEnumerator()
            Dim enumPropVals As IEnumerator = valuePropValues.GetEnumerator()

            Do While enumPropNames.MoveNext And enumPropVals.MoveNext
                Dim currentProp As String = enumPropNames.Current
                Dim currentPropVal As Object = enumPropVals.Current
                If TypeOf currentPropVal Is Object Then
                    If Not (TypeOf currentPropVal Is String) Then
                        currentPropVal = currentPropVal.ToString
```

```
            End If
        End If
        Console.WriteLine(currentProp + ":" + currentPropVal)
    Loop
End Sub


Public Function getAllListElements(ByVal testObject As TestObject) As
String()
    Dim iData As ITestDataList = testObject.GetTestData("list")
    Dim count As Integer = iData.GetElementCount()
    Dim all(count - 1) As String
    Dim iElementList As ITestDataElementList = iData.GetElements()

    For i As Integer = 0 To count - 1
        Dim iElement As ITestDataElement = iElementList.GetElement(i)
        Dim value As String = iElement.GetElement().ToString()
        all(i) = value
    Next

    Return all
End Function


Public Sub printRootNodes(ByVal tree As TestObject)
    Dim selectedNode As String = Nothing
    Dim iTreeData As ITestDataTree = tree.GetTestData("tree")
    Dim iNodes As ITestDataTreeNodes = iTreeData.GetTreeNodes()

    Dim rootNodes As ITestDataTreeNode() = iNodes.GetRootNodes()
    For i As Integer = 0 To rootNodes.length - 1
        Dim nodeData As String = rootNodes(i).GetNode.ToString
        Console.WriteLine(nodeData)
    Next
End Sub


End Class
End Namespace
```

Please note that you might need to import certain packages and namespaces (depending on whether you are using Java or VB.NET). You receive errors from the compiler that let you know that certain classes, structures, objects, and so on do not exist. In the Java version of the tool, you can usually perform a **<Ctrl> + O** keystroke combination. This imports the necessary packages. There might be instances where you have to review the error messages to get an idea of what package needs to be imported. The VB.NET version of the tool requires you to import the necessary namespace.

After you have your Helper Superclass set up, creating the desired reusable methods, you need to perform two more steps. The first is to tell your test scripts to use the new class. In other words, you want to tell your scripts about the new methods that you created. The second step is to actually call your custom methods from your script.

You can associate your new Helper Superclass either at the individual script level or at the project level. Associating your Helper Superclass at the project level causes any new script to be aware of your custom methods. If you already have scripts created, you need to associate your Helper Superclass to each of them. To associate your Superclass to your project, you do the following:

1. Right-click your project node in the Functional Test Projects view (Solution Explorer, if you're using Rational Functional .NET).

2. Click **Properties**.

3. Click **Functional Test Project** (on the left-hand side of the Properties window).

4. Click the **Browse** button next to the Script Helper Superclass property (Script Helper Base Class property if you are using Rational Functional Tester .NET).

5. Select your created Helper Superclass (Helper Base Class).

   Note: You might need to type the first few letters of the name of your Super Helper class to get it to display in the list when using the Java version of Rational Functional Tester.

6. Click the **OK** button.

Associating your Helper Superclass to individual scripts is a similar process. You need only to perform the following steps:

1. Right-click an existing script in your project node in the Functional Test Projects view (Solution Explorer, if you are using Rational Functional .NET).

2. Click **Properties**.

3. Click **Functional Test Script** (on the left-hand side of the "Properties" window).

4. Click the **Browse** button next to the Helper Superclass property.

5. Click the created Helper Superclass (Helper Base Class).

   Note: You might need to type the first few letters of the name of your Super Helper class to get it to appear in the list when using the Java version of Rational Functional Tester.

6. Click the **OK** button.

After you make the necessary Helper Superclass associations, the last thing you need to do is to actually use the custom work that you created. Referring to the methods and functions in Listings 3.17 and 3.18, you simply need to call the specific custom method(s) that you need.

Figures 3.24 and 3.25 show scripts that make calls to the custom methods contained in the Helper Superclass. This should give you an idea of how your custom work can save time for the other members on your team. They do not have to reinvent the wheel you already created. They can simply reuse the code that you built and use the method(s) that you placed in a Helper Superclass.

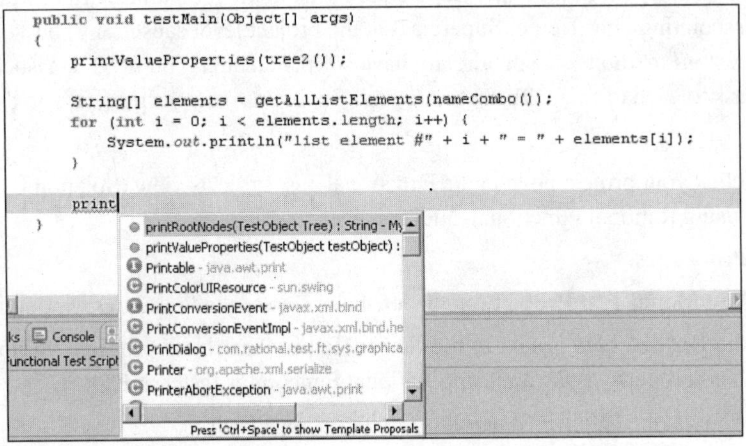

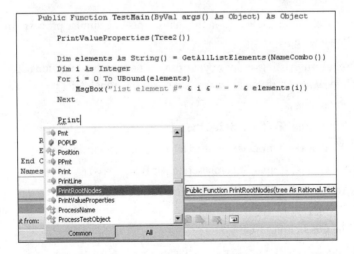

Figure 3.24   Calling custom methods in Helper Superclass—Java

Figure 3.25   Calling custom functions in Helper Base Class—VB.NET

Summary

This chapter provides you with the knowledge necessary to expand your skill set outside of the realm of record and playback test automation. You should now have the knowledge necessary to handle such tasks as synchronizing your script playback with any latency issues your application might face, acquiring data from the Windows Clipboard, manipulating data in test objects, and so on. Further, you should now possess the ability to turn your custom scripting into methods that can be reused across your project.

You should also note that this chapter provides some building blocks for more advanced code-oriented testing. The ability to create reusable methods is a commonplace task for many scripting activities you might find yourself performing in Rational Functional Tester. Further, you might find that creating custom verification points is more valuable, at times, than using the built-in ones. In any case, you should now have the level of comfort to move onto more advanced scripting tasks.

CHAPTER 4

XML and Rational Functional Tester

Jeffrey R. Bocarsly

XML is important for Rational Functional Tester users for two reasons. First, data is now frequently formulated in an XML format, either for persistence in a file, a database, or to be sent (usually via HTTP) to another application. Verifying the data content of XMLs is often an important software quality task. So, parsing XMLs to capture data to compare it to baseline data is a common software testing need. Second, Rational Functional Tester employs the XML format to persist its own data. This chapter doesn't discuss the details of Rational Functional Tester's use of XML; rather, it covers all of the core XML-handling tasks that are needed to test XML data and to manipulate Rational Functional Tester XMLs. For discussions of how Rational Functional Tester uses XML, see Chapter 10, "Advanced Scripting with Rational Functional Tester Test-Objects," and Chapter 16, "Internationalized Testing with Rational Functional Tester."

For this chapter, we assume a basic knowledge of XML, its syntax, and terminology. If you're new to XML, consult an XML primer. (See the end of the chapter for some suggestions.)

As you read this chapter, you'll see code snippets for the Java and Eclipse flavors of Rational Functional Tester and the VB.NET and Visual Studio flavors. Each language has a set of class libraries that it uses to manipulate XML. However, the implementations do differ, and there are numerous syntax differences in the same general API paradigm.

Handling XML in Rational Functional Tester

This chapter uses a simple sample XML, but one that demonstrates all the basic moves you'll need to make. It follows:

```
<?xml version="1.0"?>
<!--Sample XML 04-1-->
<ibmTools>
    <tool rxt="RFT">
        <name>Rational Functional Tester</name>
        <version>8.1.0</version>
    </tool>
    <tool rxt="RPT">
        <name>Rational Performance Tester</name>
        <version>8.1.0</version>
    </tool>
    <tool rxt="RQM">
        <name>Rational Quality Manager</name>
        <version>2.0</version>
    </tool>
</ibmTools>
```

Our discussion of XML handling in Rational Functional Tester starts with a brief overview of the two main XML-handling standards, DOM (Document Object Model) and SAX (Simple API for XML). Both DOM and SAX are W3C standards; in Java, DOM and SAX are implemented in the `org.w3c.dom` and `org.xml.sax` packages. In VB.NET, the `System.Xml` libraries implement DOM and a SAX-like parser.

DOM and SAX

DOM and SAX are fundamentally different in that the DOM loads and persists an entire XML document in memory (in a tree-structure form), whereas SAX is event-driven, meaning that a SAX parser fires off a sequence of events reflecting XML structure and content as it scans through an XML document. A SAX parser never holds a whole document in memory. You see output from a SAX parser sooner than from a DOM for equal tasks on equal documents because the SAX parser fires off its events as it encounters them during its scan. In the DOM approach, the entire document is parsed and loaded in memory before any processing can occur.

Because of this key difference in structure, the DOM demands more memory than a SAX parser does for an equivalent document. On the other hand, the DOM provides random access to all document nodes at will because they are all in memory. One of the major factors in the choice of which to use is the size and complexity of the largest document that will have to be parsed relative to the available memory. The DOM is most useful when an XML should be persisted in memory for repeated access. SAX is strongest for processing large XMLs quickly for specific data content where it is not necessary to keep the full XML in memory.

As noted previously, a major intersection of test automation and XML is data content. Code to validate the data content of XML documents is mostly what you need to write, and the most direct route to this is through the DOM. The issue is not that data content can't be validated with

SAX, but more that the DOM is the path of least resistance; the code to extract the data is simpler. So, if your XMLs do not eat up too much memory, or they are not large enough to put you in the slow processing regime, DOM is the easiest route to go. If you are parsing large documents, then SAX becomes an attractive choice.

Using the XML DOM with Rational Functional Tester

We begin our foray into the DOM with a brief summary of the logical structure of a DOM tree. An exhaustive discussion of DOM concepts is beyond the scope of this book, but this chapter discusses some of the most common structures and concepts so that the basic DOM manipulations are intelligible (see http://www.w3.org/TR/2004/REC-DOM-Level-3-Core-20040407/ for the w3C DOM specification).

From the DOM perspective, every XML document has a tree structure. The tree is composed of nodes, of which there are 12 specific types. Each node has a well-defined relationship to the surrounding nodes and is accessed through a specific interface. In addition, all nodes implement the more general Node interface. Collections of nodes are represented by the `NodeList` and `NamedNodeMap` interfaces. Table 4.1 shows the most common Node interfaces.

Table 4.1   Common XML DOM Node Interfaces and Node Collection Interfaces

Node Interface	Implementation (Java, VB.NET)	Description
Document	org.w3c.dom.Document, System.Xml.XmlDocument	Each DOM tree has a single document node. The document node must contain at least one element node, which is termed the document element and is the root of the document.
Element	org.w3c.dom.Element, System.Xml.XmlElement	Represents an element in an XML document. Elements can have child nodes and attributes.
Node	org.w3c.dom.Node, System.Xml.XmlNode	Represents any single node in the document tree (and therefore is the main type of the DOM). All specialized nodes implement the more generic Node interface.
NodeList	org.w3c.dom.NodeList, System.Xml. XmlNodeList	Represents an ordered list of nodes.

*Less commonly used Node interfaces are: `DocumentFragment`, `DocumentType`, `EntityReference`, `ProcessingInstruction`, `CDATASection`, `Entity`, `Notation`

Table 4.1 *Continued*

Node Interface	Implementation (Java, VB.NET)	Description
NamedNodeMap	org.w3c.dom.NamedNode Map, System.Xml. Xml-NamedNodeMap	Represents unordered collections of nodes that can be accessed by name.
Attribute	org.w3c.dom.Attr, System.Xml. XmlAttribute	Represents an attribute in an Element object. Attributes are *not* children of the elements with which they are associated, but are viewed as properties of their element.
Text	org.w3c.dom.Text, System.Xml.XmlText	Represents the textual content (character data, in XML lingo) of an element or attribute. It is a *child* of the node whose text it represents, not the part of the node itself.
Comment	org.w3c.dom.Comment, System.Xml.XmlComment	Represents the content of an XML comment.

*Less commonly used Node interfaces are: DocumentFragment, DocumentType, EntityReference, ProcessingInstruction, CDATASection, Entity, Notation

Loading a Document into the XML DOM

The DOM Document provides the highest-level access to the DOM object tree, and most likely, all of your DOM manipulations will start by getting a reference to a Document. Listing 4.1 shows a simple method to load an XML file on disk to the DOM using a standard factory object (in Java) or standard object creation (in VB.NET). Note that this method uses an elaborate cascade of catch clauses, illustrating the range of exceptions that might be thrown. These include parser exceptions, even though the code uses the DOM. Parsing is an underlying step that occurs prior to loading an XML into the DOM. This is clearest in the Java code, although it also reflects what is happening under the hood in VB.NET. The methods return a Document (Java) or XmlDocument (VB.NET) reference that is used for access to the Document's node tree.

Listing 4.1 Loading an XML into the DOM

Java

```
public Document loadDoc(String xmlFilePath){
    Document xmlDoc = null;
```

```
    DocumentBuilderFactory docBuilderFactory =
        DocumentBuilderFactory.newInstance();
    docBuilderFactory.setNamespaceAware(true);
    try {
      File file = new File(xmlFilePath);
      DocumentBuilder builder =
          docBuilderFactory.newDocumentBuilder();
      xmlDoc = builder.parse(file);
    } catch (SAXParseException spe) {
        spe.printStackTrace();
    } catch (SAXException sxe) {
        sxe.printStackTrace();
    } catch (ParserConfigurationException pce)
        pce.printStackTrace();
    } catch (FileNotFoundException fnf) {
        fnf.printStackTrace();
    } catch (IOException ioe) {
        ioe.printStackTrace();
    }
}

    return xmlDoc;

}
```

VB.NET

```
Public Function loadDoc(ByVal xmlFilePath As String) _
        As XmlDocument
    Dim doc As New XmlDocument
    Try
        doc.Load(xmlFilePath)
    Catch xmle As XmlException
        Console.Write(xmle.Message)
    Catch dnf As DirectoryNotFoundException
        Console.Write(dnf.Message)
    Catch ioe As IOException
        Console.Write(ioe.Message)
    End Try
    Return doc
End Function
```

It is relatively unlikely that you are going to encounter all of the exceptions illustrated here when loading a Document. In your own work, you might want to explicitly handle the more common exceptions (`SAXParseException` and `SAXException` in Java, and XmlException in VB.NET) and make the remaining exception handling more generic.

Capturing Element Values Using the XML DOM

One of the most important tasks you have to perform with XML is the extraction of data content from XML in preparation for comparing the data to baseline values, and output of the results to the Rational Functional Tester log. Data resides in XML in one of two places: either it appears as the text content of a tag (`<sometag>your_text_here</sometag>`) or it appears as an attribute on a tag (`<anothertag myattrib='attribvalue'/>`). This chapter looks at ways to pull data out of both of these locations.

Probably the most common place to find data is as the text of a tag. To start extracting the text of a tag, you build simple methods to pull target elements out of the XML structure. The simplest way to identify an element is by its tag name and its index. Remember that XML syntax allows you to have as many identically named tags as you'd like, so identifying a specific element by name isn't enough information to uniquely find a tag. Asking the DOM for an element by tag name and index fully specifies a given tag. When you specify your indices, remember that, as usual, indexing uses a zero-based count. To find the tag, use the DOM's `getElementsByTagName()` method of the Document object to generate a `NodeList` (Java) or an `XmlNodeList` (VB.NET), and then simply ask for the specified list element from the list. Listing 4.2 shows the methods.

Listing 4.2   Methods to return a specific XML Node reference based on name and index

Java
```
public Node getNode(Document doc, String tagName, int tagIndex){
    NodeList nodeList = doc.getElementsByTagName(tagName);
    if (nodeList != null){
        return nodeList.item(tagIndex);
    } else {
        return null;
    }
}
```

VB.NET
```
Public Function getNode(ByVal doc As XmlDocument, _
        ByVal tagName As String, _
        ByVal tagIndex As Integer) As XmlNode
    Dim nodeList As XmlNodeList = _
        doc.GetElementsByTagName(tagName)
    If Not (nodeList Is Nothing) Then
        Return nodeList.Item(tagIndex)
    Else
        Return Nothing
    End If
End Function
```

Note that a null reference is returned (either `null` in Java or `Nothing` in VB.NET) if the call fails. This is because `getElementsByTagName()` does not throw an exception if you specify an element that does not exist (either by invalid tag name or index). This method simply returns a null reference, indicating that no list items were returned. This makes it convenient to simply check whether the list is null or not, but of course, it places the burden for checking for nulls on the calling code.

After you find the element you want, you can capture its text content by calling the `getTextContent()` method on the `org.w3c.dom.Node` class in Java or accessing the `InnerText` property of the `System.Xml.XmlNode` class in VB.NET. This is shown in Listing 4.3.

Listing 4.3   Method to return the text of an XML Node reference

Java

```
public String getNodeText(Document doc,
        String tagName, int tagIndex){
    Node node = getNode(doc, tagName, tagIndex);
    if (node != null){
        return node.getTextContent();
    } else {
        return null;
    }
}
```

VB.NET

```
Public Function getNodeText(ByVal doc As XmlDocument, _
        ByVal tagName As String, _
        ByVal tagIndex As Integer) As String
    Dim node As XmlNode = getNode(doc, tagName, tagIndex)
    If Not (node Is Nothing) Then
        Return node.InnerText
    Else
        Return Nothing
    End If
End Function
```

The final task in this section is to capture data from the other place it might be found, in an element's attribute. The syntax around attributes is not identical to that regarding DOM nodes, but it is similar. To capture attribute data, you not only need to specify the same information as you did previously to specify an element, but you also need to then get a list of the target element's attributes, by getting a `NamedNodeMap` reference (Java) or an `XmlNamedNodeMap` (VB.NET). You then use the

`NamedNodeMap` to specify which attribute you want to get the text content of by specifying the attribute name. Attribute names must be unique in an element (unlike the element names themselves in the document), so you have to know which attribute you want by name. With the attribute name, you can call `getNamedItem()` to return a Node reference to the attribute, and then you retrieve the attribute's text data as in Listing 4.3. Listing 4.4 shows the methods.

Listing 4.4   Method to return an XML Attribute value

Java

```
public String getNodeAttribText(Document doc, String tagName,
        int tagIndex, String attribName){
    Node node = getNode(doc, tagName, tagIndex);
    NamedNodeMap nnm = node.getAttributes();
    Node attrib = nnm.getNamedItem(attribName);
    if (attrib != null){
        return attrib.getTextContent();
    } else {
        return null;
    }
}
```

VB.NET

```
Public Function getNodeAttribText(ByVal doc As XmlDocument, _
        ByVal tagName As String, ByVal tagIndex As Integer, _
        ByVal attribName As String) As String
    Dim node As XmlNode = getNode(doc, tagName, tagIndex)
    Dim nnm As XmlNamedNodeMap = node.Attributes
    Dim attrib As XmlNode = nnm.GetNamedItem(attribName)
    If Not (attrib Is Nothing) Then
        Return attrib.InnerText
    Else
        Return Nothing
    End If
End Function
```

Changing Element Data Using the XML DOM

This section briefly discusses changing element data because it can be useful for tasks such as manipulating XML configuration files. If part of your test bed setup involves XML configuration files, this type of code can be a time saver, enabling you to automate configuration changes during your test runs. In addition, as mentioned before, Rational Functional Tester persists project information in XML format and manipulation of this data in a script can sometimes provide a powerful technique for extending projects (see Chapter 16 for an example).

Listing 4.2 contains the core of what is needed to change element data. The method `getNode()` is used to obtain a reference to the node whose data you want to change. The Node reference has a method (Java) or property (VB.NET) to change its text value. Listing 4.5 shows these methods.

Listing 4.5   Modifying XML node text

Java

```java
public void setNodeText(Document doc, String tagName,
       int tagIndex, String text){
   Node node = getNode(doc, tagName, tagIndex);
   if (node != null){
       node.setTextContent(text);
   }
}
```

VB.NET

```vbnet
Public Sub setNodeText(ByVal doc As XmlDocument, _
       ByVal tagName As String, ByVal tagIndex As Integer, _
       ByVal text As String)
   Dim node As XmlNode = getNode(doc, tagName, tagIndex)
   If Not (node Is Nothing) Then
       node.InnerText = text
   End If
End Sub
```

To change attribute text, you can use exactly the same approach as you just saw for the Node text; this is shown in Listing 4.6.

Listing 4.6   Modifying XML attribute values

Java

```java
public void setNodeAttribText(Document doc, String tagName,
       int tagIndex, String attribName, String text){
   Node node = getNode(doc, tagName, tagIndex);
   NamedNodeMap nnm = node.getAttributes();
   Node attrib = nnm.getNamedItem(attribName);
   if (attrib != null){
       attrib.setTextContent(text);
   }
}
```

VB.NET

```
Public Sub setNodeAttribText(ByVal doc As XmlDocument, _
        ByVal tagName As String, ByVal tagIndex As Integer, _
        ByVal attribName As String, ByVal text As String)
    Dim node As XmlNode = getNode(doc, tagName, tagIndex)
    Dim nnm As XmlNamedNodeMap = node.Attributes
    Dim attrib As XmlNode = nnm.GetNamedItem(attribName)
    If Not (attrib Is Nothing) Then
        attrib.InnerText = text
    End If
End Sub
```

Finding Elements Using XPath

The previous discussion illustrated how to find XML nodes based on tag name and index. From the perspective of these examples, searching for specific nodes in a DOM tree is a process of iterating through all candidate nodes, and checking data or metadata, to find the ones you need. Although this works for many needs, there is a more powerful way to query XML documents for their content: XML Path language (XPath).

XPath is an XML query language based on the notion of paths through an XML tree. It does not use an XML notation, but rather a path-like notation similar to that used to describe directory paths. These paths can be modified with a range of qualifiers (which brings in considerable complexity), so that precise queries can be constructed. It can be extraordinarily useful to query XML documents with a query language format when evaluating data content. A full discussion of XPath is beyond the scope of this book (you'll see that comment a number of times in this chapter), but some of the basics and some examples that show how valuable XPath can be for the tasks involved in XML data validation are discussed.

The current XPath standard XPath 1.0 is part of Java and comes with the Eclipse version of Rational Functional Tester. Likewise, it is part of VS.NET and is available in the VB.NET flavor of Rational Functional Tester. However, XPath 2.0 and something called XQuery 1.0, both significant additions to XML query domain, are on the horizon. While current XPath 1.0 syntax should be supported in these new standards, many additional query styles and functionalities will be supported. The discussion here is based only on XPath 1.0; however, when XPath 2.0 becomes available, you'll want to check out the many new features that can enhance your testing queries.

XPath gives you the ability to query for XML elements from a document in a way broadly analogous to how you query a database with SQL for rows. The notion of a query and the syntax of XPath is, however, completely different from that of SQL. XPath queries are defined from the perspective of a specific node in a given XML. This node is called the context node. From the context node, you can move along a location path to select a specific set of nodes from a document. The grammar of location paths allows several different kinds of phrases: a *location step*, a *location path*, a *node test*, and a *predicate*.

Location Steps

A location step is a step from the context node to another node that has a specific relationship to the context node. For example, you could step from the context node to its child node. This step is considered a movement along the child "axis." XPath, in fact, defines 13 different types of axes along which location steps can be taken. Of the 13 axes, 9 can be conceptualized as "fundamental" axes, while the remaining four are composite axes, meaning that they are conceptually related to two of the fundamental axes. The XPath axes are shown in Table 4.2 along with their definitions.

Table 4.2   XPath Axes

Axis	Description
Self	The context node itself
child	All child nodes of the context node (one generation only)
descendant	All descendants of the context node (all generations)
parent	The immediate parent node of the context node
ancestor	All element nodes containing the context node up to the root element
preceding	All nodes before the context node in document order but that are not its ancestors
following	All nodes after the context node in document order but that are not its descendants
attribute	Attributes of the context node
namespace	Namespaces on the context node
descendant-or-self	The descendant axis plus the context node
ancestor-or-self	The ancestor axis plus the context node
preceding-sibling	Members of the preceding axis node set that have the same parent node as the context node
following-sibling	Members of the following axis node set that have the same parent node as the context node

The basic syntax for a location step is: *"axis::nodeName."* For example, using our sample XML, with the Document node as the context node, the following location step returns the document element:

```
"child::ibmTools"
```

If you used the following location step with the document element as context node, XPath would return all three `<tool>` nodes:

```
"descendant::tool"
```

Finally, using the first `<tool>` node as the context node, the value of the first rxt attribute is returned by the following location step:

```
"attribute::rxt"
```

Location Paths

Location steps are combined to create location paths with a forward slash ("/"). The node-set that is selected by the first location step becomes the context node-set for the second step, down through the full path. So, for example, using the `Document` node as context node, the following path returns the three `<tool>` nodes because the `<ibmTools>` node is a child of the Document node:

```
"ibmTools/tool"
```

Location paths can be made into *absolute location paths* by prepending a forward slash ("/") to the path. An absolute location path starts with the root node of a document, regardless of the context node. So, the location path used with the first `<tool>` node as context node (`"ibmTools/tool"`) returns an empty node set (because `<ibmTools>` is the document element), but the location path `"/ibmTools/tool"` (forward slash prepended) returns all three `<tool>` nodes because the search starts at the `Document` node despite the fact that a `<tool>` node is the context node.

Location paths can be used with steps. For example, you can specify a descendant of the Document node to find a child node, and then step to its attribute node. The following query returns the rxt attribute nodes on all `<tool>` nodes:

```
"descendant::tool/attribute::rxt"
```

Location paths can also be combined using the pipe operator ("|"), which indicates a logical "or." So, for example, if you wanted to return a node set that contained all `<name>` and `<version>` nodes, you could write the following XPath expression:

```
"ibmTools/tool/version|ibmTools/tool/name"
```

Node Tests

Node tests are a mechanism for limiting the nodes on an axis that are selected and returned by an XPath query. Table 4.3 shows the XPath node tests that are available.

Table 4.3   XPath Node Tests

Node Test	Description
`Name`	Matches all elements or attributes with the specified name
`*`	Matches all nodes on the specified axis
`text()`	Matches any text nodes on the specified axis
`node()`	Matches any nodes on the specified axis
`comment`	Matches any comments on the specified axis
`processing-instruction()`	Matches any processing instruction on the specified axis
`prefix:*`	Matches any element or attribute in the namespace mapped to the prefix, where prefix is the actual namespace prefix (and not the word prefix)

So, if you wanted to match all the descendants of the context node, you could write:

`"descendant::*"`

If the context node is the `Document` node, the following test returns all of the text nodes of the document:

`"descendant::text()"`

However, the following test returns nothing when used in the `Document` context because the `Document` node has no direct text children:

`"child::text()"`

XPath has an abbreviated notation for several commonly used axis and Node test expressions. A selection of the most commonly-used abbreviations follows:

- `"Name" = "child::Name"`
- `"@Name" = "attribute::Name"`
- `"." = "self::node()"`
- `".." = "parent::node()"`
- `"//" = "descendant-or-self::node()"`

Predicates

A predicate is a logical XPath expression that is evaluated for each node selected by a location step. If a predicate evaluates to true for a specific node, the node is retained in the returned node set; otherwise, it is omitted. Predicates are enclosed in square brackets.

Sample XPath queries that use predicates include the following (the `Document` node is the context node):

- `"descendant::tool[1]"`—returns the first `<tool>` node
- `"descendant::tool[child::name='Rational Performance Tester']"`—Returns the `<tool>` node that has a `<name>` child with text Rational Performance Tester
- `"descendant::*[@rxt]"`—Returns all three descendant nodes with an `rxt` attribute
- `"//tool[attribute::rxt='RFT']"`—Returns all `<tool>` nodes whose `rxt` attribute is RFT
- `"//version[text()='8.1.0']"`—Returns all `<version>` nodes whose text is 8.1.0

Code for XPath Searches

The code required for XPath searching is relatively straightforward, especially if namespaces are not involved. There are a number of packages that offer XPath searching; however, our illustrations are with the core classes that distribute with the tool languages (`javax.xml.xpath.*`, `System.Xml`). Listing 4.7 shows the basic form of the invocation for searches on namespace unaware XMLs.

Listing 4.7   A simple XPath search implementation

Java

```java
public NodeList xpath(Node contextNode, String xpathQuery){
        NodeList nodeList = null;
    try {
        XPath xpath = XPathFactory.newInstance().newXPath();
        nodeList = (NodeList)xpath.evaluate(xpathQuery,
            contextNode, XPathConstants.NODESET);
        return nodeList;
    } catch (XPathExpressionException xpe) {
        System.out.println(xpe.getMessage());
        return null;
    }
}
```

VB.NET

```vbnet
Public Function xpath(ByVal contextNode As XmlNode, _
        ByVal pathExpression As String) As XmlNodeList
    Dim nodeList As XmlNodeList
    Try
        nodeList = contextNode.SelectNodes(pathExpression)
        Return nodeList
    Catch ex As XPathException
```

```
        Console.WriteLine("XMLException: " + ex.Message)
        Return Nothing
    End Try

End Function
```

In Listing 4.7, note that the results of the XPath queries are always returned as list objects, even if only a single node in the result is expected. This is done purely for the sake of simplicity. If you want to write some additional `xpath()` method implementations that return only a single node instead of a list, you can do it easily—in Java, by passing `XPathConstants.NODE` to the `execute()` method, and in VB.NET, by calling the method `SelectSingleNode()` on the context node in place of `SelectNodes()`.

Visual Studio has another mechanism for handling XPath queries—a set of classes that are optimized for fast query execution. These classes do not load the full functionality of the XML DOM objects, so memory is not wasted on unneeded instructions when the main focus is on querying the XML. The approach starts with the `XPathNavigator` class, a reference to which is obtained by calling the `CreateNavigator()` method on a regular DOM object. Following is a simple method that illustrates this coding approach to XPath queries.

```
    Public Function xpathNav(ByVal contextNode As _ XmlNode, ByVal
    pathExpression As String) As _ XPathNodeIterator
        Dim pathNav As XPathNavigator
        Dim pathNodeIter As XPathNodeIterator
        Try
            pathNav = contextNode.CreateNavigator()
            pathNodeIter = _
            pathNav.Select(pathExpression)
            Return pathNodeIter
        Catch ex As XPathException
            Console.WriteLine(ex.Message)
            Return Nothing
        End Try
    End Function
```

A Word about Namespaces

XML uses the concept of a namespace as a mechanism to avoid name collisions between XML documents designed by different organizations employing tags with the same name. A *namespace* is simply a unique identifier (typically based on an organization's URL) that can be applied to any or all tags or attributes in an XML. A namespace can be declared as a default namespace, applying to all children of the element in which it is declared. A namespace can also be declared as a nondefault namespace with a tag name prefix, and namespace members include only those elements using the prefix with their tag names. Namespaces are declared using special attributes on an element; in the following example, the namespace `rt` is declared on the root of the sample XML: `<ibmTools xmlns:rt="http://www.ibm.com"/>`. The namespace declaration is composed of the `xmlns` designation, the namespace prefix (`rt`), and the namespace URI (Universal Resource Indicator, "http://www.ibm.com"). The URI provides uniqueness to the namespace.

To apply the `rt` namespace to an XML element, `rt` is used as a colon-separated prefix to the tag name (for example, `<rt:tool rt:rxt="RQM">`. When an element is included in a namespace, its tag name without the prefix is referred to as the local name (`tool` is the local name in this example). Either elements or attributes can be namespace members, as in: `<tool rt:rxt="RQM">`.

All of the XPath examples thus far are *not* namespace-aware. XPath, of course, does support namespace-aware queries. Some of the mechanisms of support have already been mentioned: there is a `namespace` axis (Table 4.2) and a `prefix:*` node test (Table 4.3).

If your XML uses namespaces, your XPath queries will, of course, have to reflect the namespace a given node belongs to. So, for example, if you modify the sample XML to declare the `rt` namespace in the root tag, and put the final `<tool>` element and its `<name>` child in the namespace, you get the following XML, which is used to illustrate some common namespace-aware queries.

```
<?xml version="1.0"?>
<!--Sample XML 04-2-->
<ibmTools xmlns:rt="http://www.ibm.com/">
    <tool rxt="RFT">
        <name>Rational Functional Tester</name>
        <version>8.1.0</version>
    </tool>
    <tool rxt="RPT">
        <name>Rational Performance Tester</name>
        <version>8.1.0</version>
    </tool>
    <rt:tool rxt="RQM">
        <rt:name>Rational Quality Manager</rt:name>
        <version>2.0</version>
    </rt:tool>
</ibmTools>
```

The first query to consider uses a simple location path. Using the document element as context, the following query returns the `tool` node in the `rt` namespace (i.e., `<rt:tool>`):

```
"ibmTools/rt:tool"
```

An equivalent query that returns the same result can be built with an axis:

```
"descendant::rt:tool"
```

The following related query (again, with the `Document` element as the context node) returns all of the nodes in the `rt` namespace:

```
"descendant::rt:*"
```

This query returns two nodes: `<rt:tool>` and `<rt:name>`.

Finally, there is an XPath function called `local-name()`, so that if you wanted to write a query to return nodes that are in a namespace, but without using the namespace prefix, you could write:

```
"descendant::*[local-name()='tool']"
```

This query returns all nodes on the descendant axis whose local name equals `'tool'`. In our case, three nodes are returned: two `<tool>` nodes and one `<rt:tool>` node.

Note that if you request the following, the XPath engine returns to you the `rxt` attribute `rxt=RQM`:

```
"ibmTools/rt:tool/attribute::rxt"
```

However, if you request the following, then nothing is returned, because the `rt` namespace on the `<tool>` tag is not automatically inherited by the tag's attribute.:

```
"ibmTools/rt:tool/attribute::rt:rxt"
```

Code for Namespace-Aware XPath Searches

For namespace-aware XMLs in Java, there are some complexities that must be dealt with. First, you must make sure that your XML documents are loaded using a `DocumentBuilderFactory` that is has namespace-awareness 'turned on'. This appears in the `loadDoc()` method shown in Listing 4.1 in the following line:

```
docBuilderFactory.setNamespaceAware(true);
```

It is important to check this line of code because if it is omitted, the default is false, and the parser ignores any namespaces you use. Setting the value to true has no effect for namespace-*un*aware XML shown earlier, so leaving `setNamespaceAware(true)` should be safe.

Another important note in setting up namespace-aware XPath searching is that Java 5 and Java 6 (also known as 1.5 and 1.6) require you to supply a helper class for namespace-aware XPath queries. This class must implement the interface `NamespaceContext`, which enables the XPath engine to look up prefixes from URIs and URIs from prefixes. Without a `NamespaceContext` implementation, the exception `XPathStylesheetDOM3Exception` is thrown when you try to execute your query. (In an upcoming Java release, there should be a default `NamespaceContext` implementation, so eventually, you will not have to supply this class). After you have built an implementation for `NamespaceContext`, you can write code to execute your namespace-aware XPath queries. Listing 4.8 shows code for a simple version of the `NamespaceContext`-implementing class (it persists only one `namespace` per XML), and Listing 4.9 shows calling code for a namespace-aware XPath query.

Listing 4.8 `NamespaceContextImpl`: implementation of interface `NamespaceContext`

Java

```java
public class NamespaceContextImpl implements NamespaceContext {
    private HashMap<String, String> prefixUri = null;
    private HashMap<String, String> uriPrefix = null;

    public NamespaceContextImpl() {
        prefixUri = new HashMap<String, String>();
        uriPrefix = new HashMap<String, String>();
        // values defined in the NamespaceContext javadoc
        prefixUri.put(XMLConstants.XML_NS_PREFIX,
            XMLConstants.XML_NS_URI);
        prefixUri.put(XMLConstants.XMLNS_ATTRIBUTE,
            XMLConstants.XMLNS_ATTRIBUTE_NS_URI);
        uriPrefix.put(XMLConstants.XML_NS_URI,
            XMLConstants.XML_NS_PREFIX);
        uriPrefix.put(XMLConstants.XMLNS_ATTRIBUTE_NS_URI,
            XMLConstants.XMLNS_ATTRIBUTE);
    }
    public String getNamespaceURI(String prefix) {
        String uri = (String)prefixUri.get(prefix);
        if (prefix.equals("")){ //DEFAULT_NS_PREFIX
            return XMLConstants.NULL_NS_URI;
        } else if (uri.equals("")){//unbound prefix
            return XMLConstants.NULL_NS_URI;
        } else if (prefix == null){//null
            throw new IllegalArgumentException();
        } else {
            return uri; //bound prefix
        }
    }
    public String getPrefix(String uri) {
        String prefix = (String)uriPrefix.get(uri);
        if (uri.equals("")){ //default Namespace URI
            return XMLConstants.DEFAULT_NS_PREFIX;
        } else if (prefix.equals("")){//unbound Namespace URI
            return XMLConstants.NULL_NS_URI;
        } else if (uri == null){//null
            throw new IllegalArgumentException();
        } else {
```

```
            return prefix; //bound Namespace URI
        }
    }
    public void setNamespace(String prefix, String uri){
        prefixUri.put(prefix, uri);
        uriPrefix.put(uri, prefix);
    }
    public void setNamespace(HashMap<String,String> prefixUri){
        Iterator<String> it = prefixUri.keySet().iterator();
        String prefix = null;
        String uri = null;
        while (it.hasNext()){
            prefix = (String)it.next();
            uri = (String)prefixUri.get(prefix);
            this.prefixUri.put(prefix, uri);
            this.uriPrefix.put(uri, prefix);
        }
    }
    public Iterator getPrefixes(String uri) {
        return null;//no implementation needed
    }
}
```

As noted earlier, Listing 4.9 shows calling code for a namespace-aware XPath query. The signature of this method differs from the one shown in Listing 4.7 because namespace-aware queries require the namespaces in use to be explicitly set. This is done using a HashMap in Java or a Hashtable in VB.NET, so that the calling code (in Java) for a query on our sample XML looks like the following:

```
HashMap<String,String> ns = new HashMap<String,String>();
ns.put("rt", "http://www.ibm.com/");
NodeList xpsearchNS = xpath(xmlDocNS, "ibmTools/rt:tool", ns);
```

Listing 4.9   Sample calling code for a namespace-aware XPath query

Java

```
public NodeList xpath(Node contextNode, String xpathQuery,
        HashMap<String,String> ns){
    NodeList nodeList = null;
    try {
        XPath xpath = XPathFactory.newInstance().newXPath();
        NamespaceContext namespaceContext = new
```

```
            NamespaceContextImpl();
        ((NamespaceContextImpl)
            namespaceContext).setNamespace(ns);
        xpath.setNamespaceContext(namespaceContext);
        nodeList = (NodeList)xpath.evaluate(xpathQuery,
            contextNode, XPathConstants.NODESET);
        return nodeList;
    } catch (XPathExpressionException xpe){
        System.out.println(xpe.getMessage());
        return null;
    }
}
```

VB.NET

```
Public Function xpath(ByVal contextNode As XmlNode, _
        ByVal pathExpression As String, _
        ByVal ns As Hashtable) As XmlNodeList
    Dim nodeList As XmlNodeList
    Dim doc As XmlDocument
    Try
        doc = getDocRef(contextNode)
        Dim xmlnsMgr As XmlNamespaceManager = New _
            XmlNamespaceManager(doc.NameTable)
        ' Add the namespaces
        Dim it As IDictionaryEnumerator = ns.GetEnumerator
        While (it.MoveNext())
            xmlnsMgr.AddNamespace(it.Entry.Key, it.Entry.Value)
        End While
        nodeList = contextNode.SelectNodes( _
            pathExpression, xmlnsMgr)
        Return nodeList
    Catch ex As XPathException
        Console.WriteLine("XMLException: " + ex.Message)
        Return Nothing
    Catch nre As NullReferenceException
        Console.WriteLine("Null context ref: " + nre.Message)
        Return Nothing
    End Try
End Function
Private Function getDocRef(ByVal node As XmlNode) As XmlDocument
```

```
      Dim doc As XmlDocument
      If (TypeOf node Is XmlDocument) Then
          doc = CType(node, XmlDocument)
      Else
          doc = node.OwnerDocument
      End If
      Return doc
End Function
```

This discussion should give you a sense of the power that XPath has for test automation. This is not a complete discussion of XPath; so if you are inclined to use it, get more resources! Broad queries can be made that return large node sets, and highly specific queries can be made that return just a small number of desired nodes. The tremendous flexibility of XPath can make the job of XML data validation much quicker, with code that is more readable and maintainable.

Serializing XML to a String or to a File

One of the more practical and useful things you need to do is to take an XML DOM involved in a test and change it into a form in which it can either be saved or printed. This is useful for debugging a test or for documenting defects. In other words, you need to serialize your DOM either to a file on disk or to a String. This can be done easily with the `XMLSerializer` class (named the same in Java and VB.NET). In Java, you use an `OutputStream` to achieve serialization. (`Writers` can be used, but they do not let you handle internationalized characters.) In VB.NET, `StringWriter` or `StreamWriter` can be used. A core method that takes a generic `OutputStream` argument (Java) or `XmlTextWriter` argument (VB.NET) is shown in Listing 4.10. Note that in both cases, you must check whether the node you are serializing is an Attribute node because these require special handling.

Listing 4.10   Serializing XML nodes via a Writer

Java
```java
public void serializeXml(Node node, OutputStream outputStream) {
    OutputFormat format = null;
    try {
        format = new OutputFormat("xml", "UTF-8", true);
        XMLSerializer serializer =
            new XMLSerializer(outputStream, format);
        if(!Attr.class.isInstance(node)){
        if (node instanceof Attr){
            serializer.asDOMSerializer();
            if (node instanceof Document){
                serializer.serialize((Document)node);
            } else {
```

```java
            serializer.serialize((Element)node);
        }
    } else {
        Attr attr = (Attr)node;
        StringBuilder sb =
            new StringBuilder(
                attr.getNodeName() + "=" +
                attr.getNodeValue());
        outputStream.write(
            sb.toString().getBytes("UTF-8"));
    }
} catch (IOException ioe) {
    System.out.println(ioe.getMessage());
    }
}
```

VB.NET

```vbnet
Public Sub serializeXml(ByVal node As XmlNode, _
        ByVal writer As XmlTextWriter)
    Try
        If (node.NodeType = XmlNodeType.Element) Or _
            (node.NodeType = XmlNodeType.Document) Then
            Dim serializer As New XmlSerializer(node.GetType())
            serializer.Serialize(writer, node)
        ElseIf (node.NodeType = XmlNodeType.Text) Then
            writer.WriteString(node.InnerText)
        ElseIf (node.NodeType = XmlNodeType.Attribute) Then
            Dim attr As XmlAttribute = CType(node, XmlAttribute)
            writer.WriteAttributeString(attr.Name, attr.Value)
        End If
    Catch ex As Exception
        Console.WriteLine(ex.Message)
    End Try
End Sub
```

You can write some wrapper methods for serializeXml() that set up the kind of object you are going to use and handle the output. Note that because our output handles the actual output, there is no return value from serializeXml(). Listing 4.11 shows method calls for string and file output.

Listing 4.11   Serializing XML to a file or a string

Java

```java
public void serializeXmlToFile(Node node, String outputPath){
    try {
        FileOutputStream fos =
            new FileOutputStream(outputPath);
        serializeXml(node, fos);
    } catch (FileNotFoundException fnf) {
        System.out.println("Error: File Not Found");
    }
}
public String serializeXmlToString(Node node){
    ByteArrayOutputStream baos = new ByteArrayOutputStream();
    serializeXml(node, baos);
    try {
        return baos.toString("UTF-8");
    } catch (UnsupportedEncodingException uee){
        return baos.toString();
    }
}
```

VB.NET

```vbnet
Public Sub serializeXmlToFile(ByVal node As XmlNode, _
        ByVal filePath As String)
    Dim xw As XmlTextWriter = New XmlTextWriter(filePath, _
        System.Text.Encoding.UTF8)
    serializeXml(node, xw)
    xw.Close()
End Sub
Public Function serializeXmlToString(ByVal node As XmlNode) _
        As String
    Dim sw As New StringWriter
    Dim xw As XmlTextWriter = New XmlTextWriter(sw)
    serializeXml(node, xw)
    Return sw.ToString
End Function
```

As a side note, for convenience, you can easily override `serializeXmlToFile()` to take a `File` argument instead of a `String` argument.

Processing XML with SAX in Rational Functional Tester

As previously mentioned, SAX parsing requires a more elaborate setup than DOM parsing of XML, but it becomes attractive when you are dealing with large XMLs. What constitutes a large XML depends on your box's hardware spec, of course, but if you are using a box of relatively recent vintage, large is probably somewhere in the multiple megabyte range, and small is in the range of hundreds of kilobytes or smaller. Because setting up DOM code is simpler, it is probably wisest to try that first on your largest XMLs and see if the performance outcome is acceptable. If you need something faster, SAX is recommended.

Before delving into SAX, it is important to note that SAX is chiefly a creature of Java. While there is an open-source port of the SAX API specification to C# (see http://sourceforge. net/projects/saxdotnet), the .NET framework itself doesn't contain an implementation of SAX. Rather, it comes with a parser implemented in the `System.Xml.XmlReader` class (a pull parser instead of SAX's push parser). For this reason, this chapter does not examine SAX in .NET, but it does include a short example using `XmlReader`.

Implementing with SAX

To use SAX, you need to build custom classes that contain event handlers for the various SAX events. The SAX parser calls these handlers as it scans through an XML document, firing off events in response to document contents.

> **NOTE** You can keep up with new developments in SAX at the SAX website www. saxproject.org/, if that is where your interests or needs take you.

There are six SAX handler classes, four of which are considered standard classes, and two of which are extensions to SAX; Table 4.4 lists the SAX handler classes.

To handle standard XML-related testing tasks, you need to implement only SAX event-handling methods that help to pull data out of target XMLs. This can be done with just two classes: one that implements both the `ContentHandler` and `LexicalHandler` interfaces and one that implements the `ErrorHandler` interface. For the methods not needed for data-related testing tasks, you can provide stubs. (You could also implement with a `DefaultHandler`; the approach shown here is selected because it is simpler.)

Typically, actual transactional data in XML is found either in element text (as character text or as a CDATA section) or in element attributes. It is also possible that data that might be significant for testing could appear in a processing instruction or in an XML comment. Data from all of these different element types can be captured with five event handlers: three are specified by the `ContentHandler` interface [element name, text, attributes, and processing instructions are handled with `ContentHandler` methods `startElement()`, `characters()`, and `processingInstruction()`], and the other two by the `LexicalHandler` with comments and CDATA sections being handled by `LexicalHandler` events `endCDATA()` and `comment()`.

Table 4.4   SAX 2.0 Handler Classes

Class	Import	Description
ContentHandler	org.xml.sax.ContentHandler	Handles element text, attribute callbacks, and others
ErrorHandler	org.xml.sax.ErrorHandler	Handles parser error notifications
EntityResolver	org.xml.sax.EntityResolver	Handles parser entity resolution notifications
DTDHandler	org.xml.sax.DTDHandler	Handles DTD unparsed entity and notation callbacks
LexicalHandler	org.xml.sax.ext.LexicalHandler	Handles lexical callbacks (comment, CDATA, DTD, and so on)
DeclHandler	org.xml.sax.ext.DeclHandler	Handles DTD element, attribute, and entity callbacks

*SAX also offers a DefaultHandler (org.xml.sax.helpers.DefaultHandler), which contains implementations of the first four interfaces in this table. You can extend the DefaultHandler in a custom class and override just the methods you need.

The class RFTSAXContentHandler will implement the ContentHandler and LexicalHandler interfaces and will provide implementations of the five data-capture event handlers. The five events that will handle the capture of XML data are startElement(), characters(), processingInstruction(), endCDATA(), and comment().

The ErrorHandler-implementing class is RFTSAXErrorHandler. The ErrorHandler interface requires three methods: warning(), error(), and fatalError().

Before examining the actual RFTSAXContentHandler code, there is a small design consideration: how to handle the XML data when the SAX parser fires its events. The data needs to be packaged as the SAX engine parses it on the fly. To do this, we'll use a simple class, in which all of the data for any specific XML element can be held. The data for each XML element is loaded into an object of this type on parsing, and the full data set from a parsing run is managed with an ArrayList of these objects. A simple class that meets these requirements is the Tag class shown in Listing 4.12.

Listing 4.12 The Tag class

Java

```
public class Tag {
    public String name = null;
    public String content = null;
    public String type = null;
    public HashMap<String,String> attr =
        new HashMap<String,String>();
}
```

The Tag class contains a set of fields sufficient to describe the data from a single XML tag. The name field corresponds to the element name in the case of a tag, the target in the case of a processing instruction or "comment" for comment tags. The content field holds whatever content is associated with the tag, either text, processing instruction data, or an XML comment. The type field keeps an indication of the data type (use the standard DOM type notations, #text, #cdata-section, and #comment, and add #processing-instruction). Finally, attr is a HashMap to store any attributes found.

To manage Tag objects, you need some custom members of RFTSAXContentHandler. These are shown in Listing 4.13.

Listing 4.13 Custom members of RFTSAXContentHandler for management of Tags

Java

```
private ArrayList<Tag> tags = new ArrayList<Tag>();
private Tag tag = null;
private void setupParseCapture() {
    tag = new Tag();
    tags.add(tag);
}
public ArrayList<Tag> getTagData() {
    return tags;
}
```

The private field tag that you'll see in RFTSAXContentHandler corresponds to the current Tag instance holding the data of the XML element currently being parsed; the tags ArrayList is the container in which all the Tag instances for a parsing run are loaded for return to the calling class. The setupParseCapture() method creates a new Tag instance and loads it into the tags ArrayList. This method has to appear in any event handler that fires at the beginning of a tag reading. Finally, the class needs a method to return the tags ArrayList to the calling class: getTagData().

This example does not explicitly deal with namespace issues, but as you can see from the `startElement()` signature, the SAX parser includes namespace information in its callbacks. If you need to work with namespaces, you can handle them with some fairly straightforward changes to the sample code shown in this discussion. With these custom bits in hand, you can look at the key event handlers in the `RFTSAXContentHandler` class, which is shown in Listing 4.14.

Listing 4.14   Event handlers in `RFTSAXContentHandler` (implements `ContentHandler` and `LexicalHandler`)

Java

```
public class RFTSAXContentHandler implements ContentHandler,
     LexicalHandler {
  /* ContentHandler methods */
  public void startElement(String namespaceURI,
     String localName, String qName, Attributes attr) {
     setupParseCapture();
     tag.name = localName;
     for (int n = 0; n < attr.getLength(); n++) {
         tag.attr.put(
         attr.getLocalName(n), attr.getValue(n));
     }
  }
  public void characters(char[] ch, int start, int length) {
     String output = new String(ch, start, length);
     if (output.trim().length() != 0) {
         tag.type = "#text";
         tag.content = output;
     }
  }
  public void processingInstruction(String target,
         String data) {
     setupParseCapture();
     tag.name = target;
     tag.type = "#processing-instruction";
     tag.content = data;
  }
  /* LexicalHandler methods */
  public void comment(char[] ch, int start, int length) {
     String output = new String(ch, start, length);
     setupParseCapture();
     tag.name = null;
```

```
        tag.type = "#comment";
    tag.content = output;
    }
    public void endCDATA() {
        tag.type = "#cdata-section";
    }
}
```

Some comments about these methods are necessary. First, it is interesting to note that in `startElement()`, the tag *text content* is not reported; only the tag name and attributes are. Text content is handled by the `characters()` method.

The `characters()` callback has some interesting behavior. First, the content data is passed back to the event handler as a `char` array, along with start and length parameters. The parser is required only to ensure that the data for the event is *within* the reported length. The `char` array might legally be longer than the reported length, and if you read past the length indicated, you might get "gibberish" data back. Furthermore, parsers have the option of passing back element content in either one call to `characters()` or in multiple calls. Calls can also include whitespace. You should become familiar with your parser implementation on these points, so that you can fashion your methods to interact properly with the parser behavior.

The final `ContentHandler` method is `processingInstruction()`. This callback method receives a processing instruction target and data. The target is defined as the first term in the processing instruction; the rest is data, regardless of the punctuation used.

There are two `LexicalHandler` methods: one for XML comments and the other for CDATA notifications. The `comment()` method works much like the `characters()` method. Finally, if you parse a CDATA-containing tag, the tag content is captured by `characters()`, and you can use `endCDATA()` to change the tag type from #text to #cdata-section. Note that neither `endCDATA()` nor `startCDATA()` handle the actual content from the CDATA section.

Finally, note that the `ContentHandler` and `LexicalHandler` interfaces require several more methods each than what is shown in Listing 4.14. These are stubbed in the full `RFTSAXContentHandler` class; they are omitted from Listing 4.14 for clarity. This ends the work implementing `ContentHandler` and `LexicalHandler` callbacks. All you need to do next is implement an `ErrorHandler`, and you are ready to parse. Listing 4.15 shows the code for `RFTSAXErrorHandler`.

Listing 4.15   Class RFTSAXErrorHandler (implements ErrorHandler)

Java
```
public class RFTSAXErrorHandler implements ErrorHandler {
    public void warning(SAXParseException e) {
        System.out.println("***Warning***\n" +
            "line: " + e.getLineNumber() + ", " +
```

```
                e.getSystemId() + ", " +
                e.getMessage());
    }
    public void error(SAXParseException e) {
        System.out.println("***Nonfatal Error***\n" +
                "line: " + e.getLineNumber() + ", " +
                e.getSystemId() + ", " +
                e.getMessage());
    }
    public void fatalError(SAXParseException e) {
        System.out.println("***Fatal Error***\n" +
                "line: " + e.getLineNumber() + ", " +
                e.getSystemId() + ", " +
                e.getMessage());
    }
}
```

The SAX `ErrorHandler` interface specifies three callbacks for three levels of errors: a warning, a nonfatal error, and a fatal error. Each of these events receives a `SAXParserException`, which returns the line number where the error occurred, the document URI, and an error message. All three `ErrorHandler` methods can be implemented with identical code, as shown in Listing 4.15.

With the `ErrorHandler` implemented, you are ready to write some parsing code. To start a parser, four tasks need to be accomplished:

- An `XMLReader` must be created with the `createXMLreader()` method.
- Instances of the handler classes must be created.
- Handlers must be registered.
- An `InputSource` must be identified.

When these tasks are finished, you are ready to parse. You can place all three classes designed in this exercise in the same file as your TestScript class, or you can place them in separate files in the same package in the classpath. A basic calling script for parsing with the required exception handling is shown in Listing 4.16.

Listing 4.16   An RFT script for SAX parsing

Java
```
try {
    /* create reader */
    XMLReader reader = XMLReaderFactory.createXMLReader();
    /* create handler instances */
    RFTSAXContentHandler saxContentHandler =
```

```
        new RFTSAXContentHandler();
    RFTSAXErrorHandler saxErrorHandler =
        new RFTSAXErrorHandler();
    /* register ContentHandler */
    reader.setContentHandler(saxContentHandler);
    /* register ErrorHandler */
    reader.setErrorHandler(saxErrorHandler);
    /* register LexicalHandler */
    reader.setProperty(
        "http://xml.org/sax/properties/lexical-handler",
        saxContentHandler);
    /* identify InputSource */
    File uriFile = new File(uri);
    FileInputStream fis = new FileInputStream(uriFile);
    InputSource inSource = new InputSource(fis);
    /* parse! */
    reader.parse(inSource);
    /* get return data as an ArrayList of Tag objects */
    tags = saxContentHandler.getTagData();
    for (int n = 0; n < tags.size(); n++){
        String tagName =((Tag)tags.get(n)).name;
        String text = ((Tag)tags.get(n)).content;
        String tagType = ((Tag)tags.get(n)).type;
        HashMap<String,String> attr = ((Tag)tags.get(n)).attr;
        System.out.println(tagName + ", " + text + ", " +
            tagType + ", " + attr);
    }
} catch (SAXException saxe) {
    System.out.println(saxe.getMessage());
} catch (IOException ioe) {
    System.out.println("IOException: " + ioe.getMessage());
}
```

As discussed previously, there is more going on with SAX than what is described in this introduction. If you're interested in pursuing a broader understanding of SAX, there are excellent publications available (some of them are found in the literature section at the end of this chapter) and in resources on the Web.

Implementing with .NET's XmlReader

As noted previously, SAX emerged from the Java world and is not part of the .NET world, at least as far as the standard .NET libraries are concerned. Instead, .NET provides a conceptually related but different implementation for fast parsing in the `XmlReader` class. Setting up a basic parsing routine with `XmlReader` is simpler than with SAX—custom classes do not need to be supplied. Instead, all you need is to instantiate an `XmlReader`, and use a few of its methods to trap XML tag values as the parser scans through them. You can capture tag values in a VB.NET structure (an extension of the concept of a C-type struct) and return tag data as an array of structures. Listing 4.17 shows the structure and a simple parsing method.

Listing 4.17   A simple XmlReader implementation

VB.NET

```
Structure TAG
    Public name As String
    Public content As String
    Public type As String
    Public attr As Hashtable
End Structure
Public Function readXml(ByVal pathToXmlFile As String) As TAG()
    Dim ctr As Short = 0
    Dim attrCtr As Short = 0
    Dim content As String
    Dim tags() As TAG = Nothing
    Dim reader As New XmlTextReader(pathToXmlFile)
    Try
        While reader.Read
            ReDim Preserve tags(ctr)
            content = reader.ReadString
            tags(ctr).name = reader.Name
            ' clean up any <cr><lf> in the content
            tags(ctr).content = content.Replace(vbCrLf, "")
            tags(ctr).type = reader.NodeType.ToString
            ' handle attributes on a tag
            If (reader.HasAttributes) Then
                tags(ctr).attr = New Hashtable
                For attrCtr = 0 To reader.AttributeCount - 1
                    reader.MoveToAttribute(attrCtr)
                    tags(ctr).attr.Add(reader.Name, reader.Value)
                Next
```

```
        End If
        ctr = ctr + 1
    End While
    Return tags
Catch npe As NullReferenceException
    Return Nothing
End Try
End Function
```

Summary

As you can see, XML manipulation for testing purposes can range across the entire XML universe; almost every aspect of XML can come into play when it comes to testing. Using the techniques described in this chapter, you can compare test XMLs against baseline XMLs or against data from Rational Functional Tester datapools, flat files, SQL calls, or practically any data source or repository to which you have access. With XML testing using Rational Functional Tester, you are limited by little beyond your imagination.

For Further Information

Harold, Rusty Eliotte and W. Scott Means. *XML in a Nutshell*, Third Edition. Sebastopol, CA: O'Reilly Media, Inc., 2004.

Kay, Michael. *XPath 2.0 Programmer's Reference*. Indianapolis, IN: Wrox, 2004.

Bornstein, Niel M. *.NET and XML*. Sebastopol, CA: O'Reilly Media, Inc., 2003.

Wahlin, Dan. *XML for ASP.NET Developers*. Indianapolis, IN: Sams Publishing, 2001.

Harold, Eliotte Rusty. *Processing XML with Java*. Boston, MA: Addison-Wesley Professional, 2002.

## CHAPTER 5

Managing Script Data

Chip Davis, Daniel Chirillo, Fariz Saracevic

In this chapter, you learn how Rational Functional Tester can manage script data. You start with in depth coverage of Rational Functional Tester datapools, followed by techniques to access databases from Java and .NET, and you learn how to handle user-specific runtime variables.

Accessing Rational Functional Tester Datapools

The easiest and most common way of managing test data in your scripts is to use *datapools*. Datapools are essentially just tables of data that are represented in Rational Functional Tester as simple test elements, along with the scripts and maps. You can have multiple datapools and these can be shared by multiple test scripts.

Although simple datapool usage is easy, you can do more sophisticated things with datapools to handle test data in automated testing. For basic data-driven testing involving reading test data from a datapool and sending to the application under test during playback, you can rely on the wizards to create the datapool commands in the test scripts. For more powerful manipulation of datapools, you can use several methods in the Rational Functional Tester Application Programming Interface (API). These methods are in the package `com.rational.test.ft.datapool`, which is fully documented in the product Help.

You might want to use more than one datapool with a particular script. You might want to control the rows of data that are read while the script executes. You might even want to add data to a datapool while a test is running, instead of just reading data. All of this requires adding code into your test scripts and the examples in this section show you how to do this.

Datapool Basics

Datapools are essentially just tables of data that have special functions that enable Rational Functional Tester to work with them more easily. When you use datapools, you do not have to concern yourself with file locations or SQL statements to retrieve test data the way you would using files or database tables. You also do not need to use another application or editor, such as a spreadsheet or database tool, to work with your test data. You work with your datapools in Rational Functional Tester just like you work with scripts, object maps, and other test assets.

A datapool is made up of columns and rows of data. The columns are called *variables* and they have a type to represent the data in that column, such as a string or a float. Note that the default type is always a string. The rows are called *records*, and each row contains a value, which could be null, for every variable. You read a datapool row by row, meaning that there is always a pointer, called the *cursor*, to a particular record at a given point in time. When Rational Functional Tester reads from a datapool, it reads a variable from the current record.

How Do I Read from a Datapool?

When you use the data-driven wizards to automatically generate datapool script code, you see only one method in the script to read from the datapool. This is the `dpString` method, and you will probably see this often in scripts with datapools. An example of this is:

```
expirationDateText().setText(dpString("ExpirationDateText"));
```

Other methods required to open and iterate through the datapool exist, but these are not shown in the test script. When you want to control and program these functions yourself, you add them into the test script.

Rational Functional Tester always reads a datapool value into a string by default, even for numbers. You can use several other methods to read different types of data, such as dpInt, dpFloat, and dpValue. You use these methods the same way you use dpString, for example:

```
Integer quantity = dpInt("Quantity");
// Perform some math calculation with quantity
quantityText().setText(quantity.toString());
```

For this code to work correctly, the datapool variable `"Quantity"` must be of type `integer`, as shown in Figure 5.1.

You normally use the name of the datapool variable, or column, with these methods to read a particular value. The variable name is contained in quotes as shown in the previous two examples. These methods always retrieve the current row of the datapool. Instead of using the variable name, you can use the index number to indicate which column value to read. The index starts at zero and increases from left to right. For example, if you wanted to read the fourth column of the current record, you would use:

```
creditCombo().setText(dpString(3));
```

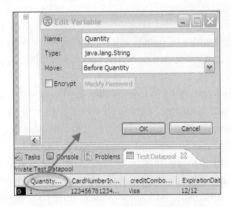

Figure 5.1   Datapool variable—setting the variable type to integer

Multiple Scripts, Multiple Datapools

Typically, when you use the Rational Functional Tester data-driven wizards, you have a one-to-one relationship between a test script and a datapool. You are also likely to create a shared datapool at some point, which means multiple scripts use the same datapool. In both of these cases, a given test script is using only one particular datapool. You do not see any explicit lines of code in the scripts showing which datapool is accessed or how the records are incremented because the Rational Functional Tester handles this automatically. You can view the association between test scripts and their datapools by opening test scripts and looking in the Script Explorer. You can also view this association without opening test scripts by right-clicking on a test script from the Project Explorer and selecting Properties, and then clicking on Functional Test Script, as shown in Figure 5.2.

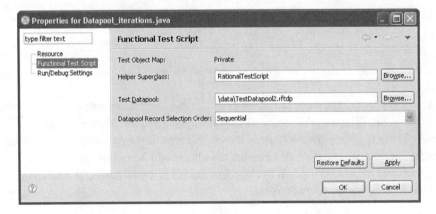

Figure 5.2   Test script properties—viewing the associated datapool

You might want to use more than one datapool with a given test script, in which case you will need to manually add code to the script. Whenever you have more than one datapool per test script, you need to explicitly state the name of the datapools to open them in the script. Figure 5.3 shows a simple test script that reads data from two different datapools: FirstDatapool and SecondDatapool. Note that you see only the association to the first, or default, datapool in the Rational Functional Tester Script Explorer as shown in Figure 5.3; the association to the second datapool is not shown graphically.

Figure 5.3   Script Explorer showing the default associated datapool

To open a second datapool, you must add several lines of code to open the file, load the datapool, and open the iterator (controls the cursor or row pointer) for the datapool. After you create the new datapool and iterator in your script, you can use the same methods to work with the datapool as the default datapool by using the iterator or datapool object prefix. This is shown in Listing 5.1, which gets a phone number from the first datapool (shown in the script explorer) and then a credit card number from the second datapool.

TEST ASSETS IN RATIONAL FUNCTIONAL TESTER

To clarify the test assets discussed here: test script contains the test procedure (the steps) and the verification (pass or fail) points, and the datapool contains data (numbers, names, values, and so on) that is used in the tests. Although some scripts might always use the same set of data (a one-to-one relationship), some might not (one-to-many, many-to-one, or many-to-many). For this reason, the scripts and datapools are kept as separate test assets.

Listing 5.1   Example How to Add Second Datapool

```
...
import org.eclipse.hyades. execution.runtime.datapool.IDatapool;
import org.eclipse.hyades.execution.runtime.datapool.IDatapoolIterator;
...


// Get a value from the first (script) datapool
String phone = dpString("PhoneText");


// Open a second datapool
java.io.File dpFile = new java.io.File(
                           (String)
getOption(IOptionName.DATASTORE),
                              "SecondDatapool.rftdp");
IDatapool dp2 = dpFactory().load(dpFile, true);
IDatapoolIterator dp2I = dpFactory().open(dp2, null);
dp2I.dpInitialize(dp2);


// Get a value from the second datapool
String ccNum = dp2I.dpString("CardNumber");


// ... use the values in the test script here
logInfo("The first datapool's phone number is: "+phone);
logInfo("The second datapool's credit card number is: "+ccNum);
```

Setting the Datapool Row

Typically, Rational Functional Tester automatically handles which record (row) of a datapool is being read. It also automatically increments the cursor that points to a row for each datapool iteration (see the section, "Handling User-Specific Runtime Variables," later in this chapter) or when another script reads from the same datapool. However, there are times when you might need to manipulate this yourself through script code. You might want to count a certain number of times to the desired row, or you might want to look for a particular variable value.

The following example shows how to set the datapool cursor to a particular row. In this example, you loop through each row of the datapool until you find a specific value, and then you reset the cursor back to the beginning.

```
// continued from previous example
...


// Set the datapool cursor to the row with quantity of 3
```

```
dp2I.dpInitialize(dp2);
while (dp2I.dpInt("Quantity") < 3) // Quantity is an integer in datapool
{
      dp2I.dpNext();
}
ccNum = dp2I.dpString("CardNumber");     // This is 1st row Quantity is 3

// ... use the value in the test script here
logInfo("The credit card number with a quantity of 3 is: "+ccNum);


dp2I.dpReset();    // move the cursor back to the beginning
```

Adding Rows to a Datapool During Test Playback

So far, you examined several examples of how to read values from datapools. You might usually think of test data as being fixed at the time you are ready to execute tests. However, you might want to add value into a datapool while a test is running. You might do this to retrieve some value from the application under test and store it back into a datapool for another test to use. To do this, you create an equivalence class from the datapool and then use the `constructRecord` and `appendRecord` methods to create the new row. You then use dpFactory to save the record into the datapool.

In Listing 5.2, you create a new record, copy the values from the first record into the new record, and then save the record into the datapool.

Listing 5.2   Example of Adding Rows to a Datapool

```
...
import org.eclipse.hyades.edit.datapool.IDatapoolCell;
import org.eclipse.hyades.edit.datapool.IDatapoolEquivalenceClass;
import org.eclipse.hyades.edit.datapool.IDatapoolRecord;
import org.eclipse.hyades.execution.runtime.datapool.IDatapool;
import org.eclipse.hyades.execution.runtime.datapool.IDatapoolIterator;
...


// continued from previous example
...


// Add a new record to the second datapool
IDatapoolEquivalenceClass equivalenceClass = (IDatapoolEquivalenceClass)
      dp2.getEquivalenceClass(dp2.getDefaultEquivalenceClassIndex());
IDatapoolRecord dpRecord = equivalenceClass.constructRecord();
```

```
// Set values of new record copying the first record
String dpCellValue = "";
for (int i = 0; i < dp2I.getDatapool().getVariableCount(); ++i)
{
     dpCellValue = dp2I.dpString(
                         dp2I.getDatapool().getVariable(i).getName());
     IDatapoolCell dpCell = (IDatapoolCell) dpRecord.getCell(i);
     dpCell.setCellValue(dpCellValue);
}
equivalenceClass.appendRecord(dpRecord);
DatapoolFactory dpFactory = DatapoolFactory.get();
dpFactory.save((org.eclipse.hyades.edit.datapool. IDatapool) dp2);


// You could also use dp2I.getDatapool().getRecordCount()
```

Adding Columns to a Datapool During Test Playback

Like the values in a datapool, you normally define the columns in a datapool while you are developing the tests, and they are then fixed when you begin running the tests. However, you might want to add a new variable to a datapool during test execution. You might want to do this for similar reasons when adding values during test execution. To do this, use the dpFactory addVariable method to create a new variable for the datapool.

In the following example, you create a new variable called "CellPhone" and copy the value from the "Phone" variable into the new record. Note that this simple example applies the same phone value into the new variable for all records in the datapool, which might not be realistic. This is equivalent to using the Copy and Paste commands in a spreadsheet to fill an entire blank column with the same value.

```
// continued from previous example
...


// Add a new variable to the second datapool
dpFactory.addVariable((org.eclipse.hyades.edit.datapool.IDatapool) dp2,
                                            "CellPhone", phone);
dpFactory.save((org.eclipse.hyades.edit.datapool.IDatapool) dp2);
// A different IDatapool interface is used than earlier statements
```

Listing 5.3 is the complete test script combining each of the previous examples.

Listing 5.3   *Complete Test Script Combining Previous Examples*

```
import resources.Ch5_DatapoolsHelper;
import com.rational.test.ft.*;
import com.rational.test.ft.datapool.DatapoolFactory;
import com.rational.test.ft.object.interfaces.*;
import com.rational.test.ft.script.*;
import com.rational.test.ft.value.*;
import com.rational.test.ft.vp.*;
import org.eclipse.hyades.edit.datapool.IDatapoolCell;
import org.eclipse.hyades.edit.datapool.IDatapoolEquivalenceClass;
import org.eclipse.hyades.edit.datapool.IDatapoolRecord;
import org.eclipse.hyades.execution.runtime.datapool.IDatapool;
import org.eclipse.hyades.execution.runtime.datapool.IDatapoolIterator;

...
public void testMain(Object[] args)
{
      // Read from this first datapool
      String phone = dpString("PhoneText");
      // ... use the value in the test script here

      // Open a second datapool
      java.io.File dpFile = new java.io.File(
                           (String)getOption(IOptionName.DATASTORE),
                           "SecondDatapool.rftdp");
      IDatapool dp2 = dpFactory().load(dpFile, true);
      IDatapoolIterator dp2I = dpFactory().open(dp2, null);
      dp2I.dpInitialize(dp2);

      // Set the datapool cursor to the row with quantity of 3
      dp2I.dpInitialize(dp2);
      while (dp2I.dpInt("Quantity") < 3)
            dp2I.dpNext();
      // Get value from second datapool
      String ccNum = dp2I.dpString("CardNumber");
      // ... use the value in the test script here
      dp2I.dpReset();
```

```
    // Add a new record to the second datapool
    IDatapoolEquivalenceClass equivalenceClass =
                    (IDatapoolEquivalenceClass) dp2.getEquivalenceClass(
                    dp2.getDefaultEquivalenceClassIndex() );
    IDatapoolRecord dpRecord = equivalenceClass.constructRecord();

    // Set values of new record copying the first record
    String dpCellValue = "";
    for (int i = 0; i < dp2I.getDatapool().getVariableCount(); ++i) {
        dpCellValue = dp2I.dpString(
                    dp2I.getDatapool().getVariable(i).getName());
        IDatapoolCell dpCell = (IDatapoolCell) dpRecord.getCell(i);
        dpCell.setCellValue(dpCellValue);
    }
    equivalenceClass.appendRecord(dpRecord);
    DatapoolFactory dpFactory = DatapoolFactory.get();

    // Add a new variable to the second datapool
    dpFactory.addVariable((org.eclipse.hyades.edit.datapool.IDatapool)
                                    dp2, "CellPhone", phone);
    dpFactory.save((org.eclipse.hyades.edit.datapool.IDatapool) dp2);
}
```

Database Access from Java and .NET

This section looks at how to create Rational Functional Tester test scripts for both Java and the Visual Basic .NET environment to access information from databases. There are a number of possible ways to implement database access in Visual Basic; however, you examine the most common way to do this in the .NET environment using ActiveX Data Objects (ADO).

This section shows the basic functions used to work with data in databases for use in Rational Functional Tester test scripts. This section does not explain SQL queries or other database-specific information. You have to know the database connection strings and the SQL queries to get the information you need for your tests. After you have this information, you can use the examples shown here as a reference to make your own specific Rational Functional Tester scripts.

JDBC Overview

Java Database Connectivity (JDBC) is an Application Programming Interface (API) that defines how a client can access a database. It provides methods for accessing databases, sending SQL statements, and processing results. There are two major sets of interfaces provided by JDBC API. One is for application writers, and the second is the lower-level JDBC driver API for driver writers. There are four different JDBC driver categories:

- JDBC Type 1—JDBC-ODBC Bridge plus Open Database Connectivity (ODBC) Driver
- JDBC Type 2—A native API partly Java technology-enabled driver
- JDBC Type 3—Pure Java Driver for Database Middleware
- JDBC Type 4—Direct-to-Database Pure Java Driver

You use JDBC APIs to create automated test scripts, and you might need to add lower-level JDBC driver developed by Relational Database Management Systems (RDBMS) or third-party vendors. If you are interested to learn more about JDBC, please visit http://java.sun.com/products/jdbc/overview.html.

ADO Overview

ADO, not to be confused with Data Access Objects (DAO), which was a previous technology used with Visual Basic, is a flexible way to develop database access code that can then be used for different data sources. This enables you to create an application, or in this case, automated test scripts, with a simple database such as Microsoft Access® and later change to an enterprise level database such as IBM DB2® or Microsoft SQL Server with barely any changes to the implementation. In Rational Functional Tester Visual Basic scripting, you can add classes for ADO.NET from the `System.Data.dll` library.

Setting Up a Rational Functional Tester Project to Access a Database

The first step to access a database from your Rational Functional Tester project is creating the connection and opening the database. This is similar regardless of the kind of database you have, although the details vary.

As a prerequisite, you must ensure that every workstation that executes these test scripts has access to the database(s). This might require the installation of database drivers for Rational Functional Tester to gain access. You might also have to determine if special database users or login credentials are used by the automated test scripts. Basically, if you cannot manually connect to the database from a particular workstation, then Rational Functional Tester is not able to either.

The general steps to establish a connection to a database in the test scripts follow:

1. Create the connection using a known connect string.
2. Open the database.
3. Interact with the database, which can include:
   - Executing queries using known SQL statements
   - Inserting or deleting rows of data

- Firing database triggers by executing SQL statements

4. Close the database.

Several similar but distinct classes are available in the .NET framework to connect to different types of databases. The following list shows the commands you can use in Visual Basic depending on the type of database to which you are connecting:

- If you have IBM DB2 or other databases with Object Linking and Embedding (OLE) access, you can use OleDbConnection and OleDbCommand in the System.Data.OleDb namespace.

- If you have Microsoft SQL Server, you can use the SqlConnection and SqlCommand objects in the System.Data.SqlClient namespace.

- For Oracle, you use the OracleConnection and OracleCommand objects in the System.Data.OracleClient namespace.

You use a simple Microsoft Access database for the example in this section. You do not need Microsoft Access to execute this test script, you need only the database file (with the .mdb file extension) and the Access drivers, which are included in most Windows installations.

Java

In the next example, you use the `DriverManager` to load JDBC driver in memory and `getConnection()` method along with a specific connection string to connect to the database. If you use a different database type, your connection string is different. If you are interested in establishing a connection to DB2, see the developerWorks article "Establishing an IBM DB2 database connection in IBM Rational Functional Tester" at http://www.ibm.com/developer-works/rational/library/07/1120_saracevic-narasappa/index.html and for Oracle, see the article "Establishing a Database Connection in IBM Rational Functional Tester Scripts" at http://www-128.ibm.com/developerworks/rational/library/05/saracevic/.

```
public void testMain(Object[] args)
{
    // Different databases would use different connection strings
    String connectStr = "jdbc:odbc:Driver=" +
                    "{Microsoft Access Driver (*.mdb)};" +
                    "DBQ=C:/temp/xtreme.mdb;" +
                    "DriverID=22;READONLY=true};";

    // Create the connection to the database
    Connection connection = DriverManager.getConnection(connectStr,"","");

    // The database is now open for commands!
}
```

VB.NET

In the next example, you use the `OleDbConnection` class along with a specific connection string, followed by the `Open()` method to connect to the database. If you use a Microsoft SQL Server database, then you use the `SqlConnection` class instead. Likewise, if you use an Oracle database, then you would use the `OracleConnection` class. If you use an IBM DB2 database, then the only difference is the content of the connection string.

```
Public Function TestMain(ByVal args() As Object) As Object


    ' Different databases would use different connection strings
    Dim connectStr As String = "Provider=Microsoft.Jet.OLEDB.4.0;
                            Data Source=C:\temp\xtreme.mdb;
                            Persist Security Info=True"


    ' Create the connection to the database
    Using connection As New OleDbConnection(connectStr)

        ' Open the connection
        connection.Open()

        ' The database is now open for commands!

    End Using ' Automatically closes the connection

    Return Nothing

End Function
```

Querying a Database

Often, one of the first things you do after connecting to a database is execute a query. This is not required, but it is common because querying is how you get information out of a database. The results from a query can be a set of values or it can be a single value. The data you get from each query can then be used in the Rational Functional Tester script as part of the automated test. You can use a database for test data instead of, or in combination with, datapools.

A query is made up of SQL statements, which are stored in a string in the Rational Functional Tester script. The value of the query string can be hard coded in the script, generated from other values, passed as an argument, or come from another source into the script. Putting together a SQL query programmatically can be accomplished using simple string functions. In the example, you just hard code the SQL query string that you use.

Java

The next example shows you how to execute a SQL query against a database and read the result into the script. You use the `createStatement` method to execute a SQL query or statement, which is linked to the database connection. You then use the `execute` method to execute a query that returns rows of data to a `ResultSet` object. You use the `next()` method to extract values from the return set. Because you know that the one column value you are retrieving (PO#) is a string value, you can use the `getString` method to assign this to a local script variable. You can use many methods and techniques to get values from the reader object to use in your test script.

```java
public void testMain(Object[] args)
{
  String connectStr = "jdbc:odbc:Driver=" +
                      "{Microsoft Access Driver (*.mdb)};" +
                      "DBQ=C:/temp/xtreme.mdb;" +
                      "DriverID=22;READONLY=true};";


  // Create the SQL statement
  // We want to get the PO # for Order ID 1011
  String readQuery = "SELECT Orders.[PO#] FROM Orders " +
                     "WHERE ([Order ID] = 1011)";

  // Create the connection to the database
  Connection connection = DriverManager.getConnection(connectStr,"","");

  // Create a statement to execute the query
  Statement statement = connection.createStatement();

  // Query the database
  statement.execute(readQuery);

  // get results that came from our query
  ResultSet dbReader = statement.getResultSet();

  // Loop until nothing left to read
  while (dbReader.next())
  {
          String PO = "";                // Initialize script variable
          PO = dbReader.getString(0);    // Assign value to script variable
```

```
        // ... use the values in the test script here


    }
    connection.close();  // close the connection to the database
  }
```

VB.NET

The next example shows you how to execute a SQL query against a database and read the result into the script. You use the `OleDbCommand` method to execute a SQL query or statement, which is linked to the database connection. You then use the `ExecuteReader` method to execute a query that returns rows of data to an `OleDbDataReader` object. You then use the `Read` method to extract values from the return set. Because you know that the one column value you are retrieving (PO#) is a string value, you can use the `GetString` method to assign this to a local script variable. You can use many methods and techniques to get values from the reader object to use in your test script.

```
Public Function TestMain(ByVal args() As Object) As Object
    Dim connectStr As String = "Provider=Microsoft.Jet.OLEDB.4.0;
                                Data Source=C:\temp\xtreme.mdb;
                                Persist Security Info=True"

    Using connection As New OleDbConnection(connectStr)

        ' Create the SQL statement
        ' We want to get the PO # for Order ID 1011
        Dim readQuery As String = "SELECT Orders.[PO#] FROM Orders
                                WHERE ([Order ID] = 1011)"

        ' Create a command to execute the query
        Dim queryCommand As New OleDbCommand(readQuery, connection)

        ' Open the conenction
        connection.Open()

        ' Query the database
        Dim dbReader As OleDbDataReader = queryCommand.ExecuteReader()

        ' Loop until nothing left to read
        While dbReader.Read()
```

```
        Dim PO As String = ""        ' Initialize script variable
        PO = dbReader.GetString(0)   ' Assign value to script variable

        ' ... use the values in the test script here

     End While

     dbReader.Close() ' Close the reader

  End Using ' Automatically closes the connection
  Return Nothing
End Function
```

Inserting Rows into a Database Table

One common reason for linking a Rational Functional Tester script to a database is to store data produced or obtained from the test procedure. The information might be stored for logging purposes or the data might be used in other automated tests. You put information into a database by inserting new rows of data into a table. To do this, you must already know which table to use and its design (the data types of each table column). To modify the particular table, you must have the required database permissions obtained from the connection string user name and password. After you know the table you want to modify, adding a row is simple in Rational Functional Tester.

Java

The following example shows you how to insert a row into a table. You do this by using SQL statements just like the query you created to read data from the table. The difference is that the SQL statement you execute does not return any data from the database.

```java
public void testMain(Object[] args)
{
   String connectStr = "jdbc:odbc:Driver=" +
                       "{Microsoft Access Driver (*.mdb)};" +
                       "DBQ=C:/temp/xtreme.mdb;" +
                       "DriverID=22;READONLY=true};";

   // Add a row to the Credit table, using these values
   // Note that Order ID and Product ID must be unique each time
   String insertStatement = "INSERT INTO [Orders Detail] " +
             "([Order ID], [Product ID], [Unit Price], Quantity)" +
```

```
                          "VALUES (9999, 8888, 9.95, 2)";
     // Create the connection to the database
     Connection connection = DriverManager.getConnection(connectStr,"","");
     Statement statement = connection.createStatement();

     // Insert a row into a table
     statement.execute(insertStatement);

     connection.close();  // close the connection to the database
  }
```

VB.NET

The following example shows you how to insert a row into a table. You do this by using SQL statements just like the query you created to read data from the table. The difference is that the SQL statement you execute does not return any data from the database. Because of this, you use the ExecuteNonQuery method instead of ExecuteReader. You do not have to assign return data into the script, but you can use the return value of this method, which is the number of rows affected by the statement execution, for error checking.

```
Public Function TestMain(ByVal args() As Object) As Object
    Dim connectStr As String = "Provider=Microsoft.Jet.OLEDB.4.0;
                                Data Source=C:\temp\xtreme.mdb;
                                Persist Security Info=True"
    Using connection As New OleDbConnection(connectStr)

        ' Add a row to the Credit table, using these values
        ' Note that Order ID and Product ID must be unique each time
        Dim insertStatement As String = "INSERT INTO [Orders Detail]
                    ([Order ID], [Product ID], [Unit Price], Quantity)
                    VALUES (9999, 8888, 9.95, 2)"

        ' Insert a row into a table
        Dim insertCommand As New OleDbCommand(insertStatement, connection)
        connection.Open()
        insertCommand.ExecuteNonQuery() ' Execute the statement

    End Using ' Automatically closes the connection
    Return Nothing
End Function
```

> **INSERTING ROWS INTO TABLES WITH UNIQUE KEYS**
>
> Many database tables have keys, or specific column values, which must be unique for each row. You have to manage the values in an SQL INSERT statement to ensure that you are not attempting to add duplicate keys. The example shown here might not be realistic because the values are hard-coded in the script.

Deleting Rows from a Database Table

In addition to inserting rows to a database table, you can also make a Rational Functional Tester script delete rows. You likely have to do this to manipulate the test data used by your automated tests. Just like inserting rows, you must already know which table and have the required database permissions. After you have this information, deleting a row is easy to do in Rational Functional Tester.

Java

The following example shows you how you can delete a row from a table. You do this by using SQL statements just like in the previous examples. The only difference between inserting and deleting rows is the SQL statement used. You also have to consider which data and rows you want to mark for deletion from the database. In the example shown, you delete the row that was inserted from the previous example, using a hard-coded filter ([Order ID] = 9999).

```
public void testMain(Object[] args)
{
    String connectStr = "jdbc:odbc:Driver=" +
                        "{Microsoft Access Driver (*.mdb)};" +
                        "DBQ=C:/temp/xtreme.mdb;" +
                        "DriverID=22;READONLY=true};";

    // Delete the row from the Credit table with the Order ID of 9999
    String deleteQuery = "DELETE FROM [Orders Detail] " +
                        "WHERE ([Order ID] = 9999)";

    // Create the connection to the database
    Connection connection = DriverManager.getConnection(connectStr,"","");
    Statement statement = connection.createStatement();

    // Delete a row from a table
    statement.execute(deleteQuery);

    connection.close();  // close the connection to the database
}
```

VB.NET

The following example shows you how you can delete a row from a table. You do this by using SQL statements just like in the previous examples. Like inserting rows, the SQL statement you execute does not return any data from the database. The only difference between inserting and deleting rows is the SQL statement used. You also have to consider which data and rows you want to mark for deletion from the database. In the example shown, you delete the row that was inserted from the previous example, using a hard-coded filter ([Order ID] = 9999).

```
Public Function TestMain(ByVal args() As Object) As Object
    Dim connectStr As String = "Provider=Microsoft.Jet.OLEDB.4.0;
                                Data Source=C:\temp\xtreme.mdb;
                                Persist Security Info=True"

    Using connection As New OleDbConnection(connectStr)

        ' Delete the row from the Credit table with the Order ID of 9999
        Dim deleteQuery As String = "DELETE FROM [Orders Detail]
                                WHERE ([Order ID] = 9999)"

        ' Delete a row from a table
        Dim deleteCommand As New OleDbCommand(deleteQuery, connection)
        connection.Open()
         deleteCommand.ExecuteNonQuery() ' Execute the query

    End Using ' Automatically closes the connection
    Return Nothing
End Function
```

Fire a Database Trigger

Database triggers automatically make something happen in the database when a particular event occurs. These are special types of stored procedures, which are like functions that run inside the database. There are different kinds of events that can fire (cause it to execute); the trigger and the trigger can do various things in the database. For example, a database might have a trigger that fires when a row is inserted into a particular table, which then causes the trigger to update other tables.

Although possible, you are not likely to create or modify database triggers from a Rational Functional Tester script. You might, however, want to fire a trigger. Causing a trigger to fire is just a matter of making whatever change is necessary in the database through SQL statements, such as an INSERT, an UPDATE, or a DELETE command. Therefore, you can fire a trigger from a test script by invoking the appropriate SQL statement with the right data and possibly at the right time or sequence. This obviously requires knowledge of the triggers you might want to fire and the database schema design, which you can get from a database administrator (DBA). One possible scenario in which you would fire a trigger in an automated test procedure follows:

1. Get some values from the application under test as part of the test procedure.

2. Put these values into the database that is part of, or linked to, the application under test. Do this by executing a SQL statement, such as an INSERT, which fires a database trigger to update data in other tables (which is part of the application's functionality).

3. Read the new information from the database by executing a query to read the tables updated by the trigger.

4. Use the new values from the query as test data in the test procedure.

Java

In Listing 5.4, Java code shows one possible example how to fire a trigger as described in the previous section.

Listing 5.4   Java Example of How to Fire a Database Trigger

```
public void testMain(Object[] args)
  // ... record initial test steps here

  // Get values from the application under test (recorded)
  String orderID = OrderIDField().getProperty("text");
  String prodID = ProductIDField().getProperty("text");

  // Connect to the application's database
  String connectStr = "jdbc:odbc:Driver=" +
                      "{Microsoft Access Driver (*.mdb)};" +
                      "DBQ=C:/temp/xtreme.mdb;" +
                      "DriverID=22;READONLY=true};";


  // This INSERT will fire the database trigger
  String insertStatement = "INSERT INTO [Orders Detail] " +
                      "([Order ID], [Product ID]) " +
                      "VALUES (" + orderID + "," + prodID + ")";

  // Create the connection to the database
  Connection connection =
DriverManager.getConnection(connectStr,"","");
  Statement statement = connection.createStatement();
  // Insert a row into a table
```

```
    statement.execute(insertStatement);

    // ------------------
    // At this point the database trigger fires, updating other tables
    // ------------------

    // Read the table updated by the trigger
    String readQuery = "SELECT Orders.[PO#] FROM Orders " +
                       "WHERE ([Order ID] = 1011)";

    // Query the database
    statement.execute(readQuery);

    // get results that came from our query
    ResultSet dbReader = statement.getResultSet();

    String newPO = "";      // Initialize in case read fails
    // Get the new PO number from the trigger's update
    while (dbReader.next())
    {
        newPO = dbReader.getString(0);  // Assign value to script variable
    }
    dbReader.close();       // Close the reader

    // ... use the new values in the test script here
    PONumberText().setProperty("text", newPO);

    connection.close();  // close the connection to the database
}
```

VB.NET

In Listing 5.5, VB.NET code shows you one possible example how one would fire a trigger as described earlier in this section.

Listing 5.5 VB.NET Example of How to Fire a Database Trigger

```
Public Function TestMain(ByVal args() As Object) As Object
    ' ... record initial test steps here

    ' Get values from the application under test (recorded)
    Dim orderID As String = OrderIDField().GetProperty("text")
    Dim prodID As String = ProductIDField().GetProperty("text")
```

```
' Connect to the application's database
Dim connectStr As String = "Provider=Microsoft.Jet.OLEDB.4.0;
                            Data Source=C:\temp\xtreme.mdb;
                            Persist Security Info=True"

Using connection As New OleDbConnection(connectStr)

    ' This INSERT will fire the database trigger
    Dim insertStatement As String = "INSERT INTO [Orders Detail]
                            ([Order ID], [Product ID])
                            VALUES (" + orderID + "," + prodID + ")"

    Dim insertCommand As New OleDbCommand(insertStatement, connection)
    connection.Open()
    insertCommand.ExecuteNonQuery() ' Execute the statement

    ' -------------------
    ' At this point the database trigger fires, updating other tables
    ' -------------------

    ' Read the table updated by the trigger
    Dim readQuery As String = "SELECT Orders.[PO#] FROM Orders
                            WHERE ([Order ID] = 1011)"

    Dim queryCommand As New OleDbCommand(readQuery, connection)
    connection.Open()
    Dim dbReader As OleDbDataReader = queryCommand.ExecuteReader()

    Dim newPO As String = "null"      ' Initialize in case read fails
    ' Get the new PO number from the trigger's update
    While dbReader.Read()
        newPO = dbReader.GetString(0) ' Assign value to script variable
    End While
    dbReader.Close() ' Close the reader

    ' ... use the new values in the test script here
    PONumberText().SetProperty("text", newPO)

End Using ' Automatically closes the connection
Return Nothing
End Function
```

Handling User-Specific Runtime Variables

Often, when you run sets of automated tests, you need to run tests with varying options. These options might set different test environments or configurations, or they might set the number of times various parts of the tests are run. There are many other possible uses of these values. The difference between the test values discussed in this section from test data stored in datapools is that these parameters are typically assigned or picked at the time of execution. However, there might not always be a clear "border" or rule where you might put a value in a datapool or pass a value as a user-specific runtime variable.

The following four sections describe and give examples of four different ways to set these user-specific runtime variables. Also related to this is passing variables between scripts as arguments, which is covered in Chapter 7, "Managing Script Execution."

Playback Options

The simplest way to pass runtime parameters to a test script is using the Rational Functional Tester playback options. There are two different playback options: the run arguments and the datapool iteration count. You can assign values to these during the `second step` of the playback wizard, shown in Figure 5.4.

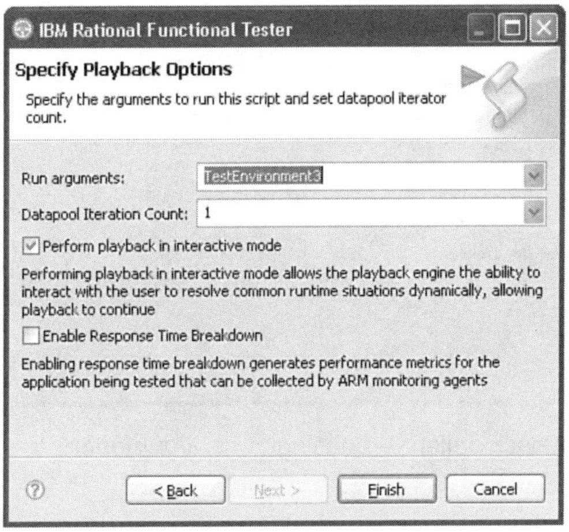

Figure 5.4   Playback options—passing arguments to a test script

The `run` argument is passed to the test script's `testMain()` as the `args` value. This argument is always declared as an `Object` type, but you can cast it as a `String` or other type as needed. You can then use the `args` variable, containing the runtime argument, in the script. The following simple example illustrates a run argument used in a script.

```
public void testMain(Object[] args)
{
        //...
        logInfo("The run argument used is: "+args[0]);
```

PASSING A STRING WITH SPACES

If the run argument you want to pass to the test script is a string with spaces, you must enclose the argument with double quotes.

If you need to pass multiple values, you can enter them into a string separated by spaces or other separator character, and then parse the string in the script as shown in Figure 5.5. The following code shows how to pass a string and a numeric value to a script.

Figure 5.5   Example playback options—passing three arguments

```
public void testMain(Object[] args)
{
      // Get the run arguments, store in local string
      String runtime_variable = (String) args[0];

      if (runtime_variable.length() > 0) {
            // Parse argument values, format is: "string,string,number"
            String testURL = runtime_variable.substring( 0,
```

```
runtime_variable.indexOf(','));
            String server = runtime_variable.substring(
runtime_variable.indexOf(',')+1,
runtime_variable.lastIndexOf(','));
            String job_number = runtime_variable.substring(
      runtime_variable.lastIndexOf(',')+1);
            // Note that this code assumes no comma's in the URL

            // ... use the values in the test script here

            // Record the arguments used in the test log
            logInfo("URL used is: "+testURL);
            logInfo("Server used is: "+server);
            logInfo("Job number used is: "+job_number);
    }
    }
```

The second Rational Functional Tester playback option is the datapool iteration count. This option is available only if a test script has datapool associated with it; otherwise, it is disabled. This value controls how many rows of the datapool are retrieved when the test is run. The test script repeats the lines of code based on datapool iteration count. For example, the following code illustrates a test script getting values from a datapool (from a single row) and entering them into the application under test.

```
public void testMain(Object[] args)
{
      startApp("ClassicsJavaA");
      // Frame: ClassicsCD
      placeOrder().click();
      // Frame: Member Logon
      ok().click();

      // Data Driven Code
      CardNumberText().setText(dpString("CardNumberText"));
expirationDateText().setText(dpString("ExpirationDateText"));
      placeOrder2().click();

      // Order confirmation
      ok2().click();
      // Frame: ClassicsCD
      classicsJava(ANY,MAY_EXIT).close();
}
```

If you run this test script and enter a datapool iteration count of 5, the script runs from beginning to end five times to retrieve five datapool rows. If the datapool has less than five rows, it repeats some rows. Another playback option for the datapool iteration count is to select Iterate until done, which repeats as many times as needed to get to the end of the datapool, without repeating any rows.

Using the playback options is the easiest way to pass user runtime variables to a test script because it requires minimal lines of code and no files to manage. The disadvantage is that you have to manually enter the values every time you execute the script.

Java Properties Files

A Java properties file is an easy way for Java programs to get data, typically application configuration parameters, that is in stored files. The advantage of using properties files in Java is that classes and methods make it much easier to read and parse the files without having to write detailed code for file input and output. These files are simple text files, and they always have the file extension .properties. The basic format is a list of data, each having a name and the value, referred to as key/value pairs. The classes to use Java properties files are in the package `java.util.Properties`.

If you use Rational Functional Tester with Java scripting, you can use Java properties files to store configuration data for your test scripts. As long as you follow the correct format for these files, you can get the values into your test script using only a few lines of code. You can learn more about the file format and classes that implement this at http://java.sun.com.

The following is an example of a Rational Functional Tester script using a Java properties file. In this example, you start with a properties file containing three values, which are used as test parameters. The properties file contents are shown in Listing 5.6.

Listing 5.6   Example Java properties file contents

```
Filename: "test_config_data.properties"
# These values can be set prior to each test run
# The # and ! indicate comments in Java properties files
#
test_URL = http://www.testurl.com/notarealurl/test_this.html
server = testserver1
job_number = 8
```

Next, you add lines of code to retrieve these values from the file into the test script. In this example, the file is named test_config_data.properties and it is saved at the root of the C: drive. There are only three lines of code required to do this: declaring a new Properties object, opening the file with the `load()` method, and getting the value using the key name with the `getProperty()` method.

```
    ...


    import java.io.FileInputStream;   // Add these after the other imports
    import java.io.IOException;        // Add these after the other imports
    import java.util.Properties;       // Add these after the other imports


    ...


    public void testMain(Object[] args)
    {
        Properties properties = new Properties();
        try {
            properties.load( new FileInputStream("c:\\test_config_data.properties"));

            // Get values from properties file
            String testURL = properties.getProperty("test_URL");
            String server = properties.getProperty("server");
            String job_num = properties.getProperty("job_number");

        // ... use the values in the test script here

        // Record the properties used in the test log
        logInfo("URL used is: "+testURL);
        logInfo("Server used is: "+server);
        logInfo("Job number used is: "+job_num);
        } catch (IOException ioe) {
                System.out.println("IOException error: " +
    ioe.getMessage());
    }
```

The previous example simply assigns these values to local script variables and writes them to the test log. Realistically, you use the variables as part of a test procedure in the middle of the previous example.

XML Files

Similar to the way Java programmers use properties file, .NET programmers can use XML files to store configurable parameters for applications. Like properties files, the advantage of using XML configuration files in .NET is that there are classes and methods that make it much easier to read and parse the files without having to write detailed code for file input and output. XML files are a common file format used to transfer data between many system components and applications. XML files can have any extension, but the .config extension is frequently used for storing application configuration parameters. You can use `XmlTextReader` from the `System.Xml` package in the .NET Framework class library to work with XML files.

If you use Rational Functional Tester with Visual Basic scripting, you can use XML files to store configuration data for your test scripts. As long as you follow XML syntax for these files, you can get the values into your test script using only a few lines of code. You can learn more about the file format and classes that implement this at http://www.w3.org/.

The following is an example of a Rational Functional Tester script using an XML configuration file. Like the previous example, you start with a configuration file containing three values that will be used as test parameters. The file contents are shown in Listing 5.7.

Listing 5.7   Example XML configuration file contents

```
File name: "test_data.config"
<!-- These values can be set prior to each test run -->
<!-- These are comments in XML files -->
<configuration
            testURL='http://www.testurl.com/notarealurl/test_this.html'
            server='testserver2' jobnumber='9'>
    </configuration>
```

You now add lines of code to retrieve these values from the XML file into the test script. In this example, the file is named `"test_data.config"` and it is saved at the root of the C: drive. There are only three lines of code required to do this: declaring a new reader (file) object, accessing the file contents with the `MoveToContent()` method, and getting the value using the key name with the `GetAttribute()` method.

You can use the `System.Xml` library; however, Rational Functional Tester does not support importing the .NET System package into a Visual Basic test script. Instead, you must copy the required dynamic link library (DLL) file into the Rational Functional Tester customization directory. Copying the DLL files automatically adds the methods references to the Rational Functional Tester projects. This customization directory is located by default in the following locations:

- Windows Vista at C:\Users\All Users\IBM\RFT\customization
- All other Windows at C:\Documents and Settings\All Users\Application Data\IBM\ RFT\customization

The DLL files you need are located by default in the framework installation directory, for example: C:\WINDOWS\Microsoft.NET\Framework\v3.0.

You need to copy the files that contain the classes you need and any dependent assemblies (more files). For example, the `XmlReader` function shown in the following code is contained in the `system.xml.dll`, so this file gets copied to the Rational Functional Tester customization folder. Refer to the Microsoft .NET framework documentation and references for more information on the .NET System package contents.

REQUIREMENT FOR THIS CUSTOMIZATION

This customization is per machine, so you have to repeat this for every machine that executes the test scripts requiring the System packages.

```
Public Function TestMain(ByVal args() As Object) As Object
        Dim reader As System.Xml.XmlTextReader = Nothing

    Try
            'Load the reader with the XML file.
            reader = New
System.Xml.XmlTextReader("C:\test_data.config")

            'Read the attribute.
            reader.MoveToContent()
            Dim test_URL As String = reader.GetAttribute("testURL")
            LogInfo("URL used is: " & test_URL)
            Dim server As String = reader.GetAttribute("server")
            LogInfo("Server used is: " & server)
            Dim jobnumber As String = reader.GetAttribute("jobnumber")
            LogInfo("Job number used is: " & jobnumber)

            ' ... use the values in the test script here

    Finally
            If Not (reader Is Nothing) Then
                    reader.Close()
            End If
    End Try

        Return Nothing
    End Function
```

The previous example simply assigns these values to local script variables and writes them to the test log. Realistically, you use the variables as part of a test procedure in the middle of the script.

Simple Flat Files

In this last example, you examine passing runtime parameters to a test script that involves using simple flat files. This method refers to storing data in any file format and adding code to the test script to read from the file. This method enables the greatest flexibility, because you do not have to use a particular format or file extension, but it can also be the most complex and require the most amount of work to implement. You are most likely to use this approach in situations where you have to use existing files containing test parameters and cannot change the file format.

There are many different possibilities for file formats and even more possibilities for how to read data from these files. You look at only one possible example to illustrate the strategy. The general strategy to get data into a test script from a file is as follows:

1. Open the file.
2. Read a line from the file.
3. Parse the line for the specific data you need.
4. Repeat getting lines to get the particular data you need.
5. Close the file.

JAVA AND .NET, PROPERTIES, AND XML

Although it is not typical, it is possible to use a .properties file with a Visual Basic test script or you can use an XML file with a Java test script. In these cases, you do not use the built-in classes, but instead, you use a strategy similar to reading simple flat files, which is described in the following section.

In Listing 5.8, the simple example reads a file that has three parameters of data on each line of the file. The methods used in this example are typical functions in Java for reading and parsing files. The comments in the test script code explain many of the specific steps.

Listing 5.8   Example of How to Read a File

```
...
import java.io.File;                     // Add these to the imports
import java.io.FileNotFoundException;    // Add these to the imports
import java.io.FileReader;               // Add these to the imports
import java.io.IOException;              // Add these to the imports
import java.io.StreamTokenizer;          // Add these to the imports
// import java.io.*   // Also works but is less efficient
...
public void testMain(Object[] args)
{
```

```
// Initialize variables
String testURL = "";
String server = "";
String job_num = "";

// The following file must exist in the specified location
File cfgFile = new File("c:\\test_config_data.txt");
FileReader in;
try {
      in = new FileReader(cfgFile);
      // Read the file using StreamTokenizer
      StreamTokenizer st = new StreamTokenizer(in);
      st.commentChar('*');      // Use * for a comment line
      st.wordChars('/','_');    // Consider characters as normal
      int tokenType;
      do {
            tokenType = st.nextToken();
            if (st.sval != null) {
                  if (st.sval.equals("test_URL")) {
                        tokenType = st.nextToken();
                        if ((char)tokenType == '-') {
                              tokenType = st.nextToken();
                              testURL = st.sval;
                        }
                  }
                  if (st.sval.equals("server")){
                        tokenType = st.nextToken();
                        if ((char)tokenType == '-'){
                              tokenType = st.nextToken();
                              server = st.sval;
                        }
                  }
                  if (st.sval.equals("job_number")) {
                        tokenType = st.nextToken();
                        if ((char)tokenType == '-') {
                              tokenType = st.nextToken();
                              //Double djob_num = st.nval;
                              Integer djob_num = (int) st.nval;
                              job_num = djob_num.toString();
                        }
```

```
                            }
                    }
            } while (tokenType != StreamTokenizer.TT_EOF);
            if (in!=null) {
                    in.close();
            }
        } catch (FileNotFoundException fnfe) {
            System.out.println("File not found error: " +
fnfe.getMessage());
        }
        catch (IOException ioe) {
            System.out.println("IOException error: " +
ioe.getMessage());
        }

        // ... use the values in the test script here

        logInfo("URL used is: "+testURL);
        logInfo("Server used is: "+server);
        logInfo("Job number used is: "+job_num);
}
```

The file used for this example can have data as follows:

```
* These values can be set prior to each test run
* The * character is set as a comment indicator in the test script
*
test_URL - http://www.testurl.com/notarealurl/test_this.html
server - testserver3
job_number - 10
```

Like the previous examples, this example simply assigns these values to local test script variables and writes them to the test log. Realistically, you should use the variables as part of a test procedure in the middle of the test script.

Summary

As you can see, Rational Functional Tester gives you various options to manage data. Using datapools enhances your test scripts with an elegant and a simple mechanism. The openness of Rational Functional Tester enables you to access databases and how it handles user-specific runtime variables. This chapter pointed to the most common implementation for managing data. Either you can embrace one of these implementations or you can create a hybrid that would fit the needs of your organization.

Debugging Scripts

Chip Davis, Daniel Chirillo, Daniel Gouveia

Soon after you begin creating your scripts, you might find yourself in a situation where a script you develop isn't doing what you want it to do and your first debugging tool—watching script execution and reading the RFT log—does not provide enough useful information for you to pin-point the root cause of the problem.

Eclipse and Visual Studio have powerful, integrated debuggers. You might want to take advantage of the many features offered in both. We limit our discussion here to the critical features you need to start using your IDE's debugger. If you've never used a debugger before, you might feel intim-idated at first. That's normal. We encourage you to practice using the debugger; in many cases, it can save you the tremendous time it costs to identify the causes of problems.

Common Debugging Concepts

This chapter shows the Eclipse and Visual Studio debuggers. It begins with an explanation of some concepts that are common to debugging in both environments.

To make describing these concepts easier, refer to the following theoretical script that consists of these method calls:

```
startApplication()
login()
enterItemSearchCriteria()
selectItems()
placeItemsInCart()
checkout()
completePurchase()
```

Imagine that your script has a problem. Before looking at Eclipse and Visual Studio debuggers in action, defining some key terms that are used in both development environments is helpful. In the discussion of these terms in the following sections, the method names in this theoretical script are referenced.

Breakpoints

A *breakpoint* is a statement in your script before you want to pause. A script can have any number of breakpoints. You can put them in methods that are called by scripts and to which the source code is available. Typically, you put breakpoints where you have problems or suspect a problem might occur.

Stepping

Stepping though a script refers to executing the script one statement at a time. As described in this chapter, there are two variations on a definition of a *single* statement.

Step Over

The term *step over* can sometimes be misleading to people who are new to using a debugger. To the untrained ear, step over might be interpreted as "skip this statement" or "step over, i.e., don't execute this statement." This is not the case. To step over a statement means to execute that statement (or, the first method that's called in a *single* statement that contains multiple method calls) in its entirety. For example, if you put a breakpoint on the line that contains the call to login(), when you run the debugger, Rational Functional Tester pauses before executing login(). When it pauses, you have the opportunity to examine the current values of variables. You can also execute the next statement, login(). Stepping over login() executes all of login(), which internally, consists of multiple method calls. You step *over* a method call when you're not interested in examining what occurs *within* that method.

Step Into

What if you have a breakpoint on the line in your script that calls login() and you suspect that the source of your current problem might be related to something that occurs within the login() method? In that case, if you have the source to login(), then, if you *step into* (instead of stepping over) it, you are brought into the source of the login() method. You then see the first statement in login(). At this point, you can choose to step over or into methods called in the login() method. After the last statement is executed, you are brought back to your script, and execution is paused at enterItemSearchCriteria().

What happens if you step into a method to which you don't have the source? For example, what if you try to step into a Rational Functional Tester method such as the following?

```
startApp( "ClassicsJavaA" )
```

In Visual Studio, the effect is that of a step over. You get no complaints; Rational Functional Tester simply executes the method in its entirety. In Eclipse, if you step into a method to which you don't have the source, you see what's shown in Figure 6.1.

Figure 6.1   Eclipse's Source not found class file

Do not worry. If this happens, all you need to do is execute a *step return* (discussed in the next section).

Step Return

If you step return, Rational Functional Tester executes the rest of the current method (pausing at any breakpoints along the way that might be set) and brings you back (*returns*) to the method from which you stepped into the current method. After you've returned, you can continue stepping though the code.

Debugging in Eclipse

Rational Functional Tester provides a rich debugging environment in the Eclipse shell. You have the ability to set breakpoints, step through individual lines in your script, set hit counts for loops, and change variables at runtime. Working with these capabilities is easy, and they provide you with the necessary information to quickly debug any issues in your scripts. This section introduces you to the Rational Functional Tester's debugging environment in the Eclipse development environment.

Before any debugging begins, the first thing you need to do is set at least one breakpoint. You set a breakpoint by following these steps:

1. Find the line of code in your script at which you wish to pause execution.
2. Right-click in the vertical editor ruler (located on the far left of the editor).
3. Select **Toggle Breakpoint**.

Alternatively, you can set a breakpoint by clicking on the desired line and selecting **Run →
Toggle Breakpoint** from the RFT menu.

Doing this places a small blue dot in the gray column on the left side of the script. Figure 6.2 shows the process of setting a breakpoint.

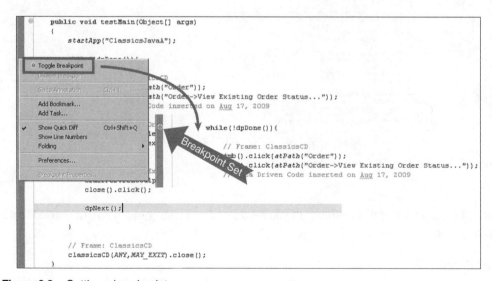

Figure 6.2   Setting a breakpoint

After your breakpoint is set, you can begin the process of debugging your scripts. This requires you to run your script in "debug" mode. You do this by selecting **Script > Debug**. Alternately, you can press the **Shift + F11** keystroke combination. In either case, your script starts as it usually does. When the breakpoint in your script is hit, you receive a dialog box asking you to switch to the **Functional Test Debug** perspective (see Figure 6.3). Click the **Yes** button and Rational Functional Tester switches to the debug perspective.

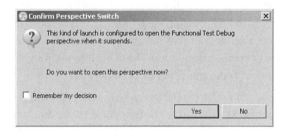

Figure 6.3   Confirm Perspective Switch dialog box

The Functional Test Debug perspective contains multiple views. One view that you work with often is the Debug view. This view is used with the Script editor, usually found in the middle of the Functional Test Debug perspective. The Script editor displays the contents of your script, using a blue arrow and highlighting to reveal the line that is currently under review. The idea is for you to watch this view as you utilize the step commands in the Debug view to execute individual statements in your script. This helps you pinpoint which line in your script is causing the issue.

Figure 6.4 highlights Script and Debug views. The callout arrow shows how the debugger flags the current line under review, using a small blue arrow (on the left side) and highlighting. The box at the top of the figure highlights the buttons that engage the step commands. These commands are discussed in the introduction to this chapter. They enable you to step into, step out of, and step over individual lines of scripts. The Eclipse debugger also provides a means to set up step filters, helping to expedite the debugging process.

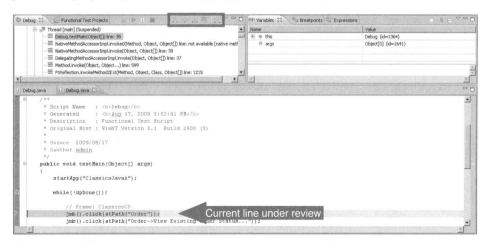

Figure 6.4   Functional Test Debug perspective—Debug and Script views

While using the debugger, you control the statements you want to step into/over/return from using the buttons in the Debug View:

- The first button in the box is the `Step Into` command. Clicking this button lets you step into the method the current line of code is trying to execute. You can also engage the `Step Into` command by pressing the **F5** key. This lets you dive deeper into what a particular line in your script does. For instance, if a line calls out to a method to which you have the source code, the `Step Into` command lets you jump into that method and step through each line of code, analyzing its behavior.

- The second button in the box is the `Step Over` command. You can either click this button or press your **F6** key to engage the functionality. As discussed earlier in the chapter, stepping over a line of code enables it to execute normally and move on to the next statement in your script. You use this command when you are confident that a certain line isn't the problem. It prevents you from diving deeper into what the method does. Using the example in the preceding paragraph, you use the `Step Over` command if you are confident that your method works correctly. This enables the line in your script that calls out to the method to execute without actually entering into the method.

- The third button in the box is the `Step Return` command. This enables you to jump out of a method that you stepped into. It is useful when you dive deep into Rational Functional Tester's base methods or even the base methods of any Java classes that you are using. You click on this button to return back to the point in your debug session where you clicked the **Step Into** button.

- The fifth button in the box is the `Step Filters` command. This is an advanced capability that enables you to filter out certain elements that you do not wish to step through. You use this if you know that your script issue doesn't lie within a certain class or package. There are two steps to follow to use `Step Filters`. The first is to click on the **Step Filters** button. This tells the debugger to filter out the classes, packages, and user-specified filters listed in the Step Filtering preferences. The second step is to specify the filters. You do this by right-clicking the Debug view and selecting the **Edit Step Filters** option. This opens the Step Filtering preferences dialog box (shown in Figure 6.5). If you click the **Add Filter** button, you can specify a pattern to filter. For instance, if you didn't want to step through any part of your script that dealt with text fields, you could specify ***TextGuiTestObject*** as your pattern. The Add Class button lets you select a specific class to skip over when stepping through script. For instance, instead of specifying a pattern, you can simply type `TextGui` in the class field and it displays the `TextGuiTextObject` in the list box. You can then select that class, adding it to the filter list. Lastly, the **Add Package** button lets you omit an entire set of classes. Perhaps you don't want to deal with stepping through Rational Functional Tester's datapool classes. You can type `com.rational.test.ft.data`. This displays the packages that match your search string, `com.rational.test.ft.datapool` being one of them. You select this package, adding it to the filter list. These are displayed as the checked boxes in Figure 6.5. Ultimately, you use `Step Filters` to hone in on the problem by skipping over the pieces you know aren't part the issue, such as the `com.rational.test.ft.datapool` package and the `TextGuiTestObject` class. The goal of this capability is to expedite your debugging session.

Figure 6.5 Step Filters preferences—Step Filtering list

The Functional Test Debug perspective also offers a Variables view (see Figure 6.6). You can use this view with the step commands. This view enables you to see what the current values of your variables are. When you execute a line in your script that modifies a variable, you can watch to see if the value was set correctly. This becomes a valuable view when your script (or custom method) deals with setting and passing variables. You can watch values being assigned to your variables, looking for proper assignments.

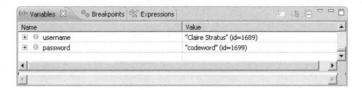

Figure 6.6 Functional Test Debug perspective—Variables view

Sometimes issues occur within a loop. For instance, you may have a `while` loop that parses a file of usernames, line-by-line, and enters them into your application. You notice that toward the end of the file, Rational Functional Tester places an incorrect name into the application. Typically, you step through your script (or method), looking for the issue. This is tedious because you know you have to step through the loop a number of times before you get to the point where you can start investigating where the actual problem is. The Eclipse debugger provides a way to alleviate this. You can edit the breakpoint properties and provide a hit count. Hit counts tell functional tester to pause the execution after the *nth* time the breakpoint is hit.

To set a hit count, right-click on your breakpoint (remember the blue dot?) and select **Breakpoint Properties**. This opens a dialog box that displays the breakpoint's properties. You then need to place a check in the **Hit Count** checkbox and provide an integer (this is the number of times Rational Functional Tester executes the breakpoint before it pauses playback). Figure 6.7 shows the execution is suspended after the fourth time the breakpoint is hit. If the breakpoint is set on the `while` line in your script, the loop is executed four times before the breakpoint is engaged and execution is paused. This is a useful feature for getting to the necessary point in your loop for debugging, without having to uselessly step through the loop multiple times (or modify the source code to simply keep debugging).

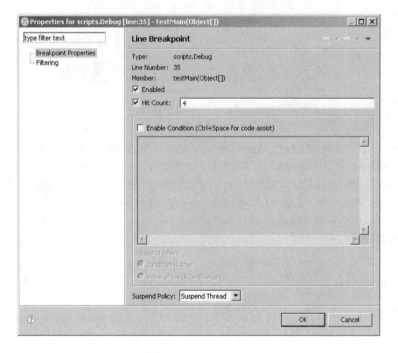

Figure 6.7   Breakpoint properties—Hit Count

Rational Functional Tester's debugger offers another means to save time during your debug sessions. It enables you to change the values of your variables while debugging your script. This is a great feature to test different values to use with your script's variables *without* having to stop the debugger, set a new variable value, and restart the debugger. Here's how to change a variable value while debugging:

1. Right-click on the variable that you want to change (in the Variables view).
2. In the **Change Object Value** window, replace the old value with a new one.
3. Click the **OK** button.

Figure 6.8 shows these steps. The username variable was initially set to `Jack Thompson`. Using these steps, the value was changed to `John Doe`. This is while the script is being debugged.

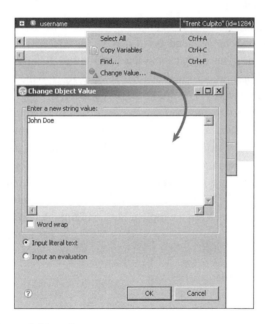

Figure 6.8   Editing variable values

Adding Breakpoints While Debugging

Sometimes, as you step through a script in debug mode looking for problems, you discover a place where you want to add a breakpoint (for the next time you execute the script in debug mode or for the next time you enter a loop). You can add one while you're debugging (you don't need to be in edit mode). Right-click in the vertical editor ruler and select **Toggle Breakpoint**.

Removing, Disabling, and Enabling Breakpoints

If you decide that you don't need one of your breakpoints, you can remove or disable it. Disabling it is useful when you think you might want to restore that breakpoint at some point in the future. Disabling a breakpoint preserves a visual marker in IDE. If you need to use the breakpoint again, you can enable it.

To remove a breakpoint, right-click and select **Toggle Breakpoint**.

To disable a breakpoint, right-click and select **Disable Breakpoint**. The breakpoint marker turns from blue to white.

To enable a breakpoint, right-click and select **Enable**; the marker becomes blue again.

You can remove all breakpoints in a single step by selecting **Run > Remove All breakpoints** from the RFT menu.

Debugging in Visual Studio

This section discusses debugging Rational Functional Tester Visual Basic .NET test scripts. This section assumes that you already understand basic debugging concepts, such as breakpoints, stepping, and variable watching. These topics are discussed in the "Common Debugging Concepts" section of this chapter. For more information on this topic, refer to the Microsoft Developer Network (MSDN®) Developing with Visual Studio.NET (building, debugging, and testing).

Like most debugging environments, you must execute your program in debug mode to enable the debugging features, such as breakpoints. Furthermore, you must execute Rational Functional Tester scripts from the Debug Functional Test Script playback mode, *not* the normal Visual Studio debug playback. If you run a test script from normal test playback mode or from the Visual Basic .NET debug mode, you cannot debug your test script. You can initiate Debug Functional Test Script playback from the **Script > Debug** menu shown in Figure 6.9, *not* the Debug menu. You can also debug test scripts from the toolbar button highlighted in Figure 6.10.

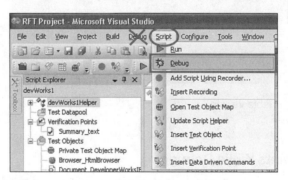

Figure 6.9   Debugging functional test scripts in Visual Studio

> **NOTE**   Rational Function Tester Java scripting in Eclipse provides a Test Debug Perspective, which is referenced in online documentation. There is no such perspective in Visual Studio.NET.

Figure 6.10 Debugging functional test scripts toolbar button

Setting Breakpoints

Setting a breakpoint enables you to pause execution of a test script when it is run in Debug Functional Test Script playback. You can set and remove breakpoints in several ways: using the Debug menu, pressing **F9**, clicking in the left margin (next to the line number if shown) or clicking a toolbar button (not added by default). In addition to adding and removing breakpoints, Visual Studio enables you to enable and disable breakpoints. When a breakpoint is disabled, it leaves a placeholder at the specific line in the script without actually breaking when run. This can help make debugging easier because it lets you remove breakpoints without forgetting where you initially set them.

Visual Studio also has a Breakpoints window that lists all the breakpoints currently set in your script and helps you monitor and manage them (see Figure 6.11). You can access the Breakpoints window from the **Debug > Windows > Breakpoints** menu, pressing **Ctrl+Alt+B**, or by adding a toolbar button.

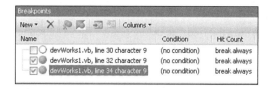

Figure 6.11 Managing breakpoints in Visual Studio

Step Into, Step Over, and Step Out

As previously mentioned, you cannot start debugging a Rational Functional Tester script from the Visual Studio Debug toolbar or the Debug menu. (You must use the Debug Functional Tester Script button.) However, after you begin the debug playback, you can use the Visual Studio menu or toolbar to control debugging, including stepping. Stepping enables line-by-line control of the script playback (see Figure 6.12).

The most common debug stepping you will probably use is step over, which moves the line pointer to the next line of the test script. The keyboard shortcut, which can be useful when debugging to step over, is Shift+F8. The reason this is called step *over* is that it skips the underlying code of the test script line and moves to the next line of the test script. For example, if you use

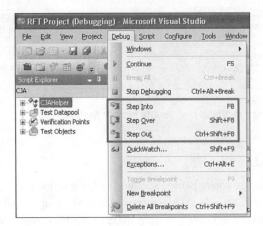

Figure 6.12   Stepping through a test script playback

step over from the following line, the debug pointer does *not* move into the SubScript1 test script but continues on to the next line in the current script:

```
CallScript("SubScript1")
```

If you have scripts that call other scripts, you might use step into. You might also use this if you have a tricky test playback problem, although this is not common. Step into moves the debug pointer into the module of the line being executed. For example, if you use step over from the following line, the debug pointer moves into the first line of the SubScript2 test script:

```
CallScript("SubScript2")
```

If you used step into from the following line, the debug pointer moves into the first line of the script helper class, into the function for the test object PlaceAnOrder (you are not likely to do this):

```
PlaceAnOrder().InputChars("12345")
```

If you have used step into to move the debug pointer into another script or class, then you might use step out. Step out returns the line pointer back to the calling class script. For example, if you debug a script that was called from another script, step out moves the debug pointer back out to the calling test script.

If you use step out from the highest level, or the initial calling test script, or if you run a single test script that is not called from another, step out acts the same as if you selected **Debug > Continue**. Whenever you no longer want to step through a test script, you can press **F5** to continue playback to the next breakpoint, or to the end of the test.

Changing Variable Values at Runtime

When you debug a Rational Functional Tester script, you can use the Watch window to monitor the values of any variables you have in your script. These might be simple counters, datapool values, or any other script variable. You might need to see what the value is at a particular point in the script or you might want to change the value during playback. You can manage up to four different Watch windows to help organize the variables you want to monitor.

The easiest way to monitor a variable is to right-click on the variable (anywhere in the variable name) while paused at a breakpoint and select **Add Watch**. This automatically shows the Watch window with the variable along with its current value. Note that you can do this only while the script is playing back in debug mode, although Visual Studio remembers variables that were added from previous debug runs. As you step through the script or pause at breakpoints, the Watch window shows the current variable values at that point in the script (see Figure 6.13).

Figure 6.13   Viewing the value of a script variable

You can change the value of script variables while executing a script in debug mode from the Watch window. Right-click on the variable you want to change and select **Edit Value**. You can change the values of test data, captured from or input to the application under test. You might also do this with a counter value to skip to the end of a looping structure.

You can add a datapool value to a Watch window similarly to the way that you add a script variable. You must select the entire field DpString("*name*") to get the value of the datapool. If you only set the cursor in this field, or if you select only part of the function name, the Watch window does not display the correct value from the datapool (see Figure 6.14).

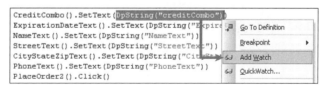

Figure 6.14   Viewing a datapool value during debug

Note that you cannot change a datapool value as you can other script variables. This is because the value is read from a file (not traditional file input/output) directly into the test script. If you need to change values taken from a datapool, either as part of normal test execution or for debugging, you must set the datapool value into an intermediate variable first, and then use this variable in place of the datapool call (e.g., dim creditCard as String = DpString ("creditCombo").

Adding Breakpoints While Debugging

Sometimes, as you step through a script in debug mode looking for problems, you discover a place where you want to add a breakpoint (for the next time you execute the script in debug mode or for the next time your code enters a loop or method). You can add one while you're debugging (you don't need to be in edit mode). Right-click in the vertical editor ruler and select **Toggle Breakpoint**.

Summary

Debugging is a critical skill that you develop with time and experience. Like any skill, you need to exercise it to develop it. Hopefully, this chapter has helped give you the confidence and knowledge to use the debugger in your development environment.

## CHAPTER 7

Managing Script Execution

Daniel Chirillo, Daniel Gouveia

Managing script execution consists of tasks such as manipulating playback settings, using conditional and looping logic to optimize the flow of your scripts, handling errors your scripts encounter, building regression scripts (for example, scripts that call other scripts), and executing your scripts outside of the Rational Functional Tester environment. This chapter takes you through each of these tasks and teaches you how to enhance your scripts further. You are armed with an arsenal of techniques that can help you transform your recorded scripts into robust functional testing assets.

Setting Execution Options Within Your Scripts

Previous chapters discussed setting some of the playback options via Rational Functional Tester's global settings. These enable you to adjust logging, tweak the ScriptAssure™ logic, and tune different delays. The problem that teams encounter when working with these global settings is that they are specific to an instance of Rational Functional Tester. This means that if you change your settings to get a script to successfully play back, everybody on your team needs to modify their settings to match yours—if they want to play your script back or include it in their regression test. The way to escape this dependency is by manipulating the outside of Rational Functional Tester's global playback settings. Rational Functional Tester enables you to set execution options right in your scripts.

This chapter teaches you how to release your dependency on global playback settings. You learn how you can set these from within your scripts. This enables you and your team to work within an environment where you are all not constantly adjusting your playback settings to run other team members' scripts.

Manipulating Playback Options Within Scripts

Rational Functional Tester provides programmatic access for manipulating execution options. These enable you to adjust playback settings right within the body of your script. This provides an excellent means for you to control the behavior of your scripts without depending on Rational Functional Tester's global playback settings.

If you find that your script is struggling at certain points—perhaps facing synchronization issues with your application—you first should adjust the global playback settings in Rational Functional Tester. This helps to easily pinpoint the necessary option that would fix the playback of your script. The idea is to adjust the value of one option, re-execute your script, and see if that fixes the problem. After you find the right setting, make a note of it along with the value that you provided. You can then reset it back to its original value (easily accomplished by clicking the **Restore Defaults** button). This information enables you to work with Rational Functional Tester's Application Programming Interface (API) to modify that particular setting in your script. The first thing you need to understand is the IOptionName interface, which is a simple means to access the different options that enable you to control your script's behavior. The complete list of fields (options) and their descriptions for this interface can be found in the *Rational Functional Tester API Reference*.

The basic means of working with this interface is to explicitly call it with the desired option name. For example, a call to this, in either version of the tool (VB.NET or Java), looks similar to the following example:

```
IOptionName.USE_DEFAULT_LOG_INFO
```

Using the information you garnered from your experiments with the global playback settings, you peruse the IOptionName field settings in the *Rational Functional Tester API Reference* and find which one matches the option you found to fix your problem. You would then reference it and select it from the content assist dialog, shown in Figure 7.1.

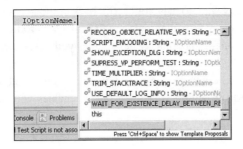

Figure 7.1   IOptionName—field choices

IOptionName provides you with only the options you need to work with. You manipulate them using one of three methods: getOption, setOption, and resetOption. These enable you to adjust your scripts' behaviors at any point.

As its name suggests, getOption enables you to retrieve the current value of a given option. This comes in handy if you want to create some logic in your script that first acquires a given playback setting's value and then adjusts execution accordingly. Listing 7.1 provides code examples that show the basic usage pattern of getOption.

Listing 7.1   Using getOption() in the context of a script

Java
```
public void testMain(Object[] args)
{
      Object myOption = getOption(IOptionName.DELAY_AFTER_WINDOW_ACTIVATE);
      System.out.println(myOption.toString());
}
```

VB.NET
```
Public Function TestMain(ByVal args() As Object) As Object
      Dim myOption As Object =
GetOption(IOptionName.DELAY_AFTER_WINDOW_ACTIVATE)
      System.Console.WriteLine(myOption.ToString)
      Return Nothing
End Function
```

The sample scripts in Listing 7.1 acquire the current value of the **Delay after top level window activates** setting. If you run these scripts, the return value of the getOption/GetOption is displayed in the console window. In this case, **0.5** is returned. This is the default value for the **Delay after top level window activates** setting (see Figure 7.2).

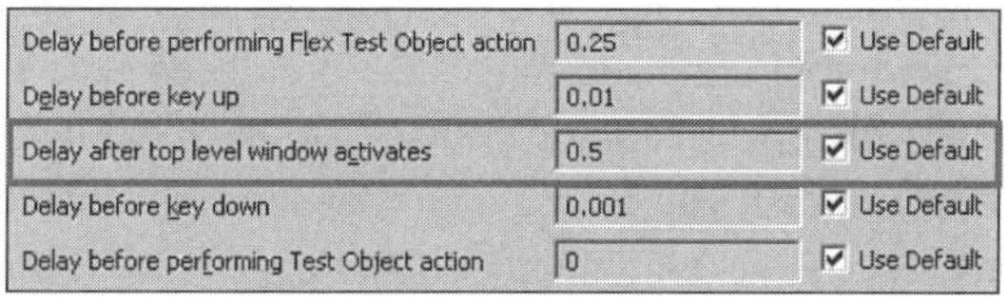

Delay before performing Flex Test Object action	0.25	☑ Use Default
Delay before key up	0.01	☑ Use Default
Delay after top level window activates	0.5	☑ Use Default
Delay before key down	0.001	☑ Use Default
Delay before performing Test Object action	0	☑ Use Default

Figure 7.2   Global playback settings—other delays and Delay after top level window activates

Changing the value of an IOptionName field is accomplished using setOption. The basic usage pattern for this method is to specify the option you wish to change and the value to which you wish to change it. For example, if your application has touchy mouse-over menus that take less than a second to display one minute and five seconds to display another minute, you can set the MOUSE_HOVER_TIME option to address this.

Java

```
setOption(IOptionName.MOUSE_HOVER_TIME, 5.0);
```

VB.NET

```
SetOption(IOptionName.MOUSE_HOVER_TIME, 5.0)
```

This ensures Rational Functional Tester hovers over the necessary region of your application and waits five seconds for the mouse-over menu to display. Using `setOption` enables you to tweak small pieces of your script without having to use the global playback options.

Finally, Rational Functional Tester's API also provides a `resetOption` method. This enables you to turn off your overrides and default back to the values residing in the global playback settings. This is useful for optimizing the behavior of your scripts. For instance, if you increase your mouse delays to handle a tricky drag-and-drop action, you might want to reset them so that you don't slow down *every* mouse action in your script. Using `resetOption` is quite easy. You simply make a call to it, specifying the option you wish to reset. An example of this is shown in the following line of code:

```
resetOption(IOptionName.DELAY_BEFORE_MOUSE_UP);
```

This result in your script defaulting back to the value set for this option in the global playback settings. The behavior of your script would be such that it would delay only for the necessary drag-and-drop action and return to normal mouse speeds for the duration of playback.

Flow Control

Recording your scripts enables you to capture the actions necessary for navigation and verification. There are times when you need to build flow control into your scripts to handle errors and decisions. The latter are typically brought about by the need for things such as role-based testing, negative testing, and testing for Graphical User Interface (GUI) standards. The prior are instances that are neither predictable nor controllable.

Loops and conditional logic enable you to adjust the flow of your scripts based off things such as decisions you need your scripts to make, data you need your scripts to read, role-based scenarios you need to test for, error handling you need to flush out, and so on. With some clever recording and basic programming, you can modify your scripts so that they can handle these situations. This also helps reduce the overall number of scripts you have to maintain.

The basic idea of error handling is to recover from issues that arise during playback, or at least terminate with grace! Rational Functional Tester throws exceptions when it encounters errors. These are typically what drive the creation and continued growth of your error handling. Whether it is continuing script execution after playback or simply terminating it with detailed logging, handling errors is a key capability your scripts should have.

This chapter addresses flow control. It helps to answer the questions surrounding decision and error handling in your scripts. By the end of the next section, you should have a good feel for how to develop your script so it's adaptable to different situations that might arise in your project.

Handling Positive and Negative Testing in the Same Script

Developing a script that handles positive and negative testing is a multistep process. It involves multiple recordings and manual editing. It requires a dataset to work with that can include a database, external file, or native datapool. The general idea is that you record the basic flow through your application. You then amend your script with the necessary steps to test for and handle the alternate flows (for example, when you enter "bad" data).

The first thing you need to do is figure out where and when the error handlers are invoked in the application you are testing. This enables you to figure out how to design your script. After you have that done, record the base script. Essentially, this is a recording of the "happy day" scenario, using positive data. Finally, you need to set your application's state to the point where the error handler is invoked. This is where you insert a recording into your script that captures the steps needed to deal with the handler. Depending on the number of error handlers you try to capture for your script, you might need to iterate this process the appropriate number of times.

To exemplify this, you can use the `ClassicsJavaA` application that comes pre-configured with Rational Functional Tester. When looking at testing the process of ordering a single CD, note that two error handlers can be invoked. One is engaged when the quantity field is not populated. The other is engaged when the credit card number or expiration date is left empty. When you record the "happy day" scenario, you look to test to make sure that the order confirmation message dialog box displays after placing your order (see Figure 7.3). You then perform a secondary verification to make sure the order confirmation message is correct.

Listing 7.2 shows what the recorded "happy day" scenario would look like in Java and VB.NET when connected to a datapool for quantity and credit card information.

Figure 7.3 Order Confirmation dialog box

Listing 7.2 Happy day scenario for ClassicsJavaA

Java
```
public void testMain(Object[] args)
{
```

```
startApp("ClassicsJavaA");

// Frame: ClassicsCD
tree2().click(atPath("Composers->Haydn->Location(PLUS_MINUS)"));
tree2().click(atPath("Composers->Haydn->Symphonies Nos. 99 & 101"));
placeOrder().click();

// Frame: Member Logon
nameCombo().click();
nameCombo().click(atText("Susan Flontly"));
passwordText().click(atPoint(9,16));
memberLogon().inputChars("PASSWORD");
ok().click();
// Data Driven Code inserted on Sep 6, 2008

// Frame: Place an Order
quantityText().setText(dpString("Quantity"));
cardNumberIncludeTheSpacesText().setText(dpString("CardNumber"));
creditCombo().setText(dpString("CardType"));
expirationDateText().setText(dpString("ExpirationDate"));

// Frame: Place an Order
placeOrder2().click();

// POSITIVE DATA SCENARIO - TEST FOR ORDER CONFIRMATION DIALOG

yourOrderHasBeenReceivedYourOr().performTest(VerifyOrderConfirmationVP());
ok2().click();

// Frame: ClassicsCD
classicsJava(ANY,MAY_EXIT).close();
}
```

VB.NET

```
Public Function TestMain(ByVal args() As Object) As Object
    StartApp("ClassicsJavaA")

    ' Frame: ClassicsCD
    Tree2().Click(AtPath("Composers->Haydn->Location(PLUS_MINUS)"))
    Tree2().Click(AtPath("Composers->Haydn->Symphonies Nos. 99 & 101"))
    PlaceOrder().Click()

    ' Frame: Member Logon
    NameCombo().Click()
```

```
NameCombo().Click(AtText("Susan Flontly"))
PasswordText().Click(AtPoint(71,13))
MemberLogon().InputKeys("PASSWORD")
OK().Click()
' Data Driven Code inserted on Sep 6, 2008

' Frame: Place an Order
QuantityText().SetText(DpString("Quantity"))
CardNumberIncludeTheSpacesText().SetText(DpString("CardNumber"))
CreditCombo().SetText(DpString("CardType"))
ExpirationDateText().SetText(DpString("ExpirationDate"))
PlaceOrder2().Click()

' POSITIVE DATA SCENARIO - TEST FOR ORDER CONFIRMATION DIALOG
YourOrderHasBeenReceivedYourOr().PerformTest(VerifyOrderConfirmationVP())
OK2().Click()

' Frame: ClassicsCD
ClassicsJava(ANY,MAY_EXIT).Close()
Return Nothing
End Function
```

Referring to the basics steps outlined in the second paragraph, the next thing you do is set ClassicsJavaA to the state where the quantity error handler is invoked. Please refer to the error dialog box in Figure 7.4.

Figure 7.4   Error handler #1—missing quantity value

After performing that step, you need to locate the place in your script where this error dialog box is launched. In this case, it is the following line:

```
placeOrder2().click();
```

Upon playback, your script executes this line and places the order into the database. If the quantity field is empty, ClassicsJavaA pops open the error handler (shown in Figure 7.4). You need to insert a recording after this line in your script. This is where you capture the steps for handling this dialog box. In this case, you record a verification point (VP) to ensure the proper message is displayed in the error dialog. You also record the action to dismiss the handler (for example, clicking the **OK** button). Listing 7.3 displays the result.

Listing 7.3   Dealing with the quantity field error handler

Java
```
// DEAL WITH QUANTITY ERROR HANDLER
aQuantityIsRequiredToPlaceAnOr().performTest(VerifyQuantityErrorHandlerVP());
ok3().click();
cancel().click();
```

VB.NET
```
' DEAL WITH QUANTITY ERROR HANDLER
AQuantityIsRequiredToPlaceAnOr().PerformTest(VerifyQuantityErrorHandlerVP())
OK3().Click()
Cancel().Click()
```

You need to iterate through this process again and deal with the second error handler. This is the one that is engaged when the credit card number or expiration date is left blank. You can see an example of this error dialog in Figure 7.5.

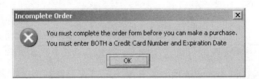

Figure 7.5   Error Handler #2—missing credit card number or expiration date

The steps for this are identical. You need to insert a recording that verifies the correct error message displays and handles getting rid of the error dialog. The code shown in Listing 7.4 looks similar to the lines that dealt with the first error handler in your script.

Listing 7.4   Dealing with the Credit Card Number/Expiration Data Field error handler

Java
```
// DEAL WITH QUANTITY ERROR HANDLER
youMustEnterBOTHACreditCardNum().performTest(VerifyCardInfoErrorHandlerVP());
ok4().click();
cancel().click();
```

VB.NET
```
' DEAL WITH CREDIT CARD NUMBER/EXPIRATION DATE ERROR HANDLER
AQuantityIsRequiredToPlaceAnOr().PerformTest(VerifyQuantityErrorHandlerVP())
OK4().Click()
Cancel().Click()
```

After the necessary pieces are recorded for the three scenarios, you need to add the flow control. This requires conditional branching. The basic logic is something like: "If the quantity error handler was launched, handle it. If the card information error handler was launched, handle that. Otherwise, just deal with the normal scenario, testing for the order confirmation message." Converting that to code, you get something similar to the two scripts in Listing 7.5.

Listing 7.5   Flow control

Java

```java
if(aQuantityIsRequiredToPlaceAnOr().exists()){
     // DEAL WITH QUANTITY ERROR HANDLER
     aQuantityIsRequiredToPlaceAnOr().performTest(VerifyQuantityErrorHandlerVP());
     ok3().click();
     cancel().click();

} else if(youMustEnterBOTHACreditCardNum().exists()){
     // DEAL WITH CREDIT CARD NUMBER/EXPIRATION DATE ERROR HANDLER
     youMustEnterBOTHACreditCardNum().performTest(VerifyCardInfoErrorHandlerVP());
     ok4().click();
     cancel().click();

} else{
     // POSITIVE DATA SCENARIO - TEST FOR ORDER CONFIRMATION DIALOG
     yourOrderHasBeenReceivedYourOr().performTest(VerifyOrderConfirmationVP());
     ok2().click();
}
```

VB.NET

```vbnet
If (AQuantityIsRequiredToPlaceAnOr().Exists) Then
     ' DEAL WITH QUANTITY ERROR HANDLER
     QuantityIsRequiredToPlaceAnOr().PerformTest(VerifyQuantityErrorHandlerVP())
     OK3().Click()
     Cancel().Click()

ElseIf (YouMustEnterBOTHACreditCardNum().Exists) Then
     ' DEAL WITH CREDIT CARD NUMBER/EXPIRATION DATE ERROR HANDLER
     YouMustEnterBOTHACreditCardNum().PerformTest(VerifyCardInfoErrorHandlerVP())
     OK4().Click()
     Cancel().Click()
```

```
Else
        ' POSITIVE DATA SCENARIO - TEST FOR ORDER CONFIRMATION DIALOG
        YourOrderHasBeenReceivedYourOr().PerformTest(VerifyOrderConfirmationVP())
        OK2().Click()
End If
```

The last piece to complete this script is tying things together with the datapool. The datapool not only contains the data to enter into your application's fields, but it also contains a column letting the script know if a row of data is a positive or negative test. Please refer to Figure 7.6 for an example of a datapool that handles both positive and negative testing.

	CardType::String	CardNumber::S...	ExpirationDate:...	Quantity::String	TestType::String
0	Visa	1111 1111 111...	12/2009	3	POSITIVE
1	Amex	2222 2222 222...		10	NEGATIVE
2	Mastercard		1-2010	1	NEGATIVE
3	Mastercard	3333 3333 333...	08/2011		NEGATIVE
4	Amex	4444 4444 444...	6/2012	5	POSITIVE
5	Visa	1111 2222 333...	5-2009		NEGATIVE
6	Visa	1111 2222 333...	5-2009		NEGATIVE
7	Visa			1	NEGATIVE

Figure 7.6   Datapool for positive and negative testing

This column enables you to avoid false positives and negatives. For example, if an error handler is launched while testing a normal "happy day" scenario (for example, valid data is provided), you need to log the error and, at some point, submit a defect. This demands that you amend your script to check to see if it currently runs through a positive or negative test, providing for error logging, if necessary. Listing 7.6 provides sample code snippets that show how to edit the quantity error handler to check for the test type (such as whether it is a positive or negative test).

Listing 7.6   Checking for a positive or negative test type

Java
```java
if(aQuantityIsRequiredToPlaceAnOr().exists()){
        // CHECK FOR TEST TYPE
        if(dpString("TestType").equals("POSITIVE")){
                logError("Error Handler Launched For Positive Test!",
                aQuantityIsRequiredToPlaceAnOr().getScreenSnapshot());
        }
        // DEAL WITH QUANTITY ERROR HANDLER
        aQuantityIsRequiredToPlaceAnOr().performTest(VerifyQuantityErrorHandlerVP());
        ok3().click();
        cancel().click();
}
```

VB.NET
```
If (AQuantityIsRequiredToPlaceAnOr().Exists) Then
     ' CHECK FOR TEST TYPE
    If (DpString("TestType").Equals("POSITIVE")) Then
          LogError("Error Handler Launched For Positive Test",
          AQuantityIsRequiredToPlaceAnOr().GetScreenSnapshot)
    End If
    ' DEAL WITH QUANTITY ERROR HANDLER
    AQuantityIsRequiredToPlaceAnOr().PerformTest(VerifyQuantityErrorHandlerVP())
    OK3().Click()
    Cancel().Click()
End If
```

The basic idea here is that the script checks for the test type and, if necessary, logs the error message, complete with an image of the error handler that was incorrectly launched. You need to modify the other two pieces of your conditional branching (that is, the normal scenario and the credit card information error handler) in a similar manner. Again, the point is to avoid false positives and negatives. The result of your script editing looks like Listing 7.7.

Listing 7.7   Complete positive and negative testing script for ClassicsJavaA

Java
```
public void testMain(Object[] args)
{

     startApp("ClassicsJavaA");

     // Frame: ClassicsCD
     tree2().click(atPath("Composers->Haydn->Location(PLUS_MINUS)"));
     tree2().click(atPath("Composers->Haydn->Symphonies Nos. 99 & 101"));
     placeOrder().click();

     // Frame: Member Logon
     nameCombo().click();
     nameCombo().click(atText("Susan Flontly"));
     passwordText().click(atPoint(9,16));
     memberLogon().inputChars("PASSWORD");
     ok().click();

     // Frame: Place an Order
     quantityText().setText(dpString("Quantity"));
     cardNumberIncludeTheSpacesText().setText(dpString("CardNumber"));
```

```
creditCombo().setText(dpString("CardType"));
expirationDateText().setText(dpString("ExpirationDate"));

// Frame: Place an Order
placeOrder2().click();

        if(aQuantityIsRequiredToPlaceAnOr().exists()){
        // CHECK FOR TEST TYPE
        if(dpString("TestType").equals("POSITIVE")){
            logError("Error Handler Launched For Positive Test!",
            aQuantityIsRequiredToPlaceAnOr().getScreenSnapshot());
}
        // DEAL WITH QUANTITY ERROR HANDLER
        aQuantityIsRequiredToPlaceAnOr().performTest
        (VerifyQuantityErrorHandlerVP());
        ok3().click();
        cancel().click();

} else if(youMustEnterBOTHACreditCardNum().exists()){
        // CHECK FOR TEST TYPE
        if(dpString("TestType").equals("POSITIVE")){
            logError("Error Handler Launched For Positive Test!",
            yourOrderHasBeenReceivedYourOr().getScreenSnapshot());
        }
        // DEAL WITH CREDIT CARD NUMBER/EXPIRATION DATE ERROR HANDLER
        youMustEnterBOTHACreditCardNum().performTest
        (VerifyCardInfoErrorHandlerVP());
        ok4().click();
        cancel().click();

} else{
        // CHECK FOR TEST TYPE
        if(dpString("TestType").equals("NEGATIVE")){
            logError("Error Handler Was NOT INVOKED For Negative Test!");
}
        // POSITIVE DATA SCENARIO - TEST FOR ORDER CONFIRMATION DIALOG
        yourOrderHasBeenReceivedYourOr().performTest
        (VerifyOrderConfirmationVP());
        ok2().click();
}
// Frame: ClassicsCD
classicsJava(ANY,MAY_EXIT).close();
}
```

VB.NET

```vb
Public Function TestMain(ByVal args() As Object) As Object
    StartApp("ClassicsJavaA")

    ' Frame: ClassicsCD
    Tree2().Click(AtPath("Composers->Haydn->Location(PLUS_MINUS)"))
    Tree2().Click(AtPath("Composers->Haydn->Symphonies Nos. 99 & 101"))
    PlaceOrder().Click()

    ' Frame: Member Logon
    NameCombo().Click()
    NameCombo().Click(AtText("Susan Flontly"))
    PasswordText().Click(AtPoint(71, 13))
    MemberLogon().InputKeys("PASSWORD")
    OK().Click()
    ' Data Driven Code inserted on Sep 6, 2008

    ' Frame: Place an Order
    QuantityText().SetText(DpString("Quantity"))
    CardNumberIncludeTheSpacesText().SetText(DpString("CardNumber"))
    CreditCombo().SetText(DpString("CardType"))
    ExpirationDateText().SetText(DpString("ExpirationDate"))
    PlaceOrder2().Click()

    If (AQuantityIsRequiredToPlaceAnOr().Exists) Then
        ' CHECK FOR TEST TYPE
        If (DpString("TestType").Equals("POSITIVE")) Then
            LogError("Error Handler Launched For Positive Test",
            AQuantityIsRequiredToPlaceAnOr().GetScreenSnapshot)
        End If
        ' DEAL WITH QUANTITY ERROR HANDLER
        AQuantityIsRequiredToPlaceAnOr().PerformTest
        (VerifyQuantityErrorHandlerVP())
        OK3().Click()
        Cancel().Click()

    ElseIf (YouMustEnterBOTHACreditCardNum().Exists) Then
        ' CHECK FOR TEST TYPE
        If (DpString("TestType").Equals("POSITIVE")) Then
            LogError("Error Handler Launched For Positive Test",
            YouMustEnterBOTHACreditCardNum().GetScreenSnapshot)
        End If
        ' DEAL WITH CREDIT CARD NUMBER/EXPIRATION DATE ERROR HANDLER
```

```
        YouMustEnterBOTHACreditCardNum().PerformTest
        (VerifyCardInfoErrorHandlerVP())
        OK4().Click()
        Cancel().Click()

Else
        ' CHECK FOR TEST TYPE
        If (DpString("TestType").Equals("NEGATIVE")) Then
             LogError("Error Handler Was NOT INVOKED For Negative Test!")
        End If
        ' POSITIVE DATA SCENARIO - TEST FOR ORDER CONFIRMATION DIALOG
        YourOrderHasBeenReceivedYourOr().PerformTest
        (VerifyOrderConfirmationVP())
        OK2().Click()
End If


    ' Frame: ClassicsCD
    ClassicsJava(ANY, MAY_EXIT).Close()
    Return Nothing
End Function
```

Localizing the Looping of a Datapool to a Certain Section of a Script

Rational Functional Tester's datapool capability is useful for testing sections of your application that require data entry. For instance, you can quickly iterate through all the possible positive and negative data combinations that are required to test user registration, user logon, order entry, and so on. It is easy to create datapools, especially when you import existing data. It is simple to connect a datapool to your scripts. However, as powerful and easy to use as datapools are, they do have one slight issue that can affect you. The lowest level of granularity they work at is the script level.

When you execute a script associated to a datapool, it plays back the specified number of iterations. It loops through the datapool and pulls out a row of data to use each time. It then uses that row's individual values to plug into the application that you test. Each iteration through the datapool, in fact, starts the script from the beginning—every single time! In most cases, this isn't an issue. When it does become an issue for people, there are simple ways around it. One of the best ways to deal with this is to use the datapool methods in a loop.

The easiest way to do this is to set up a `while` loop that iterates through the entire datapool. Calling `dpDone()` enables your loop to know when it is finished. The following line of code shows what this looks like in Java:

```
while(!dpDone())
```

If you use VB.NET, it mimics the following line:

```
While (Not (DpDone()))
```

To move to the next row, you simply call the dpNext() method. Lastly, to obtain the individual values of the current datapool row, you call the dpXXX() for the value's data type. For instance, you call dpString() for string values, dpInt() for integer values, dpFloat() for floating point integers, and so on. You need to pass the datapool column index or column name to these methods. For instance, calling the dpString() method, using a column name, looks something like following:

```
dpString("ColumnName").
```

The VB.NET version would resemble the following:

```
DpString("ColumnName").
```

Using column indices is as simple as passing the column number to the method—*dpString(1)* / *DpString(1)* for Java and VB.NET, respectively.

The previous section covered controlling the flow of your script with conditional logic. It showed how to use a single script to accomplish both positive and negative testing for ordering a CD. It was connected to a datapool containing both good and bad data. Playing it back results in your script iterating through the datapool, opening and closing the ClassicsJavaA application each time. If you strategically place a while loop into this script and make the necessary datapool method calls, you can avoid opening and closing the application for each iteration. The end result looks similar to the Java and VB.NET scripts found in Listing 7.8.

Listing 7.8   Enhancing the "Error-Handling" script by looping through a datapool

Java
```
public void testMain(Object[] args)
{

    startApp("ClassicsJavaA");

    while(!dpDone()){

        // Frame: ClassicsCD
        tree2().click(atPath("Composers->Haydn-
        >Location(PLUS_MINUS)"));
        tree2().click(atPath("Composers->Haydn->Symphonies Nos. 99 & 101"));
        placeOrder().click();

        // Frame: Member Logon
        nameCombo().click();
        nameCombo().click(atText("Susan Flontly"));
        passwordText().click(atPoint(9,16));
        memberLogon().inputChars("PASSWORD");
        ok().click();
        // Data Driven Code inserted on Sep 6, 2008
```

```
// Frame: Place an Order
quantityText().setText(dpString("Quantity"));
cardNumberIncludeTheSpacesText().setText(dpString("CardNumber"));
creditCombo().setText(dpString("CardType"));
expirationDateText().setText(dpString("ExpirationDate"));


// Frame: Place an Order
placeOrder2().click();

if(aQuantityIsRequiredToPlaceAnOr().exists()){
     // CHECK FOR TEST TYPE
     if(dpString("TestType").equals("POSITIVE")){
          logError("Error Handler Launched For Positive Test!",
          aQuantityIsRequiredToPlaceAnOr() getScreenSnapshot());
     }
     // DEAL WITH QUANTITY ERROR HANDLER
          aQuantityIsRequiredToPlaceAnOr().performTest
          (VerifyQuantityErrorHandlerVP());
          ok3().click();
          cancel().click();


} else if(youMustEnterBOTHACreditCardNum().exists()){
     // CHECK FOR TEST TYPE
     if(dpString("TestType").equals("POSITIVE")){
          logError("Error Handler Launched For Positive Test!",
          yourOrderHasBeenReceivedYourOr().getScreenSnapshot());
     }
     // DEAL WITH CREDIT CARD NUMBER/EXPIRATION DATE ERROR HANDLER
          youMustEnterBOTHACreditCardNum().performTest
          (VerifyCardInfoErrorHandlerVP());
          ok4().click();
          cancel().click();


} else{
     // CHECK FOR TEST TYPE
     if(dpString("TestType").equals("NEGATIVE")){
          logError("Error Handler Was NOT INVOKED For Negative
          Test!");
     }
          // POSITIVE DATA SCENARIO - TEST FOR ORDER CONFIRMATION
          DIALOG
          yourOrderHasBeenReceivedYourOr().performTest
          (VerifyOrderConfirmationVP());
          ok2().click();
```

```
            }

        dpNext();
    }


    // Frame: ClassicsCD
    classicsJava(ANY,MAY_EXIT).close();
}
```

VB.NET

```
Public Function TestMain(ByVal args() As Object) As Object
    StartApp("ClassicsJavaA")

    While (Not (DpDone()))

        ' Frame: ClassicsCD
        Tree2().Click(AtPath("Composers->Haydn-Location(PLUS_MINUS)"))
        Tree2().Click(AtPath("Composers->Haydn->Symphonies Nos. 99 & 101"))
        PlaceOrder().Click()

        ' Frame: Member Logon
        NameCombo().Click()
        NameCombo().Click(AtText("Susan Flontly"))
        PasswordText().Click(AtPoint(71, 13))
        MemberLogon().InputKeys("PASSWORD")
        OK().Click()
        ' Data Driven Code inserted on Sep 6, 2008

        ' Frame: Place an Order
        QuantityText().SetText(DpString("Quantity"))
        CardNumberIncludeTheSpacesText().SetText(DpString("CardNumber"))
        CreditCombo().SetText(DpString("CardType"))
        ExpirationDateText().SetText(DpString("ExpirationDate"))
        PlaceOrder2().Click()

        If (AQuantityIsRequiredToPlaceAnOr().Exists) Then
            ' CHECK FOR TEST TYPE
            If (DpString("TestType").Equals("POSITIVE")) Then
                LogError("Error Handler Launched For Positive Test",
                AQuantityIsRequiredToPlaceAnOr().GetScreenSnapshot)
```

```
                    End If
                    ' DEAL WITH QUANTITY ERROR HANDLER
                    AQuantityIsRequiredToPlaceAnOr().PerformTest
                    (VerifyQuantityErrorHandlerVP())
                    OK3().Click()
                    Cancel().Click()


          ElseIf (YouMustEnterBOTHACreditCardNum().Exists) Then
                    ' CHECK FOR TEST TYPE
                    If (DpString("TestType").Equals("POSITIVE")) Then
                         LogError("Error Handler Launched For Positive Test",
                         YouMustEnterBOTHACreditCardNum().GetScreenSnapshot)
                    End If
                    ' DEAL WITH CREDIT CARD NUMBER/EXPIRATION DATE ERROR
                    HANDLER
                    YouMustEnterBOTHACreditCardNum().PerformTest
                    (VerifyCardInfoErrorHandlerVP())
                    OK4().Click()
                    Cancel().Click()


          Else
                    ' CHECK FOR TEST TYPE
                    If (DpString("TestType").Equals("NEGATIVE")) Then
                         LogError("Error Handler Was NOT INVOKED For
                         Negative Test!")
                    End If
                    ' POSITIVE DATA SCENARIO - TEST FOR ORDER
                    CONFIRMATION DIALOG
                    YourOrderHasBeenReceivedYourOr().PerformTest
                    (VerifyOrderConfirmationVP())
                    OK2().Click()


          End If


          DpNext()
     End While


     ' Frame: ClassicsCD
     ClassicsJava(ANY, MAY_EXIT).Close()
     Return Nothing
End Function
```

The scripts in Listing 7.8 adjust the flow control of the default datapool loop (for example, the internal loop that occurs by simply using a datapool). In fact, they actually override the looping mechanism of Rational Functional Tester's datapool functionality. When you execute these scripts, they work with the `while` loops that you embedded into them. This is an important thing to note when you begin developing scripts that call other scripts (sometimes referred to as *shell* scripts). This is covered in the "Developing Regression Scripts" section.

Preventing Script Execution from Stopping If an Exception Is Thrown

To quote a colleague, "Hope for the best; plan for the worst." Unexpected events, despite how hard your work, almost certainly occur. In this section, you examine techniques that you can use to handle problems in three ways:

- Find out that a problem has occurred.
- Prevent, if you choose, script execution from suddenly coming to an end; meaning, enabling yourself the opportunity to clean up and end gracefully.
- Handle the problem and go back and try and repeat the thing that caused the problem.

As you probably know, without adding anything to a script, any exception thrown during script execution time causes the execution of your script (or suite of scripts) to come to an abrupt end. In the log, there is mention of an "unhandled exception."

Various Rational Functional Tester-specific exceptions can occur at runtime. The root class of many of these problems is RationalTestException, which is inherited by many subclasses (see Figure 7.7).

The (arguably) most commonly thrown exceptions are `ObjectNotFoundException` and `AmbiguousRecognitionException` (which, incidentally, inherits from `ObjectNotFound Exception`).

You can use two techniques (either one of the following or a combination of the two) to handle exceptions:

- Add a `try/catch`.
- Override `RationalTestScript` events that are automatically called by the playback engine when (or right before) an exception is thrown.

For readers who might be new to `try/catch`, we start off with an example that simply illustrates how a `try/catch` is used and the flow of control. In this contrived example, you have a single statement: a click on a button. The button is not present, though. To prevent Rational Functional Tester from waiting 20 seconds for the object (you know it's not there) and from displaying the Exception dialog box, you add two calls to `setOption()`. Please refer to the examples in Listing 7.9.

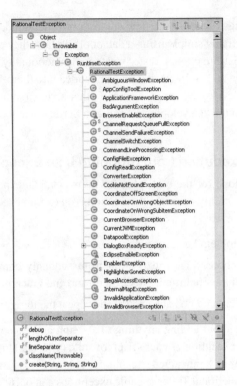

Figure 7.7   Test exception hierarchy

Listing 7.9   Simple `try`/`catch` example

Java
```java
public void testMain(Object[] args) {

    setOption(IOptionName.MAXIMUM_FIND_OBJECT_TIME, 2);
    setOption(IOptionName.INTERACTIVE, false);

    try {
        button_logOnsubmit().click();
        logInfo("After attempt to click"); // Not executed
    } catch (ObjectNotFoundException notFoundExc) {
        logInfo("In catch");
    }

        logInfo ("After catch");
}
```

VB.NET
```
Public Function TestMain(ByVal args() As Object) As Object

  SetOption(IOptionName.MAXIMUM_FIND_OBJECT_TIME, 2)
  SetOption(IOptionName.INTERACTIVE, False)

  Try

     Button_LogOnsubmit.Click()
     LogInfo("after attempt to click") ' Not executed

  Catch notFoundExc As ObjectNotFoundException
     LogInfo("In catch")
  End Try

  LogInfo("After catch")

  Return Nothing
End Function
```

If you execute this script, you should notice a couple of things:

- Two of the three messages were written to the log. The statement immediately following the click() was not executed.

- There's no failure in the log. The log makes it appear that the script executed successfully. In a sense, it did. Script execution halts when an *unhandled* exception is thrown. Catching the exception is considered handling it (the fact you didn't handle it in a meaningful way is another story).

Next task: What would you do if you wanted your script to handle multiple exceptions, for example, a PropertyNotFoundException (which is thrown if you try to get a property that doesn't exist from a test object) and an ObjectNotFoundException? Easy—use multiple catch blocks.

In the following example, you have two statements that could potentially cause an exception to be thrown:

- You attempt to get the age property from the browser (of course there is no such property).

- You try to click on a button that is not present.

Listing 7.10 shows examples of using catch blocks to tell your script what to do when one of the two previously listed statements causes an exception to occur.

Listing 7.10   Using catch blocks to handle exceptions

Java
```
public void testMain(Object[] args) {
  setOption(IOptionName.MAXIMUM_FIND_OBJECT_TIME, 2);
  setOption(IOptionName.INTERACTIVE, false);

  try {
    browser_htmlBrowser().getProperty("age");
    button_logOnsubmit().click();
  } catch (ObjectNotFoundException notFoundExc) {
      logInfo(notFoundExc.getMessage());
  } catch ( PropertyNotFoundException noPropExc ) {
      logInfo(noPropExc.getMessage());
  }
  logInfo("After catch");
}
```

VB.NET
```
  Public Function TestMain(ByVal args() As Object) As Object
    SetOption(IOptionName.MAXIMUM_FIND_OBJECT_TIME, 2)
    SetOption(IOptionName.INTERACTIVE, False)
      Try
        Browser_HtmlBrowser().GetProperty("age")
        Button_LogOnsubmit.Click()
        LogInfo("after attempt to click")
      Catch notFoundExc As ObjectNotFoundException
        LogInfo(notFoundExc.Message)
      Catch noPropExc As PropertyNotFoundException
        LogInfo(noPropExc.Message)
      End Try

      LogInfo("After catch")

      Return Nothing
  End Function
```

As in the previous example, the script completes successfully. In this example, you write a more interesting message to the log within the catch, you retrieve and write the exception message to the log, which in this case includes "Property age not found." If the age property did exist, the second exception would have been caught for the absent Logon button, writing the appropriate message to the log.

Many types of exceptions can be thrown. If you wanted to catch *any* type of Rational Functional Tester runtime exception, you can be generic and just catch `RationalTestScriptException`, shown in Listing 7.11.

Listing 7.11 Using the generic `RationalTestScriptException` to catch any exception

Java

```java
public void testMain(Object[] args) {
  setOption(IOptionName.MAXIMUM_FIND_OBJECT_TIME, 2);
  setOption(IOptionName.INTERACTIVE, false);

  try {
    browser_htmlBrowser().getProperty("age");
    button_logOnsubmit().click();
  } catch (RationalTestScriptException ratlException) {
      logInfo(ratlException.getMessage());
  }
  logInfo("After catch");
}
```

VB.NET

```vbnet
  Public Function TestMain(ByVal args() As Object) As Object
    SetOption(IOptionName.MAXIMUM_FIND_OBJECT_TIME, 2)
    SetOption(IOptionName.INTERACTIVE, False)
    Try
      Browser_HtmlBrowser().GetProperty("age")
      Button_LogOnsubmit.Click()
      LogInfo("after attempt to click")

    Catch ratlException As RationalTestScriptException
      LogInfo(ratlException.Message)
    End Try

    LogInfo("After catch")

    Return Nothing
  End Function
```

Wouldn't it be helpful if you could not only catch the exception but also *fix* the problem? Of course, it would. You can fix the problem in the catch, but the challenge is then going back to the statement that caused the exception to be thrown. There are a couple of ways to do this:

- Put a loop around the try/catch block. The loop enables you to attempt to execute a statement (or series of statements) several times. You end up with something like the pseudocode in Listing 7.12.

Listing 7.12   Placing a loop around a `try/catch` block

Java
```java
boolean exceptionThrown = false;
for (int attempt = 1; attempt <= 3; attempt++ ) {
    try {
        // Code that might throw and exception


    } catch ( ObjectNotFoundExcepion  e ) {
        exceptionThrown = true;

        // Try to fix the problem



    }
    if( exceptionThrown == false ) {
        break;
    }
}
```

One issue with this approach is that you might end up with many blocks of code like this.

- Don't use a `try/catch` at all; instead, override a `RationalTestScript` event.

You can override seven exception-related events. Your scripts never call these events. These are:

```
onAmbiguousRecognition

onCallScriptException

onObjectNotFound

onSubitemNotFound

onTestObjectMethodException

onUnhandledException

onVpFailure
```

These events are defined in the `RationalTestScript` class. The implementation defined in `RationalTestScript` is to write a message to the log and to allow execution to come to a halt. You have the option of overriding this behavior. You can override any `RationalTestScript` even in a test script or in a `HelperSuper` class.

Next, you look at `onObjectNotFound`. The first thing you should know about these events is that, unlike `try/catch` blocks, unless you *do something* in your event-handling code, the exception is thrown again after your own code is executed and execution is abruptly stopped.

To illustrate this point, override the `onObjectNotFound` event. If you're using Eclipse, right-click anywhere in your script editor and select **Source > Override/Implement Methods**. Then, in the dialog that displays, under `RationalTestScript`, select **onObjectNotFound** and click **OK**. Eclipse inserts an event stub into your script. In Visual Studio, you need to type the code.

As in the first example, you have a script with a single statement—a click on an object that you purposefully make sure isn't present when you execute. When Rational Functional Tester fails to find the test object, execution automatically leaves `testMain()` and goes to the `onObjectNotFound` event, in this case to the overridden `onObjectNotFound` event. The first thing you do is put a single statement in the event—one that writes to the log—just to prove that the code is being executed and just having the event code doesn't prevent the exception from being thrown. Refer to the code samples in Listing 7.13 for the respective Java and .NET implementations of this proposed solution.

Listing 7.13   Example of overriding the `onObjectNotFound` event

Java

```java
public void testMain(Object[] args) {

    setOption(IOptionName.MAXIMUM_FIND_OBJECT_TIME, 2);
    setOption(IOptionName.INTERACTIVE, false);

    button_logOnsubmit().click();
    logInfo("After attempt to click");

    }

    public void onObjectNotFound(ITestObjectMethodState testObjectMethodState) {

        logInfo("in onObjectNotFound()");
    }
}
```

VB.NET

```vbnet
Public Function TestMain(ByVal args() As Object) As Object

    SetOption(IOptionName.MAXIMUM_FIND_OBJECT_TIME, 2)
    SetOption(IOptionName.INTERACTIVE, False)

    Button_LogOnsubmit.Click()
    LogInfo("after attempt to click")

    Return Nothing

End Function
```

```
Public Overrides Sub OnObjectNotFound( _
        ByVal testObjectMethodState As ITestObjectMethodState )

   LogInfo("In our event handler")

End Sub
```

If you execute either of the scripts in Listing 7.13, you see your log message and a failure in the log. You do not see the "after attempt to click" log message. Playback comes to a halt.

How do you prevent playback from bombing? The Rational Functional Tester API documentation for onObjectNotFound has the following statement: "If this event is not handled and the testObjectMethodState is not modified, an ObjectNotFoundException is thrown." So *two* things must occur to prevent the exception from being thrown:

1.   Override the event (which you're doing).
2.   Modify the testObjectMethodState.

So how do you modify the testObjectMethodState? If you look up ITestObjectMethod-State in the API, you see (among others) three methods: findObjectAgain(), setFoundTestObject(), and setReturnValue(). Calling any of these methods prevents the exception from being thrown. Use setReturnValue(). Setting any return value other than a null (nothing in VB.NET) is sufficient to prevent the exception from being thrown. Listing 7.14 shows how to implement this in Java and VB.NET.

Listing 7.14   Preventing exceptions from being thrown, terminating script execution

Java
```
public void testMain(Object[] args) {

     setOption(IOptionName.MAXIMUM_FIND_OBJECT_TIME, 2);
     setOption(IOptionName.INTERACTIVE, false);

     button_logOnsubmit().click();
     logInfo("After attempt to click");

     }


public void onObjectNotFound(ITestObjectMethodState testObjectMethodState) {

        logInfo("in onObjectNotFound()");
        testObjectMethodState.setReturnValue(new Integer(0));
     }
}
```

VB.NET

```
Public Function TestMain(ByVal args() As Object) As Object

    SetOption(IOptionName.MAXIMUM_FIND_OBJECT_TIME, 2)
    SetOption(IOptionName.INTERACTIVE, False)

    Button_LogOnsubmit.Click()
    LogInfo("after attempt to click")

    Return Nothing

End Function

Public Overrides Sub OnObjectNotFound( _
        ByVal testObjectMethodState As ITestObjectMethodState )

  LogInfo("In our event handler")
  testObjectMethodState.SetReturnValue(0)
End Sub
```

If you execute, you can see that not only did script playback not come to an end, but after your event was fired, execution flow went back to testMain() and resumed with the next statement. In many cases, continuing execution after an exception has occurred might not be reasonable. What's neat is that Rational Functional Tester's execution apparatus makes that possible for you if you need it.

Now for the big finish: Try to fix the problem and instruct Rational Functional Tester to execute the method call that caused this situation. Although powerful, this can be challenging to implement in real life. To fix the problem, the event has to somehow know (or figure out) what should be done to right the wrong that's taken place. A simple example follows. Assume, for the purposes of this example, that if the button is not present, this indicates that something caused the application process to die, for example, you've probably seen Internet Explorer suddenly disappear. In this case, to right the wrong, all you need to do is launch the browser and navigate to a particular URL. That's a single statement, startBrowser(). Directing Rational Functional Tester to execute the code that caused the event handler to fire is also a single method call: You call findObjectAgain() on the ITestObjectMethodState argument to the event. This is illustrated in Listing 7.15.

Listing 7.15   Fixing the problem in the onObjectNotFound event handler

Java

```
    public void testMain(Object[] args) {
```

```
    setOption(IOptionName.MAXIMUM_FIND_OBJECT_TIME, 2);
    setOption(IOptionName.INTERACTIVE, false);

    button_logOnsubmit().click();
    logInfo("After attempt to click");

    }

    public void onObjectNotFound(ITestObjectMethodState estObjectMethodState) {

        logInfo("in onObjectNotFound()");
        startBrowser( <some URL> );
        testObjectMethodState.findObjectAgain();

    }
}
```

VB.NET

```
    Public Function TestMain(ByVal args() As Object) As Object

        SetOption(IOptionName.MAXIMUM_FIND_OBJECT_TIME, 2)
        SetOption(IOptionName.INTERACTIVE, False)

        Button_LogOnsubmit.Click()
        LogInfo("after attempt to click")

        Return Nothing

    End Function

    Public Overrides Sub OnObjectNotFound( _
            ByVal testObjectMethodState As ITestObjectMethodState )

    LogInfo("In our event handler")
    startBrowser( <some url> )
    testObjectMethodState.FindObjectAgain
End Sub
```

Adding a Screenshot to the Log If a Verification Point Fails

Sometimes it can be a challenge to convince others that an application is exhibiting defective behavior. Pictures can sometimes help you make a stronger case.

Rational Functional Tester makes adding screenshots to the log trivial. You can capture a screenshot by invoking `getScreenSnapshot()` on the `RootTestObject`. The image is returned as a `BufferedImage` (`System.Drawing.Bitmap` in Visual Basic.NET)

```
BufferedImage image = getRootTestObject().getScreenSnapshot();
```

In addition, each of the logging methods—`logInfo()`, `logWarning()`, and `logError()`—is overloaded. The two-argument version takes a `String` and a `BufferedImage`. What if you want a screenshot added to the log if a verification point (or all verification points) fails? Well, the long way to achieve this is to look at the return value of verification point (`performTest()` returns a Boolean). This is shown in Listing 7.16.

Listing 7.16   Checking for a verification point failure before logging a screenshot

Java
```
boolean vpResult = someVP().performTest();
if( vpResult == false ) {
   logInfo( "Screen when VP failed",getRootTestObject.getScreenSnapshot());

}
```

VB.NET
```
Dim vpResult As Boolean = someVP().PerformTest()
If (vpResult = False) Then
  LogInfo("Screen when VP failed",GetRootTestObject.GetScreenSnapshot)
End If
```

To prevent the need to check the return value of each verification point, override `onVpFailure` (shown in Listing 7.17).

Listing 7.17   Overriding `onVPFailure` to log a screenshot

Java
```
public void onVpFailure(IFtVerificationPoint vp) {
     logInfo( "Screen when VP failed",
getRootTestObject.getScreenSnapshot());
}
```

VB.NET
```
Public Overrides Sub OnVpFailure( ByVal vp As IFtVerificationPoint )
     LogInfo("Screen when VP Failed", _
                        GetRootTestObject.GetScreenSnapshot)
End sub
```

For this event to be applied to every script, put it in a Helper Superclass (see Chapter 3, "General Script Enhancements").

Passing Arguments to a Script from the Rational Functional Tester User Interface

Rational Functional Tester enables you to set playback options prior to executing a script. One of these options is the ability to pass arguments to your script upon playback. To do this, you need to follow two steps: specifying the arguments and handling those arguments in the scripts.

Passing arguments to your scripts is similar to passing arguments to UNIX/Linux shell scripts or Windows batch files. You simply provide the desired arguments, separating them by spaces. Figure 7.8 illustrates an example of this.

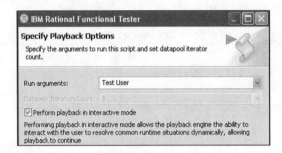

Figure 7.8   Specify playback options—Run Arguments

Figure 7.8 shows `Test` and `User` as the two arguments being passed to the script. Upon playback, these are passed into your script in an object array. You need to edit your script so it can handle these arguments. Listing 7.18 shos a simple example of handling these arguments.

Listing 7.18   Handling arguments passed to the script from the Rational Functional Tester playback options

Java
```java
public void testMain(Object[] args)
{
      String firstName = args[0].toString();
      String lastName = args[1].toString();

      System.out.println("Hello, " + firstName + " " + lastName);
}
```

VB.NET
```vbnet
Public Function TestMain(ByVal args() As Object) As Object
      Dim firstName As String = args(0).ToString
      Dim lastName As String = args(1).ToString

      System.Console.WriteLine("Hello, " & firstName & " " & lastName)
```

```
      Return Nothing
End Function
```

You need to parse the object array. As shown in Listing 7.18, the first cell of the array contains the first name—either `arg[0]` when using Java or `arg(0)` when using VB.NET. The second cell of the array holds the last name, `arg[1]` or `arg(1)`. The net result of these scripts is a `Hello` message displayed in the console window (Figure 7.9 for Eclipse and Figure 7.10 for .NET).

Figure 7.9   Script output in console window—Java

Figure 7.10   Script output in output window—VB.NET

This is an oversimplified example. However, the concept remains the same for much more complex scripting. For example, you might wish to pass in the specific web server or database server to test against on a given day. You simply specify the server information in the playback options and ensure that you have the code to handle them in your script, capturing the data from the object array that contains your argument(s). In other words, you do the same thing exemplified in the scripts found in Listing 7.18, substituting a first and last name for a web server and database server.

Passing Arguments to Scripts Invoked from Other Scripts

The previous topic discussed how you pass arguments into your scripts from Rational Functional Tester's playback options. This is a useful technique for dealing with such dynamics as testing against different web servers, database servers, and so on. What about the scenario of dealing with dynamics between scripts? How do you develop your scripts to manage consistency throughout your application? Rational Functional Tester provides for this by passing arguments to other scripts, using the `callScript(RationalTestScript script, Object[] args)` method. This enables you to invoke another script from within the currently executing script, passing information to it in an Object array. The VB.NET version of this is `CallScript(scriptFullName As String, args() As Object)`.

Imagine you want to test for the following scenario, using the `ClassicsJavaA` application:

1. Launch the `ClassicsJavaA` application.
2. Order a CD.
3. Verify the order is successfully placed.
4. Verify the order exists in the order history portion of the application.
5. Cancel the order.
6. Close the `ClassicsJava` application.

This can be accomplished in a single script. In fact, if this were a real automation project, you would probably already have a script that handles the testing of placing an order in this application. What happens if another member on your team already created a script to handle the testing of reviewing that an order exists in the `ClassicsJavaA` order history section? Would you rerecord that functionality into your existing script? Ideally, you would not. You would reuse the piece that already exists, making the necessary modifications to make the two scripts work together.

The two scripts in Listing 7.19 show the recording of launching `ClassicsJavaA`, ordering a CD, verifying the order was placed (using the order message), and closing the application.

Listing 7.19   PlaceCDOrder

Java
```
public void testMain(Object[] args)
{
        startApp("ClassicsJavaA");

        // Frame: ClassicsCD
        tree2().click(atPath("Composers->Schubert->Location(PLUS_MINUS)"));
        tree2().click(atPath("Composers->Schubert->Die schone Mullerin, Op. 25"));
        placeOrder().click();

        // Frame: Member Logon
        nameCombo().click();
        nameCombo().click(atText("Claire Stratus"));
        passwordText().click(atPoint(37,13));
        memberLogon().inputChars("password");
        ok().click();
```

```
// Frame: Place an Order
cardNumberIncludeTheSpacesText().click(atPoint(33,10));
placeAnOrder().inputChars("1111 1111 1111 1111");
expirationDateText().click(atPoint(22,10));
placeAnOrder().inputChars("12/09");
placeOrder2().click();

//
yourOrderHasBeenReceivedYourOr().performTest(VerifyOrderMessageVP());
ok2().click();

// Frame: ClassicsCD
classicsJava(ANY,MAY_EXIT).close();
}
```

VB.NET

```
Public Function TestMain(ByVal args() As Object) As Object
    StartApp("ClassicsJavaA")

    ' Frame: ClassicsCD
    Tree2().Click(AtPath("Composers->Schubert->Location(PLUS_MINUS)"))
    Tree2().Click(AtPath("Composers->Schubert->Die schone Mullerin, Op. 25"))
    PlaceOrder().Click()

    ' Frame: Member Logon
    NameCombo().Click()
    NameCombo().Click(AtText("Claire Stratus"))
    PasswordText().Click(AtPoint(59,7))
    MemberLogon().InputChars("password")
    OK().Click()

    ' Frame: Place an Order
    CardNumberIncludeTheSpacesText().Click(AtPoint(41,10))
    PlaceAnOrder().InputChars("1111 1111 1111 1111")
    ExpirationDateText().Click(AtPoint(19,10))
    PlaceAnOrder().InputChars("12/09")
    PlaceOrder2().Click()

    '
    YourOrderHasBeenReceivedYourOr().PerformTest(VerifyOrderPlacedVP())
    OK2().Click()

    ' Frame: ClassicsCD
```

```
      ClassicsJava(ANY, MAY_EXIT).Close()
      Return Nothing
End Function
```

The next set of scripts (located in Listing 7.20) shows what a script might look like for reviewing the order history in ClassicsJavaA. The scripts simply access the order history, select the desired order row in the history table, verify it, cancel the order, and close out the order history window (see Listing 7.20).

Listing 7.20 ReviewOrderHistory

Java
```
public void testMain(Object[] args)
{

      // Frame: ClassicsCD
      jmb().click(atPath("Order"));
      jmb().click(atPath("Order->View Existing Order Status..."));

      // Frame: View Order Status
      nameComboB().click();
      nameComboB().click(atText("Claire Stratus"));
      passwordText().click(atPoint(65,9));
      viewOrderStatus().inputChars("PASSWORD");
      ok().click();

      // Frame: View Existing Orders
      existingTable().click(atCell(atRow("ORDER ID", "11", "ORDER DATE",
            "13/09/08", "STATUS",
            "Order Initiated"),
            atColumn("ORDER ID")),
            atPoint(38,5));
      // SELECT SPECIFIC ORDER BY COMPOSER AND COMPOSITION
      existingTable().performTest(VerifyOrderTableVP());
      cancelSelectedOrder().click();
      close().click();
}
```

VB.NET
```
Public Function TestMain(ByVal args() As Object) As Object

      ' Frame: ClassicsCD
      Jmb().Click(AtPath("Order"))
```

```
Jmb().Click(AtPath("Order->View Existing Order Status..."))
' Frame: View Order Status
NameComboB().Click()
NameComboB().Click(AtText("Claire Stratus"))
PasswordText().Click(AtPoint(69,10))
ViewOrderStatus().InputChars("password")
OK().Click()

' Frame: View Existing Orders
ExistingTable().Click(AtCell(AtRow("ORDER ID", "11", "ORDER DATE", _
       "13/09/08", "STATUS", _
       "Order Initiated"), _
       AtColumn("ORDER ID")), _
       AtPoint(38, 6))

' SELECT ROW BY COMPOSER AND COMPOSITION
ExistingTable().PerformTest(VerifyOrderTableVP())
CancelSelectedOrder().Click()
Close().Click()
Return Nothing
End Function
```

Mentioned previously, the `ReviewOrderHistory` script might be something that a team member already recorded. Working together, you and your teammate can make simple modifications to this script and enable it to communicate with and pass data to your `PlaceCDOrder` script. Only three things are needed:

1. Modify the `"PlaceCDOrder"` script to capture the necessary data for properly selecting the correct row in the Order History window.

2. Modify the `"PlaceCDOrder"` script to invoke the `"ReviewOrderHistory"` scripting, passing this information gathered in step #1.

3. Modify the `"ReviewOrderHistory"` script to use the data that was captured in the `"PlaceCDOrder"` script (see step #1).

To accomplish step #1, you need to investigate the `"ReviewOrderHistory"` script. This lets you know what you need to capture in the `"PlaceCDOrder"` script. You are looking for the line where the desired order row is selected. It looks like the following code snippet in Java:

```
existingTable().click(atCell(atRow("ORDER ID", "11", "ORDER DATE",
       "13/09/08", "STATUS",
       "Order Initiated"),
       atColumn("ORDER ID")),
       atPoint(38,5));
```

VB.NET looks like the following:

```
ExistingTable().Click(AtCell(AtRow("ORDER ID", "11", "ORDER DATE", _
      "13/09/08", "STATUS", _
      "Order Initiated"), _
      AtColumn("ORDER ID")), _
                                    AtPoint(38, 6))
```

Rational Functional Tester clicks on the row specified by a particular ORDER ID, ORDER DATE, and STATUS (11, 13/09/08, and Order Initiated, respectively). Looking at Figure 7.11, you can see that these are the table columns.

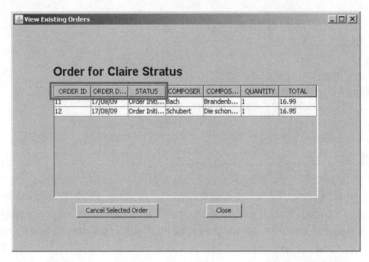

Figure 7.11   View existing orders window

Basically, Rational Functional Tester identifies a row by certain columns. In step #1, you need to figure out which of these columns is the best to use for identifying your order. For the purpose of this example, you use the COMPOSER and COMPOSITION columns. You should take note that you need to modify the previous line of code for the third step of this process.

With the information you garner from the `"ReviewOrderHistory"` script, you can easily accomplish the first step by inserting a recording into your `"PlaceCDOrder"` using Rational Functional Tester's Verification Point and Action Wizard. Chapter 1, "Overview of Rational Functional Tester," discussed how you can use this wizard's **Get a Specific Property Value** option to capture a property value for a particular object on your application. Before inserting the recording for this, you need to first open the `ClassicsJavaA` application to the point where the *Place an Order* window is open, displaying the composer and composition data (see Figure 7.12).

You also need to find the proper place to put the newly recorded lines of code in your script. You can do this at any point in your script that deals with the Place an Order window. For this example, you can insert the recording after the lines in your script that log into `ClassicsJavaA` as Claire Stratus. Please see Listing 7.21.

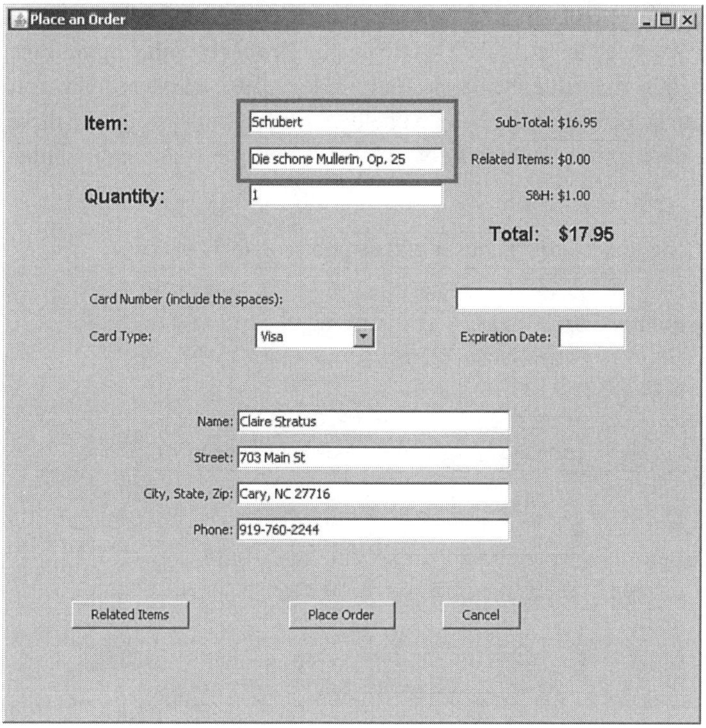

Figure 7.12   Place an Order window

Listing 7.21   Login steps found in script snippet for ClassicsJavaA

Java

```
nameCombo().click();
nameCombo().click(atText("Claire Stratus"));
passwordText().click(atPoint(37,13));
memberLogon().inputChars("password");
ok().click();
```

VB.NET

```
NameCombo().Click()
NameCombo().Click(AtText("Claire Stratus"))
PasswordText().Click(AtPoint(59,7))
MemberLogon().InputChars("password")
OK().Click()
```

After you place your cursor after the last line in login steps (for example, `ok().click()`), you can insert a recording into your script. You want to engage the Verification Point and Action Wizard, pointing the Object Finder Tool at the composer text field, residing on the Place an Order window. You need to select the **Get a Specific Property Value** option, specifying the *text* property. This grabs the value that is currently in the `composer` text field. You need to repeat this process against the `composition` text field. After you finish recording these two steps, ideally supplying descriptive comments for each one, you see something similar to the code in Listing 7.22.

Listing 7.22   Code to acquire composer and composition text field data

Java
```
// USE VERIFICATION POINT WIZARD TO CAPTURE THE 'TEXT'
// PROPERTIES OF THE COMPOSER & COMPOSITION TEXT FIELDS
// ON ORDER WINDOW
String composer = (String)itemText().getProperty("text");
String composition = (String)_1695Text().getProperty("text");
```

VB.NET
```
' USE VERIFICATION POINT WIZARD TO CAPTURE THE 'TEXT'
' PROPERTIES OF THE COMPOSER & COMPOSITION TEXT FIELDS
' ON ORDER WINDOW
Dim composer As String = ItemText().GetProperty("text")
Dim composition As String = _1695Text().GetProperty("text")
```

The second step you need to do is provide the code that invokes the `ReviewOrderHistory` script, passing in the composer and composition data. The opening paragraph in this section discussed using the `callScript(RationalTestScript script, Object[] args)` method and `CallScript(scriptFullName As String, args() As Object)` function. They are simple to use. You need to create a couple of lines of code to create the object array for storing the composer and composition data in it. You then call this method, passing in the name of the script you want, `ReviewOrderHistory` in this case and the array you created. Much like inserting a recording into your script, you need to properly locate this code. If you look at the flow of your `PlaceCDOrder` script, you note that the last two steps verify and close the order confirmation message and then close the `ClassicsJavaA` application. You want to place your code in between these sections. The final result looks like the code in Listing 7.23.

Listing 7.23   `callScript(RationalTestScript script, Object[] args)`

Java
```
yourOrderHasBeenReceivedYourOr().performTest(VerifyOrderMessageVP());
ok2().click();
```

```
// SET UP ARRAY TO PASS TO "ReviewOrderHistory" SCRIPT
Object[] composerData = {composer, composition};

// INVOKE "ReviewOrderHistory" SCRIPT, PASSING ARRAY IN
callScript("ReviewOrderHistory",composerData);

// Frame: ClassicsCD
classicsJava(ANY,MAY_EXIT).close();
```

VB.NET
```
YourOrderHasBeenReceivedYourOr().PerformTest(VerifyOrderPlacedVP())
OK2().Click()

' SET UP ARRAY TO PASS TO "ReviewOrderHistory" SCRIPT
Dim composerData() As Object = {composer, composition}

' INVOKE "ReviewOrderHistory" SCRIPT, PASSING ARRAY IN
CallScript("ReviewOrderHistory", composerData)

' Frame: ClassicsCD
ClassicsJava(ANY, MAY_EXIT).Close()
```

The examples in Listing 7.23 show that your `PlaceCDOrder` script now invokes the `ReviewOrderHistory` script, passing it the composer name and composition as an array. Remember, you captured the `composer` and `composition` values by following the first step in this process.

The third and final step of this process is to modify the `ReviewOrderHistory` script so that it can use the composer information in a meaningful way. Remember the mental note that you were supposed to make in Step 1? You were supposed to remember that you need to modify the line in your script that makes the order row selection, substituting the different column names and values. Doing so results in the following line in your Java script:

```
existingTable().click(atCell(atRow("COMPOSER", args[0].toString(),
        "COMPOSITION", args[1].toString()),
        atColumn("ORDER ID")),
    atPoint(38,5));
```

... and in VB.NET:

```
ExistingTable().Click(AtCell(AtRow("COMPOSER", args(0).toString, _
        "COMPOSITION", args(1).toString), _
        AtColumn("ORDER ID")), _
    AtPoint(38, 6))
```

The previous lines of script—Java and VB.NET respectively—reference the 0 and 1 cells of the `args` array. The 0 cell represents the composer text, whereas the 1 cell represents the composition text. This is because you set the array up in the `PlaceCDOrder` script in that order. It is important to keep track of how data gets stored in one script so you know the order in which to access it in another.

The steps covered up to this point take you through passing data between scripts. Listing 7.24 shows the final product of `PlaceCDOrder`, incorporating the necessary changes for invoking the `ReviewOrderHistory` script.

Listing 7.24   PlaceCDOrder—the final product

Java
```java
public void testMain(Object[] args)
{
       startApp("ClassicsJavaA");

       // Frame: ClassicsCD
       tree2().click(atPath("Composers->Schubert->Location(PLUS_MINUS)"));
       tree2().click(atPath("Composers->Schubert->Die schone Mullerin, Op. 25"));
       placeOrder().click();

       // Frame: Member Logon
       nameCombo().click();
       nameCombo().click(atText("Claire Stratus"));
       passwordText().click(atPoint(37,13));
       memberLogon().inputChars("password");
       ok().click();

       // USE VERIFICATION POINT WIZARD TO CAPTURE THE 'TEXT'
       // PROPERTIES OF THE COMPOSER & COMPOSITION TEXT FIELDS
       // ON ORDER WINDOW
       String composer = (String)itemText().getProperty("text");
       String composition = (String)_1695Text().getProperty("text");

       // Frame: Place an Order
       cardNumberIncludeTheSpacesText().click(atPoint(33,10));
       placeAnOrder().inputChars("1111 1111 1111 1111");
       expirationDateText().click(atPoint(22,10));
       placeAnOrder().inputChars("12/09");
       placeOrder2().click();

       //
       yourOrderHasBeenReceivedYourOr().performTest(VerifyOrderMessageVP());
       ok2().click();
```

```
      // SET UP ARRAY TO PASS TO "ReviewOrderHistory" SCRIPT
      Object[] composerData = {composer, composition};

      // INVOKE "ReviewOrderHistory" SCRIPT, PASSING ARRAY IN
      callScript("ReviewOrderHistory",composerData);

      // Frame: ClassicsCD
      classicsJava(ANY,MAY_EXIT).close();
}
```

PlaceCDOrder—VB.NET

```
Public Function TestMain(ByVal args() As Object) As Object
      StartApp("ClassicsJavaA")

      ' Frame: ClassicsCD
      Tree2().Click(AtPath("Composers->Schubert->Location(PLUS_MINUS)"))
      Tree2().Click(AtPath("Composers->Schubert->Die schone Mullerin, Op. 25"))
      PlaceOrder().Click()

      ' Frame: Member Logon
      NameCombo().Click()
      NameCombo().Click(AtText("Claire Stratus"))
      PasswordText().Click(AtPoint(59, 7))
      MemberLogon().InputChars("password")
      OK().Click()

      ' USE VERIFICATION POINT WIZARD TO CAPTURE THE 'TEXT'
      ' PROPERTIES OF THE COMPOSER & COMPOSITION TEXT FIELDS
      ' ON ORDER WINDOW
      Dim composer As String = ItemText().GetProperty("text")
      Dim composition As String = _1695Text().GetProperty("text")

      ' Frame: Place an Order
      CardNumberIncludeTheSpacesText().Click(AtPoint(41, 10))
      PlaceAnOrder().InputChars("1111 1111 1111 1111")
      ExpirationDateText().Click(AtPoint(19, 10))
      PlaceAnOrder().InputChars("12/09")
      PlaceOrder2().Click()

      '
      YourOrderHasBeenReceivedYourOr().PerformTestVerifyOrderPlacedVP())
      OK2().Click()
```

```
      ' SET UP ARRAY TO PASS TO "ReviewOrderHistory" SCRIPT
      Dim composerData() As Object = {composer, composition}

      ' INVOKE "ReviewOrderHistory" SCRIPT, PASSING ARRAY IN
      CallScript("ReviewOrderHistory", composerData)

      ' Frame: ClassicsCD
      ClassicsJava(ANY, MAY_EXIT).Close()
      Return Nothing
End Function
```

Listing 7.25 displays the updated contents of the ReviewOrderHistory script, including the modification that was made to parse and use the data passed to it via its args array.

Listing 7.25   ReviewOrderHistory

Java
```java
public void testMain(Object[] args)
{
      // Frame: ClassicsCD
      jmb().click(atPath("Order"));
      jmb().click(atPath("Order->View Existing Order Status..."));
      // Frame: View Order Status
      nameComboB().click();
      nameComboB().click(atText("Claire Stratus"));
      passwordText().click(atPoint(65,9));
      viewOrderStatus().inputChars("PASSWORD");
      ok().click();

      // Frame: View Existing Orders
      existingTable().click(atCell(atRow("COMPOSER", args[0].toString(),
            "COMPOSITION", args[1].toString()),
            atColumn("ORDER ID")),
            atPoint(38,5));

      // SELECT SPECIFIC ORDER BY COMPOSER AND COMPOSITION
      existingTable().performTest(VerifyOrderTableVP());
      cancelSelectedOrder().click();
      close().click();
}
```

VB.NET

```
Public Function TestMain(ByVal args() As Object) As Object

    ' Frame: ClassicsCD
    Jmb().Click(AtPath("Order"))
    Jmb().Click(AtPath("Order->View Existing Order Status..."))

    ' Frame: View Order Status
    NameComboB().Click()
    NameComboB().Click(AtText("Claire Stratus"))
    PasswordText().Click(AtPoint(69, 10))
    ViewOrderStatus().InputChars("password")
    OK().Click()

    ' Frame: View Existing Orders
    ExistingTable().Click(AtCell(AtRow("COMPOSER", args(0).ToString, _
        "COMPOSITION",args(1).ToString), _
        AtColumn("ORDER ID")), _
        AtPoint(38, 6))

    ' SELECT ROW BY COMPOSER AND COMPOSITION
    ExistingTable().PerformTest(VerifyOrderTableVP())
    CancelSelectedOrder().Click()

    Close().Click()
    Return Nothing
End Function
```

The next section, "Returning Values from My Scripts," covers returning data from scripts. This is the last section you need to understand before learning about regression scripts. The section, "Developing Regression Scripts," ties this topic with the next one into a nice neat package. You see how to create one script that simply invokes other scripts and catches return values from some and passes those as arguments to others.

Returning Values from My Scripts

Rational Functional Tester provides you with the valuable ability to return values from your scripts. Returning values from your scripts enables you to share data across scripts, without the need for external files or global variables. You need to do a few basic things to return data from your scripts.

The first step is to specify the data type you want your script to return. The return type that you choose depends on what you want to share with another script. You need to remember that scripts catch return values as objects. Therefore, you want to specify an object or a data type based off of an object (for example, integer, string, and so on). Do you simply want to pass a 1 or 0 back to signify that your script did (or didn't do) what you wanted? You want to pass it back as an integer. Do you need to pass along an Order ID? You might try passing it back as a string. Ultimately, you need to orchestrate how you want your scripts to run together. This enables you to figure out the return values you need for sharing data among your scripts. In any case, you need to modify the basic script's `testMain()` method signature to specify the return value.

Whenever you create a script (either an empty one or a recorded one), it has a `testMain()` method. This is the method that drives the execution of Rational Functional Tester scripts. The following lines of code show what the Java and VB.NET signatures look like for this `testMain()`.

Script Signature—Java

```
public void testMain(Object[] args)
```

Script Signature—VB.NET

```
Public Function TestMain(ByVal args() As Object) As Object
```

By default, the Java version of this method returns nothing (for example, void), whereas the VB.NET version returns an object. To change the return value of `testMain()`, you simply need to supplant the default value with the Object type that you need. Examples follow:

Script Signature—Java

```
public String testMain(Object[] args)
```

Script Signature—VB.NET

```
Public Function TestMain(ByVal args() As Object) As String
```

Looking at the signatures in the previous lines of code, you can see that the `testMain()` method now returns a string. What is the string that it needs to return? This is up to you, which brings us to the second step.

After you specify the return type in your script's `testMain()` signature, you need to modify the script to return the corresponding data value. This is a two-part process. The first part requires you to capture the data in the body of your script. The second part is where you construct the return statement. The return statement is as simple as typing "return" and specifying the data to return.

Return Statement—Java

```
return "This is a return value";
```

Return Statement—VB.NET

```
Return "This is a return value"
```

The prior statements return a string value. You can also pass a variable to the return statement. Looking at the coding examples in Listing 7.26, you can see how all these steps come together, specifying the new return value in the `testMain()` signature, capturing the desired data and constructing the proper return statement.

Listing 7.26   Simple return example

Java

```
public String testMain(Object[] args)
{
     String s = "This is a return value";
     return s;
}
```

VB.NET

```
Public Function TestMain(ByVal args() As Object) As String
     Dim s As String = "This is a return value"
     Return s
End Function
```

These are oversimplified examples. They basically create a string and return it. The next set of examples provides you with context. They modify a recorded script to return an order message. This script places an order for a CD, using ClassicsJavaA. Please refer to Listing 7.27.

Listing 7.27   Returning data from a recorded script

Java

```
public String testMain(Object[] args)
{
     startApp("ClassicsJavaA");

     // Frame: ClassicsCD
     tree2().click(atPath("Composers->Haydn->Location(PLUS_MINUS)"));
     tree2().click(atPath("Composers->Haydn->Symphonies Nos. 99 & 101"));
     placeOrder().click();

     // Frame: Member Logon
     nameCombo().click();
     nameCombo().click(atText("Tony Miatta"));
     passwordText().click(atPoint(65,12));
     memberLogon().inputChars("password");
     ok().click();

     // Frame: Place an Order
     cardNumberIncludeTheSpacesText().click(atPoint(33,7));
     placeAnOrder().inputChars("1111 1111 1111 1111");
     expirationDateText().click(atPoint(33,11));
     placeAnOrder().inputChars("01/09");
     placeOrder2().click();
```

```
// USE THE "VERIFICATION POINT AND ACTION WIZARD" TO CAPTURE
// THE ORDER CONFIRMATION MESSAGE'S TEXT PROPERTY
// THIS WILL GIVE THE ORDER MESSAGE, INCLUDING ORDER ID
String orderMessage = (String)yourOrderHasBeenReceivedYourOr()
.getProperty("text");

//
ok2().click();

// Frame: ClassicsCD
classicsJava(ANY,MAY_EXIT).close();

// RETURN ORDER MESSAGE
return orderMessage;
}
```

VB.NET

```
Public Function TestMain(ByVal args() As Object) As String
    StartApp("ClassicsJavaA")

    ' Frame: ClassicsCD
    Tree2().Click(AtPath("Composers->Haydn->Location(PLUS_MINUS)"))
    Tree2().Click(AtPath("Composers->Haydn->Symphonies Nos. 99 & 101"))
    PlaceOrder().Click()

    ' Frame: Member Logon
    NameCombo().Click()
    NameCombo().Click(AtText("Tony Miatta"))
    PasswordText().Click(AtPoint(19, 12))
    MemberLogon().InputChars("password")
    OK().Click()

    ' Frame: Place an Order
    CardNumberIncludeTheSpacesText().Click(AtPoint(18, 10))
    PlaceAnOrder().InputChars("1111 1111 1111 1111")
    ExpirationDateText().Drag(AtPoint(14, 8), AtPoint(14, 7))
    PlaceAnOrder().InputChars("01/09")
    PlaceOrder2().Click()

    ' USE THE "VERIFICATION POINT AND ACTION WIZARD" TO CAPTURE
    ' THE ORDER CONFIRMATION MESSAGE'S TEXT PROPERTY
    ' THIS WILL GIVE THE ORDER MESSAGE, INCLUDING ORDER ID
    Dim orderMessage As String = _
```

```
          YourOrderHasBeenReceivedYourOr().GetProperty("text")

     '
     OK2().Click()

     ' Frame: ClassicsCD
     ClassicsJava(ANY, MAY_EXIT).Close()

     ' RETURN ORDER MESSAGE
     Return orderMessage
End Function
```

The next few sections discuss different scenarios for shell scripts. These are scripts that primarily just call other scripts. You examine how you combine the past two topics—passing arguments and returning data—and create robust shell scripts for regression testing.

Developing Regression Scripts

Rational Functional Tester enables you to create scripts whose job is simply to invoke other scripts. These are sometimes referred to as *shell scripts*. This section refers to them simply as *regression scripts*. The ultimate goal of the scripts is to cover the testing of an application or each of its subsystems.

The next couple of sections show basic to advanced usage of this capability. You gain an understanding of the different techniques for passing data between scripts, dynamically adding calls to newly created scripts, and managing the flow of your regression scripts.

Creating a Simple Regression Script

The previous section mentioned that a regression script is one that simply invokes other scripts. This is done using the `callScript()` methods. You were exposed to a flavor of this method in the "Passing Arguments to Scripts Invoked from Other Scripts" section in this chapter. In reality, many ways to create regression scripts exist. They range from simplistic implementations that simply call other scripts to extremely robust implementations that manage the handling errors within scripts and passing data between them.

The most simplistic regression script is one that uses the `callScript()` method without any arguments. Its purpose is to invoke the necessary scripts and let them do what they were created to do. It neither passes arguments to the scripts it invokes nor catches return values from them. If you look at the scenario of placing an order in the `ClassicsJavaA` application, it might look something like this:

1. Launch `ClassicsJavaA`.
2. Place an order for a CD.

3. Review that the order exists in the database.

4. Close ClassicsJavaA.

You can almost envision having a one-to-one mapping of scripts to steps. That is, you have a script that launches the application (`StartClassicsJavaA`), one that orders the CD (`PlaceCDOrder`), one that reviews the order in the database (`ReviewOrderHistory`), and one that closes the application (`CloseClassicsJavaA`). To create a regression script that invokes these other scripts, you need to:

1. Create an empty script (**File > New > Empty Functional Test Script**). Note that for Rational Functional Tester VB.NET, you select **File > New > Add Empty Script**.

2. Place the cursor in the body of your newly created script.

3. Right-click on the script you want to invoke (the "StartClassicsJavaA" script would be good one to start with!) and select **Insert as "callScript."**

4. Repeat Steps 3 and 4 as many times as necessary to include your scripts (in this case, it is three more times, calling the remaining three scripts).

Figure 7.13 provides you with a visual representation of this process using the Eclipse version of Rational Functional Tester.

```
public class SimpleRegressionScript extends SimpleRegressionScriptHelper
{
    /**
     * Script Name   : <b>SimpleRegressionScript</b>
     * Generated     : <b>Aug 17, 2009 9:11:30 AM</b>
     * Description   : Functional Test Script
     * Original Host : WinNT Version 5.1  Build 2600 (S)
     *
     * @since  2009/08/17
     * @author admin
     */
    public void testMain(Object[] args)
    {
        callScript("scripts.StartClassicsJavaA");
        callScript("scripts.PlaceOrder");
        callScript("scripts.ReviewOrderHistory");
        callScript("scripts.CloseClassicsJavaA");
    }
}
```

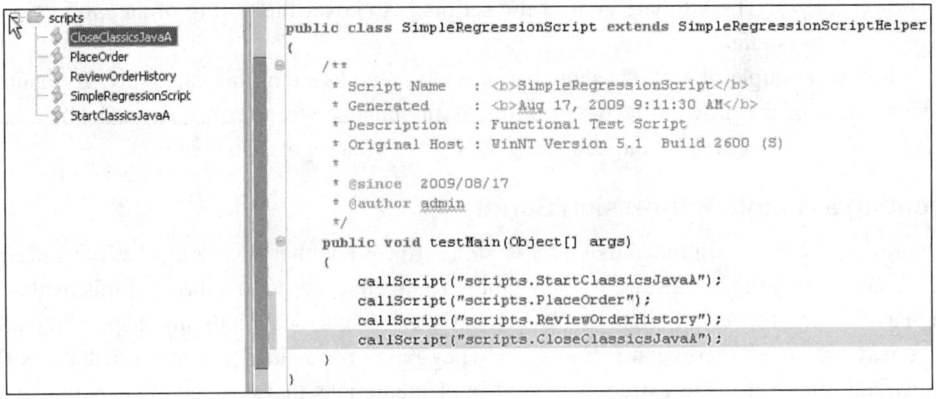

Figure 7.13   Creating a simple regression test—Java

Figure 7.14 shows what these steps look like in the VB.NET flavor of Rational Functional Tester.

One important factor that you need to consider is the ordering of the scripts. In the prior example, you had four scripts that accomplished the scenario of ordering a CD in the `ClassicsJavaA` application. Each script carries out a small task, relying on other scripts to successfully get the application to the necessary state for it to work with. This is considered modular

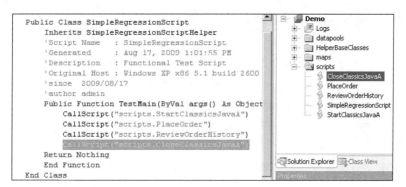

```
Public Class SimpleRegressionScript
    Inherits SimpleRegressionScriptHelper
    'Script Name   : SimpleRegressionScript
    'Generated     : Aug 17, 2009 1:01:55 PM
    'Description   : Functional Test Script
    'Original Host : Windows XP x86 5.1 build 2600
    'since  2009/08/17
    'author admin
    Public Function TestMain(ByVal args() As Object
        CallScript("scripts.StartClassicsJavaA")
        CallScript("scripts.PlaceOrder")
        CallScript("scripts.ReviewOrderHistory")
        CallScript("scripts.CloseClassicsJavaA")
    Return Nothing
    End Function
End Class
```

Figure 7.14   Creating a simple regression test—VB.NET

scripting. This type of scripting helps to keep your scripts small and focused and eases the cost of script maintenance. It does require you to ensure that your regression scripts call these modular scripts in the proper sequence. If you do not, you will soon find that your regression scripts error out. Refer to Figures 7.13 and 7.14 and note that the sequence has been ordered correctly. If you don't want to worry about setting up the proper sequence in a regression script, you can create your other scripts so that they are self-reliant. In other words, you create your scripts so that they get the application into the state it needs to be in and then carry out its designated task. They don't have to rely on another script to do this. Some people refer to this as creating *round-trip scripts*. If you wish to pursue this path, there is a useful strategy for creating regression scripts to support this. This is covered in the "Creating Regression Scripts That Dynamically Include Scripts As They Are Created" section.

You should now know how to create simple regression scripts. The process is simple. In fact, many people skip the GUI-supported means of calling scripts. They simply create the empty scripts, type the first **callScript("SomeScript")** command, and then copy and paste it as many times as they need, replacing the old script name with the new one. The next section covers how to take advantage of catching return values and passing arguments in your regression scripts. These were discussed earlier in the "Returning Values from My Scripts" section. They are discussed in more detail in the context of managing data between your scripts.

Managing Data in Regression Scripts

The previous section showed you how to create basic regression scripts. These can be useful. Chances are, however, that you need to share data among your scripts. This section expands on your knowledge of passing arguments to scripts, sending them back and catching return values from scripts, and developing regression scripts.

The example in the previous section covered the simple scenario of placing an order for a CD using the ClassicsJavaA application. The resulting regression script that was built looks like the scripts in Listing 7.28.

Listing 7.28   Simple regression script

Java
```java
public void testMain(Object[] args)
{
      callScript("StartClassicsJavaA");
      callScript("PlaceCDOrder");
      callScript("ReviewOrderHistory");
      callScript("CloseClassicsJavaA");
}
```

VB.NET
```vbnet
Public Function TestMain(ByVal args() As Object) As Object
      CallScript("StartClassicsJavaA")
      CallScript("PlaceCDOrder")
      CallScript("ReviewOrderHistory")
      CallScript("CloseClassicsJavaA")
      Return Nothing
End Function
```

What if `StartClassicsJavaA` encounters an error that didn't enable it to complete execution? You might want your regression script to terminate playback, which prevents other scripts from trying to launch. You want `StartClassicsJavaA` to return a success/failure flag and your regression script to catch it. This is a key example of how to control the flow and manage data in your regression scripts. `StartClassicsJavaA` should be a straightforward script. Its only purpose is to launch the application. Unless you add a verification point to check that the application launched, it should ultimately be one line. Listing 7.29 shows the basic version of the `StartClassicsJavaA` script.

Listing 7.29   StartClassicsJavaA

Java
```java
public void testMain(Object[] args)
{
      startApp("ClassicsJavaA");
}
```

VB.NET
```vbnet
Public Function TestMain(ByVal args() As Object) As Object
      StartApp("ClassicsJavaA")
      Return Nothing
End Function
```

With some clever scripting, you can enhance your scripts so that they can deal with errors that occur during playback. For instance, you can add a small amount of code to the StartClassicsJavaA script that checks to see if the window exists or the process was started, returning an integer that specifies whether it executed successfully or not. You can also add log messages to your script, citing any errors. This is shown in Listing 7.30.

Listing 7.30   Simple Regression Script Enhancement #1, Return Success Value

Java

```java
public Integer testMain(Object[] args)
{
      startApp("ClassicsJavaA");

      try{
            // WAIT FOR MAIN WINDOW TO LAUNCH TO PREPARE FOR
            // NEXT SCRIPT
            classicsJava().waitForExistence(120.0, 1.0);
            return new Integer(1);
      } catch(ObjectNotFoundException onfe){
            // MAIN WINDOW DIDN'T LAUNCH
            LogError("Error!  ClassicsJavaA Did Not Launch!");
            return new Integer(0);
      }
}
```

VB.NET

```vbnet
Public Function TestMain(ByVal args() As Object) As Integer
      StartApp("ClassicsJavaA")

      Try
            ' WAIT FOR MAIN WINDOW TO LAUNCH TO PREPARE FOR
            ' NEXT SCRIPT
            ClassicsJava().WaitForExistence(120.0, 1.0)
            Return 1
      Catch onfe As ObjectNotFoundException
            ' MAIN WINDOW DIDN'T LAUNCH
            LogError("Error!  ClassicsJavaA Did Not Launch!")
            Return 0
      End Try
      Return Nothing

End Function
```

The net result is that you now have a script that attempts to launch the `ClassicsJavaA` application. It waits for the main window to open. If it opens in two minutes (120 seconds), then it completes successfully, returning the integer "1." If the main window doesn't open within two minutes, the script assumes the application encountered an error trying to launch and writes an error message to the log file. It also returns the Integer "0." You need to modify your shell script so that it catches the integer returned from the `StartClassicsJavaA` script and allows it to control the remaining flow based off of it. Please refer to Listing 7.31 for an example of this scripting.

Listing 7.31 Simple regression script enhancement #2, catch return value

Java

```java
public void testMain(Object[] args)
{
        Integer scriptSuccess;
        scriptSuccess = (Integer)callScript("StartClassicsJavaA");

        if(scriptSuccess.intValue() == 1){
            callScript("PlaceCDOrder");
            callScript("ReviewOrderHistory");
            callScript("CloseClassicsJavaA");
        } else
            logError("StartClassicsJavaA terminated unsuccessfully!
            Stopping playback!");
}
```

VB.NET

```vbnet
Public Function TestMain(ByVal args() As Object) As Object
    Dim scriptSuccess As Integer
    scriptSuccess = CallScript("StartClassicsJavaA")

    If (scriptSuccess = 1) Then
        CallScript("PlaceCDOrder")
        CallScript("ReviewOrderHistory")
        CallScript("CloseClassicsJavaA")
    Else
        LogError("StartClassicsJavaA terminated unsuccessfully!
        Stopping playback!")
    End If
    Return Nothing
End Function
```

The regression script is now able to handle an issue with the `StartClassicsJavaA` script trying to start the `ClassicsJavaA` application. The variable `scriptSuccess` is used to catch the

Integer object returned by the StartClassicsJavaA script. If scriptSuccess equals "1," then playback can continue. If it equals "0," an error has occurred and playback terminates, writing the appropriate error message to the log. This can be enhanced to try to launch the application again.

What if you need to pass information from the PlaceCDOrder script to the ReviewOrder-History script (for example, an Order ID)? You need the PlaceCDOrder script to return the Order ID and the regression script to catch it, passing it as an argument to the ReviewOrderHistory script. This is great illustration of how to manage data consistencies among scripts.

You need to modify PlaceCDOrder, so that you can pull out the Order ID. You need to obtain the message text on the Order Confirmation dialog box. This can be done by inserting a recording into your script, using the Verification Point Wizard to capture the text on the Order Confirmation dialog box. This declares a variable and stores the text value of the label into it. You then need to parse out the actual Order ID and modify your script, so that it returns this value as a string. This is handled in the scripts contained in Listing 7.32.

Listing 7.32 PlaceCDOrder script, return Order ID

Java

```
public String testMain(Object[] args)
{

        // Frame: ClassicsCD
        tree2().click(atPath("Composers->Haydn->Location(PLUS_MINUS)"));
        tree2().click(atPath("Composers->Haydn->Violin Concertos"));
        placeOrder().click();

        // Frame: Member Logon
        nameCombo().click();
        nameCombo().click(atText("Sonia Evans"));
        passwordText().click(atPoint(50,12));
        memberLogon().inputChars("password");
        ok().click();

        // Frame: Place an Order
        cardNumberIncludeTheSpacesText().click(atPoint(25,9));
        placeAnOrder().inputChars("1111 1111 1111 1111");
        expirationDateText().click(atPoint(12,9));
        placeAnOrder().inputChars("01/10");
        placeOrder2().click();

        //
        yourOrderHasBeenReceivedYourOr().performTest(VerifyOrderMsgVP());

        // VERIFICATION POINT WIZARD OBTAINED THIS LINE
```

```
String orderMsg = (String)yourOrderHasBeenReceivedYourOr()
.getProperty("text");

// FIND THE COLON (":") AND ADD 2 TO IT TO GET START POSITION (1ST DIGIT)
int indexStart = orderMsg.indexOf(":") + 2;
// GET THE LENGTH AND SUBTRACT ONE FROM IT TO GET END POSITON (LAST DIGIT)
int indexEnd = orderMsg.length() - 1;
// GET ORDER ID SUBSTRING FROM ORDER MESSAGE
String orderID = orderMsg.substring(indexStart, indexEnd);
ok2().click();

return orderID;
}
```

VB.NET

```
Public Function TestMain(ByVal args() As Object) As String

    ' Frame: ClassicsCD
    Tree2().Click(AtPath("Composers->Haydn->Location(PLUS_MINUS)"))
    Tree2().Click(AtPath("Composers->Haydn->Violin Concertos"))
    PlaceOrder().Click()

    ' Frame: Member Logon
    NameCombo().Click()
    NameCombo().Click(AtText("Sonia Evans"))
    PasswordText().Click(AtPoint(58, 7))
    MemberLogon().InputChars("PASSWORD")
    OK().Click()

    ' Frame: Place an Order
    CardNumberIncludeTheSpacesText().Click(AtPoint(37, 8))
    PlaceAnOrder().InputChars("1111 1111 1111 1111")
    ExpirationDateText().Click(AtPoint(7, 7))
    PlaceAnOrder().InputChars("01/10")
    PlaceOrder2().Click()

    '

    YourOrderHasBeenReceivedYourOr().PerformTest(VerifyOrderMsgVP())

    ' VERIFICATION POINT WIZARD OBTAINED THIS LINE
    Dim orderMsg As String = YourOrderHasBeenReceivedYourOr().
    GetProperty("text")
```

```
    ' FIND THE COLON (":") AND ADD 2 TO IT TO GET START POSITION (1ST DIGIT)
    Dim indexStart As Integer = orderMsg.IndexOf(":") + 2
    ' GET THE LENGTH AND SUBTRACT ONE FROM THEN SUBTRACT FROM START
    ' INDEX TO GET LENGTH OF ORDER ID
    Dim subStringLength As Integer = (orderMsg.Length - 1) - indexStart
    ' GET ORDER ID SUBSTRING FROM ORDER MESSAGE
    Dim orderID As String = orderMsg.Substring (indexStart, subStringLength),
    subStringLength)

    OK2().Click()


    Return orderID
End Function
```

The second thing you need to do is catch the return value in your regression script. Because you plan on passing this into the `ReviewOrderHistory` script, you should create a single-cell array. This is because you need to pass an Object array into the `callScript()` method. After you set up your array and catch the return value into the zero cell (for example, `orderID[0]`), you should probably check if it is a null value (for example, an empty string). This enables you to prevent your script from passing in an empty string and cause issues in the `ReviewOrderHistory` script. If you do receive a null value, you might want to stop execution. You can handle this in a couple of ways. You can use Rational Functional Tester's `stop()` method. This is similar to clicking the Stop button on the script playback window. It terminates execution and writes a *User StoppedScriptError* message in the log. You can also change your regression script so that it returns an Integer object. This enables you to use the return statements to discontinue playback. It also provides the benefit of returning a success (1) or failure (0) flag. This is useful if you are creating regression scripts for each of your application's major areas of functionality and then calling those regression scripts in a large, system-level regression script. Each of the smaller regression scripts can tell the system-level one if it completed successfully or not.

You will also need to modify your regression script to pass the Order ID into the `ReviewOrderHistory` script (provided it isn't null). This is done by passing the array you created to the `callScript()` method. Refer to Listing 7.33 for the appropriate examples.

Listing 7.33 Simple regression script enhancement #3, managing the Order ID

```Java
public Integer testMain(Object[] args)
{
    Integer scriptSuccess;
    scriptSuccess = (Integer)callScript("StartClassicsJavaA");

    if(scriptSuccess.intValue() == 1){
```

```
                    String[] orderID = new String[1];
                    orderID[0] = (String)callScript("PlaceCDOrder");

                    if(orderID[0].isEmpty()){
                            logError("PlaceCDOrder Script Passed In A Null Value");
                            return new Integer(0);
                    } else{
                            callScript("ReviewOrderHistory", orderID);
                            callScript("CloseClassicsJavaA");
                            return new Integer(1);
                    }
            } else{
                    logError("StartClassicsJavaA terminated unsuccessfully!   Stopping
                    playback!");
                    return new Integer(0);
            }
    }
}
```

VB.NET
```
Public Function TestMain(ByVal args() As Object) As Integer
      Dim scriptSuccess As Integer
      scriptSuccess = CallScript("StartClassicsJavaA")

      If (scriptSuccess = 1) Then
            Dim orderID(0) As String
            orderID(0) = CallScript("PlaceCDOrder")

            If (orderID(0) = "") Then
                    LogError("PlaceCDOrder Script Passed In A Null Value")
                    Return 0
            Else
                    CallScript("ReviewOrderHistory", orderID)
                    CallScript("CloseClassicsJavaA")
                    Return 1
            End If
      Else
            LogError("StartClassicsJavaA terminated unsuccessfully!
            Stopping playback!")
            Return 0
      End If
      Return Nothing
End Function
```

Of course, you need to modify the `ReviewOrderHistory` script so that it handles the Order ID. The idea is that it is now an argument being passed in by the regression script. The Order ID itself was captured and returned by the `PlaceCDOrder` script.

Keeping in line with the other scripts, you might wish to have the `ReviewOrderHistory` and `CloseClassicsJavaA` scripts return a value, indicating its success or failure. The easiest way is to mimic the `StartClassicsJavaA` script, returning an integer value. This enables you to continue managing the flow of your regression script.

You should now have an understanding of the different techniques that can be employed for managing data and handling script failures within the context of a regression script. Please note that there are always two parts to each modification. You need to edit the regression script *and* scripts that it invokes.

Creating Regression Scripts that Dynamically Include Scripts as They Are Created

You can create dynamic regression scripts, using the `callScript()` method. This enables you to continue adding new scripts to your project, automatically including them in your regression test. This involves managing your test scripts in packages. In some cases, it also involves having your scripts be self-reliant and avoid the modular approach.

The first thing that you will want to think about is organizing your scripts. This is best done using packages (such as creating new folders in your Rational Functional Tester project). One school of thought is to look at the major areas of functionality and decompose them into separate folders. Another way you could do this is via organizing your packages by the use cases of your application. The end result is that you will have multiple packages that contain scripts to test the different pieces of your application. Figure 7.15 illustrates this.

Figure 7.15 Organizing test scripts by package

The first thing you need to do is obtain the path to your project. This is accomplished with the following line of Java:

```
File packagePath = new File(getCurrentProject().getLocation() + "\\" +
<INSERT NAME OF PACKAGE>);
```

If you use VB.NET, you need these two lines:

```
Dim packagePath As String =
System.IO.Path.GetDirectoryName(System.Reflection.Assembly.
```

```
        GetExecutingAssembly.GetModules()(0).FullyQualifiedName)
        Dim dirInfo As New System.IO.DirectoryInfo(packagePath.Replace("bin",
        <INSERT NAME OF PACKAGE>))
```

Both examples perform the same task. They obtain the location of the Rational Functional Tester project and append the name of the package (that is the folder) to it. This constructs the necessary path to the scripts that you want to execute.

After you tell the Rational Functional Tester where the package containing your scripts is, you need to obtain the list of scripts in it. The actual directory on the file system that corresponds to the package in the Rational Functional Tester GUI contains both compiled and uncompiled files. You simply need to get the list, using only one type of file. To do this with Java, you need to first create a `FileNameFilter` and then use this to obtain the array of file names that match the filter. Please see the following snippet of Java code for an example.

```
        FilenameFilter filefilter = new FilenameFilter() {
              public boolean accept(File dir, String name) {
                    // IF THE FILE EXTENSION IS .CLASS, RETURN TRUE ...
                    return name.endsWith(".class");
              }
        };


        String[] scripts = packagePath.list(filefilter);
```

VB.NET makes this much easier. You need only to call the directory object's `GetFiles()` method, specifying the extension to filter on.

```
        Dim scripts() As System.IO.FileInfo = dirInfo.GetFiles("*.testsuite")
```

In both cases, you end up with an array of files. You can set up a `for` loop to access each script. The `callScript()` method doesn't require file extensions, so you need to remove them. Also, because you use packages, you need to preface the script name with the name of the package itself, using a period to separate them. This is shown in code snippets found in Listing 7.34.

Listing 7.34   For loop to obtain script names

Java
```
for (int i = 0; i < scripts.length; i++) {
      String scriptToInvoke = pkg + "." + scripts[i].replace (".class", "");
      callScript(scriptToInvoke);
}
```

VB.NET
```
For Each script In scripts
      Dim scriptToInvoke As String = pkg & "." & Replace(script.Name,
      script.Extension, "")
      CallScript(scriptToInvoke)
Next
```

Because you use this code multiple times and pass multiple packages to it, it makes sense to turn it into a method (or Sub) and store it in a Helper Super Class (or Helper Base Class). This is discussed in Chapter 3. The final product, including comments, looks like the examples found in Listing 7.35.

Listing 7.35 Custom method for dynamic regression testing

Java
```java
public void executeScriptsInPackage(String pkg) {
    // GET FILE PATH TO THIS PROJECT'S 'RegressionPackageUnsorted" PACKAGE
    File packagePath = new File(getCurrentProject().getLocation() + "\\" +
    pkg);

    // CREATE FILENAMEFILTER AND OVERRIDE ITS ACCEPT-METHOD
    // USE THIS TO FILTER ON JUST THE .CLASS FILES IN THE PACKAGE
    FilenameFilter filefilter = new FilenameFilter() {
        public boolean accept(File dir, String name) {
            // IF THE FILE EXTENSION IS .CLASS, RETURN TRUE ...
            return name.endsWith(".class");
        }
    };

    // GET LIST OF FILES THAT HAVE .CLASS EXTENSION (USE FILEFILTER)
    String[] scripts = packagePath.list(filefilter);

    // LOOP THROUGH FILES
    for (int i = 0; i < scripts.length; i++) {
        // SET UP SCRIPT TO INVOKE
        // SPECIFY PACKAGE NAME AND REMOVING .CLASS EXTENSION
        String scriptToInvoke = pkg + "." + scripts[i].replace(".class", "");
        // CALL SCRIPT
        callScript(scriptToInvoke);
    }
}
```

VB.NET
```vbnet
Public Sub executeScriptsInPackage(ByVal pkg As String)
    ' GET FILE PATH TO THIS PROJECT'S 'RegressionPackageUnsorted" PACKAGE
    Dim packagePath As String =
    System.IO.Path.GetDirectoryName(System.Reflection.
    Assembly.GetExecutingAssembly.GetModules()(0).FullyQualifiedName)
    Dim dirInfo As New System.IO.DirectoryInfo (packagePath.Replace("bin",
    pkg))
```

```
' GET LIST OF FILES THAT HAVE .TESTSUITE EXTENSION
Dim scripts() As System.IO.FileInfo = dirInfo.GetFiles("*.testsuite")
Dim script As System.IO.FileInfo

' LOOP THROUGH FILES
For Each script In scripts
        ' SET UP SCRIPT TO INVOKE
        ' SPECIFY PACKAGE NAME AND REMOVING .CLASS EXTENSION
        Dim scriptToInvoke As String = pkg & "." &
        Replace(script.Name, script.Extension, "")
        'Call SCRIPT
        CallScript(scriptToInvoke)
     Next
End Sub
```

Calling this method from a script is quite easy. You need only call `executeScripts-InPackage()` and pass in the name of your package as a string. For instance

```
executeScriptsInPackage("PackageA")
executeScriptsInPackage("PackageB")
executeScriptsInPackage("PackageC")
```

You can now continuously add scripts to each of these packages. The `executeScripts-InPackage()` method (or subroutine if you're using VB.NET) simply calls the newly added scripts as it loops through the packages.

One drawback, however, is that your scripts are called alphabetically (as they live in the directory). Therefore, you need to ensure that your scripts are self-reliant. They need to get the application into the state in which they need it to be. You can also add numeric prefixes to your scripts. This ensures a certain order is followed. Please refer to Figure 7.16 for what this might look like.

Figure 7.16   Numerically ordered script

You can't begin the name of your script with an integer; therefore, one solution is to use underscores. This is how the issue was addressed with the package of scripts in Figure 7.16. When it is passed to the `executeScriptsInPackage()` method, _1_*ExecuteMeFirst* will be executed before _2_*ExecuteMeSecond*, which will be executed before _3_*ExecuteMeLast*. Without the numeric prefix, *ExecuteMeLast* would be invoked before *ExecuteMeSecond*.

Executing a Functional Tester Script from the Command Line

Functional Tester has a rich command-line interface that enables you perform many Rational Functional Tester tasks, including script execution, from the command line. This discussion is limited to using the command line to recompile and execute scripts. Consult the Rational Functional Tester API documentation (the `rational_ft` class) to explore other capabilities.

Introduction to the Rational Functional Tester Command Line Interface

To use the command-line interface, your command can do two things:

<Launch RFT> <pass arguments to RFT indicating what you want done>

The Eclipse and .NET versions of Rational Functional Tester differ significantly in how Rational Functional Tester is launched. For .NET, launch Rational Functional Tester by executing either `rational_ftw.exe` (for Visual Studio version 2005) or `rational_ftw11.exe` (for Visual Studio2003). Both executables reside in the Rational Functional Tester installation directory, which can be referenced by the system variable IBM_RATIONAL_RFT_INSTALL_DIR.

For Eclipse, launch Rational Functional Tester by executing `java.exe` and passing arguments. The next two sections are devoted to showing you how to launch the Eclipse-based version of Rational Functional Tester.

Introduction to Executing Java Programs from the Command Line

We start with a primer on Java command-line options. If you're comfortable working with Java from the command line, you can skip this section.

The first thing you need to be sure of if you're going to work with Java from the command line is that java.exe is in your system path. To verify this, open a command prompt window and type **Java**. If Java is not a recognized program displays, you need to run fdsik. Just kidding. You need to add a JRE to your system path variable.

As you are probably aware, the result of compiling Java source files (.java files) are .class files. Many .class files can be packaged together into .jar files.

The entry point to any Java application is a class with a `main()` method. To launch a Java application (that requires no arguments), you use the following command:

```
java.exe <Name Of Class With Main Method>
```

For example:

```
java MyNiftyJavaProgram.
```

When you launch a Java program, you are in essence launching two programs: java.exe (the JVM) and the program of interest. Note that you don't add .class; it's assumed by the JVM (and you get an error if you include it). This is the simplest case; one in which it is assumed that the directory that contains the `MyNiftyJavaProgram.class` file is in the execution environment's (in this case, the shell's) classpath. If it is not, you need to indicate to the JVM where it should search for .class files. To tell the JVM which directories to search, you either change the system `classpath` variable or pass a `classpath` argument to java.exe. You examine the latter.

Assume that the `MyNiftyJavaProgram.class` file is in the C:\My Class Files directory. To pass this directory as a `classpath` argument to the JVM when launching the `MyNiftyJavaProgram`, you would type:

```
java -classpath "C:\My Class Files" MyNiftyJavaProgram
```

Note the double quotes. They're required if the directory you're passing to the `classpath` argument contains spaces.

To add multiple directories to the `classpath` argument, separate them with a semi-colon:

```
java -classpath "C:\My Class Files;D:\Your ClassFiles" MyNiftyJavaProgram
```

When you deal with real Java programs (even `ClassicsJavaA`), you almost always deal with .jar files and not individual .class files scattered about. If the `MyNiftyJavaProgram.class` file is in a .jar file named `Nifty.jar` in the same C:\My Class Files directory, you need to add the `Niftty.jar` file to the `classpath` to make it possible for the JVM to find the `MyNiftyJavaProgram.class` file contained within it:

```
java -classpath "C:\My Class Files\Nifty.jar" MyNiftyJavaProgram
```

Some .jar files are created in such a way that, internally, they indicate which class is the entry point (has the `main` method). These .jar files can be double-clicked to launch execution. To launch execution from the command line, you pass the `-jar` argument to java.exe. You don't need to indicate which class contains the main; that information is tucked away in the .jar file.

If MyNiftyJavaProgram were such a Java application, you could launch it like so:

```
java -jar "C:\My Class Files\Nifty.jar"
```

Now something you can try at home: `ClassicsJavaA` (and the infinitely more robust `JavaClassicsB`) are Java applications built in this way. They reside in `ClassicsJavaA.jar` and `ClassicsJavaB.jar` in the `FTSamples` directory of the Rational Functional Tester installation directory. To launch `ClassicsJavaB`, the command is:

```
java -jar  "C:\Program
Files\ibm\SDP\FunctionalTester\FTSamples\ClassicsJavaA.jar"
```

Launching Rational Functional Tester (Eclipse) from the Command Line

You launch Rational Functional Tester by passing to java.exe the name of the main class *or* the .jar file that contains the entry point for Rational Functional Tester. The entry point class is `com.rational.test.ft.rational_ft`, which resides in `rational_ft.jar`. You therefore launch Rational Functional Tester by executing either of the following:

```
java -classpath <complete path to rational_ft.jar>
com.rational.test.ft.rational_ft
```

or

```
java -jar <complete path to rational_ft.jar>
```

If you use the first variation, the JVM needs to know where the `com.rational.test.ft.rational_ft` class is located, which you can communicate by passing a `classpath` argument. The `com.rational.test.ft.rational_ft` class is in the `rational_ft.jar` file, which is located in the bin directory of your Rational Functional Tester installation directory. The complete path to the bin directory is stored in the name `IBM_RATIONAL_RFT_INSTALL_DIR` system variable. To reference the value of this system variable at the command line, place its name in a pair of `%`: `%IBM_RATIONAL_RFT_INSTALL_DIR%`.

If the path to the Rational Functional Tester installation directory contains any spaces, which it will if you accept the default installation directory of C:\Program Files...., you must put the entire classpath in double quotes.

To kick off Rational Functional Tester (without supplying any arguments, which cause it to complain), use the command:

```
java -jar "%IBM_RATIONAL_RFT_INSTALL_DIR%\rational_ft.jar"
```

Try it out. You should see the following complaint:

```
Usage: rational_ft -datastore <directory> [options] ....
```

Executing Functional Tester Java Scripts from the Command Line

To execute a script in the most straightforward manner (such as with the least number of arguments), after using the appropriate command to launch Rational Functional Tester, you need to tell it:

- Where the project is
- That you want to execute a script
- Which script to execute

Let's assume that you have a project that resides on your local area network in \\Freddy\RFT_Projects\Nifty and that you want to execute a script that resides in the root of the project called SanityTest. To execute this script, you issue the following command:

Java

```
java -jar "%IBM_RATIONAL_RFT_INSTALL_DIR%\rational_ft.jar" -datastore
\\Freddy\RFT_Projects\Nifty  -playback SanityTest
```

VB.NET

```
"%IBM_RATIONAL_RFT_INSTALL_DIR%\rational_ftw" -datastore
\\Freddy\RFT_Projects\Nifty  -playback SanityTest
```

If your `SanityTest` script resides not at the root of the project but in the scripts subdirectory, your command is:

Java

```
java  -jar "%IBM_RATIONAL_RFT_INSTALL_DIR%\rational_ft.jar" -datastore
\\Freddy\RFT_Projects\Nifty  -playback scripts.SanityTest
```

VB.NET

```
"%IBM_RATIONAL_RFT_INSTALL_DIR%\rational_ftw" -datastore
\\Freddy\RFT_Projects\Nifty  -playback scripts.SanityTest
```

Note that subdirectories are delimited by a dot, not a backslash. Also note that script names are case-sensitive. If you get the case wrong, an exception is thrown. The Eclipse version of Rational Functional Tester outputs a message to the command line. The Visual Studio version of Rational Functional Tester silently fails.

Passing Arguments to a Script from the Command Line

Listing 7.36 illustrates arguments passing with the following simple scripts.

Listing 7.36   Passing arguments to a script from the command line

Java
```java
public void testMain(Object[] args)
  if( args.length > 0 ) {
     for (int i = 0; i < args.length; i++) {
       logInfo(args[i].toString());
     }
  } else {
     logInfo("No args");
  }
}
```

VB.NET
```vbnet
public Function TestMain(ByVal args() as Object)
  If( args.length > 0 ) then
    for i as Integer = 0 to args.length - 1
       logInfo( args(i) )
    next
  else
     LogInfo( "No args" )
  End if

  Return Nothing

End Function
```

You can execute the scripts in Listing 7.36, using the following commands (Java and VB.NET respectively):

Java

```
java  -jar "%IBM_RATIONAL_RFT_INSTALL_DIR%\rational_ft.jar" -datastore
\\Freddy\RFT_Projects\Nifty  -playback scripts.SanityTest -args Good-bye
Farewell Auf Wiedersehen Good-Night
```

VB.NET

```
"%IBM_RATIONAL_RFT_INSTALL_DIR%\rational_ftw " -datastore
\\Freddy\RFT_Projects\Nifty  -playback scripts.SanityTest -args Good-bye
Farewell Auf Wiedersehen Good-Night
```

These will result in the following words being written to the log file:

```
Good-bye

Farewell

Auf

Wiedersehen

Good-Night
```

To pass Auf Wiedersehen as a single argument, place it in double quotes:

Java

```
java  -jar "%IBM_RATIONAL_RFT_INSTALL_DIR%\rational_ft.jar" -datastore
\\Freddy\RFT_Projects\Nifty  -playback scripts.SanityTest -args Good-bye
Farewell "Auf Wiedersehen" Good-Night
```

VB.NET

```
"%IBM_RATIONAL_RFT_INSTALL_DIR%\rational_ftw" -datastore
\\Freddy\RFT_Projects\Nifty  -playback scripts.SanityTest -args Good-bye
Farewell "Auf Wiedersehen" Good-Night
```

Compiling Functional Tester Scripts from the Command Line

In addition to execution, examine how to compile a script from the command line, because without this, you might run into trouble executing scripts. In particular, if someone makes a change to a script in Rational Functional Tester but doesn't execute it, depending on settings in Eclipse, you run the risk of not executing the latest version.

To compile a script from the command line, you must be sure that the standard Java compiler—javac.exe—is in your system PATH (Eclipse, incidentally, does not use javac.exe; it uses its own *incremental compiler*). When you install Functional Tester, a full JDK is installed in the main SDP directory, for example, C:\Program Files\IBM\SDP\jdk.

To compile a script, pass the following arguments to Rational Functional Tester:

```
-datastore <> -compile <script>
```

To compile your SanityTest script, use the following:

Java

```
java -jar "%IBM_RATIONAL_RFT_INSTALL_DIR%\rational_ft.jar" -datastore
\\Freddy\RFT_Projects\Nifty  -compile  scripts.SanityTest
```

VB.NET

```
"%IBM_RATIONAL_RFT_INSTALL_DIR%\rational_ftw" -datastore
\\Freddy\RFT_Projects\Nifty  -compile  scripts.SanityTest
```

No news is good news. The only output you see from compilation are compilation errors.

Passing Datapool Arguments

If your script is associated with a datapool and you want to iterate through all records, pass the `iterationCount ALL` argument:

```
java -jar "%IBM_RATIONAL_RFT_INSTALL_DIR%\rational_ft.jar" -datastore
\\Freddy\RFT_Projects\Nifty  -iterationCount ALL -playback
scripts.SanityTest
```

VB.NET

```
"%IBM_RATIONAL_RFT_INSTALL_DIR%\rational_ftw" -datastore
\\Freddy\RFT_Projects\Nifty  -iterationCount ALL -playback
scripts.SanityTest
```

If you just want to use a specific number of rows, pass that number:

Java

```
java  -jar "%IBM_RATIONAL_RFT_INSTALL_DIR%\rational_ft.jar" -datastore
\\Freddy\RFT_Projects\Nifty  -iterationCount 2 -playback
scripts.SanityTest
```

VB.NET

```
"%IBM_RATIONAL_RFT_INSTALL_DIR%\rational_ftw" -datastore
\\Freddy\RFT_Projects\Nifty  -iterationCount 2 -playback
scripts.SanityTest
```

Executing Functional Tester Scripts from a Batch File

As comfortable and confident as you might feel at the command line, you might have better things to do with your time than type long commands (especially when typos are taken into consideration). To make it easier to execute scripts from the command line, create a .bat file.

Begin by creating a modest batch script—one that is easy to use (involves little typing) but is the least flexible. It compiles and executes any single script that you want as long as it's in the Nifty Rational Functional Tester Project.

To create the batch file, enter the following commands in a plain text editor (be sure each is on a single line without a carriage return). Substitute the path here with the path to one of your Rational Functional Tester projects:

Java

```
java -classpath "%IBM_RATIONAL_RFT_INSTALL_DIR%\rational_ft.jar"
com.rational.test.ft.rational_ft -datastore
\\Freddy\RFT_Projects\Nifty  -compile %1
```

```
java -classpath "%IBM_RATIONAL_RFT_INSTALL_DIR%\rational_ft.jar"
com.rational.test.ft.rational_ft -datastore
\\Freddy\RFT_Projects\Nifty  -playback %1
```

VB.NET

```
"%IBM_RATIONAL_RFT_INSTALL_DIR%\rational_ftw" -datastore
\\Freddy\RFT_Projects\Nifty  -compile %1
```

```
"%IBM_RATIONAL_RFT_INSTALL_DIR%\rational_ftw" -datastore
\\Freddy\RFT_Projects\Nifty  -playback %1
```

The %1 token refers to the first argument passed to the batch file. Save the file in any directory that's in your system PATH under the name **runRFTScript.bat**. To execute a script, issue this command:

```
runRFTScript <script name>
```

What's inflexible about this batch file is the following:

- The path to the datastore is hard-coded.
- You can't pass arguments to the script.

If you wanted to execute a script in a different Rational Functional Tester project, you would have to either:

- Change the path in the batch file.
- Make the path a variable and allow your users to pass whatever path value in (shown in the following code).

Java

```
java -classpath "%IBM_RATIONAL_RFT_INSTALL_DIR%\rational_ft.jar"
com.rational.test.ft.rational_ft -datastore %1  -compile %2
```

```
java -classpath "%IBM_RATIONAL_RFT_INSTALL_DIR%\rational_ft.jar"
com.rational.test.ft.rational_ft -datastore %1 -playback %2
```

VB.NET

```
"%IBM_RATIONAL_RFT_INSTALL_DIR%\rational_ftw" -datastore %1  -compile %2


"%IBM_RATIONAL_RFT_INSTALL_DIR%\rational_ftw" -datastore %1 -playback %2
```

Now you can execute any script in any project, but you have to pass two arguments: The path to the Rational Functional Tester project and the script to execute is as follows:

```
runRFTScript \\Freddy\RFT_Projects\Nifty  scripts.SanityTest
```

Scheduling Script Execution

To schedule script execution, your best bet is to create a batch file that executes the desired scripts. The simplest implementation of this is to create a main Rational Functional Tester script that knows all the scripts that need to be executed (and executes them by invoking `callScript()`). Your batch file needs only to execute the main Rational Functional Tester script.

After your batch file is created, you can schedule it to run as a Windows task. To schedule a .bat file to run as a Windows task, do the following:

1. Open **Scheduled Tasks** in the Control Panel.

2. Select **Add Scheduled Task**.

3. In the list of applications, click **Browse** and select your batch file.

4. Enter a name for your task and choose how often you want it to execute. Initially, the choices seem a bit limited. If you don't see the frequency with which you want to execute (such as every day at 6:00 AM and 6:00 PM), don't fret. You can fine-tune the frequency by going into Advanced Options after the task is created.

Executing a Functional Tester Script from a Plain Java Class

You can execute Rational Functional Tester scripts from a class that's not a Rational Functional Tester script, such as from a Java `main()`, but Rational Functional Tester *must* be installed on the machine from which you're executing.

To execute from a Java `main()`, use Java's capability to execute system commands to execute a script via the command-line interface:

```
public static void main(String[] args) throws Exception {


    String FT_JAR_PATH =
"C:/Progra~1/IBM/SDP/FunctionalTester/bin/rational_ft.jar";

    String commandLineArg = "cmd /c start/wait " +
```

```
"C:/Progra~1/IBM/SDP/jdk/bin/java -classpath "
+ FT_JAR_PATH
+ " "
+ "com.rational.test.ft.rational_ft "
+ " -datastore "
+ args[0]
+ " -playback " + args[1];

Process p = Runtime.getRuntime().exec(commandLineArg);
p.waitFor();
}
```

Summary

You should now have a good sense of how to enhance your scripts for different scenarios. Whether it is dealing with errors, adjusting playback options for small snippets of your scripts, or using the command line to execute your scripts, you now know the techniques to deal with them.

## CHAPTER 8

Handling Unsupported Domain Objects

Chip Davis

This chapter discusses how you can use Rational Functional Tester with applications and systems that contain interface objects that do not automatically work well with automated tests. These objects can be from old applications, customized or modified interfaces, or less common controls that are not currently supported by Rational Functional Tester.

Rational Functional Tester and Unsupported Objects

Several things must occur for Rational Functional Tester to create and execute an automated test script that interacts with an application made up of objects:

- The test script must have a reference to a given object; this is typically created by the recorder and stored in a test object map.
- There must be at least one line of test script code to interact with or test the object.
- Rational Functional Tester must be able to find the object using recognition properties during test playback.
- Rational Functional Tester must be able to execute the correct action against the object during test playback.

If any one of these does not work correctly, you cannot effectively automate test steps against the given object. Test automation might still be possible, but there is a significant added level of effort to execute and maintain such tests.

An object that is not supported by Rational Functional Tester means that it is not able to automatically recognize the object and its properties. You cannot generate a new test object and

> ## RUNNING WITHOUT A MAP
>
> A test object map is not required for a test script if you create the object references in the script code. The examples in this chapter demonstrate how to do this.

> ## WHAT IS SUPPORTED AND WHAT IS NOT?
>
> You can find the latest list of objects supported by Rational Functional Tester in the product release notes, the Help documentation, and online at www.ibm.com/software/awdtools/tester/functional/index.html.

line of test script code using the recorder. You also cannot use any of the usual test creation wizards, such as Verification Points or data-driven commands, on the object.

In many cases, Rational Functional Tester might identify the parent object or window and record coordinates for where the object is located in this window or parent object. In these cases where coordinates are used, Rational Functional Tester is not able to determine the object's properties. It also does not know the possible actions that are available. For example, is it a drop-down list or is it a text box for entering a string? Even if you are able to use coordinates where the object is located, the test playback is likely to send incorrect actions to the object or fail to coordinate the timing required to interact with the object.

Painted Objects

Unsupported objects in this chapter are typically, but not always, visible GUI controls that are still objects in either the Windows or Linux operating systems. This accounts for most GUI controls that you use in a test procedure. However, there are some special interfaces that might look like traditional GUI controls, such as push buttons and menus, which are not objects. These interfaces *paint* controls, meaning that the appearance of the object is simply an image rendered on a larger object such as a window, region, or screen. One common example of this is an Adobe® Flash® (formerly Macromedia Flash) interface, which might contain painted objects for using parts of web-based applications.

Because painted controls are not implemented through the operating system as objects, you have to rely on coordinates (in the parent object) and other manual timing techniques to create automated test scripts.

Using Rational Functional Tester with Unsupported Objects

As previously mentioned, unsupported objects are still implemented as objects in either Windows or Linux. You can therefore still get Rational Functional Tester to interact with them even if they

---

TESTING OTHER INTERFACES

Although Rational Functional Tester might have difficulty with Adobe Flash, it does fully support Adobe Flex™. Rational Functional Tester also supports many terminal-based (sometimes called "green screen") applications, which are usually painted interfaces. Finally, you can create automated functional tests for applications through Citrix® (another painted interface) using IBM Rational Performance Tester.

---

are not officially supported. You do this by determining the object structure and hierarchy of what you are trying to test, and then manually add appropriate lines of code. These steps produce a test script that can reliably identify the object and properly interact with it for testing. The general approach to do this is as follows:

1. Determine how to best find the object: by name, location in a sequence, or other means.

2. Identify the parent object, and then search down through the object hierarchy to the desired control or interface object.

3. After you find the object to test, you can add methods to perform actions, such as sending keys against the object.

4. To create a Verification Point, you must get an actual value and manually compare it to a baseline value. You must also manually log the test result.

5. Depending on the application and test procedure, you might have to add some steps or verification to synchronize the test script with the application.

FINDING OBJECTS

You might have to add looping structures, such as do-while or other conditional structures, to find the object.

COLLABORATING WITH THE DEVELOPMENT TEAM

If you test an application interface that was developed in house or you have access to the team that developed the interface, you might consider reaching out to that team. It might be able to provide you with valuable information about the objects you are try to interact with and test. This can be an easy path to developing automated tests for unsupported objects.

The methods and script code that you use to interact with unsupported objects are in the Rational Functional Tester Application Programming Interface (API) and you add these programmatically, not using the recorder. This chapter looks at some of the key components of this API that you use to do this and shows several examples of how to do it.

The Rational Functional Tester API is well documented in the product Help.

Key Components of the Rational Functional Tester API

The Rational Functional Tester API consists of many packages, classes, and methods. Most of these are in the package `com.rational.test.ft.object.interfaces`, which enables you to work with the different types of objects that Rational Functional Tester interacts with. This section provides an overview of the parts of this API that are used to work with unsupported objects. This is not intended to fully document all possible methods that you might use, but it gives you a general sense of the API classes and methods before going into the examples.

Interface Classes

Two common interfaces you use from `com.rational.test.ft.object.interfaces` are:

- **IWindow**—Used to access the operating system's windows and objects. This can be used on either Microsoft Windows or Linux, although the same test script code will not work on both. The methods in this interface are useful in identifying and finding unsupported objects that are in windows.

- **IScreen**—A similar interface that is also used to access and interact with windows and other objects from the operating system. Just like IWindow, this applies to both Microsoft Windows and Linux.

There are several useful methods available for these interfaces; `getActiveWindow()` and `getActiveScreen()` are commonly used with unsupported applications. For example, the following line of code gets the current active window when a script is running:

```
IWindow thisIsYourActiveWindow = getScreen().getActiveWindow();
```

Key Methods

The following list describes the common methods you use; these methods are from several different interfaces and classes in the `com.rational.test.ft.object.interfaces` package. Each of these methods apply to windows and objects that exist during test execution.

- The `getScreen()` method can be used to get a screen object.
- The `getTopWindows()` method can be used to get the top-level windows available during runtime.
- The `getActiveWindow()` method can be used to get the current active window.

- The `getText()` method can be used to get values (the text for the window) from a particular window.

- The `inputKeys()` method can be used to send a string or keystroke (such as Ctrl, Alt, Shift, and so forth) to the current active window.

- The `inputChars()` method can be used to send a string value (as a sequence of key events with no special interpretation of characters) to the current active window.

Test Objects

When you develop test scripts for an unsupported application interface, there is a chance that you might need to use Rational Functional Tester's `TestObject` class. Any object you interact with this way is technically not an unsupported domain, but you might use a combination of the interface methods mentioned previously along with the `TestObject` methods. Chapter 10, "Advanced Scripting with Rational Functional Tester TestObjects," discusses this topic in greater detail.

Identifying Objects

The first example in this section shows you how you can identify the objects you want to interact with. Keep in mind that this is only one possible way to do this. This method enables the automated test script to find test objects; it is roughly equivalent to having an object stored in a test object map. We do not use the recorder or any wizard to do this; instead, we simply enter (or copy from other examples) the script code.

This example uses the IWindow interface along with the `getTopWindows`, `getText`, and other methods to find a window with a particular caption. This example finds the first Window with the caption "Adobe Reader." In this case, the window caption is known, but there are also other methods available to the `IWindows` class that can be used to match a particular window. Note also that any application running in Windows or Linux has at least a container window, so this can be used with any unsupported domain.

```
String appWindowName = "Adobe Reader"; //The window name we want to find


IWindow[] appWindows = getTopWindows(); //Get all windows into an array


for ( int i = 0; i < topWindows.length; ++i ) //Loop through all windows
{

        // getText is the window's name, see if this one matches
        if (appWindows[i].getText().equals(appWindowName))

              // appWindows[i] is the application we want to test
```

ABOUT THESE EXAMPLES: APPLICATION UNDER TEST

The examples shown here work with the Adobe Reader application, which is actually a supported domain interface (Win). You can use the normal Rational Functional Tester recorder to interact with these objects. This example was chosen as a common application that many readers on different operating systems might have.

Interacting with the Objects and Entering Data

Now that you can identify the application you want to work with, you can interact with it. By interacting, you can click, drag, send keyboard input, or perform other general window manipulations. This is how you perform test steps and procedures by exercising the application under test, and it is equivalent to capturing test steps with the recorder. Like the previous example, you do not use the recorder or any wizard to do this.

In general, it is easier to send keyboard shortcuts to an unsupported domain application rather than clicking. The reason is that clicking typically requires either coordinates or the ability to identify and manipulate objects in the window. The latter is not always possible in unsupported applications. Most applications have various keyboard shortcuts to perform various functions, and Rational Functional Tester needs only to know what the application is (which was the end result of the previous example) to use one of these shortcuts.

This next example shows you how you can make the application under test open a document as part of the test procedure. To do this, you use a keyboard shortcut to bring up the Open File dialog box. You then send a static string for the file location and verify that the document was opened. The interactions use methods such as `activate`, `inputKeys`, and `getActiveWindow` to accomplish the test steps.

```
// continued from previous example

String docLocation = "C:\\OutputReport.pdf"; // Document we want to open

appWindows[i].activate(); // Make sure our window is active

appWindows[i].inputKeys("^o"); // Ctrl+O is the shortcut for open file

    // After pressing Ctrl+O, the file open dialog becomes the active window
    IWindow openDialog = getScreen().getActiveWindow();

    // Make sure we have the right dialog by matching the name (getText)
    if (openDialog.getText().equals("Open"))
    {
```

```
openDialog.inputKeys(docLocation+"~");   // '~' is Enter

// Make sure file open dialog didn't get stuck by comparing
// the active window to our initial application window
if (getScreen().getActiveWindow().getText()
                              .equals(appWindows[i].getText()))

    // the document is now open and the file dialog is gone
```

ERROR HANDLING IN THE EXAMPLE

There is additional error-handling code that is not shown in the short examples here. This error handling is shown in the final listing of the complete example at the end of this chapter.

Getting Data and Testing an Object

The last thing you need to do to make your script into a test is to actually test something. To compare an existing state or value with an expected (correct) value, you first have to get information from the application under test. After you can get data from an application, creating a Verification Point (the test) is easy.

The technique you use to get information with Rational Functional Tester and an unsupported domain application might not be the same one that you would use if you were testing the application manually. This might also be a different technique than if you were recording supported objects with Rational Functional Tester. You need a simple and reliable way to both manipulate the application under test and get information about its behavior and the data it contains. In the example shown here, you rely on one of the application's features (the find feature) along with the state of a dialog window to automate the validation of the application's functionality. In many cases, with unsupported applications, the Clipboard Verification Point discussed in Chapter 3, "General Script Enhancements," can be easy and useful.

The document that was opened in the previous example contains a job number, presumably produced by the application being tested; this can be validated against a known correct job number. There are many ways to test an application; this example demonstrates using a function of the application under test to achieve the validation. The Find feature is used to locate the expected job number. If the value is found in the opened document, the test passes; if the value is not found, the test fails.

To do this, use some of the methods in the previous examples plus the click method and a simple if-then conditional with `logTestResult` to act as the Verification Point. Here, the click method with coordinates is used, which is sometimes necessary with unsupported domains. In actuality, the Adobe Reader application is supported by Rational Functional Tester, and you could recognize the Find toolbar object, but you are treating this as if it is an unsupported screen.

```
// continued from previous example
...
String expectedJobNum = "32896"; // This is the baseline test value

// The coordinates for the application Find field are known or measured
Point findFieldPt = new Point(540,70);

appWindows[i].maximize(); // Maximize window for consistency

// Use coordinates to click into the Find field
getScreen().click(findFieldPt);

// Enter the job number and Enter to trigger the Find
getScreen().inputKeys(expectedJobNum+"~"); // '~' is the Enter key

// If it IS found then the initial window will become active again
if (getScreen().getActiveWindow().getText()
                          .equals(appWindows[i].getText()))
    logTestResult("Job number matches", true); // Test passes

// If it is NOT found then another dialog will become active
else {
    logTestResult("Could not match job number", false); // Test fails

    // Close the not found dialog that is active
    getScreen().getActiveWindow().inputKeys("~");
}
```

MORE ABOUT THESE EXAMPLES

In addition to the script code shown here, you can also add more lines using the recorder. The examples are shown in Java, although they can also be implemented in Visual Basic. The examples were created on the Windows platform, but they could have been created on Linux.

The following is the complete test script combining each of the previous examples. Some comments and error handling have been added.

```
public void testMain(Object[] args)
{
    // Initialize the variables for script readability
    String appWindowName = "Adobe Reader";      //The window name to find
    String docLocation = "C:\\OutputReport.pdf";    // Document to open
    String expectedJobNum = "32896";    // This is the baseline test value
    Point findFieldPt = new Point(540,70);      // Coordinates are known
    boolean appFound = false;                    // Use for error logging

    // Start the application
    shellExecute(
        "C:\\Program Files\\Adobe\\Reader 8.0\\Reader\\AcroRd32.exe" );
    sleep(2);   // give it 2 seconds to open

    // Find the application window from its caption
    IWindow[] appWindows = getTopWindows(); //Get all windows into array
    for ( int i = 0; i < topWindows.length; ++i ) //Loop through windows
    {
        // getText is the window's name, see if this one matches
        if (appWindows[i].getText().equals(appWindowName))
        {
            // appWindows[i] is the application we want to test
            appFound = true; // Use for error logging

            // Open the document to verify report output
            appWindows[i].activate(); // Make sure our window is active
            appWindows[i].inputKeys("^o"); // Ctrl+O is shortcut for open

            // After pressing Ctrl+O, the file open dialog becomes active
            IWindow openDialog = getScreen().getActiveWindow();

            // Make sure we have the right dialog by matching the name
            if (openDialog.getText().equals("Open"))

            {
                openDialog.inputKeys(docLocation+"~");  // '~' is Enter

                // Make sure file open dialog didn't get stuck by comparing
                //  the active window to our initial application window
                if (getScreen().getActiveWindow().getText()
                                    .equals(appWindows[i].getText()))
                {
```

```
                 // the document is now open and the file dialog is gone
                 appWindows[i].maximize(); // Maximize for consistency

                 // Use coordinates to click into the Find field
                 getScreen().click(findFieldPt);

                 // Enter the job number and Enter to trigger the Find
                  getScreen().inputKeys(expectedJobNum+"~"); // ~ is Enter

                 // If it IS found then the initial window becomes active
                 if (getScreen().getActiveWindow().getText()
                                   .equals(appWindows[i].getText()))
                    logTestResult("Job number matches", true); // Passes

                 // If it is NOT found then another dialog becomes active
                 else
                 {  // Fails
                    logTestResult("Could not match job number", false);

                    // Close the not found dialog that is active
                    getScreen().getActiveWindow().inputKeys("~");
                 } // end else

              } //end if (Make sure file open dialog didn't get stuck)
             else
                logTestResult("File did not open correctly", false);

             } // end if (openDialog.getText().equals("Open"))
             else

                logTestResult("Unable to get open file dialog", false);

             appWindows[i].close();  // Close the application

          } // end if (appWindows[i].getText().equals(appWindowName))

       } // end for() Loop through all windows

       if (!(appFound)) // Log error if application was not found
          logTestResult("AUT window was not found.", false);
    }
```

Unsupported Objects on Windows and Linux

Although the API and methods described in this chapter can be used on both Windows and Linux operating systems, it is unlikely that a test script implemented on one platform using these methods will work on the other. However, it is even more unlikely that you would have the same unsupported objects to test on both platforms. Rational Functional Tester scripts developed in this way for unsupported objects should be considered specific to one particular platform.

Summary

Although the list of supported domains and objects keeps growing, there are always applications that are not supported by Rational Functional Tester. These might be old legacy programs or new, never-before-seen technologies. Even if Rational Functional Tester cannot automatically recognize and understand an application's objects, you can still develop automated test scripts to work with them. The strategy to do this is different from using Rational Functional Tester's recorder and object maps. With some knowledge of the application you are working with and the methods demonstrated in this chapter, you can create Rational Functional Tester scripts that interact with and test these unsupported applications.

Advanced Rational Functional Tester Object Map Topics

Jeffrey R. Bocarsly, Daniel Chirillo

The Rational Functional Tester Object Map is a mechanism to give objects in the target application visibility to each Rational Functional Tester script. In Chapter 1, "Overview of Rational Functional Tester," and Chapter 2, "Storyboard Testing," you saw the basics of the Rational Functional Tester Object Map; in this chapter, you look under the hood of the Object Map. The map isn't a single entity, but is constructed from methods that are autogenerated by Rational Functional Tester and inherited by each script. These methods return TestObjects, which serve as proxies between Rational Functional Tester and the target application objects with which each Rational Functional Tester script interacts. The recognition data for each object is persisted as an XML. All these bits must be present to have a runnable Rational Functional Tester script.

Rational Functional Tester Object Map

Your typical interaction with the Object Map is through the Script Explorer View, which appears by default on the far right of the Rational Functional Test Perspective in Eclipse and on the far left in Visual Studio .NET. The Script Explorer displays a number of script assets, including the Test Objects folder, which provides access to the Object Map. If you open the Object Map (by clicking the **Test Object Map** icon), you can see the full contents of the Map. The fact that the Script Explorer might contain only a subset of the objects in the Map hints that the Rational Functional Tester Object Map apparatus is two-tiered, and indeed, it is.

Object Map Components

In the following discussion, you survey all the standard components that make up the Rational Functional Tester Object Map. These include the Script Definition, the Object Map, and the ScriptHelper class.

The Script Definition

Each Rational Functional Tester script has a Script Definition that persists all the assets associated with a script, such as the following:

- Object Map associated with a script
- Objects from that Object Map to which the script has access
- Verification Points (VP) that the script calls
- The datapool that is associated with the script

As this list indicates, the Script Definition is more than just a part of the Object Map, because it defines the script in terms of all its assets. However, it is part of the Object Map in the sense that it delineates the part of the Map that is seen by the script. Like nearly all noncode script assets, the Script Definition is stored as an XML document. This document is persisted in the /resources directory of your project in a file named by the convention `ScriptName.rftdef`. A typical Script Definition with a single object from the Map appears in Listing 9.1.

Listing 9.1   A Script Definition, XML

```xml
<?xml version="1.0" encoding="UTF-8"?>
<ScriptDefinition L=".ScriptDefinition">
    <ScriptName>ScriptNameHere</ScriptName>
    <Language>java</Language>
    <Map>resources/ScriptNameHere.rftxmap</Map>
    <Datapool/>
    <DatapoolIterator></DatapoolIterator>
    <HelperSuper></HelperSuper>
    <ScriptNameMap L=".ScriptDefinitionNameMap">
        <TestObject L=".ScriptDefNameMapElement">
            <Name>browser_htmlBrowser</Name>
            <ID>0.5vYm2Dr5yw0:2FeZrp:LSlosoe:8WV</ID>
            <Role>Browser</Role>
            <Deleted>false</Deleted>
        </TestObject>
    </ScriptNameMap>
    <Properties L=".PropSet"></Properties>
    <ScriptEncoding>Cp1252</ScriptEncoding>
    <KeywordName></KeywordName>
</ScriptDefinition>
```

In Listing 9.1, your main interest is the `<ScriptNameMap>` tag. This `<ScriptNameMap>` tag contains a `<TestObject>` child tag in this listing (it might contain any number of such tags). These `<TestObject>` tags define the specific objects in the target application to which this script has access. The `<TestObject>` tag has the child tags `Name`, `ID`, `Role`, and `Deleted`. The value of the `<Name>` tag is the display name of the object that appears in the Test Object tree in the Script Explorer. The `<ID>` is a GUID that Rational Functional Tester generates for each object in its Map. The `<Role>` tag indicates the type of object (Browser, Frame, Button, Text, Label, ComboBox, and so on).

The Object Map

The `<TestObject>` entry in the Script Definition in Listing 9.1 tells Rational Functional Tester that this specific object is to be available to this script, so that the script can interact with the object at design-time and runtime. However, the actual information to recognize the specific object does not appear in the Script Definition; it appears in the Object Map, which, like the Script Definition, is stored in an XML format. The specific Object Map that the script uses is defined in the Script Definition XML (as you might expect), by the `<Map>` tag, which gives the path to the Object Map XML relative to the root directory of the project. This XML contains the actual object mappings and represents the central component of Rational Functional Tester's Object Map. It contains the object hierarchy and recognition properties and their values. Map XML files are named using a similar convention to Script Definition XML files. If the Map is a shared Map, its XML file is stored at the project root and is named using the convention `mapName.rftmap`. If the Map is private, its file is stored in the \resources directory and is named `ScriptName.rftxmap`. The Object Map specified in the `<Map>` tag in Listing 9.1, appears in Listing 9.2.

Listing 9.2 Object Map sample XML

```
<?xml version="1.0" encoding="UTF-8"?>
<ObjectMap L=".ObjectMap">
    <Attribute L=".Attribute">
        <Name>.NextId</Name>
        <Value>2</Value>
    </Attribute>
    <Attribute L=".Attribute">
        <Name>.LastSharedId</Name>
        <Value>-1</Value>
    </Attribute>
    <Attribute L=".Attribute">
        <Name>.TopObjs</Name>
        <Value L=".TopLevelIds">
            <Id>0.5vYm2Dr5yw0:2FeZrp:LSlosoe:8WV</Id>
        </Value>
    </Attribute>
    <Attribute L=".Attribute">
        <Name>.MtoSet</Name>
        <Value L=".ObjectMapSet">
            <MTO L=".MTO">
                <Id>0.5vYm2Dr5yw0:2FeZrp:LSlosoe:8WV</Id>
                <Name>htmlBrowser</Name>
```

```
                    <Parent/>
                    <TO>BrowserTestObject</TO>
                    <Dom>Html</Dom>
                    <Class>Html.HtmlBrowser</Class>
                    <Role>Browser</Role>
                    <Proxy>.html.HtmlBrowserProxy</Proxy>
              </MTO>
         </Value>
    </Attribute>
    <Attribute L=".Attribute">
         <Name>.PropSet</Name>
         <Value L=".MapPropertySet">
              <MapProperty L=".MapProperty">
                    <Name>rt.html_table_mapping_policy</Name>
                    <Value>Original</Value>
              </MapProperty>
         </Value>
    </Attribute>
</ObjectMap>
```

The Object Map sample XML in Listing 9.2 shows the basic features of the Map. First, every-thing in the map is a Map Attribute, which means `<Attribute>` tags contain the Map's key infor-mation, and each `<Attribute>` tag might contain a different type of information. The type of information that an `<Attribute>` tag contains is indicated by a handful of tags common to all `<Attribute>` tags: a `<Name>` tag indicates the type of data in the `<Attribute>` tag and a `<Value>` tag specifies the `<Attribute>` values. The discussion here focuses on two types of Map attributes: one that defines the top level objects in the target application (`<Name>.TopObjs</Name>`) and one that defines the objects in the target application (`<Name>.MtoSet</Name>`).

The Map attribute that holds the top-level window objects has a simple structure: a `<Value>` tag with a child `<Id>` tag that has the GUID for the top-level window. In Listings 9.1 and 9.2, the GUID is `0.5vYm2Dr5yw0:2FeZrp:LSlosoe:8WV`, and Rational Functional Tester can easily determine whether an object in the Script Definition is a top-level window object by looking its GUID up in the .TopObjs attribute of the Map.

Similarly, Rational Functional Tester uses the object GUID to look up the .MtoSet (Mapped Test Object Set) attribute for an object, and this Map attribute contains the information to recognize the object at runtime. The actual recognition information appears in the `<MTO>` tag, a child of the `<Value>` tag. The `<MTO>` tag contains several child tags of which nearly all appear on the Administrative tab of the Rational Functional Tester Test Object Map viewer:

- `Id`—The Rational Functional Tester GUID for the object
- `Name`—The Rational Functional Tester name of the object, which is typically a window caption or htmlBrowser for a browser window, or an object name

- `Parent`—Rational Functional Tester GUID of a parent object if one exists
- `TO`—The TestObject subclass of the object
- `Dom`—Domain of the object (Html, Java, Net, and so on)
- `Class`—The class of the target application object
- `Role`—The role of the object, for example, window, frame, browser, and so on
- `Proxy`—Proxy class for target object

In addition, there are certain properties, called Recognition properties, that are specific to each object class. These object-specific properties appear in `<Prop>` tags, and Rational Functional Tester uses them to recognize each object specifically (they appear on the Recognition tab of the Test Object Map viewer). For illustration, a typical set of recognition properties for a Swing `JLabel` object is shown in the following XML snippet:

```
<Prop L=".MtoProp">
    <Key>text</Key>
    <Val>Hello World</Val>
    <Wt>50</Wt>
</Prop>
<Prop L=".MtoProp">
    <Key>accessibleContext.accessibleName</Key>
    <Val>Hello World</Val>
    <Wt>100</Wt>
</Prop>
<Prop L=".MtoProp">
    <Key>.classIndex</Key>
    <Val L=".Index">
        <Index>0</Index>
    </Val>
    <Wt>50</Wt>
</Prop>
```

You can open any object in the Test Object Map viewer and compare what you find on the Recognition and Administrative tabs to the actual entries in the script's Map XML.

The ScriptHelper Class

The final part of the Object Map mechanism lies in the "ScriptHelper" class, which every script inherits from. Each ScriptHelper class is named by appending Helper to the name of your script; this name is autogenerated and cannot be changed.

NOTE ScriptHelper is capitalized in this chapter to indicate that it *represents* the name of a class; however, it does not appear in the code font because it is not a true class name.

The contents of each ScriptHelper class are also autogenerated based on how you record your script. Each ScriptHelper contains methods that instantiate the `TestObjects` that represent target application objects in your script. These methods use the object names that appear in the Script Explorer view, and in the Script Definition XML. Typically, for each object in the Script Explorer, there are two methods in the ScriptHelper class: a default method that takes no arguments and an overloaded nondefault method that takes a Rational Functional Tester anchor argument. An anchor argument is an argument of type `TestObject` that a method call is "anchored" to. For example, in the following line of code, the document `TestObject` anchor argument "anchors" the `inputKeys()` method to the browser window with this specific document loaded:

```
browser_htmlBrowser(document_ibmUnitedStates(),DEFAULT_FLAGS)
.inputChars("rational")
```

Listing 9.3 shows autogenerated code for a browser `TestObject`.

Listing 9.3   Rational Functional Tester autogenerated ScriptHelper code for a browser

```
protected BrowserTestObject browser_htmlBrowser()
{
    return new BrowserTestObject(
        getMappedTestObject("browser_htmlBrowser"));
}
protected BrowserTestObject browser_htmlBrowser(
        TestObject anchor, long flags)
{
    return new BrowserTestObject(
        getMappedTestObject("browser_htmlBrowser"), anchor, flags);
}
```

Summary of Object Map Files

Table 9.1 summarizes the files that hold the Object Map components. Note that a script can have only one Script Definition, one ScriptHelper, and either a Private or a Shared Object Map file.

You can see these underlying assets for a project simply by opening up the Eclipse Navigator View (**Window Menu > Show View > Navigator**). The Navigator view opens by default in the same pane as the Functional Test Projects View, and presents a tree view of projects. You can use this tree view to navigate all the underlying assets in your projects, including the Object Map assets.

> **NOTE**   The Simple Scripting feature in Rational Functional Tester 8.1 provides a new layer that provides access to Rational Functional Tester functionality for nontechnical users and novice Rational Functional Tester users via a set of graphical tools. Under the hood, Simple Scripting uses the entire set of standard Object Map features as described in this chapter. For a script created under the Simple Scripting paradigm, all the same apparatus described here for a standard script comes into play.

Table 9.1 Rational Functional Tester Object Map Files: File Locations and Naming Conventions

File Type	File Location	File Naming Convention
Script Definition XML file	Project resources directory	ScriptName.rftdef
Private Object Map XML file	Project resources directory	ScriptName.rftxmap
Shared Object Map XML file	Root project directory	MapName.rftmap
ScriptHelper file	Project resources directory	ScriptNameHelper.java

Rational Functional Tester Object Recognition Framework

IBM Rational designed the Object Map feature set with two features that set it apart in the market space as an exceptionally well-designed and well-engineered offering. While considering the problem of script maintenance, the architects of Rational Functional Tester incorporated two powerful concepts into the Object Map:

- ScriptAssure, a weighting mechanism for recognition properties—The ScriptAssure weighting mechanism enables the user to change the recognition weights of properties according to their volatility across builds.
- Object Map Regular Expressions, an industry-standard pattern matching (Regular Expressions) functionality—The Regular Expression implementation enables the user to write patterns for Rational Functional Tester to match instead of fixed recognition values.

No other competing tool has the power of either of these features individually. Together, these features make the Rational Functional Tester Object Map technology the most advanced on the market.

Object Recognition with ScriptAssure

The ScriptAssure weighting values can be found in the third column of the Recognition tab of the Object Map viewer. The values that you are probably most used to seeing are the default ScriptAssure weights that are applied to an object when it is inserted into the Map. Typically, the default weighting works fine, but for situations where you know the weighting needs to be optimized, you can adjust it. When you click on the ScriptAssure weight field you'd like to modify, the value becomes editable, and you can enter any value between 0 and 100 (note that weights for some properties are not editable). Simply put, the significance of the values is that the role a property plays in object recognition scales with the weighting value. A lower value means that a property is a less important factor in recognition (a zero value means that a property plays no role in recognition), and a higher value means that a property plays a role of increasing significance in recognition.

However, the actual implementation of this weighting concept is a bit more involved than that simple statement implies. The ScriptAssure algorithm works by scoring each candidate object by summing the contributions of each recognition property, scaled by the weighting scheme. As Rational Functional Tester tries to match recognition properties, if a recognition property value does *not* match to a candidate object found at runtime, the mismatch counts *against* recognition, and if it *does* match, the match contributes nothing to the total. If the total of all contributions from all properties for the candidate object exceeds a set amount, the object is not recognized by Rational Functional Tester because too many properties have failed to match. In this sense, the ScriptAssure scoring value is a measure of nonmatching because the higher the score, the poorer the match.

ScriptAssure Recognition Property Scoring—Scoring Recognition Properties

Rational Functional Tester matches objects at runtime by scoring the recognition properties of each candidate object based on matching recognition property values. The procedure works as follows: If a recognition property value for a candidate object does not match what the Map expects, the "intrinsic" match score of the property is multiplied by its ScriptAssure weight and the total of all contributions for the object's recognition properties are summed. If property values do match, no contribution to the total is made. If the sum of the scoring contributions exceeds a specific amount, the object is not recognized (see the following for a description of scoring thresholds).

The scoring contributions of different recognition properties vary based on the property and, to a lesser extent, the domain. Table 9.2 shows the intrinsic match scores of a variety of common recognition properties.

Table 9.2   ScriptAssure Match Scores for Common Recognition Properties

Object	Recognition Property	Match Score
All Java (Swing) objects	All properties, excluding `.classIndex`	100
All .NET objects	All properties, excluding `.classIndex`	100
`Html Document`	All properties, excluding `.url` and `.classIndex`	100
`Html Document`	`.url`	Scaling up to 100 based on degree of mismatch
All objects	`.classIndex`	Scaling up to 100 based on degree of mismatch

To see how this works, the following discussion takes some concrete examples and opens them up. Using the IBM home page, www.ibm.com/us/, you can capture the following slice of the object hierarchy (as of this writing):

Html: Browser: htmlBrowser: Html.HtmlBrowser

|_Html: Document: IBMUnitedStates: Html.HtmlDocument

|_Html: Html: ibmCom: Html.BODY

|_Html: Html: ibmTop: Html.DIV

|_Html: Html: ibmMasthead: Html.DIV

|_Html: Form: ibmSearchForm: Html.FORM

|_Html: Text: q: Html.INPUT.text

These objects are all on the masthead of the page. This discussion focuses on the `HtmlDocument` object near the top of the tree and the search query Text input box at its bottom. The recognition properties of these objects are shown in Table 9.3.

Table 9.3 Recognition Properties of HTML Objects with Default ScriptAssure Weights and Scores

Object	Recognition Property	Recognition Property Value	Default Weight	Match Score
HtmlDocument				
	.class	Html.HtmlDocument	100	100
	.title	IBM—United States	90	100
	.url	www.ibm.com/us/	40	scaled
INPUT.text				
	.class	Html.INPUT.text	100	100
	.classIndex	0	50	scaled
	.id	q	90	100
	.name	q	90	100
	.title		50	100
	.type	text	95	100

Let's look at the consequences for the scoring if there are mismatches between the expected values for recognition properties and the actual values captured during the recognition process at runtime. For the INPUT.Text object, if Rational Functional Tester fails to match the .id property, the scoring is:

```
90 x 100 = 9,000
```

If the match failure is on the .title property, the score is:

```
50 x 100 = 5,000
```

If Rational Functional Tester fails to match on both .id and .title for the INPUT.Text object, the score is the sum of the individual scores:

```
(90 x 100) + (50 x 100) = 14,000
```

If the INPUT.Text object's .classIndex value is off by 1, the match scoring is scaled as follows:

```
50 x 50 = 2,500
```

Look at some similar scoring numbers for the HtmlDocument object. If the .title property is mismatched, the scoring penalty is:

```
90 x 100 = 9,000
```

If the HtmlDocument's .url property is off due to some characters appended to the URL (for example, a new virtual directory level has been added to the application), the match score is scaled to 80. Using the default weighting of 40, the contribution to the total score is:

```
40 x 80 = 3,200
```

If both of these mismatches occurred, then the total score is:

```
(90 x 100) + (40 x 80) = 12,200
```

ScriptAssure Recognition Property Scoring: Scoring the Object Tree

Rational Functional Tester's concept of object matching doesn't rely on matching recognition property values of just the target object. Rather, to assure that the specific object in the target application has been located, Rational Functional Tester attempts to match the target object *and* all objects along the branch leading to the target object, up to the root of the object hierarchy (which usually is a top-level window). Moreover, the ScriptAssure scoring is *inherited*—meaning that if an object higher in the tree is scored with a mismatching property value, every object beneath the mismatched object inherits its score. This inheritance feature means that the recognition score of an object reflects its own score and the score of the inheritance tree above it.

Consider an example using the previous tree. Suppose the HtmlDocument object had a defective .url property value in the Map with a scaled match score of 90, as shown in the previous examples. Assume that, the .id property of the search query INPUT.text object is also a mismatch with a weight of 90 and a match score of 100 (see Table 9.3). The math works out on each tree node as follows:

Object Hierarchy	Object Match Score
Html: Browser: htmlBrowser: Html.HtmlBrowser	0
|_Html: Document: IBMUnitedStates: Html.HtmlDocument	40 x 80 = 3,200
|_Html: Html: ibmCom: Html.BODY	3,200
|_Html: Html: ibmTop: Html.DIV	3,200
|_Html: Html: ibmMasthead: Html.DIV	3,200
|_Html: Form: ibmSearchForm: Html.FORM	3,200
|_Html: Text: q: Html.INPUT.text	(90 x 100) + 3,200 = 12,200

All the object nodes under the `HtmlDocument` object inherit its score of 3,200 and because these objects have no mismatches, they contribute 0 additional to the score. The `INPUT.text` object contributes its own score of 9,000 due to its own mismatch, which gives it a total matching score of 12,200.

ScriptAssure Scoring Thresholds

The ScriptAssure implementation uses its scoring to achieve a more sophisticated behavior than a simple, binary match-no match conclusion does. This added sophistication is achieved through a multi-tiered set of threshold values, in which different threshold match scores are defined and are combined with recognition timeouts. The thresholds are as follows:

- Maximum acceptable recognition score—Sets the threshold score *under* which an object is recognized by Rational Functional Tester as a match candidate. The default value is 10,000.
- Warn if accepted score is greater—Defines the threshold *above* which a "weak recognition" warning is written to the log. The default value is 10,000.
- Last chance recognition score—If a match is not made in the timeout period, then this threshold defines the maximum score an object might have for Rational Functional Tester to recognize it as a candidate match. The default value is 20,000.
- Ambiguous recognition score difference—If the scores of the top candidate matches in the pool of candidates differ by less than this amount, an `AmbiguousRecognition Exception` is thrown. The default value is 1,000.

The scheme works as follows (using the default threshold values). Rational Functional Tester first looks for a pool of candidate match objects with ScriptAssure scores lower than the "Maximum acceptable recognition score." If it finds match candidates and can select one using the "Ambiguous recognition score difference" threshold, a match is made. If no candidates fit these criteria within the matching timeout, but candidates are found that are between the "Warn if accepted score is greater" and "Last chance recognition score" values, then if Rational Functional Tester can match to one using the "Ambiguous recognition score difference" threshold, a match is made. In this case, Rational Functional Tester writes a weak recognition warning to the log (and fires an `onRecognitionWarning()` event), and execution proceeds as if the object has been properly recognized. If no candidate scores below the "Last chance recognition score," then an `ObjectNotFoundException` is thrown and appropriate messages are written to the log. These relationships are schematized in Figure 9.1.

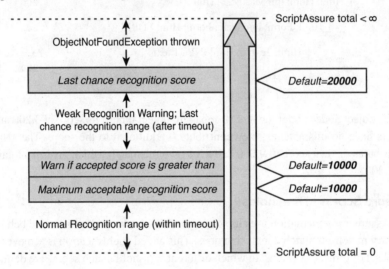

Figure 9.1   Schematic of ScriptAssure threshold cutoff values

In the previous example, the score for the `HtmlDocument`, `BODY`, `DIV`, and `FORM` objects are all 3,200 each and the score for the `INPUT.text` object is 12,200. Only the score of the `INPUT.text` object exceeds any of the default thresholds—it exceeds the "Maximum acceptable recognition score" (10,000) and the "Warn if accepted score is greater" thresholds (10,000), but not the "Last chance recognition score" (20,000). This means that the `INPUT.text` object is recognized by Rational Functional Tester during script execution, but an Object Recognition is weak warning message is written to the log for this object. None of the other objects exceeds the Maximum acceptable recognition score threshold, so they are considered to be normally recognized by Rational Functional Tester.

Usually, the default threshold values, like the default ScriptAssure weightings, work just fine for most applications. In a rare event, you might have to modify the thresholds, which can be done *globally* using the Rational Functional Tester Preferences window (select **Functional Test > Playback > ScriptAssure** in the tree view). Figure 9.2 shows the default constants by name within the threshold scheme.

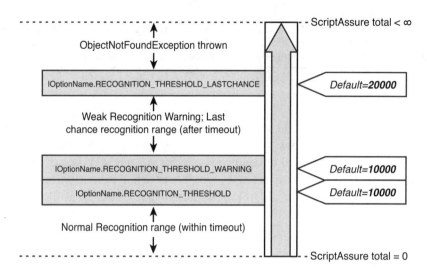

Figure 9.2   Schematic of ScriptAssure threshold constants

You also have the option of setting the threshold values in your code using the names shown in Figure 9.2, using the method `setOption()` with the `IOptionName` constants. You can set the values of any of the thresholds in your scripts at runtime using any of the following:

```
setOption(IOptionName.RECOGNITION_THRESHOLD_LASTCHANCE, thresh)
setOption(IOptionName.RECOGNITION_THRESHOLD_WARNING, thresh)
setOption(IOptionName.RECOGNITION_THRESHOLD, thresh)
```

In these examples, the variable `thresh` is the threshold value that you are setting for the execution. Note that setting ScriptAssure threshold values using `setOption()` only sets the value for the scope of the run; the default values set in your preferences are unaffected and apply normally to any other script where `setOption()` is not called.

Pattern Matching: Regular Expressions in the Object Map

The Rational Functional Tester Object Map has an additional power feature that is unequalled by any competing tool in the functional/regression automation space. This is the ability to use pattern matching, or Regular Expressions, in the Map in place of fixed values for recognition properties. If you convert a recognition property to a Regular Expression and provide an appropriate pattern, Rational Functional Tester searches for the object based on the pattern and accepts any value that matches the pattern. This feature can be extraordinarily useful in a number of situations. For example, when unique identifiers appear in recognition property values or when a series of related objects are named by a convention (and you want to handle them with a single Map entry), a Regular Expression provides a perfect solution.

> **NOTE**   In the Java flavor of Rational Functional Tester, the power of Regular Expressions was offered before they were a standard part of the Java libraries. Therefore, Rational Functional Tester uses a customized version of the Apache Regular Expression implementation. You are still free to use the Java Regular Expressions engine (released in Java 1.4) in any Java code you write in your scripts.

To illustrate how powerful Rational Functional Tester's Regular Expression implementation makes Object Map recognition, the following discussion explores some common Regular Expressions syntax to solve typical recognition issues that you might encounter. The first topic considered is how to use Regular Expression operators to define patterns. After that, Regular Expression syntax is used to solve the problem of matching a set of related URLs, a common issue that arises with web applications.

Common Regular Expression Operators

Regular Expression patterns are built out of common pieces of text along with *operators* (also called *metacharacters*) that specify a text pattern to match. Operators are typically indicated by punctuation characters. The following examples illustrate some of the Regular Expression operators that are most useful in the Object Map; a more complete discussion of Regular Expressions as implemented in Rational Functional Tester can be found in Appendix B, "Regular Expressions in Rational Functional Tester." The operators considered in this discussion are:

- . (period)—Matches any individual character (except newline).
- * (asterisk)—Matches 0 or more of the previous pattern.
- + (plus)—Matches 1 or more of the previous pattern.
- [] (square brackets)—Defines a character class. A character class describes a position in a string and a set of characters that are a match for that position.

To understand how the Regular Expressions matching engine behaves, consider the simplest kind of pattern, which is a pattern defined by a sequence of characters without any operators. For example, if you have the text "four score and seven years ago," and you try to match it with a Regular Expression pattern of "seven," the Regular Expressions engine happily matches the word "seven." This illustrates that the engine fundamentally looks for a character match for its pattern.

The next step is to examine how operators can be used to generalize a text pattern so that only the characteristics of the matching text are described and not the specific text itself. As you look through these examples, it is important to pay attention to how the operators work, and more important, to how they work *together*. Much of the power of the Regular Expression operators is in how they can modify each other. The first and simplest example is to look at how the asterisk operator works. The asterisk modifies the pattern that precedes it and matches the preceding pattern any number of times, including 0 times. For example, in the pattern `'a*'`, the asterisk modifies the pattern `'a'`. The `'a*'` pattern matches but it also matches `'aa'` and `'aaa'` and `'aaaa'` and `'aaaaa'`, or any number of `'a'`s (because * matches any number of the pattern it modifies). It matches `'b'` as well, because * matches as few as 0 of the pattern it modifies. Now, consider the combination of the asterisk with the period, ' . * '. In this ' . * ' pattern, the period matches *any single character* (except newline), and the asterisk therefore matches *any number of any character* (including no characters). The ' . * ' pattern is thus the most promiscuous pattern, matching nearly anything, *including nothing*.

Let's look at a closely related pattern to ' . * ', the pattern ' . + '. The only difference between the ' * ' operator and the ' + ' operator is that the '+' operator requires a minimum of one of the previous pattern for there to be a match. This pattern would match any set of characters of any size, but it would not match 0 characters as ' . * ' would. The ' . + ' pattern therefore requires at least one character to match.

The final Regular Expression operator considered here is the square brackets, ' [] ', which define character classes. As noted previously, a character class specifies a set of characters that are matches for a specific position in a string. Consider a simple example—you want to write a pattern to match a word that has two spellings: gray and grey. Start by composing your pattern with the letters that both spellings agree with, the g, r, and the final y. The position after the r, which is the position at which the two spellings diverge is defined with a character class. The class is composed of the two possible letters that might occupy the position, a and e, producing the pattern gr[ae]y. This pattern translates as: match any character sequence where the first position is a 'g', the second position is an 'r', the third position is *either* an 'a' or an 'e', and the final position is a 'y'.

Character classes have some additional syntax features. Although you can explicitly specify all characters of a class, ranges of characters can be specified by a simple shorthand notation. For example, ' [0-9] ' means a class including all the numeric characters between 0 and 9 inclusive. Similarly, the class ' [3-6] ' is equivalent to the class ' [3456] '. Likewise, ' [a-z] ' includes the lowercase alphabet and ' [A-Z] ' is the uppercase alphabet. Shorthand notations can be combined in a single class: ' [a-zA-Z] ' includes both lowercase and uppercase alphabets.

Just as you saw with the ' . ', character classes can be modified by the ' * ' and ' + ' operators. So, the pattern ' [0-9]+ ' matches any number of digit characters, as long as there is at least one digit. The related pattern ' [0-9]* ' would match any number of digit characters (including no digits, of course). The pattern ' [0-9A-F]+ ' would match any number denoted in hexadecimal notation.

Now that you have examined some basic Regular Expression operators, look at some common situations where they might be used in the Object Map. To apply the Regular Expression syntax, consider the situation in which you have some related URLs from a web application that you want to represent with a single object in your Map:

```
http://www.etailer.com/products/75013_HCAAC_8B0F570C/index
http://www.etailer.com/products/75018_HCABX_8B0F570D/index
http://www.etailer.com/products/75018_HCBBX_8B0F570D/index
```

These URLs all start with the same character string http://www.etailer.com/products/. They end with an instance identifier, a sequence of letters and number in three fields separated by underscores. The first field is all numbers, the second all uppercase letters, and the third is a mixture of the two. Think about some possible patterns that could be used to match the URLs. The simplest pattern, as suggested earlier, is simply to use the characters common to all three URLs:

```
http://www.etailer.com/products/
```

This matches all the URLs, and this type of match probably works for many of your Object Map patterns. However, imagine that you might in the future need to distinguish between URLs that end with /index and those that end differently. You can modify this pattern to include this by employing the most general metacharacter pattern, .*:

```
http://www.etailer.com/products/.*/index
```

This matches your URLs, and the approach is quick to implement. However, note that .* can be *too* powerful—it can match more than you intend. A less general, more specific pattern can avoid unintended consequences due to an overly broad pattern. In this case, it is easy to write one. You can write a character class that contains all the permitted characters (all numbers, all uppercase letters, and the underscore character), and modify it with the + operator to require at least one member of the class:

```
http://www.etailer.com/products/[0-9A-Z_]+/index
```

Again, you can ask whether this pattern is overly broad. You can certainly use your knowledge of the URLs and Regular Expressions to write an even more specific pattern because you can specify the three fields in the instance identifier separately. The pattern is:

```
http://www.etailer.com/products/[0-9]+_[A-Z]+_[0-9A-Z]+/index
```

In this pattern, the first field is constrained to be at least one number, the second field to be at least one uppercase letter, and the third field to be at least one character from the set of numbers and uppercase letters. Note that in this final pattern, if you have a letter in your first field or a number in your second field, the Regular Expressions engine does not find a match. This pattern opens the door for even more granular specificity in the match. If you wanted, for example, to match only URLs where the second field ends in X, you can write:

```
http://www.etailer.com/products/[0-9]+_[A-Z]+[X]_[0-9A-Z]+/index
```

There is one additional subtlety in the previous three patterns that is worth mentioning. As will all URLs, the server name uses a period (www.server.com). However, the period is also an operator! Because the period operator matches any single character, it matches itself, and your pattern matches as expected. However, the pattern matches *any* character appearing where the periods appear in the server name (www!server!com would match, for example). If you want to, you can escape the period operator and tell the Regular Expression engine to treat the period as a normal character and not a metacharacter. Escaping operators is done by enclosing the operator in square braces (or preceding them with backslashes). The final pattern would therefore look like:

```
http://www[.]etailer[.]com/products/[0-9]+_[A-Z]+_[0-9A-Z]+/index
```

Note that in most cases, the first and simplest pattern is sufficient for Object Map purposes. There are cases, however, where a simple but general pattern might be too broad for the need, and in this case, the additional syntax becomes useful. The downside of writing a highly specific pattern is that you may exclude cases that you don't want to—always be sure that your pattern does the work you need it to. For convenience, several of the regular expressions in the previous discussion are collected in Table 9.4.

Table 9.4 Summary of Regular Expression Examples

Pattern	Matching Example	Nonmatching Example
a*	a, aa, aaa, aaaa, b, c, etc.	—
.*	Matches everything	—
.+	Requires at least one character	No characters
gr[ae]y	gray, grey	gry, gr@y, groy, gr6y, etc.
[0-9]	Any single digit	Any single letter or punctuation character
[A-Z]	Any single upper case letter	Any single lower case letter, digit, punctuation
[a-z]	Any single lower case letter	Any single upper case letter, digit, punctuation
[a-zA-Z]	Any single letter of any case	Any single digit or punctuation
[3-6]	Any one of 3, 4, 5, 6	0, 1, 2, 7, 8, 9
[0-9A-F]+	Any hexadecimal number	Any string containing lower case letters, upper case letters above F, punctuation characters
[0-9A-Z_]+	75013_HCAAC_8B0F570C, 75018_HCABX_8B0F570D, 75018_HCBBX_8B0F570D	#75013-HCAAC-8B0F570C
[0-9]+_[A-Z]+_[0-9A-Z]+	75013_HCAAC_8B0F570C, 75018_HCABX_8B0F570D, 75018_HCBBX_8B0F570D	A5013_HCAAC_8B0F570C, 75018_HC1BX_8B0F570D
[0-9]+_[A-Z]+[X]_[0-9A-Z]+	75018_HCABX_8B0F570D, 75018_HCBBX_8B0F570D	75013_HCAAC_8B0F570C

Customizing Recognition Properties and Weights

Under most circumstances, Rational Functional Tester's default recognition properties and weights meet your needs (particularly when regular expressions are used). If you find yourself in a situation where you need to modify them—add or remove recognition properties or change their weights—Rational Functional Tester makes this possible.

Remove a Recognition Property for an Individual Test Object

To remove a recognition property from the Object Map for a Test Object, open the Map and either set the property's weight to zero (the recommended choice) or delete the property entirely by right-clicking on the property and selecting **Delete** in the context menu.

Add a Recognition Property for an Individual Test Object

To add a recognition property to the Object Map, you must first make the Test Object available to the Object Map. After you do this, click the Test Object in the Object Map and select **Test Object > Update Recognition Properties** from the Object Map menu. Rational Functional Tester highlights the object on your desktop, captures its current (live) property values, and displays the dialog box shown in Figure 9.3; recognition property discrepancies are automatically pointed out.

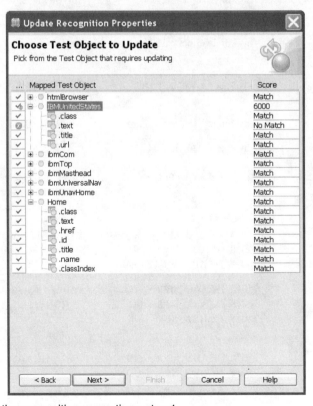

Figure 9.3   Updating recognition properties—step 1

Now click the **Next** button; the dialog box shown in Figure 9.4 appears.

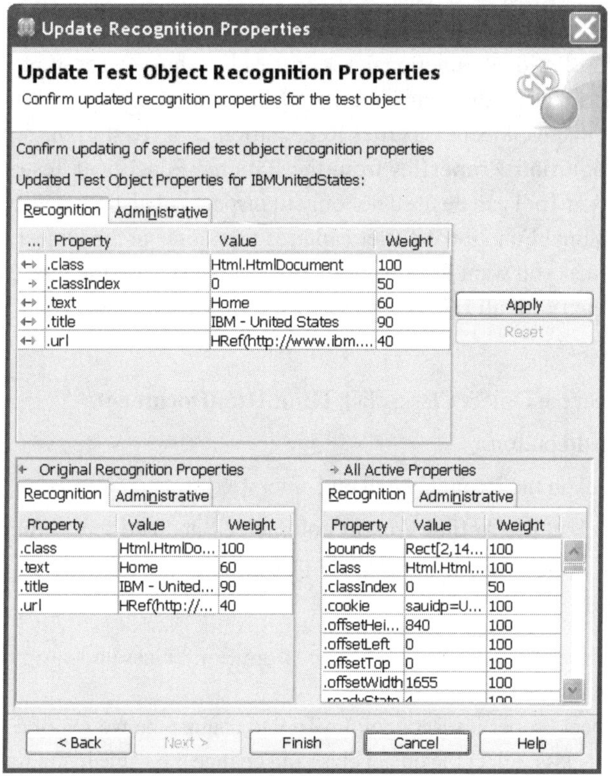

Figure 9.4   Updating recognition properties—step 2

This dialog has three lists of properties and values: all the recognition properties *currently* stored in the Object Map (Original Recognition Properties on the bottom left), all the Test Object's current mappable (value class) property values (All Active Properties on the bottom right), and the properties and property values that are added, removed, or modified to the Map.

To add a recognition property to the Map, follow these steps:

1. Double-click the desired property in the **All Active Properties** list (or right-click on it and select **Add to Unified Test Object Properties**).

2. The property immediately appears in the Updated Properties list at the top of the dialog box.

3. If you accidentally add the wrong property, click the **Reset** button or right-click it and delete it. You can change the property values and weights.

4. After you add all the properties you want to add to the Map for the selected test object, click **Finish**.

Changing Default Recognition Properties and Property Weights with the Object Properties Recognition Tool

For each test domain-object class combination (for example, `Java/java.awt.Frame` and `Html/Html.Table`), Rational Functional Tester tries to capture a set of recognition properties. The properties it captures and the weights it assigns to each property for each type of Test Object are exposed to you via the Object Properties Recognition Tool. To start the tool, select **Configure > Configured Recognition Properties** from the Rational Functional Tester menu. The Object Properties Recognition Tool can be used not only to inspect but also to modify the default properties and weights Rational Functional Tester captures and stores in the Object Map.

If you decide that you want Rational Functional Tester to use the `.text` property by default as a recognition property for all HTML documents, follow these steps:

1. Select **Html**.

2. Under Select the Object Class, click **Html.HtmlDocument**.

3. Click the **Add** button.

4. Double-click in the **Property** cell and enter **.text**.

5. Double-click in the **Actual Weight** column cell and add the weight you want Rational Functional Tester to assign to the .text property.

6. Click **Finish**.

If you add the `.text` property to the `Html.HtmlDocument` class and assign a weight of 90, you see what's shown in Figure 9.5.

To use the Object Properties Recognition Tool to change the weight of a recognition property used by a Test Object class, select the object class and change the value in the Actual Weight column.

Note that any customizations you make using the Object Properties Recognition Tool do not take effect in any Test Objects already in the Object Map unless you run the Update Recognition Properties utility described earlier in this section for each Test Object.

To remove your customizations at any point, that is, to go back to using Rational Functional Tester's default properties and weights, select the Test Object class and click the **Restore** button.

Renaming Test Objects (ScriptHelper Methods)

Unclear or ambiguous method names make code difficult to understand and, therefore, to maintain. In some cases, the ScriptHelper method names generated by Rational Functional Tester's recording engine do not make it obvious to the reader which objects they reference. In such cases, it is wise to rename them.

The simplest technique you can use to change the name of a Test Object (this amounts to changing the name of a ScriptHelper method) is to rename the Test Object from the Script Explorer view. Right-click on the Test Object, select **Rename**, and enter a new name. Eclipse automatically renames all calls in the current script to that ScriptHelper method. This is both

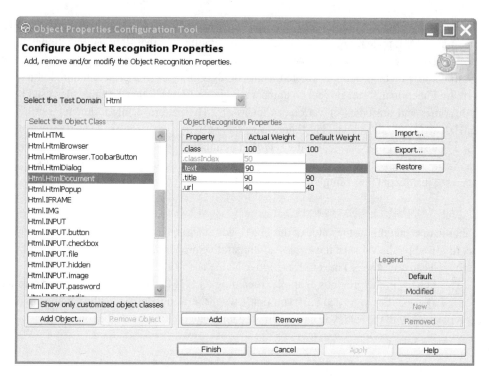

Figure 9.5   Adding a recognition property

simple and convenient, but the name change is made to the current script only. If the script in which you rename a test object is associated with a shared map and that test object has been added to multiple scripts, the new name is not reflected in any other scripts. Luckily, Rational Functional Tester has a mechanism you can use to rename a Test Object in multiple scripts at once.

To rename a Test Object in multiple scripts (that share the same test Object Map) in a single bound, do the following:

1. Highlight the test object's node in the Object Map Viewer.

2. Change the test object's Descriptive Name on the Administrative tab to the name you want to use.

3. Select **Test Object > Renew Name in Associated Script(s)**.

4. Modify the name if desired.

5. Click **Finish**. Rational Functional Tester renames the ScriptHelper methods in all scripts (associated with the given Object Map) that contain the Test Object.

Depending on the application domain of the Test Object you rename (for example, HTML, Java, .NET), the method name you entered in Step 2 might be slightly different from the name Rational

Functional Tester presents to you see in Step 4. For example, if you changed the Descriptive Name of an HTML table to `customersTable`, the default name that Rational Functional Tester generates and presents to you in Step 4 is `table_customersTable`. The reason for this is that the ScriptHelper method name is created using an algorithm set in a project template file. The root of the Functional Tester project contains a templates directory that contains files used to set default names and attributes of various script assets. The pattern or algorithm for setting the ScriptHelper method name is found in the `ft_script_<domain>_object_name.java.rfttpl` file. For example, for the HTML domain, the file is `ft_script_html_object_name.java.rfttpl`. If you open the `ft_script_html_object_name.java.rfttpl` file, you can see that it contains a single line:

```
%map:#role%^_%map:#name%^
```

You should interpret this as the value of the `#role` administrative property, followed by an underscore, followed by the value of the `#name` administrative property. If you look at the Administrative tab, you can see (`#name`) next to Descriptive Name and (`#role`) next to Role.

This is why, in the previous example (renaming an HTML table), the default name generated is `table_customersTable`. If you don't want the ScriptHelper method names of html objects prefixed with the role, you can modify the template file to contain the following:

```
%map:#name%^
```

Searching the Object Map

The Object Map editor offers the following four ways to search the map for Test Objects. Think of them as queries, as shown in Figure 9.6.

- Find Test Objects that scripts use.
- Find Test Objects that no scripts use.
- Find Test Objects using a simple query.
- Find Test Objects using a custom query.

Figure 9.6   Object Map find menu

Searvching for Test Objects Used and Not Used by Scripts

In the context of the Object Map, a *used Test Object* is a Test Object that either appears in the Test Objects folder of a script's Script Explorer or is an ancestor within the Test Object hierarchy in a script's Script Explorer. For example, if you perform a single action in a new script, such as a click on the link to IBM Rational at http://www.ibm.com/developerworks, the Script Explorer contains just one Test Object: the link. However, if you open the Object Map, you see what's shown in Figure 9.7.

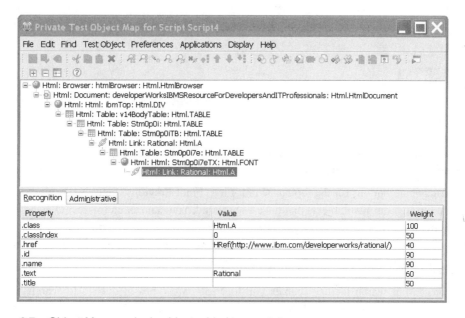

Figure 9.7 Object Map—a single object added to a script

As discussed in previous sections of this chapter, to find the link, Rational Functional Tester must find all the link's ancestors that display in the Object Map. From Rational Functional Tester's perspective, therefore, all the Test Objects shown in Figure 9.7 are *used by* the script.

To search for Test Objects that scripts use, select **Find Used** in the Object Map's Find menu. Rational Functional Tester finds Test Objects required by any scripts associated with the given Object Map and presents the results of the search to you by making three changes to the map editor (see Figure 9.8):

- An arrow appears to the left of each used Test Object.
- The font color of each found Test Object changes to blue.
- Navigation buttons are enabled on the toolbar.

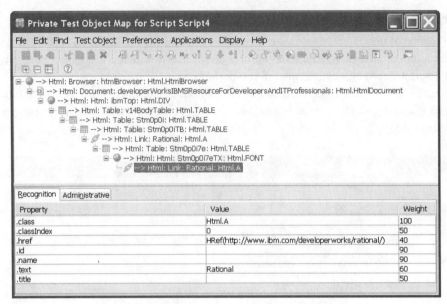

Figure 9.8   Object map search results

Use the navigate buttons on the toolbar (Find: First; Find: Previous; Find: Next; Find: Last) to navigate through the Test Objects that have been found. You can search for Test Objects that are not required by any of the Object Map's associated scripts by selecting **Find Not Used** under the Find menu. The results of the search are presented in the same manner described previously.

Searching for Test Objects Using Filters

The Object Map search facility enables you to create two types of queries to search for Test Objects: a simple query (**Find > Quick Find**) and a complex query (**Find > Find by Filters**).

Searching for Test Objects Using Quick Find

The Quick Find search utility enables you to search for objects using a simple Regular Expression (one without any operators) that can be a Test Object's recognition property name, recognition property value, or either of these (see Figure 9.9).

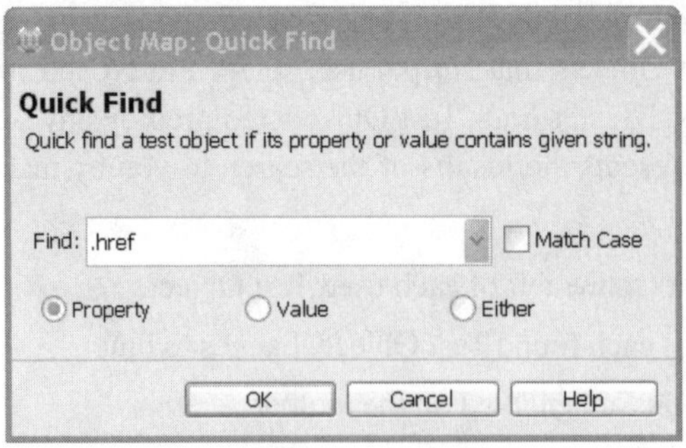

Figure 9.9   Quick Find

If you're familiar with SQL queries, think of the Quick Find utility as a way to create any of the following queries:

- `SELECT * from TestObjects WHERE PropertyName like % <>%`

- `SELECT * from TestObjects WHERE PropertyValue like %<>%`

- `SELECT * from TestObjects WHERE PropertyName like %<>% OR PropertyValue like %<>%`

For example, imagine that an HTML hyperlink has a .href property. If you want to find all the hyperlinks in the map, enter **.href** in the Find field, select **Property** to indicate that you want to find Test Objects with a .href Property, and click **OK**. If you want to find all Test Objects that contain *Rational* anywhere within any recognition (or administrative) property value, enter **Rational** in the Find field, select **Value**, and click **OK**.

Searching for Test Objects Using Find by Filters

To search the Map using multiple filters, select **Find > Find by Filters**. The dialog box shown in Figure 9.10 displays.

Figure 9.10   Find by Filters

The Find Filter Names contains queries already created. To create a query, follow these steps:

1. Click the **Create** button. In the dialog box that displays, select the properties you want to include as query filters. By default, the wizard groups the properties you select under an AND operator (thus creating a query filter of *roughly* WHERE x = <> **AND** y = <>, etc.). If you want to change the operator to OR, right-click **AND** and select **OR**. After you select all the properties you want to use in your query, click the **Next** button.

2. In the Define Find Filter Relationships dialog, set the filter values you want to use for each of the properties used in your query. Select a property in the filter tree and then set the expression you want to express about that property. The wizard allows you to select one of three operators for each filter: IsNull, Exists, and Equals. Equals is what is used most often. In addition to these operators, you can negate the expression by selecting **NOT Relationship**. You can also use a Regular Expression in the value by clicking the Regular Expression button.

3. After you create expressions for each property, click the **Next** button.

4. The last step is to give your query a name. Enter a name and click **Finish**.

5. Your query now appears in the list of Filter Names. To execute your search, select it and click **OK**.

6. If you want to change your filter, select it and click the **Edit** button. You can then add or remove filter properties and change the expressions used for each.

Sharing Test Objects Between Multiple Scripts

A question that is often asked is, "How do you add a Test Object to multiple scripts?" The next question that's asked is, "How do you share Test Objects between multiple scripts?" Recall that making a mapped Test Object available to a script requires not only that the Test Object be added to the script's associated test Object Map, but also that the Test Object be added to the script. This second step is the potentially expensive operation. Even if you had a single shared Object Map for all your scripts and you wanted a Test Object to be capable of being referenced in all scripts, you have to add the Test Object to the map only once, but you then need to manually add the Test Object to each script from the Object Map. Without any scripting, this is your only option. With coding, you have more options.

Scripts access mapped Test Objects through the ScriptHelper methods. If ScriptA has a Test Object added to it, ScriptB can access the Test Object if it can invoke ScriptA's ScriptHelper method. The challenge here is that the ScriptHelper methods are, by default, `protected`, which means they can only be called by classes in the same package as the ScriptHelper class and inheriting classes. The challenge is now how to give other script classes access to protected methods. The following sections explore two possible solutions.

Solution 1

Make the protected ScriptHelper methods `public`. This is by far the simplest route. The ScriptHelper classes are maintained by Rational Functional Tester. In fact, they're recreated every time you record in a script or insert a Test Object or verification point. If you change the access modifier from `protected` to `public` in the ScriptHelper class directly, your changes persist only until the ScriptHelper class is regenerated by Rational Functional Tester. Even if you could change the signatures directly, it could potentially be a huge task: there are two methods created for each

Test Object that's added to a script (a no-argument version and a version that takes an anchor argument and a state flag).

As it turns out, changing the signatures of potentially hundreds of ScriptHelper methods in your Rational Functional Tester project is amazingly simple. The helpers' signatures are controlled by a project template file (located in the templates directory of the Rational Functional Tester project): `ft_scripthelper_method.java.rfttpl` (`ft_scripthelper_method.vb.rfttpl` in Visual Studio). Here are the contents of this file in Eclipse:

```
/**
 * %map:description% with default state.
 *          %map:properties%
 */
protected %helper:testObjectInterfaceName% %helper:methodName%()
{
    return new %helper:testObjectInterfaceName%(
        getMappedTestObject("%helper:methodName%"));
}
/**
 * %map:description% with specific test context and state.
 *          %map:properties%
 */
protected %helper:testObjectInterfaceName% %helper:methodName%(TestObject
anchor, long flags)
{
    return new %helper:testObjectInterfaceName%(
        getMappedTestObject("%helper:methodName%"), anchor, flags);
}
```

If you want the helpers to be `public`, all you need to do is replace `protected` with `public` and regenerate the ScriptHelper classes:

```
/**
 * %map:description% with default state.
 *          %map:properties%
 */
public %helper:testObjectInterfaceName% %helper:methodName%()
{
    return new %helper:testObjectInterfaceName%(
        getMappedTestObject("%helper:methodName%"));
}
/**
 * %map:description% with specific test context and state.
 *          %map:properties%
 */
```

```
public %helper:testObjectInterfaceName% %helper:methodName%(TestObject
anchor, long flags)
{
    return new %helper:testObjectInterfaceName%(
        getMappedTestObject("%helper:methodName%"), anchor, flags);
}
```

To regenerate a script's ScriptHelper class, open the script and select **Script > Update Script Helper** from the Rational Functional Tester menu.

Solution 2

Create `public` wrapper methods in script classes around the `protected` ScriptHelper methods. This solution involves more work and maintenance because it requires that you create the `public` wrappers for every Test Object you want to share. Because the `public` methods are created by you, this does give you the opportunity to set the method names to whatever name you see fit.

If you choose this approach, you can have Eclipse do a lot (though not all) of the grunt work. Specifically, you can use one of Eclipse's wizards to generate the wrappers for you. They just won't be `public`. To use this wizard, right-click anywhere in a script and select **Source > Override/Implement Methods**. In the dialog box that displays, select the methods in the ScriptHelper class for which you want to create wrappers and click **OK**. Eclipse inserts methods that call the ScriptHelper class' methods. For example:

```
@Override
protected GuiTestObject link_rational() {
    // TODO Auto-generated method stub
    return super.link_rational();
}
@Override
protected GuiTestObject link_rational(TestObject anchor, long flags) {
    // TODO Auto-generated method stub
    return super.link_rational(anchor, flags);
}
```

Be sure you leave `super.<ScriptHelperMethodName>`. If you're satisfied with the method names, the only modification you need to make to each method is to change the access modifier from `protected` to `public`. If you want to change method names, you can, but you need to remove the `@Override` annotation.

Whichever approach you choose (making the ScriptHelper methods `public` or creating `public` wrappers), any script that wants to access a publicized Test Object would do so by first creating an instance of the script class that exposes the ScriptHelper method and then invoking its public methods that return mapped test objects. For example:

```
SomeClassicsScript script = new SomeClassicsScript();
TextGuiSubitemTestObject creditCardField =
```

```
        script.cardNumberIncludeTheSpacesText();
    creditCardField.setText( "5555 5555 5555 5555" );
    script.creditCardField().setText( "5555 5555 5555 5555" );
```

If you want to reduce the number of test object variables in your scripts you have to declare, you can use a style in which you chain your calls:

```
    SomeClassicsScript script = new SomeClassicsScript();
    script.creditCardField().setText( "5555 5555 5555 5555" );
```

All these approaches give you a range of options for making objects in your Maps more broadly available than they are in the standard Object Map use of Rational Functional Tester. Because you are working with the internals of a Rational Functional Tester project with the template-based approach, be careful! Back up your project or export it before you modify any templates.

Summary

In this chapter, you took a tour of the Rational Functional Tester Object Map internals to become familiar with the building blocks from which the Rational Functional Tester Object Map is assembled. You looked at how object recognition works in the Rational Functional Tester and investigated Rational Functional Tester's powerful ScriptAssure and pattern-matching technologies. You also looked at practical power features, such as renaming objects, searching the Map, and sharing mapped objects across a project. With the underlying features of the Object Map in hand, you have the foundation to discuss `TestObjects` at an advanced level (see Chapter 10, "Advanced Scripting with Rational Functional Tester TestObjects").

Advanced Scripting with Rational Functional Tester TestObjects

Jeffrey R. Bocarsly

Objects in a target application are represented in Rational Functional Tester scripts by objects derived from class TestObject. TestObjects *are customarily used for two tasks in your Rational Functional Tester script implementation activities: manipulating Graphical User Interface (GUI) objects (administering clicks, performing data entry, and so on) and capturing data for verification against a baseline. This chapter examines some of the advanced features of the* TestObject *Application Programming Interface (API) that are relevant to these tasks. Because much of this discussion reflects aspects of how the Rational Functional Tester Object Map works, you might review Chapter 9, "Advanced Rational Functional Tester Object Map Topics," before reading this chapter.*

This chapter discusses five broad topics that should familiarize you with some of the layers underlying Rational Functional Tester's TestObjects *and the ways you can take advantage of* TestObjects *to extend the reach of your scripts. The first two topics address some of Rational Functional Tester's basic design concepts underlying the* TestObject *classes, and some of the key requirements for using advanced* TestObject *technology. The third topic provides an extended discussion about how you can use key features of* TestObjects *to handle dynamic scripting situations where you need to exceed the constraints of the Rational Functional Tester Object Map. From there, the chapter moves on to the use of* TestObjects *to handle third-party controls. Finally, the discussion ends with a review of all of the different data-capture techniques available within Rational Functional Tester. Because these topics do build conceptually on one another, they are best read in the order in which they are presented.*

Mapped TestObjects and Unmapped TestObjects

The normal `TestObject` that you are used to working with during recording and script enhancement activities is a mapped `TestObject`. The term not only describes the fact that you access these `TestObjects` via the Object Map, but also serves to underscore the central concept of this chapter: in addition to referencing objects through the Object Map, Rational Functional Tester also allows you to reference *un*mapped objects. In other words, Rational Functional Tester gives you the option, through its API, of accessing objects completely *outside* of the Object Map.

Unmapped objects have a few different names in the Rational Functional Tester documentation—in addition to the term unmapped reference, they are also called bound or found references. This terminology refers to the fact that these references are `TestObject` references that are bound or found outside the Object Map apparatus. In permitting the user to go outside the Map apparatus, Rational Functional Tester provides you with tremendous flexibility, but it also places the burden on you to provide your scripts with what the Map provides under the hood: the setup for finding specific objects and the teardown to clean up after you are finished with your off-map `TestObjects`. For reasons that are mentioned in the next section in this chapter, the usual rule of letting garbage collection take care of your objects after you are done with them doesn't apply when unmapped objects are used. When you go off-map, you are not only responsible for finding your objects, you also are responsible for cleaning up after you are done with those objects.

Unregistering TestObjects

Each time you create a *mapped* `TestObject` by calling a method from the Object Map, you invoke the standard Rational Functional Tester mechanism for attaching to an object in the target application and manipulating or interrogating it. Whenever you do this, Rational Functional Tester takes care of all setup and teardown activities, including disconnecting any `TestObjects` from their targets to let the remote Java Virtual Machine (JVM) or Common Language Runtime (CLR) release any memory resources via garbage collection that might be tied up by Rational Functional Tester. Although `TestObjects` are regular objects (in the JVM or CLR sense), they are unusual in that they can hold references to their target objects in the (remote) target application process. Because of this atypical arrangement, special care is required when destroying `TestObjects`, due to the following possibility: if Rational Functional Tester holds on to a reference to a target object when the target application has abandoned that object to garbage collection, *the garbage collector will not collect the object due to Rational Functional Tester's reference to it*. Memory is not released, which ultimately can lead to unpredictable behavior. Under normal recording and playback circumstances, all the required cleanup activity is handled under the hood by Rational Functional Tester.

However, when you create your own unmapped references, Rational Functional Tester assumes that you are taking responsibility for all aspects of `TestObject` management, including cleanup activities. Termination of script execution in this case *does not* automatically result in cleanup of bound references. If you do not handle bound reference cleanup in your code, the situation described previously with Rational Functional Tester holding on to bound references to remote objects that are not garbage collected by their own virtual machines can occur. This problem happens with any number of bound references, but it can become especially pronounced if your script creates a large number of bound references that are not cleaned up. In this case, a large amount of memory might be involved, which results in resource constraints and the unpredictable behavior already mentioned. This is why bound references must be explicitly cleaned up, or *unregistered*.

Bound references are unregistered by calling one of the `unregister` methods (`obj.unregister()`, `unregister(Object[])`, or `unregisterAll()`). These method calls mean that you can release bound references on an individual basis, in groups, or all at once. Individual bound references are released using the `obj.unregister()` method call, where `obj` is a bound reference. If you have an array of bound references, the `unregister(Object[])` method is used; all current bound references can be released with `unregisterAll()`. It is also useful to note that the method `getRegisteredTestObjects()` returns an array of all currently bound `TestObject` references.

Finding Objects Dynamically

There are a number of reasons why you might want to discover objects dynamically. Typically, the need to do this occurs when target objects are in some way created on the fly, and there is no way to capture key recognition properties in the Object Map at design time, because they are not determined until run time. In this situation, a strategy that works well is to record into the Object Map a stable non-dynamic parent object, and then to use one of the methods in the Rational Functional Tester API to dynamically hook the interesting objects that have instance-based recognition properties.

Obtaining Bound TestObject References

The Rational Functional Tester API contains multiple methods that dynamically return bound references:

```
getChildren()
getMappableChildren()
getParent()
getMappableParent()
getTopParent()
getTopMappableParent()
getOwnedObjects()
getOwner()
find()
getSubitem()
getTopObjects()
```

Before you look at these methods in detail, a few concepts need to be defined. On looking at this list, you can see that three of the methods contain the term Mappable. As noted in Chapter 3,

"General Script Enhancements," Rational Functional Tester has a concept of a `mappable` object, which does not mean that an object can or cannot be mapped; rather, a `mappable` object refers to an object that is *useful* to have mapped. In other words, objects that are not *interesting* from a Rational Functional Tester perspective are not considered mappable. Usually, objects are not mappable because they do not hold interesting application data or controls.

Another concept from the list of methods is that of the `top` object, or the top-level window. The top-level window of an application is the window at the root of the application window hierarchy. In the Windows operating system, top-level windows are windows that technically are not child windows of other windows but *are* parent windows of other windows (however top-level windows act in some ways as children of the desktop window). Each top-level window is the parent of its' application window hierarchy.

A final concept that appears implicitly in the names of the methods in the list is the idea of owned and owner objects and parent and child objects. These two sets of terms reflect two parallel hierarchies that exist together in the Windows operating system, the owner/owned and the parent/child hierarchies. In the parent/child hierarchy, children are contained by parents and inherit from their parents. Windows that are owned are not constrained by their owners in this way—ownership is typically a relationship *between* top-level windows (for example, usually a dialog is owned by a top-level window, but is not its child; both the dialog and its owner are top-level windows). Owned windows, however, have to follow certain state rules that rely on the state of their owners.

With these concepts, it becomes easy to understand what most of the methods in our list do. For example, `getChildren()` returns an array of `TestObjects` representing all of an object's children, whereas `getMappableChildren()` children returns a `TestObject` array of just the mappable children. A similar relationship exists for the pair `getParent()` and `getMappableParent()` and the pair `getTopParent()` and `getTopMappableParent()`. The methods `getOwner()` and `getOwnedObjects()` likewise return `TestObjects` representing an object's owner and owned objects.

All the methods discussed are methods of the `TestObject` class, and calls into these methods are straightforward: none of them takes an argument, and they return a `TestObject` reference or an array of `TestObject` references.

The remaining methods in the "bound reference" list are a bit special, and they require a more detailed examination. The first of these is the `find()` method, which has a couple of overloaded versions that make it a powerful tool for obtaining references to `TestObjects`. In its simplest form, you can call `find()` with no arguments on any `TestObject`, and it returns a bound reference to that object. However, if you provide `find()` with a `Subitem` argument defining search criteria, it acts as a powerful search engine to *find* objects that satisfy your search criteria.

To see how this version of `find()` works, consider the problem of a table in a web page that contains variable links—imagine the links represent files that are uploaded by users for other users to download. Figure 10.1 shows a sample page that can be used to illustrate this—the links change every time the page is loaded (the page is included in the Supplementary material for the text at www.ibm.com/developerworks/rational/library/09/testengineeringrft/index.html).

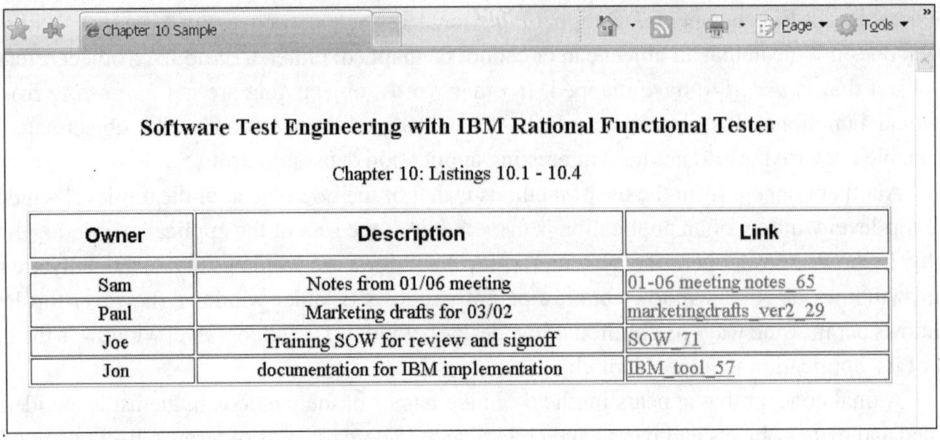

Figure 10.1   A sample web page with variable links

Because the names of the links are unpredictable, you have to search for the links that are children of the HTML table in order to click on a specific link. To construct your search, `find()` takes a `Subitem` argument that specifies the search criteria. There are 16 different types that inherit from `Subitem`: `Anchor`, `Button`, `Cell`, `Column`, `Date`, `Id`, `Index`, `List`, `Location`, `Position`, `Property`, `Row`, `Separator`, `Value`, `Week`, and `Weekday`.

However, `find()` executes with only three of them (`Anchor`, `Property`, and `List`); otherwise, it throws an `InvalidSubitemException` exception. For `find()`, the relevant `SubitemFactory` methods (with the types of their return values) are:

```
atChild() - Anchor
atDescendant() - Anchor
atProperty() - Property
atList() - List
```

You might construct a search with the `find()` method using two properties, the. `"class"` and the. `"classIndex"` properties, as shown in Listing 10.1.

Listing 10.1   A first call to `find()`

Java
```
TestObject [] links = htmlTable().find(atDescendant(
    ".class", "Html.A", ".classIndex", new Integer(0)));
((GuiTestObject)links[0]).click();
```

VB.NET
```
Dim links() As TestObject = htmlTable().Find(AtDescendant( _
        ".class", "Html.A", ".classIndex", 0))
Dim link As GuiTestObject = CType(links(0), GuiTestObject)
link.Click()
```

In Listing 10.1, `find()` searches for a ".class" property of value `Html.A` and a ".classIndex" of 0. Note that the numeric is passed as an `Integer`. The exact same effect can be achieved with a `Property` object, as shown in Listing 10.2.

Listing 10.2   Calling `find()` with a **Property** object

Java
```
Property [] props = {
    new Property(".class", "Html.A"),
    new Property(".classIndex", new Integer(1))};
TestObject [] links = htmlTable().find(atDescendant(props));
((GuiTestObject)links[0]).click();
```

VB.NET
```
Dim props() As Rational.Test.Ft.Script.Property = _
    {New Rational.Test.Ft.Script.Property(".class", "Html.A"), _
    New Rational.Test.Ft.Script.Property(".classIndex", 1)}
Dim links() As TestObject = htmlTable().Find(AtDescendant(props))
Dim link As GuiTestObject = CType(links(0), GuiTestObject)
link.Click()
```

This second syntax using a `Property` object enables you to define as many properties as you would like to use as constraints for your search. The first syntax relies on overloaded versions of `atDescendant()`, which takes at most two pairs of property arguments.

> **NOTE**   In the VB.NET listing (Listing 10.2), the fully qualified name for the Rational **Property** class is required, as .NET has a **Property** namespace, and the compiler cannot distinguish between the two, even with an explicit **Imports** statement.

It is worth noting that there is a significant difference between passing a pair of property-value arguments to `atDescendant()` (as in Listing 10.1) and passing a list of `atDescendant()` arguments using `atList()` (shown in the following code snippet). In the snippet below, `find()` does *not* find *any* target objects, because this search is looking for a link descendant of the HTML table that *itself* has a descendant with a .classIndex property of 0. In Listing 10.1, the search is looking for a descendant of the HTML table with both a .class property of value `Html.A` *and* a .classIndex property of value 0.

```
TestObject [] links = htmlTable().find(atList(
    atDescendant(".class", "Html.A"),
    atDescendant(".classIndex", new Integer(0))));
```

There is another dimension to the use of `find()` that makes it even more powerful than what you have already seen. This is the ability to specify the target value for a property not as an actual value, but rather as a regular expression. To use this functionality, the regular expression pattern is defined using the `RegularExpression` class and is then passed in to the `Subitem` call as an argument. For example, if you want to find the link or links that contain the phrase "marketing-drafts" in the link name, you can call `find()` with a `RegularExpression` argument as shown in Listing 10.3.

Listing 10.3   Calling **`find()`** with a **`RegularExpression`** argument

Java
```
RegularExpression findRe = new RegularExpression(
    "<a.*>marketingdrafts.*</a>", false);
TestObject [] links = htmlTable().find(atChild("outerHtml", findRe));
((GuiTestObject)links[0]).click();
```

VB.NET
```
Dim findRe As RegularExpression = _
    New RegularExpression("<a.*>marketingdrafts.*</a>", False)
Dim links() As TestObject = htmlTable().Find( _
    AtChild("outerHtml", findRe))
Dim link As GuiTestObject = CType(links(0), GuiTestObject)
link.Click()
```

As you can see, the `RegularExpression` constructor takes two arguments in this example. The first is the regular expression pattern, and the second is a boolean specifying whether the comparison is to be case sensitive or not. In Listing 10.3, the comparison is not case sensitive. This enables you to use a simpler regular expression than otherwise; for example, you don't have to specify in your regular expression whether to accept tag names that are both capitalized and not capitalized with the second argument set to `false`. If you want to control every aspect of the matching from your regular expression, just set this argument to `true`. Finally, as a side note, although the `RegularExpression` constructor used here is the one you are most likely to use, it is overloaded—see the `RegularExpression` class documentation for the other versions (Rational Functional Tester Help menu > Functional Test API Reference).

Rational Functional Tester provides another route to locating objects on the fly, and this is the method `getSubitem()`. `getSubitem()` is found in all classes implementing the `IGraphicalSubitem` interface (`StatelessGuiSubitemTestObject` and its descendants) and a few of the classes that inherit from `Subitem`. The method takes `Subitem` arguments that define a location in an object. Usually, the objects this approach is appropriate for are data-rich objects such as menus, lists, and tables. A menu path is defined using the method `atPath()`, whereas a list position is defined using `atIndex()`, and a cell location on a table is identified using `atCell()` in conjunction with `atRow()` and `atColumn()`. With these methods, `getSubitem()` can be used to solve the same problem solved in Listing 10.1 and Listing 10.2 with `find()`—how to click on the link in an HTML table cell without knowing the actual link text at design time. Listing 10.4 shows the code.

Listing 10.4   Using getSubitem()

Java
```
GuiTestObject cell = (GuiTestObject)htmlTable().getSubitem(
    atCell(atRow(4), atColumn(2)));
TestObject [] cellLinks = cell.getMappableChildren();
((GuiTestObject)cellLinks[0]).click();
```

VB.NET
```
Dim obj As Object = htmlTable().GetSubitem( _
    AtCell(AtRow(4), AtColumn(2)))
Dim cell As GuiTestObject = CType(obj, GuiTestObject)
Dim cellLinks() As TestObject = cell.GetMappableChildren
Dim link As GuiTestObject = CType(cellLinks(0), GuiTestObject)
link.Click()
```

Listing 10.4 shows how you can define the cell that you're interested in by its coordinates (4, 2), and then query for its mappable children. Assuming that the only mappable child is its link child, you can use standard Rational Functional Tester code to click on the target link. If there are multiple mappable children, you might want to combine the getSubitem() approach with a find() on the resulting cell to filter out the cell children that are uninteresting.

There is one final method from the list of methods that return bound references for you to review. This is the method getTopObjects(). This method returns all the top-level objects (windows) in a domain that Rational Functional Tester supports, as an array of TestObjects. The ability to access top-level objects in a domain gives the Rational Functional Tester user a way to access all the objects in that domain without recourse to the Rational Functional Tester Object Map. This method is discussed in the next section.

Living Off the Map

Rational Functional Tester, in addition to all the advanced functionality of its Object Map, provides you with the ability to go off-Map completely. This amounts to building your own map, but it certainly is a good option to have, and in some cases, the amount of extra effort required to build an implementation is justified.

The process starts by obtaining a set of objects that represent the running Rational Functional Tester domains. These are a set of special TestObjects called DomainTestObjects. The method getDomains() returns an array of DomainTestObjects that represent all domains that are currently running. Note that there can be more domains running than you are aware of, because, for example, Rational Functional Tester connects to the Internet Explorer browser through its Java plugin, so when you are working in the HTML domain with Internet Explorer, both the HTML and the Java domains are in use. In addition, Rational Functional Tester creates DomainTestObjects for its own purposes, so there are usually DomainTestObjects running that you are not actually using.

You can identify the specific `DomainTestObject` that you need by calling the method `getName()` on each `DomainTestObject` and selecting based on the name. For example, you select the `Html` domain for a web application, the `Java` domain for a Swing application, the `Net` domain for a .NET application, and so on. Listing 10.5 shows a method that implements a simple domain search.

Listing 10.5   Getting a domain's `DomainTestObject`

Java
```java
private DomainTestObject getDomainTestObj(String domainName){
    DomainTestObject [] dtos = getDomains();
    DomainTestObject retDomain = null;
    for (int n = 0; n < dtos.length; n++){
        if(((String)dtos[n].getName()).equalsIgnoreCase(domainName)){
            retDomain = dtos[n];
            break;
        }
    }
    return retDomain;
}
```

VB.NET
```vbnet
Private Function getDomainTestObj(ByVal domainName As String) _
        As DomainTestObject
    Dim dtos() As DomainTestObject = GetDomains()
    Dim retDomain As DomainTestObject = Nothing
    Dim n As Short
    For n = 0 To dtos.Length - 1
        If (dtos(n).GetName = domainName) Then
            retDomain = dtos(n)
            Exit For
        End If
    Next
    Return retDomain
End Function
```

After you have the correct `DomainTestObject`, you can call `getTopObjects()`, and this supplies you with an array of `TestObjects` for all the top-level windows in the domain. When you have your domain's top-level objects, you are living off the Map. Listing 10.6 illustrates how simple this is with the method `getDomainTestObj()` from Listing 10.5.

Listing 10.6   Getting the top-level windows of a domain

Java
```
DomainTestObject htmlDomain = getDomainTestObj("Html");
TestObject [] topWins = htmlDomain.getTopObjects();
```

VB.NET
```
Dim htmlDomain As DomainTestObject = getDomainTestObj("Html")
Dim topWins() As TestObject = htmlDomain.GetTopObjects()
```

With the top-level windows in a domain in hand, you are ready to search the object tree underneath the top-level windows for specific objects. To illustrate, consider the same problem that was solved previously—finding a link of unknown text in an HTML table. The top-level window in this case is the browser, and one way to capture an element of a page would be to use `find()` on the top-level window to obtain a `TestObject` reference to one of its descendants. Listing 10.7 shows how this can be done.

Listing 10.7   Getting descendants of a top-level window

Java
```
private TestObject findMappableDescendant(TestObject parent,
       Property [] props){
   TestObject [] children = parent.find(atDescendant(props), true);
   TestObject childTestObject = children[0];
   return childTestObject;
}
```

VB.NET
```
Private Function findMappableDescendant(ByVal parent As TestObject, _
   ByVal props() As Rational.Test.Ft.Script.Property) As TestObject
   Dim children() As TestObject = parent.Find( _
       AtDescendant(props), True)
   Dim childTestObject As TestObject = children(0)
   Return childTestObject
End Function
```

A few comments about the `findMappableDescendant()` method in Listing 10.7. In this method, the search criteria are assumed to be specific so that only one child is found, and a reference to that child is returned. That might not always be true, and you might want to extend your own code to include other possibilities. Second, the search criteria are defined by an array of `Property` references instead of a single property-value pair, so that you can use multiple criteria. Finally, the code is set up to search only for descendants of our `parent` argument, which is the broadest search—using `atChild()` limits the search to immediate children of the `parent` object and would execute more quickly.

It is worthwhile to reflect for a moment on the use of `find()`. As noted, `find()` is a powerful tool, but on complex web pages or forms, invoking `find()` (especially with an `atDescendant()` argument) might mean that you perform a full (recursive) search of the object tree every time you call your method. That can involve a serious amount of overhead, especially if you use a high-level `parent` object relative to your actual search target. Performing a large search every time you execute can make your scripts run slowly. If you plan to shape your solution this way, test the implications of your approach carefully before deploying your test suite.

You can use the method `findMappableDescendant()` to find a specific HTML table (for example, you can uniquely identify an HTML table in a page by its `.classIndex` property). Once you have the table reference you need, you can identify a specific cell using `getSubitem()` and hook its link (a child of the cell) with `find()`. This is shown in Listing 10.8.

Listing 10.8   Getting a table cell and its children

Java
```
private GuiTestObject getCellChild(
      StatelessGuiSubitemTestObject table, int row, int col,
      String property, String value){
   GuiTestObject cell = (GuiTestObject)table.getSubitem(
      atCell(atRow(row), atColumn(col)));
   // find the cell's child
   TestObject [] cellChildren = cell.find(atProperty(
      property, value));
   GuiTestObject child = (GuiTestObject)cellChildren[0];
   return child;
}
```

VB.NET
```
Private Function getCellChild( _
      ByVal table As StatelessGuiSubitemTestObject, _
      ByVal row As Short, _
      ByVal col As Short, _
      ByVal prop As String, _
      ByVal value As String) As GuiTestObject
   Dim obj As Object = table.GetSubitem( _
      AtCell(AtRow(row), AtColumn(col)))
   Dim cell As GuiTestObject = CType(obj, GuiTestObject)
   Dim cellChildren() As TestObject = cell.Find( _
      AtProperty(prop, value))
   Dim child As GuiTestObject = CType(cellChildren(0), GuiTestObject)
   Return child
End Function
```

The methods assembled provide a simple, live Map implementation, which you can use to build a script for your application. Sample code to find a specific link by cell coordinates (row 3, column 2) and click on the link is shown in Listing 10.9. Listing 10.9 starts with the code from Listing 10.6 and calls the methods developed in Listings 10.7 and 10.8.

Listing 10.9 A sample off-map script

Java
```
// get the domain
DomainTestObject htmlDomain = getDomainTestObj("Html");
TestObject [] topWins = htmlDomain.getTopObjects();
// create the properties
Property [] props = {new Property(".class", "Html.TABLE"),
    new Property(".classIndex", new Integer(0))};
// find the table and cast its ref to StatelessGuiSubitemTestObject
StatelessGuiSubitemTestObject tbl = (StatelessGuiSubitemTestObject)
    findMappableDescendant(topWins[0], props);
// get the cell and its link child and click()
GuiTestObject link = getCellChild(tbl, 3, 2, ".class", "Html.A");
link.click();
unregisterAll(); // don't forget to unregister your bound refs!
```

VB.NET
```
' get the domain
Dim htmlDomain As DomainTestObject = getDomainTestObj("Html")
Dim topWins() As TestObject = htmlDomain.GetTopObjects()
' create the properties
Dim props() As Rational.Test.Ft.Script.Property = _
    {New Rational.Test.Ft.Script.Property(".class", "Html.TABLE"), _
    New Rational.Test.Ft.Script.Property(".classIndex", 0)}
' find the table and cast it's ref to StatelessGuiSubitemTestObject
Dim tObj As TestObject = findMappableDescendant(topWins(0), props)
Dim tbl As StatelessGuiSubitemTestObject = CType(tObj, _
    StatelessGuiSubitemTestObject)
' get the cell and its link child and click()
Dim link As GuiTestObject = getCellChild(tbl, 3, 2, ".class", _
    "Html.A")
link.Click()
' don't forget to unregister your bound refs!
UnregisterAll()
```

As you can see, the methods in the Rational Functional Tester API that make it possible for you to search for TestObjects on the fly give you a powerful set of tools for dynamically working with objects in your target application. As a final (cautionary) thought about dynami-cally tracking `TestObjects`, before you spend time and effort building a full custom implemen-tation, consider whether you can use the Rational Functional Tester Object Map for your needs. The Rational Functional Tester Object Map with its feature set is a robust, flexible solution to the problem of tracking objects, and you might be able to meet your needs with it, rather than expending the effort of building your own custom framework.

> **NOTE**   Remember, all the `TestObject` references used in this discussion are bound ref-erences; therefore, you will need to unregister each of them with one of the unregister methods at the appropriate place in your code. Typically, this can be done at the end of a script; however, if your code generates a large number of bound references relative to the amount of memory you have available, you might have to be more aggressive about man-aging your bound references.

Handling Third-Party Controls

Third-party controls have long been a challenge for automated testing. This is because although the tool vendors have always committed to supporting the standard controls supplied by the IDE vendors and perhaps a selection of the most popular third-party controls, there are always more third-party control packages available than can be conveniently supported by the tool vendors. If your project uses an unsupported third-party control package, you have often been out of luck. With Rational Functional Tester, you are frequently *in luck* because Rational Functional Tester offers you an API to handle third-party controls.

To illustrate how to handle a third-party control with Rational Functional Tester, the fol-lowing discussion uses an open-source .NET control. This is the DevAge SourceGrid control (copyright www.devage.com), which is a flexible and powerful .NET winforms grid control writ-ten in C#. The examples that follow use SourceGrid version 4.11 with the DevAge reference application (you can download the reference application with the DevAge package and run the examples on it without having to write your own application). One presentation of the Source-Grid control is shown in Figure 10.2 (this is Sample Grid 1 in the reference application); the fol-lowing example focuses on this grid.

The General Strategy

When you handle a third-party control that is unhandled by the standard Rational Functional Tester mechanisms, the general approach is to discover the native methods and properties of the unhandled control with the Rational Functional Tester API to learn how to either manipulate the control for testing purposes (for example, create a click event on the control) or to capture control data. Similar to other tools in its class, Rational Functional Tester gives you direct access to the control object and its children. Rational Functional Tester does this not by giving you a live refer-ence to the control in your script, but rather by giving you a bound `TestObject` reference to the

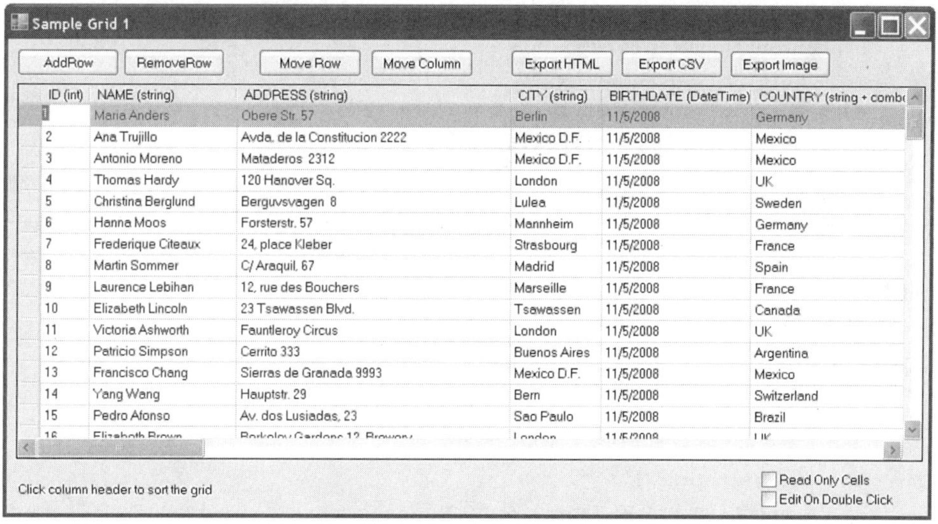

Figure 10.2 The DevAge SourceGrid control

control, just as you saw in the previous section. You can use these bound references to call the native methods and properties of the target control.

Scoping Out the Third-Party Object Hierarchy

The first task with any third-party control is to scope out the object hierarchy, so that you have the information you need about the control to use a bound reference to it. You need to understand what the relationships are between the objects from which the control is composed and the methods on each object that are available for you to call. The simplest way to start doing this is with Rational Functional Tester's Test Object Inspector tool. The Test Object Inspector tool gives a fast and direct way to get a complete picture of object methods and properties. The Test Object Inspector has a significant limitation, however, and that is that it only gives you information about specific objects in the hierarchy. Objects that are deeper in the hierarchy are not visible with the Inspector, so you have to explore the object tree by hand. You can explore with a few simple tools built from the Rational Functional Tester API. The key API method to start with is the `TestObject` method `getMethods()`, which returns an array of `MethodInfo` references that describe the methods each object exposes. You can use `getMethods()` to build a simple method-spy method, which is shown in Listing 10.10.

Listing 10.10 A spy method to spy methods on unhandled objects

Java

```
private void getMethodList(TestObject obj){
    System.out.println("class: " + obj.getObjectClassName());
    MethodInfo [] methodList = obj.getMethods();
```

```
for (int n = 0; n < methodList.length; n++){
    System.out.println(n + ". " +
    methodList[n].getName() + ": " +
    methodList[n].getSignature() + "\t" +
    methodList[n].getDeclaringClass());
    }
}
```

VB.NET
```
Private Sub getMethodList(ByVal obj As TestObject)
    Console.writeline("class: " & obj.GetObjectClassName())
    Dim methodList() As MethodInfo = obj.GetMethods()
    Dim n As Short
    For n = 0 To methodList.Length - 1
        Console.WriteLine(n & ". " & _
            methodList(n).GetName() & ": " & _
            methodList(n).GetSignature() & vbTab & _
            methodList(n).GetDeclaringClass())
    Next
End Sub
```

The getMethodList() method in Listing 10.10 prints each method, its signature, and its class to the Eclipse console. You can use this list to find methods that are likely to help you drill down into the control to obtain references to interesting and useful child objects.

To make this process more concrete, the following discussion works through an example. The example comes from the DevAge SourceGrid (Figure 10.2). The process starts by exploring what grid objects can be captured into the Rational Functional Tester Object Map. This turns out to be only the winform container of the grid control. If you use getMethodList() and pass in a reference to the winform object in the object map, 1,028 methods are returned for the form. Several methods look like they might provide access to the controls on the form (for example, get_ActiveControl, get_TopLevelControl, and get_Children), but the most promising is get_Controls, which returns a reference to the form's controls collection.

After you know the name of the method you're interested in calling, the mechanism by which you get access to target object methods is by calling the TestObject method invoke(). The invoke() method is overloaded, but this example requires only the simplest version, in which invoke() takes a single argument: the name of the method you want to call. When you pass in get_Controls as the argument, invoke() returns a TestObject that wraps the form's controls collection. Because the controls collection is a collection object, you can expect that it has methods to return references to individual members of the collection. In Rational Functional Tester parlance, this is called an indexer, and you can use the method getIndexers() on your TestObject reference (which returns an array of IndexerInfo references) to get information about the indexers that are available on the collection. Listing 10.11 illustrates a call to `invoke()` to get a control collection from the grid's form and a query of the returned collection reference for indexers.

Listing 10.11 A simple `invoke()` example

Java
```
TestObject controls =
    (TestObject)sampleGrid1window().invoke("get_Controls");
IndexerInfo [] controlsIndexer = controls.getIndexers();
for (int n = 0; n < controlsIndexer.length; n++){
    System.out.println(n + ")"+ controlsIndexer[n].getIndexerSig());
}
```

VB.NET
```
Dim controls As TestObject = _
    CType(SampleGrid1Window().Invoke("get_Controls"), TestObject)
Dim controlsIndexer() As IndexerInfo = controls.GetIndexers()
Dim n As Short
For n = 0 To controlsIndexer.Length - 1
    Console.WriteLine(n & ")" + controlsIndexer(n).GetIndexerSig())
Next n
```

In Listing 10.11, the mapped `TestObject` for the application winform (returned by `sampleGrid1window()`) is used to invoke the form's `get_Controls` method. The code then gets a list of the control collection's indexers by calling `getIndexers()` on the returned `TestObject` reference, and each indexer method's signature is printed to the console—indexers are really just enumeration methods. The following indexer information is printed by this code:

```
0) Item(I)
1) Item(LSystem.String;)
```

This output tells you that there are two overloaded indexer methods to call—one takes an `Integer` argument, and the other a `String` (the notation used is discussed in the "JNI Signature Types" sidebar). The first signature offers the convenience of iterating through the collection using an index. By iterating through the collection the collection members can be interrogated for their class names, and if they are `TestObjects`, the class that each `TestObject` wraps. Listing 10.12 shows this approach.

Listing 10.12 Interrogating a collection object with an indexer

Java
```
for (int n = 0; ; n++){
    try {
```

```java
        Object o = controls.getIndexer("Item", new Integer(n));
        if (o instanceof TestObject){
            System.out.println(n + ". " +
            o.getClass().toString() + "; " +
            ((TestObject)o).getObjectClassName());
        } else {
            System.out.println(n + ". " + o.getClass());
        }
    } catch (WrappedException wre) {
        System.out.println(wre.getMessage() );
        break;
    }
}
```

VB.NET

```vbnet
Do
    Try
        Dim o As Object = controls.GetIndexer("Item", m)
        If (TypeOf o Is TestObject) Then
            Dim testObj As TestObject = CType(o, TestObject)
                Console.WriteLine(m & ". " & _
                    o.GetType.ToString() & "; " & _
                    testObj.GetObjectClassName())
        Else
            Console.WriteLine(m & ". " + o.GetType().ToString)
        End If
        m += 1
    Catch wre As WrappedException
        Console.WriteLine(wre.Message)
        Exit Do
    End Try
Loop
```

Listing 10.12 has a couple of interesting features. First, indexers do not broadcast the size of their collection, so the size is unknown at the outset. This is handled in Listing 10.12 by catching a `WrappedException`. This is the second interesting feature in Listing 10.12—what is wrapped by Rational Functional Tester's `WrappedException` class? This is typically an exception class on the *target*. In this case, it is the .NET exception `System.ArgumentOutOfRangeException`. As you can see from the code in Listing 10.12, this exception is caught regardless of whether you use the Java flavor or the VB.NET flavor of Rational Functional Tester.

The output from the code in Listing 10.12 is rewarding because it shows you just the information that is needed (the output is abbreviated slightly to make it more readable):

```
class GuiSubitemTestObject; SourceGrid.Grid
class GuiTestObject; System.Windows.Forms.Button
class ToggleGUITestObject; System.Windows.Forms.CheckBox
class ToggleGUITestObject; System.Windows.Forms.CheckBox
class GuiTestObject; System.Windows.Forms.Button
class GuiTestObject; System.Windows.Forms.Button
class GuiTestObject; System.Windows.Forms.Label
class GuiTestObject; System.Windows.Forms.Button
class GuiTestObject; System.Windows.Forms.Button
class GuiTestObject; System.Windows.Forms.Button
class GuiTestObject; System.Windows.Forms.Button
```

From this output, you can see the `TestObject` types that wrap references to the target application GUI objects. In addition, you can see by class exactly what the target objects are, and this list tells you that the first entry is what you want—a reference to the `SourceGrid` control. With this information, it is straightforward to write some code to pull a reference out of the control collection corresponding to the `SourceGrid`, as shown in Listing 10.13.

Listing 10.13   Using an indexer to search a collection

Java
```
TestObject srcGrid = null;
Integer collectionCount = (Integer)controls.invoke("get_Count");
for (int n = 0; n < collectionCount; n++){
    Object o = controls.getIndexer("Item", new Integer(n));
    if (o instanceof TestObject){
        String cntrlClass = ((TestObject)o).getObjectClassName();
        if(cntrlClass.equals("SourceGrid.Grid")){
            srcGrid = (TestObject)o;
            break;
        }
    }
}
```

VB.NET
```
Dim srcGrid As TestObject = Nothing
Dim collectionCount As Integer = _
    CType(controls.Invoke("get_Count"), Integer)
For n = 0 To collectionCount - 1
    Dim o As Object = controls.GetIndexer("Item", n)
    If (TypeOf o Is TestObject) Then
        Dim testObj As TestObject = CType(o, TestObject)
        Dim cntrlClass As String = o.getObjectClassName()
        If (cntrlClass = "SourceGrid.Grid") Then
            srcGrid = CType(o, TestObject)
```

```
        Exit For
    End If
End If
Next n
```

Listing 10.13 uses an approach that is similar to that in Listing 10.12. However, in Listing 10.13, the `get_Count` method is invoked on the controls collection object to retrieve the number of control references in the collection. This removes the requirement for any exception handling inside the loop because the exact number of members is known.

It is also worthwhile to note that Listings 10.11–10.13 are at least partly for purposes of illustration of how to cull through an object tree. You could accomplish the same thing using a call to `find()` on your mapped `TestObject`:

```
TestObject [] srcGrid = sampleGrid1window().find(
    atProperty(".class", "SourceGrid.Grid"), false);
```

However, if you use this approach, you bear the cost of calling `find()` every time you run your script. With the code shown in Listings 10.11–10.13, you need only to search through the controls collection, which might be a much more limited search, depending on where your target object is in the overall control hierarchy.

With the grid reference obtained in Listing 10.13, you are now ready to see how to capture grid data and otherwise manipulate the grid via a bound reference.

Capturing SourceGrid Cell Data

Now that you have a bound reference to the SourceGrid, you can use it to explore the grid control and how to capture data from the control. If you use `getMethodList()` on the grid, you find among the 970 grid methods a method called `GetCell`. This sounds just like what you want in order to get a bound reference to a cell object from the grid control.

To call `GetCell`, you have to learn about an overloaded `invoke()` method call, which takes not one but three arguments. The first argument of the three is the same as the argument to the one-argument version of `invoke()`—the remote method name. The second argument is a description of the remote method signature (see the "JNI Signature Types" sidebar), and the final argument is an `Object` array of arguments to pass to the remote method call.

The remote method call `GetCell` has the signature "`(II)LSourceGrid.Cells.ICellVirtual;`" according to the output from `getMethodList()`. This means that the remote method call takes two `int` arguments and returns a reference to the SourceGrid type `SourceGrid.Cells.ICellVirtual`. Listing 10.14 shows how to set up this call, using an arbitrary cell (the 5, 3 cell of the grid) for purposes of illustration.

Listing 10.14   Three-argument **invoke()**

Java
```
Object [] rowcol = {new Integer(5), new Integer(3)};
TestObject cell = (TestObject) srcGrid.invoke(
    "GetCell", "(II)LSystem/Object;", rowcol);
```

VB.NET

```
Dim rowcol() As Object = {5, 3}
Dim cell As TestObject = CType(srcGrid.Invoke( _
    "GetCell", "(II)LSystem/Object;", rowcol), TestObject)
```

The first argument to `invoke()` is just the name of the remote method call, as you saw previously. The second argument is more subtle. According to the output from `getMethodList()`, this argument should be: "`(II)LSourceGrid/Cells/ICellVirtual;`". However, with reference types in the return value signature, Rational Functional Tester might throw an `InvalidSignatureException` exception if it doesn't have a reference to the type (even where the signature is clearly correct based on the `getMethodList()` output). This is true even if you use the .NET flavor of Rational Functional Tester for a .NET application because the target application has referenced the type, not Rational Functional Tester. There are two solutions to this problem: one is simply to omit the return type from the signature (which is legal), and the other is to use a completely general typing— "`LSystem/Object;`" for this case. Both appear to work equally well. This gives the full signature "`(II)LSystem/Object;`" for the call to `GetCell` (or more simply: "`(II)`" without the return type) indicating that the method takes two `int` arguments and returns an object reference.

The final argument to `invoke()` is an Object array containing the values to be passed as arguments to the remote call. Listing 10.14 uses the arbitrarily chosen 5, 3 cell in the grid, employing an array of type `Object` containing the `Integers` 5 and 3 to specify the cell to the remote call.

Now that you have a `TestObject` reference to a grid cell (Listing 10.14), you can perform the final step in data capture from the grid. If you run `getMethodList()` on a cell object containing text, the output shows that the cell class is `SourceGrid.Cells.Cell` and has 42 methods. One of those methods is `get_Value` a good candidate method for retrieving the text data from a cell. If you hunt around the grid and check cells in different columns (by invoking `get_Value` and calling `getClass().toString()` on the returned type), you see that `invoke()` returns a variety of different data types (all value classes): `String`, `Integer`, `Double`, `Boolean`, and `DateWrapper`, depending on the data type of the cell you hooked. To handle these different data types, we write a small filter to check for each data type and cast it to a `String`, because `String` is frequently the most useful form to evaluate data with. Listing 10.15 shows the call to `get_Value` and the handling for the return value.

Listing 10.15   Getting values from cells

Java
```
Object data = cell.invoke("get_Value");
String value = null;
if (data instanceof String){
    value = (String)data;
```

```
} else if (data instanceof Integer){
    value = ((Integer)data).toString();
} else if (data instanceof Double){
    value = ((Double)data).toString();
} else if (data instanceof Boolean){
    value = ((Boolean)data).toString();
} else if (data instanceof DateWrapper){
    value = ((DateWrapper)data).toString();
}
```

VB.NET
```
Dim data As Object = cell.Invoke("get_Value")
Dim value As String = Nothing
If (TypeOf data Is String) Then
    value = CType(data, String)
ElseIf (TypeOf data Is Integer) Then
    value = CType(data, Integer).ToString
ElseIf (TypeOf data Is Double) Then
    value = CType(data, Double).ToString
ElseIf (TypeOf data Is Boolean) Then
    value = CType(data, Boolean).ToString
ElseIf (TypeOf data Is DateWrapper) Then
    value = CType(data, DateWrapper).ToString
End If
```

A couple of aspects of the code in Listing 10.15 are worth noting. The data type returned depends on the data that the cell holds, so you need to handle whatever data types your grid might contain. The SourceGrid example has cells that contain the standard numerical types `Integer` and `Double`, along with cells that contain `String` data. In addition, the grid contains cells that have checkboxes, and the data from these cells is returned as `Boolean` data. Rational Functional Tester considers these value classes. One of the types of data returned by the SourceGrid does not appear to be a standard value class, and this is the `DateWrapper` type. In this case, Rational Functional Tester provides its own custom wrapper of a "standard" value class in order to add additional functionality. `DateWrapper` overrides some of the `Date` methods to provide more powerful ways to compare date values.

Manipulating SourceGrid Cell Objects

In addition to data capture, another important implementation task you might encounter is a manipulation of a GUI object. This might mean any of the standard GUI actions, such as entering data into an object, dragging an object, or clicking an object. In addition to presenting data in a

JNI TYPE SIGNATURES

Method signatures for `invoke()` are indicated using *Java Native Interface (JNI)* type signatures. (JNI is Java's mechanism for connecting into "native," or C, platform code.) JNI method signatures use the Java Virtual Machine's [JVM] type encoding. The signature formalism is summarized in Table 10.1.

Table 10.1   JNI Type Signatures*

Type Signature	Java Type
Z	Boolean
B	byte
C	char
S	short
I	int
J	long
F	float
D	double
V	Void
Lfully/qualified/class;**	Fully/qualified-class
[type	type[]

*Available from java.sun.com/j2se/1.3/docs/guide/jni/spec/types.doc.html#597

**Note that the trailing semicolon is part of the signature of any fully qualified class.

These type signatures are assembled into method signatures using the following formalism: `(argType1argType2 ... argTypen)returnType`. There is no delimiter between types in the signature, as there is in Java syntax. Inclusion of the `returnType` in the signature is optional, but inclusion of the trailing semi-colon for object types is not. To clarify the usage, here are some examples*** of JNI method signatures and their Java counterparts:

```
String f();                "()Ljava/lang/String;"
long f(int i, Boolean b);  "(ILjava/lang/Boolean;)J"
void f(long n, int[] arr)  "(J[I)V"
```

***Java Native Interface: Programmer's Guide and Specification, Chapter 12. Sec. 12.3 (java.sun.com/docs/books/jni).

grid format, the sample `SourceGrid` has GUI objects embedded in its cells (checkboxes, dropdowns, and links), and these cells can be employed to illustrate how to use the Rational Functional Tester API to manipulate GUI objects instead of data capture.

Checkboxes

Column 8 of the SourceGrid contains checkboxes instead of text data. There are generally two tasks you need to achieve with checkboxes: data capture to identify the state of the checkbox and direct manipulation of the state of the checkbox. You can capture the state of the checkbox by invoking `get_Value` on the cell object (as previously noted); a `Boolean` is returned that indicates the checkbox state. The following discussion addresses how to alter the state of the checkbox between checked and unchecked.

You can start this task by noting that the class of the cell object for these checkbox-containing cells is different than the class of a regular text-containing cell. A regular text cell is of class `SourceGrid.Cells.Cell`, but the checkbox cells are of class `SourceGrid.Cells.CheckBox` (as shown by `getObjectClassName()`). This suggests that there might be some specific methods for checkboxes in this type of cell, and if you check with `getMethodList()`, you find that indeed there are. Among its specific methods, there are `get_Checked` and `set_Checked`. You can use `get_Checked` and `set_Checked` to manipulate the checkboxes, as shown by the toggle code in Listing 10.16.

Listing 10.16   Manipulating a checkbox

Java
```
if (cell.getObjectClassName().equals("SourceGrid.Cells.CheckBox")){
    Boolean checked = (Boolean)cell.invoke("get_Checked");
    if (checked){
        Object [] arg = {false};
        cell.invoke("set_Checked", "(LSystem/Boolean;)V", arg);
    } else {
        Object [] arg = {true};
        cell.invoke("set_Checked", "(LSystem/Boolean;)V", arg);
    }
}
```

VB.NET
```
If (cell.GetObjectClassName() = "SourceGrid.Cells.CheckBox") Then
    Dim checked As Boolean = CType( _
            cell.Invoke("get_Checked"), Boolean)
    If (checked) Then
        Dim arg() As Object = {False}
        cell.Invoke("set_Checked", "(LSystem/Boolean;)V", arg)
    Else
```

```
      Dim arg() As Object = {True}
      cell.Invoke("set_Checked", "(LSystem/Boolean;)V", arg)
   End If
End If
```

Note that the checkbox object has both `get_Value` and `set_Value` methods, which return or accept the state of the checkbox as `System.Object`, not as `System.Boolean`.

Links

The final column of the sample SourceGrid contains HTML links. For testing purposes, it might be necessary simply to capture the link text and that can be captured, as you saw previously, by invoking the cell's `get_Value` method. However, it might also be required to click a link as part of executing an application transaction. Here, the path you choose depends completely on what methods the cell and grid objects expose. Some cell objects might expose a `click()` method, although this is unlikely to be part of a cell's design, and SourceGrid cells do not. More likely, a cell object might expose a method that returns the cell's coordinates, which can be used to execute a click method. Again, unfortunately, the SourceGrid cell does not. A final strategy would be to iterate through rows and columns and sum their heights and widths to calculate the coordinates of the cell. This supposes, of course, that there are methods to call that enable you to traverse rows and columns and obtain their sizes. However, these types of methods—methods that return row and column collections, row and column objects, and widths and heights—are often part of grid design, and the SourceGrid is no different.

The approach illustrated in the following discussion is to build a small library of methods that can be used to generate the coordinates of the center of a cell, based on the grid's *visible* rows and columns. (Recall that grids frequently have members that are not currently visible due to the scroll position of the grid's window.) This library requires a method that generates the visible rows and columns, a method that takes the visible rows and columns as input and calculates the center of a target cell (which must be visible, of course), and a method that generates a click on the cell.

The first of these methods to generate the grid's visible rows and columns is shown in Listing 10.17. The SourceGrid has a convenient set of methods that reports out the visible grid members *by index*. That is, object references to the visible members are not returned—just the index numbers are, the first column being column 0, the second, column 1, and so on, with the rows handled in the same fashion.

In Listing 10.17, the arguments to the method are a reference to the cell `TestObject` and an `int` value (`ROWCOL`) that tells the method whether you want to deal with a row or a column. This `ROWCOL` argument is used to choose the remote grid methods you invoke.

Listing 10.17   Capturing SourceGrid's visible rows and columns

Java
```
private ArrayList<Integer> getVisibleGridRowsColsByIndex(
    TestObject cell, int ROWCOL) {
```

```
    String rowColMethod = null;
    String rowColVisibleMethod = null;
    TestObject grid = (TestObject)cell.invoke("get_Grid");
    // get the grid row or column method names
    switch (ROWCOL) {
    case 1:
        rowColMethod = "get_Row";
        rowColVisibleMethod = "GetVisibleRows";
        break;
    case 2:
        rowColMethod = "get_Column";
        rowColVisibleMethod = "GetVisibleColumns";
        break;
    default:
        return null;
    }
    TestObject rowCol = (TestObject)cell.invoke(rowColMethod);
    Integer rowColIndex = (Integer)rowCol.invoke("get_Index");

    Object [] rowcolarg = {true};
    // get the visible rowcol indices
    TestObject visibleRowColColl = (TestObject)grid.invoke(
        rowColVisibleMethod, "(Z)LSystem.Object;", rowcolarg);
    // get the count of visible rows/cols
    Integer visibleRowColCt =
        (Integer)visibleRowColColl.invoke("get_Count");
    // iterate to get the indexes of the visible rows/cols
    ArrayList<Integer> visibleRowsCols = new ArrayList<Integer>();
    Integer currRowItem = new Integer(0);
    for (int n = 0;
        (n < visibleRowColCt) && (currRowItem < rowColIndex); n++){
        Object [] arg = {n};
        Integer item = (Integer)visibleRowColColl.invoke(
            "get_Item", "(I)LSystem.Object;", arg);
        currRowItem = item;
        visibleRowsCols.add(item);
    }
    return visibleRowsCols;
}
```

VB.NET
```
Private Function getVisibleGridRowsColsByIndex( _
    ByVal cell As TestObject, ByVal ROW_COL As Short) As ArrayList
Dim rowColMethod As String
```

```
Dim rowColVisibleMethod As String
Dim n As Integer
Dim grid As TestObject = _
    CType(cell.Invoke("get_Grid"), TestObject)
    ' get the grid row or column method names
    Select Case (ROW_COL)
        Case 1
            rowColMethod = "get_Row"
            rowColVisibleMethod = "GetVisibleRows"
        Case 2
            rowColMethod = "get_Column"
            rowColVisibleMethod = "GetVisibleColumns"
        Case Else
            Return Nothing
    End Select
Dim rowCol As TestObject = _
    CType(cell.Invoke(rowColMethod), TestObject)
Dim rowColIndex As Integer = _
    CType(rowCol.Invoke("get_Index"), Integer)
    Dim rowcolarg() As Object = {True}
    ' get the visible rowcol indices
    Dim visibleRowColColl As TestObject = _
        CType(grid.Invoke(rowColVisibleMethod, _
        "(Z)LSystem.Object;", rowcolarg), TestObject)
    ' get the count of visible rows/cols
    Dim visibleRowColCt As Integer = _
        CType(visibleRowColColl.Invoke("get_Count"), Integer)
    ' iterate to get the indexes of the visible rows/cols
    Dim visibleRowsCols As ArrayList = New ArrayList
    Dim currRowItem As Integer = New Integer()
    Dim item As Integer
    Do While ((n < visibleRowColCt) And (currRowItem < rowColIndex))
        Dim arg() As Object = {n}
        item = CType(visibleRowColColl.Invoke("get_Item", _
            "(I)LSystem.Object;", arg), Integer)
        currRowItem = item
        visibleRowsCols.Add(item)
        n = n + 1
    Loop
    Return visibleRowsCols
End Function
```

Now that you have a list of visible rows or columns, a method is needed that can use the visible row or column information, along with the specifics of the cell to determine the coordinates of the center of the cell. Listing 10.18 shows how to do this. As with Listing 10.17, the code is designed to take a `TestObject` argument corresponding to the target cell and an `int` ROWCOL argument that identifies whether the method is to return the horizontal (ROW) or vertical (COL) midpoint of the cell. The method also takes an `ArrayList` argument that contains the return value from `getVisibleGridRowsColsByIndex()` (Listing 10.17). The strategy is to access either the rows collection object or the columns collection object (via get_Rows, get_Columns) and use the `ArrayList` of *visible* rows and columns to obtain references to each visible row or column object (get_Row, get_Column). The heights or widths of each row or column are used to obtain the vertical or horizontal coordinate of the center of the target cell (with special handling for the dimensions of the target cell itself).

Listing 10.18 Finding a cell's vertical or horizontal center

Java
```java
private int getRowColCoords(
        TestObject cell, ArrayList<Integer> visibleRowsCols,
        int ROWCOL){
    String rowsColsMethod = null;
    String heightWidthMethod = null;
    TestObject grid = (TestObject)cell.invoke("get_Grid");
    // get the grid row or column method names
    switch (ROWCOL) {
    case ROW:
        rowsColsMethod = "get_Rows";
        heightWidthMethod = "get_Height";
        break;
    case COL:
        rowsColsMethod = "get_Columns";
        heightWidthMethod = "get_Width";
        break;
    default:
        return -1;
    }
    TestObject rowColColl = (TestObject)grid.invoke(rowsColsMethod);
    int cellRowColCtr = 0;
    // iterate through the visible row/col objs
    // summing their heights/widths
    for (int n = 0; n < visibleRowsCols.size(); n++){
        Object [] arg = {visibleRowsCols.get(n)};
        TestObject item = (TestObject)rowColColl.invoke(
            "get_Item", "(I)LSystem.Object;", arg);
```

```
        Integer rowColHeightWidth =
                (Integer)item.invoke(heightWidthMethod);
        if (n < visibleRowsCols.size() - 1){
            cellRowColCtr += rowColHeightWidth;
        } else {
            cellRowColCtr += (rowColHeightWidth / 2);
        }
    }
    return cellRowColCtr;
}
```

VB.NET

```
Private Function getRowColCoords( ByVal cell As TestObject, _
        ByVal visibleRowsCols As ArrayList, _
        ByVal ROW_COL As Integer) As Integer
    Dim n As Integer
    Dim rowsColsMethod As String
    Dim heightWidthMethod As String
Dim grid As TestObject = _
        CType(cell.Invoke("get_Grid"), TestObject)
    ' get the grid row or column method names
    Select Case (ROW_COL)
        Case 1
            rowsColsMethod = "get_Rows"
            heightWidthMethod = "get_Height"
        Case 2
            rowsColsMethod = "get_Columns"
            heightWidthMethod = "get_Width"
        Case Else
            Return -1
    End Select

    Dim rowColColl As TestObject = _
        CType(grid.Invoke(rowsColsMethod), TestObject)
    Dim cellRowColCtr As Integer = 0
    ' iterate through the visible row/col objs
    ' summing their heights/widths
    For n = 0 To visibleRowsCols.Count - 1
        Dim arg() As Object = {visibleRowsCols.Item(n)}
        Dim item As TestObject = _
            CType(rowColColl.Invoke("get_Item",
                "(I)LSystem.Object;", arg), TestObject)
        Dim rowColHeightWidth As Integer = _
            CType(item.Invoke(heightWidthMethod), Integer)
```

```
        If (n < visibleRowsCols.Count - 1) Then
            cellRowColCtr += rowColHeightWidth
        Else
            cellRowColCtr += (rowColHeightWidth / 2)
        End If
    Next
    Return cellRowColCtr
End Function
```

Note that `getRowColCoords()` in Listing 10.18 is designed to return either a horizontal (column) coordinate or a vertical (row) coordinate, so two calls to the method are required to determine the actual center point of the target cell (one for the horizontal coordinate and one for the vertical). This set of tandem calls is shown on Listing 10.19.

Listing 10.19 Calculate the center point of a cell

Java
```
private Point getVisibleCellCtrPt(TestObject cell){
    ArrayList<Integer> visibleRows =
        getVisibleGridRowsColsByIndex(cell, ROW);
        int cellVertCtr= getRowColCoords(cell, visibleRows, ROW);
    ArrayList<Integer> visibleCols =
      getVisibleGridRowsColsByIndex(cell, COL);
    int cellHorizCtr = getRowColCoords(cell, visibleCols, COL);
    return new Point(cellHorizCtr, cellVertCtr);
}
```

VB.NET
```
Private Function getVisibleCellCtrPt(ByVal cell As TestObject) _
        As Point
    Dim visibleRows As ArrayList = _
    getVisibleGridRowsColsByIndex(cell, ROW)
    Dim cellVertCtr As Integer = _
        getRowColCoords(cell, visibleRows, ROW)

    Dim visibleCols As ArrayList = _
        getVisibleGridRowsColsByIndex(cell, COL)
    Dim cellHorizCtr As Integer = _
        getRowColCoords(cell, visibleCols, COL)
    Return New Point(cellHorizCtr, cellVertCtr)
End Function
```

After obtaining the coordinates of the target cell's center, there is a final task to complete in order to deliver a click to a cell, which involves noting a subtle difference between the grid and cell references. In Listing 10.13, when the grid object is fished out from the form's controls collection, it is cast as `TestObject` with no further examination. Similarly, in Listing 10.14, when a cell reference is obtained from the grid, the procedure again is to cast it as `TestObject` with no further investigation. However, if you interrogate each `TestObject` (grid or cell) using `getObjectClassName()`, you would find that the grid reference is really a `GuiTestObject` reference, whereas the cell reference is a `TestObject` reference. This difference is crucial, because `TestObject` has no `click()` method, but `GuiTestObject` does. Thus, you cannot use the cell reference to click on the cell; you must use the grid reference to do so. This is accomplished by downcasting the grid reference from `TestObject` to `GuiTestObject` and using the cell center point (either `java.awt.Point` or `System.Drawing.Point`) with the overloaded `click()` method (in Java):

```
Point pt = getVisibleCellCtrPt(cell);
((GuiTestObject)srcGrid).click(pt);
```

or (in VB.NET):

```
Dim pt As Point = getVisibleCellCtrPt(Cell)
Dim grid As GuiTestObject = CType(srcGrid, GuiTestObject)
grid.Click(pt)
```

Listboxes

The manipulation of listbox cells in the SourceGrid is a relatively simple matter, because although Rational Functional Tester does not recognize the grid itself natively, it does recognize the `listbox`. So, the Object Map can be used as normal and recording works as normal. The only issue to be dealt with is how to create the `listbox` object so that the Rational Functional Tester can manipulate it. In regular use, this is done with a click on the cell, so you can simply use the solution developed in Listings 10.17—10.19. Although this code was developed to click on a cell with a link, the code makes no reference to the link itself and can be used to deliver a click to any cell.

How Many Different Ways Are There to Capture Data from a Control in Rational Functional Tester?

At this point, you have seen a variety of ways to effect data capture using the Rational Functional Tester API from a target application. In previous chapters, you've seen full discussions of how to use `getProperty()` and the `ITestData` interface manifold for data capture. In this chapter, the additional option of using the `invoke()` method to invoke remote data-related methods on the target was added. In addition to these three key approaches, there is an additional one that is not really a different approach but rather is a combination of techniques you have already seen—the use of an indexer to find an object reference followed by `getProperty()` to capture its data. Listing 10.20 shows the approach using the SourceGrid.

Listing 10.20 Using an indexer with `getProperty()`

Java
```
private String getCellValueByIndexer(TestObject obj, int x, int y){

    Object data = null;
    String value = null;

    Object [] cellCoords = {new Integer(x), new Integer(y)};
    Object o = obj.getIndexer("Item", cellCoords);
    if (o instanceof TestObject){
        data = ((TestObject)o).getProperty("Value");
    }
    if (data instanceof String){
        value = (String)data;
    } else if (data instanceof Integer){
        value = ((Integer)data).toString();
    } else if (data instanceof Double){
        value = ((Double)data).toString();
    } else if (data instanceof Boolean){
        value = ((Boolean)data).toString();
    } else if (data instanceof DateWrapper){
        value = ((DateWrapper)data).toString();
    }
    return value;
}
```

VB.NET
```
Private Function getCellValueByIndexer( _
        ByVal obj As TestObject, _
        ByVal x As Integer, _
        ByVal y As Integer) As String
    Dim data As Object = Nothing
    Dim value As String = Nothing
    Dim cellCoords() As Object = {x, y}
    Dim o As Object = obj.GetIndexer("Item", cellCoords)
    If (TypeOf data Is String) Then
        value = CType(data, String)
    ElseIf (TypeOf data Is Integer) Then
        value = CType(data, Integer).ToString
    ElseIf (TypeOf data Is Double) Then
```

```
        value = CType(data, Double).ToString
    ElseIf (TypeOf data Is Boolean) Then
        value = CType(data, Boolean).ToString
    ElseIf (TypeOf data Is DateWrapper) Then
        value = CType(data, DateWrapper).ToString
    End If
    Return value
End Function
```

Summary

All the handling developed in this chapter gives you the tools to discover target objects dynamically, to work off-Map if you need to, and to capture data from unsupported third-party controls and to manipulate those controls with GUI actions. All these techniques provide extraordinary power for dealing with challenging object architectures that different target applications might offer. However, this chapter's discussion of third-party controls has not included any mention of how it might be possible to use the full Rational Functional Tester mechanism—including the recording engine—against an unsupported control. This topic is examined in Chapter 13, "Building Support for New Objects with the Proxy SDK," where you look at the Rational Functional Tester Proxy SDK.

For Further Reading

Liang, S. *Java Native Interface: Programmer's Guide and Specification*. Reading, MA: Addison-Wesley Pub. Co., 1999.

Gordon, R., Gordon, R., McClellan, A. *Essential JNI*. Upper Saddle River, NJ: Prentice Hall, 1998.

## CHAPTER 11

Testing Specialized Applications

Fariz Saracevic, Lee B. Thomas

Rational Functional Tester is capable of testing a large variety of application types. In most cases, you use Rational Functional Tester in exactly the same manner, even though the applications can be built using different technologies. However, in some cases, you need to provide a lot of capability out of the box (for example, Swing, SWT, HTML, .NET, and so on) because there are instances in which capabilities need to be extended. This chapter helps you understand how to take advantage of these extended capabilities to test applications that are terminal-based or are written using the SAP, Siebel, or Adobe Flex technologies.

Why Rational Functional Tester Won't Test Every Application

Just like other automated testing tools, Rational Functional Tester is somewhat at the mercy of the application. If the application is built in such a way that the internals of the application are exposed, then Rational Functional Tester can interact with it in a rich way. If, on the other hand, the internals are hidden, then Rational Functional Tester can do little when recording its interactions with the application, and playback is likely to fail. In such a case, playback is likely to fail even when the ScriptAssure™ settings are adjusted because the original recording might have ambiguous references to objects.

By way of analogy, imagine a visually impaired person trying to use a completely screen-based, self-service checkout at a store. It might be possible for the person to learn where the buttons are on the screen, carefully pressing at x, y coordinates, starting from some particular corner of the screen. However, if the application is changed and the location and size of the buttons change, the person needs to learn all over again. That's the equivalent of throwing out your recorded Rational Functional Tester script and rerecording.

Contrast this with that same person using a standard 10-key keypad with a raised bump on the number 5. Even if the machine is replaced with a new model and the entire keypad is moved, the fact that the buttons are raised, the number and position of buttons are unchanged, and the raised bump contributes to help the person interact successfully with the machine.

In a similar way, Rational Functional Tester needs a special interface for some classes of applications. Otherwise Rational Functional tester would need to learn how to interact with these types of applications (for example, SAP, Siebel, and so on) by means of x, y coordinates. In all the cases in this chapter, an additional component is used along with Rational Functional Tester, and in all but the first one of the cases, something must be installed and configured prior to making a recording with Rational Functional Tester.

The technologies covered in this chapter are terminal-based applications (sometimes referred to as mainframe applications), SAP applications, Siebel applications, and applications built on Adobe Flex technology.

Extension for Terminal-Based Applications

Terminal-based applications are built on application frameworks that assume the end user has a terminal on his desk, not a desktop or laptop computer. The terminal is connected by a special cable to a mainframe or midrange computer. The terminal would have a limited set of display capabilities and a specialized set of input functions controlled by the keyboard. The display area is divided into a grid of rows and columns, with cells of the grid combined into fields and attributes (such as read-only or foreground and background colors) applied to those fields. Some keystrokes can be entered into any writable field, whereas other keystrokes clear the field of characters, or even send the data. In many applications, the user presses the Tab key to navigate from one field to the next and presses the Enter key to send the data. The application is in a locked state, refusing input, until the response is prepared and transmitted, at which time, the application is unlocked. All transmissions occur over specialized data lines, using a unique protocol that supports the locking and unlocking actions.

However, today most users have replaced their terminals with computers. To connect with terminal-based applications without rewriting them, users use a *terminal emulator* program. This program interacts with the application just as a terminal would and also behaves like a native application on the user's desktop.

To control and verify the application, Rational Functional Tester must interact with the terminal emulator. In turn, the terminal emulator must expose the attributes of the application to RFT and must also allow Rational Functional Tester to send any specialized input characters to the application. Because the terminal emulator program does not alter the way the application works, RFT's Extension for Terminal-based Applications installs its own emulator. This enables the interactions between Rational Functional Tester and the terminal emulator to be optimal.

Prerequisites

The Extension for Terminal-based Applications is supported only for the Microsoft Windows platform for both recording and playback. It is not possible to record or play back these types of scripts on Linux. To use Rational Functional Tester to test a terminal-based application, you must satisfy the following prerequisites:

1. Install and license of Rational Functional Tester version 7.0 or newer.

2. Purchase a license for the Extension for Terminal-based Applications for Rational Functional Tester versions older than the 8.0 version.

You should also collect the following connection settings that your terminal emulator uses to connect to the application:

- The Host name (the name of the mainframe) where the application runs. You can also use the IP address, which is typically in the form of four sets of numbers separated by dots, as in 192.168.1.1.

- The Port used to connect to the application. This is a number of typically two to four digits, with a default of 23.

- The Terminal type, such as TN3270, TN3270E (where the E stands for Extended), TN5250, or VT100.

  - For a Terminal type of TN3270E, also collect the Logical Unit (LU) or pool name.

  - For a Terminal type of TN5250, also collect the Workstation ID.

- The Code page, which controls the types of characters that the terminal accepts and displays. For United States English, this is the default of 037.

- The Screen size, which is the number of rows and columns of characters. This defaults to 24x80, ignoring the mode line.

You might need settings in addition to these, depending on your Terminal type.

Setup Instructions

To use the Extension for Terminal-based Applications, you must create a connection. Refer to the data you gathered:

1. Launch the terminal emulator by clicking on the Extension for Terminal-based Applications icon.

2. In the Connection Configuration dialog box, enter the following information you collected earlier:

Required:

- A name for the configuration in the Connection Configurations dropdown box.
- The name or IP address of the mainframe in the Host name box.
- The type of terminal from the Terminal type dropdown.

Your choice of Terminal Type might cause one of the two grayed-out fields to become active. For TN3270E, you might specify the LU or pool name. For TN5250, you might specify the Workstation ID.

Possibly Required:

- The Port, if it is different from the default of 23.
- The **Code page**, if it is different from the default of 037 United States.
- The **Screen size**, if it is different from the default of 24x80.
- Click the **Advanced** tab, and investigate the Advanced Settings area to see if any of the settings need to be changed.

3. On the toolbar of the Connection Configuration dialog box, click on the **Connect** icon ⚡ to attempt to connect to the mainframe.

4. If you see a successful connection in the Terminal Area, click the **OK** button to save this configuration. If you do not see a successful connection, check the settings you entered above to see if you need to enter additional data or change some of the data you entered.

5. Click the **Disconnect** icon 🔌 to disconnect from the mainframe.

6. Close the Extension for Terminal-based Applications window by clicking the **X** in the top-right corner.

Recording the Test Script

You are ready to start recording the test script against your mainframe application. To start recording the Rational Functional Tester script, follow these steps:

1. Click the **Record a Functional Test Script** button or **File > New > Functional Test Script Using Recorder**.

2. Enter the script name, select the script folder location, and click **Finish** (see Figure 11.1).

3. Click **Start Application** in the recording window to select the **Extension for Terminal-based Applications** option (see Figure 11.2).

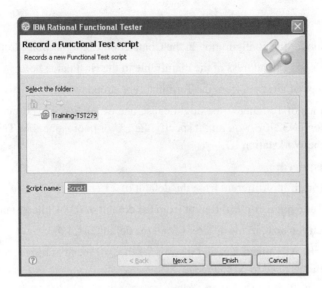

Figure 11.1   Rational Functional Tester Record window

Figure 11.2   Start Application window

4. When the Extension for Terminal-based Applications window opens, select the configuration you defined previously via the Connection, and then click the **OK** button (see Figure 11.3).

5. You can now perform the actions to connect to the mainframe, start your application, and interact with your application (see Figure 11.4).

6. When you have finished interacting with the application and logged off the mainframe, click the **Disconnect** button.

7. Close the Extension for Terminal-based Applications window by clicking the **X** in the top-right corner.

8. Click the **Stop Recording** button on the toolbar.

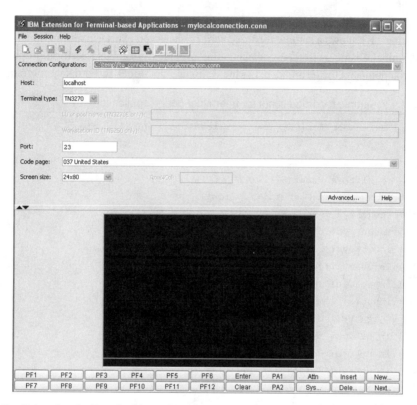

Figure 11.3 Extension for Terminal-based Applications window

Figure 11.4 Extension for Terminal-based Applications connected to an application

You have now completed this test scenario. When you stop the recording, the test script is generated. Listing 11.1 shows a sample recorded script, where you can see confirmation of recognition of the terminal objects with their corresponding events. You can also perform property and data verification points on the terminal, using the Rational Functional Tester data pool framework.

Listing 11.1   Sample recorded script for a terminal-based application

```
startApp("Extension for Terminal Applications - java");

TFrame().maximize();
Host_Text().click(atPoint(82,10));
ConnectUsingtheCurrentConnecti().click();
TFrame().inputKeys("cicsa{ENTER}");
TFrame().inputKeys("cicsa{ENTER}");
TFrame().inputKeys("cicsa{ENTER}");
TFrame().inputKeys("cicsa{ENTER}");
TFrame().inputKeys("mylogin{TAB}");
TFrame().inputKeys("mypass{ENTER}");
Field_6_40_textVP().performTest();
TFrame().inputKeys("myapplication{ENTER}");
TFrame().inputKeys("John{TAB}");
TFrame().inputKeys("Smith{ENTER}");
PF2().click();
disconnectFromTheHost().click();
tFrame().close();
```

You are ready to play back the test script. The procedure is the same as you would use to play back a Rational Functional Tester script against an application that is not terminal-based.

SAP

Rational Functional Tester helps deliver successful functional testing on an application's build on the SAP framework. SAP is designed to help organizations quickly and confidently deliver expected application functionality and reliability to meet the business needs of the on-demand organization.

STILL USING RATIONAL FUNCTIONAL TESTER VERSION 7.X?

If you are using Rational Functional Tester version 7, refer to the "Test Terminal-based Applications with Rational Functional Tester" article on developerWorks (http://www.ibm.com/developerworks/edu/r-dw-r-termbased.html).

There are two SAP access implementations supported by Rational Functional Tester: SAP GUI for Windows and HTML (mySAP). The supported versions of SAP GUI are 7.1, 6.40, and 6.20 with patch level 52 or more. SAP GUI has its own controls that Rational Functional Tester needs to understand. mySAP is accessed via standard browsers (Internet Explorer, Firefox), and special mySAP objects are added to the application. These objects have many dynamically changing properties. Therefore, Rational Functional Tester needs to provide a mechanism to handle the value of dynamically changing objects.

Rational Functional Tester enables you to record and play back test scripts against the SAP UI with reliable recognition against SAP controls, including customized data verification of SAP controls. Rational Functional Tester support is built on top of SAP's GUI scripting framework, exposing all scripting capabilities provided by SAP and adding significant value through the inherent capabilities of Rational Functional Tester.

Prerequisites

To test an application built on the SAP framework, you must satisfy the following prerequisites:

1. Install Rational Functional Tester version 8.0.

2. Support the version of the SAP GUI and if needed, support the patch level.

   You can check the patch level by clicking on the top-left corner of the SAP Logon dialog box and selecting **About SAP Logon** (see Figure 11.5).

Figure 11.5 Checking the patch level

3. SAP client-side and server-side environments need to be configured for the object recognition to work. Nothing extra needs to be installed; however, a SAP Administrator needs to enable some settings on the server-side. There are two approaches:

- You can enable scripting temporarily from the SAP client. The value set using this procedure is lost when the system is restarted. The following procedure is used to enable scripting temporarily from the SAP client:

    a. Start the SAP Logon program and log in to the SAP server.

    b. Start a RZ11 transaction.

    c. Type sapgui/user_scripting in the Maintain Profile Parameters window.

    d. Click Display.

    e. Click Change value in the Display Profile Parameter Attributes window.

    f. Type TRUE in the New value field.

    g. Save the settings and log off the SAP GUI.

    h. Exit the SAP Logon program.

- If the administrator edits the application server profile of the SAP sever to include sapgui/user_scripting = TRUE, scripting is enabled by default when the server is restarted. After the server side is enabled, the SAP GUI (client) needs to be restarted. Rational Functional Tester enables client-side scripting automatically when the recorder starts up.

NOTE   See the "Using Rational Functional Tester to Test SAP applications" technote for additional details (www-01.ibm.com/support/docview.wss?uid=swg21255820).

Setup Instructions

When you test a SAP application, you first need to define the SAP system that SAP GUI client connects to. This example uses SAP GUI version 7.1.

Defining the SAP System

To define the SAP, follow these steps:

1. Open the SAP Logon view and select the **Systems** tab.

2. Click **New Item** and you should get a window like the one shown in Figure 11.6.

3. Select the system that you are looking for or specify parameters in the Search to find it. If you are not able to find your system, but you have system details, click the **Next** button.

4. You need to populate the Description, Application Server, System Number, and System ID fields (see Figure 11.7).

5. Click Finish and test that you can connect to the SAP system.

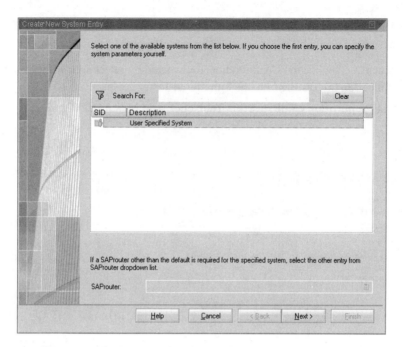

Figure 11.6 Create New System entry

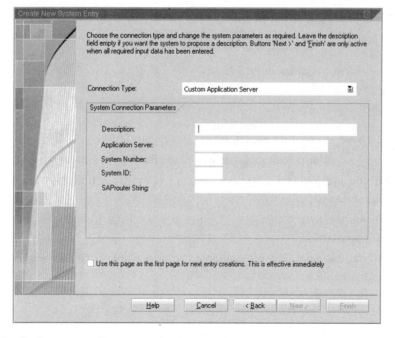

Figure 11.7 System connection parameters

Configuring the SAP GUI for Testing

You need to configure the SAP GUI for testing by completing the following steps:

1. Launch the Application Configuration Tool wizard by selecting **Configure > Configure Application for Testing** from the **Functional Tester** perspective.
2. In the **Application Configuration Tool**, click **Add** button (see Figure 11.8).

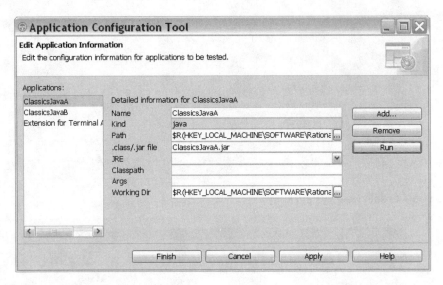

Figure 11.8   Application Configuration Tool

3. Select **SAP Application** and click **Next** (see Figure 11.9).
4. Specify .sal or .sap file or saplogon files or use the Browse button (see Figure 11.10).
   - If you use SAP GUI 7.1, saplogon.exe is available from `C:\Program Files\ sappc\SapGui`.
   - If you use SAP GUI 6.4, saplogon.exe is available from `C:\program files\ sappc\SAPGUI`.
   - If you use SAP GUI 6.2, saplogon.exe is available from `C:\program files\ SAP\FrontEnd\SAPGUI`.

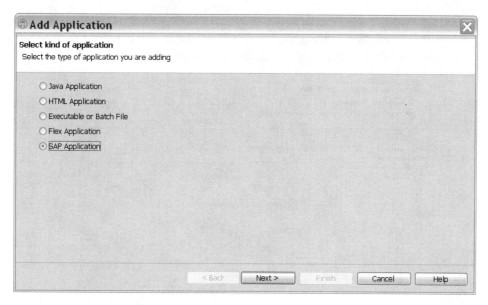

Figure 11.9 Add Application

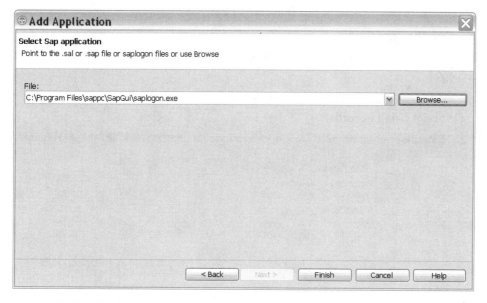

Figure 11.10 Add Application: select SAP Application

5. Click **Finish**. Notice that **saplogon** displays in the Applications list in the Application Configuration Tool. You can provide a different name at this point. For this exercise, select SAP Logon. An example of this is shown in Figure 11.11.

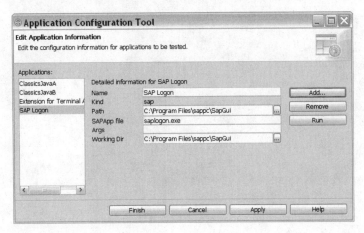

Figure 11.11 Application Configuration Tool with the SAP Logon choice

6. Click either **Finish** or **Apply** to save your changes.

Recording the Test Script

You are ready to start recording the test script against your SAP application. To do so, follow these steps:

1. Click the **Record a Functional Test Script** button or **File > New > Functional Test Script Using Recorder**.

2. Enter the script name, select the script folder location, and then click **Finish** (see Figure 11.12).

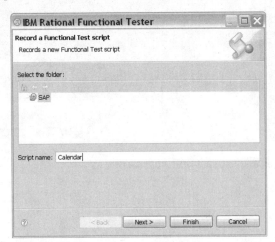

Figure 11.12 Rational Functional Tester Record window

3. Click **Start Application** in the recording window to select the **SAP Logon** that was defined previously (see Figure 11.13).

Figure 11.13 Start Application window

4. From the SAP Logon window that opens, select the system that you want to test, and then click the **Log On** button (see Figure 11.14).

Figure 11.14 SAP Logon window

5.   Enter your user credentials in the SAP Welcome screen (see Figure 11.15).

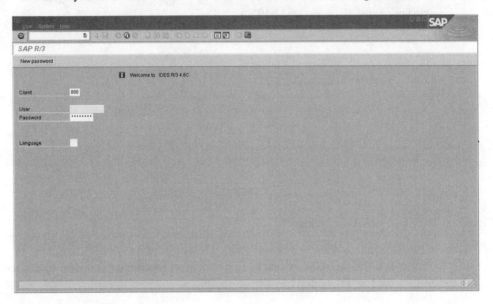

Figure 11.15   SAP Welcome screen

6.   After supplying your user credentials, you can perform actions against the application
under test. For this demonstration, select the **Own calendar** under **Appointment
Calendar** (see Figure 11.16).

Figure 11.16   Selections available under Appointment Calendar

7. Close the appointment calendar by clicking the round red icon with the X. Then close SAP by clicking the X in the top-right corner.

8. Select **Yes** in the Log Off window (see Figure 11.17).

Figure 11.17 Log Off window

You have completed this test scenario. When you stop the recording, the test script is generated. Listing 11.2 shows a recorded sample test script, where you can see confirmation of recognition of the SAP GUI objects, with their corresponding events. You can also perform property and data verification points on the SAP GUI, using the Functional Tester data pool framework.

Listing 11.2 Sample recorded script for a SAP application

```
startApp("SAP Logon");

// Window: saplogon.exe: SAP Logon 710
_LogOnbutton().click(atPoint(35, 18));

// Window: SAPR3
window_sapR3().resizeWorkingPane(166, 25, false);
text_rsystbname().setText("user0001");
text_rsystbcode().setText("********");
text_rsystbcode().setFocus();
text_rsystbcode().setCaretPosition(3);
button_enter().press();

// Window: SAPEasyAccess
tree_sapTableTreeControl1().expandNode(atPath("SAP menu->Office"));
tree_sapTableTreeControl1().expandNode(
               atPath("SAP menu->Office->Appointment Calendar"));
```

```
tree_sapTableTreeControl1().setSelectedNode(
            atPath("SAP menu->Office->Appointment Calendar->Own"));
tree_sapTableTreeControl1().setTopNode(atPath("Favorites"));
tree_sapTableTreeControl1().doubleClickNode(
            atPath("SAP menu->Office->Appointment Calendar->Own"));

// Window: DisplayAppointmentsFirstName_User000LastName_User000
calendar_sapCalendarControl1().setFirstVisibleDate(atDate(5, 12, 2008));
button_exit().press();

// Window: SAPEasyAccess
button_logOff().press();

// Dialog: LogOff
button_yes().press();

// Window: saplogon.exe: SAP Logon 710
sapLogon710window(ANY, MAY_EXIT).close();
```

As you can see, SAP password is recorded as `text_rsystbcode().setText(********)`. Rational Functional Tester tool records the password entered as it appears in the password field, and it cannot read the encrypted value. Therefore, before playing back the script, be sure to **replace** the recorded password with the actual password in the script.

You are ready to play back the test script. The procedure is the same as when using the Rational Functional Tester against non-SAP applications.

Enabling SAP Support for Preexisting Rational Functional Tester Projects

You can use Rational Functional Tester SAP support for a project that was created using the earlier versions of Rational Functional Tester. You must add two new templates (one for script headers and one for script helper headers) to the project. You will also need to update the build or reference information for the project. You can use the following steps to enable SAP support for pre-existing Rational Functional Tester projects:

1. In the Rational Functional Test Projects view, right-click the project and select the **Properties** option.
2. In the Properties dialog box, select **Functional Test Script Templates** from the navigation list.

3. Select the template type **Script Helper: Header of the file**.

4. If you have not customized this template, you can upgrade it by clicking the **Restore Defaults** button.

5. Add the line `import com.rational.test.ft.object.interfaces.SAP.*;` in the import section of the template.

6. After modifying the template, click the **Apply** button.

7. Select the template type **Script: Header of the file** and add the same line in the import section of the template.

8. Finally, right-click the project again in the Functional Test Projects view and click Reset Java Build Path.

Each member of your team must perform this last step, because the **Java Build Path** is local to each project on each machine.

> **NOTE** If you are using Rational Functional Tester version 7, refer to the "Effectively Use the IBM Rational Functional Tester Extension for SAP Solutions" article on developerWorks (http://www.ibm.com/developerworks/rational/library/07/0126_saracevic/).

Siebel

Rational Functional Tester helps deliver successful functional testing on an applications build on the SAP framework. SAP is designed to help organizations quickly and confidently deliver expected application functionality and reliability to meet the business needs of the on-demand organization.

When you interact with a Siebel application, the Siebel system downloads ActiveX controls into your browser. These are special Siebel controls that do not behave like the standard HTML controls you would use to interact with any non-Siebel website. Because these controls are special, Rational Functional Tester must be assisted to work with them. Otherwise, your scripts will record successfully, but will not play back correctly.

You can obtain a package known as Siebel Test Automation which will permit Rational Functional Tester to interact with the Siebel ActiveX controls, as seen in the diagram contained in Figure 11.18.

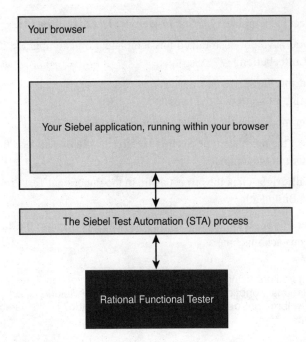

Figure 11.18   Siebel Test Automation architecture

The Siebel ActiveX controls come in two types: Standard Interactivity (SI) and High Inter-activity (HI) objects. The Rational Functional Tester Extension supports both types. The HI objects can be referenced in one of two ways; see the "Recording the Test Script" section. HI support also requires an additional framework to be downloaded to your browser.

Prerequisites

To use Rational Functional Tester to test an application built on the Siebel framework, you must satisfy these prerequisites:

- Rational Functional Tester for Siebel requires Rational Functional Tester 7.0 or greater. The capability to record and play back against Siebel applications is included in Rational Functional Tester itself; you do not need to download or install an extension for Rational Functional Tester or modify your Rational Functional Tester installation in any way.

- Rational Functional Tester for Siebel only works for Rational Functional Tester running on Windows. You cannot use Rational Functional Tester on Linux to either record or play back against your Siebel application, because the Siebel Test Automation package only works on Windows.

- Using Rational Functional Tester to record a script for a Siebel application requires that you buy a license, the Siebel Test Automation license from Oracle, and correctly make the Siebel Test Automation package available on the Siebel server. Rational Functional Tester itself is not modified.

- Rational Functional Tester can test applications running under Siebel versions 7.7, 7.8, and 8.0.

- You must have the Java Runtime Engine (JRE) installed and enabled in your browser. If this is not the case, you will receive an error when trying to record with Rational Functional Tester. However, the error dialog will instruct you in how to download and configure the correct JRE.

Setup Instructions

When you are testing a Siebel application, you first need to install and enable the STA on the Siebel server. You must also activate test automation on the Siebel server. Finally, you Install and Enable the STA on the Siebel Server. To do this, refer to your documentation from Oracle.

Activating Test Automation on the Siebel Server

To activate test automation on the Siebel server, open the **.CFG** file for the applications that you are testing, and set the **EnableAutomation** and **AllowAnonUsers** switches to TRUE in the **SWE** section:

```
[SWE]
...
EnableAutomation = TRUE
AllowAnonUsers = TRUE
...
```

Configuring a New Application for Testing Within RFT

Within RFT, configure your application for testing by following these steps:

1. Create a new entry from the Configure menu.
2. Select Configure Applications for Testing.
3. Add a new browser-based application.

On the end of the URL you normally use to access your application, add "?SWECmd=AutoOn." This tells the Siebel Web Engine to generate test automation information for Siebel applications. So, if your original URL looks like this:

http://hostname/callcenter/start.swe

enter this as the URL in the Configure Applications for Testing dialog:

http://hostname/callcenter/start.swe?SWECmd=AutoOn

If the STA and SWE are installed correctly on your Siebel server, and if you have correctly changed the URL that Rational Functional Tester will use, then the first time you try to create a recording against your Siebel application, the SWE and STA will combine to download and install STA components from the Siebel server to the workstation where Rational Functional Tester is running. This one-time installation may take a few minutes. You can confirm that it has occurred successfully by looking in the Task Manager on the Windows system where Rational Functional Tester is installed; you should see an entry for SiebelAx_Test_Automation_ *nnnnn*.exe, where the value of *nnnnn* will depend on your version of the STA. It should look similar to what is displayed in Figure 11.19.

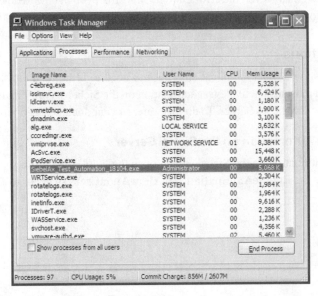

Figure 11.19   Process table showing STA running on Rational Functional Tester workstation

Recording the Test Script (Siebel)

When you are ready to record, you need to make one more decision. By default, the Rational Functional Tester tool records using the repository name, but it can record Siebel HI controls by using the name of the user interface (UI). You might prefer to use the UI name because it makes your script easier to compare to the application. See Figure 11.20.

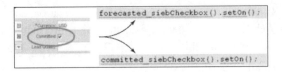

Figure 11.20   Repository name ("forecasted") versus UI name ("committed') for the Committed checkbox

If you want to have your scripts use the UI name, use `regedit` to create a new registry key named `HKEY_CURRENT_USER/Software/Rational Software/Rational Test/8` of type `REG_DWORD`, and set its Data value to `1`.

Security Warning Window

When you start the Rational Functional Tester tool with your Siebel application for the first time, the Siebel High Interactivity Framework might be loaded. If a Security Warning dialog box displays, select Yes to install and run the Siebel High Interactivity Framework.

Siebel Browser Check

If you do not have the JRE configured to run with your browser, a window titled Siebel Browser Check displays, stating that you do not have the Sun Java Runtime Environment 1.4.1.02 or higher installed. If that happens, you need to install a supported version of the Java Runtime Engine (see the Details section in the Siebel Browser Check window).

To record the Functional Tester script, follow these steps:

1. Click the **Record a Functional Test Script** button or choose **File > New > Functional Test Script Using Recorder**.
2. Enter the script name, select the script folder location, and click **Finish**.
3. Click **Start Application** in the recording window to select the new application that you configured previously.
4. Interact with your Siebel application under test exactly as you would if you were not recording in Rational Functional Tester.
5. Log out of your Siebel application and close it as you normally would do.
6. Stop the Rational Functional Tester recording.

You have completed this test scenario. When you stop the recording, the test script is generated. Listing 11.3 shows a recorded sample test script, where you can see confirmation of recognition of the Siebel GUI objects with their corresponding events. You can also perform property and data verification points on the Siebel GUI, using the Functional Tester data pool framework.

Listing 11.3   Portion of a recorded script for a Siebel application

```
pageTabList_siebPageT
abs().gotoScreen("Contacts Screen");
pageTabList_siebPageTabs().gotoView("Visible Contact List View");
button_newRecord().performAction();
text_firstName().setText("John");
text_lastName().setText("Smith");
text_emailAddress().performTest(EmailAddress_TextVP());
```

You are ready to play back the test script. The procedure is the same as when using the Rational Functional Tester against nonSiebel applications.

NOTE   If you are using Rational Functional Tester version 7, refer to the "IBM Rational Functional Tester Extension for Siebel Solutions" article on developerWorks (www.ibm.com/developerworks/rational/library/07/0109_saracevic/).

Troubleshooting

Two common troubleshooting issues are the timeout that is too short for client automation and the need to use Siebel 7.8 scripts for a Siebel 7.7 installation. These issues are addressed next.

Configuring the Client Automation Server Timeout

The Client Automation Server (CAS) provides a mechanism to configure a timeout on calls that can result in a stalled system. By default, this timeout is set to one second, but you can configure this in the ivory.properties file, which is found in your Rational Functional Tester installation folder, by setting the `rational.test.ft.siebel.cas_submit_timeout` to the value that you prefer.

Reverting to Siebel 7.7 with Your Siebel 7.8 Rational Functional Tester Scripts

Rational Functional Tester V7.0 does not recognize Siebel 7.7 controls if you revert your server installation back to Siebel 7.7 from Siebel 7.8. When you start Siebel 7.8, Microsoft Internet Explorer® installs the latest Microsoft ActiveX® objects for Siebel. Therefore, if you try to record by using the Rational Functional Tester tool on Siebel 7.7 after you have used Siebel 7.8, the software cannot recognize the Siebel 7.7 controls.

The workaround for this situation is to remove the Siebel ActiveX objects (for example, Siebel High Interactivity Framework, Siebel Test Automation) from the C:\WINDOWS\Downloaded Program Files folder, and then try recording with the Siebel 7.7 application again.

Adobe Flex

Adobe Flex is an application framework that enables developers to create Rich Internet Applications. Flex applications are usually written using either Adobe MXML™, the Flex markup language, or the Adobe ActionScript® language. A .mxml or .as file can be compiled, and then linked with the Flex SDK libraries to produce an Adobe Shockwave® (.swf) file, which is the executable application. This .swf file can run in the AdobeFlash player, but is typically embedded in an HTML wrapper file.

By default, Flex does not expose its controls so that they can be used by Rational Functional Tester. There are two ways to use Rational Functional Tester with a Flex application:

- **Compile-time automation support**—This method requires that a developer compile the application with the Flex SDK libraries, Flex Automation Framework libraries, and Rational Functional Tester adapter. However, multiple Flex applications that have each been compiled using this method can all be tested simultaneously; this is useful if your website uses several applications, particularly if they also communicate with one another. In fact, all the application SWF files can even be embedded into a single HTML page to avoid pagination during testing. This method works if the application is deployed on a web server machine that is different from the machine where Rational Functional Tester is executed, or if they are both on the same machine. This method has three different techniques that can be used to enable the application. The URL is unchanged. Note that the application that is tested by Rational Functional Tester is identical to the applications that are deployed into production because they are created by different builds.

- **Run-time automation support**—This method does not require any recompile of the application, but does require the one-time compilation of the RuntimeLoader.mxml file with Flex SDK libraries, Flex Automation Framework libraries, and Rational Functional Tester adapter according to the Flex SDK version. After the mxml is compiled to RuntimeLoader swf, it can be used to test any Flex application The user can test one or more Flex applications by passing the name(s) of the application(s) as a list of comma-separated .swfs in the URL. The applications must be deployed to a machine different from the one where Rational Functional Tester is installed. The method consists of a single technique. The URL must include an additional parameter. Because the applications are not rebuilt, the production builds can be tested with this method.

Prerequisites

You need to validate a few prerequisites to ensure that Rational Functional Tester can test an application built on the Flex framework:

- A supported version of the Adobe Flex framework is installed
- The Flex Automation Package is deployed on the web server
- You use Flex® Builder™ 2.0.1 or later
- You use Flex SDK 2.0 or later
- You have installed the Flex Automation Framework

Setup Instructions

Rational Functional Tester requires an enablement library to test a Flex application. You have two options:

- Recompile the application to include the enablement library
- Use a runtime version of the enablement library

If you recompile the application, you can test it without using a web server. If you do deploy to a web server, you can use the same process as you would if the application had not been recompiled. In addition, you can test multiple enabled Flex applications using a single HTML page.

If you cannot recompile the application (as is the case if you do not have access to the source) or simply prefer not to recompile it, you can use the runtime enablement library. With this method, you must deploy the application to a web server, but you must also change the deployment process to include the enablement library.

The following sections describe each option for enabling your application. There are two to recompile your application, whereas using the runtime enablement library has only a single method.

Recompiling the Application

You can recompile your application using one of two methods:

- Using Flex Builder
- Using the Flex command-line compiler

When you have recompiled it, you need to embed the application in an HTML wrapper (if it does not already have one). If you use a web server instead of testing locally, you need to deploy all the recompiled components. The following sections describe these actions.

Recompiling the Application Using Flex Builder

If you have Flex Builder, you can configure it to compile your Flex application with the enablement libraries included. To recompile your application, you need to add files to the Flex build environment:

1. Copy the `automation_agent.swc` file from the *<flex automation install folder>*/frameworks/libs directory to the *<flex builder install folder>*/Flex SDK 2/frameworks/libs directory.

2. Copy the `automation_agent_rb.swc` file from the *<flex automation install folder>*/frameworks/locale/en_US directory to the *<flex builder install folder>*/Flex SDK 2/frameworks/locale/en_US directory.

   This path is for the en_US locale (U.S. English). If you use a different locale, replace en_US with that locale. By default, the Flex automation install directory is C:\Program Files\Adobe\Flex Automation, and the Flex builder install directory is C:\Program Files\Adobe\Flex Builder 2.

3. Start Flex Builder.

4. Create or select your Flex project.

5. Click **Select Project > Properties > Flex Compiler**.

6. Enter the following code in the Additional compiler arguments field:

```
-Include-libraries "<Flex Builder install folder>\<Flex SDK folder>
\frameworks\libs\automation.swc" "<Flex Builder install folder>\<Flex
SDK folder>
```

```
\frameworks\libs\automation_agent.swc" "<Flex Builder install
folder>\<Flex SDK folder>
\frameworks\libs\automation_charts.swc" "<RFT install folder>\Functional
Tester\bin\rft.swc"
```

NOTE You need the `automation_charts.swc` file only if the application contains charting controls.

---

7. Click **OK** to save your changes.

8. Click **OK** to close the Properties dialog box.

9. Compile your Flex sample application.

10. Open the application's .mxml file in Flex Builder. (Use the example filename `compiletime.mxml`.)

The output files from the compilation are `compiletime.swf` and `compiletime.htm`. The .htm file is an HTML wrapper that is generated by Flex Builder in the applications directory. This HTML is ready to be tested by Rational Functional Tester.

Recompiling the Application Using the Command Line

If you do not have Flex Builder, you can compile the source with the Flex SDK libraries, Flex Automation libraries, and Rational Functional Tester adapter via the command line. You do this by running the batch file buildapplicationwithadaptor.bat that can be found in the `RFT install folder>\FunctionalTester\Flex` folder:

1. Copy this batch file to the same directory as your .mxml file.

2. In a command shell, change to that directory and run the batch file with the mxml filename as the argument. For example, if your application is `compiletime.mxml`, type the following command at the command prompt:

```
Buildapplicationwithadapter.bat compiletime.mxml
```

This compilation results in a .swf file. (For the example before it is `compiletime.swf`.)

Embedding the Recompiled Flex Application in an HTML Wrapper

Before you can use Rational Functional Tester to test the Flex application, the application must be embedded in an HTML page. If the page does not already exist or you do not want to modify an existing page, you can create one. For the previous `compiletime.mxml` application, Listing 11.4 shows sample HTML code that you can save in a .html file. You can name the file `compiletime.html`, for example.

Listing 11.4   HTML wrapper for Flex application

```
<HTML>
<HEAD><TITLE>Flex Sample Application Testing</TITLE>
</HEAD>

<BODY>
<HR>
<object classid="clsid:D27CDB6E-AE6D-11cf-96B8-444553540000"
id="myapp" width="100%" height="100%"
codebase="http://download.macromedia.com/pub/shockwave/cabs/flash/swflash.cab">
<param name="movie" value="compiletime.swf" />
<param name="quality" value="high" />
<param name="bgcolor" value=#CCCCCC />
<param name="allowScriptAccess" value="sameDomain" />
<embed src="compiletime.swf" quality="high" bgcolor=#CCCCCC
width="100%" height="100%" name="myapp" align="middle"
play="true"
loop="false"
quality="high"
allowScriptAccess="sameDomain"
type="application/x-shockwave-flash"
plug-inspage="http://www.macromedia.com/go/getflashplayer">
</embed>
</object>

</BODY>
</HTML>
```

The SWF name has been passed as parameter. You can use this same HTML page to test other enabled applications simply by changing the .swf filename.

Deploying the Recompiled Application

You can test your application on the same machine where you compiled it. If you prefer to use a web server, you need to deploy all of the following files:

- Application file (SWF)
- HTML wrapper and wrapper files (the wrapper files can include SWF files, JavaScript files, and other files)
- Module files (SWF)

- RSL files (SWC)
- Helper files such as theme SWC files, style SWF files, and image, video, and sound files

Using Runtime Automation Support

If you cannot or do not want to rebuild your application's .swf file, you can use the runtime enablement library. The runtime enablement library is available in the `<RFT install folder>\`
`FunctionalTester\Flex` folder, and is named `runtimeLoader.swf`.

If you use a version of the Flex SDK other than the 2.0 version, you might need to recompile the runtime enablement library. The source for the runtime enablement library is named `runtimeLoader.mxml` and is also available in the `<RFT install folder>\Functional-`
`Tester\Flex` folder. The `runtimeLoader.mxml` file needs to be compiled with Flex SDK libraries, Flex Automation Framework libraries, and Rational Functional Tester adapter to create the `runtimeLoader.swf` file, using either of the methods mentioned previously.

To use runtime automation support, you need to deploy the runtime enablement library along with the application. For example, if you use Apache for your web server, you copy the `runtimeLoader.swf` file to your `apache\htdocs` directory.

Configuring the Application for Testing by RFT

To configure your application for testing, follow these steps:

1. Select **Configure > Configure Application for Testing** from the Functional Tester perspective.
2. In the Application Configuration Tool, click the **Add** button. See Figure 11.21.

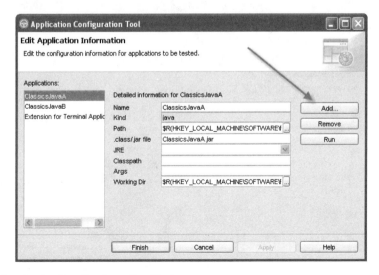

Figure 11.21   Application Configuration Tool

3. Select **Flex Application** as in Figure 11.22, and click **Next**.

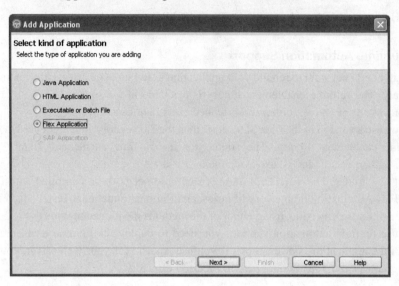

Figure 11.22   Add application

4. For an application accessed via a URL, you would click the radio button for Add URL of Flex Application, enter the URL, and click **Finish**. For a locally installed application, click the radio button Configure Flex application setup, and then click **Next**. See Figure 11.23.

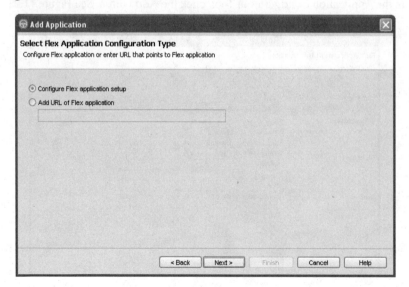

Figure 11.23   Add Application—Select the type of Flex application

5. In the Flex Application Configuration dialog box, enter the parameters for your application. The application name is passed to the HTML page as a query parameter:

    http://localhost/runtime.html?automationswfurl=runtime.swf

    Multiple applications can be passed as follows:

    http://localhost/runtimeLoadingTestMultipleSwfs.html?automationswfurl=runtime.
    swf, runtime2.swf,runtime3.swf

    See Figure 11.24.

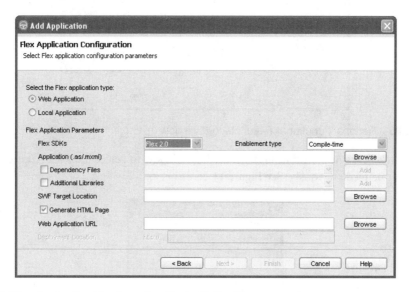

Figure 11.24   Application Configuration Tool with the Flex parameters

6. Click **Finish** to save your changes.

Recording the Test Script (Flex)

You are ready to start recording the test script against your Flex application. Follow these steps:

1. Click the **Record a Functional Test Script** button or **File > New > Functional Test Script Using Recorder**.

2. Enter the script name, select the script folder location, and then click **Finish**. See Figure 11.25.

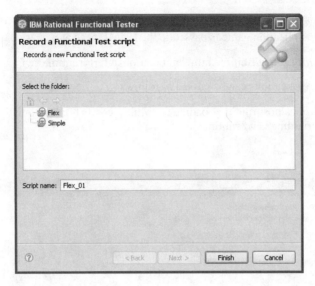

Figure 11.25   Rational Functional Tester Record window

3. Click **Start Application** in the recording window to select the **Flex Application** that was defined previously. See Figure 11.26.

Figure 11.26   Start Application window

4. Perform actions against the application under test.
5. Exit the application as you normally would.
6. Close the browser window.

You have completed this test scenario. When you stop the recording, the test script is generated. Listing 11.5 shows a recorded sample test script, where you can see confirmation of recognition of the SAP GUI objects with their corresponding events. You can also perform property and data verification points on the SAP GUI using the Functional Tester data pool framework.

Listing 11.5   A sample recorded script for a Flex application

```
startApp("Flex Application");

button_customizedButton().click();
button_pressEnter().click();
application_myapp()scroll(atPosition(364),
FlexScrollDirections.SCROLL_VERTICAL,
FlexScrollDetails.THUMBPOSITION);

checkBox_milk().click();
colorChooser_colorpick().open();
colorChooser_colorpick().change("#cc3333");
application_myapp()scroll(atPosition(939),
FlexScrollDirections.SCROLL_VERTICAL,
FlexScrollDetails.THUMBPOSITION);
calendar_index0().change("Mon Nov 03 2008");
```

You are ready to play back the test script. The procedure is the same as when using the Rational Functional Tester against a nonFlex application.

Troubleshooting

If any of the following errors occur, you can resolve them easily yourself.

Security Warning

A security violation notice comes up when the Flex application is started (see Figure 11.27).

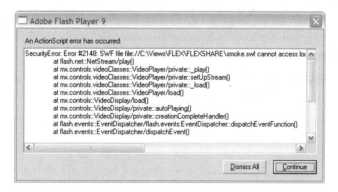

Figure 11.27   Adobe Flash error notification

Make sure that the Flex applications that you test are run from a trusted folder.

1. You can add the OUT directory to the Flex file in the FlashPlayerTrust folder.

2. You can create a FlashPlayerTrust folder in the C:\Windows\System32\Macromed\Flash\ directory:

   a. Create a .txt file and add the path of the application to be tested to this file.

   b. Save this file as Flex with no extension. You can add any number of directories to this TXT file. For example, if the `testMyApp.swf` and `testMyApp.html` files are in the `C:\FlexTutorial` directory, you can add that path to the Flex file.

Flex Plug-in Call Failed Alert

When the application is run from the localhost/IIS server, you might get a notice saying that the plug-in call failed (see Figure 11.28).

Figure 11.28   Adobe Flex error notification

If this happens, check the local security settings of the Internet Explorer ActiveX and plug-ins:

1. Open Internet Explorer.

2. Select **Tools > Internet Options** from the menu bar.

3. Click the **Security** tab.

4. Select the appropriate web content zone. For example, select **Local Intranet** if you have set up Apache or IIS on the local machine.

5. Select **Custom Level**.

6. From the Reset to list, select **Medium-low**.

7. Under Initialize and script ActiveX controls not marked as safe, click the **Enable** radio button.

8. Click **OK**.

NOTE   If you use Rational Functional Tester version 7, refer to the Testing Flex applications with the Rational Functional Tester 7.0.1 article on developerWorks (www.ibm.com/developerworks/rational/library/08/0819_awasthy/).

Summary

You now know how to use extensions to Rational Functional Tester to test terminal-based, SAP, Siebel, and Adobe Flex applications. In some instances, you needed to work with a separate user interface (for example, terminal-based applications). In other instances, it is simple a matter of configuring Rational Functional Tester a certain way (for example, SAP, Siebel, and Adobe Flex). In any case, you now have the knowledge to test these technologies, using Rational Functional Tester.

## CHAPTER 12

Extending Rational Functional Tester with External Libraries

Larry Quesada, Daniel Gouveia, Marc van Lint

Rational Functional Tester is much more than a record and playback automated testing tool. Because Rational Functional Tester is based on industry standard, object-oriented programming languages, you can extend its capabilities in powerful ways. One way you do this is to leverage open source libraries. This chapter covers examples of how to extend Rational Functional Tester to:

- *Test PDF files using PDFBox, google-diff-match-patch libraries, and IKVM.NET.*
- *Create a custom logging solution using log4j and log4net.*
- *Create an Excel® reporting utility using Jawin and Microsoft Interop libraries.*

Examples are provided in both Java and .NET.

Testing PDF Files

Many applications today generate reports in PDF format. PDF files don't readily expose their information, requiring the Adobe Acrobat Reader software to view them. This presents a challenge to many automation tools. The Acrobat Reader is akin to a box, hiding the information that it contains. Test automation tools can see only the box, not what is in it. The good news for automation engineers using Rational Functional Tester is there is an open source package that can access the information in PDF files. This package is so aptly named PDFBox. You can access the text of a PDF file from a Rational Functional Tester script by calling the PDFBox methods for loading PDF files and extracting data from them. In this section, you learn how to use PDFBox to create a custom verification point (VP), which compares the text of two PDF files. You use an open source package called google-diff-match-path to compare the two blocks of plain text. For the .NET version of the verification point, you use a third open source package called IKVM.NET to convert the Java JAR files to .NET assemblies.

To use this verification point, you create a test script and set the helper super class to be the class `PdfBoxHelperSuperClass`. The verification points for PDF text you create in your test script look and feel like any other Rational Functional Tester verification points. The example test script, shown in Listing 12.1, uses the new verification point to compare two PDF files. These files differ in that the expected PDF file uses RFT and the actual PDF file sometimes uses Rational Functional Tester. Further, the PDF file contains the current date in the footer and this date is different in the two files. The test script runs the test twice. The first verification point is a straight comparison. The second verification point uses a mask to ignore dates. Both verification points fail, but the second verification point does not mark the dates in the footer as a difference.

Listing 12.1   Example PDF compare test script

Java
```
package testScripts;
import resources.testScripts.pdfboxExampleHelper;

public class pdfboxExample extends pdfboxExampleHelper
{
  public void testMain(Object[] args)
  {
    String expected = "pdfFiles\\Expected PDF.pdf";
    String actual = "pdfFiles\\Actual PDF.pdf";

    vpPdfText("PDF",expected,actual).performTest();
    vpPdfText("PDF Date Mask",expected,actual,
        MASK_DATE, MASK_DATE_NAME).performTest();
  }
}
```

VB.NET
```
Namespace testScripts
  Public Class pdfBoxExample
    Inherits pdfBoxExampleHelper

    Public Function TestMain(ByVal args() As Object) As Object
      Dim expected As String
      expected = "pdfFiles\\Expected PDF.pdf"
      Dim actual As String
      actual = "pdfFiles\\Actual PDF.pdf"

      vpPdfText("PDF", expected, actual).PerformTest()
```

```
    vpPdfText("PDF Date Mask", expected, actual, _
      MASK_DATE, MASK_DATE_NAME).PerformTest()


    Return Nothing
   End Function
  End Class
End Namespace
```

Figures 12.1 and 12.2 show the results of running the `pdfBoxExample` test script. You can graphically see the differences between the text of the expected and actual PDF files. In the results of the first verification point, the date in the footer is marked as a difference. In the results of the second verification point, the date in both the expected and actual text is replaced with the text ***MM/DD/YYYY*** and is not marked as a difference.

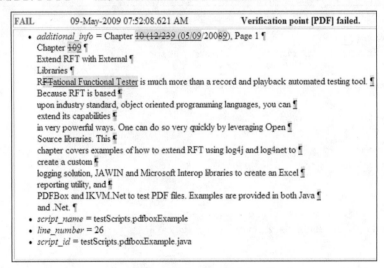

Figure 12.1　Test log for `pdfBoxExample`—PDF verification point

Setting Up the PDFBox Example for Rational Functional Tester Java

Follow the instructions in this section to set up the PDF compare example for Rational Functional Tester Java. You can download the example code from www.ibm.com/developerworks/rational/library/09/testengineeringrft/index.html. Unzip the file Chapter12.zip into a directory. The setup steps assume you unzipped into the directory C:\.

Importing the Example into an Existing Project

Follow these instructions to import the example into an existing project:

1. Create a new Rational Functional Tester project (or use an existing one).
2. From RFT, select **Import** from the File menu.

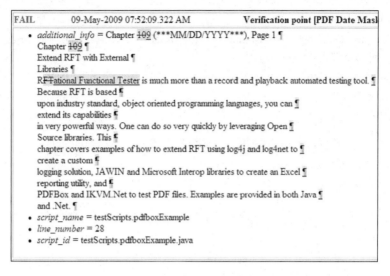

FAIL   09-May-2009 07:52:09.322 AM   **Verification point [PDF Date Mask**

- *additional_info* = Chapter ~~109~~ (***MM/DD/YYYY***), Page 1 ¶
  Chapter ~~109~~ ¶
  Extend RFT with External ¶
  Libraries ¶
  ~~RFT~~ational Functional Tester is much more than a record and playback automated testing tool. ¶
  Because RFT is based ¶
  upon industry standard, object oriented programming languages, you can ¶
  extend its capabilities ¶
  in very powerful ways. One can do so very quickly by leveraging Open ¶
  Source libraries. This ¶
  chapter covers examples of how to extend RFT using log4j and log4net to ¶
  create a custom ¶
  logging solution, JAWIN and Microsoft Interop libraries to create an Excel ¶
  reporting utility, and ¶
  PDFBox and IKVM.Net to test PDF files. Examples are provided in both Java ¶
  and .Net. ¶
- *script_name* = testScripts.pdfboxExample
- *line_number* = 28
- *script_id* = testScripts.pdfboxExample.java

Figure 12.2 Test Log for `pdfBoxExample`—PDF Date Mask verification point

3.   In the Import dialog box, expand the Other folder and select **Functional Test Project Items** (see Figure 12.3).

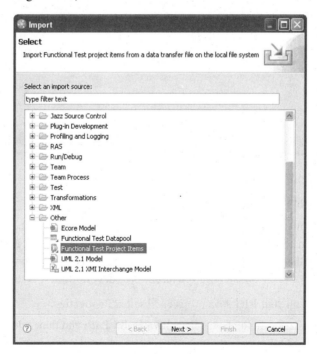

Figure 12.3 Import Rational Functional Tester Java project items

4. Select **Next**.

5. Next to **Transfer File**, select the file **pdfBox.rftjdtr** from the directory \Ch12 Downloads\RFT Java.

6. Under **Select the import location**, select the destination RFT Java project (see Figure 12.4).

7. Select **Finish.**

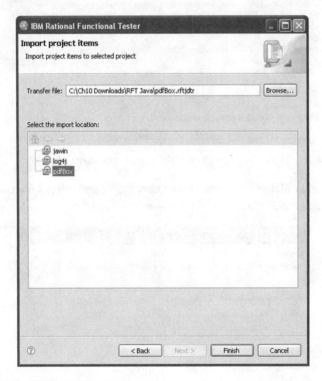

Figure 12.4   Import pdfBox.rftjdtr

Configuring the RFT Java Project to Use PDFBox

To set up PDFBox in a new RFT Java project, you add a reference to the PDFBox JAR files (PDFBox-0.7.3.jar and FontBox-0.1.0-dev.jar) in the Java Build Path of your RFT Java project. You can either download them from the Apache Software Foundation (www.pdfbox.org) or you can use the JAR files contained in the transfer file you just imported. Follow these instructions:

1. Right-click on your RFT Java project and select **Properties.**

2. In the **Properties** dialog box, select **Java Build Path** and then select the **Libraries** tab (see Figure 12.5).

3. Select the **Add External JARs** button.

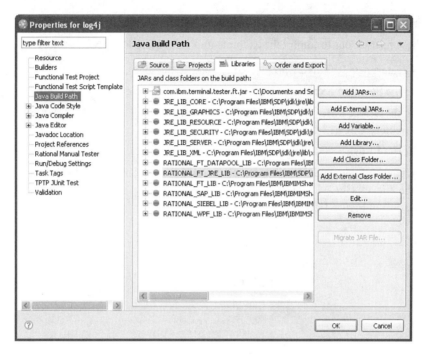

Figure 12.5 The Java Build Path

4. Navigate to the **jars** directory in your RFT Java Project. Select the JAR files **PdfBox-0.7.3.jar** and **FontBox-0.1.0-dev.jar**.

5. Select **OK.**

Configuring the RFT Java Project to Use google-diff-match-patch libraries

Google packages google-diff-match-patch libraries as source code, which you can download from http://code.google.com/p/google-diff-match-patch. To use it, you need to either import the source code into your RFT Java project or create a JAR file and reference the JAR file. A JAR file called google-diff-match-patch.jar in the transfer file you imported is provided. It is in the folder called jars. You can use it by adding it to the Java Build Path of your project. Follow the instructions outlined previously to do so.

Setting Up the PDFBox Example for RFT .NET

Follow the instructions in this section to set up the PDF compare example for RFT .NET. You can download the example code from www.ibm.com/developerworks/rational/library/09/testengineeringrft/index.html. Unzip the file Chapter12.zip into a directory of your choosing. The setup steps assume you unzipped into the directory C:\.

Importing the Example into an Existing RFT .NET Project

Follow these instructions to import the example into an existing RFT .NET project:

1. Create a new RFT .NET project (or use an existing one).

2. In the **Solution Explorer** view, right-click on your project and select **Import**.

3. In the **Select Data Transfer File** dialog box, select the file **pdfbox.rftvdtr**. It is in the directory C:\Ch12 Downloads\RFT .NET\.

4. Select **Finish**.

5. Copy the folders **pdfFiles** into the RFT .NET Project directory. This folder is located in the file C:\Ch12 Downloads\RFT .NET\pdfBox.zip. Your project should appear as shown in Figure 12.6.

Figure 12.6   RFT .NET project after importing PDFBox example

Configuring the RFT .NET Project to use PDFBox

Because PDFBox does not support .NET, you need to convert the Java libraries to .NET assemblies. You do this using an open source project called IKVM.NET. IKVM provides tools to enable Java and .NET interoperability. Alternatively, you can find the converted libraries in the file C:\Ch12 Downloads\RFT .NET\assemblies.zip. The assemblies you want are called PDFBox-0.7.3.dll and FontBox-0.1.0-dev.dll.

You also need several additional IKVM assemblies to run the Java code in .NET. You can download these from the IKVM site (www.ikvm.net). They are also provided in the assemblies.zip file:

- ..\ikvm\bin\IKVM.Runtime.dll

- ..\ikvm\bin\IKVM.OpenJDK.ClassLibrary.dll

- ..\PDFBox\bin\IKVM.GNU.Classpath.dll

To create references from your RFT .NET project to the assemblies just discussed, perform the following tasks:

1. Copy PDFBox-0.7.3.dll, IKVM.OpenJDK.ClassLibrary.dll, and IKVM.GNU.Classpath.dll into the RFT customization directory (C:\Documents and Settings\All Users\ Application Data\IBM\RFT\customization).

   Rational Functional Tester loads them when it launches, providing your test project access to their contents.

2. Copy PDFBox-0.7.3.dll, FontBox-0.1.0-dev.dll, IKVM.GNU.Classpath.dll, IKVM. Runtime.dll, and IKVM.OpenJDK.ClassLibrary.dll into the bin directory located in your RFT .NET project.

   This enables the DLLs to find each other and, more specifically, their objects and methods, at runtime.

If you want to convert the Java JAR files to .NET assemblies, you need a tool called IKVMC, which you can find in the bin directory of the download of IKVM. From a command line, run the following commands to complete the conversion:

```
C:\> C:\ikvm\bin\ikvmc -target:library PDFBox-0.7.3.jar
C:\>  C:\ikvm\bin\ikvmc -target:library FontBox-0.1.0-dev.jar
```

These commands assume the current directory of the command line contains all of the JAR files to convert and outputs the files PDFBox-0.7.3.dll and Fontbox.0.1.0-dev.dll. Note that the PDFBox download contains versions of the PDFBox and FontBox assemblies, but do not use these because they are not compatible with the google-diff-match-patch assembly.

Configuring the RFT .NET to Use google-diff-match-patch libraries

Like PDFBox, google-diff-match-patch libraries does not support .NET. You need to convert the Java libraries to .NET assemblies. You find the converted assembly in the file C:\Ch12 Downloads\RFT .NET\assemblies.zip. The assembly you want is called diff-match-patch.dll. Copy it into the RFT customization directory (C:\Documents and Settings\All Users\Application Data\IBM\RFT\customization) and the bin directory of your project. Finally, restart Rational Functional Tester.

If you are not using the assembly supplied with the chapter download, run the following command to complete the conversion. We provide the google-diff-match-patch.jar file in the transfer file C:\Ch12 Downloads\RFT Java\pdfBox.rftjdtr.

```
C:\>  C:\ikvm\bin\ikvmc -target:library google-diff-match-patch.jar
```

This command assumes the current directory of the command line contains the JAR file to convert and outputs the file google-diff-match-patch.dll.

Understanding the Code

The solution consists of several parts. Most of the work is done in a class called PDFTextVerificationPoint. It represents the verification of the text of a PDF file. In addition to extracting the text from the PDF file using the PDFBox classes, this class implements the IFtVerificationPoint interface. It provides methods such as performTest and `compare`, which use the `Diff Match Patch` classes to intelligently compare the text of the expected and actual PDF files. To account for text that would always differ between to PDF files, such as a date, you can provide a mask. We use regular expressions to implement the mask. The `performTest` and `compare` methods ignore any text, which match the regular expression. There is also a class called `PdfBoxHelperSuperClass`. This helper super class has methods and constants that make it simple to create a PDF text verification point in a test script. See Figure 12.7.

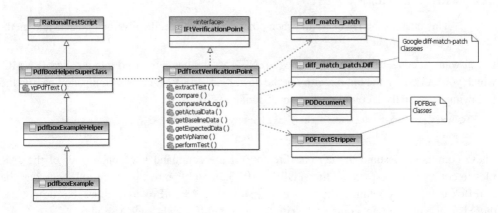

Figure 12.7   pdfBoxExample class diagram

The rest of this section describes how the PDF verification point works. The `PdfTextVerificationPoint` class is reviewed first, and then the `PdfBoxHelperSuperClass`.

Import Statements

You need to import a number of libraries in the `PdfTextVerificationPoint` class to easily access methods from PDFBox, google-diff-match-patch libraries, `IftVerificationPoint`, and some utility classes. Refer to Listing 12.2.

Listing 12.2   Import statements

Java
```
import java.util.Calendar;
import java.util.LinkedList;
import name.fraser.neil.plaintext.diff_match_patch;
import name.fraser.neil.plaintext.diff_match_patch.Diff;
import org.pdfbox.pdmodel.PDDocument;
import org.pdfbox.util.PDFTextStripper;
import com.rational.test.ft.script.RationalTestScript;
import com.rational.test.ft.vp.IFtVerificationPoint;
```

VB.NET
```
Imports System
Imports System.Text.RegularExpressions
Imports name.fraser.neil.plaintext
Imports org.pdfbox.pdmodel
Imports org.pdfbox.util
Imports Rational.Test.Ft.Script
Imports Rational.Test.Ft.Vp
```

Data Members and Constructors

The `PdfTextVerificationPoint` class keeps track of a number of data items. It has a verification point name, expected text, and actual text. Of course, it also needs to keep track of the location of the expected PDF file and the actual PDF file. Finally, the `PdfTextVerificationPoint` has a mask and a mask name. A *mask* is a regular expression that represents text that should be ignored during a comparison. The mask name is used in place of all text that matches the mask. A good example is the current date. If the current date appears in the expected and actual PDF files, you don't want the verification point to fail when the dates differ because they may always be different. By replacing all instances of the date (as defined by the mask regular expression) with the mask name, the verification point effectively ignores all dates in the two files.

The `PdfTextVerificationPoint` class has two constructors. One of the constructors passes in a mask and mask name, and the other does not. Both constructors update member data with the passed in parameters and call a method called `extractText` to extract the text from the expected and actual PDF files. Refer to Listing 12.3.

Listing 12.3   Data members and constructors

Java
```java
private String vpName;
private String expectedFilename;
private String actualFilename;
private String expectedText;
private String actualText;
private String mask;
private String maskName;

public PdfTextVerificationPoint(String vpName,
    String expectedFilename,
    String actualFilename) {
  super();
  this.vpName = vpName;
  this.expectedFilename = expectedFilename;
  this.actualFilename = actualFilename;
```

```
    this.mask = "";
    this.maskName = "";
    this.expectedText = "";
    this.actualText = "";

    //Get the text from the pdf files.
    extractText();
}

public PdfTextVerificationPoint(String vpName,
    String expectedFilename,
    String actualFilename,
    String mask,
    String maskName) {
  super();
  this.vpName = vpName;
  this.expectedFilename = expectedFilename;
  this.actualFilename = actualFilename;
  this.mask = mask;
  this.maskName = maskName;
  this.expectedText = "";
  this.actualText = "";

    //Get the text from the pdf files.
    extractText();
}
```

VB. NET
```
Private vpName As String
Private expectedFilename As String
Private actualFilename As String
Private expectedText As String
Private actualText As String
Private mask As String
Private maskName As String

Public Sub New(ByVal vpName As String, _
    ByVal expectedFilename As String, _
    ByVal actualFilename As String)
  Me.vpName = vpName
  Me.expectedFilename = expectedFilename
  Me.actualFilename = actualFilename
  Me.mask = ""
```

```
  Me.maskName = ""
  Me.expectedText = ""
  Me.actualText = ""

  'Get the text from the pdf files.
  extractText()
End Sub

Public Sub New(ByVal vpName As String, _
   ByVal expectedFilename As String, _
   ByVal actualFilename As String, _
   ByVal mask As String, ByVal maskName As String)
  Me.vpName = vpName
  Me.expectedFilename = expectedFilename
  Me.actualFilename = actualFilename
  Me.mask = mask
  Me.maskName = maskName
  Me.expectedText = ""
  Me.actualText = ""

  'Get the text from the pdf files.
  extractText()
End Sub
```

Extracting Text from the PDF Files

The `PdfTextVerificationPoint` class needs to extract the text from the expected and actual PDF files. You can write this code easily by using classes from the PDFBox libraries. The `PDDocument` class represents the PDF file, and the `PDFTextStripper` knows how to extract the text from the PDF files. After you extract the text, you then replace all instances of text that match the mask with the mask name (if a mask is required). Both Java and .NET provide methods for working with strings and regular expressions to accomplish this task. Refer to Listing 12.4.

Listing 12.4   Extracting text

Java
```
/*
 * Description: Extracts the text from the expected and actual pdf
 * files. If a mask is defined, all occurrences of the substring
 * the mask defines are replaced with the text maskName.
 */
private void extractText()
{
```

```java
try
{
  //Load the PDF files
  PDDocument expectedDoc = PDDocument.load(expectedFilename);
  PDDocument actualDoc = PDDocument.load(actualFilename);

  //Extract the text from the PDF file.
  PDFTextStripper stripper = new PDFTextStripper();
  expectedText = stripper.getText(expectedDoc);
  actualText = stripper.getText(actualDoc);

  //Use the mask, if it is defined. Replace all substrings,
  //which match the regular expression, mask with maskName
  if(mask != "")
  {
    expectedText = expectedText.replaceAll(mask, maskName);
    actualText = actualText.replaceAll(mask, maskName);
  }

  //Close the PDF files.
  expectedDoc.close();
  actualDoc.close();
  }
catch (Exception e)
{
  RationalTestScript.logException(e);
  RationalTestScript.stop();
}
}
```

VB.NET

```vbnet
' Description: Extracts the text from the expected and actual
' pdf files. If a mask is defined, all occurrences of the
' substring the mask defines are replaced with the text in
' maskName
Private Sub extractText()
  'Load the PDF files
  Dim expectedDoc As PDDocument
  Dim actualDoc As PDDocument
  expectedDoc = PDDocument.load(expectedFilename)
  actualDoc = PDDocument.load(actualFilename)

  'Extract the text from the PDF file.
```

```
Dim stripper As PDFTextStripper
stripper = New PDFTextStripper()
expectedText = stripper.getText(expectedDoc)
actualText = stripper.getText(actualDoc)

'Use the mask, if it is defined. Replace all substrings,
'which match the regular expression, mask with maskName
If Not mask.Equals("") Then
  'Replace all text matching the mask with maskName
  Dim r As Regex = New Regex(mask)
  expectedText = r.Replace(expectedText, maskName)
  actualText = r.Replace(actualText, maskName)
End If

'Close the PDF files.
expectedDoc.close()
actualDoc.close()
End Sub
```

Performing the Test

The PdfTextVerification point now has everything it needs to test the text of the expected and actual PDF files. Comparing large amounts of text with any kind of sophistication is not a trivial task. Fortunately, the google-diff-match-patch library can do the work for you. With only a couple of lines of code, you can retrieve a list that represents the differences between the two blocks of text. Further, the google-diff-match-patch library can output the results in a "pretty" HTML format, which graphically displays the differences. You can take advantage of these capabilities to write a simple, yet effective performTest method as shown in Listing 12.5.

Listing 12.5   performTest

Java
```
public boolean performTest(boolean compareTrueEqualsPass) {

  /*
   * Get a linked list representing the difference between
   * the text. Each node represents text which is the
   * same (EQUAL), text which was added to the actual text
   * (INSERT), or text which was deleted from expected text
   * (DELETE).
   */
  diff_match_patch dmp = new diff_match_patch();
```

```
LinkedList<Diff> diffList =
  dmp.diff_main(expectedText,actualText,true);
dmp.diff_cleanupSemantic(diffList);

//Perform the test and log the results.
if(expectedText.equals(actualText) == compareTrueEqualsPass) {
  RationalTestScript.logTestResult(
    "Verification point [" + vpName + "] passed.",
    true,
    dmp.diff_prettyHtml(diffList));
  return true;
}
else
{
  RationalTestScript.logTestResult(
    "Verification point [" + vpName + "] failed.",
    false,
    dmp.diff_prettyHtml(diffList));
  return false;
}
}
```

VB.NET

```
Public Function PerformTest( _
    ByVal compareTrueEqualsPass As Boolean) _
    As Boolean Implements _
    Rational.Test.Ft.Vp.IFtVerificationPoint.PerformTest

  ' Get a linked list representing the difference between the text.
  Dim dmp As diff_match_patch
  dmp = New name.fraser.neil.plaintext.diff_match_patch()
  Dim diffList As Object
  diffList = dmp.diff_main(expectedText, actualText, True)
  dmp.diff_cleanupSemantic(diffList)

  If (expectedText.Equals(actualText) = compareTrueEqualsPass) Then
    RationalTestScript.LogTestResult( _
      "Verification point [" + vpName + "] passed.", _
      True, _
      dmp.diff_prettyHtml(diffList))
    Return True
  Else
    RationalTestScript.LogTestResult( _
```

```
      "Verification point [" + vpName + "] failed.", _
      False, _
    dmp.diff_prettyHtml(diffList))
  Return False
End If
End Function
```

Taking into Account Variable PDF Generation Times

It is possible that the application under test takes a variable amount of time to generate a PDF file. The `IftVerificationPoint` interface contains instances of the `performTest` and `compare` methods, which take this into account. The caller provides the maximum test time (in seconds) and the delay between retries (also in seconds). These methods then repeat the test at the interval defined by the delay until either time runs out or the verification point passes. Listing 12.6 shows one possible way to implement this capability.

Listing 12.6   Compare and performTest with retry

Java
```java
public boolean compare(double delayBetweenRetries,
    double maximumTestTime) {
  //Get the end time for the test.
  long endTime = (long) (Calendar.getInstance().getTimeInMillis()
    + (maximumTestTime * 1000));

  //perform the test until time runs out or the test passes.
  boolean result = compare();
  long nextTime = (long) (Calendar.getInstance().getTimeInMillis()
    + (delayBetweenRetries * 1000));

  while((nextTime < endTime) && result == false)
  {
    RationalTestScript.sleep(delayBetweenRetries);
    extractText();
    result = compare();
    nextTime = (long) (Calendar.getInstance().getTimeInMillis()
      + (delayBetweenRetries * 1000));
  }
  return result;
}

public boolean performTest(double delayBetweenRetries,
    double maximumTestTime, boolean compareTrueEqualsPass) {
```

```java
//Get the end time for the test.
long endTime = (long) (Calendar.getInstance().getTimeInMillis()
   + (maximumTestTime * 1000));

//perform the test until time runs out or the test passes.
boolean result = (compare() == compareTrueEqualsPass);
long nextTime = (long) (Calendar.getInstance().getTimeInMillis()
   + (delayBetweenRetries * 1000));

while((nextTime < endTime) && result == false)
{
   RationalTestScript.sleep(delayBetweenRetries);
   extractText();
   result = (compare() == compareTrueEqualsPass);
   nextTime = (long) (Calendar.getInstance().getTimeInMillis()
      + (delayBetweenRetries * 1000));
}
return performTest(compareTrueEqualsPass);
}
```

VB.NET

```vbnet
Public Function Compare(ByVal delayBetweenRetries As Double, _
    ByVal maximumTestTime As Double) _
    As Boolean Implements _
    Rational.Test.Ft.Vp.IFtVerificationPoint.Compare

 'Get the end time for the test.
 Dim endTime As System.DateTime
 Dim maxTimeSpam As TimeSpan
 maxTimeSpam = New TimeSpan(0, 0, maximumTestTime)
 endTime = DateTime.Now.Add(maxTimeSpam)

 'perform the test until time runs out or the test passes.
 'perform the test until time runs out or the test passes.
 Dim result As Boolean
 Dim nextTime As DateTime
 Dim nextTimeSpam As TimeSpan
 nextTimeSpam = New TimeSpan(0, 0, delayBetweenRetries)

 result = Compare()
 nextTime = DateTime.Now.Add(nextTimeSpam)
```

```
  Do While ((nextTime < endTime) And (result = False))
    RationalTestScript.Sleep(delayBetweenRetries)
    extractText()
    result = Compare()
    nextTime = DateTime.Now.Add(nextTimeSpam)
  Loop

  Return result

End Function

Public Function PerformTest( _
    ByVal delayBetweenRetries As Double, _
    ByVal maximumTestTime As Double, _
    ByVal compareTrueEqualsPass As Boolean) _
    As Boolean Implements _
    Rational.Test.Ft.Vp.IFtVerificationPoint.PerformTest

  'Get the end time for the test.
  Dim endTime As System.DateTime
  Dim maxTimeSpam As TimeSpan
  maxTimeSpam = New TimeSpan(0, 0, maximumTestTime)
  endTime = DateTime.Now.Add(maxTimeSpam)

  'perform the test until time runs out or the test passes.
  Dim result As Boolean
  Dim nextTime As DateTime
  Dim nextTimeSpam As TimeSpan
  nextTimeSpam = New TimeSpan(0, 0, delayBetweenRetries)

  result = (Compare() = compareTrueEqualsPass)
  nextTime = DateTime.Now.Add(nextTimeSpam)
  Do While ((nextTime < endTime) And (result = False))
    RationalTestScript.Sleep(delayBetweenRetries)
    extractText()
    result = (Compare() = compareTrueEqualsPass)
    nextTime = DateTime.Now.Add(nextTimeSpam)
  Loop

  Return PerformTest(compareTrueEqualsPass)
End Function
```

Completing the Remaining Methods

The remaining methods of the IftVerificationPoint interface, shown in Listing 12.7, are trivial. There are some get methods, some additional instances of the performTest method, and some compare methods.

Listing 12.7   Trivial methods

Java
```java
public boolean compare() {
  return expectedText.equals(actualText);
}


public boolean compareAndLog() {
  return compareAndLog(true);
}


public boolean compareAndLog(boolean compareTrueEqualsPass) {


  if(expectedText.equals(actualText) == compareTrueEqualsPass) {
    RationalTestScript.logTestResult(
      "Verification point [" + vpName + "] passed.",
      true);
    return true;
  }
  else
  {
    RationalTestScript.logTestResult(
      "Verification point [" + vpName + "] failed.",
      false);
    return false;
  }
}


public Object getActualData() {
  return actualText;
}


public Object getBaselineData() {
  return null;
}


public Object getExpectedData() {
  return expectedText;
```

```
}

public String getVPName() {
    return vpName;
}

public boolean performTest() {
    return performTest(true);
}

public boolean performTest(double delayBetweenRetries,
        double maximumTestTime) {

    return performTest(delayBetweenRetries,maximumTestTime,
        true);
}
```

VB.NET

```
Public Function Compare() As Boolean Implements _
    Rational.Test.Ft.Vp.IFtVerificationPoint.Compare

  Return expectedText.Equals(actualText)
End Function

Public Function CompareAndLog() As Boolean Implements _
    Rational.Test.Ft.Vp.IFtVerificationPoint.CompareAndLog
  Return CompareAndLog(True)
End Function

Public Function CompareAndLog(ByVal compareTrueEqualsPass As Boolean) _
    As Boo lean Implements _
    Rational.Test.Ft.Vp.IFtVerificationPoint.CompareAndLog

  If (expectedText.Equals(actualText) = compareTrueEqualsPass) Then
    RationalTestScript.LogTestResult( _
      "Verification point [" + vpName + "] passed.", _
      True)
    Return True
  Else
    RationalTestScript.LogTestResult( _
      "Verification point [" + vpName + "] failed.", _
      False)
    Return False
```

```
     End If
End Function

Public Function GetActualData() As Object Implements _
     Rational.Test.Ft.Vp.IFtVerificationPoint.GetActualData
   Return actualText
End Function

Public Function GetBaselineData() As Object Implements _
     Rational.Test.Ft.Vp.IFtVerificationPoint.GetBaselineData
   Return Nothing
End Function

Public Function GetExpectedData() As Object Implements _
     Rational.Test.Ft.Vp.IFtVerificationPoint.GetExpectedData
   Return expectedText
End Function

Public Function GetVPName() As String Implements _
     Rational.Test.Ft.Vp.IFtVerificationPoint.GetVPName
   Return vpName
End Function

Public Function PerformTest() As Boolean Implements _
     Rational.Test.Ft.Vp.IFtVerificationPoint.PerformTest
   Return PerformTest(True)
End Function

Public Function PerformTest( ByVal delayBetweenRetries As Double, _
     ByVal maximumTestTime As Double) _
     As Boolean Implements _
     Rational.Test.Ft.Vp.IFtVerificationPoint.PerformTest
   Return PerformTest(delayBetweenRetries, _
     maximumTestTime, _
     True)
End Function
```

Helper Super Class

This solution has a helper super class called PDFBoxHelperSuperClass, which contains a pre-defined mask for a date field, and some helper functions for returning a PDF text verification point. This class, shown in Listing 12.8, makes using the new PDF text verification point easy.

Listing 12.8   PdfBoxHelperSuperClass

Java
```java
package util;

import com.rational.test.ft.script.RationalTestScript;
import com.rational.test.ft.vp.IFtVerificationPoint;

/**
 * Description    : This Super class contains methods which may
 * be used to compare pdf files.
 *
 *  * @since  November 26, 2008
 */
public abstract class PdfBoxHelperSuperClass extends RationalTestScript
{
  /*
   * This regular expression matches a date time stamp in
   * the format mm/dd/yyyy hh:mm PM (or AM). It may be used
   * to mask the date from the expected and actual text of a
   * pdfTextVp.
   *
   */
  public static final String MASK_DATE = "[0-9]{2}/[0-9]{2}/[0-9]{4}";
  public static final String MASK_DATE_NAME = "***MM/DD/YYYY***";

  /*
   * Description:  This method returns a verification point
   * for the text of a pdf file. It replaces any text in the
   * expected and actual files, which match the regular
   * expression defined in the mask parameter with maskName.
   * One can use the mask to remove text from the vp, which
   * would cause the vp to fail incorrectly. A date would be
   * a good example of text which could be masked.
   *
   */
  protected IFtVerificationPoint vpPdfText(String vpName,
      String expected,
      String actual,
      String mask,
      String maskName)
  {
    return new PdfTextVerificationPoint(vpName,
      expected,actual,mask, maskName);
  }
```

```
/*
 * Description:  This method returns a verification point
 * for the text of a pdf file.
 */
protected IFtVerificationPoint vpPdfText(String vpName,
    String expected,
    String actual)
{
   return new PdfTextVerificationPoint(vpName,expected,actual);
}
}
```

VB.NET

```
Imports Rational.Test.Ft.Script
Imports Rational.Test.Ft.Vp

Namespace util


  'Description   : Base class for script helper
  'since  November 30, 2008

  Public MustInherit Class PdfBoxHelperSuperClass
      Inherits RationalTestScript

    'This regular expression matches a date time stamp in
    ' the format mm/dd/yyyy hh:mm PM (or AM). It may be used
    ' to mask the date from the expected and actual text of a
    ' pdfTextVp.
    '
    Public Const MASK_DATE As String = "[0-9]{2}/[0-9]{2}/[0-9]{4}"
    Public Const MASK_DATE_NAME As String = "***MM/DD/YYYY***"

    ' Description:  This method returns a verification point
    ' for the text of a pdf file. It replaces any text in the
    ' expected and actual files, which match the regular
    ' expression defined in the mask parameter with maskName
    ' One can use the mask to remove text from the vp, which
    ' would cause the vp to fail incorrectly. A date would be
    ' a good example of text which could be masked.
    Protected Function vpPdfText(ByVal vpName As String, _
```

```
        ByVal expected As String, _
        ByVal actual As String, _
        ByVal mask As String, _
        ByVal maskName As String) As IFtVerificationPoint

        Return New PdfTextVerificationPoint(vpName, _
            expected, actual, mask, maskName)
    End Function


    ' Description:  This method returns a verification point
    ' for the text of a pdf file.
    Protected Function vpPdfText(ByVal vpName As String, _
        ByVal expected As String, _
        ByVal actual As String) As IFtVerificationPoint

        Return New PdfTextVerificationPoint(vpName,expected, actual)
    End Function


    End Class
End Namespace
```

Writing to a Custom Log File with Log4j and Log4net

Log4j and Log4net are open source utilities for writing log files from a Java program or a .NET program. They provide an easy-to-use powerful set of classes. You log data using hierarchical categories and levels, and you can control the behavior of your logging in powerful ways from a configuration file. This way, you can change how you log without changing your test scripts. You can, for example, turn on trace logs only for one test script in a suite. You can control the level of information, the output destination (the console, a file, a socket, and so on), and the layout of the log. All of this behavior can be specified by categories that you define.

This section describes how to use Log4J and Log4net in the context of Rational Functional Tester. We start with a simple Rational Functional Tester test script that writes logs to the console by calling log methods. The Java version of the script is called log4jExample1 and the VB.NET version of the script is called log4netExample1. Both are located in the testScripts folder. If you run the .NET version of this script, execute the script by selecting Debug Functional Test Script instead of Run Functional Test Script (the bug icon instead of the green triangle). Otherwise, you do not see anything in the output view. When you run the script, you get the following output:

```
    INFO  testScripts.log4jExample1:20 - Starting Script!
    INFO  testScripts.log4jExample1:22 - Do something.
    DEBUG testScripts.log4jExample1:23 - Log Debug Data
```

```
WARN  testScripts.log4jExample1:24 - Something bad might have happened!
ERROR testScripts.log4jExample1:25 - Something bad happened!
FATAL testScripts.log4jExample1:26 - That's all she wrote!
ERROR testResult.testScripts.log4jExample1:27 - FAIL
INFO  testScripts.log4jExample1:29 - Script Ended!
```

You now explore manipulating the logging output of the test script by changing the configuration file. We change the log level (although the messages logged from this script are the same), the format of the log messages, and the destination of the log messages. When you run the Example1 test script using the new configuration file, the script writes logs to the console and to the files logs\log.txt and logs\results.txt. The following is output to both the console and to the log.txt:

```
11/09/2008 09:31:04,testScripts.log4jExample1:20,INFO,Starting Script!
11/09/2008 09:31:04,testScripts.log4jExample1:22,INFO,Do something.
11/09/2008 09:31:04,testScripts.log4jExample1:23,DEBUG,Log Debug Data
11/09/2008 09:31:04,testScripts.log4jExample1:24,WARN,Something bad may
have happened!
11/09/2008 09:31:04,testScripts.log4jExample1:25,ERROR,Something bad
happened!
11/09/2008 09:31:04,testScripts.log4jExample1:26,FATAL,That's all she
wrote!
11/09/2008 09:31:04,testResult.testScripts.log4jExample1:27,ERROR,FAIL
11/09/2008 09:31:04,testScripts.log4jExample1:29,INFO,Script Ended!
```

The following is output to the file logs\results.txt:

```
09/02/2008 01:05:16,testResult.testScripts.log4jExample1,FAIL
```

Finally, you create your own custom logging solution that automatically writes the result of running a test script (pass, fail, or warning) to a summary log (logs\results.txt) and that writes detailed logs to the file logs\log.txt. The only change you have to make to the test script is to set its helper super class to be util.LogHelperSuperClass. No changes need to be made to the code in the script.

A test script is provided; it uses the logging solution. The Java version of the script is called log4jExample2, and the .NET version is called log4netExample2. Again, both are located in the testScripts folder. This script, shown in Listing 12.9, tests the ClassicsJavaA application. It selects and purchases a CD. Along the way, it verifies that the purchase price is correct and also that the confirmation message is correct. Because the confirmation message has a one up number in it, this verification point fails.

Listing 12.9   Log example test script

Java
```
public void testMain(Object[] args)
{
  startApp("ClassicsJavaA");
```

```
    // Frame: ClassicsCD
    tree2().click(atPath("Composers->Bach->Location(PLUS_MINUS)"));
    tree2().click(atPath(
      "Composers->Bach->Brandenburg Concertos Nos. 1 & 3"));
    placeOrder().click();

    // Frame: Member Logon
    ok().click();

    // Frame: Place an Order
    _1799().performTest(order_total_textVP());
    cardNumberIncludeTheSpacesText().click(atPoint(60,9));
    placeAnOrder().inputChars("123456789");
    expirationDateText().click(atPoint(37,14));
    placeAnOrder().inputChars("12/12");
    placeOrder2().drag();

    yourOrderHasBeenReceivedYourOr().
      performTest(order_confirmation_textVP());
    ok2().drag();

    // Frame: ClassicsCD
    classicsJava(ANY,MAY_EXIT).close();
}
```

VB.NET

```
Public Function TestMain(ByVal args() As Object) As Object
  StartApp("ClassicsJavaA")

  ' Frame: ClassicsCD
  Tree2().Click(AtPath("Composers->Bach->Location(PLUS_MINUS)"))
  Tree2().Click(AtPath( _
    "Composers->Bach->Brandenburg Concertos Nos. 1 & 3"))
  PlaceOrder().Click()

  ' Frame: Member Logon
  OK().Click()

  ' Frame: Place an Order
  CardNumberIncludeTheSpacesText().Drag(AtPoint(52,13), AtPoint(52,12))
  PlaceAnOrder().InputChars("123456789")
  ExpirationDateText().Click(AtPoint(12,8))
  PlaceAnOrder().InputChars("12/12")
```

```
_1799().PerformTest(OrderTotalVP())
PlaceOrder2().Click()
YourOrderHasBeenReceivedYourOr().PerformTest(OrderConfirmationVP())
OK2().Click()


' Frame: ClassicsCD
ClassicsJava(ANY,MAY_EXIT).Close()
Return Nothing
End Function
```

When you execute the test script, and pass in build1 as a run argument, the following is output to the console and appended to the file logs\log.txt:

```
11/03/2008 15:52:37,testScripts.log4jExample2,INFO,Starting Script!
11/03/2008 15:52:41,testScripts.log4jExample2,INFO,Testing vp
[order_total_text]
11/03/2008 15:52:42,testScripts.log4jExample2,INFO,Testing vp
[order_confirmation_text]
11/03/2008 15:52:47,testScripts.log4jExample2,WARN,WARNING on line 51
11/03/2008 15:52:47,testScripts.log4jExample2,WARN,Weak recognition for
[OptionPane.label] with a score of [15000]
11/03/2008
15:52:47,testScripts.log4jExample2.order_confirmation_text,ERROR,FAIL on
line 51
11/03/2008
15:52:47,testScripts.log4jExample2.order_confirmation_text,ERROR,expected
[Your order has been received!  Your order number is: 60.]
11/03/2008
15:52:47,testScripts.log4jExample2.order_confirmation_text,ERROR,actual
[Your order has been received!  Your order number is: 19.]
11/03/2008 15:52:49,testResult.testScripts.log4jExample2,ERROR,build1,FAIL
11/03/2008 15:52:49,testScripts.log4jExample2,INFO,Script Ended!
```

You also get the following appended to the logs\results.txt file:

```
11/03/2008
15:52:49,testResult.testScripts.log4jExample2,build1,FAIL
```

Setting Up the Logging Example for RFT Java Projects

Follow the instructions in this section to set up the logging example. You can download the example code from www.ibm.com/developerworks/rational/library/09/testengineeringrft/index.html. Unzip the file Chapter12.zip into a directory of your choosing. The setup steps assume you unzipped into the directory C:\.

Importing the Example into an Existing RFT Java Project

Follow these instructions to import the example into an existing RFT Java project:

1. Create a new RFT Java project (or use an existing one).

2. From RFT, select **Import** from the File menu.

3. In the Import dialog box, expand the Other folder and select **Functional Test Project Items** (see Figure 12.8).

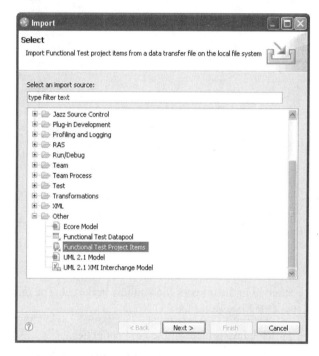

Figure 12.8   Import RFT Java project items

4. Select **Next**.

5. Next to **Transfer File**, select the file **log4j.rftjdtr** from the directory \Ch12 Downloads\RFT Java.

6. Under **Select the import location**, select the destination RFT Java project (see Figure 12.9).

7. Select **Finish**.

Configuring the RFT Java Project to Use log4j

To set up log4j in a new RFT Java project you add a reference to the JAR file log4j-1.2.15.jar. You can either download it from the Apache Software Foundation (http://logging.apache.org/) or you

Figure 12.9   Import log4j.rftjdtr

can use the JAR file contained in the transfer file you just imported. The instructions that follow assume you are using the JAR file we provided.

1. Right-click your RFT Java project and select **Properties.**

2. In the **Properties** dialog box, select **Java Build Path**, and then select the **Libraries** tab (see Figure 12.10).

3. Select the **Add External JARs** button.

4. Navigate to the **jars** directory now in your RFT Java project. Select the JAR file **log4j-1.2.15.jar**.

5. Select **OK.**

Setting Up the Logging Example for RFT .NET

Follow the instructions in this section to set up the logging example. You can download the example code from www.ibm.com/developerworks/rational/library/09/testengineeringrft/index.html. Unzip the file Chapter12.zip into a directory of your choosing. The setup steps assume you unzipped into the directory C:\.

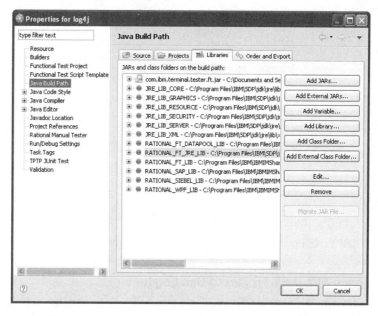

Figure 12.10   The Java build path

Importing the Example into an Existing RFT .NET Project

Follow these instructions to import the example into an existing RFT .NET project:

1. Create a new RFT .NET project (or use an existing one).

2. In the Solution Explorer view, right-click on your project and select **Import**.

3. In the Select Data Transfer File dialog box, select the file **log4net.rftvdtr**. It is in the directory C:\Ch12 Downloads\RFT .NET\.

4. Select **Finish**.

5. Copy the folders config and logs into the RFT .NET Project directory. These folders are located in the file C:\Ch12 Downloads\RFT .NET\log4net.zip. Your project should appear as follows as shown in Figure 12.11.

6. Open the file **log4NetExample3.xml** (located in the config folder).

7. Change line `<file value="c:\temp\logs\log.txt"/>` to point to the log.txt file now in your RFT .NET project. For example, it might read `<file value="C:\ Documents and Settings\YOU\My Documents\Visual Studio 2005 \ Projects\ log4net\log4net\logs\log.txt"/>`.

8. Change line `<file value="c:\temp\logs\results.txt"/>` to point to the results.txt file now in your RFT .NET project. For example, it might read `<file value="C:\Documents and Settings\YOU\My Documents\Visual Studio 2005\Projects\log4net\log4net\logs\results.txt"/>`.

9. Repeat steps 6–8 for the file **log4NetExample4.xml**.

Figure 12.11   RFT .NET project after importing log4net example

Configuring the RFT .NET Project to Use Log4net

To set up log4net in a new RFT .NET project, you add a reference to the assembly log4net.dll. You can either download it from the Apache Software Foundation (http://logging.apache.org/) or you can use the assembly provided in the file C:\Ch12 Downloads\RFT .NET\assembiles.zip.

1. Copy the assembly file **log4net.dll** into the RFT .NET customization directory. By default, this directory is located at C:\Documents and Settings\All Users\Application Data\IBM\RFT\customization.

2. Restart Rational Functional Tester.

Understanding the Simple Example

This section starts by explaining the simple example.

Reading the Configuration File

The examples use configuration files to control logging behavior. This way, you can alter your logging without changing any script code. Listing 12.10 shows how to read an XML configuration file, which is located in the config folder of the RFT .NET project:

Listing 12.10   Reading the configuration file

Java
```
//Configure logging behavior from xml configuration file.
DOMConfigurator.configure("config\\log4jExample1.xml");
```

VB.NET
```
'Configure logging behavior from properties file.
Dim xmlFile As String
xmlFile = "config\\log4netExample2.xml"
XmlConfigurator.Configure(New System.IO.FileInfo(xmlFile))
```

Setting Up Loggers

You write messages to your log using a class called `Logger`. When you create a `Logger` object, you give that logger a name. A good best practice is to use the name of the test script as the name of any logger in that test script. You create two loggers. One logger is for logging what happens in the test script. This one has the name of the test script. The other logger is for logging the overall results of the test script. In Listing 12.11, this logger is given the name `testResult.scriptName` so that all of the test script results in the log can be easily found.

Listing 12.11   Setting up Loggers

Java
```
Logger logger = Logger.getLogger(getScriptName());
Logger resultsLog = Logger.getLogger("testResult." + getScriptName());
```

VB.NET
```
'Set up loggers
Dim ISI As Rational.Test.Ft.Script.Impl.IScriptInternal = Me
Dim logger As ILog
logger = LogManager.GetLogger(ISI.GetScriptName())
```

Logging Some Messages

Finally, let's log some messages. You can log six levels of messages: trace, debug, info, warning, error, and fatal. In Listing 12.12, you log the start and ending of the script, and some information messages, warning messages, and error messages.

Listing 12.12   Logging some messages

Java
```
logger.info("Starting Script!");

logger.info("Do something.");
logger.debug("Log Debug Data");
logger.warn("Something bad might have happened!");
logger.error("Something bad happened!");
```

```
logger.fatal("That's all she wrote!");
resultsLog.error("FAIL");

logger.info("Script Ended!");
```

VB.NET
```
logger.Info("Starting Script!")

logger.Info("Do something.")
logger.Debug("Log Debug Data")
logger.Warn("Something bad might have happened!")
logger.Error("Something bad happened!")
logger.Fatal("That's all she wrote!")
resultsLog.Error("FAIL")

logger.Info("Script Ended!")
```

The Configuration File

XML is used in Listing 12.13 for this example. Logs are sent to the console using the defined layout. You look at the configuration file more in the next section.

Listing 12.13   The configuration file

log4j
```
<?xml version="1.0" encoding="UTF-8" ?>
<!DOCTYPE log4j:configuration SYSTEM "log4j.dtd">
<log4j:configuration xmlns:log4j="http://jakarta.apache.org/log4j/">

  <appender name="console" class="org.apache.log4j.ConsoleAppender">
    <param name="Target" value="System.out"/>
    <layout class="org.apache.log4j.PatternLayout">
      <param name="ConversionPattern" value="%-5p %c:%L - %m%n"/>
    </layout>
  </appender>

  <root>
    <priority value ="debug" />
    <appender-ref ref="console" />
  </root>

</log4j:configuration>
```

Log4net

```
<log4net>
  <appender name="Console" type="log4net.Appender.ConsoleAppender">

    <!-- A1 uses PatternLayout -->
    <layout type="log4net.Layout.PatternLayout">
      <conversionPattern value="%-5p %c:%L - %m%n" />
    </layout>
  </appender>

  <root>
    <level value="DEBUG" />
    <appender-ref ref="Console" />
  </root>
</log4net>
```

Changing Log Behavior via the Configuration File

Log4j and log4net enable you to configure the logging behavior in powerful ways. You can configure which logs get written and which get ignored based upon log level. You can configure where a log message goes. Finally, you can configure the layout of the messages in the logs. This section provides a brief description for how to configure log4j and log4net within the context of Rational Functional Tester. For a detailed description of the configuration options, refer to the documentation.

Configuring the Log Level

You control which messages are logged and which are ignored by setting the log level. The level can be set to TRACE, DEBUG, INFO, WARN, ERROR, or FATAL. Only messages that have a level equal to or greater than the set level get output. The lowest level is TRACE and the highest is FATAL. If, for example, we set the log level to INFO, all trace and debug messages are ignored. One useful way to filter logs in Rational Functional Tester is to turn on debug logging for a single test script, whereas other test scripts ignore debug logs. In Listing 12.14, you change the configuration file so that the level of the root logger is set to INFO. This means all TRACE and DEBUG log messages are ignored. However, we also set the log level of the testScripts.log4jExample1 Logger to DEBUG. Because you use the test script name as the name of the logger, the log4jExample1 test script in the testScripts folder outputs DEBUG log messages.

Listing 12.14   Configuring the log level

log4j

```
<?xml version="1.0" encoding="UTF-8" ?>
<!DOCTYPE log4j:configuration SYSTEM "log4j.dtd">
<log4j:configuration xmlns:log4j="http://jakarta.apache.org/log4j/">
```

```
<appender name="console" class="org.apache.log4j.ConsoleAppender">
  <param name="Target" value="System.out"/>
  <layout class="org.apache.log4j.PatternLayout">
    <param name="ConversionPattern" value="%-5p %c:%L - %m%n"/>
  </layout>
</appender>

<logger name="testScripts.log4jExample1">
  <level value ="debug" />
</logger>

<root>
  <priority value ="info" />
  <appender-ref ref="console" />
</root>
</log4j:configuration>
```

log4net
```
<log4net>
  <appender name="Console" type="log4net.Appender.ConsoleAppender">

    <!-- A1 uses PatternLayout -->
    <layout type="log4net.Layout.PatternLayout">
      <conversionPattern value="%-5p %c:%L - %m%n" />
    </layout>
  </appender>

  <logger name="testScripts.log4netExample1">
    <level value="DEBUG" />
  </logger>

  <root>
    <level value="INFO" />
    <appender-ref ref="Console" />
  </root>
</log4net>
```

Configuring the Output Destination

You can control the destination of log messages by configuring appenders. There are many options to choose from including the console, files, and remote socket servers. You can send messages to one or multiple destinations. In the logging example, you want to parse out the overall verdict of each test script from the log file. You can simply change the logging configuration to send all test result verdicts to a separate file. In the configuration file shown in Listing 12.15, you extend the example to contain three appenders. The console appender sends log messages to the console, the LogFile appender sends logs messages to the file log.txt, and the ResultsFile appender sends messages to the file results.txt. Further, you define that all loggers whose name starts with testResult send messages to the result.txt file.

Listing 12.15   Configuring the output destination

log4j

```
<?xml version="1.0" encoding="UTF-8" ?>
<!DOCTYPE log4j:configuration SYSTEM "log4j.dtd">
<log4j:configuration xmlns:log4j="http://jakarta.apache.org/log4j/">
  <appender name="console" class="org.apache.log4j.ConsoleAppender">
    <param name="Target" value="System.out"/>
    <layout class="org.apache.log4j.PatternLayout">
      <param name="ConversionPattern" value="%-5p %c:%L - %m%n"/>
    </layout>
  </appender>

 <appender name="LogFile" class="org.apache.log4j.FileAppender">
    <param name="File" value="logs\\log.txt"/>
    <layout class="org.apache.log4j.PatternLayout">
      <param name="ConversionPattern" value="%-5p %c:%L - %m%n"/>
    </layout>
  </appender>

 <appender name="ResultsFile" class="org.apache.log4j.FileAppender">
    <param name="File" value="logs\\results.txt"/>
    <layout class="org.apache.log4j.PatternLayout">
      <param name="ConversionPattern" value="%-5p %c:%L - %m%n"/>
    </layout>
  </appender>

  <logger name="testResult">
    <level value ="info" />
    <appender-ref ref="ResultsFile" />
  </logger>

  <logger name="testScripts.log4jExample1">
    <level value ="debug" />
  </logger>
```

```
  <root>
    <priority value ="info" />
    <appender-ref ref="console" />
    <appender-ref ref="LogFile" />
  </root>
</log4j:configuration>
```

log4net

```
<log4net>
  <appender name="Console" type="log4net.Appender.ConsoleAppender">

    <!-- A1 uses PatternLayout -->
    <layout type="log4net.Layout.PatternLayout">
      <conversionPattern value="%-5p %c:%L - %m%n" />
    </layout>
  </appender>

  <appender name="LogFile" type="log4net.Appender.FileAppender">
    <file value="C:\temp\logs\log.txt" />
    <appendToFile value="true" />

    <layout type="log4net.Layout.PatternLayout">
      <conversionPattern value="%-5p %c:%L - %m%n" />
    </layout>
  </appender>

  <appender name="ResultsFile" type="log4net.Appender.FileAppender">
    <file value="C:\temp\logs\results.txt" />
    <appendToFile value="true" />

    <layout type="log4net.Layout.PatternLayout">
      <conversionPattern value="%-5p %c:%L - %m%n" />
    </layout>
  </appender>

  <root>
    <level value="DEBUG" />
    <appender-ref ref="LogFile" />
    <appender-ref ref="Console" />
  </root>

  <logger name="testResult">
    <level value="INFO" />
```

```
       <appender-ref ref="ResultsFile" />
   </logger>
</log4net>
```

Configuring the Format

You can control the format of log messages for each appender using pattern layouts. The pattern used so far is `%-5p %c:%L - %m%n`. When a message is sent to an appender, each conversion specifier (`%` followed by format modifiers and a conversion character) is replaced with information about the message. In this case, p is the log priority (INFO, WARN, ERROR, and so on), c is the category, L is the line number, m is the message, and n is a new line. In the Rational Functional Tester logging example, you output all log messages delimited by commas. This makes it easy to parse the logs using applications such as Microsoft Excel. You also add the date and time to the logs. The pattern is `%d{MM/dd/yyyy HH:mm:ss},%c:%L,%p,%m%n`. Refer to the log4j and log4net documentation for a complete list of all format modifiers and conversion characters. Listing 12.16 shows the completed configuration file with the updated layouts:

Listing 12.16   Configuring the format

log4j
```
<?xml version="1.0" encoding="UTF-8" ?>
<!DOCTYPE log4j:configuration SYSTEM "log4j.dtd">
<log4j:configuration xmlns:log4j="http://jakarta.apache.org/log4j/">
   <appender name="console" class="org.apache.log4j.ConsoleAppender">
     <param name="Target" value="System.out"/>
     <layout class="org.apache.log4j.PatternLayout">
       <param name="ConversionPattern"
value="%d{MM/dd/yyyy HH:mm:ss},%c:%L,%p,%m%n"/>
     </layout>
   </appender>

  <appender name="LogFile" class="org.apache.log4j.FileAppender">
     <param name="File" value="logs\\log.txt"/>
     <layout class="org.apache.log4j.PatternLayout">
       <param name="ConversionPattern"
value="%d{MM/dd/yyyy HH:mm:ss},%c:%L,%p,%m%n"/>
     </layout>
   </appender>

   <appender name="ResultsFile" class="org.apache.log4j.FileAppender">
     <param name="File" value="logs\\results.txt"/>
     <layout class="org.apache.log4j.PatternLayout">
       <param name="ConversionPattern"
value="%d{MM/dd/yyyy HH:mm:ss},%c,%m%n"/>
```

```
    </layout>
  </appender>

  <logger name="testResult">
    <level value ="info" />
    <appender-ref ref="ResultsFile" />
  </logger>

  <logger name="testScripts.log4jExample1">
    <level value ="debug" />
  </logger>

  <root>
    <priority value ="info" />
    <appender-ref ref="console" />
    <appender-ref ref="LogFile" />
  </root>
</log4j:configuration>
```

log4net

```
<log4net>
  <appender name="Console" type="log4net.Appender.ConsoleAppender">

    <!-- A1 uses PatternLayout -->
    <layout type="log4net.Layout.PatternLayout">
     <conversionPattern value="%d{MM/dd/yyyy HH:mm:ss},%c:%L,%p,%m%n" />
    </layout>
  </appender>

  <appender name="LogFile" type="log4net.Appender.FileAppender">
    <file value="C:\temp\logs\log.txt" />
    <appendToFile value="true" />

    <layout type="log4net.Layout.PatternLayout">
     <conversionPattern value="%d{MM/dd/yyyy HH:mm:ss},%c:%L,%p,%m%n" />
    </layout>
  </appender>

  <appender name="ResultsFile" type="log4net.Appender.FileAppender">
    <file value="C:\temp\logs\results.txt" />
    <appendToFile value="true" />
```

```
    <layout type="log4net.Layout.PatternLayout">
      <conversionPattern value="%d{MM/dd/yyyy HH:mm:ss},%c,%m%n" />
    </layout>
  </appender>

  <root>
    <level value="DEBUG" />
    <appender-ref ref="LogFile" />
    <appender-ref ref="Console" />
  </root>

  <logger name="testResult">
    <level value="INFO" />
    <appender-ref ref="ResultsFile" />
  </logger>
</log4net>
```

Understanding the LogHelperSuperClass

In this section, you generalize the solution so the start of a test script, the end of a test script, verification points, and the test script result are logged automatically as the script runs. You do this by creating a helper super class called `LogHelperSuperClass` and by taking advantage of the many callback methods available for Rational Functional Tester test scripts. A *callback method* is a method that Rational Functional Tester calls when a specific event happens. You can override a callback method to extend the behavior of RFT. This capability is used to write logging code that gets called when a script initializes, when a verification point starts, when a verification point fails, and when a script terminates. The Java and .NET implementations are essentially the same. There are some minor differences in the names of the log4j and log4net classes and the format of the logging configuration file, but the concepts and approaches are identical. Refer to Figure 12.12 for a Unified Modeling Language (UML) representation of the Java logging solution, and refer to Figure 12.13 for a UML representation of the .NET solution.

Script Initialization

Rational Functional Tester calls a method called `onInitialization` before it runs `testMain`. Here is where you initialize the logging framework and read the configuration file. It is possible that many test scripts might be called in a single run (using `callScript`), and you need to make sure the properties file is read only once. Similar to the simple example, you log the fact that the test script has started. Finally, you set the build of the test run by assigning

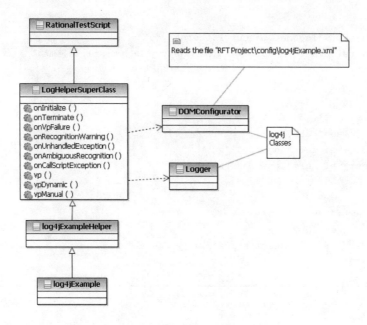

Figure 12.12   Class diagram of log4jExample

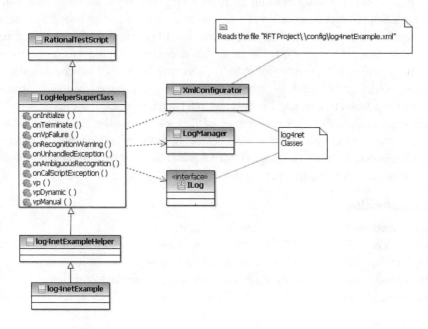

Figure 12.13   Class diagram of log4netExample

the first argument passed into the script to be the build. If no arguments are passed, the build is set to unspecified. See Listing 12.17.

Listing 12.17   Script initialization

Java

```java
/**
 * Description: This method is called automatically at the start of
 * every script. Initialize log4j,
 * if not already completed. Log the start of the script. Set the
 * build, if it was passed into the
 * script (first argument).
 */
public void onInitialize()
{
  //Read log4j property file, if not already completed.
  if(!log4jInitialized)
  {
    log4jInitialized = true;
    DOMConfigurator.configure("config\\log4jExample4.xml");
  }

  //Log the start of the test script.
  Logger logger = Logger.getLogger(getScriptName());
  logger.info("Starting Script!");

  //Set the build to be the first parameter. If no parameter,
  //use the default (unspecified)
  Object [] args = getScriptArgs();
  if(args.length > 0)
    build = (String) args[0];
}
```

VB.NET

```vbnet
'Description  :  This method is called automatically at the
'start of every script. Initialize log4j,
'if not already completed. Log the start of the script. Set the
'build, if it was passed into the script (first argument).
Public Overrides Sub onInitialize()

  'Read log4net property file, if not already completed.
  If (Not log4netInitialized) Then
    log4netInitialized = True
```

```
  'Configure logging behavior from properties file.
  Dim xmlFile As String
  xmlFile = "config\\log4netExample4.xml"
  XmlConfigurator.Configure(New System.IO.FileInfo(xmlFile))


End If



'Log the start of the test script.
Dim logger As ILog = LogManager.GetLogger(getScriptName())

logger.Info("Starting Script!")

'Set the build to be the first parameter. If no parameter, use
'the default (unspecified)
Dim args() As Object
args = GetScriptArgs()
If (args.Length > 0) Then
  build = args(0)
End If


MyBase.OnInitialize()
End Sub
```

Script Termination

You can complete similar actions when a script completes by overriding the `onTerminate` method. This method is called whenever a script completes. In Listing 12.18, you log the results (which you calculate as the script runs), and you log the fact that the script ended.

Listing 12.18   Script termination

Java
```
/**
* Description: This method is called automatically at the end of
* every script. Log the test result and
* log the end of the script.
*/
public void onTerminate()
{
  //Get the results Logger.
  Logger resultsLog = Logger.getLogger("testResult." + getScriptName());

  //Log the result based upon the verdict.
```

```
  if(verdict == PASS_INT)
  {
    resultsLog.info(build + "," + PASS_STRING);
  }
  else if(verdict == WARN_INT)
  {
    resultsLog.warn(build + "," + WARN_STRING);
  }
  else
  {
    resultsLog.error(build + "," + FAIL_STRING);
  }

  //Log the end of the script.
  Logger logger = Logger.getLogger(getScriptName());
  logger.info("Script Ended!");
}
```

VB.NET

```
'Description: This method is called automatically at the end of every
'script. Log the test result and log the end of the script.
Public Overrides Sub onTerminate()

  'Get the results Logger.
  Dim resultsLog As ILog
  resultsLog = LogManager.GetLogger("testResult." + getScriptName())

  'Log the result based upon the verdict.
  If (verdict = VERDICT_ENUM.PASS) Then
    resultsLog.Info(build + "," + PASS_STRING)
  ElseIf (verdict = VERDICT_ENUM.WARN) Then
    resultsLog.Warn(build + "," + WARN_STRING)
  Else
    resultsLog.Error(build + "," + FAIL_STRING)
  End If


  'Log the end of the script.
  Dim logger As ILog = LogManager.GetLogger(getScriptName())
  logger.Info("Script Ended!")

  MyBase.OnTerminate()
End Sub
```

Logging Failures

Now you need a way to log verification point results and to calculate the overall result of running a test script. For the overall result, you use a simple approach. If all verification points pass, the overall verdict is PASS. If the test script recognizes an object, but the recognition score is greater than the threshold, the verdict is WARN. If any verification point in the test script fails, the overall verdict is FAIL.

Rational Functional Tester provides a callback method called `onVpFailure`, which is called any time a verification point fails. In Listing 12.19, you override this method in order to log a message about the failure and to indicate the test script has an overall verdict of fail.

Listing 12.19   onVpFailure

Java
```java
/**
* Description:  Called when a verification point fails to complete
* successfully. Log a failure and set
* the verdict of the test script to FAIL_INT.
*/
public void onVpFailure(IFtVerificationPoint vp)
{
  //Set verdict.
  verdict = FAIL_INT;

  //Get logger.
  Logger logger = Logger.getLogger(getScriptName() + "." +
    vp.getVPName());


  //Get the expected data.
  Object expected =  vp.getExpectedData();
  String expectedString;

  //The expected data may be a string if the VP is from vpManual.
  if(expected.getClass().toString().contains("String"))
    expectedString = (String) expected;
  else
  {
    //Extract expected data.
    ITestData expectedTestData = (ITestData) expected;
    expectedString = expectedTestData.getData().toString();
  }

  //Get actual data.
```

```
Object actual =  vp.getActualData();
String actualString;

//Actual data may be a string if the VP is from vpManual.
if(actual.getClass().toString().contains("String"))
  actualString = (String) actual;
else
{
  //Extract actual data.
  ITestData actualTestData = (ITestData) actual;
  actualString = actualTestData.getData().toString();
}

//Log VP failure.
logger.error("FAIL on line " + getLineNumber());
logger.error("expected [" +
    expectedString + "]");
logger.error("actual [" +
    actualString + "]");

super.onVpFailure(vp);
}
```

VB.NET
```
'Description:  Called when a verification point fails to complete
'successfully. Log a failure and set the verdict of the test script
'to FAIL_INT.
Public Overrides Sub OnVpFailure(ByVal vp As
Rational.Test.Ft.Vp.IFtVerificationPoint)
  'Set verdict.
  verdict = VERDICT_ENUM.FAIL

  'Get logger.
  Dim logger As ILog = LogManager.GetLogger(getScriptName() + "." _
    + vp.GetVPName())

  'Get the expected data.
  Dim expected As Object
  expected = vp.GetExpectedData()
  Dim expectedString As String

  'The expected data may be a string if the VP is from vpManual.
  If (expected.GetType().ToString().Contains("String")) Then
```

```
    expectedString = expected
  Else
    'Extract expected data.
    Dim expectedTestData As Rational.Test.Ft.Vp.ITestData
    expectedTestData = expected
    expectedString = expectedTestData.GetData.ToString
  End If

  'Get the actual data.
  Dim actual As Object
  actual = vp.GetActualData()
  Dim actualString As String

  'The actual data may be a string if the VP is from vpManual.
  If (actual.GetType().ToString().Contains("String")) Then
    actualString = actual
  Else
    'Extract expected data.
    Dim actualTestData As Rational.Test.Ft.Vp.ITestData
    actualTestData = actual
    actualString = actualTestData.GetData.ToString
  End If

  'Log VP failure.
  logger.Error("FAIL on line " + GetLineNumber().ToString)
  logger.Error("expected [" + expectedString + "]")
  logger.Error("actual [" + actualString + "]")

  MyBase.OnVpFailure(vp)
End Sub
```

Logging Warnings

Whenever a test script finds an object, but the object's recognition score exceeds the warning threshold, Rational Functional Tester calls the onRecognitionWarning method. In Listing 12.20, you override this method to set the verdict to WARNING. Note that if the verdict is already FAIL, you leave it as is.

Listing 12.20   onRecognitionWarning

Java
```
/**
* Description: This method is called whenever an object is found, but
* the recognition score is higher
```

```
* than the warning threshold. Set the verdict to WARN_INT and log
* the error.
*/
public void onRecognitionWarning(ITestObjectMethodState
      testObjectMethodState, TestObject foundObject, int score)
{
  //Do not reset verdict, if test script already has a failure.
  if (verdict == PASS_INT)
    verdict = WARN_INT;

  Logger logger = Logger.getLogger(getScriptName());
  logger.warn("WARNING on line " + getLineNumber());
  logger.warn("Weak recognition for [" +
      foundObject.getProperty("name") +
      "] with a score of [" + score + "]");

  super.onRecognitionWarning(testObjectMethodState,
    foundObject, score);
}
```

VB.NET

```
'Description: This method is called whenever an object is found, but
'the recognition score is higher than the warning threshold. Set the
'verdict to WARN_INT and log the error.
Public Overrides Sub OnRecognitionWarning(ByVal testObjectMethodState As
Rational.Test.Ft.Script.ITestObjectMethodState, ByVal foundObject As
Rational.Test.Ft.Object.Interfaces.TestObject, ByVal score As Integer)

  'Do not reset verdict, if test script already has a failure.
  If (verdict = VERDICT_ENUM.PASS) Then
    verdict = VERDICT_ENUM.WARN
  End If

  Dim logger As ILog = LogManager.GetLogger(getScriptName())
  logger.Warn("WARNING on line " + GetLineNumber().ToString)
  logger.Warn("Weak recognition for [" + _
    foundObject.GetProperty("name") + "] with a score of [" + _
    score.ToString + "]")

  MyBase.OnRecognitionWarning(testObjectMethodState, foundObject, _
    score)
End Sub
```

Handling Additional Callbacks

There are many other callback methods that are called when a Rational Functional Tester test script throws an exception. In Listing 12.21, you override these methods to set the verdict to FAIL and to log the event.

Listing 12.21   Additional callbacks

Java
```java
/**
* Description: This method is called when a test object cannot be
* found. Set the verdict of the test
* script to FAIL_INT and log the error.
*/
public void onObjectNotFound(ITestObjectMethodState
    testObjectMethodState)
{
  verdict = FAIL_INT;
  Logger logger = Logger.getLogger(getScriptName());
  logger.error("Object not found at line " + getLineNumber() +
      ". ");

  super.onObjectNotFound(testObjectMethodState);
}


/**
* Description: This method is called whenever an exception is
* thrown from testMain. Set the verdict of the test
* script to FAIL_INT and log the error.
*/
public boolean onUnhandledException(java.lang.Throwable e)
{
  verdict = FAIL_INT;
  Logger logger = Logger.getLogger(getScriptName());
  logger.error("Call Script exception at line " + getLineNumber()
      + ": " + e.getMessage());
  return super.onUnhandledException(e);
}


/**
* Description: This method is called whenever RFT is looking for an
* object and finds 2 that match. Set
* the verdict to FAIL_INT and log the error.
*/
public void onAmbiguousRecognition(ITestObjectMethodState
  testObjectMethodState, TestObject[] choices, int[] scores)
```

```java
{
  verdict = FAIL_INT;

  Logger logger = Logger.getLogger(getScriptName());
  logger.error("Ambigious Recognition at line " +
    getLineNumber());
  for(int i=0;i<choices.length;i++)
    logger.error("Test Object " + i + ": " +
      choices[i].getProperty("name") + " score: "
      + scores[i]);

  super.onAmbiguousRecognition(testObjectMethodState, choices,
    scores);
}


/**
* Description: This method is called whenever an exception from
* callScript. Set the verdict of the test
* script to FAIL_INT and log the error.
*/
public boolean onCallScriptException(java.lang.RuntimeException e)
{
  verdict = FAIL_INT;
  Logger logger = Logger.getLogger(getScriptName());
  logger.error("Call Script exception at line " + getLineNumber()
    + ": " + e.getMessage());

  return super.onCallScriptException(e);
}
```

VB.NET

```vbnet
'Description: This method is called when a test object cannot be
'found. Set the verdict of the test script to FAIL_INT and log the
'error.
Public Overrides Sub OnObjectNotFound(ByVal testObjectMethodState As
Rational.Test.Ft.Script.ITestObjectMethodState)
  verdict = VERDICT_ENUM.FAIL
  Dim logger As ILog = LogManager.GetLogger(getScriptName())
  logger.Error("Object not found at line " + _
  GetLineNumber().ToString + ". ")

  MyBase.OnObjectNotFound(testObjectMethodState)
End Sub


'Description: This method is called whenever an exception is thrown
```

```vbnet
'from testMain. Set the verdict of the test script to FAIL_INT and
'log the error.
Public Overrides Function OnUnhandledException(ByVal e As System.Exception) As
Boolean
  verdict = VERDICT_ENUM.FAIL
  Dim logger As ILog = LogManager.GetLogger(getScriptName())
  logger.Error("Call Script exception at line " + _
    GetLineNumber().ToString + ": " + e.Message)

  Return MyBase.OnUnhandledException(e)
End Function

'Description: This method is called whenever RFT is looking for an
'object and finds 2 that match. Set the verdict to FAIL_INT and log 'the error.
Public Overrides Sub OnAmbiguousRecognition(ByVal testObjectMethodState As
Rational.Test.Ft.Script.ITestObjectMethodState, ByVal choices() As
Rational.Test.Ft.Object.Interfaces.TestObject, ByVal scores() As Integer)
  verdict = VERDICT_ENUM.FAIL

  Dim logger As ILog = LogManager.GetLogger(getScriptName())
  logger.Error("Ambigious Recognition at line " + _
    GetLineNumber().ToString)

  Dim i As Integer
  For i = 0 To choices.Length - 1
    logger.Error("Test Object " + i.ToString + ": " + _
      choices(i).GetProperty("Name").ToString + " score: " + _
      scores(i).ToString)
  Next i

  MyBase.OnAmbiguousRecognition(testObjectMethodState, choices, _
    scores)
End Sub

'Description: This method is called whenever an exception from 'callScript. Set
the verdict of the test script to FAIL_INT and log
'the error.
Public Overrides Function OnCallScriptException(ByVal e As
System.SystemException) As Boolean
  verdict = VERDICT_ENUM.FAIL
  Dim logger As ILog = LogManager.GetLogger(getScriptName())
  logger.Error("Call Script exception at line " + _
    GetLineNumber().ToString + ": " + e.Message())

  Return MyBase.OnCallScriptException(e)
End Function
```

Logging a Pass

No callback methods execute when a verification point passes. You can add code after each verification point to check the results and log PASS, but this is too intrusive. Instead, you override the vp method and log a message to indicate that the verification point is about to be executed. This method, shown in Listing 12.22, is called whenever a test script prepares to execute a verification point. You then pass control back to the API so that processing continues as before. With this approach, if the log says a verification point executed and there are not failure logs, the verification point has passed.

Listing 12.22   Logging a pass

Java
```java
/**
* Description: Log the start of a verification point, and then pass
* to the API.
*/
protected  IFtVerificationPoint vp(java.lang.String vpName, TestObject anchor)
{
  Logger logger = Logger.getLogger(getScriptName());
  logger.info("Testing vp [" + vpName + "]");

  return super.vp(vpName,anchor);
}
```

You also need to handle manual and dynamic verification points. You do so in a similar way:
```java
/**
* Description: Log the start of a verification point, and then pass
* to the API.
*/
protected  IFtVerificationPoint vpDynamic(java.lang.String vpName)
{
  Logger logger = Logger.getLogger(getScriptName());
  logger.info("Testing vp [" + vpName + "]");

  return super.vpDynamic(vpName);
}


/**
* Description: Log the start of a verification point, and then pass
* to the API.
*/
protected  IFtVerificationPoint vpDynamic(java.lang.String vpName,
    TestObject objectUnderTest)
{
```

```java
  Logger logger = Logger.getLogger(getScriptName());
  logger.info("Testing vp [" + vpName + "]");

  return super.vpDynamic(vpName,objectUnderTest);
}


/**
 * Description: Log the start of a verification point, and then pass
 * to the API.
 */
protected  IFtVerificationPoint vpManual(java.lang.String vpName,
    java.lang.Object actual)
{
  Logger logger = Logger.getLogger(getScriptName());
  logger.info("Testing vp [" + vpName + "]");

  return super.vpManual(vpName, actual);
}


/**
 * Description: Log the start of a verification point, and then pass
 * to the API.
 */
protected  IFtVerificationPoint vpManual(java.lang.String vpName,
    java.lang.Object expected, java.lang.Object actual)
{
  Logger logger = Logger.getLogger(getScriptName());
  logger.info("Testing vp [" + vpName + "]");

  return super.vpManual(vpName,expected,actual);
}
```

VB.NET

```vbnet
'Description: Log the start of a verification point, and then pass to
'the API.
Protected Overrides Function Vp(ByVal vpName As String, ByVal anchor As
Rational.Test.Ft.Object.Interfaces.TestObject) As
Rational.Test.Ft.Vp.IFtVerificationPoint
  Dim logger As ILog = LogManager.GetLogger(getScriptName())
  logger.Info("Testing vp [" + vpName + "]")
  Return MyBase.Vp(vpName, anchor)
End Function
```

```
'Description: Log the start of a verification point, and then pass to
'the API.
Protected Overrides Function VpDynamic(ByVal vpName As String) As
Rational.Test.Ft.Vp.IFtVerificationPoint
   Dim logger As ILog = LogManager.GetLogger(getScriptName())
   logger.Info("Testing vp [" + vpName + "]")
   Return MyBase.VpDynamic(vpName)
End Function

'Description: Log the start of a verification point, and then pass to
'the API.
Protected Overrides Function VpDynamic(ByVal vpName As String, ByVal
objectUnderTest As Rational.Test.Ft.Object.Interfaces.TestObject) As
Rational.Test.Ft.Vp.IFtVerificationPoint
   Dim logger As ILog = LogManager.GetLogger(getScriptName())
   logger.Info("Testing vp [" + vpName + "]")
   Return MyBase.VpDynamic(vpName, objectUnderTest)
End Function

'Description: Log the start of a verification point, and then pass to
'the API.
Protected Overrides Function VpManual(ByVal vpName As String, ByVal expected As
Object, ByVal actual As Object) As Rational.Test.Ft.Vp.IFtVerificationPoint
   Dim logger As ILog = LogManager.GetLogger(getScriptName())
   logger.Info("Testing vp [" + vpName + "]")
   Return MyBase.VpManual(vpName, expected, actual)
End Function

'Description: Log the start of a verification point, and then pass to
'the API.
Protected Overrides Function VpManual(ByVal vpName As String, ByVal actual As
Object) As Rational.Test.Ft.Vp.IFtVerificationPoint
   Dim logger As ILog = LogManager.GetLogger(getScriptName())
   logger.Info("Testing vp [" + vpName + "]")
   Return MyBase.VpManual(vpName, actual)
End Function
```

Interfacing with COM Scriptable Components

It is sometimes useful to call a COM scriptable component from RFT. The application under test might be a COM-based application and you want to write a custom test harness, or you might want to write a utility that uses a COM component. In this section, you learn how to interface to a commonly used COM scriptable component, Microsoft Excel. You use Jawin to interface to Excel from RFT Java, and .NET Com Interop classes to interface to Excel from RFT .NET. Jawin is an open source library that stands for the Java/Win32 integration project. It enables you to easily make calls to COM components and Win32 .dlls from a Java program. You can use JNI for the same purpose, but Jawin requires much less work and produces cleaner code. The .NET COM Interop classes are .NET libraries, which encapsulate the interface to applications such as Excel. They enable you to manipulate Excel from your Rational Functional Tester scripts using a reference to the Excel Object Model.

You start by developing a simple script that creates an Excel workbook with the text Hello World in the first cell. When you run this script, it creates an Excel workbook as pictured in Figure 12.14.

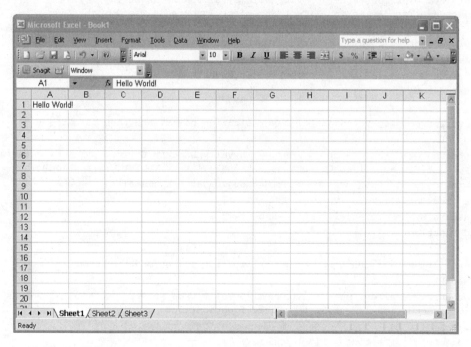

Figure 12.14   A simple Excel workbook created from a Rational Functional Tester script

Next, you explore an example of a utility Rational Functional Tester script, which creates a Chart in Excel from the results.txt file. This file is an output from the logging solution described in the section "Writing to a Custom Log File with Log4j and Log4net." The chart can be generated automatically after running a large set of Rational Functional Tester scripts. The Java version of the test script is called jawinExample2, and the .NET version is called MSInteropExample2. Both are located in the testScripts folder. When you execute this test, it creates a new Excel workbook similar to the one shown in Figure 12.15.

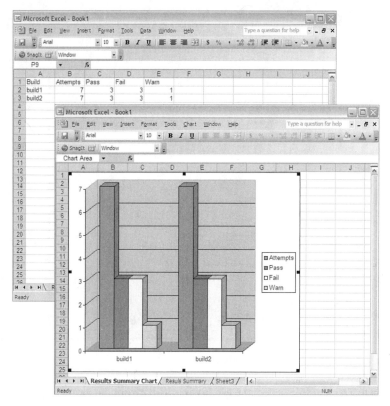

Figure 12.15   Result data and chart in Excel

Setting Up the Charting Example for RFT Java

Follow the instructions in this section to set up the charting example. You can download the example code from www.ibm.com/developerworks/rational/library/09/testengineeringrft/index.html. Unzip the file Chapter12.zip into a directory of your choosing. The setup steps assume you unzipped into the directory C:\.

Importing the Example into an Existing RFT Java Project

Follow these instructions to import the example into an existing RFT Java project:

1. Create a new RFT Java project (or use an existing one).
2. From RFT, select **Import** from the File menu.
3. In the Import dialog box, expand the Other folder and select **Functional Test Project Items** (see Figure 12.16).
4. Select **Next**.

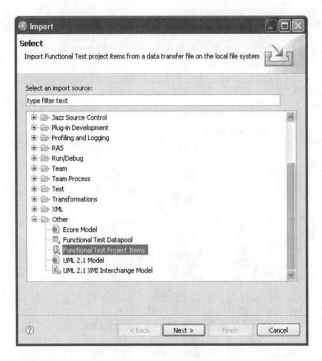

Figure 12.16   Import RFT Java project items.

5. Next to Transfer File, select the file **jawin.rftjdtr** from the directory
    \Ch12 Downloads\RFT Java.

6. Under Select the import location, select the destination RFT Java project (see
    Figure 12.17).

7. Select **Finish**.

Configuring the RFT Java Project to Use Jawin

To set up Jawin in a new RFT Java project, you add a reference to the JAR file jawin.jar. You also
load the Jawin native code in the file jawin.dll. To do so, you need to place the jawin.dll file in a
directory that is referenced from the standard java.library path property. RFT sets this property to
include the directory <installation dir>\jdk\jre\bin, so simply copy the jawin.dll into that directory. You can download the latest versions of jawin.jar and jawin.dll from the Apache Logging
Services Project web page (`http://logging.apache.org/`), or you can use files provided in the
transfer file you just imported. The instructions that follow assume you are using the files
provided.

1. Right-click on your RFT Java project and select **Properties.**

2. In the Properties dialog, select **Java Build Path**, and then select the **Libraries** tab (see
    Figure 12.18).

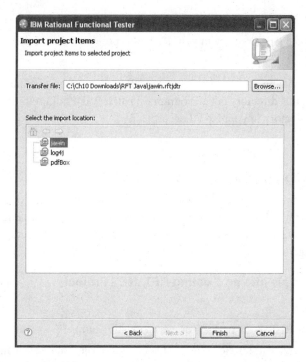

Figure 12.17   Import jawin.rftjdtr

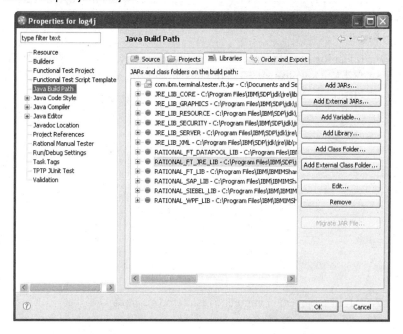

Figure 12.18   The Java Build Path

3. Select the **Add External Jars** button.

4. Navigate to the jars directory in your RFT Java project. Select the JAR file **jawin.jar**.

5. Select **OK.**

6. Copy the file jawin.dll into the directory <RFT installation dir>\jdk\jre\bin (in a standard install, this directory is C:\Program Files\IBM\SDP\jdk\jre\bin). The dll is located in the jars directory in your RFT Java project.

7. Restart RFT.

Setting Up the Logging Example for RFT .NET

Follow the instructions in this section to set up the logging example. You can download the example code from www.ibm.com/developerworks/rational/library/09/testengineeringrft/index.html. Unzip the file Chapter12.zip into a directory of your choosing. The setup steps assume you unzipped into the directory C:\.

Importing the Example into an Existing RFT .NET Project

Follow these instructions:

1. Create a new RFT .NET project (or use an existing one).

2. In the Solution Explorer view, right-click on your project and select **Import**.

3. In the Select Data Transfer File dialog box, select the file **msinterop.rftvdtr**. It is in the directory C:\Ch12 Downloads\RFT .NET\.

4. Select **Finish**.

5. Copy the folder logs into the RFT .NET Project directory. This directory is contained in the file C:\Ch12 Downloads\RFT .NET\msinterop.zip. Your project should appear as shown in Figure 12.19.

Figure 12.19   RFT .NET project after importing MsInterop example

Configuring the RFT .NET Project to Use Microsoft Office Interop

To set up Microsoft Office Interop in a new RFT .NET project, you add a reference to the assembly Microsoft.Office.Interop.Excel.dll. You can either download it from Microsoft (www.msdn.com), or you can use the assembly provided in the file C:\Ch12 Downloads\RFT .NET\assembiles.zip.

1. Copy the assembly file Microsoft.Office.Interop.Excel.dll into the RFT .NET customization directory. By default, this directory is located at C:\Documents and Settings\All Users\Application Data\IBM\RFT\customization.

2. Restart Rational Functional Tester.

Understanding the Simple Example

In this section, you learn how to develop the Hello World Excel-RFT script. Because this script makes calls to the Excel COM API, it is useful for you to familiarize yourself with that interface and to have the interface documentation available. You can find this documentation on the MSDN website (http://msdn.microsoft.com). Search for Excel Object Model. This uses Microsoft Excel 2003.

Simple Example in VBA

A trick to understanding how to use the Excel COM interface is to use the macro recording capability of Excel and then to examine the generated VBA code. If you record a macro from Excel to generate the VBA code for this example, your code would look something like Listing 12.23.

Listing 12.23 Hello World

```VBA
Sub Macro2()
  Workbooks.Add
  ActiveCell.FormulaR1C1 = "Hello World!"
End Sub
```

Let's see what you need to do to convert this code to Java using Jawin and to .NET using the Microsoft Excel Primary Interop assembly.

Simple Example in Java

Jawin provides an interface for invoking methods in COM and Win32 .dlls. It is simple and does not require you to write any native code. To use Jawin from a Rational Functional Tester script, you must initialize the COM library. When you are done you uninitialize the library. You also need to either catch or throw the COMException. Listing 12.24 is a skeleton of what your Rational Functional Tester script might look like when calling Jawin code. Note that `throws` `COMException` is added to the `testMain` method declaration.

Listing 12.24   Initializing COM library

Java
```
package testScripts;
import org.jawin.COMException;
import org.jawin.win32.Ole32;

public class jawinExample extends jawinExampleHelper
{
  public void testMain(Object[] args) throws COMException
  {
    //Setup COM libraries.
    Ole32.CoInitialize();

    /*JAWIN Code*/

    //Tear down COM libraries.
    Ole32.CoUninitialize();
  }
}
```

You use the `DispatchPtr` class from the Jawin library to interface to any scriptable COM object. You first need to get a handle for the top-level object, and then you can invoke methods, get properties, and set properties per the object's published interface. Listing 12.25 is the code for accessing the top-level COM object for Excel.

Listing 12.25   Getting the top-level `DispatchPtr`

Java
```
//Get a handle for Excel Application
DispatchPtr app = new DispatchPtr("Excel.Application");
```

Now that you have access to Excel, you can open a new workbook. In the recorded example, you see that you can add a new workbook by calling `Workbooks.Add`. A review of the Excel Object Model shows that the Application object has a `Workbooks` property that represents all open workbooks. You can therefore add a new workbook by getting a handle for the `Workbooks` property and calling its `Add` method. In this example, you can access the `Workbooks` property by calling the `get` method of the `DispatchPtr` class that represents the Excel Application object. This call returns another instance of the `DispatchPtr` class. You can call the `Add` method of the `Workbooks` property by calling `invoke` from the `DispatchPtr` class that represents the `Workbook` property. The Java code in Listing 12.26 completes these actions. Note that the code also sets the `Visible` property to true. This causes Excel to display the workbook so you can see the automation as it happens.

Listing 12.26   Creating a new workbook

Java
```
app.put("Visible", true);

//Create a new Excel Workbook.
DispatchPtr workbooks = (DispatchPtr) app.get("Workbooks");
workbooks.invoke("Add");
```

To complete the example, you need to set the `FormulaR1C1` property of the `ActiveCell` object. Similar to the previous example, you can accomplish this by getting a handle on the `ActiveCell` object, and then setting its `FormulaR1C1` property. Listing 12.27 is the Java code that completes this step.

Listing 12.27   Writing Hello World in a cell

Java
```
//Set some text.
DispatchPtr activeCell;
activeCell = (DispatchPtr) app.get("ActiveCell");
activeCell.put("FormulaR1C1", "Hello World!");
```

The Simple Example in .NET

Writing this example in a RFT .NET script is straightforward. You first create an instance of the `Application` class. This gives you access to both the `Workbooks` and `ActiveCell` properties. You can create a new workbook by calling the `Add` method of the `Workbooks` property, and you can set the value of the first cell by setting the `Value` property of `ActiveCell`. Listing 12.28 shows the RFT .NET example script:

Listing 12.28   The Hello World Rational Functional Tester script

VB.NET
```
#Region " Script Header "
Imports Microsoft.Office.Interop.Excel
```

```vbnet
#End Region
Namespace testScripts

  Public Class MsInteropExample
    Inherits MsInteropExampleHelper
    Public Function TestMain(ByVal args() As Object) As Object

      'Get a handle for Excel Application
      Dim xlApp As New Application()
      xlApp.Visible = True

      'Create a new Excel Workbook.
      Dim workbooks As Workbooks = xlApp.Workbooks
      workbooks.Add()

      'Set some text
      xlApp.ActiveCell.Value = "Hello World!"
      Return Nothing
    End Function
  End Class
End Namespace
```

Understanding the Results Chart Example

Now that you understand the basics, let's move on. This section takes you through how to write a script that takes the contents of the results.txt file and places them an Excel workbook, creating a three-dimensional chart in the process.

For the Java implementation, you start by calling Jawin directly. Later, you move those calls into a set of classes that encapsulates the interface to Excel. Jawin provides a mechanism to generate a set of classes from a COM component for this purpose. You also created a class called BuildResults to represent a count of verdicts (pass, fail, warning) for each build and managed these results in the Java LinkedHashMap class. Figure 12.20 shows the example test script along with the generated classes, utility classes, Java classes, and Jawin classes.

The .NET version of this example looks similar to the Java example, except you did not have to write the classes that encapsulate the interface to Excel. Like the Java example, you create a class called BuildResults to represent a count of verdicts and manage these results in the Hashtable class. Figure 12.21 shows the example test script along with the Excel COM Interop classes, utility classes, and .NET API classes.

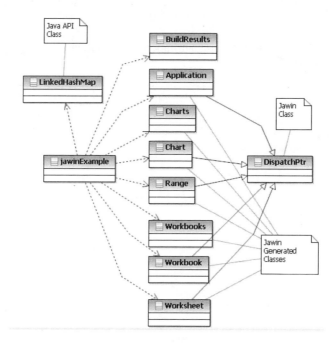

Figure 12.20   Class diagram of jawinExample

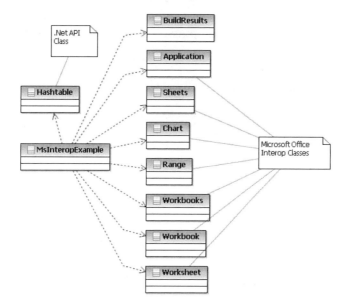

Figure 12.21   Class diagram of MsInteropExample

Imports

The first thing you need to do is to set up your imports as in Listing 12.29.

Listing 12.29   Imports

Java
```
import java.io.File;
import java.util.Iterator;
import java.util.LinkedHashMap;

import org.jawin.COMException;
import org.jawin.DispatchPtr;
import org.jawin.win32.Ole32;
```

VB.NET
```
Imports System.Collections
Imports System.IO
Imports Microsoft.Office.Interop.Excel
```

Initialize and Break Down the COM Library (Java Only)

Recall from the Simple Example in Java that you need to initialize and break down the COM library. You also need to catch or throw the COMException. This step, shown in Listing 12.30, is not required for .NET.

Listing 12.30   Initialize and break down COM library

Java
```
public void testMain(Object[] args) throws COMException
{
  //Setup COM libraries.
  Ole32.CoInitialize();

  //Tear down COM libraries.
  Ole32.CoUninitialize();
}
```

Accessing the Excel Application

To access Excel's methods, properties, and child objects, you need to access the top-level COM object, the Excel application. It is nice to see Excel as your script manipulates it, and you can do so by setting the Visible property to true. Refer to Listing 12.31.

Listing 12.31 Accessing the Excel application

Java
```
//Get a handle for Excel Application
DispatchPtr app = new DispatchPtr("Excel.Application");
app.put("Visible", true);
```

VB.NET
```
Dim xlApp As New Application()
xlApp.Visible = True
```

Accessing the Workbooks Collection

You need to gain access to the Excel workbooks collection. This enables you to create a new workbook to store the contents of `results.txt`. This is accomplished using the `Workbooks` property on your top-level object. You can then call the `Add()` function on the workbooks collection you just acquired, as shown in Listing 12.32.

Listing 12.32 Accessing the workbooks collection

Java
```
//Create a new Excel Workbook.
DispatchPtr workbooks = (DispatchPtr) app.get("Workbooks");
DispatchPtr newWorkkbook = (DispatchPtr) workbooks.invoke("Add");
```

VB.NET
```
Dim workbooks As Workbooks = xlApp.Workbooks
Dim newWorkbook As Workbook = workbooks.Add()
```

Parsing Results.txt

The new workbook that you created is used to store the contents of your text file. It also serves to generate a three-dimensional chart. The next step you need to perform in this example is acquiring the data from results.txt. Because this is a comma-separated file, you can take advantage of the `OpenText` method exposed by the workbooks collection. This method, shown in Listing 12.33, opens results.txt as a new workbook, parsing each comma-separated value into its own cell. You need to gain control of the worksheet that contains the actual data. This is done using the Worksheets collection of the Excel application. You need to pass the name of the worksheet you want to this collection. This is the name of the file you opened, minus the file extension. Figure 12.22 shows the current state of the Excel objects after completing this step.

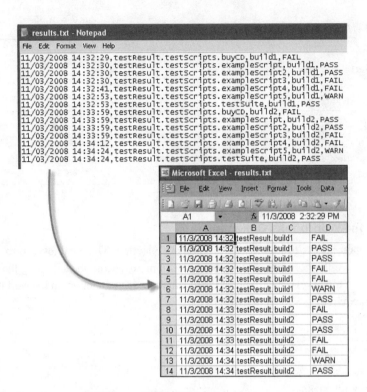

Figure 12.22   Opening results.txt in an Excel workbook

Listing 12.33   Parsing results.txt

Java

```java
//Open the results.txt file as a comma delimited file.
String resultsFile = Directory.GetCurrentDirectory() +
  "\\logs\\results.txt";
workbooks.invokeN("OpenText", new Object[] {
  resultsFile, //Filename
  new Integer(437), //Origin - xlWindows
  new Integer(1), //StartRow
  new Integer(1), //DataType - xlDelimited
  new Integer(1),   //Text Qualifier - xlTextQualifierDoubleQuote
  "true", //ConsequtiveDelimiter
  "false", //Tab,
  "false", //Semicolon,
  "true" //Comma,                                }
);
```

```
//Get a handle of results worksheet.
DispatchPtr resultsSheet =
  (DispatchPtr) app.get("Worksheets","results");
```

VB.NET
```
workbooks.OpenText("C:\results.txt", _
  XlPlatform.xlWindows, _
  1, _
  XlTextParsingType.xlDelimited, _
  XlTextQualifier.xlTextQualifierDoubleQuote, _
  "True", _
  "False", _
  "False", _
  "True")
Dim resultsSheet As Worksheet = xlApp.Worksheets("results")
```

Note several things regarding invoking the `OpenText` method in Java. You can skip this paragraph if you care only about VB.NET. Many of the parameters are of type `Variant`. You have to read the text in the API to determine what type to use in your code. Further, some of the parameters are enumerations. You can use `Integer` to represent an enumeration, and the API tells you what number represents each value. Finally, most of the parameters are optional and may be ignored.

Formatting the Data

After you have control over the results data worksheet, you can now format how you want the data displayed. Returning back to the original workbook you created, newWorkbook, you will want to rename the first worksheet, sheet1, to something more intuitive such as Results Summary. You also want to create column headers to represent the build names, execution attempts per build, and results per execution. These can be created in the initial row of the first five columns, A through E. Your worksheet that now looks like Figure 12.23 contains the summary of the results captured from the results worksheet. Refer to Listing 12.34.

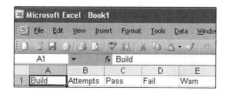

Figure 12.23   Column headers for Results Summary worksheet

Listing 12.34   Formatting the data

Java
```
//Rename "Sheet1" to "Results Summary" in new workbook
DispatchPtr rsltSummaryWorksheet =
  (DispatchPtr) newWorkkbook.get("Sheets","Sheet1");
rsltSummaryWorksheet.put("Name","Results Summary");

//Set column headings in Results Summary Sheet
DispatchPtr cell;
cell = (DispatchPtr) rsltSummaryWorksheet.get("Range","A1");
cell.put("FormulaR1C1", "Build");

cell = (DispatchPtr) rsltSummaryWorksheet.get("Range","B1");
cell.put("FormulaR1C1", "Attempts");

cell = (DispatchPtr) rsltSummaryWorksheet.get("Range","C1");
cell.put("FormulaR1C1", "Pass");

cell = (DispatchPtr) rsltSummaryWorksheet.get("Range","D1");
cell.put("FormulaR1C1", "Fail");

cell = (DispatchPtr) rsltSummaryWorksheet.get("Range","E1");
cell.put("FormulaR1C1", "Warning");
```

VB.NET
```
Dim rsltSummaryWorksheet As Worksheet = newWorkbook.Worksheets("sheet1")
rsltSummaryWorksheet.Name = "Results Summary"

rsltSummaryWorksheet.Range("A1").Value = "Build"
rsltSummaryWorksheet.Range("B1").Value = "Attempts"
rsltSummaryWorksheet.Range("C1").Value = "Pass"
rsltSummaryWorksheet.Range("D1").Value = "Fail"
rsltSummaryWorksheet.Range("E1").Value = "Warn"
```

The Build Results Utility Class

Recall the results can be found in the resultsSheet object you created earlier. A utility class shown in Listing 12.35 will help you facilitate the tallying and summarization of these results. It is used to capture the build names found in the original results.txt file. It also encapsulates the methods for incrementing, calculating, and returning the number of execution attempts per build and the results per execution attempt.

Listing 12.35   The Build Results Utility class

Java
```java
package util;
/**
 * Description   : Utility class used to track the results of a set of tests for
a build.
 */
public class BuildResults {
  private int attempts = 0;
  private int pass = 0;
  private int fail = 0;
  private int warn = 0;
  private String buildName;

  public BuildResults(String name)
  {
    buildName = name;
  }

  public int getAttempts() {
    return attempts;
  }

  public int getPass() {
    return pass;
  }

  public int getFail() {
    return fail;
  }

  public int getWarn() {
    return warn;
  }

  public String getBuildName() {
    return buildName;
  }

  public void addResult(String verdict)
  {
    attempts++;
```

```
    if(verdict.equals("PASS"))
      pass++;
    else if(verdict.equals("FAIL"))
      fail++;

    else if(verdict.equals("WARN"))
      warn++;
  }
}
```

VB.NET
```
Public Class BuildResults

  Private attempts As Integer = 0
  Private pass As Integer = 0
  Private fail As Integer = 0
  Private warn As Integer = 0
  Private buildname As String

  Public Sub New(ByVal name As String)
    buildname = name
  End Sub

  Public Function getAttempts() As Integer
    Return attempts
  End Function

  Public Sub setAttempts(ByVal a As Integer)
    attempts = a
  End Sub

  Public Function getPass() As Integer
    Return pass
  End Function

  Public Sub setPass(ByVal p As Integer)
    pass = p
  End Sub

  Public Function getFail() As Integer
    Return fail
```

```
   End Function

   Public Sub setFail(ByVal f As Integer)
     fail = f
   End Sub

   Public Function getWarn() As Integer
     Return warn
   End Function

   Public Sub setWarn(ByVal w As Integer)
     warn = w
   End Sub

   Public Function getBuildName() As String
     Return buildname
   End Function

   Public Sub addResult(ByVal verdict As String)
     attempts = attempts + 1

     Select Case verdict
       Case "PASS"
         pass = pass + 1
       Case "FAIL"
         fail = fail + 1
       Case "WARN"
         warn = warn + 1
     End Select
   End Sub
End Class
```

Filtering results.txt by Build

This `BuildResults` utility class is first used to filter the results.txt data by build. This is accomplished by `iterating` through a `For` loop, based off of the number of populated rows in the result worksheet (in the results.txt workbook). The build names are used as keys in a hashtable called `resultsSummary`. If a build name does not exist in the hashtable, it is added; otherwise, it is ignored. This prevents duplicate keys. The `addResult()` method, of the `BuildResults` class is then called to increment the number of passes, failures, and warnings found for each execution attempt per build. Refer to Listing 12.36.

Listing 12.36   Filtering results.txt by build

Java
```
//Get the number of rows in the results sheet.
DispatchPtr usedRange =
   (DispatchPtr) resultsSheet.get("UsedRange");
DispatchPtr rows = (DispatchPtr) usedRange.get("Rows");
int numRows = ((Integer)rows.get("Count")).intValue();

//Count the number of attempts, passes, fails and warning
// verdicts.
LinkedHashMap<String, util.BuildResults> resultsSummary =
   new LinkedHashMap<String, util.BuildResults>();
for(int i=1;i<= numRows;i++)
{
  //Parse the build name and the verdict from the current row.
  DispatchPtr buildCell =
     (DispatchPtr) resultsSheet.get("Range","C" + i);
  DispatchPtr verdictCell =
     (DispatchPtr) resultsSheet.get("Range","D" + i);

  //Retrieve the build results record for the build. If there
  //is no record, add it.
  util.BuildResults b =
   resultsSummary.get(buildCell.get("FormulaR1C1").toString());
  if(b == null)
  {
    b = new util.BuildResults(
        buildCell.get("FormulaR1C1").toString());
    resultsSummary.put(buildCell.get("FormulaR1C1").toString(),b);
  }

  //Update verdict totals.
  b.addResult(verdictCell.get("FormulaR1C1").toString());
}
```

.NET
```
Dim numRows As Long = resultsSheet.UsedRange.Rows.Count
Dim resultsSummary As New Hashtable

Dim i As Long
For i = 1 To numRows
  Dim buildCell As Range = resultsSheet.Range("C" & i)
  Dim verdictCell As Range = resultsSheet.Range("D" & i)
```

```
  Dim b As util.interop.excel.BuildResults = _
    resultsSummary(buildCell.FormulaR1C1.ToString())

  If (b Is Nothing) Then
    b = New util.interop.excel.BuildResults( _
      buildCell.FormulaR1C1.ToString())
    resultsSummary.Add(buildCell.FormulaR1C1.ToString(), b)
  End If

    b.addResult(verdictCell.FormulaR1C1.ToString)
Next
```

Populating the Result Summary Sheet

The utility class is then used within a `While` loop. The `resultsSummary` hashtable is revisited to acquire its values enumerator. This drives the number of iterations in the `While` loop. Each iteration solicits the `BuildResults` class, obtaining build names, execution attempts, and execution results. Refer to Listing 12.37.

Listing 12.37   Populating the Result Summary sheet

Java
```
//iterate through build records, and output build results (attempts,
//passes, fails, warnings).
Iterator<util.BuildResults> itr = resultsSummary.values().iterator();
int i = 2;
while(itr.hasNext())
{
  util.BuildResults b = itr.next();

  DispatchPtr summaryBuildCell =
    (DispatchPtr) rsltSummaryWorksheet.get("Range","A" + i);
  summaryBuildCell.put("FormulaR1C1", b.getBuildName());

  DispatchPtr attemptsCell =
    (DispatchPtr) rsltSummaryWorksheet.get("Range","B" + i);
  attemptsCell.put("FormulaR1C1",
    String.valueOf(b.getAttempts()));

  DispatchPtr passCell =
    (DispatchPtr) rsltSummaryWorksheet.get("Range","C" + i);
  passCell.put("FormulaR1C1", String.valueOf(b.getPass()));

  DispatchPtr failCell =
```

```
    (DispatchPtr) rsltSummaryWorksheet.get("Range","D" + i);
  failCell.put("FormulaR1C1", String.valueOf(b.getFail()));

  DispatchPtr warnCell =
      (DispatchPtr) rsltSummaryWorksheet.get("Range","E" + i);
  warnCell.put("FormulaR1C1", String.valueOf(b.getWarn()));

  i++;
}
```

VB.NET
```
Dim e As IEnumerator = resultsSummary.Values.GetEnumerator()
i = 2

While (e.MoveNext)
  Dim b As util.interop.excel.BuildResults = e.Current
  rsltSummaryWorksheet.Range("A" & i).Value = b.getBuildName
  rsltSummaryWorksheet.Range("B" & i).Value = b.getAttempts
  rsltSummaryWorksheet.Range("C" & i).Value = b.getPass
  rsltSummaryWorksheet.Range("D" & i).Value = b.getFail
  rsltSummaryWorksheet.Range("E" & i).Value = b.getWarn
  i = i + 1
End While
```

Creating the Chart

The last piece of this example, shown in Listing 12.38, is creating the chart. After selecting the cells that you populated in the results summary worksheet, you need to gain access to the charts collection in the first workbook you created (that is, newWorkbook). This collection enables you to add a new chart using its Add() method. You are allowed to specify the chart's name, type, and whether it is plotted by columns or rows.

Listing 12.38   Creating the chart

Java
```
//Select cells in the results summary sheet so they may be
//charted.
DispatchPtr cells =
  (DispatchPtr)  rsltSummaryWorksheet.get("UsedRange");
newWorkkbook.invoke("Activate");
cells.invoke("Select");

//Add a new chart.
DispatchPtr charts = (DispatchPtr) newWorkkbook.get("Charts");
```

```
DispatchPtr resultsChart = (DispatchPtr) charts.invoke("Add");
resultsChart.put("Name","Results Summary Chart");

//Set chart properties.
resultsChart.put("PlotBy", new Integer(2));        //xlColumns
resultsChart.put("ChartType",new Integer(54));     //xl3DColumnClustered
```

VB.NET
```
newWorkbook.Activate()
rsltSummaryWorksheet.Cells.Select()

Dim charts As Sheets = newWorkbook.Charts
Dim chart As Chart = charts.Add

chart.Name = "Results Summary Chart"
chart.ChartType = XlChartType.xl3DColumnClustered
chart.PlotBy = XlRowCol.xlColumns
```

Encapsulating Jawin Code in a Set of Classes

Using Jawin to interface to a scriptable COM component from Java is powerful because the Jawin code is simple and generic. However, the code is so generic that it is ugly, difficult to understand, and difficult to maintain. One area of concern is the parameters passed to the methods in Excel are not type safe. It is recommended that you encapsulate the Jawin code in a set of wrapper classes, which in turn invoke Excel methods.

The Jawin project comes with an application called the `TypeBrowser`, which can be used to generate wrapper classes. You point it to a .dll or an executable and it produces the code. Refer to the `TypeBrowser` documentations for instructions to generate code to access Excel. The generated code is a useful starting point, but also has many issues:

- The generated code does not compile because there are many classes that are referenced, but not generated. There are also many instances where a class is defined as `_ClassName`, but referenced as `Class` (`_Application` vs `Application`). Finally, some methods use variables that are undefined.

- Many of the parameters to methods are of type `Variant`. Using this type is cumbersome and not beneficial in terms of maintaining type safety.

- Many of the method signatures include unnecessary parameters. The Excel Object Model has many methods with long lists of optional parameters. Although the API supports ignoring optional parameters, the generated code uses each one. The generated code for Workbooks.OpenText, for example, has 18 parameters (only 1 is required). Calling a method with this many parameters is ugly.

Despite all of the issues, using the generated code is much better than starting from scratch. After you understand the Jawin interface and the interface of the Com object you are interfacing to, it is a simple matter of altering the code to be more useful. As an example, Listing 12.39 is a Rational Functional Tester test script that accomplishes the same task as the previous simple example. This script uses classes that are generated using the `TypeBrowser` and then altered to correct the issues just described.

Listing 12.39   Hello World Rational Functional Tester script using classes to encapsulate Jawin

Java
```java
package testScripts;

import org.jawin.COMException;
import org.jawin.win32.Ole32;
import util.jawin.excel.Application;
import util.jawin.excel.Workbooks;
import resources.testScripts.jawinExample3Helper;

public class jawinExample2 extends jawinExample2Helper
{
  public void testMain(Object[] args) throws COMException
  {

    //Setup COM libraries.
    Ole32.CoInitialize();

    //Get a handle for Excel Application
    Application app = new Application("Excel.Application");
    app.put("Visible", true);

    //Create a new Excel Workbook.
    Workbooks workbooks = app.getWorkbooks();
    workbooks.Add();

    //Set some text.
    app.getActiveCell().setValue("Hello World!");

    //Tear down COM libraries.
    Ole32.CoUninitialize();
  }
}
```

Listing 12.40 shows the `Application` class used in the `jawinExample2` test script. Only the methods used in the test script are shown.

Listing 12.40 The `Application` class

Java
```java
package util.jawin.excel;

import org.jawin.COMException;
import org.jawin.DispatchPtr;
import org.jawin.GUID;
import org.jawin.IdentityManager;

public class Application extends DispatchPtr {
  public static final GUID DIID =
    new GUID("{000208d5-0000-0000-C000-000000000046}");
  public static final int IID_TOKEN;
  static {
    IID_TOKEN = IdentityManager.registerProxy(DIID,
            Application.class);
  }

  public Application() {
    super();
  }

  public Application(String progid) throws COMException {
    super(progid, DIID);
  }

    public Workbooks getWorkbooks() throws COMException
    {
        Workbooks res = new Workbooks();
          DispatchPtr dispPtr = (DispatchPtr)get("Workbooks");
          res.stealUnknown(dispPtr);
          return res;
    }

    public Range getActiveCell() throws COMException
    {
      Range res = new Range();
          DispatchPtr dispPtr = (DispatchPtr)get("ActiveCell");
          res.stealUnknown(dispPtr);
          return res;
    }
}
```

Listing 12.41 shows the `Workbooks` class used in the `jawinExample2` test script. Only the methods used in the test script are shown.

Listing 12.41   The `Workbooks` class

Java

```
package util.jawin.excel;

import org.jawin.COMException;
import org.jawin.DispatchPtr;
import org.jawin.GUID;
import org.jawin.IdentityManager;

public class Workbooks extends DispatchPtr {
  public static final GUID DIID =
    new GUID("{000208db-0000-0000-C000-000000000046}");
  public static final int IID_TOKEN;
  static {
    IID_TOKEN = IdentityManager.registerProxy(DIID,
            Workbooks.class);
  }

  public Workbooks() {
    super();
  }

  public Workbooks(String progid) throws COMException {
    super(progid, DIID);
  }

    public Workbook Add() throws COMException
    {
      Workbook res = new Workbook();
        DispatchPtr dispPtr = (DispatchPtr)invoke("Add");
        res.stealUnknown(dispPtr);
        return res;
    }
}
```

Listing 12.42 shows the `Range` class used in the `jawinExample2` test script. Only the methods used in the test script are shown.

Listing 12.42   The Range class

Java

```java
package util.jawin.excel;

import org.jawin.COMException;
import org.jawin.DispatchPtr;
import org.jawin.GUID;
import org.jawin.IdentityManager;

public class Range extends DispatchPtr {
  public static final GUID DIID =
    new GUID("{00020846-0000-0000-C000-000000000046}");
  public static final int IID_TOKEN;
  static {
    IID_TOKEN = IdentityManager.registerProxy(DIID, Range.class);
  }

  public Range() {
    super();
  }

  public Range(String progid) throws COMException {
    super(progid, DIID);
  }

  public void setValue(String newValue) throws COMException
  {
    put("FormulaR1C1", newValue);
  }

  public String getValue() throws COMException
  {
    return get("FormulaR1C1").toString();
  }

  public int getCount() throws COMException
  {
    return ((Integer)get("Count")).intValue();
  }

  public Range getRows() throws COMException
```

```
    {
    Range res = new Range();
        DispatchPtr dispPtr = (DispatchPtr)get("Rows");
        res.stealUnknown(dispPtr);
    return res;

    }


    public Object Select() throws COMException
    {
       return invokeN("Select", new Object[] {});
    }

}
```

Summary

This chapter covers several examples of how you can extend the capability of Rational Functional Tester using existing external libraries. You now have an understanding of how you might use PDFBox to load a PDF file and extract the text from it. This extracted text is the basis for a custom verification point using the google-diff-match-patch library as the comparison algorithm. You learned how to create a logging framework that leverages the configuration capabilities of log4j and log4net. Finally, you learned how to interface to Excel to create a charting utility, which can be run from a Rational Functional Tester script. This utility reads the output from the logs in the logging example. You can run large sets of tests, and then execute the charting script to automatically create a chart suitable for your test report.

You can easily build on these examples to create powerful test automation capabilities. You can create a logging solution that sends logs to a central log server. You can create a framework for testing Excel-based applications. You can explore other pieces of PDFBox that you can take advantage of such as highlighting words, wrapping stripped text in simple HTML, and stripping text from a specified region. You might instead choose to work with other external libraries. The possibilities are endless.

## CHAPTER 13

Building Support for New Objects with the Proxy SDK

Daniel Gouveia

Automating custom controls usually ends up with one of two things happening: You either create a series of custom scripting methods or abandon the piece of your automation project that contains the custom controls. Rational Functional Tester actually provides a third option—building support for your control(s) directly into its record and playback capabilities. This provides a great benefit to you and the rest of your team. They do not have to work at the code-level and call the methods that you constructed to handle custom controls. Instead, they can continue engaging Rational Functional Tester's record and playback engine, automating the application's custom control(s) much like everything else they automated. This chapter, along with the documentation in Rational Functional Tester's Help files, should provide you with a good starting point for building new capabilities for custom controls into Rational Functional Tester.

Creating record and playback support for custom control(s) is handled through the Proxy SDK. This chapter introduces you to it and covers topics at a higher and hopefully easier level to understand. It is broken down so that you can understand the information as it relates to the following three typical tasks you automate:

- *Verifying object properties*
- *Verifying object data*
- *Clicking via object information*

You also encounter some supporting tasks for creating a new proxy project, building it, "plugging" it into Rational Functional Tester, and debugging it. You do not need to read this chapter straight through. You are welcome to skip around to the different sections. However, you might want to acquaint yourself with the first two sections. They cover the content for understanding proxies and creating the proxy projects inside of Eclipse and .NET Studio.

The final thing to note is that proxies are developed using either Java or Visual C#®. Java is used to develop proxies for Abstract Windows Toolkit (AWT), Swing, Standard Widget Toolkit (SWT), and Applet controls. For .NET, Win32, Siebel, and SAP controls, you use C#. Rational Functional Tester's help files provide the list of software requirements to carry out this task. Just look under the Proxy Development Environment topic.

Figuring Out Which Proxy to Extend

The first step to creating a proxy is gaining an understanding of the Graphical User Interface (GUI) control that you actually try to create a proxy for. The control is either created from a base class or the base class itself. A *base class* is the unit that Rational Functional Tester understands. When you hear people talking about Rational Functional Tester supporting .NET, Java, and so on, it means that Rational Functional Tester understands and can interact with the base classes that represent the .NET and Java (and other) GUI controls. The base class is the key piece of information that you need to figure out. Acquiring knowledge of it can give you an understanding of the Rational Functional Tester proxy class that you need to extend. The out-of-the-box proxy classes give Rational Functional Tester its capability to work with the technologies it supports. For instance, clicking a .NET button, navigating a JTable, entering text into an HTML input field, and so on are performed with proxy classes that are part of Rational Functional Tester. Extending these standard proxies simply means that you build on top of their capabilities. An example of this might involve extending a proxy to add a new data test. The original out-of-the-box proxy works just fine; you just need to add a new way of testing data in your control.

In most cases, Rational Functional Tester provides a shortcut to base class information via its Test Object Map. An example to illustrate this is the SWT `DateTime` control. It is part of the Eclipse SWT control-set (see Figure 13.1).

Figure 13.1   `DateTime` control

Rational Functional Tester is able to recognize this control. However, it is unable to capture data or execute a data verification point (VP) for it. Therefore, you seek to extend the out-of-the-box capabilities that Rational Functional Tester interacts with this `DateTime` by adding the ability to test its data (see Figure 13.2).

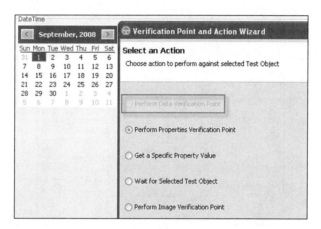

Figure 13.2   Verification Point Wizard—no data verification point

Further, when looking at the properties, you can see that a selected date type of property does not exist for this control. This is another area that you should extend, adding capability to the original proxy so Rational Functional Tester can test for a selected date (see Figure 13.3).

You can create a custom proxy to add these capabilities to Rational Functional Tester's Verification Point Wizard. As mentioned in this section's opening paragraph, you first need to understand which proxy to extend for this control. You can acquire useful information by placing this control in Rational Functional Tester's Test Object Map (for example, start recording and simply click on it). The Administrative properties, for this control, contain the `Proxy Class Name` (`#proxy`) property. This property lets you know what proxy Rational Functional Tester uses to work with the `DateTime` control (see Figure 13.4).

You can see that Rational Functional Tester uses the `CompositeProxy` to work with it. It does not have an explicit proxy to interact with the `DateTime` control (that is no DateTime-Proxy). If it did, you would have seen it in the `Proxy Class Name` (`#proxy`) property, instead of the `CompositeProxy`. You now know that the `CompositeProxy` is the base proxy you need to extend, adding the necessary verification point capabilities mentioned previously.

There are some cases where Rational Functional Tester won't recognize the control at all. In other words, it isn't able to add it to the map, capture properties, test for data, and so on. It is almost as if it is invisible to Rational Functional Tester. In these instances, you are not able to use the Test Object Map shortcut to understand which proxy to extend. This is where you need to figure out the base class for the control using other sources.

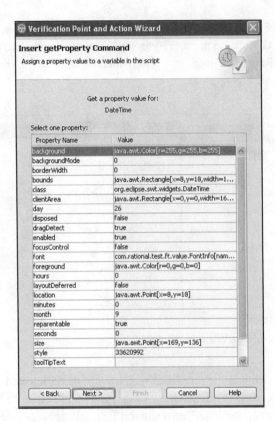

Figure 13.3   Verification Point Wizard—no selected date type of property

A good place to start figuring out which Rational Functional Tester proxy to extend is by looking for information about the target control class. Control developers, the control's API documentation, and the actual source code itself can provide this information. Developers are usually able to provide you with the quickest answer. They have an intimate understanding of the source code with which they are working. A quick email, instant message, or phone call usually results in the information that you need—the base class.

If you don't have access to the development staff, perusing the API documentation can be helpful. It can also be daunting. You can shorten your search by simply looking at the hierarchy information for the class that your GUI control instantiates. For instance, in the Java world, you can use the Javadoc. You can find similar API documentation for other controls; for instance, you can search MSDN for Win32 and .NET control information. Regardless of the documentation you need to use, you should be able to find the class hierarchy for your control. Figure 13.5 shows what this information would look like for the DateTime control.

Traversing the DateTime hierarchy shows you that the org.eclipse.swt.widgets. DateTime class is derived from the org.eclipse.swt.widgets.Composite class, which is derived from the org.eclipse.swt.widgets.Scrollable class, and so on. Starting at the

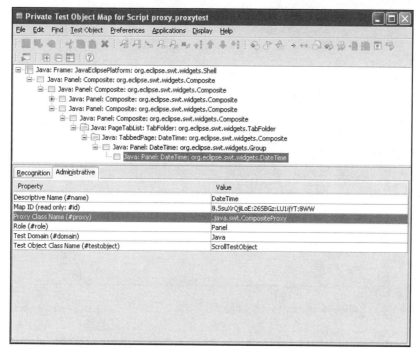

Figure 13.4   Test Object Map—DateTime object's administrative properties

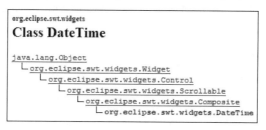

Figure 13.5   Javadoc for DateTime control—hierarchy

bottom of the list with the `DateTime` class, you want to see which Rational Functional Tester proxy matches up. Looking in Rational Functional Tester's help files, you can find the list of proxies for the SWT domain.

Figure 13.6 shows that a proxy does not exist for the `DateTime` control. It also shows that a proxy does, however, exist for the Composite control (outlined in the red box). This matches up against the `org.eclipse.swt.widgets.Composite` class in the `DateTime` control's hierarchy.

The last means of finding hierarchical information is the source code. If you have access to it, you can find the source files that contain the class your custom control is built from. Depending on your ability to read source files, this can be a difficult or easy task. It can almost seem like you are connecting the dots, looking at each class signature to see what other class it extends, and stopping only when you have found the base class.

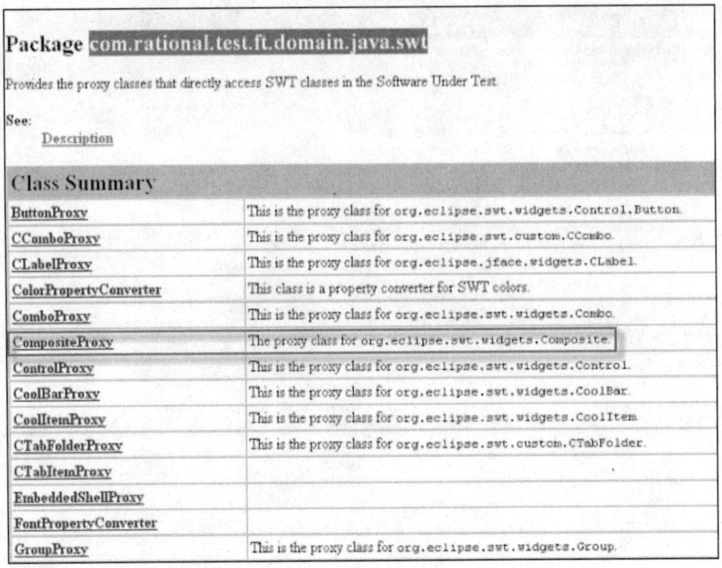
Package com.rational.test.ft.domain.java.swt

Provides the proxy classes that directly access SWT classes in the Software Under Test.

See:
Description

Class Summary	
ButtonProxy	This is the proxy class for org.eclipse.swt.widgets.Control.Button.
CComboProxy	This is the proxy class for org.eclipse.swt.custom.CCombo.
CLabelProxy	This is the proxy class for org.eclipse.jface.widgets.CLabel.
ColorPropertyConverter	This class is a property converter for SWT colors.
ComboProxy	This is the proxy class for org.eclipse.swt.widgets.Combo.
CompositeProxy	The proxy class for org.eclipse.swt.widgets.Composite.
ControlProxy	This is the proxy class for org.eclipse.swt.widgets.Control.
CoolBarProxy	This is the proxy class for org.eclipse.swt.widgets.CoolBar.
CoolItemProxy	This is the proxy class for org.eclipse.swt.widgets.CoolItem.
CTabFolderProxy	This is the proxy class for org.eclipse.swt.custom.CTabFolder.
CTabItemProxy	
EmbeddedShellProxy	
FontPropertyConverter	
GroupProxy	This is the proxy class for org.eclipse.swt.widgets.Group.

Figure 13.6 SWT proxies—`CompositeProxy`

A good example of this is DevAge's `SourceGrid` control package, also covered in Chapter 10, "Advanced Scripting with Rational Functional Tester TestObjects" (see Figure 13.7). The `SourceGrid` is a C# package that uses a `Grid` class to represent a GUI control similar to a base .NET grid.

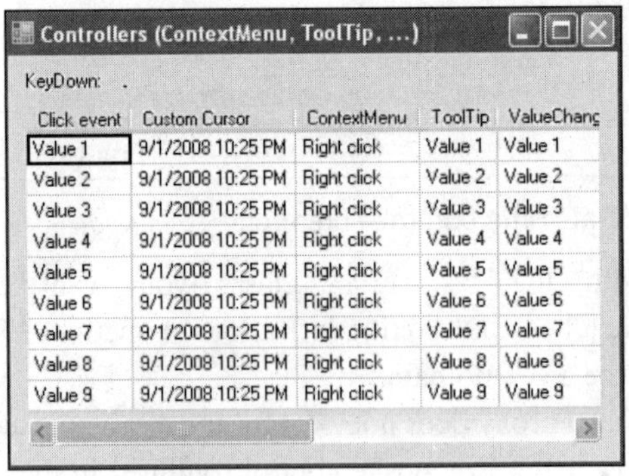

Figure 13.7 `SourceGrid`

Rational Functional Tester has no understanding of this. In fact, it won't even see it or map it (for example, you do not see the red box and tool tip around it when you are recording a verification point against it). Building a proxy for this requires that you gain an understanding of the base class. You can use the source code to "connect the dots," starting with the `Grid` class, until you find it.

You can see in Figure 13.8 that the `SourceGrid` `Grid` class extends the `GridVirtual` class. This is another part of the `SourceGrid` package. Looking further, you find that the `GridVirtual` class extends another custom `SourceGrid` class, `CustomScrollControl`. This class extends the `System.Windows.Forms.Panel` class. The System.Windows.Forms namespace tips you off that the Panel class is, indeed, the base class you are looking for. You can look in Rational Functional Tester's Help files to find list of proxies for the .NET domain. This list would show that an out-of-the-box `PanelProxy` exists (see Figure 13.9).

```
public partial class Grid : GridVirtual
       public abstract class GridVirtual : CustomScrollControl
              public abstract class CustomScrollControl : System.Windows.Forms.Panel
```

Figure 13.8   SourceGrid class hierarchy

Figure 13.9   .NET proxies— `PanelProxy`

Creating a Proxy Project

After you know what proxy to extend, you need to create a project for it. If you are building a proxy for a Java GUI control, you can take advantage of the Java development environment that lives in the same Eclipse shell as Rational Functional Tester. If you need to create a proxy for a .NET control, you need to build it using C#. This might be part of the .NET Studio 2003 or 2005 instance you installed Rational Functional Tester into.

Java Project

The first thing to state from the start: You must not use proxies that were compiled with a version of Java that is newer than Rational Functional Tester's version of Java. This causes Unsupported-ClassVersionError issues. Now that you know this, on with the proxy project topic. The Eclipse SWT `DateTime` GUI control example requires a Java proxy. This is handled by switching to the Java perspective in Rational Functional Tester's Eclipse shell. You can do this by selecting: **Window > Open Perspective > Other > Java**. You then create a new Java project by selecting:

File > New > Java Project. The New Java Project wizard displays. You can simply provide a name and location for your project and click the **Finish** button.

The project stores the proxy that you create. This is actually a Java class file. Prior to creating this new class file, Java development best practices suggest you create a package to store it in. This is done by right-clicking on your project and selecting **New > Package**. You call the package for your `DateTime` project **sdk.custom.swt**. This represents the custom SWT proxies you build.

Finally, you can create the new class by right-clicking on the **sdk.custom.swt** package and selecting **New > Class**. This invokes the New Java Class wizard. Aside from providing the necessary package and class name information in this wizard, you need to specify the correct Superclass to extend. In this case, it is the `CompositeProxy` Superclass (for example, what your research returned). To make the change, do the following (see Figure 13.10):

1. Click the **Browse** button next to the Superclass text field; this launches the **Superclass Selection** dialog box.

2. Type **Composite** in the Choose a type: text field; this lists the classes that match your entry.

Figure 13.10 Set `CompositeProxy` as Superclass

3. Select the **CompositeProxy** class that is part of the **com.rational.test.ft. domain.java.swt** package.

NOTE If the CompositeProxy class does not show up, you need to add a reference to the RATIONAL_FT_LIB variable. (For example, click the Add Variable button on your project's Java Build Path.)

---

4. Click the **OK** button.

The last thing that you need to do in the New Java Class wizard, is select the **Constructors from superclass** checkbox. This ensures that the appropriate constructor method(s)—from the CompositeProxy class—are used (see Figure 13.11).

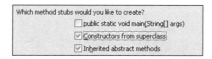

Which method stubs would you like to create?
☐ public static void main(String[] args)
☑ Constructors from superclass
☑ Inherited abstract methods

Figure 13.11 New Java class wizard—constructors from superclass checkbox

Click the **Finish** button to complete the class creation. Listing 13.1 shows what the resulting proxy class looks like.

Listing 13.1 ExtendedCompositeProxy class

```
package sdk.custom.swt;

import com.rational.test.ft.domain.java.swt.CompositeProxy;

public class ExtendedDateTimeProxy extends CompositeProxy {

    public ExtendedDateTimeProxy(Object theObjectInTheSUT) {
        super(theObjectInTheSUT);
        // TODO Auto-generated constructor stub
    }
}
```

The code in Listing 13.1 shows you three things. First, it shows that an import statement to the com.rational.test.ft.domain.java.swt.CompositeProxy class is automatically created. Secondly, it gives the skeleton of your ExtendedDateTimeProxy class. Finally, it shows the constructor that was created from the CompositeProxy superclass. These provide the tools for extending the capabilities of the out-of-the-box CompositeProxy class with your own.

C# Project

You need to create a C# proxy project for the `SourceGrid` GUI control. This is done by selecting **File** > **New Project** to engage the New Project wizard (see Figure 13.12). You need to select **Visual C#** as your project type. You then need to choose **Windows Control Library** as the template.

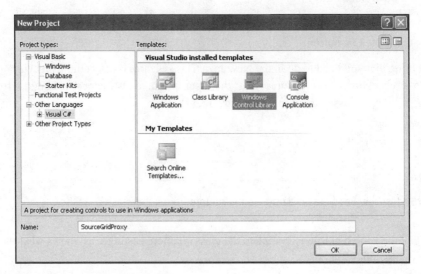

Figure 13.12   New C# Project wizard

Provide a project name and click the **OK** button to complete the process of creating your proxy project. There are still a few setup tasks to accomplish before the proxy is ready for developing. These steps ensure that your project recognizes the different proxy objects you reference.

The first thing that you need to do is to add a reference to the rtxftnet.dll file (see Figure 13.13). This enables you to see all of the proxy information available to the .NET domain. Right-clicking on your project and selecting **Add Reference** (or selecting **Project** > **Add Reference**) displays the **Add Reference** dialog box. You need to click the **Browse** tab and then navigate to the rtxftnet.dll file found in Rational Functional Tester's bin directory.

Click the **OK** button to add the reference to your project. This enables you to select the original out-of-the-box Rational Functional Tester proxy that you need to extend. In this case, it is the `PanelProxy`. This gives the basis for your new proxy class.

You need to find some method information for the `PanelProxy`. Specifically, you need to find out what constructor your class should use. The first step here is to open the **Object Browser**. You can select **View** > **Object Browser**. This lists all the object references for this project. One of those references is the .rtxftnet assembly. Expanding the .rtxftnet reference shows the different namespaces it contains. You're interested in the `Rational.Test.Ft.Domain.Net` namespace (see Figure 13.14).

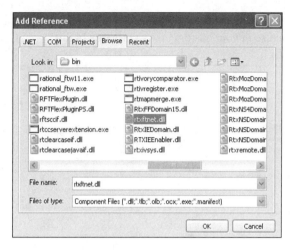

Figure 13.13   Add project reference—rtxftnet.dll

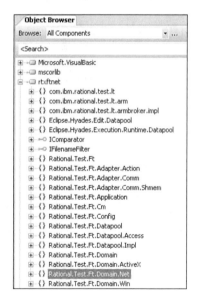

Figure 13.14   `Rational.Test.Ft.Domain.Net`

This contains the list of proxies that you can extend. Referring back to the first section in this chapter, "Figuring out Which Proxy to Extend," your research shows that the `PanelProxy` is the out-of-the-box proxy class that you want to extend. If you expand the `Rational.Test.Ft.Domain.Net` namespace, you find that the `PanelProxy` class exists in it. Further, selecting this class and viewing its *members* (such as properties, methods, and so on) reveals the constructor you need to use in your custom proxy class (see Figure 13.15).

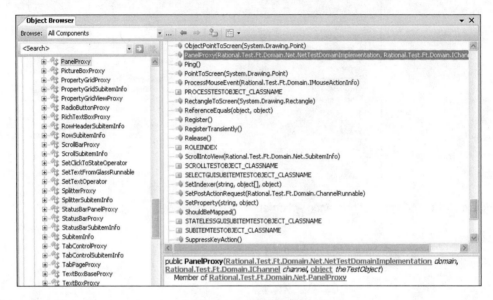

Figure 13.15 `PanelProxy class`—constructor to use

All the information that you have collected up to this point enables you to quickly create the skeleton of your proxy class. This is done by right-clicking the project and selecting **Add > Class**. You can select the **C# Class**, provide a name for it, and click the **Add** button (see Figure 13.16). This gives you a starting point. Framework code is shown in Listing 13.2.

Listing 13.2   Initial class creation

```
using System;
using System.Text;

namespace SourceGridProxy
{
    class SourceGridControlProxy
    {
    }
}
```

You need to modify this so that you can begin adding custom capabilities. This involves adding "using" statements for the `Rational.Test.Ft.Domain` and `Rational.Test.Ft.Domain.Net` namespaces. These namespaces provide you with access to the necessary classes for your constructor.

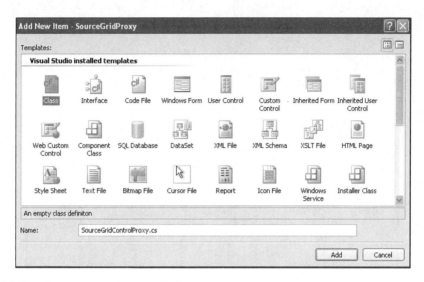

Figure 13.16   Create proxy class—called `SourceGridControlProxy`

```
using Rational.Test.Ft.Domain;
using Rational.Test.Ft.Domain.Net;
```

You also need to extend the `Rational.Test.Ft.Domain.Net.PanelProxy` class. This provides you access to all the methods to override. You can accomplish this by adding this class to the end of your class definition, separating the two by a colon. An example of what this looks like is shown in the following line of code:

```
class SourceGridControlProxy :
Rational.Test.Ft.Domain.Net.PanelProxy
```

The next thing is to provide the constructor information. You can copy and paste this from the `PanelProxy` constructor. This is easily done by returning to the Object View, expanding the `Rational.Test.Ft.Domain.Net` namespace, selecting `PanelProxy`, scrolling to and selecting the `PanelProxy` constructor, and copying and pasting from its definition from the bottom of the browser. You need to change the name of the constructor method from `PanelProxy` to the name of the proxy you are building. In your case, it is `SourceGridControlProxy`. The following code listing shows what your constructor should look like.

```
public SourceGridControlProxy(NetTestDomainImplementation domain,
                        IChannel channel, object theTestObject)
                : base(domain, channel, theTestObject)

{
}
```

Figure 13.17 shows what your initial class should look like.

```
using System;
using System.Collections.Generic;
using System.Text;

using Rational.Test.Ft.Domain;
using Rational.Test.Ft.Domain.Net;

namespace SourceGridProxy
{
    class SourceGridControlProxy : Rational.Test.Ft.Domain.Net.PanelProxy
    {
        #region constructor

        public SourceGridControlProxy(NetTestDomainImplementation domain,
                                IChannel channel, object theTestObject)
                                : base(domain, channel, theTestObject)

        {
        }

        #endregion
    }
}
```

Figure 13.17   Initial class after modifications

One last thing to consider at this point is adding a reference to the SourceGrid.dll and DevAge.Core.dll files (found in the `SourceGrid` installation's bin directory). It is not imperative that it is done at this point. However, this enables you to avoid any missing class issues as you go through the different sections.

You should now have a basis for what it takes to create a new proxy. The next step is to build out your proxy by overriding the methods found in the out-of-the-box proxy class. This would be the `CompositeProxy` class for the `DateTime` control and the `PanelProxy` class for the `SourceGrid Grid` control. This is done by creating your own custom Java or C# code for these methods. You also find that you end up creating your own custom methods to handle certain supporting tasks.

Adding Object Recognition

Rational Functional Tester might or might not recognize custom controls in your application. If it does, it usually is able only to give you limited information and provide limited capabilities for the control. This is true for the `DateTime` example. Rational Functional Tester recognizes it. However, it does not provide a verification point for its object data nor does it have a selected date property. In your (.NET) example, on the other hand, the `SourceGrid Grid` control isn't even recognized by Rational Functional Tester. In fact, Rational Functional Tester sees only the top-level form object that this control lives on. This mean you can't even get basic information or capabilities for it without a proxy.

When you encounter instances like these, you need to coax Rational Functional Tester into recognizing (or further recognizing) your object. This is done with the four methods found in Table 13.1.

Table 13.1   Proxy Development: Object Recognition Methods to Override

Java	C#
getDescriptiveName()	GetDescriptiveName()
getRole()	GetRole()
getTestObjectClassName()	GetTestObjectClassName()
shouldBeMapped()	ShouldBeMapped()

getDescriptiveName() / GetDescriptiveName()

This method provides name capabilities for Rational Functional Tester. The name (as a string) that you return from this method is the initial name provided for the `TestObject` that gets created when you record against the application's custom control.

getRole() / GetRole()

This method tells Rational Functional Tester the type of control that it is dealing with. This sets the icon that Rational Functional Tester uses to describe the `TestObject` that communicates with your proxy.

getTestObjectClassName()

Overriding this method tells Rational Functional Tester what type of `TestObject` a script should use to represent your control.

shouldBeMapped() / ShouldBeMapped()

This method tells Rational Functional Tester that it should map the custom control, providing a `TestObject` wrapper class for the proxy class. Basically, this puts the custom control into the Test Object Map.

Overriding these methods in your proxy class enables Rational Functional Tester to do more with the custom control than it can using the out-of-the-box proxy.

Java—Using the DateTime Example

The Eclipse Java perspective makes it easy to override methods. You can simply select **Source > Override/Implement Methods**. You are presented with a dialog box (see Figure 13.18) where you select the methods that you want to override (or implement). Select the methods and click the

OK button, which puts the stub code into your proxy for you. It is then up to you to change the definition of the method (that is override it).

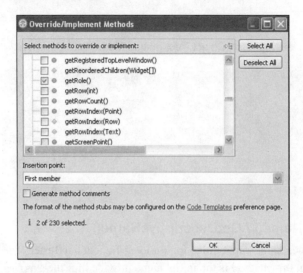

Figure 13.18   Override and implement methods

Because the `DateTime` example is recognized by Rational Functional Tester, it is safe to say that it is being mapped. You just want to make some changes so you can help Rational Functional Tester understand a little more about it. Therefore, you can simply override the `getDescriptiveName()`, `getRole()`, and `getTestObjectClassName()` methods.

getDescriptiveName()

Here is how the `getDescriptiveName()` method was overridden for your `ExtendedDate TimeProxy` class. You tell Rational Functional Tester that the `TestObject` for the `DateTime` class should be named `SWT DateTime Control`.

```
public String getDescriptiveName() {
    return "SWT DateTime Control";
}
```

In the preceding example, the initial name for the TestObject is `swtDateTimeControl` (see Figure 13.19).

When Rational Functional Tester records and maps the `DateTime` control, it causes the following two mapping behaviors to occur (see Figure 13.20):

1. The Descriptive Name displays in the tooltip when you place your cursor on the object in your script.

2. The name you provide is placed in the Administrative Properties of the Test Object Map.

Figure 13.19   Initial name of `TestObject`

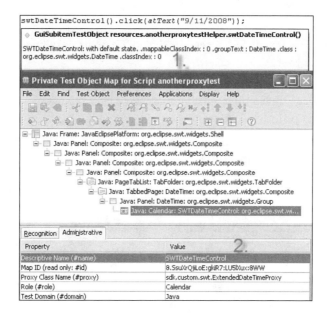

Figure 13.20   Result of `getDescriptiveName()`

getRole()

Here is how the `getRole()` method is overridden in your proxy. You tell Rational Functional Tester that the `TestObject` that is created for the `DateTime` control should be a calendar.

```
public String getRole() {
    return com.rational.test.ft.domain.TestObjectRole.ROLE_CALENDAR;
}
```

When Rational Functional Tester interacts with and maps the `DateTime` control, it does two things (see Figure 13.21). First, it associates a calendar icon with the `DateTime` Test Object it created. Second, it captures its role in the Administrative Properties of the `TestObject` Map.

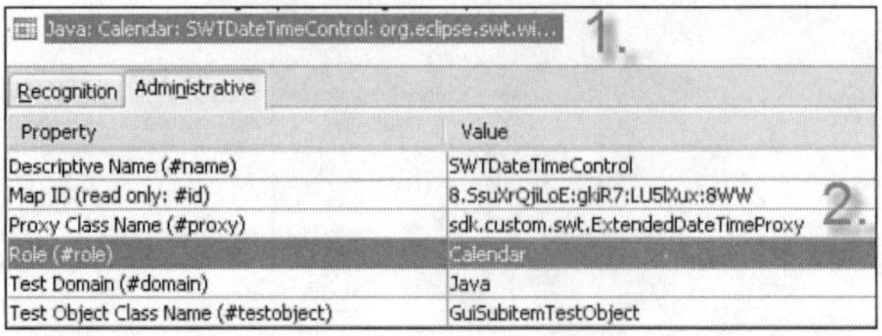

Figure 13.21   Result of overriding `getRole()`

getTestObjectClassName()

Here is the example for overriding the `getTestObjectClassName` for your `DateTime` proxy. You tell Rational Functional Tester that it should treat the resulting `TestObject` as a `GuiSubItemTestObject`.

```
public String getTestObjectClassName() {
    return ProxyTestObject.GUISUBITEMTESTOBJECT_CLASSNAME;
}
```

This gives it capabilities that can be taken advantage of later. For example, it allows for Subitems to be passed to its `click()` methods (for example, `atText()`, `atCell()`, `atIndex()`, and so on). Like the other two methods you overrode, this information gets stored in the Administrative Properties of the `TestObject` Map (see Figure 13.22).

Figure 13.22   Result of overriding `getTestObjectClassName()`

Note that you might need to import the `ProxyTestObject` class if it isn't initially recognized (for example, an error marker shows up on the line). You can do this by right-clicking the error marker and choosing Quick Fix. You can also engage the **CTRL+SHIFT+O** keystroke combination. This imports any necessary packages/classes into your class files. In this case, it imports the `com.rational.test.ft.domain.ProxyTestObject` into your proxy class file. Moving forward with this chapter, you might need to import the necessary packages and classes as you go. The keystroke combination mentioned previously helps you deal with these imports.

C#—Using the SourceGrid Grid Example

The proxy you build for the `SourceGrid Grid` control is somewhat similar to the previous Java example. You override the `GetDescriptiveName()`, `GetRole`, and `GetTestObjectClass Name()` methods. One key difference is that you also override the `ShouldBeMapped()` method. If you recall from the first section in this chapter, "Figuring Out Which Proxy to Extend," Rational Functional Tester is unable to recognize and map this control. Overriding this method enables you to change that behavior.

The C# editor in Visual Studio makes it easy to override methods. You simply need to type out the keyword **override**, press the Space key, and start typing the name of a method (see Figure 13.23). This shows you the list of methods that you can override for your proxy.

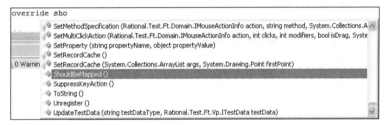

Figure 13.23   Overriding in C#

GetDescriptiveName()

You can return "`DevAge SourceGrid`" here. This provides the initial name for the `TestObject` that is recorded, as well as set up the Administrative properties (see Figure 13.24).

```
public override string GetDescriptiveName()
{
    return "DevAge SourceGrid";
}
```

Figure 13.24   Result of overriding GetDescriptiveName()

GetRole()

Providing the following code enables your proxy to inform Rational Functional Tester that it
should treat the resulting `TestObject` as a table. This provides a table icon for the `TestObject`.
It also updates the Administrative Properties in the Test Object Map (see Figure 13.25).

```
public override string GetRole()
{
    return Rational.Test.Ft.Domain.TestObjectRole.ROLE_TABLE;
}
```

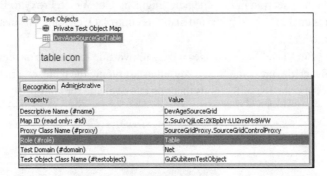

Figure 13.25 Result of overriding `GetRole()`

GetTestObjectClassName()

This example for overriding the `getTestObjectClassName()` tells Rational Functional Tester
that it should treat the resulting `TestObject` as a `GuiSubItemTestObject`. This enables you
to add some more functionality, such as using Subitems (`atIndex()`, `atCell()`, `atText()`,
and so on) to your clicks if you need to (see Figure 13.26).

```
public override string GetTestObjectClassName()
{
    return ProxyTestObject.GUISUBITEMTESTOBJECT_CLASSNAME;
}
```

Recognition	Administrative	
Property		Value
Descriptive Name (#name)		DevAgeSourceGrid
Map ID (read only: #id)		2.SsuXrQjiLoE:2KBpbY:LU2rr6M:8WW
Proxy Class Name (#proxy)		SourceGridProxy.SourceGridControlProxy
Role (#role)		Table
Test Domain (#domain)		Net
Test Object Class Name (#testobject)		GuiSubitemTestObject

Figure 13.26 Result of overriding `GetTestObjectClassName()`

ShouldBeMapped()

Overriding this method is quite simple. You return true, telling Rational Functional Tester that it should map this control, providing a `TestObject` class wrapper.

```
public override bool ShouldBeMapped()
{
    return true;
}
```

As you can see in Figures 13.24, 13.25, and 13.26, overriding this method to return true resulted in the `SourceGrid.Grid` class getting mapped. Rational Functional Tester now gives you a `TestObject` class for this.

At this point, you should understand how to develop your proxy to instruct Rational Functional Tester how to recognize (or better recognize) your application's custom control. This is a good place to start when first building a proxy. In some instances, it sets the stage for other pieces of your proxy development (for example, working with click actions and using Subitems).

Verifying Object Properties

Adding custom verifications is a big part of proxy development. Sometimes it is the only reason you build a custom proxy. The out-of-the-box proxy doesn't provide the verification that you want to implement; therefore, you need to extend it to accommodate the test you want to perform. One way to do this is by overriding the following two methods in Table 13.2.

Table 13.2   Proxy Development: Object Property Methods to Override

Java	C#
`public Hashtable getProperties()`	`public override Hashtable GetProperties()`
`public Object getProperty(String propertyName)`	`public override object GetProperty(string propertyName)`

These methods are used to add new properties to the list exposed by the `TestObject`. Overriding the `getProperties()`/`GetProperties()` method enables you to expose your own custom properties to Rational Functional Tester's Verification Point Wizard. Further, you are able to use the Test Object Inspector to see these properties when you hover over your custom control. The `getProperty()`/`GetProperty()` method enables you to create your own custom properties, making them accessible through the `TestObject` API method `getProperty()`/`GetProperty()`. The following examples show that you can combine these methods in a clever way so that `getProperties()`/`GetProperties()` uses `getProperty()`/`getProperty()` to do its work.

Java—Using the DateTime Example

The first section in this chapter, "Figuring Out Which Proxy to Extend," mentioned that the `DateTime` GUI control did not contain a selected date property. If you use an Object Properties Verification Point with the out-of-the-box property, you do not see a property that tells you what the selected date is (see Figure 13.27).

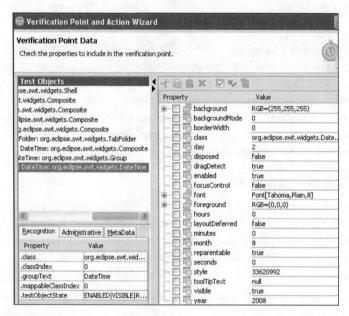

Figure 13.27 Object Properties Verification Point—no "selected date" property

Overriding the `getProperties()` and `getProperty()` methods in a proxy enable you to create a new property, `selectedDate`, and add it to the list of properties Rational Functional Tester can test for. See Listing 13.3.

Listing 13.3 Overridden methods that create a new property

getProperties()
```
public Hashtable getProperties(){
        Hashtable properties = super.getProperties();
   try{
      properties.put("selectedDate", getProperty("selectedDate"));
   } catch (Throwable e){
      debug.error("MYCUSTOMPROXY: " + e.getMessage());
   }

   return properties;
}
```

getProperty()

```
public Object getProperty(String propertyName){
    if (propertyName.equals("selectedDate"))
        return getDateAsString();
    return super.getProperty(propertyName);
}
```

Reviewing the two code listings shows that getProperty() services getProperties(). The code for getProperties() is simple. It makes a call to the out-of-the-box proxy's getProperties() method to get the list of properties it normally captures. It stores this in a Hashtable, aptly called properties. This enables you to manage the list of properties as a list of names and values. The getProperties() method then adds your custom property to the properties Hashtable. It uses selectedDate as the name and calls the getProperty() method to get the value. If it is successful on adding the new property() to the Hashtable, it returns it. It if is not successful, it writes out a debug message, returns the original set of properties, and ignores your attempt to synthesize your own property.

The overridden getProperty() method is straightforward to understand. It accepts the property name as a string argument called propertyName. In your example, this is selectedDate. If the propertyName argument equals selectedDate, it calls another method, getDateAsString(), to handle attaining the property value to return. If the propertyName argument is not selectedDate, it calls the out-of-the-box proxy's getProperty() method, passing in propertyName and returning the value it acquires.

You saw that the overridden getProperty() method called out to another method to do its work, getDateAsString(). It is a custom method written for the express purpose of returning the value of a selected date (see Listing 13.4).

Listing 13.4 getDateAsString()—custom method

```
public String getDateAsString(){
    try{
        int day = ((DateTime)this.theTestObject).getDay();
        // month is 0-based (e.g. 0 = jan) add 1 to it
        int month = ((DateTime)this.theTestObject).getMonth() + 1;
        int year = ((DateTime)this.theTestObject).getYear();

        return month + "/" + day + "/" + year;
    } catch(ClassCastException cce){
        cce.printStackTrace();
    } catch(Exception e){
        e.printStackTrace();
    }
    return null;
}
```

The first thing `getDateAsString()` does is try to cast the object reference that is being manipulated as a `DateTime` class. When you see `this.theTestObject`, you use a stolen reference to the control object for which you write the proxy. This is the GUI object that Rational Functional Tester records against. Casting it to the `DateTime` class enables you to call the methods needed to get the day, month, and year that are currently selected. These are `getDay()`, `getMonth()`, and `getYear()`, respectively. To use the `DateTime` class, you need to place the swt.jar file in your proxy project's Java Build Path (see Figure 13.28).

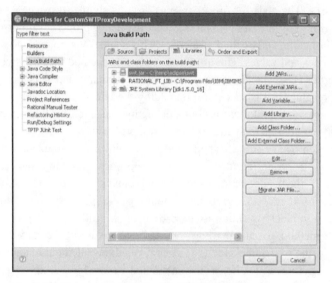

Figure 13.28   swt.jar added to proxy project's Java Build Path

The cast also requires you to add the following imports statement at the top of your class file:

```
import org.eclipse.swt.widgets.DateTime;
```

If the cast is successful, you are able to manipulate the different methods of the `DateTime` class. If it isn't successful, the `ClassCastException` is caught and handled, printing out the stack trace.

Because the goal of this method is to return a selected date value, you can use the following `DateTime` methods: `getDay()`, `getMonth()`, and `getYear()`. They each return an integer that represents their specific piece of the date that was selected by the end user. For instance, if `getDay()` returns 15, it represents that the 15th day of the year was selected. The `getYear()` method is self-explanatory, returning the selected four-digit year. Finally, the `getMonth()` method requires a little bit of extra processing. This is because it returns the selected month based off a 0-based numbering. In other words, 0 represents January, 1 represents February, and so on. This is easily resolved by adding one to the selected month. The return value for this method is a string. This string gets constructed and returned as the following "selected date" format: month/day/year.

Successfully overriding these methods results in Rational Functional Tester adding the custom `selectedDate` property to its Object Properties Verification Point wizard. To see your custom property in the list, you need to uncheck the **Use standard properties** checkbox (see Figure 13.29).

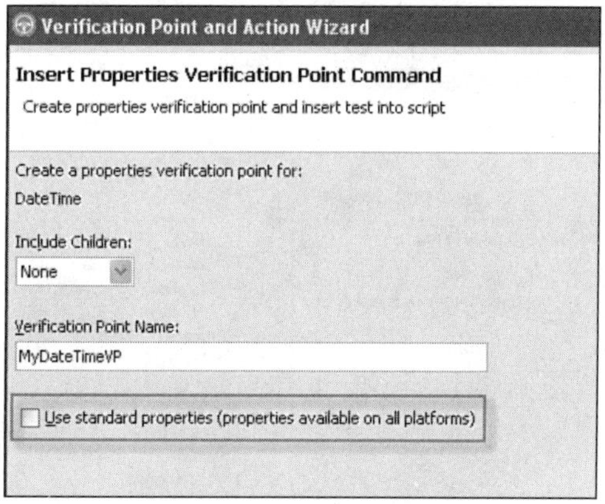

Figure 13.29   Uncheck the Use standard properties checkbox

This shows you all the properties that you can test for, including your own custom property (see Figure 13.30).

You are also able to obtain the value of this property using the `getProperty()` and `getProperties()` TestObject API scripting methods (see Listing 13.5).

Listing 13.5   `TestObject` API methods

```
swtDateTimeControl().getProperties();
swtDateTimeControl().getProperty("selectedDate");
```

C#—Using the SourceGrid Grid Example

The `SourceGrid` control suffers a similar fate as the `DateTime` control. A key property is missing (see Figure 13.31).

You can see that simply by using the out-of-the-box proxy's properties Hashtable, you can get key values such as row count, column count, object name, and so on. Unfortunately, a property does not exist to tell you which cell is currently selected. This can easily be addressed by overriding the `GetProperty()` and `GetProperties()` methods (see Listing 13.6).

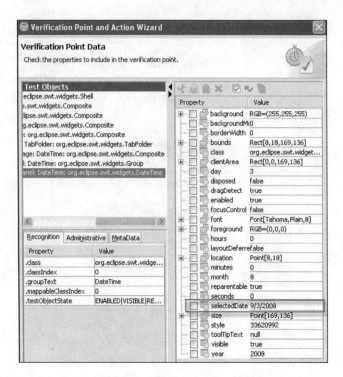

Figure 13.30   Object Properties Verification Point—selectedDate property

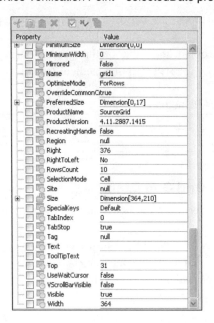

Figure 13.31   Object Properties Verification Point—missing selected cell property

Listing 13.6   Overridden property handling methods

GetProperties()

```
public override System.Collections.Hashtable GetProperties()
{
    System.Collections.Hashtable props = base.GetProperties();
    props.Add("selected cell", GetProperty("selected cell"));
    return props;
}
```

GetProperty()

```
public override object GetProperty(string propertyName)
{
    if (propertyName.Equals("selected cell"))
        return GetSelectedCellValue();
    else
        return base.GetProperty(propertyName);
}
```

The behavior of this is similar to the Java example. The `GetProperties()` method makes an initial call out to the out-of-the-box proxy method `GetProperties()`. This returns the list of properties that the base proxy can acquire for you. It stores things in a Hashtable called props, so you can cache the base name and value pairs. It then adds a synthetic property to the props Hashtable, passing "selected cell" in for the name and calling `GetProperty()` to get the value. It passes "selected cell" to the `GetProperty()` method.

The `GetProperty()` method accepts one argument: `propertyName`. This is a string. It checks to see if the `propertyName` string matches "selected cell". If it does, it calls the `GetSelectedCellValue()` method to acquire the actual value of the selected cell. If it doesn't match, this method passes the `propertyName` string to the base class `GetProperty()` method, returning the value that was obtained.

The `GetSelectedCellValue()` method is the helper that handles acquiring the value for a selected cell. It is not an overridden method. It is a custom method created specifically to help with the other two overridden methods: `GetProperties()` and `GetProperty()`.

Listing 13.7   `GetSelectedCellValue()` —custom method

```
private string GetSelectedCellValue()
{
    SourceGrid.Cells.ICellVirtual cv =
        ((Grid)base.theTestObject).GetCell(
        ((Grid)base.theTestObject).Selection.ActivePosition);
    string val = cv.ToString();
    if (val == "")
```

```
      return "NO VALUE";
else
      return val; }
```

The first thing this method does is create a `SourceGrid.Cells.ICellVirtual` variable called `cv`. It then casts the stolen object reference—currently being manipulated by Rational Functional Tester—as a `SourceGrid.Grid` class twice: first to call the Grid's `getCell()` method and second to pass the `"Section.ActivePosition"` property as the argument to the `getCell()` method. To do this, you need to add the following using statement at the top of your class:

```
using SourceGrid;
```

By overriding the `GetProperty()` and `GetProperties()` methods and using a custom method to acquire the selected cell value, you are able to record an Object Properties Verification Point that contains a `"selected cell"` property (see Figure 13.32).

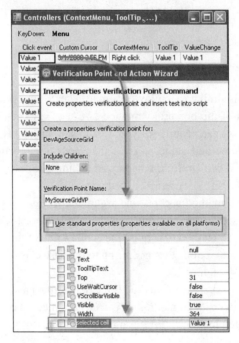

Figure 13.32   Object Properties Verification Point—selected cell property exists

You are also able to obtain the value of this property using the `getProperty()` and `getProperties()` TestObject API scripting methods (Listing 13.8).

Listing 13.8   TestObject API methods

```
swtDateTimeControl().GetProperties()
swtDateTimeControl().GetProperty("selected cell")
```

At This Point

The basic concept for adding custom property tests to your proxies is overriding two base class methods and creating any necessary method(s) to handle the data acquisition. It is critical that you have an in-depth understanding of the custom control for which you are creating the proxy. You should make sure that you have a copy of the custom control's API documentation. It behooves you to stay friendly with the development team. This increases your ability to quickly find answers to your questions.

Verifying Object Data

A popular task you might run into while developing your proxy is adding a custom Object Data Verification Point. The control you are working with might not provision its data to Rational Functional Tester in a typical manner. In other words, when you record your script and go to create an Object Data Verification Point, a data type (for example, the type of date test you are looking to use) doesn't exist for what you are looking to do. You might even run into the instance where the Verification Point Wizard doesn't even give you the option to test for object data (see Figure 13.33).

Figure 13.33   No Object Data Verification Point

You can add this functionality into your proxy teaching, Rational Functional Tester how to record an Object Data Verification Point for your control, by overriding the two methods shown in Table 13.3.

Table 13.3   Proxy Development: Object Data Methods to Override

Java	C#
public Hashtable getTestDataTypes()	public override Hashtable GetTestDataTypes()
public ITestData getTestData(String testDataType)	pubic override ITestData GetTestData(string testDataType)

Java—Using the DateTime Example

You need to start with the `getTestDataTypes()` method. This is how you tell Rational Functional Tester what types of object data tests you want to see in the Verification Point Wizard. Using class-level constants in your proxy class enables you to capture and reference the data types you want. You can accomplish this with string variables, making them private, static, and final. This helps you when you need to refer to your test types in other parts of the proxy (that is the two data methods you are going to override). You don't have to worry about typing the same strings each time. You can simply refer to the variables that you create. Referring back to the `DateTime` object referenced in the first section of this chapter, you might use the following:

```
private static final String SELECTED_DATE = "Date";
private static final String SELECTED_DATE_DESC = "Selected Date";

private static final String MONTH_YEAR = "Month/Year";
private static final String MONTH_YEAR_DESC = "Selected Month and Year";
```

The code listing tells Rational Functional Tester that you want to create two data tests. The first is for the data currently selected in the `DateTime` control. The second captures the currently selected month and year in the header of control. Note that there are two lines for each test type. The first is the actual type. The second is the description of the type. The description shows up in the Verification Point Wizard as the test selection (see Figure 13.34).

Figure 13.34   Object Data Verification Point—custom data tests

After creating the data types, you now simply override the `getTestDataTypes()` method. This is accomplished by first making a call to the `getTestDataTypes()` method that belongs to the base class. This is the proxy that you are extending. In the `DateTime` example, it is the `com.rational.test.ft.domain.java.swt.CompositeProxy` class. Calling this method returns any data types that might exist for the base class. These are stored in a Hashtable. The next thing you need to do is add your new data types to the Hashtable. Lastly, you simply return the Hashtable (as required by the `getTestDataTypes()` signature). Listing 13.9 shows how this is implemented for the `DateTime` example.

Listing 13.9 `getTestDataTypes()` —overridden method

```
public Hashtable getTestDataTypes() {
    Hashtable datatypes = super.getTestDataTypes();
    datatypes.put(SELECTED_DATE, SELECTED_DATE_DESC);
    datatypes.put(MONTH_YEAR, MONTH_YEAR_DESC);

    return datatypes;
}
```

The next thing you need to do is override the `getTestData()` method. This method actually captures and returns the data from your control and displays it in the Object Data Verification Point. This method returns an `ITestData` object. This object contains the values that you want to display in the Object Data Verification Point. Overriding this method is actually simple. It is a matter of creating the conditional logic that figures out the test data type that is selected in the Verification Point Wizard. You can easily handle this with an `if...then...else` block. Listing 13.10 shows this for the `DateTime` control example with which you have been working.

Listing 13.10 The `getTestData()` —overridden method

```
public ITestData getTestData(String testDataType) {
    if (testDataType.equals(SELECTED_DATE)) {
        return getSelectedDateTime();
    } else if(testDataType.equals(MONTH_YEAR)) {
        return getMonthYear();
    } else {
        return super.getTestData(testDataType);
    }
}
```

The previous code listing shows that the conditional logic checks to see which data type was chosen in the Verification Point Wizard. If it is either of your custom date types—SELECTED_DATE or MONTH_YEAR, respectively—it calls out to a secondary method to capture and return the requested data. If the selected value was something else (such as you hit the "else" piece of your logic); it calls out to the `getTestData()` method of the base class, returning its value if it exists. Note the bulk of the work is handled in another method. Overriding the `getTestDataTypes()` method is just a matter of figuring out which other method you need to write and then invoke to acquire and return the appropriate data.

In the case of the SELECTED_DATE type chosen, you need to capture and return the currently chosen date with a method similar to Listing 13.11.

Listing 13.11   `getSelectedDate()` —custom method

```
public ITestDataText getSelectedDateTime() {
    String date = getDateAsString();
    return VpUtil.getTestData(date);
}
```

The `getselectedDate()` method relies on the `getDateAsString()` method that was defined in the "Verifying Object Properties" section. As a refresher, the `getDateAsString()` method builds a date in the format of month/day/year, returning it as a string. This value is passed to `VpUtil.getTestData`, creating and returning an `ITestDataText` object to the invoking `getTestData()` method.

You also need a method to handle the `MONTH_YEAR` data type as well. This is something like what you can see in Listing 13.12.

Listing 13.12   The `getMonthYear()` —custom method

```
public ITestDataText getMonthYear(){
    String s_month;
    int i_month = ((DateTime)this.theTestObject).getMonth();
    switch(i_month){
        case 0: s_month = "January"; break;
        case 1: s_month = "February"; break;
        case 2: s_month = "March"; break;
        case 3: s_month = "April"; break;
        case 4: s_month = "May"; break;
        case 5: s_month = "June"; break;
        case 6: s_month = "July"; break;
        case 7: s_month = "August"; break;
        case 8: s_month = "September"; break;
        case 9: s_month = "October"; break;
        case 10: s_month = "November"; break;
        case 11: s_month = "December"; break;
        default: s_month = "INVALID MONTH"; break;
    }
    int year = ((DateTime)this.theTestObject).getYear();
    String monthyear = s_month + ", " + year;

    return VpUtil.getTestData(monthyear);
}
```

This method behaves similarly to the `getDateAsString()` method. It casts the stolen reference to a `DateTime` reference. To reiterate, the cast occurs so you can access the methods necessary for obtaining certain information from the `DateClass` GUI Object that Rational Functional Tester is recording against. In this case, you want to capture and return the month and year that are currently displayed in the control's header. A switch statement is used to convert the month from an integer (returned by the `getMonth()` method) to a string, starting with 0 to represent January and ending with 11 to represent December.

Rational Functional Tester now has two Object Data Verification Points that it can use (see Figure 13.35). One tests for the selected month and year. The other tests for the selected date.

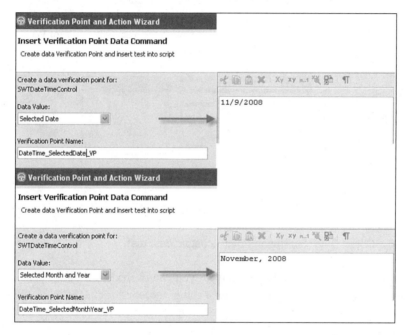

Figure 13.35   New Object Data Verification Points

C#—Using the SourceGrid Example

The first method to override is `getTestDataTypes()`. This method instructs Rational Functional Tester on the types of object data tests to perform. You can use class-level constants in your proxy to capture and reference the data types you want. This is accomplished using string variables with the `private` and `const` modifiers. Doing this helps you when you need to refer to your test types in other parts of the proxy (that is the two data methods you are going to override). It is also beneficial if you need to change the string itself. You only have to change it in one location.

The `SourceGrid` example is missing a data test for the selected cell. You can create four constants to inform Rational Functional Tester that there two new data tests: `"selected cell"` and `"contents"`.

```
private const string SOURCEGRID_SELECTED = "selected cell";
private const string SOURCEGRID_SELECTED_DESC = "Selected Grid Cell";


private const string SOURCEGRID_CONTENTS = "contents";
private const string SOURCEGRID_CONTENTS_DESC = "SourceGrid Contents";
```

Rational Functional Tester is now aware that there are new data tests for its Object Data Verification Point. Note that there are two lines for each test type. The first is the actual type. The second is the description of the type. The description shows up in the Verification Point Wizard as the test selection (see Figure 13.36).

Figure 13.36   Object Data Verification Point—custom data test

Now that you have the data test specified, you can override the `GetTestDataTypes()` method. This is accomplished by first making a call to the `GetTestDataTypes()` method that belongs to the base out-of-the-box proxy class. This is the `PanelProxy` for this example. Calling this method returns any data types that might exist for the base class. These are stored in a Hashtable, called `datatypes`. You can place new test types into the `datatypes` using its `Add()` method. The last step is to return the `datatypes` Hashtable. Listing 13.13 represents the steps you just discussed.

Listing 13.13   `GetTestDataTypes()`—overridden method

```
public override System.Collections.Hashtable GetTestDataTypes()
{
    System.Collections.Hashtable datatypes = base.GetTestDataTypes();
    datatypes.Add(SOURCEGRID_SELECTED, SOURCEGRID_SELECTED_DESC);
    datatypes.Add(SOURCEGRID_CONTENTS, SOURCEGRID_CONTENTS_DESC);
    return datatypes;
}
```

The next step is to override the `GetTestData()` method. This method captures and returns the data from your control and displays it in the Object Data Verification Point. It returns this data as an `ITestData` object and contains the values that you want to display in the Object Data Verification Point. Overriding this method is a matter of creating conditional logic that figures out the data test that the Verification Point Wizard requests. You can easily handle this with a switch statement (see Listing 13.14).

Listing 13.14   The `GetTestData()`—overridden method

```
public override Rational.Test.Ft.Vp.ITestData GetTestData(
                        string testDataType)
{
    Rational.Test.Ft.Vp.ITestData testData = null;
    switch (testDataType)
    {
        case SOURCEGRID_SELECTED:
            string selectedcellval = GetSelectedCellValue();
            testData = new Rational.Test.Ft.Vp.Impl.TestDataText(
                selectedcellval);
            break;
        case SOURCEGRID_CONTENTS:
            testData = GetTableDataAsString();
            break;
        default:
            testData = base.GetTestData(testDataType);
            break;
    }
    return testData;
}
```

Your overridden version of the `GetTestData()` method seeks to collect the string representation of a selected cell value and return it as an `ITestData` object, called `testData`. This object is initialized with `null`. However, it is assigned a new value after execution reaches the switch statement. This statement first checks to see if the `testDataType` string (the argument passed into the `GetTestData()` method) matches the SOURCEGRID_SELECTED constant string (also known as the `"selected cell"`). If it does match, it calls `GetSelectedCellValue()` to obtain the value of the selected cell and return it as a string. This value is stored in `testData`. You head down a similar path if `testDataType` matches the SOURCEGRID_CONTENTS constant. The `GetTableDataAsString()` method is invoked and returns the contents of the SourceGrid control. If `testDataType` does not match either SOURCEGRID_SELECTED or SOURCEGRID_ CONTENTS, it calls the out-of-the-box proxy's `GetTestData()` method, passing `testDataType` along to it and storing the value that comes back into `testData`. Finally, the method returns `testData` and displays the results in the Object Data Verification Point.

Your overridden `GetTestData()` method relies on `GetSelectedCellValue()` to capture and return the desired date. This is the same method that is used in the "Verifying Object Properties" section. It is used to populate the custom object property, `"selected cell"`. It can be reused here to capture the value to display in your data verification point. These three methods (see Figure 13.37) enable Rational Functional Tester to invoke your desired data verification.

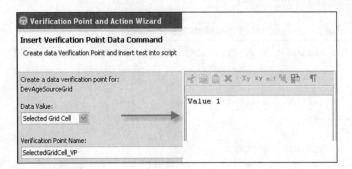

Figure 13.37   New Object Data Verification Point—selected cell value

`GetTestData()` also invokes another helper method, `GetTableDataAsString()`, to obtain the contents of the `SourceGrid` Grid (see Listing 13.15).

Listing 13.15 `GetTableDataAsString()`—custom method

```
private Rational.Test.Ft.Vp.ITestData GetTableDataAsString()
{
    Rational.Test.Ft.Vp.Impl.TestDataTable tstdatatbl =
        new Rational.Test.Ft.Vp.Impl.TestDataTable();

    int rowCount = ((Grid)base.theTestObject).RowsCount;
    int colCount = ((Grid)base.theTestObject).ColumnsCount;

    string[] rowElements = new string[colCount];

    for(int row = 1; row < rowCount; row++)
    {
        for(int col = 0; col < colCount; col++)
        {
            SourceGrid.Cells.ICellVirtual cv =
                ((Grid)base.theTestObject).GetCell(row,col);

            rowElements[col] = cv.ToString();
        }
```

```
        tstdatatbl.Add(rowElements);
    }

    String[] colHeaders = new string[colCount];
    for (int i = 0; i < colCount; i++)
    {
        SourceGrid.Cells.ICellVirtual cv =
            ((Grid)base.theTestObject).GetCell(0, i);

        colHeaders[i] = cv.ToString();
    }

    tstdatatbl.SetColumnHeaders(colHeaders);

    tstdatatbl.AddComparisonRegion(
    Rational.Test.Ft.Vp.Impl.TestDataTableRegion.AllCells());

    tstdatatbl.SetCompareBothByLeftRegions(true);

    return tstdatatbl;
}
```

GettestDataTableAsString() starts off by creating a new TestDataTable class called tstdatatbl. This is used to capture and return the contents of the grid. It then captures the grid's row and column counts and casts the TestObject reference to a SourceGrid Grid class. The column count is used to initialize the number of cells for your rowElements array. This array is used to store the string values of each cell in the grid. A for loop is employed to access the rows of the grid. It is important to note that the loop starts with the second row of the grid (**int row** = 1). The first row contains the column headers. This information is garnered from reviewing the documentation for this control. For each row encountered, another for loop is used to walk through each column of the row, pulling out the string values and storing them in the rowElements array along the way. Every row is added to tstdatatbl. Ultimately, when the for loops end, the grid data is fully represented in this TestDataTable class.

The next thing your method does is set the column headers of tstdatatbl. This is done by looping through the first row of the grid. As mentioned in the preceding paragraph, this information is obtained from reviewing the control's documentation.

After the grid data and column header information is set, you need to set a couple of flags. The first flag says that you want to look at all the cells in the grid. The second flag states that you want to compare the data by using the comparison regions of both left and right values.

The end result of this method, in conjunction with the overridden GetTestDataTypes() and GetTestData() methods, is a verification point that looks like Figure 13.38.

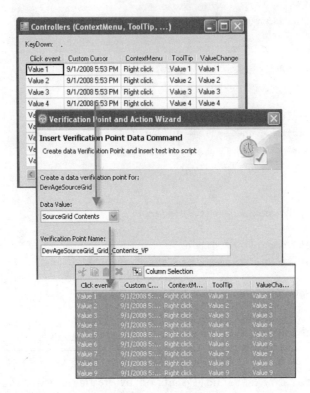

Figure 13.38   New Object Data Verification Point—grid contents

At This Point

As you can see, the general idea behind adding custom data tests to your proxies is a matter of overriding two base class methods and creating your own custom method(s) to handle the majority of the data acquisition. A key facet of this is having an understanding of the class to which you are casting the `TestObject` wrapper class. This provides you with the necessary methods needed to capture the data that satisfies your test. You should make sure that you have a copy of the custom control's API documentation. Another channel for gaining this knowledge is your development team. Keeping lines of communication open with them greatly enhances your ability to quickly find answers to your questions.

Executing a Click Using Object Information

Object-oriented clicking is a primary need for automation tools. It makes an action relative to a piece of the object, for instance, clicking on a particular cell (row, column) of a table, selecting an item in a combobox by its text, and so on. This eliminates the dependencies on screen or top-level object coordinates for navigation. It ultimately enables an automation tool to find an object, regardless of where it has moved to on its parent control (for example, a Windows form, HTML document, and so on).

You usually find that if you need to build a proxy so that Rational Functional Tester can recognize and interact with your control, you need to add object-oriented clicking to your to do list The implementation of this is somewhat similar to the other tasks that you have seen. You need to override a series of methods in the base out-of-the-box proxy to tell Rational Functional Tester how to handle object-oriented clicking for your custom control.

Java—Using the DateTime Example

Rational Functional Tester can navigate only the `DateTime` control via coordinate-based clicking. When you select a particular date, you see a line in your script similar to the following:

```
dateTime().click(atPoint(112,81));
```

This is what is meant by coordinate-based clicking. Rational Functional Tester maps the `DateTime` control, creating a `TestObject` class-wrapper for it. Unfortunately, it can't figure out how to tell you what date it clicked on. You need to add capability to your proxy to help teach Rational Functional Tester how to do this. You need to override methods for both record and playback.

There are different record mouse event methods that you can override. For example, you can choose `ProcessMouseEvent()`, `ProcessSingleMouseEvent()`, `ProcessHoverMouse Event()`, and so on. The method(s) that you choose are dependent upon the control for which you are writing the proxy. This requires you to have a good understanding of your control. You need to know the different methods that you can use to help provide object-oriented information for a click event.

The purpose of overriding the mouse event methods is to convert a point—clicked on by Rational Functional Tester while recording—to an object-oriented subitem. This can be an index, text string, table cell, and so on. The `DateTime` doesn't readily expose methods that enable you to relate a point to it, extracting the object-oriented information that you want. You can spend time researching how to accomplish this task, working with developers, reading through Javadoc, and experimenting. To keep things simple, you can cheat some here using the `DateTime`'s internal methods for aggregating the day, time, and year pieces of the date that was clicked on. This task is handled by overriding the `processSingleMouseEvent()` and `getActionArgs()` methods (see Listings 13.16 and 13.17, respectively).

Listing 13.16 `processSingleMouseEvent()`—overridden method

```
public void processSingleMouseEvent(IMouseActionInfo action) {
    currentMethod = "click";
    Vector clickArgs = getActionArgs(new Point());

    MethodSpecification methSepc = MethodSpecification.proxyMethod(this,
        currentMethod, clickArgs.toArray());

    action.setActionMethodSpecification(methSepc);
}
```

Overriding the `processSingleMouseEvent()` method involves skipping over the point-to-object-oriented information conversion. Instead, after setting current method to a click, it makes a call to the `getActionArgs()` method, passing in an arbitrary point. In other words, it invokes the method without a true need for the point. It takes the returned `clickArgs` vector and uses it along with the `currentMethod` string (`"click"`) and current proxy test object (`this`) to create a new method for the recorded event.

The `processSingleMouseEvent()` method relies on `getActionArgs()` to provide the object-oriented information for the click event to use (see Listing 13.17). Your proxy bases your click off the selected date.

Listing 13.17   `getActionArgs()`—overridden method

```
protected Vector getActionArgs(Point point) {
    Vector args = new Vector();
    String s = getDateAsString();
    Subitem subitem = new Text(s);
    args.add(subitem);
    return args;
}
```

Overriding this extensible method is quite simple, at least for your purposes. You basically create a new vector and call the `getDateAsString()` method. The `getDateAsString()` method was defined in the "Verifying Object Properties" section. It stores the selected date in the format month/day/year in a string variable called s. You then create a new `Subitem` class, aptly named `subitem`, and store a new Text object in it, based off your string variable s. This is ultimately the `atText("month/day/year")` subitem that you want to see in your recorded click statements.

Defining a custom, object-oriented means of recording a click requires you to create a custom means of playing it back. You simply work your way backward. This means that for the `DateTime` control, you break the date string into its individual day, month, and year parts and set the selected calendar date with them. Because you cheated the record methods, you can cheat the playback. You need only develop a custom `click()` method (see Listing 13.18).

Listing 13.18   `click()`—custom method

```
public void click(Subitem subitem){
        String date = ((Text)subitem).getText();
    String[] monthdayyear = date.split("/");
    ((DateTime)this.theTestObject).setMonth(new Integer(
        monthdayyear[0]).intValue() - 1);
    ((DateTime)this.theTestObject).setDay(new Integer(
        monthdayyear[1]).intValue());
    ((DateTime)this.theTestObject).setYear(new Integer(
        monthdayyear[2]).intValue());
}
```

This method converts the subitem argument into a text string. This is the month/day/year string found in your object-oriented click. You can easily parse this string into its separate day, month, and year pieces using the `split()` method. This returns an array that contains the individual parts. You use these parts as arguments to the `DataTime` methods for setting the month, day, and year. This is accomplished by casting the stolen reference to your control object (that is, `this.theTestObject`) as a `DateTime` class. Doing this exposes `setMonth()`, `setDay()`, and `setYear()`. Passing in the respective array values as arguments to these methods sets the calendar to the date on which you clicked.

These three methods provide you with a means to eliminate the coordinate-based clicks. You now see the following type of click instead:

```
swtDateTimeControl().click(atText("11/11/2008"));
```

C#—Using the SourceGrid Grid Example

You most likely need to implement object-oriented clicking in your proxy. You can come to this conclusion based off the simple fact that Rational Functional Tester won't recognize the `SourceGrid Grid` control without your proxy. You had to override the `ShouldBeMapped()` method to tell Rational Functional Tester that it should include this control in its map. If you need to validate your assumption, start recording a script and click on the `SourceGrid` control. This results in the following line generated in your test script:

```
DevAgeSourceGridTable().Click(AtPoint(24,104))
```

You can see that Rational Functional Tester clicks on the control via coordinates. Having confirmed your initial thoughts, you can add object-based clicking in your proxy. For your purposes, you need some out-of-the-box proxy methods. You can break these down into the following two categories:

Record Methods

```
ProcessMouseEvent()

ProcessPreDownMouseEvent()

getActionArgs()
```

Playback Methods

```
GetSubitemRect
```

You need also to create a custom `Click()` method to tell Rational Functional Tester what you want it to do.

The reason you break things down into record and playback methods is due to the fact that you need to construct how you tell Rational Functional Tester to record the click against your custom control and then how to play those clicks back. Let's start with the record methods.

Record Methods

The ProcessMouseEvent() is the first method that gets called when you record a mouse event. At a high level, it just sorts through the type of event that was just recorded. Questions to ask include: Was it a hover event? Was it an event prior to a mouse button being depressed? You can probably guess that the method contains logic to figure this out (see Listing 13.19).

Listing 13.19   ProcessMouseEvent()

```
public override void ProcessMouseEvent(IMouseActionInfo action)
{
    switch (action.GetEventState())
    {
        case MouseActionStates.PRE_DOWN:
            if (action.GetClickCount() == 1)
                ProcessPreDownMouseEvent(action);
            break;
        case MouseActionStates.PRE_UP:
            if (action.GetClickCount() != 1 || action.IsDrag())
                ProcessPreUpMouseEvent(action);
            break;
        case MouseActionStates.HOVER:
            ProcessHoverMouseEvent(action);
            break;
    }
}
```

The primary logic is contained in a switch statement. This looks at the event state of the mouse action and matches it to one of three cases. If the event state is a PRE_DOWN state (prior to the mouse button being fully depressed), the number of clicks is collected and then the ProcessPreDownMouseEvent() is called. A similar series of actions occur if you hit a PRE_UP state, testing for the click count and even testing if you encounter a drag action prior to the mouse button be released. The ProcessPreUpMouseEvent() methods gets called in this case. The HOVER case simply calls out to its event handling method, ProcessHoverMouseEvent. Because you are concerned with capturing object-related clicks, you can focus on collecting them as the mouse button is depressed. Therefore, you override the ProcessPreDownMouseEvent() method (see Listing 13.20).

Listing 13.20   ProcessPreDownMouseEvent()

```
protected override void ProcessPreDownMouseEvent(
        IMouseActionInfo action)
{
    IMouseEventInfo mouseevent = action.GetEventInfo(0);
```

```
    int eventcount = action.GetEventCount() - 1;
I   MouseEventInfo mouseEvent = action.GetEventInfo(eventcount);

    System.Drawing.Point firstPoint =
        new System.Drawing.Point(mouseevent.GetX(), mouseevent.GetY());

    SetRecordCache();

    currentMethod = "click";
    clickArgs = GetActionArgs(firstPoint);
    preDownState = GetScriptCommandFlags();

    SetMethodSpecification(action, currentMethod,
        SetClickArgs(mouseevent.GetModifiers()), preDownState);
}
```

Overriding this method relies on you gathering information from the mouse event. To do this, you instantiate the `IMouseEventInfo mouseevent` interface and store the mouse action's event information in it. You then take `mouseevent`'s X and Y coordinates to create the point—called firstPoint—where you click. This point is passed into the `GetActionArgs()` method for the purpose of capturing the actual object-based information derived from `firstPoint`. The object-based click arguments that get returned from `GetActionArgs()` are used along with the `currentMethod` variable (set to click) and `preDownstate` variable (containing the originating script's command flags) to create a new method specification for Rational Functional Tester, telling it how to use the information your overridden method collected.

The method that actually specifies the object-based click action is the `GetActionArgs()` method (see Listing 13.21). You need to override this to specify the object-based action arguments you want for your `SourceGrid` control. This is the row index and column index for which cell in the grid to click on.

Listing 13.21 `GetActionArgs()`

```
protected override System.Collections.ArrayList GetActionArgs(
            System.Drawing.Point point)
{
    System.Collections.ArrayList args =
        new System.Collections.ArrayList();

    System.Drawing.Point clientPt =
        ((Grid)base.theTestObject).PointToClient(point);

    SourceGrid.Position pos =
        ((Grid)base.theTestObject).PositionAtPoint(clientPt);
```

```
    int row = -1;
    int col = -1;
    row = pos.Row;
    col = pos.Column;

    if (row == -1 || col == -1)
    {
        base.GetActionArgs(point);
    }
    else
    {
        Rational.Test.Ft.Script.Row atRow =
            new Rational.Test.Ft.Script.Row(row);

        Rational.Test.Ft.Script.Column atCol =
            new Rational.Test.Ft.Script.Column(col);

        Rational.Test.Ft.Script.Subitem subitem =
            new Rational.Test.Ft.Script.Cell(atRow, atCol);

        args.Add(subitem);
    }

    return args;

}
```

Overriding the GetActionArgs() methods essentially translates the point where Rational Functional Tester is clicking while recording. The first thing you need to do is create a new ArrayList, called args. This is used to store object-oriented information for the Click() method. After this is created, you can go about the business of translating the original click point to a row index and column index.

The original click point is passed to GetActionArgs() as an argument. You can use the native SourceGrid Grid control to get some more interesting data. You need to cast the reference to your TestObject (for example, base.theTestObject) as a SourceGrid Grid class. This enables you access to the PointToClient() method. Passing the point argument to this method enables you to capture the click point relative to the grid control itself. In other words, instead of having a point relative to the screen, you have a point relative to the actual SourceGrid control. This new point, called clientPt, is used to capture and return a SourceGrid Position structure called pos. This is where the translation begins. The pos object knows what row and column in the SourceGrid control relates back to clientPt. You can simply call pos.Row and pos.Column to get the integer values that represent a cell in the grid. This is a critical thing to understand. You used the SourceGrid Grid class methods to take the original point from the Rational Functional Tester recorder, turn it into a point, relative to the grid, and then turn that into the row and column indices that represent a cell in the grid.

The last part of this method is simple. You need to create the following three subitems:

- `Rational.Test.Ft.Script.Row`
- `Rational.Test.Ft.Script.Column`
- `Rational.Test.Ft.Script.Cell`

The `Row` subitem represents the row index in a cell. The `Column` subitem represents the column portion of the cell. The `Cell` subitem is the combination of the `Row` and `Column`. This is what gets passed back to the `ProcessPreDownMouseEvent()` as the click arguments.

The result of overriding these three record methods is the following, newly recorded click statement:

```
DevAgeSourceGridTable().Click(AtCell( _
                                   AtRow(AtIndex(3)), _
                                   AtColumn(AtIndex(0))))
```

A more industrious version of this method would add the name of the column and perhaps text that is in the cell. This is something that can be addressed by tweaking the `GetActionArgs()` method to get more data out of the `SourceGrid` control.

Playback Methods

Overriding the methods for telling Rational Functional Tester how to record an object-oriented click is only half of the equation. You need to tell Rational Functional Tester how to play back the Click() action using your newly created object-oriented information. There are a few implementations for handling this. You traverse the path that creates a custom implementation of the `Click()` method and override the `GetSubitemRect()` method.

Your Click() implementation is somewhat of an inverse to the record methods you overrode. It takes object-oriented information and turns it into a point to click in the `SourceGrid` Grid (see Listing 13.22).

Listing 13.22 `Click()`

```
public new void Click(Rational.Test.Ft.Script.Subitem subitem)
{
    System.Drawing.Rectangle rectangle = GetSubitemRect(subitem);
    int x_midpoint = rectangle.X + rectangle.Width / 2;
    int y_midpoint = rectangle.Y + rectangle.Height / 2;
    System.Drawing.Point clickPt =
        new System.Drawing.Point(x_midpoint, y_midpoint);
    Rational.Test.Ft.Domain.BaseChannelScreen.Click(
        Rational.Test.Ft.Script.MouseModifiers.Left(),clickPt);
}
```

The first thing your `Click()` method does is take the object-oriented information, passed in as the subitem argument, and passes it to the `GetSubitemRect()` method. This returns a `System.Drawing.Rectangle` class called `rectangle`. You then calculate the X and Y midpoints of `rectangle`. These are used to create a new `System.Drawing.Point` class called `clickPt`. You have essentially calculated the center point of the cell you want to click, derived from the object-oriented information contained in `subitem`. The final thing you do is perform the click action, stating that it should be a left click at the point defined by `clickPt`.

The actual conversion of the object-oriented information to `System.Drawing.Rectangle` is handled via the `GetSubitemRect()` method. You need to override the out-of-the-box proxy's implementation of this method to make it understand how to convert the information you collected in the recording methods of your proxy (see Listing 13.23).

Listing 13.23   `GetSubitemRect()`

```
protected override System.Drawing.Rectangle GetSubitemRect(
        Rational.Test.Ft.Script.Subitem subitem)
{
    Rational.Test.Ft.Script.Column col =
        ((Rational.Test.Ft.Script.Cell)subitem).GetColumn();

    Rational.Test.Ft.Script.Row row =
        ((Rational.Test.Ft.Script.Cell)subitem).GetRow();

    SourceGrid.Position p =
        new SourceGrid.Position(row.GetIndex().GetIndex(),
    col.GetIndex().GetIndex());

    System.Drawing.Rectangle clientRect = (
        (Grid)base.theTestObject).PositionToRectangle(p);

    System.Drawing.Rectangle screenRect = base.GetScreenRectangle();

    System.Drawing.Rectangle rectToClick =
        new System.Drawing.Rectangle((clientRect.X + screenRect.X),
            (clientRect.Y + screenRect.Y),
            clientRect.Width,
            clientRect.Height);

    return rectToClick;
}
```

As stated previously, you perform the inverse of what you did with the recording methods. You take the argument `subitem` and parse out the children that it contains. If you recall, you created Row and `Column` subitems in your overridden `GetActionArgs()` method. You just pull them out here and use them to calculate their position in the `SourceGrid control`. You do this by creating a `SourceGrid.Position` class called p, passing in the integer values contained in the `Row` and `Column` subitems. You cast your `TestObject` reference again to a `SourceGrid` Grid class. This enables you to call the `PositionToRectangle()` method, passing p in as the argument. The return value of this method is a `System.Drawing.Rectangle` class that you named `clientRect`. This represents the cell's area on the grid control. You are not quite done yet. You want to pass back a rectangle that represents the cell's area, relative to the screen. You call the base proxy's `GetScreenRectangle()` method to obtain the screen's rectangle, called `screenRect`. You then create a third `System.Drawing.Rectangle` called `rectToClick`, which is instantiated with the fusion of `screenRect` and `clientRect`. You finally return `rectToClick` back to the invoking `Click()` method.

At This Point

A good way to view this process, be it done in Java or C#, is that you need to undo what you do. You saw that first you need to define the object-oriented information for Rational Functional Tester's recorder to understand how to click within a custom control. This involved converting the point that was clicked into object-oriented information—a text string, table cell, and so on. You then handled the reverse of that. You took the object-oriented information and converted it back into the necessary point to click. You can view this as pseudo-template for adding more object-oriented `click()` actions to future proxies.

Building the Proxy

You need to build and export your proxy after you finish coding it. This results in a .jar file, if your proxy is written in Java or a .dll file, if it was developed in C#. This file is the final product that Rational Functional Tester uses when interacting with the control for which you build the proxy.

Building the Java Proxy

Building your proxy in the Eclipse environment is as simple as selecting **Project > Build Project** from the menu (see Figure 13.39).

Figure 13.39 Build project

It shouldn't take long to build your project. The process lets you know if any errors exist in your proxy code. After you have completed building your proxy project, you can export that class into a .jar file. You can right-click on your class file and choose **Export** from the right-click menu. This engages the Export Wizard (see Figure 13.40).

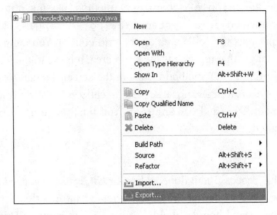

Figure 13.40 Begin export process

The first page of the wizard asks you to select the export destination. You first need to expand the Java folder. This exposes the list of export options it contains. You want to select the **JAR file** option (see Figure 13.41).

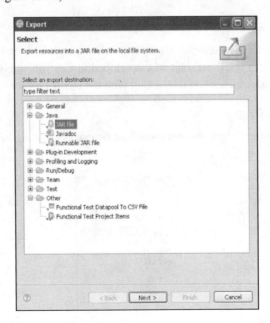

Figure 13.41 Java folder—JAR file option

The next page of the wizard, the JAR File Specification (see Figure 13.43), shows you what you are exporting. Feel free to expand the selected project in the left side of the Select resources to export list box until you see the package that you created. Selecting the package shows you which class you are exporting (see Figure 13.42).

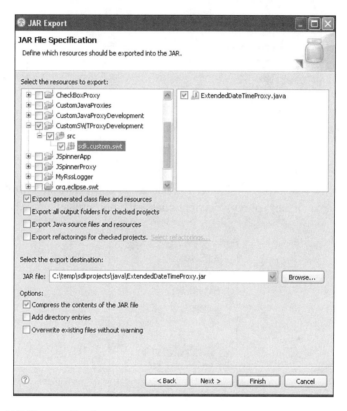

Figure 13.42   JAR file specification

You need to provide a directory path and file name in the JAR file text field. After doing so, you can click the **Finish** button. This generates the .jar file you specified.

The directory where the resulting file is created is arbitrary. After the .jar file is created, you need to deploy it to the Rational Functional Tester customization directory—C:\Documents and Settings\All Users\Application Data\IBM\RFT\customization for typical installations of Rational Functional Tester (see Figure 13.43).

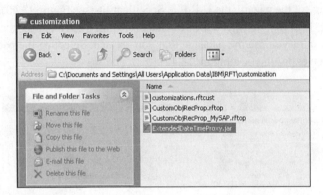

Figure 13.43   Completed proxy—.jar file in Rational Functional Tester customization directory

Building the C# Proxy

The process to build your proxy is simple. You can either choose **Build > Build SourceGrid-Proxy** (or the name of any proxy) or right-click on your project and choose **Build** (see Figure 13.44).

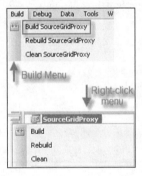

Figure 13.44   Build options

It takes a short amount of time for your proxy to build. You are informed of any errors. You are required to correct all errors prior to your proxy being built. If you do not receive any error messages, your proxy is built. You should see a success message at the bottom of Visual Studio, and you end up with a .dll file (see Figure 13.45).

If your build is a success, you can enter into your project's bin directory. The proxy .dll file is in the Release directory (unless you specify a debug build). You should see all the supporting .dll files that you referenced in your project (see Figure 13.46).

Notice that the name of the .dll file comes from the name of your project, SourceGrid Proxy, not the SourceGridControlProxy class. This is the difference between building a C# proxy and building a Java proxy (which exports the class file as a .jar).

Figure 13.45   Build succeeded

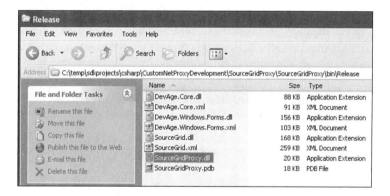

Figure 13.46   Build Proxy—SourceGridProxy.dll

You can move the SourceGridProxy.dll to the Rational Functional Tester customization directory. This is C:\Documents and Settings\All Users\Application Data\IBM\RFT\customization for typical installations of Rational Functional Tester (see Figure 13.47).

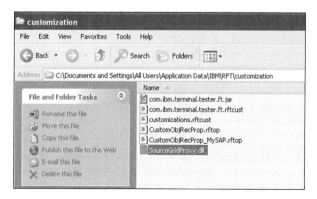

Figure 13.47   Completed Proxy—.dll file in Rational Functional Tester Customization directory

At This Point

This completes the process for creating a custom proxy. If you have made it to this point without any errors, your proxy should be loaded and engaged by Rational Functional Tester. There is one final step, covered in the next section, to make this happen.

Mapping the Proxy

You need to create a mapping file for your proxy after you complete the custom coding and building of it. This involves creating an XML file, specifying information about your proxy and the control it was built for. The end result is a file that shares the same name as your proxy file but has a .rftcust extension.

You do not have to create this file from scratch. If you browse to the Rational Functional Tester customization directory, C:\Documents and Settings\All Users\Application Data\IBM\ RFT\customization in most install instances, you find a file called customizations.rftcust. This is the starting point of your mapping file (see Figure 13.48).

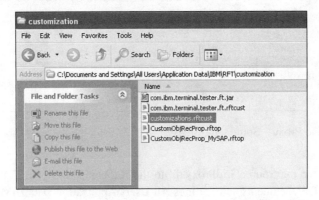

Figure 13.48   Rational Functional Tester customization directory—customizations.rftcust

The XML shown in Listing 13.24 contains the skeletal XML tags that you can use to get started. It is broken down into multiple sections.

Listing 13.24   customizations.rftcust

```
<?xml version="1.0" encoding="UTF-8"?>
<ConfigFile L=".ConfigFile">
    <Section L=".ConfigFileSection">
        <Name>proxies</Name>
        <Val L=".ProxyManager">
            <DomainImplementation L=".DomainImplementation">
                <Name>Java</Name>
            </DomainImplementation>
```

```
            <DomainImplementation L=".DomainImplementation">
                <Name>Html</Name>
            </DomainImplementation>
        </Val>
    </Section>
    <Section L=".ConfigFileSection">
        <Name>valueManagers</Name>
        <Val L=".ValueManagerManager">
            <ComponentModel L=".ComponentModel">
                <Name>Java</Name>
            </ComponentModel>
        </Val>
    </Section>
    <Section L=".ConfigFileSection">
        <Name>valueConverters</Name>
        <Val L=".ValueConverterManager">
        </Val>
    </Section>
    <Section L=".ConfigFileSection">
        <Name>options</Name>
        <Val L=".Options">
        </Val>
    </Section>
    <Section L=".ConfigFileSection">
        <Name>propertyConverters</Name>
        <Val L=".PropertyConverterManager">
            <ComponentModel L=".ComponentModel">
                <Name>Java</Name>
            </ComponentModel>
        </Val>
    </Section>
</ConfigFile>
```

This chapter focuses only on the first section. This is where you list your proxy and the control it supports. It is broken down into subsections. These are identified by the <DomainImplementation> tags. They define the different technology domains with which Rational Functional Tester works. By default, only Java and HTML are listed. You use this framework to initialize your own file. There are four steps for creating your initial mapping file:

1. Create a new text file in the Rational Functional Tester customization directory, provide the same name as your .jar or .dll, and give it an extension of .rftcust. Continuing with the DateTime proxy example, your file would be ExtendedDateTimeProxy.rftcust. Continuing with the SourceGrid Grid example, your file would be SourceGridProxy.rftcust.

2. Open both the new file and the customizations.rftcust file. You can use your favorite text editor for this.

3. Copy the contents of the customizations.rftcust file into your newly created .rftcust file.

4. Save your .rftcust file (close customizations.rftcust because you are done with it). After completing these four steps, you should end up with a new .rftcust file that maps your proxy to the Rational Functional Tester's recorder (see Figure 13.49).

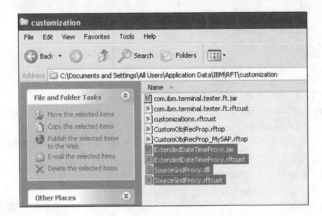

Figure 13.49 Rational Functional Tester customization directory—
ExtendedDateTimeProxy.rftcust

The last thing that you need to do is edit the mapping file to tell Rational Functional Tester to use your custom proxy for the specific control for which you built it. This requires you to make a couple of small edits. These changes only take place in the first section, which is the one that covers the domains. It was mentioned previously that the original customization.rftcust file only contained the Java and HTML domains. If you need to add a new domain, for instance, in .NET, you supply the following lines:

```
<DomainImplementation L=".DomainImplementation">
    <Name>Net</Name>
</DomainImplementation>
```

These three lines enable you to list proxies that you have developed for the .NET technology platform, such as the `SourceGrid proxy`. You can place these lines anywhere in the domain section. The location doesn't matter. They come before the Java domain lines, after them, or even after the HTML domain lines. If you want to get a better feel for the structure of domains and the proxies that are listed for them, you can look at the rational_ft.rftcust file. This is found in Rational Functional Tester's bin directory. It shows you the different domains that are supported, listing the base proxies built that support different controls out of the box. You extend these base proxies when you create your own proxies. You need to list your proxy in the appropriate domain.

Mapping for DateTime Proxy

The `DateTime` proxy needs to be listed in the Java domain. This is accomplished by providing the XML that defines a proxy object. You need to specify the classname of the proxy and the classname of the control by which your proxy is used. Looking at the example for the `DateTime` class, you see:

```
<Obj L=".Proxy">
    <ClassName>sdk.custom.swt.ExtendedDateTimeProxy</ClassName>
    <Replaces/>
    <UsedBy>org.eclipse.swt.widgets.DateTime</UsedBy>
</Obj>
```

The five lines in the preceding code listing are what wire your proxy to Rational Functional Tester's recording engine. Figure 13.50 shows you what these five lines look like in the context of the Java domain.

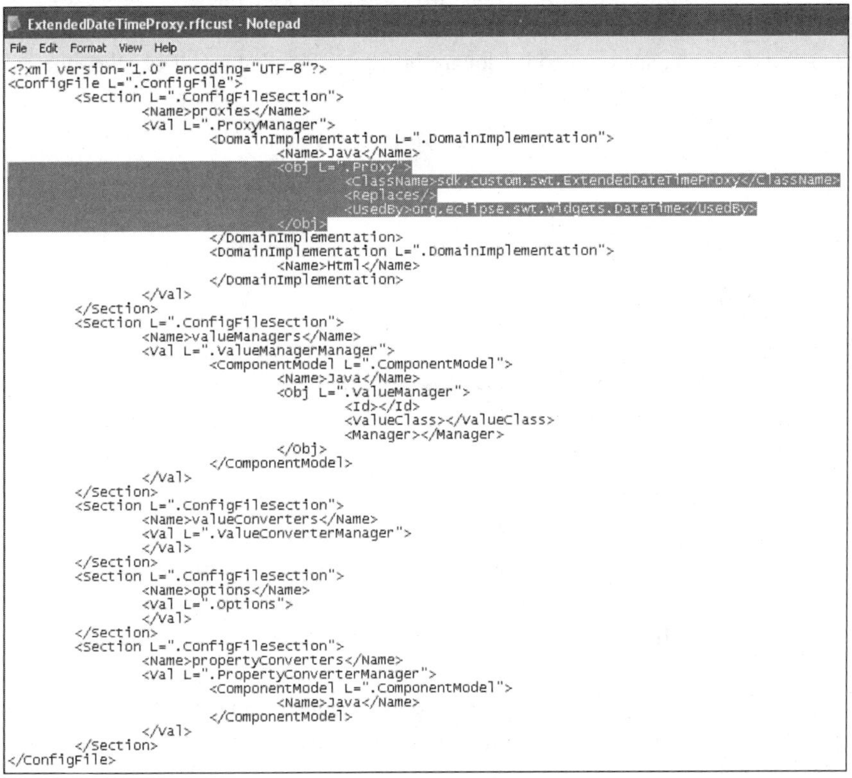


```
<?xml version="1.0" encoding="UTF-8"?>
<ConfigFile L=".ConfigFile">
        <Section L=".ConfigFileSection">
                <Name>proxies</Name>
                <Val L=".ProxyManager">
                        <DomainImplementation L=".DomainImplementation">
                                <Name>Java</Name>
                                <Obj L=".Proxy">
                                        <ClassName>sdk.custom.swt.ExtendedDateTimeProxy</ClassName>
                                        <Replaces/>
                                        <UsedBy>org.eclipse.swt.widgets.DateTime</UsedBy>
                                </Obj>
                        </DomainImplementation>
                        <DomainImplementation L=".DomainImplementation">
                                <Name>Html</Name>
                        </DomainImplementation>
                </Val>
        </Section>
        <Section L=".ConfigFileSection">
                <Name>valueManagers</Name>
                <Val L=".ValueManagerManager">
                        <ComponentModel L=".ComponentModel">
                                <Name>Java</Name>
                                <Obj L=".ValueManager">
                                        <Id></Id>
                                        <ValueClass></ValueClass>
                                        <Manager></Manager>
                                </Obj>
                        </ComponentModel>
                </Val>
        </Section>
        <Section L=".ConfigFileSection">
                <Name>valueConverters</Name>
                <Val L=".ValueConverterManager">
                </Val>
        </Section>
        <Section L=".ConfigFileSection">
                <Name>options</Name>
                <Val L=".Options">
                </Val>
        </Section>
        <Section L=".ConfigFileSection">
                <Name>propertyConverters</Name>
                <Val L=".PropertyConverterManager">
                        <ComponentModel L=".ComponentModel">
                                <Name>Java</Name>
                        </ComponentModel>
                </Val>
        </Section>
</ConfigFile>
```

Figure 13.50 Contents of ExtendedDateTimeProxy.rftcust

OPTIONAL CONSIDERATIONS FOR THE .NET DOMAINIMPLEMENTATION SECTION

Note that the assembly prefix for the <UsedBy> element entries is not required. It is optional. This is due to the fact that the control classnames are unique in the world and, therefore, do not need to be prefixed by the name of the .dll files (for example, assemblies) they live in. In the off chance that there are multiple custom controls with the same classname, the assemblies can be prepended to delineate between them.

Mapping for SourceGrid Proxy

The SourceGrid proxy needs to be listed in the Net domain. You need to add the appropriate lines (mentioned previously) and then add the XML that defines your proxy object. Similar to the DateTime example, you need to specify the classname of the proxy and the classname of the control that uses the proxy. One slight variation exists. You specify the name of the assemblies (for example, .dll files) that contain key class files (for example, custom control and your proxy classes). This is accomplished by prepending the <ClassName> and <UsedBy> element entries with the assembly name, surrounded by square brackets. The end result of all of this is the following XML:

```
<DomainImplementation L=".DomainImplementation">
    <Name>Net</Name>
    <Obj L=".Proxy">
        <ClassName>
            [SourceGridProxy]SourceGridProxy.SourceGridControlProxy
        </ClassName>
        <Replaces/>
        <UsedBy>[SourceGrid]SourceGrid.Grid</UsedBy>
    </Obj>
</DomainImplementation>
```

These lines tell Rational Functional Tester to use your proxy when interacting with the custom control you built it for. The full SourceGrid.rftcust file is displayed in Figure 13.51.

The creation of the .rftcust mapping file is the last step in creating a custom proxy. Whenever you launch rational Functional Tester, it looks in C:\Documents and Settings\All Users\Application Data\IBM\RFT\customization to see if there are any custom proxies to load. It sees your .rftcust file, opens it, and reads the XML, telling it to use the proxy you created. An important thing to note is that after you have your .jar/.dll and .rftcust in place, you need to close and reopen both Rational Functional Tester and the application you were automating for your mapping to take place.

```
SourceGridProxy.rftcust - Notepad
File  Edit  Format  View  Help
<?xml version="1.0" encoding="UTF-8"?>
<ConfigFile L=".ConfigFile">
        <Section L=".ConfigFileSection">
                <Name>proxies</Name>
                <Val L=".ProxyManager">
                        <DomainImplementation L=".DomainImplementation">
                                <Name>Java</Name>
                        </DomainImplementation>
                        <DomainImplementation L=".DomainImplementation">
                                <Name>Net</Name>
                                <Obj L=".Proxy">
                                        <ClassName>
                                        [SourceGridProxy]SourceGridProxy.SourceGridControlProxy
                                        </ClassName>
                                        <Replaces/>
                                        <UsedBy>[SourceGrid]SourceGrid.Grid</UsedBy>
                                </Obj>
                        </DomainImplementation>
                        <DomainImplementation L=".DomainImplementation">
                                <Name>Html</Name>
                        </DomainImplementation>
                </Val>
        </Section>
</ConfigFile>
```

Figure 13.51   Contents of SourceGridProxy.rftcust

Taking an Easier Path

Rational Functional Tester v8.1 introduces two wizards to facilitate proxy development. They are presently available only for the Eclipse flavor of Rational Functional Tester. The wizards enable you to create the base project structure and the skeleton for the code that you need to complete. Further, they create a template for the .rftcust file needed for mapping the proxy to Rational Functional Tester's recorder. The first wizard you execute is for the project setup (see Figure 13.52).

Figure 13.52   New Proxy Project wizard

The second is for creating the skeletons for any proxy classes you need to build. Ultimately, if you are using Java to create a proxy, you still need to follow the steps in the prior sections in this chapter *minus* the steps in the "Creating a Proxy Project" section in this chapter.

The first step to creating proxies using the wizards is to create the project itself. You initiate the wizard with the following steps:

1. Select **File > New > Other** (this opens the New dialog).

2. On this dialog, simply select **Functional Test > Proxy Project** (shown in Figure 13.52).

These steps invoke the basic New Proxy Project wizard. You have to provide only a project name here. Optionally, you can provide a new location in which to create the project. By default, the project is created in your workspace (see Figure 13.53).

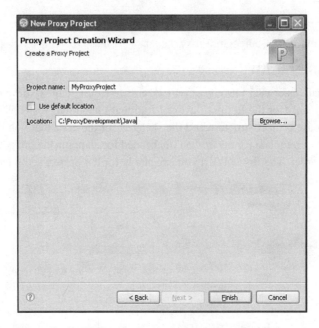

Figure 13.53   New Proxy Project Wizard—name and location provided

The end result of providing this data and clicking the **Finish** button is a new project, ready for your proxy development. You need to access the Java Perspective's Package Explorer View to see your project (see Figure 13.54).

If you expand the `src` folder in your project structure, you find that a .rftcust file is created for you. This gives you the template needed to create the mapping discussed in the previous section, "Mapping the Proxy." You can come here to fill in the necessary data for any proxy class that you develop in this project.

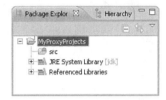

Figure 13.54   Java Perspective's Package Explorer View—New Proxy Project

You are able to engage the second wizard when you create a new proxy project. Follow these steps:

1. Select **File > New > Other** (this opens the New dialog box).

2. In this dialog box, simply select **Functional Test > Proxy Class** (shown in Figure 13.55).

Figure 13.55   New Proxy Class wizard

3. You need to fill out the **Source folder**, **Package**, **Proxy Class Name**, and **Control Class Name** fields. The Proxy Class Name is what you call your proxy. The Control Class Name is the actual control that you want to build the proxy for (for example, in this example—`org.eclipse.swt.widgets.DateTime`). See Figure 13.56 for an

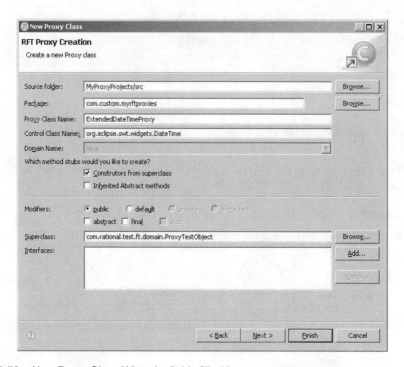

Figure 13.56   New Proxy Class Wizard—fields filled in

example of these fields filled out. You can click the **Browse** button and select an existing package or type in the name of a new package (for example, com.custom. myrftproxies) to store your proxy class in.

4. The next thing that you need to do is extend the proxy class that you researched earlier. For example, the SWT example from the "Figuring Out Which Proxy to Extend" section in this chapter is the CompositeProxy. Extending this class is done by clicking the **Browse** button for the Superclass field. This launches the Superclass Selection dialog box. You can find the proxy class you want to extend by typing the name of it in the Choose a type field (see Figure 13.57).

5. Verify that the Superclass field is populated with the proxy class you selected in Step 4. This is shown in Figure 13.58.

6. Click the wizard's **Next** button. This takes you to the Proxy Feature Page.

7. You need to select the methods you want to override.

NOTE   You might not see every method you need. For example, the CompositeProxy class provides only a subset of the methods that you need to override (see Figure 13.59).

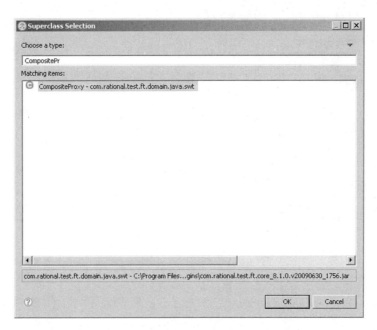

Figure 13.57   New Proxy Class Wizard—extending the proxy class

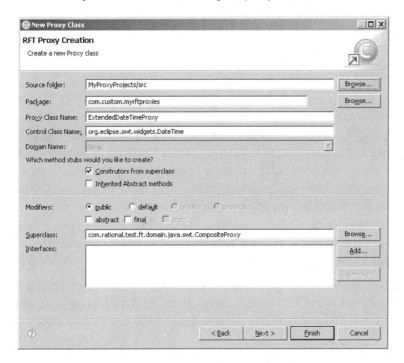

Figure 13.58   New Proxy Class Wizard—Superclass field populated

Figure 13.59   New Proxy Class Wizard—extending the proxy class

The previous sections regarding the Java SWT proxy example showed that you need to have the following methods: `processSingleMouseEvent()`, `getTestData()`, `getTestDataTypes()`, `getProperties()`, `getProperty()`, `getDescriptive-Name()`, `getRole()`, `getTestObjectClassName()`, and `getActionArgs()`. Figure 13.59 shows that the methods to override for the `CompositeProxy` class are only a subset of what is needed (for example, only the first five methods, in the preceding list, are available). Therefore, you still need to include the other methods in your proxy class, using the means that were detailed in the previous sections.

   8. After selecting the methods to override, click the **Finish** button. This completes the New Proxy Class Wizard and creates the skeleton of the proxy you need. This is displayed in Figure 13.60.

As you can see, the wizards help to expedite proxy development. They provide you with the pieces to quickly get you started in your efforts. However, as nice as the wizards are, you still need to fill in most of the coding—the content that accomplishes the actual work.

```
ExtendedDateTimeProxy.java

   package com.custom.myrftproxies;

   import com.rational.test.ft.domain.IMouseActionInfo;
   import com.rational.test.ft.domain.java.swt.CompositeProxy;
   import com.rational.test.ft.vp.ITestData;


   public  class ExtendedDateTimeProxy extends CompositeProxy
   {

     public ExtendedDateTimeProxy(java.lang.Object theObjectInTheSUT) {
          super(theObjectInTheSUT);
     }

   public void processSingleMouseEvent(IMouseActionInfo action){
        // TODO Auto-generated method stub
       super.processSingleMouseEvent(action);
     }
   public ITestData getTestData(String type){
          // TODO Auto-generated method stub
          return super.getTestData(type);
     }
   public java.util.Hashtable getTestDataTypes(){
          // TODO Auto-generated method stub
          return super.getTestDataTypes();
     }
   public java.util.Hashtable getProperties(){
          // TODO Auto-generated method stub
          return super.getProperties();
     }
   public Object getProperty(String propertyName){
          // TODO Auto-generated method stub
          return super.getProperty(propertyName);
     }
     }
```

Figure 13.60   New Proxy Class Wizard—completed proxy class skeleton

Debugging a Proxy

You most likely need to debug your proxy at least once. Rational Functional Tester provides a means to do this through a debug log. To use this log for your purposes, you need to specify a few options in the ivory.properties file.

The ivory.properties file is found in the ..\FunctionalTester\bin directory. Opening it reveals a myriad of options. You want to focus on the `Debugging Options` section (see Figure 13.61).

```
###
### Debugging options
###
# The following propeties are used to control the debugging output generated by the FT
# product.  In production versions this output is minimal, limited primarily to error
# and warning level information.
rational.test.ft.debug.enabled=true      1.
rational.test.ft.debug.native_to_file=false
rational.test.ft.debug.clear_on_init=false
rational.test.ft.debug.filename=c:/ivDebug.txt     2.
# filter levels: error,0;warning,1;debug,2;verbose,3
rational.test.ft.debug.filter=default,1;rational_ft,1;wsw.rftuiplugin,1;native,3;mycustomproxy,3;     3.
```

Figure 13.61   The ivory.properties file—debugging options

The numbered boxes highlight the three properties with which you need to work. First, you want to ensure that the debugging is actually enabled. Therefore, you need to make sure that the `rational.test.ft.debug.enabled` property is set to a value of true. Secondly, you control what to name your debug log and where to write it. You can do this by setting the `rational.test.ft.debug.filename` property to your desired value. By default, it is set to `c:/ivDebug.txt`. Finally, you want to make sure that you can easily identify your proxy messages. You can add in a custom filter for your proxy by adding it to the `rational.test.ft.debug.filter` property. Figure 13.61 shows this in the third box, highlighting the `mycustomproxy` filter. The number 3, that follows the filter, tells Rational Functional Tester to log all the messages coded into the proxy, not just the warnings and errors it encounters. After making the appropriate edits to the ivory.properties file, you can save the changes and close it. You have now enabled logging for your proxy.

To write messages from your proxy to the log, you first need to add the following line to the beginning of your proxy class:

```
protected static FtDebug debug = new FtDebug("mycustomproxy");
```

This line is the same whether or not you use C# or Java to create your proxy. However, you need to ensure that you have imported the appropriate package into your proxy class. Using Java, your import looks like the following:

```
import com.rational.test.ft.util.FtDebug;
```

If you create a proxy in C#, you need:

```
using Rational.Test.Ft.Util;
```

Essentially, you create a new `FtDebug` object that writes your desired messages to the `mycustomproxy` filter. You write to the log using one of the following messages types:

- `trace`
- `verbose`
- `warning`
- `error`

It behooves you to prefix any of your messages with some sort of identifier. For instance, you might use the name of your proxy filter (see Listing 13.25).

Listing 13.25   Debug messages

Java
```
debug.trace("MYCUSTOMPROXY: THIS IS A TRACE MESSAGE");
debug.verbose("MYCUSTOMPROXY: THIS IS A VERBOSE MESSAGE");
debug.warning("MYCUSTOMPROXY: THIS IS A WARNING MESSAGE");
debug.error("MYCUSTOMPROXY: THIS IS AN ERROR MESSAGE");
```

C#

```
debug.Trace("MYCUSTOMPROXY: THIS IS A TRACE MESSAGE");
debug.Verbose("MYCUSTOMPROXY: THIS IS A VERBOSE MESSAGE");
debug.Warning("MYCUSTOMPROXY: THIS IS A WARNING MESSAGE");
debug.Error("MYCUSTOMPROXY: THIS IS AN ERROR MESSAGE");
```

A lot of information outside of the proxy messages is recorded in the log file. Using a prefix, in conjunction with the filter name, helps you quickly locate your proxy messages. This helps you find and solve your issues faster.

As you can see in Figure 13.62, the custom proxy messages are identified by their filter name and prefix (contained in the red outline). Depending upon the type of debug message you are writing, a code might be associated with it. For instance, a trace message has a code of Dbg, a warning message has a code of Wrn, and an error message has a code of Err. A verbose message does not have a code.

Figure 13.62   ivDebug.txt file

You can use these to help you identify the types of messages you want to place in your proxy code. You can place error messages in catch statements, use verbose messages to identify the start and completion of methods, and so on. The idea is to thread your messages throughout your code to have the most robust means to debug your proxy issues.

If you don't see your debug messages in the log file, Rational Functional Tester might not have successfully loaded your proxy. To check for this, you want to look for lines that are similar to the following:

```
10:50:58:343 PM    1868    3932  Wrn  rational_ft  File: C:\Documents and
Settings\All Users\Application
Data\IBM\RFT\customization\ExtendedDateTimeProxy.jar added to custom list


10:50:58:343 PM    1868    3932  Wrn  rational_ft  File: C:\Documents and
Settings\All Users\Application
Data\IBM\RFT\customization\ExtendedDateTimeProxy.rftcust added to custom list
```

These two lines show that the .jar and .rftcust files are engaged by Rational Functional Tester. If you do not see these, you need to check your .rftcust file for syntax errors. It is not uncommon to mis-spell the name of your class. You also want to make sure the name of your .rftcust file matches the name of your .jar file. In the previous example, they are both called `ExtendedDateTimeProxy`. If they do not match or you have a typo inside of your .rftcust file, Rational Functional Tester does not engage your proxy.

Summary

This chapter took a high-level view of Rational Functional Tester's Proxy SDK. It provided samples to give you an idea of what is involved with creating your own custom proxies and the tools available in Rational Functional Tester to help you build proxies. You should have a feel for what level of effort is involved with this type of project. You should also assume that your project shares some similarities with the examples here but also differs in many aspects. Your proxy development is dictated by the GUI control(s) you automate.

## CHAPTER 14

Developing Scripts in the VB.NET Environment

Larry Quesada

In this chapter, you find information on the Visual Studio version of Rational Functional Tester. Other chapters provide examples of concepts in both VB.NET and Java, so you do not find a lot of detail here. However, you do find a few discussions about using Rational Functional Tester in Visual Studio, which are not covered in other parts of the book.

Installing Rational Functional Tester into Visual Studio .NET

To install the VB.NET version of Rational Functional Tester, you must first install Visual Studio. At the time of this writing, Rational Functional Tester supports Visual Studio Net 2003 with .NET Framework 1.1 and Visual Studio Net 2005 with .NET Framework 2.0. You begin the installation of Rational Functional Tester by starting the launch pad program, either from the CD or an electronic image. From the launch pad, click **Install IBM Rational Functional Tester**. Select either **install** or **modify** depending on your situation, and then follow the instructions in the wizard to complete the installation process. On the wizard screen that prompts you to select the features to install, select either **.NET 2003 Scripting** or **.NET 2005 Scripting**. Complete the installation and you are done!

Locating Projects on Network Shares

For various reasons, you might want to locate your Rational Functional Tester .NET project on a network share. This section describes what you need to do to get a Rational Functional Tester .NET project to work on a share.

Code Access Security

The .NET common language runtime has a code access security system, which determines an assembly's permissions to access protected resources. The location of the assembly helps to determine what permissions the assembly has. If the permission set associated to the Rational Functional Tester .NET project is sufficiently strict, you get errors when using Rational Functional Tester in Visual Studio.

If you attempt to create a Rational Functional Tester .NET project in a network share and the security associated to the network location is not FullTrust, you get the error shown in Figure 14.1.

Figure 14.1   Error when creating Rational Functional Tester.NET project on a network share without FullTrust

Further, anytime you open the project, you get the warning shown in Figure 14.2.

Figure 14.2   Warning when opening Rational Functional Tester .NET project on a network share without FullTrust

Finally, when you play back a script, you might receive this message: FullTrust security policy needed to run script [Script1].

Selecting **Yes**, as the dialog box in Figure 14.1 recommends, does not actually change the security policy. To fix this problem, you can either adjust the zone security on your computer or adjust the security for your Rational Functional Tester project.

Adjusting Local Zone Security

You can change the security of your computer by network zone. To do so, follow these steps:

1. Open the Administrative Tools of your operating system.
2. Open the Microsoft .NET Framework <version> Configuration.
3. Right-click **Runtime Security Policy**, and then select **Adjust Security**.
4. Click the option button to make changes to this computer.
5. Set the Local Intranet security policy to **Full Trust**.

Depending upon where your share is, you might have to adjust the policy of the other zones, too, but usually Local Intranet is sufficient. You need to perform this step on any computer that uses the Rational Functional Tester project.

If you continue to have issues, try configuring security in Internet Explorer with the following steps:

1. Click **Tools > Internet Options** in the Internet Explorer window.
2. In the Security tab, select **Local intranet** zone.
3. Click **Sites**.
4. In the Local Intranet dialog box, click **Advanced**.
5. Uncheck **Require server verification (https:) for all sites in this zone**.
6. Specify the project path, and click **Add**.
7. Click **OK**.

Adjusting the Security of a Rational Functional Tester Project

Alternatively, you can adjust the security of the Rational Functional Tester project. Again, this must be done on each computer. IBM provides a utility called rational_ft in the directory C:\Program Files\IBM\SDP\FunctionalTester\bin\NetCommandLine, which you can use for this purpose.

If your Rational Functional Tester project is located in the share <\\computerName\projects\rft book\Example14\Example14>, then you run the following command:

```
rational_ft -datastore "\\name\projects\rft
book\Example14\Example14" -addfulltrust
```

After completing this command, your Rational Functional Tester project functions correctly, although you might still receive the *project location is not trusted* warning.

Reusing Code

One of the powerful capabilities of Rational Functional Tester is the capability to reuse code. You can make calls to any managed code, written in any .NET language from a Rational Functional Tester script in Visual Studio. This section describes how to do this.

Using External .NET Assemblies in a Rational Functional Tester.NET Project

In an out-of-the-box Visual Studio project, you can add a reference to an external assembly or project by right-clicking on your project and selecting **Add Reference**. Rational Functional Tester, however, does not support adding a reference in this way. Instead, Rational Functional Tester automatically creates a reference to any assembly located in the Rational Functional Tester customization directory. By default, the customization directory is located at C:\Documents and Settings\All Users\Application Data\IBM\RFT\customization. Rational Functional Tester immediately senses any changes you make to the customization directory.

The easiest way to share assemblies is to place them in a directory that all computers used to develop and run scripts can access. You can change the location of the Rational Functional Tester customization directory by altering the registry key located at HKEY_LOCAL_MACHINE\ SOFTWARE\Rational Software\Rational Test\8. The Rational Functional Tester customization direction is stored in the string value called Rational FT Customization Directory. The easiest way to share assemblies is to place the assemblies in your configuration management system. You can then create views on each computer your team users to develop scripts and point the Rational FT Customization Directory to the appropriate directory in your view.

Another way you can add a reference to an assembly is to place the assembly in the Rational Functional Tester bin directory located in the Rational Functional Tester installation directory. When using this technique, you must also add the name of the Dynamic Link Library (DLL) to the netAssembliesForCompiler.txt in the same directory and restart Rational Functional Tester.

Be careful that you do not have any folders or classes in your Rational Functional Tester project that are the same as any namespaces or classes in your external assembly. If you do, your scripts might not compile or run.

Using the .NET Foundation Class Library

You can incorporate classes from the .NET Foundation Class Library into your scripts, and the scripts do compile. However, when you try to run the scripts, you might get the error displayed in Figure 14.3.

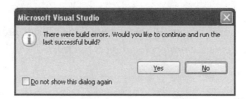

Figure 14.3   Error when running a Rational Functional Tester.NET Script when Foundation Assembly is not found

The problem here is again about references. You can not create a reference from your Rational Functional Tester project to the appropriate .NET assembly. Instead, you need to find the assembly that contains the namespace you want to use and either copy the assembly to the customization directory or place it in the Rational Functional Tester bin directory. Don't forget to update the netAssembliesForCompiler.txt if you use the bin directory route. You find the .NET Foundation library in the directory C:\windows\Microsoft.NET\Framework\<framework version>. You can use some Foundation namespaces, such as `System` and `System.IO`, without copying the assembly. For other namespaces, such as `System.data` and `System.XML`, you must copy the assembly.

Sharing Scripts Between Rational Functional Tester.NET Projects

One way to share code between Rational Functional Tester.NET projects is to refactor your code and extract those pieces that you want to reuse. You can then place these classes in an external assembly and share that assembly as described previously.

You cannot share some Rational Functional Tester test artifacts in this way. You cannot, for example, define a `Helper Base` Class in an external assembly nor can you run a test script from one Rational Functional Tester project that is defined in another Rational Functional Tester project. The best way to share these kinds of objects is to keep everything in one Rational Functional Tester project and partition the project with folders. You might also consider putting your project under a source control system, such as IBM Rational ClearCase.

Summary

This chapter covered some topics specific to using Rational Functional Tester in Visual Studio .NET that were not covered in other parts of the book. We explored installation, adjustment of security to locate a project on a network share, and reuse of code.

CHAPTER 15

Using Rational Functional Tester in a Linux Environment

Chip Davis, Lee B. Thomas, Marc van Lint

This chapter describes how to use Rational Functional Tester (RFT) on a Linux system. There is one significant difference: There is no "Red button" to record. This chapter describes the steps to install Rational Functional Tester and create a basic script. For details on all other topics, use the Java examples that are provided throughout this book.

Although this chapter uses the term "Linux," IBM does not provide support for using Rational Functional Tester on all Linux distributions. At the time of this writing, particular versions of Red Hat Enterprise Linux and SUSE Linux (SLES and SLED) are supported. This chapter shows examples for Red Hat Enterprise Linux.

Installation

You should already have installed a Linux distribution that is a supported operating system (OS) for Rational Functional Tester. In that installation, you need to proceed with the following steps:

1. Install additional Linux software required by Rational Functional Tester.
2. Install Java and enable it in Firefox.
3. Install IBM Installation Manager.
4. Install Rational Functional Tester via IBM Installation Manager.

All these actions must be performed with root access.

Installing Additional Linux Software Required by Rational Functional Tester

A full and up to date description of the components needed on the Linux operating system can be found in the installation documentation for Rational Functional Tester. Still, there are two components that require attention:

- Graphical Internet
- Legacy Software Development

To add these components, follow these steps:

1. Select **System Settings > Add/Remove Applications**. See Figure 15.1.

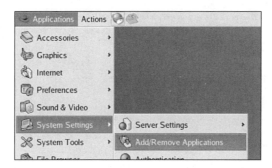

Figure 15.1 The Linux Add/Remove programs

2. Select the **Graphical Internet** group and select **Details**. See Figure 15.2.

Figure 15.2 Graphical Internet group in the list of optional components

3. Confirm that the Firefox browser is installed. See Figure 15.3.

Figure 15.3 Legacy Software Development group

4. Confirm that the GNU Image Manipulation Program Toolkit (GTK+), Version 2.2.1 or later, and its associated libraries (Glib and Pango) are installed. See Figure 15.4.

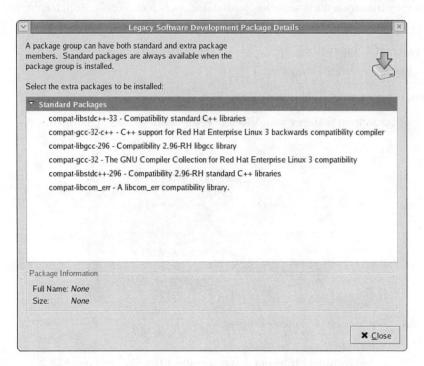

Figure 15.4   The needed compatibility libraries for Rational Functional Tester

Installing Java and Enabling Java in Firefox

Rational Functional Tester requires a Java Runtime Environment (JRE), which can be obtained from www.java.com. You should refer to the instructions on that site for how to download and install the JRE, and refer to your Rational Functional Tester online documentation for version compatibility.

Installing IBM Installation Manager

Eclipse-based Rational products are installed from IBM Installation Manager (IIM). IBM Installation Manager takes care of any dependencies among packages to be installed and the environment already available. IBM Installation Manager operates in the same manner on both Windows and Linux. You enter a Linux path to identify the location of the repository, as shown in Figure 15.5.

To install the IBM Installation Manager, follow these steps:

1. Double-click the **install icon**, as shown in Figure 15.6.

2. Select **Next**. See Figure 15.7.

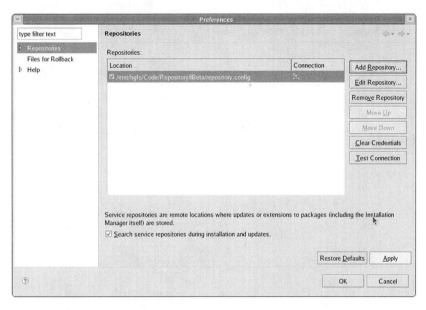

Figure 15.5   The directory where the code for IIM is available

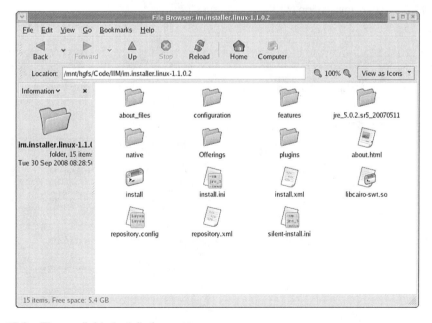

Figure 15.6   The available installation manager

3. Select the **I accept the terms in the license agreements** radio button.

4. Select **Next**. See Figure 15.8.

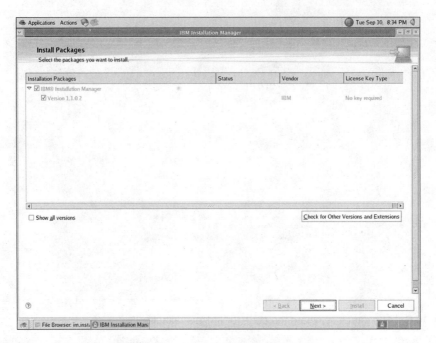

Figure 15.7   Accept installation of IBM Installation Manager.

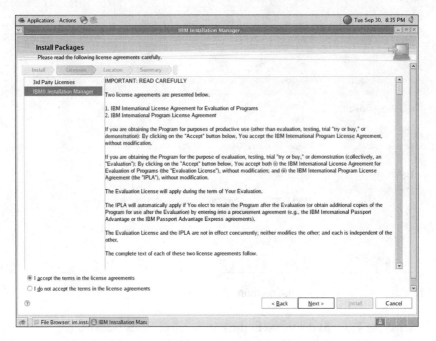

Figure 15.8   Accept the terms and conditions before IBM Installation Manager.

5. Assuming this default directory is acceptable, Select **Next**. See Figure 15.9.

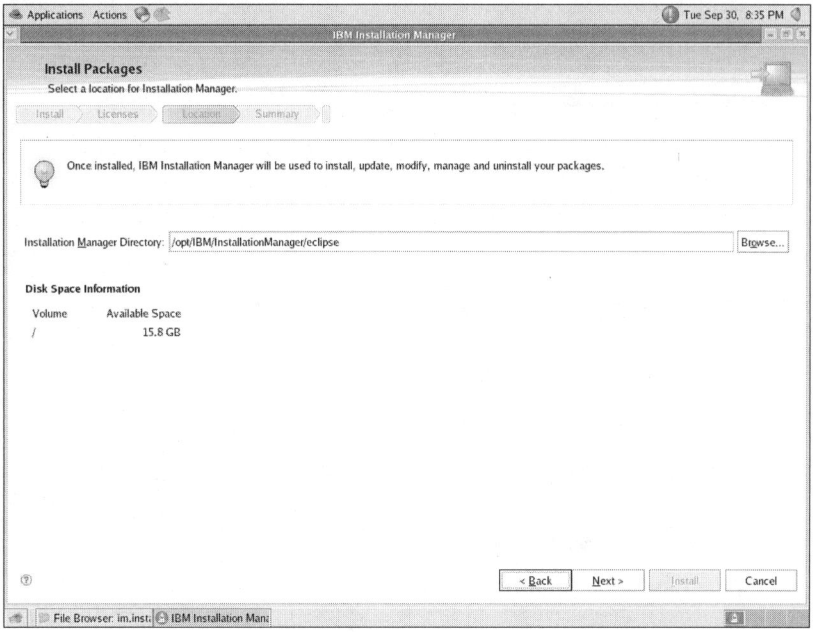

Figure 15.9   A check on the settings for the installation of IBM Installation Manager

6. Select **Install**. See Figure 15.10.

7. Select **Finish**.

You can start IBM Installation Manager from the menu. Select **Applications > System Tools > IBM Installation Manger**, as shown in Figure 15.11.

Installing Rational Functional Tester

With IBM Installation Manager installed, you can install Rational Functional Tester. Define the location of the repository of the code to be used. Select **File > Preferences**. See Figure 15.12.

Using Rational Functional Tester

This section gives you the basic steps for creating an automated test script in Rational Functional Tester in a Linux environment:

- Start Rational Functional Tester.
- Enable environments for testing.
- Configure applications for testing.

Figure 15.10   Check for settings and install.

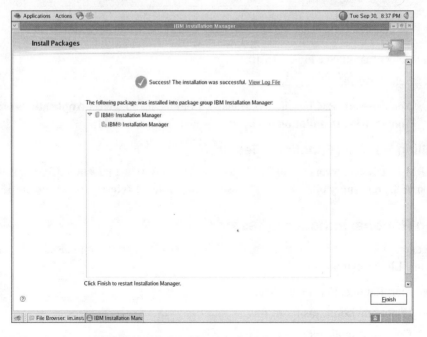

Figure 15.11   A successful IBM Installation Manager installation

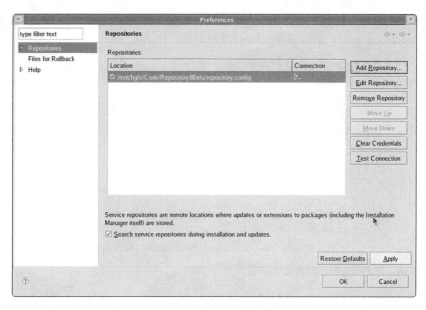

Figure 15.12   The definition of the source of the installation files

- Create an empty script.
- Insert a Test Object.
- Insert a Verification Test Object.
- Insert `waitForExistence`.
- Create an entire script.

Starting Rational Functional Tester

1. Start Rational Functional Tester by selecting **Applications > Programming > IBM Rational Functional Tester**. See Figure 15.13.

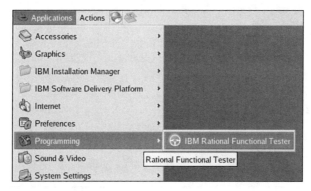

Figure 15.13   Starting Rational Functional Tester

2.   Rational Functional Tester prompts for the location of the workspace, which is the area
     where temporary settings are stored. See Figure 15.14.

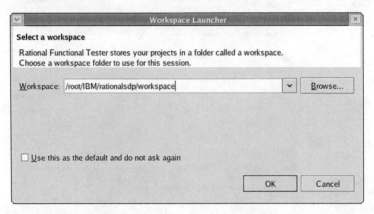

Figure 15.14   Defining the workspace

3.   If it appears, you can close the Welcome view. However, it is highly recommended that
     you return to it by the menu **Help > Welcome**, to review the material there. If you do not
     see the Functional Test perspective at this point, open it via **Window > Perspective >
     Other > Functional Test.**

4.   Create a project, which is the area where all artifacts are stored. Select **File > New >
     Functional Test Project**. See Figure 15.15.

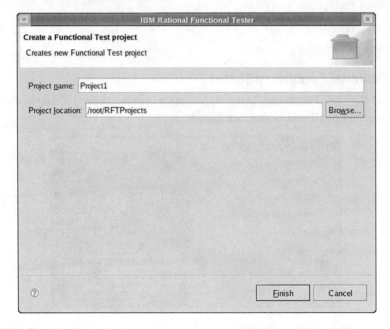

Figure 15.15   Creating the project

Enabling Environments for Testing

You have to set your environments or at least check to see if they are set correctly. See Figure 15.16.

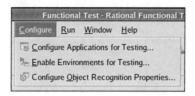

Figure 15.16   The configuration of applications and environments

1. If you are testing a browser-based application, you need to define the browsers used. See Figure 15.17.

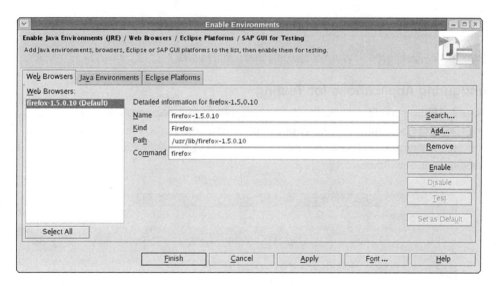

Figure 15.17   Define the browsers that can be used.

2. Select the **Search** option to automatically search for all browsers.
3. Select the **Search All** and **Search** to add any browsers.
4. Select the **Java Environments** tab. See Figure 15.18.
5. Select the **Search** option again.
6. Enable the appropriate Java Runtime and make it the default.

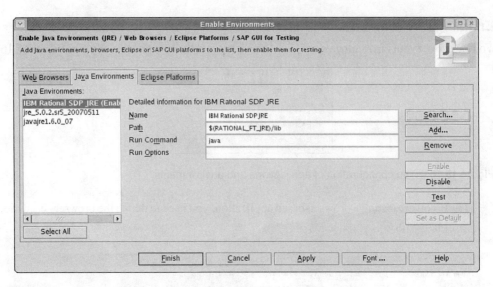

Figure 15.18   Define the Java environments that can be used.

Configuring Applications for Testing

In Rational Functional Tester, you can define the applications under test. This can be done via the menu **Configure > Configure Applications for Testing**. You can add the application to test. For this exercise, you use the Java application ClassicsJavaA and the browser-based application www.ibm.com. See Figure 15.19.

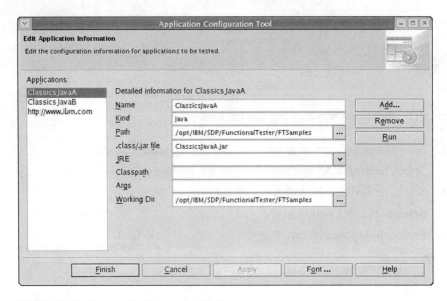

Figure 15.19   Define the application under test.

Creating an Empty Script

In the Linux version of IBM Rational Functional Tester, there is no "Record" button available. You create the script by entering code into an empty script.

1. Create an empty script by selecting the menu item **File > New**. See Figure 15.20.

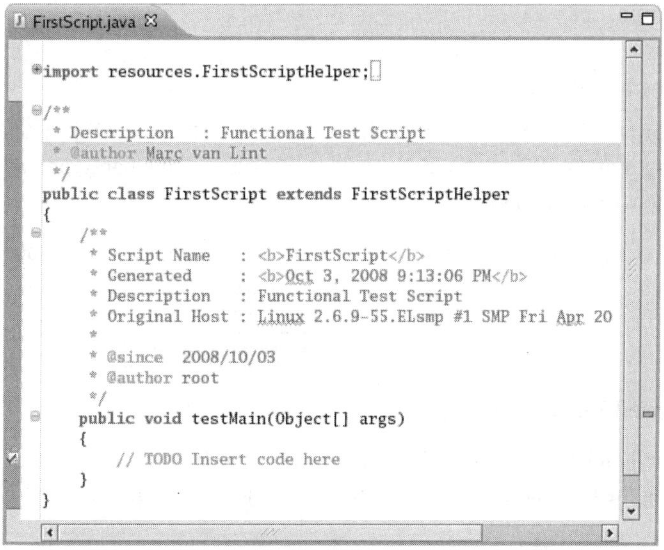

Figure 15.20   An empty script

2. To gain familiarity with the Eclipse-editing features, deliberately add an erroneous `startApplication` statement. If you make a coding error, the syntax and logic checking of Eclipse assist you. You can immediately see that the statement is incorrect if you look at the highlighting feature. Rational Functional Tester proposes quick fixes to correct the error. See Figure 15.21.

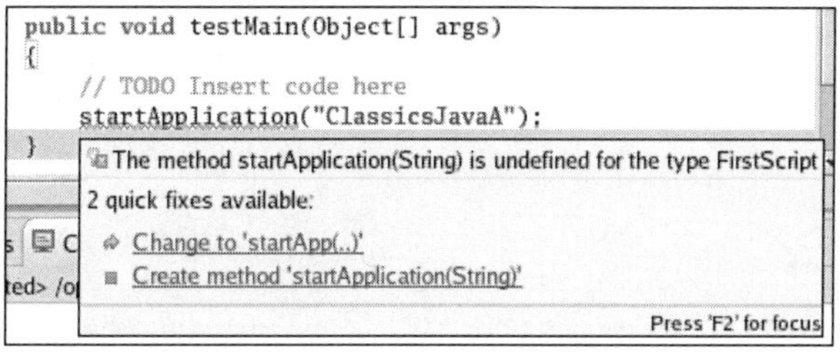

Figure 15.21   An example of assistance in correcting errors

The majority of statements in a test script consist of two parts: identifying the object to be acted upon and specifying the action to perform. In more detail, the parts are:

1. **Insert an object**—Points to the object in the application under test. This results in an entry in the Test Object Map, which enables actions against that object.

2. **Action on an object**—The object in the script complemented with an action such as a click action.

Inserting a Test Object

Creating a test script is done by inserting a Test Object from the Test Object Map into the script, and then selecting a method for the action, such as click(). This paragraph describes the steps to add a Test Object to the Test Object Map.

1. The Test Objects are added with the Insert Test Object icon. See Figure 15.22.

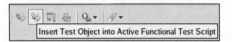

Figure 15.22   Insert Test Object.

2. Drag the hand cursor to the object to be activated (for example, a tree or a button). By releasing the hand cursor, you can select the object that is highlighted. See Figure 15.23.

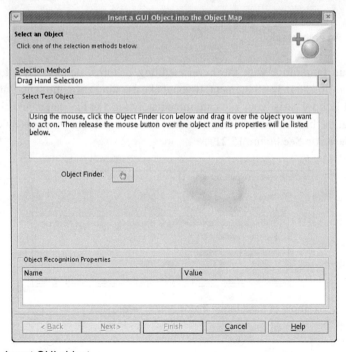

Figure 15.23   Insert GUI object.

3. You can verify you've selected the correct object by investigating the Object Recognition Properties (see Figure 15.24). Select **Finish.**

Figure 15.24   Verify the object recognition properties.

4. Reference the object in the test script. For example, you can enter the following:

```
placeOrder()
```

As you type, the Code Assist feature proposes the methods that are available. Methods such as click, focus, and so on are shown, and if you select one, you are shown the patterns for arguments that can be passed.

Inserting a Verification Point

You can create Verification Points much like you create actions on objects.

1. Place the cursor at the correct location in the script and select the **Insert Verification Point** icon. See Figure 15.25.

Figure 15.25   The Insert Verification Point icon

2. The Insert Verification Point Action Wizard displays, as shown in Figure 15.26.

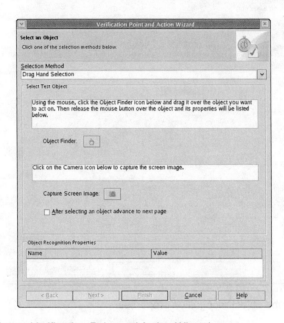

Figure 15.26   The Insert Verification Point and Action Wizard

3. Drag the hand to the object to test by holding down the left mouse button. Rational Functional Tester draws a red square around the object that is selected when you release the mouse button. Selection is done when the cursor is released. See Figure 15.27.

4. Select **Next,** or reselect the object to test. See Figure 15.28.

0

Figure 15.27 The identified object can be verified by checking the object properties.

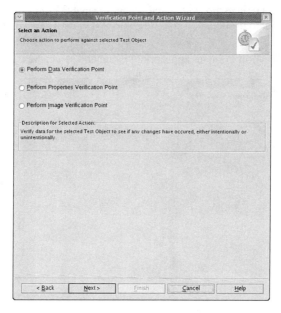

Figure 15.28 The various types of Verification Points. Note that waitForExistence is not available for Linux through this dialog.

5. Select the appropriate type of test. Here a Data Verification Point is selected. See Figure 15.29.

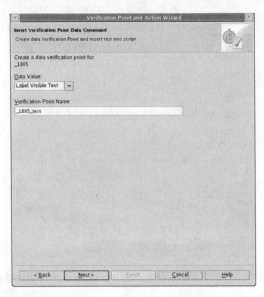

Figure 15.29   The panel to give the Verification Point a sensible name. This name is not meaningful as a datapool reference.

6. Give the Verification Point an appropriate name and select **Next**. See Figure 15.30.

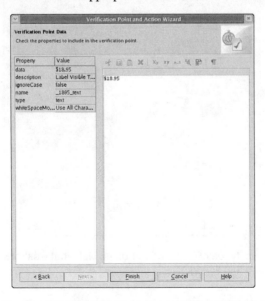

Figure 15.30   The Verification Point Wizard where the baseline of the Verification Point can be defined in hard-coded manner as a regular expression or as a datapool reference.

7. Select **Finish.** The following line is inserted into the code:

```
placeOrder().performTest( PlaceOrder_textVP() );
```

Inserting waitForExistence

You can add `waitForExistence` for a Test Object by inserting the object, and adding the method via Eclipse's Code Assist feature. The way to create is as follows:

1. Insert the Test Object into your script that Rational Functional Tester should wait for to ensure that it exists.

2. Add the `.waitForExistence()` method to the object's reference.

Creating an Entire Script

On Linux, Rational Functional Tester does not provide a way for you to record your script. This section shows how you create a script from start to finish, using the `ClassicsJavaA` application.

1. Create an empty functional test script via the Rational Functional Test menu by selecting **File > New > Empty Functional Test Script**. See Figure 15.31.

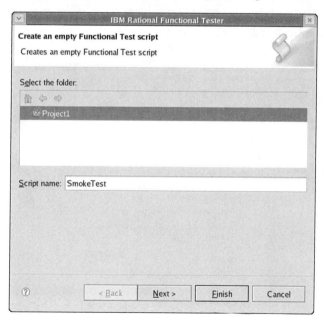

Figure 15.31   Starting a new script

2. Enter a meaningful script name and Select **Next**.

3. Accept the script assets. Select **Finish.** See Figure 15.32. The RFT main screen displays. See Figure 15.33.

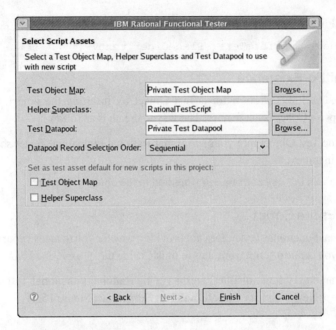

Figure 15.32   Acceptance of default script assets

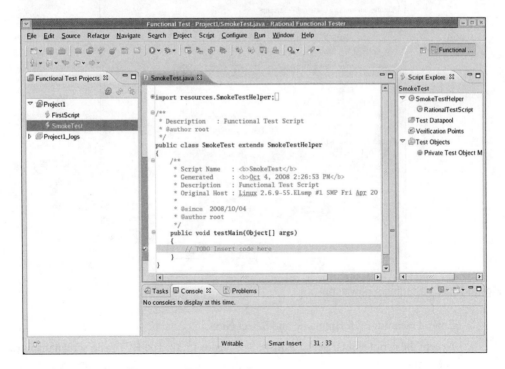

Figure 15.33   Rational Functional Tester overview

4. Start your application from the Enable Application for Testing menu.

5. Type the following code, making use of Eclipse's Code Assist feature to help you. Create the Test Objects and Verification Points as described in the sections "Inserting a Test Object" and "Inserting a Verification Point" earlier in this chapter.

```java
public void testMain(Object[] args)
    {
        startApp("ClassicsJavaA");

        // Frame: ClassicsCD
        tree2().click(atPath("Composers->Haydn->Location(PLUS_MINUS)"));
        tree2().click(atPath("Composers->Haydn->Symphonies Nos. 94 & 98"));
        placeOrder().click();

        // Frame: Member Logon
        nameCombo().click();
        nameCombo().click(atText("Susan Flontly"));
        ok().click();

        // Frame: Place an Order
        cardNumberIncludeTheSpacesText().click(atPoint(5,5));
        placeAnOrder().inputChars("1");
        expirationDateText().click(atPoint(5,5));
        placeAnOrder().inputChars("12/12");

        // Frame: Place an Order
        placeAnOrder().waitForExistence();
        // Frame: Place an Order
        placeOrder2().performTest(PlaceOrder_textVP());
        placeOrder2().click();

        // Select OK
        ok2().click();

        classicsJava(ANY, MAY_EXIT).close();
    }
}
```

Summary

This chapter showed how to use Rational Functional Tester to create automated scripts on a Linux system. The Code Assist feature of Eclipse and the many wizards in Rational Functional Tester make this a straightforward task.

Internationalized Testing with Rational Functional Tester

Jeffrey R. Bocarsly

Both Java and VB.NET handle the full range of international character sets, and Rational Functional Tester and its objects do, too. With growing frequency, applications are built to handle a range of languages and the language-related customs that accompany internationalized applications. This chapter shows how to set Rational Functional Tester up to test applications that feature internationalized Graphical User Interfaces (GUIs).

Internationalized testing setup does involve working with script internals for those scripts that you want to execute with multilanguage support. You might want to review Chapter 4, "XML and Rational Functional Tester," Chapter 9, "Advanced Rational Functional Tester Object Map Topics," and Chapter 10, "Advanced Scripting with Rational Functional Tester TestObjects," before reading this chapter, so that the details are fresh in your mind. Furthermore, because this topic is considered an advanced topic, we treat it only from the perspective of the "regular" functional scripting apparatus (Java and VB.NET), and not from the perspective of the graphical Storyboard Testing option (released in Rational Functional Tester 8.1), which is meant to make Rational Function Tester more broadly accessible to nontechnical and novice users.

Unicode and Rational Functional Tester

Application software, especially Internet-enabled software, increasingly is internationalized for global commerce. This means that systems are built so that their GUIs can display in a range of character sets and locales. The expanded character sets required for internationalized applications fall under the rubric of the Unicode standard. Unicode is the name of a major effort to standardize all human character sets, past and present, together under one system of platform-independent unique character mappings. At the time of this writing, Unicode 5.1.0 is the current release; it contains over 100,000 characters. The Unicode standard is under continual expansion, and new mappings for additional character sets are added regularly.

> **NOTE**   The Unicode Consortium is the organization that develops the Unicode standard. You can get the flavor of the range of activities that the Consortium is involved in and look up character sets at the Unicode home page (www.unicode.org).

Having a single character mapping for all characters, regardless of language, is only part of the answer. For the set of numbers representing each of these characters, there must be an encoding scheme. Numerous encoding schemes have been proposed, but the current *de facto* Internet standard is called UTF-8, which typically uses up to four bytes to encode a Unicode character (but may use up to six).

> **NOTE**   A complete description of UTF-8 and how it encodes Unicode code points can be found at www.faqs.org/rfcs/rfc2279.html. An excellent summary appears at www.wikipedia.org/wiki/UTF-8.

To make this a bit more concrete, let's look at some examples of Unicode on the Internet. The IBM website is internationalized, and it can easily be viewed in numerous languages. If you examine the title tag for the home page in English and in Russian, you see the following:

```
<title>IBM  - United States</title>
<title>IBM  - в России и странах СНГ</title>
```

Each of these title characters can be represented by corresponding Unicode values, and by the UTF-8 encoding of the Unicode code point. Table 16.1 shows selections of these values.

Table 16.1   Unicode and UTF-8 Sample Values

Character	Unicode Code Point	UTF-8 Encoding
I	73	49
B	66	42
M	77	4D
U	85	55

Table 16.1 Unicode and UTF-8 Sample Values

Character	Unicode Code Point	UTF-8 Encoding
n	110	6E
i	105	69
t	116	74
e	101	65
d	100	64
S	83	53
a	97	61
s	115	73
В	1074	D0 B2
Р	1056	D0 A0
о	1086	D0 BE
с	1089	D1 81
и	1080	D0 B8
т	1090	D1 82
р	1088	D1 80
а	1072	D0 B0
н	1085	D0 BD
х	1093	D1 85
С	1057	D0 A1
Н	1053	D0 9D
Г	1043	D0 93

For the most part, with current text editors, you won't have to deal with Unicode values directly or with the UTF-8 encodings. You just need the native fonts and texts for setting up an internationalized testing scheme. Of course, this likely requires access to resources fluent in each language, so the assembly of test data still won't be as simple as with a single-language automation project (but you shouldn't have to deal with collecting data as code points).

Handling Internationalized Data in Rational Functional Tester

Microsoft Windows offers broad language and locale support (a *locale* is the collection of writing practices and symbols used by a cultural group—for example, the United States locale uses the English alphabet, formats dates in the order month-day-year with either a dash or a slash delimiter, and for numbers, it uses a comma to separate thousands, a point to indicate the decimal place, and the dollar symbol ($) to signify money, and so on). You can have multiple languages and locales loaded on Windows at any given time. For information about how to set up internationalized support on Windows, read the article "Enabling International Support in Windows XP/Server 2003 Family" (http://www.microsoft.com/globaldev/handson/user/xpintlsupp.mspx). Numerous articles on the Microsoft website and on the Internet describe how to enable language support on Windows. For performing internationalized testing on Windows, setting up Windows with the different language-locale combinations that you need is the first step.

Language Support in Windows and the Windows Language Bar

After you have set up language support, you can access the different language-locale combinations you have chosen through the Windows Language bar (which displays as a floating toolbar or as a static toolbar next to the system tray, depending on your configuration choices). Using the Language bar, there is one additional Windows feature used in the implementation described in this chapter. Windows enables you to associate specific hotkeys with specific *keyboard* selections. This is done with the Windows Language bar Settings window (Text Services and Input Languages). You use the Key Settings button in the Preferences section of the window (see Figure 16.1 for the dialog window). This chapter uses the keystroke sequence Left+Alt+Shift+num for each keyboard/language, where the value of num uniquely identifies each language.

Language Support in Rational Functional Tester

Language support in Rational Functional Tester is present by default. It's already set up! All Rational Functional Tester objects (except the Console Views in both Eclipse and Visual Studio) can display internationalized text, whether you capture it in a script by recording, for example, or whether you type it in a datapool.

File Formats for Handling Unicode Data

Unicode data can be handled with any file format, either standard or custom, as both Java and VB.NET handle Unicode characters natively. As XML increasingly becomes a standard for storing data in files on disk (this is the .NET approach, and the Rational Functional Tester approach, too), the XML format is used for this chapter's discussion.

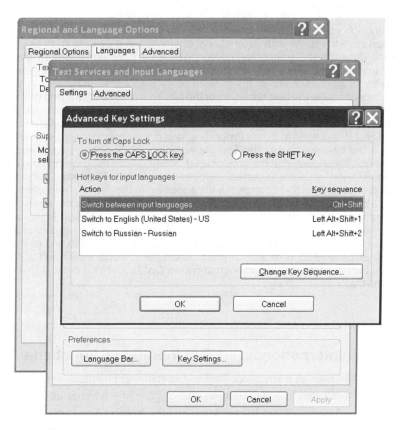

Figure 16.1   The Windows Language bar hotkey configuration dialog

Unicode Editors and Files on Windows

On the Windows platform, Unicode text is most simply handled using Notepad, WordPad, or any of a variety of other Unicode-enabled text editors. If you plan to use Notepad, simply remember to save your file using the UTF-8 encoding. WordPad saves in Rich Text Format or Unicode text format, both of which handle Unicode characters. Because XML format is used for this work, you can use any XML editor that handles Unicode or any text editor (such as Notepad) that is Unicode-enabled.

You can type internationalized characters in your editor window by changing the editor window's keyboard using the Windows Language bar to any international keyboard that you have loaded. You may have to change the file encoding to a suitable choice (UTF-8, Unicode text, Rich Text Format, and so on) when you save to properly save your internationalized text.

NOTE   Although you can capture internationalized names in a script, this does not mean that you can save the script with international characters in it by default. In Eclipse, this is because the default text file encoding on Windows is Cp1252, and it is likely that many or all of your international characters will not map to this encoding, which triggers the error when you try to save your script. If you want to save Unicode characters in your script class, you must change the text encoding of the file. This is done at any one of three levels: You can change the encoding for just the script, for the entire Rational Functional Tester project, or for the Eclipse instance. To modify just the script, right-click on the script in the Functional Test Projects view, select Properties, and in the script Properties window, select Resource in the treeview and in the Text file encoding section, change the encoding. To change the text file encoding at the project level, right-click on the project in the Functional Test Projects view, select Properties, and in the project Properties window, select Resource in the treeview and change the file encoding in the Text file encoding section. If you want to change the file encoding at the level of the Eclipse instance, open the Eclipse Preferences window (Window Menu > Preferences), and then navigate in the treeview to General > Workspace. You make the change, as before, in the Text file encoding section. At any of these levels, you can set your text file encoding to UTF-8 (or to one of a number of encodings) to be able to save with Unicode characters. Visual studio will automatically prompt you to change a file's default encoding from Cp1252 when it detects Unicode characters in the file.

Setting Up an Internationalized Test in Rational Functional Tester

To illustrate how to set up an internationalized test in Rational Functions Tester, pages from the IBM website are used; they can be configured to display in a number of languages. For the examples shown in this chapter, the United States English homepage and the Russian homepage are used (see Figures 16.2 and 16.3). Simple data verifications on the page along with some standard object manipulations are performed to illustrate the setup for an internationalized testing project.

Note that one critical assumption for the setup discussed here is that each language version of the application must have the same object hierarchy (see Figures 16.4 and 16.5). This might be true of your application; if it is not, you need to take object hierarchy differences into your automation strategy. Be aware that this can add significant additional work to your project.

Rational Function Tester Script Files

The overall strategy for implementing internationalized testing involves the following Rational Functional Tester script files. Rational Functional Tester can use up to four general types of supporting XML files for each script to persist script data. (There are actually six file extensions because both Object Maps and Datapools each have two sub-types.) XML file locations and extensions are shown in Table 16.2.

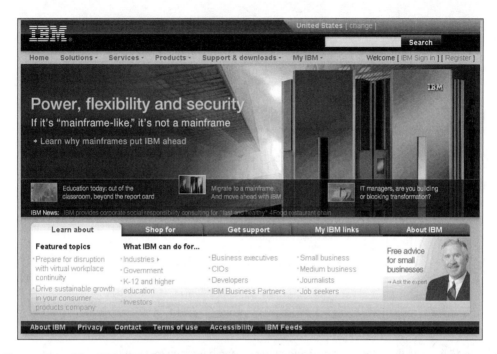

Figure 16.2 The IBM United States English homepage

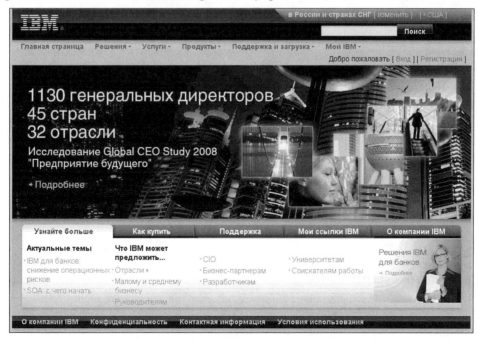

Figure 16.3 The IBM Russian Federation Russian homepage

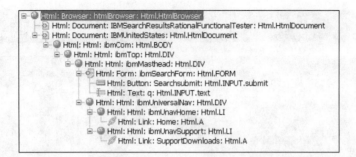

Figure 16.4   The IBM United States homepage Object Map hierarchy (partial)

Figure 16.5   The IBM Russian homepage Object Map hierarchy (partial)

Table 16.2   Rational Functional Tester Script Files: File Locations and Extensions

File Type	File Location	File Extension
Script Definition XML file	Project resources directory	.rftdef
Private Object Map XML file	Project resources directory	.rftxmap
Shared Object Map XML file	Root project directory	.rftmap
Verification Point XML file	Project resources directory	.rftvp
Private Datapool XML file	Project resources directory	.rftxdp
Shared Datapool XML file	Root project directory	.rftdp

The Script Definition and Object Map files are discussed in Chapter 9. The other two types of files—the Verification Point XML and the Datapool XML—persist for each script its Verification Point (VP) data or Datapool data for the script. A script might have multiple Verification Points, and therefore, multiple Verification Point files associated with it. Only a single Datapool can be associated with a script, just as only a single Object Map can be associated with a script.

Of the four types of files, only three (the Object Map, the Verification Point, and the Datapool) contain actual object data that might use internationalized characters.

Custom Internationalized XML for Unicode Testing Data

To set up an internationalized testing implementation, object or transaction data in each of the Rational Functional Tester script files must be changed to suit each language version of the target application. This means simply that if you're testing the English version of the application, all the data values must be in English, and if you're testing the Russian version, all the corresponding values must be changed to their Russian equivalents, and so on for other languages. Because this chapter extends the Rational Functional Tester approach of using an XML format to store data, the approach described here needs a simple XML grammar to support the storage of the Unicode test data.

The XML grammar used here is illustrated in Listing 16.1. The `<i18n>` root tag has two attributes: One designates the language of the character data in the XML by its two-letter ISO code, and the other identifies the unique hotkey number to activate the language keyboard for the specified application window. This number is used as part of the hotkey keystroke sequence for each language configured using the Windows Language bar. You can see the full list of ISO language codes at (see http://www.loc.gov/standards/iso639-2/php/code_list.php).

Beyond the root tag, there are just four child tags: `<url>`, `<obj>`, `<dp>`, and `<vp>`. The `<url>` tag holds the language-specific URL for each version of the application; the `<obj>` tags contain the language-specific object information, and the `<dp>` and `<vp>` tags contain the Datapool and Verification Point data. A couple of additional comments are in order. The `<obj>` and `<vp>` tags each must have an `id` attribute that identifies the `TestObject` involved. There can be either one of two types of data in an `id` attribute: the object name as it appears in the Rational Functional Tester Script Explorer (and therefore, in the Script Definition XML) or the Rational Functional Tester GUID identifier for the object (which appears in the Object Map XML, the Script Definition XML, and as the Map ID property on the Administrative tab of the Object Map tool). The reason that both of these object identification types are supported is because you might have to manipulate the property value for an object that is not in your script's Script Explorer, but *is* in the hierarchy of an object that is in your Script Explorer (see Chapter 9). The `type` attribute of the `<obj>` tag indicates which kind of `id` is used by each `<obj>` tag; if the `type` attribute has a value of 'name', the Script Explorer object name is used, and if it has a value of `'id'`, the Rational Functional Tester GUID is used.

You can avoid the use of the Rational Functional Tester GUID by putting the parents of all objects explicitly in the Script Explorer, but there is a downside to loading the Test Objects folder in your Script Explorer with a large number of objects; as the underlying Script Definition XML grows, the time required to look up objects in this XML grows. For relatively short Script Definition XMLs, adding several additional objects might not make much difference; however, eventually you might slow your script execution significantly.

Listing 16.1　Custom internationalized Rational Functional Tester XMLs

English Version

```
<i18n lang="en" key="1">
    <url>http://www.ibm.com/us/</url>
    <obj type="id" id="1.1JiZT3aEcY98:1SZfIB:LWukDhH:8WW" key=".title">
        IBM - United States</obj>
    <obj type="id" id="1.1JiZT3aEcY98:1SZfIB:LWukDhH:8WW" key=".url">
        http://www.ibm.com/us/</obj>
    <obj type="name" id="link_home" key=".text">Home</obj>
    <obj type="name" id="link_home" key=".href">http://www.ibm.com/us/en/</obj>
    <obj type="name" id="link_supportDownloads" key=".text">
        Support &amp; downloads</obj>
    <obj type="name" id="link_supportDownloads"
        key=".href">http://www.ibm.com/support/us/en/</obj>
    <obj type="name" id="button_searchsubmit" key=".value">Search</obj>
    <dp>
        <record>
            <cell>Rational Functional Tester</cell>
            <cell>2000</cell>
        </record>
        <record>
            <cell>Rational Quality Manager</cell>
            <cell>1000</cell>
        </record>
    </dp>
    <vp id="Home_text">Home</vp>
    <vp id="SupportDownloads_text">Support &amp; downloads</vp>
</i18n>
```

Russian Version

```
<i18n lang="ru" key="2">
    <url>http://www.ibm.com/ru/ru/</url>
    <obj type="id" id="1.1JiZT3aEcY98:1SZfIB:LWukDhH:8WW" key=".title">
        IBM - в России и странах СНГ</obj>
    <obj type="id" id="1.1JiZT3aEcY98:1SZfIB:LWukDhH:8WW" key=".url">
        http://www.ibm.com/ru/ru/</obj>
    <obj type="name" id="link_home" key=".text">Главная страница</obj>
    <obj type="name" id="link_home" key=".href">http://www.ibm.com/ru/ru/</obj>
    <obj type="name" id="link_supportDownloads" key=".text">
        Поддержка и загрузка</obj>
    <obj type="name" id="link_supportDownloads"
        key=".href">http://www.ibm.com/support/ru/ru/</obj>
    <obj type="name" id="button_searchsubmit" key=".value">Поиск</obj>
```

```
<dp>
    <record>
        <cell>автоматизация тестирования</cell>
        <cell>2000</cell>
    </record>
    <record>
        <cell>Менеджер по качеству</cell>
        <cell>1000</cell>
    </record>
</dp>
<vp id="Home_text">Главная страница</vp>
<vp id="SupportDownloads_text">Поддержка и загрузка</vp>
</i18n>
```

The whole internationalized testing game at this point resolves to building code to take the data from the custom internationalized XMLs in Listing 16.1 and save it to the appropriate Rational Functional Tester XML file. The example here uses a simple design for housing this code: a driver script that handles all of the data copying, changing, and saving, and that also calls the "testing" script(s), each of which runs multiple times using different internationalized underlying data for each execution run, with no changes to the actual script code.

Internationalized Driver Script Design

As noted previously, the driver script needs to accomplish two broad tasks for each language it handles. It needs to move language-specific Unicode character data from the custom internationalized XML files to the Rational Functional Tester XML files for each specific "testing" script and it needs to call that script; then it needs to move data for the next language into the "testing" script XML files and call the script again, until it cycles through all the languages that are queued up and all the "testing" scripts that are queued up.

Driver Script Utility Methods

To start setting this up, this chapter's example takes advantage of Rational Functional Tester's XML file naming convention and extends it to use convention-based names for the custom internationalized XML files that are developed as part of this implementation, such as those in Listing 16.1. To implement, a library of methods are needed that can generate the file paths for the XML files and load the XMLs into the XML DOM, so that scripts can modify the XMLs as necessary. For this latter work, the example developed here relies on methods discussed in Chapter 4. (You may want to refer back to that chapter while you read this material.) All the utility methods that are developed here to support internationalized scripts are housed in a utility class in a project called I18NUtils.

WARNING The code you explore in this chapter operates directly on underlying Rational Functional Tester and Project files. These files are normally manipulated only by Rational Functional Tester. Back up all files that the code touches before you execute any of these methods!

Start with a couple of simple methods that return the path to the current project directory and to the project's resources directory (see Listing 16.2). These methods are straightforward and are just wrappers for methods from the Rational Functional Tester API.

Listing 16.2 Methods to return project directory locations

Java
```
public String getProjectPath() {
    ITestProject proj = getCurrentProject();
    return proj.getLocation() + "\\";
}
public String getResourcePackagePath() {
    ITestProject proj = getCurrentProject();
    return proj.getLocation() + "\\resources\\";
}
```

VB.NET
```
Public Function GetProjectPath() As String
    Dim filePath As String = GetOption(IOptionName.DATASTORE)
    Return filePath
End Function
Public Function getResourcePackagePath() As String
    Return getProjectPath() + "\resources\"
End Function
```

Constructing the path for a given XML file is relatively straightforward. We start by getting the file path from one of the methods in Listing 16.2. The Rational Functional Tester file-path convention is simple: for the Private Object Map, Script Definition, and Private Datapool XML files, the file location is in the project resources directory, and the XML file naming convention is the script name followed by the XML extension. (See Table 16.2 for details.) For a Shared Object Map or a Shared Datapool, the file location is at the root project directory, and the files appear with their own unique extensions (Table 16.2). For these Shared Map or Datapool files, the file-naming convention is the Map or Datapool name with a file extension identifying the type of XML. For Verification Point files, which are found in the project resources directory, the file-naming convention changes slightly; the script name is followed by the Verification Point name with a period delimiter, followed by the ".base" designation, and ends with the Verification Point extension (Table 16.2). These naming conventions are summarized in Table 16.3. The file types,

Table 16.3 Rational Functional Tester Script XML File Naming Conventions

File Type	File Location	Naming Convention	Variable Name
Script Definition XML file	Project resources directory	`scriptName.rftdef`	DEF_XML
Private Object Map XML file	Project resources directory	`scriptName.rftxmap`	PRV_MAP_XML
Shared Object Map XML file	Root project directory	`mapName.rftmap`	SHD_MAP_XML
Verification Point XML file	Project resources directory	`scriptName.vpName.base.rftvp`	VP_XML
Private Datapool XML file	Project resources directory	`scriptName.rftxdp`	PRV_DP_XML
Shared Datapool XML file	Root project directory	`datapoolName.rftdp`	SHD_DP_XML

locations, and variable names used in the code Listings that hold the file extensions are also shown in Table 16.3.

The methods in Listing 16.2 are used as building blocks (along with methods from Chapter 4) for methods to load the required XML files (both Rational Functional Tester script XMLs and custom internationalized XMLs). The first of these methods has the following design: It constructs the file path for a chosen Rational Functional Tester script XML file and uses the method `loadDoc()` (from Chapter 4) to load the XML file into the XML DOM, and then returns a reference to the DOM. In addition, an overloaded method is shown that adds an argument to return the constructed path to the calling routine, so that the path to any file is available to the calling code for file management purposes. Listing 16.3 shows these overloaded methods.

The sample project uses a Private Object Map and a Private Datapool, so all the files are in the Rational Functional Tester project resource package. The methods in Listing 16.3 for obtaining the complete file path for each file type are simple. These methods require just the script name, an optional field name (for the extra field that Verification Point filenames have), and the file type to build any of the XML filenames.

Listing 16.3 Overloaded Rational Functional Tester script XML file loading methods

Java
```
public Document loadRftXml(String script, String xmlType) {
    String filePath =
        getResourcePackagePath() + script + "." + xmlType;
    Document xmlDoc = loadDoc(filePath);
```

```java
    return xmlDoc;
}
public Document loadRftXml(String script, String xmlType,
        StringBuilder retFilePath) {
    String filePath =
        getResourcePackagePath() + script + "." + xmlType;
    retFilePath.append(filePath);
    Document xmlDoc = loadDoc(filePath);
    return xmlDoc;
}
public Document loadRftXml(String script, String name, String xmlType,
        StringBuilder retFilePath) {
    String filePath = getResourcePackagePath() +
        script + "." + name + "." + xmlType;
    retFilePath.append(filePath);
    Document xmlDoc = loadDoc(filePath);
    return xmlDoc;
}
```

VB.NET

```vbnet
Public Function loadRftXml(ByVal script As String, _
        ByVal xmlType As String) As XmlDocument
Dim filePath As String = _
    getResourcePackagePath() + script + "." + xmlType
    Dim xmlDoc As XmlDocument = loadDoc(filePath)
    Return xmlDoc
End Function
Public Function loadRftXml(ByVal script As String, ByVal xmlType _
        As String, ByVal retFilePath As StringBuilder) As XmlDocument
Dim filePath As String = _
    getResourcePackagePath() + script + "." + xmlType
    retFilePath.Append(filePath)
    Dim xmlDoc As XmlDocument = loadDoc(filePath)
    Return xmlDoc
End Function
Public Function loadRftXml(ByVal script As String, _
    ByVal name As String, ByVal xmlType As String, _
    ByVal retFilePath As StringBuilder) As XmlDocument
Dim filePath As String = _
    getResourcePackagePath() + script + "." + name + "." + xmlType
    retFilePath.Append(filePath)
    Dim xmlDoc As XmlDocument = loadDoc(filePath)
    Return xmlDoc
End Function
```

The final method needed for this part of the work is a method to load the custom interna-tionalized XMLs (Listing 16.1). For convenience, the custom files are stored in the project root directory with the script .java files (not in the resource directory with the script XML files). The advantage this affords is that Eclipse automatically picks up the presence of these files and shows them in the Project Explorer, and they can be viewed or modified using Eclipse's convenient XML viewer. The naming convention for these custom files is ScriptName.la.xml, where the field "la" corresponds to the two-letter ISO language code. To keep this method parallel in structure to similar methods in Listing 16.3, it takes three arguments: the script name, the language code, and the file extension. Listing 16.4 shows the method.

Listing 16.4   Custom internationalized XML `load` method

Java
```
public Document loadI18nXml(String script, String lang,
        String xmlType) {
    String filePath =
        getProjectPath() + script + "." + lang + "." + xmlType;
    Document xmlDoc = loadDoc(filePath);
    return xmlDoc;
}
```

VB.NET
```
Public Function loadI18nXml(ByVal script As String, _
        ByVal lang As String, ByVal xmlType As String) As XmlDocument
Dim filePath As String = _
    getProjectPath() + script + "." + lang + "." + xmlType
    Dim xmlDoc As XmlDocument = loadDoc(filePath)
    Return xmlDoc
End Function
```

The Driver Script Framework

With the utilities illustrated in the previous sections, the driver script framework can be built. The driver script framework handles looping through scripts and languages, moving Unicode data into the supporting Rational Functional Tester script files in the resources directory, executing the internationalized script under each language, and performing file management so that the under-lying files are protected from accidental deletion and the internationalized script is returned to its original language at the end of script execution.

For convenience, the driver framework is illustrated using just a single target international-ized "testing" script and just two languages (English and Russian). The driver framework must handle the following detailed tasks:

- Looping through scripts
- Looping through languages

- Loading Rational Functional Tester script XML documents
- Copying the original Rational Functional Tester script XMLs for safekeeping
- Modifying the configurations.rftcfg file for each i18n URL
- Modifying the Object Map, Verification Point, and Datapool XMLs with Unicode data
- Executing the script for each language configuration
- Cleaning up and returning the script to its original language configuration

The driver script starts with arrays and loops in the script `testMain()` method to handle the looping through scripts and languages. Listing 16.5 shows this basic framework. Two arrays—`scripts` and `langs`—are needed to hold the names of the testing scripts called by the driver (script `I18n_homepage`, in this example) and the languages that the scripts run under (English and Russian). An `ArrayList` (called `rftResourcFiles`) is also created that is used to track the names of the Rational Functional Tester XML files.

Listing 16.5   Basic framework of Driver script for internationalized testing

Java

```
public void testMain(Object[] args) {
    // array of scripts to internationalize and run
    String[] scripts = { "I18n_homepage" };
    // array of languages to run scripts
    String[] langs = {"en", "ru"};
    // track source files for file management
    ArrayList<File> rftResourcFiles = new ArrayList<File>();
    for (int n = 0; n < scripts.length; n++) {
        for (int j = 0; j < langs.length; j++) {
            // framework i18n handling
        }
    }
}
```

VB.NET

```
Public Function TestMain(ByVal args() As Object) As Object
    Dim n As Int16 = 0
    Dim j As Int16 = 0
    ' array of scripts to internationalize and run
    Dim scripts As String() = {"I18n_homepage"}
    ' array of languages to run scripts
    Dim langs As String() = {"en", "ru"}

    ' track source files for file management
    Dim rftResourceFiles As ArrayList = New ArrayList()
```

```
For n = 0 To scripts.Length - 1
    For j = 0 To langs.Length - 1
        ' framework i18n handling
    Next j
Next n
Return Nothing
End Function
```

The next step in building the framework is to handle loading the XML documents that are needed. This is the first task in the inner loop. To do this, the script uses methods from Listings 16.3 and 16.4. For the files that are modified with Unicode data, the file path is captured in the driver code so that the driver can manage the files during execution (by copying the original files to a safe location during runtime, and restoring the original files at the end of execution). Listing 16.6 shows the code.

Listing 16.6   Loading the Rational Functional Tester Script XMLs and the custom internationalized XML

Java
```
Document i18nXmlDoc = loadI18nXml(scripts[n], langs[j], I18N_XML);
Document defXmlDoc = loadRftXml(scripts[n], DEF_XML);
StringBuilder mapFilePath = new StringBuilder();
Document mapXmlDoc = loadRftXml(scripts[n], PRV_MAP_XML, mapFilePath);
StringBuilder dpFilePath = new StringBuilder();
Document dpXmlDoc = loadRftXml(scripts[n], PRV_DP_XML, dpFilePath);
```

VB.NET
```
Dim i18nXmlDoc As XmlDocument = _
    loadI18nXml(scripts(n), langs(j), I18N_XML)
Dim defXmlDoc As XmlDocument = loadRftXml(scripts(n), DEF_XML)
Dim mapFilePath As StringBuilder = New StringBuilder()
Dim mapXmlDoc As XmlDocument = _
    loadRftXml(scripts(n), PRV_MAP_XML, mapFilePath)
Dim dpFilePath As StringBuilder = New StringBuilder()
Dim dpXmlDoc As XmlDocument = _
    loadRftXml(scripts(n), PRV_DP_XML, dpFilePath)
```

For the next task, the framework needs to protect the original XML files by copying the files to a safe location. The framework does this by prepending the string "orig_" to the filenames and copying the files to their home directory (the resources directory) under the modified names. In addition, the filenames are captured to the `ArrayList` created for this purpose (`rftResourceFiles`) so that later the driver script can perform file management on the files to return the Rational Functional Tester script to its original state. Listing 16.7 shows a method for these steps.

Listing 16.7   Copying the original Rational Functional Tester script XML files for safekeeping

Java
```java
public void copyXmlScriptFiles(StringBuilder mapFilePath,
        StringBuilder dpFilePath, String script,
        ArrayList<File> rftResourceFiles){
    File mapFileI18n = new File(mapFilePath.toString());
    StringBuilder mapFilePathPrefixed =
        new StringBuilder(mapFilePath);
    mapFilePathPrefixed.insert(
        mapFilePathPrefixed.indexOf(script), "orig_");
    File mapFileOrig = new File(mapFilePathPrefixed.toString());
    copyFile(mapFileI18n, mapFileOrig, false);
    rftResourceFiles.add(mapFileOrig);
    StringBuilder dpFilePathPrefixed =
        new StringBuilder(dpFilePath);
    File dpFileI18n = new File(dpFilePath.toString());
    dpFilePathPrefixed.insert(
        dpFilePathPrefixed.indexOf(script), "orig_");
    File dpFileOrig = new File(dpFilePathPrefixed.toString());
    copyFile(dpFileI18n, dpFileOrig, false);
    rftResourceFiles.add(dpFileOrig);
}
```

VB.NET
```vbnet
Public Sub copyXmlScriptFiles(ByVal mapFilePath As StringBuilder, _
        ByVal dpFilePath As StringBuilder, ByVal script As String, _
        ByVal rftResourceFiles As ArrayList)
    Dim mapFile As New FileInfo(mapFilePath.ToString)
Dim mapFilePathPrefixed As String = _
        mapFile.FullName.Insert(mapFile.FullName.IndexOf( _
        mapFile.Name), "orig_")
    Dim dpFile As New FileInfo(dpFilePath.ToString)
Dim dpFilePathPrefixed As String = _
        dpFile.FullName.Insert(dpFile.FullName.IndexOf( _
        dpFile.Name), "orig_")
    Try
        mapFile.CopyTo(mapFilePathPrefixed)
        dpFile.CopyTo(dpFilePathPrefixed)
    Catch e As Exception
        Console.WriteLine(e.Message)
```

```
    Finally
        rftResourceFiles.Add(mapFilePathPrefixed)
        rftResourceFiles.Add(dpFilePathPrefixed)
    End Try
End Sub
```

In Listing 16.7, in Java, the file copy is performed using the method `copyFile()`, which employs the efficient Java "new I/O" classes (`java.nio.*`) to copy the files (for discussion, see http://java.sun.com/developer/JDCTechTips/2002/tt0507.html; full code can be found in the supplementary materials, of course). In VB.NET, the `CopyTo()` method of the `FileInfo` class is used.

The next task for the driver is a bit off the beaten track. This is a modification of the configurations.rftcfg file. This file (in Windows, it is found at C:\Documents and Settings\All Users\Application Data\IBM\RFT\configuration\configurations.rftcfg; in the code listings, this path is denoted by the variable `configXmlPath`) is where Rational Functional Tester persists information about applications configured for testing. Because we're going to launch each language version of the application as a separate application instance, we need to modify this file so that the correct language version of the application is launched for each language. It is worthwhile to pause a moment to note that you don't actually have to use this approach; you can configure each language version as a separately configured application and pass each configured application name into each script. This is a perfectly reasonable solution; however the approach of modifying the configurations.rftcfg in code is used here to provide an example of how this can be done.

The key thing to be aware of for modifying application configuration data in the configurations.rftcfg XML is that the critical information for the application configurations appears in `<Application>` tags. In the example, the configured application is named 'ibm homepage,' so we're looking for an `<Application>` tag with a child `<Name>` tag with a value of 'ibm homepage.' Rational Functional Tester won't let you create two configured applications with the same name, so the value of this tag must be unique. After a reference to the correct `<Application>` tag has been found, all that needs to be done is to modify its child `<Path>` tag to hold the proper URL for each specific language version of the application, which is stored in the custom internationalized XML. In making this change to the `<Path>` tag value, the code should also capture the original value of the tag (in the `origUrl` variable) so that it can be reset when the driver performs housekeeping tasks. Finally, this is the first Rational Functional Tester XML that the driver modifies, so once the XML is loaded into the DOM, it should be saved to disk. This is performed with the method `serializeXmlToFile()` from Chapter 4. Listing 16.8 shows the method.

Listing 16.8   Method to modify the Rational Functional Tester configurations.rftcfg file

Java

```
public HashMap<String,Object> modRftcfgAppPath(String appName,
        Document i18nXmlDoc, Document configDoc){
    HashMap<String, Object> ret = new HashMap<String, Object>();
```

```
Node configPathNode = xpath(configDoc,
    "//Application[child::Name[text()='" + appName + "']]/Path")
        .item(0);
String origUrl = configPathNode.getTextContent();
Node url = xpath(i18nXmlDoc, "//url").item(0);
configPathNode.setTextContent(url.getTextContent());
serializeXmlToFile(configDoc, configXmlPath);
ret.put("origUrl", origUrl);
ret.put("configPathNode", configPathNode);
return ret;
}
```

VB.NET

```
Public Function modRftcfgAppPath(ByVal appName As String, _
        ByVal i18nXmlDoc As XmlDocument, _
        ByVal configDoc As XmlDocument) As Collection
    Dim ret As Collection = New Collection
    Dim configPathNode As XmlNode = xpath(configDoc, _
        "//Application[child::Name[text()='" + appName + "']]/Path")
            .Item(0)
    Dim origUrl As String = configPathNode.InnerText
    Dim url As XmlNode = xpath(i18nXmlDoc, "//url").Item(0)
    configPathNode.InnerText = url.InnerText
    serializeXmlToFile(configDoc, configXmlPath)
    ret.Add(origUrl, "origUrl")
    ret.Add(configPathNode, "configPathNode")
    Return ret
End Function
```

With regard to the driver framework, there are two more tasks that the framework needs to support: the actual execution of the target internationalized script and housekeeping tasks. The execution of the script is performed as usual with the `callScript()` method using the target script name (from the `scripts[]` array, see Listing 16.5); however, the called script must be passed an argument—the hotkey number that the script can use to change the keyboard of the application window to the desired language keyboard. You might recall that these key numbers are set up using the Windows Language bar functionality as part of configuring Windows to handle multiple input languages (see the section "Handling Internationalized Data in Rational Functional Tester" for details). The hotkey numbers for each language are kept in the custom internationalized XML, in the `key` attribute of the root `<I18n>` tag. In the driver script, the key value is passed in as an argument to the script; the script has to handle the argument in its implementation. Listing 16.9 shows the script calling code.

Listing 16.9   Calling the target internationalized script

Java
```
String key = xpath(i18nXmlDoc.getDocumentElement(),
    "attribute::key").item(0).getTextContent();
Object [] scriptargs = {key};
callScript(scripts[n], scriptargs);
```

VB.NET
```
Dim key As String = xpath(i18nXmlDoc.DocumentElement, _
    "attribute::key").Item(0).InnerText
Dim scriptargs As Object() = {key}
CallScript(scripts(n), scriptargs)
```

As noted, the housekeeping tasks make up the last part of the framework. The variable `origUrl` holds the original URL for the application (Listing 16.8) and the `rftResourceFiles` `ArrayList` holds the file paths for the original script files; these are used to return the script to its original state. Listing 16.10 shows a method for these tasks.

Listing 16.10   Housekeeping method for the internationalization driver script

Java
```
public void cleanupFileChanges(ArrayList<File> rftResourceFiles,
        String origUrl, Node configPathNode, Document configDoc){
    for (int m = 0; m < rftResourceFiles.size(); m++){
        File origResourceFile = rftResourceFiles.get(m);
        String rebuildRFTNamePath =
            origResourceFile.getPath().replaceFirst("orig_", "");
        File rebuildRFTNameFile = new File(rebuildRFTNamePath);
        copyFile(origResourceFile, rebuildRFTNameFile);
    }
    // cleanup configurations.rftcfg file
    configPathNode.setTextContent(origUrl);
    serializeXmlToFile(configDoc, configXmlPath);
}
```

VB.NET
```
Public Sub cleanupFileChanges(ByVal rftResourceFiles As ArrayList, _
        ByVal origUrl As String, ByVal configPathNode As XmlNode, _
        ByVal configDoc As XmlDocument)
    Dim m As Int16
    For m = 0 To rftResourceFiles.Count - 1
        Dim origResourceFile As FileInfo = _
```

```
            New FileInfo(rftResourceFiles.Item(m))
        Dim rebuildRFTNameFile As String = _
            origResourceFile.FullName.Replace("orig_", "")
        origResourceFile.CopyTo(rebuildRFTNameFile, True)
    Next m
    ' cleanup configurations.rftcfg file
    configPathNode.InnerText = origUrl
    serializeXmlToFile(configDoc, configXmlPath)
End Sub
```

Putting the Driver Script Framework Together

We've reviewed all the pieces of the driver script framework, but it can be hard to "see the forest from the trees" when there are multiple coding tasks in a block of automation. Listing 16.11 shows the full framework, with all the coded framework tasks in sequence; this example lacks only the detailed code to move Unicode data from the custom internationalized XML into each of the Rational Functional Tester script XMLs. The topics following Listing 16.11 show the Unicode data-handling tasks for the Object Map ("Modifying a Language-Specific Object Map"), for Verification Points ("Modifying Language-Specific Verification Points"), and for Datapools ("Modifying Language-Specific Datapools").

Listing 16.11   The complete driver script framework

Java

```java
public void testMain(Object[] args) {

    // array of scripts to internationalize and run
    String[] scripts = { "I18n_homepage" };
    // array of languages to run scripts
    String[] langs = {"en", "ru"};
    // track source files for file management
    ArrayList<File> rftResourceFiles = new ArrayList<File>();
    for (int n = 0; n < scripts.length; n++) {
        for (int j = 0; j < langs.length; j++) {
            // Load the RFT xml docs
            Document i18nXmlDoc =
                loadI18nXml(scripts[n], langs[j], I18N_XML);
            Document defXmlDoc = loadRftXml(scripts[n], DEF_XML);
            StringBuilder mapFilePath = new StringBuilder();
            Document mapXmlDoc = loadRftXml(
                scripts[n], PRV_MAP_XML, mapFilePath);
            StringBuilder dpFilePath = new StringBuilder();
            Document dpXmlDoc = loadRftXml(
```

```
            scripts[n], PRV_DP_XML, dpFilePath);
        // Copy the original RFT xmls for safekeeping
        copyXmlScriptFiles(mapFilePath, dpFilePath,
            scripts[n], rftResourceFiles);
        // Modify configurations.rftcfg for the i18n url
        Document configDoc = loadDoc(configXmlPath);
        HashMap<String,Object> rftCfg = modRftcfgAppPath(
            "ibm homepage", i18nXmlDoc, configDoc);
        String origUrl = (String)rftCfg.get("origUrl");
        Node configPathNode =
            (Node)rftCfg.get("configPathNode");
        /*
         * Unicode data modifying code for
         * the Object Map, Verification Points and Datapools
         */
        // Script run
        String key = xpath(i18nXmlDoc.getDocumentElement(),
            "attribute::key").item(0).getTextContent();
        Object [] scriptargs = {key};
        callScript(scripts[n], scriptargs);
        // Housekeeping - re-set to original files
        cleanupFileChanges(rftResourceFiles, origUrl,
            configPathNode, configDoc);
    }
  }
}
```

VB.NET

```
Public Function TestMain(ByVal args() As Object) As Object
    Dim n As Int16 = 0
    Dim j As Int16 = 0
    ' array of scripts to internationalize and run
    Dim scripts As String() = {"I18n_homepage"}
    ' array of languages to run scripts
    Dim langs As String() = {"en", "ru"}
    ' track source files for file management
    Dim rftResourceFiles As ArrayList = New ArrayList()
    For n = 0 To scripts.Length - 1
        For j = 0 To langs.Length - 1
            ' * Load the RFT xml docs
            Dim i18nXmlDoc As XmlDocument = _
                loadI18nXml(scripts(n), langs(j), I18N_XML)
            Dim defXmlDoc As XmlDocument = _
```

```
        loadRftXml(scripts(n), DEF_XML)
    Dim mapFilePath As StringBuilder = New StringBuilder()
    Dim mapXmlDoc As XmlDocument = _
        loadRftXml(scripts(n), PRV_MAP_XML, mapFilePath)
    Dim dpFilePath As StringBuilder = New StringBuilder()
    Dim dpXmlDoc As XmlDocument = _
        loadRftXml(scripts(n), PRV_DP_XML, dpFilePath)
    ' * Copy the original RFT xmls for safekeeping
    copyXmlScriptFiles( _
        mapFilePath, dpFilePath, scripts(n), rftResourceFiles)
    ' * Modify configurations.rftcfg for the i18n url
    Dim configDoc As XmlDocument = loadDoc(configXmlPath)
    Dim rftCfg As Collection = modRftcfgAppPath( _
        "ibm homepage", i18nXmlDoc, configDoc)
    Dim origUrl As String = rftCfg.Item("origUrl")
    Dim configPathNode As XmlNode = _
        rftCfg.Item("configPathNode")
    '/*
    ' * Unicode data modifying code for
    ' * the Object Map, Verification Points and Datapools
    ' */
    ' * Script run
    Dim key As String = xpath(i18nXmlDoc.DocumentElement, _
        "attribute::key").Item(0).InnerText
    Dim scriptargs As Object() = {key}
    CallScript(scripts(n), scriptargs)
    ' * Housekeeping - re-set to original files
    cleanupFileChanges(rftResourceFiles, origUrl, _
        configPathNode, configDoc)
        Next j
    Next n
    Return Nothing
End Function
```

Modifying a Language-Specific Object Map

Modifying the Object Map for language-specific Unicode data is a multistep process. As noted previously, objects that appear in the Script Definition can be looked up by name in the Script Definition XML, and can be cross-referenced (using each object's Rational Functional Tester GUID) to the Object Map XML. For those objects that do not appear in the Script Definition, but do have Unicode data (such as objects high in the object hierarchy that might not be in the Script Definition), their Unicode data has to be stored in the custom internationalized XML under their

Rational Functional Tester GUIDs and not under their map object names. (You can review this by looking at Listing 16.1, where some objects are identified by Script Definition name and others are identified by Object Map GUID.)

The Object Map modification starts with the structure of the custom internationalized XML (Listing 16.1). All object information—whether classified by Map object name or Rational Functional Tester GUID—is found in <obj> tags. So, the implementation starts by collecting the <obj> tags from the XML. The type attribute of the <obj> tag either has a value of 'name' if the tag describes a mapped object by name or 'id' if the tag described a mapped object by GUID. If the value of the type attribute is 'name,' the method must perform a lookup in the Script Definition XML to find the object's GUID, and if the value is 'id,' the GUID is the text value of the <obj> tag. By either route, the implementation code identifies the Rational Functional Tester GUIDs of all of the objects that are in the custom internationalized XML. There is one additional piece of information needed from the custom internationalized XML <obj> tags, and that is the value of the key attribute for each tag, which describes the Rational Functional Tester recognition property whose value changes for each language in the internationalized test (.text, .href, .value, and so on). The strategy is to use the object GUID and then to use the key value, to manipulate the target Object Map recognition property data to appear in the desired language.

The method design that implements these tasks (shown in Listing 16.12) breaks this process into two methods: The first, modifyMapValues(), handles the lookups of the XML nodes, and calls the second method, setMapValue(), which modifies the node values of the Map XML DOM. Note that neither of these methods saves the data to file; you must call serializeXmlToFile() as usual to perform a save action.

Listing 16.12   A method to modify Object Map recognition property values

Java

```java
public void modifyMapValues(Document i18nXmlDoc,
        Document defXmlDoc, Document mapXmlDoc){
    // get the obj nodes from the custom internationalized XML
    NodeList sourceNodes = xpath(i18nXmlDoc, "//obj");
    for (int m = 0; m < sourceNodes.getLength(); m++){
        String targetObjGuid = null;

        // if the node has a type attr of value 'name' lookup the
        // object by name in the script def for the guid.
        // if 'id' appears, capture the guid directly from the
        // custom i18nXml.
        Attr objType = (Attr)xpath(
            sourceNodes.item(m), "attribute::type").item(0);
        if (objType.getTextContent().equals("name")){
            Attr objName = (Attr)xpath(
                sourceNodes.item(m), "attribute::id").item(0);
```

```
                targetObjGuid = xpath(defXmlDoc,
                    "//TestObject[child::Name[text()='" +
                    objName.getTextContent() +
                    "']]/ID").item(0).getTextContent();
            } else if (objType.getTextContent().equals("id")){
                targetObjGuid = xpath(sourceNodes.item(m),
                    "attribute::id").item(0).getTextContent();
            }
            // get the target property - if the target guid exists
            if (targetObjGuid != null){
                String key = xpath(sourceNodes.item(m),
                    "@key").item(0).getTextContent();
                // find the target Value node in the map
                Node mapValueNode = xpath(mapXmlDoc,
                    "//MTO[child::Id[text()='" + targetObjGuid +
                    "']]/Prop[child::Key[text()='" + key +
                    "']]/Val").item(0);
                // check the type of value node and
                // set unicode value for the target Value node
                setMapValue(mapValueNode, sourceNodes.item(m));
            }
        }
    }
}
private void setMapValue(Node mapValueNode, Node sourceNode){
    // set unicode value for the target Value node
    Node mapValueNodeType = xpath(mapValueNode, "@L").item(0);
    if (mapValueNodeType == null){
        mapValueNode.setTextContent(sourceNode.getTextContent());
    } else if (mapValueNodeType.getTextContent().
            equals(".script.Href")){
        Node mapValueNodeChild =
            xpath(mapValueNode, "Href").item(0);
        mapValueNodeChild.setTextContent(
            sourceNode.getTextContent());
    } else if (mapValueNodeType.getTextContent().equals(".Index")){
        Node mapValueNodeChild =
            xpath(mapValueNode, "Index").item(0);
        mapValueNodeChild.setTextContent(
            sourceNode.getTextContent());
    }
}
```

VB.NET

```vb.net
Public Sub modifyMapValues(ByVal i18nXmlDoc As XmlDocument, _
        ByVal defXmlDoc As XmlDocument, _
        ByVal mapXmlDoc As XmlDocument)
    ' get the obj nodes from the custom internationalized XML
    Dim sourceNodes As XmlNodeList = xpath(i18nXmlDoc, "//obj")
    Dim m As Int16 = 0
    For m = 0 To sourceNodes.Count - 1
        Dim targetObjGuid As String = Nothing
        ' check if the node has a type attribute of value
        ' 'name' or 'id'
        ' and if 'name' appears, do a lookup in the script
        ' def for the guid. if 'id' appears, collect the
        ' guid directly from the custom i18nXml.
        Dim objType As XmlAttribute = xpath(sourceNodes.Item(m), _
            "attribute::type").Item(0)
        If (objType.InnerText = "name") Then
            Dim objName As XmlAttribute = xpath(sourceNodes.Item(m), _
                "attribute::id").Item(0)
            targetObjGuid = xpath(defXmlDoc, _
                "//TestObject[child::Name[text()='" + _
                    objName.InnerText + "']]/ID").Item(0).InnerText
        ElseIf (objType.InnerText = "id") Then
            targetObjGuid = xpath(sourceNodes.Item(m), _
                "attribute::id").Item(0).InnerText
        End If
        ' get the target property - if the target guid exists
        If Not (targetObjGuid Is Nothing) Then
            Dim key As String = xpath(sourceNodes.Item(m), _
                "@key").Item(0).InnerText
            ' find the target Value node in the map
            Dim mapValueNode As XmlNode = xpath(mapXmlDoc, _
                "//MTO[child::Id[text()='" + targetObjGuid + _
                "']]/Prop[child::Key[text()='" + key + _
                "']]/Val").Item(0)
            ' check the type of value node and
            ' set unicode value for the target Value node
            setMapValue(mapValueNode, sourceNodes.Item(m))
        End If
    Next m
End Sub
Private Sub setMapValue(ByVal mapValueNode As XmlNode, _
        ByVal sourceNode As XmlNode)
```

```vbnet
' set unicode value for the target Value node
Dim mapValueNodeType As XmlNode = _
    xpath(mapValueNode, "@L").Item(0)
If (mapValueNodeType Is Nothing) Then
    mapValueNode.InnerText = sourceNode.InnerText
ElseIf (mapValueNodeType.InnerText = ".script.Href") Then
    Dim mapValueNodeChild As XmlNode = _
        xpath(mapValueNode, "Href").Item(0)
    mapValueNodeChild.InnerText = sourceNode.InnerText
ElseIf (mapValueNodeType.InnerText = ".Index") Then
    Dim mapValueNodeChild As XmlNode = _
        xpath(mapValueNode, "Index").Item(0)
    mapValueNodeChild.InnerText = sourceNode.InnerText
    End If
End Sub
```

Because of the need to save the XML to a file after the modifications are made, the actual calling sequence for these methods in Java is as follows:

```java
modifyMapValues(i18nXmlDoc, defXmlDoc, mapXmlDoc);
File mapFileI18n = new File(mapFilePath.toString());
serializeXmlToFile(mapXmlDoc, mapFileI18n);
```

In VB.NET, this looks like the following:

```vbnet
modifyMapValues(i18nXmlDoc, defXmlDoc, mapXmlDoc)
serializeXmlToFile(mapXmlDoc, mapFilePath.ToString)
```

In these snippets, `modifyMapValues()` takes references to the three XML DOMs (the custom internationalized XML, the Script Definition XML, and the Object Map XML); the code then constructs the target file location for the modified Object Map XML (see Listing 16.6 for how the file locations are captured), and then calls `serializeXmlToFile()`.

Modifying Language-Specific Verification Points

While modifying Rational Functional Tester Verification Point XMLs for Unicode data uses many of the same techniques that modifying an Object Map XML uses (see the "Modifying a Language-Specific Object Map" section), there is one major difference. A Rational Functional Tester script has a one-to-one relationship with its Object Map, but it can have a one-to-many relationship with Verification Point XMLs. This is because each Verification Point you create in a script persists its data in a separate XML file. Because of this design, the method that is built for dealing with Unicode Verification Point data performs all its own XML DOM and file handling internally, unlike the `modifyMapValues()` method (refer to Listing 16.12). Other than that, the same general approach is used: The original files are copied under a new filename (using a prefix of "orig_" to create the new filename from the old), and the `rftResourceFiles ArrayList` is used to hold onto the new filenames. The Verification Point XML is searched for `<MP>` tags with a child `<Prop>` tag of text value 'data' to identify the nodes where Unicode data must be written. The `<Val>` sibling of the `<Prop>` tag actually holds the baseline data for the Verification Pont and therefore, it is the text value of the `<Val>` tag that is changed with each subsequent set of Unicode character data. Listing 16.13 shows the `modifyVpValues()` method.

Listing 16.13   A method to modify Verification Point baseline values

Java

```java
public void modifyVpValues(Document i18nXmlDoc, String script,
        ArrayList<File> rftResourceFiles){
    NodeList vps = xpath(i18nXmlDoc, "//vp");
    for (int m = 0; m < vps.getLength(); m++){
        Node vpNode = xpath(i18nXmlDoc, "//vp[@id]").item(m);
        String vpNameNode =
            xpath(vpNode, "@id").item(0).getTextContent();
        StringBuilder vpFilePath = new StringBuilder();
        Document vpXmlDoc = loadRftXml(
            script, vpNameNode + ".base", VP_XML, vpFilePath);
        File vpFileI18n = new File(vpFilePath.toString());
        vpFilePath.insert(vpFilePath.indexOf(script), "orig_");
        File vpFileOrig = new File(vpFilePath.toString());
        copyFile(vpFileI18n, vpFileOrig, false);
        rftResourceFiles.add(vpFileOrig);
        Node vpDataProp = xpath(vpXmlDoc,
            "//MP[child::Prop[text()='data']]/Val").item(0);
        vpDataProp.setTextContent(vpNode.getTextContent());
        serializeXmlToFile(vpXmlDoc, vpFileI18n);
    }
}
```

VB.NET

```vbnet
Public Sub modifyVpValues(ByVal i18nXmlDoc As XmlDocument, _
        ByVal script As String, ByVal rftResourceFiles As ArrayList)
    Dim vps As XmlNodeList = xpath(i18nXmlDoc, "//vp")
    Dim m As Int16 = 0

    For m = 0 To vps.Count - 1
        Dim vpNode As XmlNode = xpath(i18nXmlDoc, "//vp[@id]").Item(m)
        Dim vpNameNode As String = _
            xpath(vpNode, "@id").Item(0).InnerText
        Dim vpFilePath As StringBuilder = New StringBuilder()
```

```
    Dim vpXmlDoc As XmlDocument = loadRftXml( _
        Script, vpNameNode + ".base", VP_XML, vpFilePath)
    Dim vpFile As New FileInfo(vpFilePath.ToString)
    Dim vpFilePathPrefixed As String = vpFile.FullName.Insert( _
        vpFile.FullName.IndexOf(vpFile.Name), "orig_")
    Try
        vpFile.CopyTo(vpFilePathPrefixed)
    Catch ex As Exception
        Console.WriteLine(ex.Message)
    End Try
    rftResourceFiles.Add(vpFilePathPrefixed)
    Dim vpDataProp As XmlNode = xpath(vpXmlDoc, _
        "//MP[child::Prop[text()='data']]/Val").Item(0)
    vpDataProp.InnerText = vpNode.InnerText

    serializeXmlToFile(vpXmlDoc, vpFile.FullName)
    Next m
End Sub
```

As noted previously, because `modifyVpValues()` handles loading the Verification Point XML into the DOM internally, and file handling for the Verification Point XML files internally (which includes copying the original files and saving the Unicode-modified XML to disk), the method call itself is just a single line of code (with the trailing semicolon in Java only, of course):

```
    modifyVpValues(i18nXmlDoc, scripts[n], rftResourceFiles);
```

Modifying Language-Specific Datapools

Modification of Datapool XMLs follows much the same pattern as modification of Object Map XMLs. In the Datapool XML, data is stored in `<cell>` tags, and cell location metadata (such as the row and column values of each specific cell) are not explicitly written in the Datapool XML. Instead, row and column relationships are implicit; they emerge from the order of the tags in the XML. Each `<Record>` tag represents a row of Datapool data, and the `<cell>` descendants of the `<Record>` tags find their positions simply from their order. The tag layout used in the custom internationalized XML is much the same, so it is straightforward to correlate source data from the custom XML with the target in the Datapool XML. Listing 16.14 shows the `modifyDpValues()` methods, which implement the copying of different Unicode data sets into the Datapool XML.

Listing 16.14   A method to modify Datapool values

Java

```java
public void modifyDpValues(Document i18nXmlDoc, Document dpXmlDoc){
    NodeList dpRecords = xpath(dpXmlDoc, "//Records/Record");
    NodeList dpXmlRecords = xpath(i18nXmlDoc, "//dp/record");
    for (int m = 0; m < dpRecords.getLength(); m++){
        NodeList dpRecordCells =
            xpath(dpRecords.item(m), "./Cells/Cell");
        NodeList dpXmlRecordCells =
            xpath(dpXmlRecords.item(m), "./cell");
        for (int o = 0; o < dpRecordCells.getLength(); o++){
            dpRecordCells.item(o).setTextContent(
                dpXmlRecordCells.item(o).getTextContent());
        }
    }
}
```

VB.NET

```vbnet
Public Sub modifyDpValues(ByVal i18nXmlDoc As XmlDocument, _
        ByVal dpXmlDoc As XmlDocument)
    Dim m As Int16 = 0
    Dim n As Int16 = 0
    Dim dpRecords As XmlNodeList = xpath(dpXmlDoc, "//Records/Record")
    Dim dpXmlRecords As XmlNodeList = xpath(i18nXmlDoc, "//dp/record")
    For m = 0 To dpRecords.Count - 1
        Dim dpRecordCells As XmlNodeList = _
            xpath(dpRecords.Item(m), "./Cells/Cell")
        Dim dpXmlRecordCells As XmlNodeList = _
            xpath(dpXmlRecords.Item(m), "./cell")
        For n = 0 To dpRecordCells.Count - 1
            dpRecordCells.Item(n).InnerText = _
                dpXmlRecordCells.Item(n).InnerText
        Next n
    Next m
End Sub
```

As with the `modifyMapValues()` method (refer to Listing 16.12), file handling is outside the method body, so the calling code for `modifyDpValues()` is almost identical, with the serialization of the modified Datapool XML external to the method. In Java:

```java
modifyDpValues(i18nXmlDoc, dpXmlDoc);
File dpFileI18n = new File(dpFilePath.toString());
serializeXmlToFile(dpXmlDoc, dpFileI18n);
```

In VB.NET:

```
modifyDpValues(i18nXmlDoc, dpXmlDoc)
serializeXmlToFile(dpXmlDoc, dpFilePath.ToString())
```

A Fully Internationalized Driver Script

If you take all of the development in the previous sections and combine it with the driver framework (refer to Listing 16.11), you get the full internationalized driver script. This is shown in
Listing 16.15.

Listing 16.15   The complete internationalized driver script

Java
```
public void testMain(Object[] args) {
    // array of scripts to internationalize and run
    String[] scripts = { "I18n_homepage" };
    // array of languages to run scripts
    String[] langs = { "en", "ru"};
    // track source files for file management
    ArrayList<File> rftResourceFiles = new ArrayList<File>();

    for (int n = 0; n < scripts.length; n++) {
        for (int j = 0; j < langs.length; j++) {
            // Load the RFT xml docs
            Document i18nXmlDoc =
                loadI18nXml(scripts[n], langs[j], I18N_XML);
            Document defXmlDoc = loadRftXml(scripts[n], DEF_XML);
            StringBuilder mapFilePath = new StringBuilder();
            Document mapXmlDoc =
                loadRftXml(scripts[n], PRV_MAP_XML, mapFilePath);
            StringBuilder dpFilePath = new StringBuilder();
            Document dpXmlDoc =
                loadRftXml(scripts[n], PRV_DP_XML, dpFilePath);
            // Copy the original RFT xmls for safekeeping
            copyXmlScriptFiles(mapFilePath, dpFilePath,
                scripts[n], rftResourceFiles);
            // Modify configurations.rftcfg for the i18n url
            Document configDoc = loadDoc(configXmlPath);
            HashMap<String,Object> rftCfg = modRftcfgAppPath(
                "ibm homepage", i18nXmlDoc, configDoc);
            String origUrl = (String)rftCfg.get("origUrl");
            Node configPathNode =
```

```
                    (Node)rftCfg.get("configPathNode");
            // Modify the map for i18n
            modifyMapValues(i18nXmlDoc, defXmlDoc, mapXmlDoc);
            File mapFileI18n = new File(mapFilePath.toString());
            serializeXmlToFile(mapXmlDoc, mapFileI18n);
            // Modify VPs for i18n
            modifyVpValues(i18nXmlDoc, scripts[n],
                    rftResourceFiles);
            // Modify datapools for i18n
            modifyDpValues(i18nXmlDoc, dpXmlDoc);
            File dpFileI18n = new File(dpFilePath.toString());
            serializeXmlToFile(dpXmlDoc, dpFileI18n);
            // Script run
            String key = xpath(i18nXmlDoc.getDocumentElement(),
                    "attribute::key").item(0).getTextContent();
            Object [] scriptargs = {key};
            callScript(scripts[n], scriptargs);
            // Housekeeping - re-set to original files
            cleanupFileChanges(rftResourceFiles, origUrl,
                    configPathNode, configDoc);
        }
    }
}
```

VB.NET

```
Public Function TestMain(ByVal args() As Object) As Object
    Dim n As Int16 = 0
    Dim j As Int16 = 0
    ' array of scripts to internationalize and run
    Dim scripts As String() = {"I18n_homepage"}
    ' array of languages to run scripts
    Dim langs As String() = {"en", "ru"}
    ' track source files for file management
    Dim rftResourceFiles As ArrayList = New ArrayList()
    For n = 0 To scripts.Length - 1
        For j = 0 To langs.Length - 1
            ' * Load the RFT xml docs
            Dim i18nXmlDoc As XmlDocument = _
                loadI18nXml(scripts(n), langs(j), I18N_XML)
            Dim defXmlDoc As XmlDocument = _
                loadRftXml(scripts(n), DEF_XML)
            Dim mapFilePath As StringBuilder = New StringBuilder()
```

```
            Dim mapXmlDoc As XmlDocument = _
                loadRftXml(scripts(n), PRV_MAP_XML, mapFilePath)
            Dim dpFilePath As StringBuilder = New StringBuilder()
            Dim dpXmlDoc As XmlDocument = _
                loadRftXml(scripts(n), PRV_DP_XML, dpFilePath)
            ' * Copy the original RFT xmls for safekeeping
            copyXmlScriptFiles( _
                mapFilePath, dpFilePath, scripts(n), rftResourceFiles)
            ' * Modify configurations.rftcfg for the i18n url
            Dim configDoc As XmlDocument = loadDoc(configXmlPath)
            Dim rftCfg As Collection = modRftcfgAppPath( _
                "ibm homepage", i18nXmlDoc, configDoc)
            Dim origUrl As String = rftCfg.Item("origUrl")
            Dim configPathNode As XmlNode = _
                rftCfg.Item("configPathNode")
              ' * Modify the map for i18n
                modifyMapValues(i18nXmlDoc, defXmlDoc, mapXmlDoc)
                serializeXmlToFile(mapXmlDoc, mapFilePath.ToString)
              ' * Modify VPs for i18n
                modifyVpValues(i18nXmlDoc, scripts(n), _
                    rftResourceFiles)
              ' * Modify datapools for i18n
                modifyDpValues(i18nXmlDoc, dpXmlDoc)
                serializeXmlToFile(dpXmlDoc, dpFilePath.ToString())
              ' * Script run
            Dim key As String = xpath(i18nXmlDoc.DocumentElement, _
                "attribute::key").Item(0).InnerText
            Dim scriptargs As Object() = {key}
            CallScript(scripts(n), scriptargs)
            ' * Housekeeping - re-set to original files
            cleanupFileChanges(rftResourceFiles, origUrl, _
                configPathNode, configDoc)
        Next j
    Next n
    Return Nothing
End Function
```

A Target Script for the Internationalized Driver Script

A target script for the internationalized driver script (Listing 16.15) looks like a regular Rational Functional Tester script. The driver script needs to know its name, of course, so that it can make its call to `callScript()`, but that doesn't affect the actual target. Because all the Unicode handling is performed on the underlying script XML files before the target script is called, the target script never has to change in terms of its code, its `TestObject` names, or its Verification Points or Datapools. This example script is called `I18n_Homepage`.

The one area where a target script departs from the typical script is in the area of handling the hotkeys for the different language keyboards. Normally, a script doesn't worry about keyboard handling; it uses the default keyboard on the system. However, the internationalized test setup requires a small amount of additional handling to support testing with multiple Unicode character sets. As noted previously, when you set up language support on Windows, you should associate each keyboard with its own unique hotkey keystroke sequence, so that each sequence can be used to attach any keyboard desired to your application window. Listing 16.9 introduced the section of the driver that calls the target internationalized script, and a single argument is passed to the script—the unique keystroke (a number) to attach the required keyboard to the target application window. This argument must be handled in your target script, so that the correct keyboard is attached to the application window for the specific language iteration through the script. For most windows, it is simply a matter of a single line of code to type the keystroke sequence that assigns a keyboard to the window; in this example, the line is:

```
browser_htmlBrowser().inputKeys("%+" + args[0]);
```

This call to `inputKeys()` types the Left-Alt-Shift-num sequence followed by the numeric script argument. Listing 16.16 shows the full target script.

Listing 16.16 A target script for the internationalized driver script—I18n_Homepage

Java
```java
public void testMain(Object[] args) {
    if (!link_home().exists()){
        startApp("ibm homepage");
        document_IBMi18n().waitForExistence(60,1);
    }
    /*
     * use alt-shift-# keys you have set for each specific keyboard:
     *          left-alt-shift-1 = en
     *          left-alt-shift-2 = ru
     */
    if (args.length != 0){
        browser_htmlBrowser().inputKeys("%+" + args[0]);
    }
    // VPs on the links
    link_home().performTest(Home_textVP());
    link_supportDownloads().performTest(SupportDownloads_textVP());
    // iterate through the datapool to run searches on the site
    while (!dpDone()){
        text_q().click();
        browser_htmlBrowser(document_IBMi18n(),DEFAULT_FLAGS).
            inputChars(dpString("searchText"));
```

```
        button_searchsubmit().click();
        browser_htmlBrowser().back();
        dpNext();
    }
    browser_htmlBrowser().close();
}
```

VB.NET

```
Public Function TestMain(ByVal args() As Object) As Object
    If Not (Link_Home().Exists()) Then
        StartApp("ibm homepage")
        Document_IBMI18n().WaitForExistence(60, 1)
    End If
    '/*
    ' * use alt-shift-# keys you have set to switch to a
    ' specific keyboard.
        ' *          left alt-shift-1 = en
        ' *          left alt-shift-2 = ru
        ' */
    If Not (args.Length = 0) Then
        Browser_HtmlBrowser().InputKeys("%+" + args(0))
    End If
    ' VPs on the links
    Link_Home().PerformTest(Home_textVP())
    Link_SupportDownloads().PerformTest(SupportDownloads_textVP())
    ' iterate through the datapool to run searches on the site
    While Not (DpDone())
        Text_Q().Click()
        Browser_HtmlBrowser(Document_IBMI18n(), _
            DEFAULT_FLAGS).InputChars(DpString("searchText"))
        Button_Searchsubmit().Click()
        Browser_HtmlBrowser().Back()
        DpNext()
    End While
    Browser_HtmlBrowser().Close()
    Return Nothing
End Function
```

The Real World

The i18n scripting example illustrated in this chapter makes several simplifying assumptions. First, it assumes that the object hierarchy is identical for all target web pages regardless of language. Frequently, this is not the case for internationalized web applications, and it often does not hold for i18n thick client applications. This means that, most likely, your implementation has to use branching logic based on the language in use; additionally, extra attention might have to be directed toward Object Map maintenance. Second, the example assumes that the transaction flow is not dependent on language, but often, this is not the case either; due to differences in culture and business practice that accompany language differences, application flows often change with language. The approach shown in this chapter (using a single script for each transaction regardless of language) can be adapted by building branching logic to accommodate different transaction paths based on the language in use. Finally, other aspects of applications can change with differing language implementations, such as the graphics that the application displays. Language-based image verifications can be handled in a manner similar to the techniques shown in this chapter, because image files are stored in the resources directory like other script assets (as portable network graphics or .png files), and are simply referred to by filename in the Verification Point XML.

Summary

The approach to designing an automated internationalized test shown in this chapter is, of course, not the only way to set this type of project up. The goal of this chapter is to make the different issues that you have to deal with in designing and building an implementation clearer and to offer one set of solutions to those issues. Your own solution might differ significantly, but hopefully, this chapter has shortened your learning curve for building an internationalized test suite.

Further Information

For another approach to this problem, see www.ibm.com/developerworks/rational/library/07/0925_mirchandani-ujjwal/.

Advanced Logging Techniques

Daniel Gouveia

There are different ways to take advantage of Rational Functional Tester's logging capabilities. Chapter 9, "Advanced Rational Functional Tester Object Map Topics," covers the usage of open-source tools, including Log4J (verbose reporting). This appendix looks at ways you can expand on Rational Functional Tester's logging.

You learn tips and techniques for emailing results to yourself, using EXtensible Stylesheet Language (XSL) to transform Rational Functional Tester's XML log, and creating a new log type. XSL is not covered in detail. Neither is Java. It is assumed that you have some knowledge of these technologies and have worked with them. The goal is to provide you with the information to get your started so you can get the information you want—how you want it.

If you read this appendix topic-by-topic, you can see that you can build off of three advanced logging mechanisms. Of course, you can simply go to the topic that suits your need. It is written so that you can find the advanced logging technique that addresses your problem.

Sending Test Results Via Email

You can take advantage of the scripting languages Java and VB.NET to send an email, announcing test results. This is an excellent precursor to reviewing your actual execution log. You can make the email as robust or as simple as you wish. This section provides the information for accomplishing this capability using Simple Mail Transfer Protocol (SMTP).

The basic idea is the same for both languages. You need to set up the email structure (who it is being sent to, who it is coming from, its subject, body, and so on). You then implement the

SMTP client, specifying the host, port, and any necessary Secure Sockets Layer (SSL) connection information. Finally, you simply send the email.

Listing A.1 provides you with a Java implementation that sends simple pass/fail emails. The aim is to let the recipient know that execution has completed and what the results are. They are created as separate methods (functions). This enables you to place them into a Helper Superclass (Helper Base Class).

Listing A.1   Email method for Java

```java
public void emailTestResults(String scriptName, String[] testResults)
throws AddressException, MessagingException{

    Properties props = System.getProperties();
    props.setProperty("mail.transport.protocol", "smtp");
    props.setProperty("mail.host", "smtp.gmail.com");
    props.put("mail.smtp.auth", "true");
    props.put("mail.smtp.port", "465");
    props.put("mail.smtp.socketFactory.port", "465");
    props.put("mail.smtp.socketFactory.class", "javax.net.ssl.SSLSocketFactory");
    props.put("mail.smtp.socketFactory.fallback", "false");

    Session session = Session.getDefaultInstance(props,
                    new javax.mail.Authenticator()
    {
        protected PasswordAuthentication getPasswordAuthentication()
        { return new PasswordAuthentication("<Email Server
          Username>","<Email Server Password>");}
    });

    MimeMessage mailmsg = new MimeMessage(session);
    mailmsg.setSender(new InternetAddress("<Sender Email Address>"));
    mailmsg.setRecipients(Message.RecipientType.TO,
    InternetAddress.parse("<Email Address To Send To>", false));
    mailmsg.setSubject("Test Execution Results for: " + scriptName);
    mailmsg.setSentDate(new Date());

    String body = "";
    for(int i = 0; i < testResults.length; i++){
        body = body + testResults[i] + "\n";
    }
```

```
mailmsg.setText(body);
Transport.send(mailmsg);
}
```

The preceding code example uses JavaMail version 1.4.1. It also uses JavaBeansActivation Framework version 1.0.2. You are able to obtain both of these off of Sun's website. You download these packages as zip files and then unzip them to any directory. You just need to make sure that you have all of the .jar files listed in your Rational Functional Tester project's Java build path. The previous code sample requires the following .jar files:

- mail.jar
- mailapi.jar
- pop3.jar
- smtp.jar
- activation.jar

You also need to make the appropriate imports into your class file, as shown in Figure A.1.

```
import java.util.Date;
import java.util.Properties;

import javax.mail.Message;
import javax.mail.MessagingException;
import javax.mail.PasswordAuthentication;
import javax.mail.Session;
import javax.mail.Transport;
import javax.mail.internet.AddressException;
import javax.mail.internet.InternetAddress;
import javax.mail.internet.MimeMessage;
```

Figure A.1   Import statements

This example uses Gmail as the SMTP server. It first sets the properties that specify the mail protocol, mail (Gmail server) host, server port, and SSL settings. It then addresses the authentication mechanism that is needed. It creates a new mail session and creates the password authentication class, supplying the user credentials needed for the server. The method (emailTestResults) then creates the email message that sets the sender, send to, send date, subject, and body values. This method accepts two arguments: the name of the invoking script and an array of test results. The script name is used in the subject, letting you know which script the results are for. The method parses the results array to list the result of each subscript's execution results (in the case of a regression script). Lastly, it sends the email.

Listing A.2 is the VB.NET version of the prior email solution. It performs the same task as the prior Java example. One key difference is that you won't need to download and use separate packages. You simply import the `Mail` namespace into your class file and use the following line:

```
Imports System.Net.Mail
```

This provides access to the `SmtpClient` and `MailMessage` classes. The first thing this sample code does is set up the sent from, send to, subject, and body email fields. Like the Java code, it accepts two arguments: a script name string and test results array. The script name string is used in the subject message. The test results array is used to list the separate execution results for each script (for example, if a regression script is executed). It then creates an SMTP client, specifying a server (Gmail) and port. It sets up the SSL, providing the appropriate user credentials. The second to last thing it does is instantiate the `MailMessage` class, passing in the required email fields. Finally, it sends the email.

Listing A.2   Email function for VB.NET

```
Public Sub EmailTestResults(ByVal scriptName As String, ByVal testResults() As
String)

        Dim from As String = "<Sender Email Address>"
        Dim sendTo As String = "<Email Address To Send To>"
        Dim subject As String = "Test Execution Results for: " &
        scriptName
        Dim body As String = ""

        Dim i As Integer
        For i = 0 To UBound(testResults)
                body = body & testResults(i) & vbCrLf
        Next

        Dim smtpclient As New SmtpClient("smtp.gmail.com", 587)
        smtpclient.EnableSsl = True
        smtpclient.Credentials = New System.Net.NetworkCredential("<Email
        Server Username>", "<Email Server Password>")

        Dim mailmsg As MailMessage
        mailmsg = New MailMessage(from, sendTo, subject, body)

        smtpclient.Send(mailmsg)

End Sub
```

Calling the Mail Method

To use the method or function, you need to modify your scripts to catch the pass/fail results (in an array). You invoke the method/function and pass in the script name and test results array. The examples in Listing A.3 show how this might be done in a regression script. The scripts, invoked by the regression script, return the overall pass/fail result for them. The regression script catches the results in an array, sending them to the email method along with the name of the regression script.

Listing A.3   Invoking the Email method

Java

```java
public void testMain(Object[] args) throws AddressException, MessagingException
{

    String tempResult;
    String[] testResults = new String[3];

    tempResult = (String)callScript("PackageA.TestScript1");
    if(tempResult.equalsIgnoreCase("FAIL"))
        testResults[0] = "PackageA.TestScript1 FAILED";
    else
        testResults[0] = "PackageA.TestScript1 PASSED";

    tempResult = (String)callScript("PackageA.TestScript2");
    if(tempResult.equalsIgnoreCase("FAIL"))
        testResults[1] = "PackageA.TestScript2 FAILED";
    else
        testResults[1] = "PackageA.TestScript2 PASSED";

    tempResult = (String)callScript("PackageA.TestScript3");
    if(tempResult.equalsIgnoreCase("FAIL"))
        testResults[2] = "PackageA.TestScript3 FAILED";
    else
        testResults[2] = "PackageA.TestScript3 PASSED";

    emailTestResults("Test Regression Script", testResults);

}
```

VB.NET

```vbnet
Public Function TestMain(ByVal args() As Object) As Object

    Dim tempResult As String
```

```
    Dim testResults(2) As String

    tempResult = CallScript("PackageA.TestScript1").ToString
    If (tempResult.ToString = "FAIL") Then
          testResults(0) = "PackageA.TestScript1 FAILED"
    Else
          testResults(0) = "PackageA.TestScript1 PASSED"
    End If

    tempResult = CallScript("PackageA.TestScript2")
    If (tempResult.ToString = "FAIL") Then
          testResults(1) = "PackageA.TestScript2 FAILED"
    Else
          testResults(1) = "PackageA.TestScript2 PASSED"
    End If

    tempResult = CallScript("PackageA.TestScript3")
    If (tempResult.ToString = "FAIL") Then
          testResults(2) = "PackageA.TestScript1 FAILED"
    Else
          testResults(2) = "PackageA.TestScript1 PASSED"
    End If

    EmailTestResults("Test Regression Script", testResults)

    Return Nothing
End Function
```

The result of running one of the prior regression scripts is the creation and distribution of a simple email that shows the basic pass/fail log. It lets you know if each script, invoked in the regression test, succeeded or not. An example of this is shown in Figure A.2.

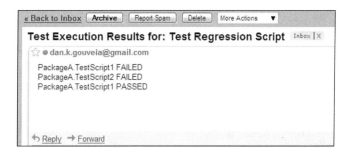

Figure A.2   Test results displayed in email

Transforming the XML Log by Using XSL

Rational Functional Tester offers you different types of logging. You can write to a text-based log, HTML-based log, and logs housed in different test-management tools. It also offers you the ability to log your script's playback events to an XML-based log. This provides you with the flexibility to develop your own custom log should you desire something different than the out-of-the-box offering. You can parse it however you want and display the information that is pertinent to you.

You can use XSL to transform the XML log into an HTML-based file. If you are interested in using a different means to parse and manipulate the XML log file, review Chapter 4, "XML and Rational Functional Tester." This section is not meant to be a tutorial on XSL. There are many good tutorials on the Web for that. Instead, this section shows you, through examples, how to use XSL to transform Rational Functional Tester's XML log into HTML.

The first thing that you want to do is acquire a utility to actually carry out the transform. Microsoft offers a utility called `msxsl.exe`, free of charge. You can also use Apache's Xalan-Java. Both of these work with the example in this section. Also, both are command-line utilities.

The next thing that you need is an XML file to look at. You can easily accomplish this by selecting the XML log type in your Rational Functional Tester Playback Preferences (see Figure A.3).

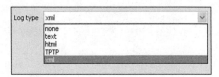

Figure A.3   Setting the Rational Functional Tester XML log

You can play back any script, preferably with a verification point (VP) in it, after you have set XML as your logging type. Listing A.4 (in both the Java and VB.NET version) generates the XML-based log shown in Figure A.4.

Listing A.4   Simple Rational Functional Tester script to generate the XML log

Java

```
public void testMain(Object[] args)
{
      startApp("ClassicsJavaA");
      classicsJava().waitForExistence(180.0, 2.0);
      // Frame: ClassicsCD
      tree2().performTest(VerifyComposerListVP());
      classicsJava(ANY,MAY_EXIT).close();
}
```

VB.NET

```
Public Function TestMain(ByVal args() As Object) As Object
     StartApp("ClassicsJavaA")
     ClassicsJava().WaitForExistence(180.0, 2.0)
     ' Frame: ClassicsCD
     Tree2().PerformTest(VerifyComposerListVP())
     ClassicsJava(ANY,MAY_EXIT).Close()
     Return Nothing
End Function
```

```
<?xml version="1.0" encoding="UTF-8" ?>
- <TestLog>
  - <Event dpIter="0">
    - <Event Timestamp="01-Sep-2008 01:14:36.265 PM" Type="Script Start" Headline="Script start [scripts.Chapter2Section1_4]"
        Result="INFORMATION">
        <Property line_number="1" />
        <Property script_iter_count="0" />
        <Property script_name="scripts.Chapter2Section1_4" />
        <Property script_id="scripts.Chapter2Section1_4.java" />
      </Event>
    - <Event Timestamp="01-Sep-2008 01:14:36.406 PM" Type="Application Start" Headline="Start application [ClassicsJavaA]" Result="PASS">
        <Property name="ClassicsJavaA" />
        <Property line_number="31" />
        <Property script_name="scripts.Chapter2Section1_4" />
        <Property script_id="scripts.Chapter2Section1_4.java" />
      </Event>
    - <Event Timestamp="01-Sep-2008 01:14:40.828 PM" Type="Verification Point" Headline="VerifyComposerList" Result="FAIL">
        <Property vp_type="object_data" />
        <Property name="VerifyComposerList" />
        <Property script_name="scripts.Chapter2Section1_4" />
        <Property line_number="36" />
        <Property script_id="scripts.Chapter2Section1_4.java" />
        <Property baseline="resources\scripts\Chapter2Section1_4.VerifyComposerList.base.rftvp" />
        <Property expected="Chapter2Section1_4.0000.VerifyComposerList.exp.rftvp" />
        <Property actual="Chapter2Section1_4.0000.0000.VerifyComposerList.act.rftvp" />
      </Event>
    - <Event Timestamp="01-Sep-2008 01:14:41.859 PM" Type="Script End" Headline="Script end [scripts.Chapter2Section1_4]" Result="FAIL">
        <Property line_number="-1" />
        <Property script_name="scripts.Chapter2Section1_4" />
        <Property script_id="scripts.Chapter2Section1_4.java" />
      </Event>
  </Event>
</TestLog>
```

Figure A.4   Rational Functional Tester XML log (same for Java or VB.NET execution)

You can use this test log as a template for building out your XSL file. Even though it is short and simple, it provides you with the hierarchal structure of Rational Functional Tester's XML logs. The basic XML log elements that you work with are:

- `<TestLog>`—The root element in the log
- `<Event>`—The datapool and script events that Rational Functional Tester logs

Putting these together enables you to construct your XSL looping and select elements. For instance, if you wanted to loop through each event, you would use:

```
<xsl:for-each select="TestLog/Event/Event">
```

This enables the transform to look at each logged event. If you just provided `TestLog/Event`, you would access only the datapool iteration events, not the data for things such as pass/fail results, script command issues, warnings, and so on.

To select a particular value from the XML log, use `<xsl:value-of>` element. If you want to simply obtain the data from an `<Event>` element, use something like the following:

```
<xsl:value-of select="@Type"/>
```

This returns the type of event, such as "Script Start," "Application Start," "Verification Point," and so on. If you wanted to acquire data from the child of an event (such as a `<Property>` element), you would place the name of the XML element in front of the @ sign.

```
<xsl:value-of select="Property/@name"/>
```

This XSL line gets the name property for an event. This is something like the name of the application you started, a verification point name, and so on. If you want to get another property ID, simply replace the value after the @ sign.

If you need to add some conditional logic, you can use the `<xsl:choose>`, `<xsl:when>`, and `<xsl:otherwise>` combination. This enables you to traverse different paths in your XSL transform. You might use this when you want to work with the different results found in your log (for example, Pass, Fail, Warning, and Information).

Listing A.5 employs conditional logic to handle the different test results. It first uses the `<xsl:choose>` element and then the `<xsl:when>` and `<xsl:otherwise>` to make the decisions. Ultimately, the code decides what color to make the table cell's background color (red, green, yellow, or blue), based off of the verification result. Further, if it encounters a verification point failure, it creates a link to call the specific verification comparator.

Listing A.5   XSL conditional logic

```
<xsl:choose>
      <xsl:when test="@Result='FAIL'">
            <td bgcolor="FF9999"><b><xsl:value-of select="@Result"/></b>
            <xsl:if test="@Type='Verification Point'">
                        <xsl:variable name="baseline"><xsl:value-of
select="Property/@baseline"/></xsl:variable>
                        <xsl:variable name="expected"><xsl:value-of
select="Property/@expected"/></xsl:variable>
                        <xsl:variable name="actual"><xsl:value-of
select="Property/@actual"/></xsl:variable>
                        -- <a
href="javascript:comparator(document.URL,'{$baseline}','{$expected}','{$actual}'
)">View Results</a>
            </xsl:if>
      </td>
```

```
        </xsl:when>
        <xsl:when test="@Result='PASS'">
                <td bgcolor="CCFF99"><b><xsl:value-of select="@Result"/></b></td>
        </xsl:when>
        <xsl:when test="@Result='WARNING'">
                <td bgcolor="FFFF99"><b><xsl:value-of select="@Result"/></b></td>
        </xsl:when>
        <xsl:when test="@Result='INFORMATION'">
                <td bgcolor="3399CC"><b><xsl:value-of select="@Result"/></b></td>
        </xsl:when>
        <xsl:otherwise>
                <td bgcolor="FFCCFF"><xsl:value-of select="@Result"/></td>
        </xsl:otherwise>
</xsl:choose>
```

After you create the XSL transform, you need to process it. That's what one of the two utilities mentioned earlier assists with. If you choose to use `msxsl.exe`, you need to specify the XML, XSL, and resulting HTML file:

```
msxsl.exe <xml file> <xsl file> -o <html file>
```

Choosing Apache's Xalan-Java requires you to place its .jar files in the `classpath`. You can do this either with an environment variable or in the command-line string. Like `msxsl.exe`, you need to specify the XML, XSL, and HTML files:

```
java -classpath serializer.jar;xalan.jar;xercesImpl.jar;xml-apis.jar
org.apache.xalan.xslt.Process -IN <xml file> -XSL <xsl file> -OUT <html
file>
```

Both utilities do the same thing. They take the specified XML file and apply the XSL transform to it. The result is an HTML representation of the original XML log. To provide more context, see Listing A.6.

Listing A.6   Complete XSL file for transforming the Rational Functional Tester XML log

```
<?xml version="1.0" encoding="ISO-8859-1"?>

<xsl:stylesheet version="1.0"
xmlns:xsl="http://www.w3.org/1999/XSL/Transform">

<xsl:template match="/">
        <html>
        <head>
        <title>RFT Execution Log</title>
```

```
        <script type="text/javascript">
            function comparator(logDir,base,exp,act){
                try{

document.ComparatorApplet.startComparatorEx(base,exp,act,logDir);
                } catch(e){
                        alert(e.name + ": " + e.message);
                        alert("CRFCN0309E: Error creating verification point
display:\nAn enabled JRE (1.3.1_02 or better) must be associated with the
browser to view VP results");
                }
            }
        </script>


        </head>
        <body>
            <h1><center><u>OVERALL EXECUTION RESULTS FOR: <xsl:value-of
select="TestLog/Event/Event/Property/@script_name"/></u></center></h1>
            <center>
            <table border="2">
                <tr>
                    <th>Script Start Time</th>
                    <th>Script End Time</th>
                    <th>Number of Scripts Executed</th>
                    <th>Overall Pass/Fail Result of Execution</th>
                </tr>
                <tr>

                    <td bgcolor="FFCCFF"><xsl:value-of
select="TestLog/Event/Event/@Timestamp"/></td>

                        <xsl:for-each select="TestLog/Event/Event">
                            <xsl:if test="@Type='Script End'">
                                <td bgcolor="FFCCFF"><xsl:value-of
select="@Timestamp"/></td>
                            </xsl:if>
                        </xsl:for-each>

                        <xsl:choose>
                            <xsl:when
```

```
test="count(TestLog/Event/Event[@Type='Call Script'])&lt;1">
                                <td bgcolor="FFCCFF">1</td>
                        </xsl:when>
                        <xsl:otherwise>
                                <td bgcolor="FFCCFF"><xsl:value-of
select="count(TestLog/Event/Event[@Type='Call Script'])"/></td>
                        </xsl:otherwise>
                </xsl:choose>

                <xsl:for-each select="TestLog/Event/Event">
                        <xsl:if test="@Type='Script End'">
                                <xsl:choose>
                                        <xsl:when test="@Result='FAIL'">
                                                <td
bgcolor="FF9999"><b><xsl:value-of select="@Result"/></b></td>
                                        </xsl:when>
                                        <xsl:when test="@Result='PASS'">
                                                <td
bgcolor="CCFF99"><b><xsl:value-of select="@Result"/></b></td>
                                        </xsl:when>
                                        <xsl:when test="@Result='WARNING'">
                                                <td
bgcolor="FFFF99"><b><xsl:value-of select="@Result"/></b></td>
                                        </xsl:when>
                                        <xsl:when
test="@Result='INFORMATION'">
                                                <td
bgcolor="3399CC"><b><xsl:value-of select="@Result"/></b></td>
                                        </xsl:when>
                                        <xsl:otherwise>
                                                <td bgcolor="FFCCFF"><xsl:value-
of select="@Result"/></td>
                                        </xsl:otherwise>
                                </xsl:choose>
                        </xsl:if>
                </xsl:for-each>
        </tr>
    </table>
    </center>


<center>============================================================</center>
```

```
            <center>
===================================================</center>
            <center>
=======================================</center>
            <center>
==============================</center>
            <xsl:choose>
                <xsl:when test="count(TestLog/Event/Event[@Type='Call
Script'])&lt;1">
                    <h3><u>Results For Script: <xsl:value-of
select="Property/@script_name"/></u></h3>
                    <table border="1">
                        <tr>
                            <th>Script Event</th>
                            <th>Time of Event</th>
                            <th>Event Result</th>
                        </tr>
                        <xsl:for-each select="TestLog/Event/Event">

                            <tr>
                                <td
bgcolor="FFCCFF"><xsl:value-of select="@Type"/>
                                    <xsl:if
test="@Type='Verification Point'">
                                            -- <b><i><xsl:value-
of select="@Headline"/></i></b>
                                    </xsl:if>
                                </td>

                                <td
bgcolor="FFCCFF"><xsl:value-of select="@Timestamp"/></td>
                                <xsl:choose>
                                    <xsl:when
test="@Result='FAIL'">
                                            <td
bgcolor="FF9999"><b><xsl:value-of select="@Result"/></b>
<xsl:if test="@Type='Verification Point'">

<xsl:variable name="baseline"><xsl:value-of
select="Property/@baseline"/></xsl:variable>

<xsl:variable name="expected"><xsl:value-of
```

```
select="Property/@expected"/></xsl:variable>

<xsl:variable name="actual"><xsl:value-of
select="Property/@actual"/></xsl:variable>

-- <a
href="javascript:comparator(document.URL,'{$baseline}','{$expected}','{$actual}'
)">View Results</a>
</xsl:if>
                                                                </td>
                                                        </xsl:when>
                                                        <xsl:when
test="@Result='PASS'">
                                                                <td
bgcolor="CCFF99"><b><xsl:value-of select="@Result"/></b></td>
                                                        </xsl:when>
                                                        <xsl:when
test="@Result='WARNING'">
                                                                <td
bgcolor="FFFF99"><b><xsl:value-of select="@Result"/></b></td>
                                                        </xsl:when>
                                                        <xsl:when
test="@Result='INFORMATION'">
                                                                <td
bgcolor="3399CC"><b><xsl:value-of select="@Result"/></b></td>
                                                        </xsl:when>
                                                        <xsl:otherwise>
                                                                <td
bgcolor="FFCCFF"><xsl:value-of select="@Result"/></td>
                                                        </xsl:otherwise>
                                                </xsl:choose>
                                        </tr>
                                </xsl:for-each>
                        </table>

<p>***************************************************</p>
                </xsl:when>
                <xsl:otherwise>
                        <xsl:for-each select="TestLog/Event/Event">
                                <xsl:if test="@Type='Call Script'">
                                        <h3><u>Results For Script:
<xsl:value-of select="Property/@name"/></u></h3>
```

```
                                <table border="1">
                                    <tr>
                                        <th>Script Event</th>
                                        <th>Time of Event</th>
                                        <th>Event Result</th>
                                    </tr>
                                    <xsl:for-each select="Event">
                                    <tr>
                                        <td
bgcolor="FFCCFF"><xsl:value-of select="@Type"/>
                                            <xsl:if
test="@Type='Verification Point'">

                                                    --
<b><i><xsl:value-of select="@Headline"/></i></b>
                                                </xsl:if>
                                            </td>

                                        <td
bgcolor="FFCCFF"><xsl:value-of select="@Timestamp"/></td>

                                        <xsl:choose>
                                                <xsl:when
test="@Result='FAIL'">
                                                        <td
bgcolor="FF9999"><b><xsl:value-of select="@Result"/></b>
<xsl:if test="@Type='Verification Point'">

<xsl:variable name="baseline"><xsl:value-of
select="Property/@baseline"/></xsl:variable>

<xsl:variable name="expected"><xsl:value-of
select="Property/@expected"/></xsl:variable>

<xsl:variable name="actual"><xsl:value-of
select="Property/@actual"/></xsl:variable>
-- <a href="javascript:comparator(document.URL,'{$baseline}','{$expected}','{
$actual}')">View Results</a>
</xsl:if>
                                                    </td>
                                            </xsl:when>
                                            <xsl:when
test="@Result='PASS'">
```

```
                                                           <td
bgcolor="CCFF99"><b><xsl:value-of select="@Result"/></b></td>
                                           </xsl:when>
                                           <xsl:when
test="@Result='WARNING'">
                                                           <td
bgcolor="FFFF99"><b><xsl:value-of select="@Result"/></b></td>
                                           </xsl:when>
                                           <xsl:when
test="@Result='INFORMATION'">
                                                           <td
bgcolor="3399CC"><b><xsl:value-of select="@Result"/></b></td>
                                           </xsl:when>
                                           <xsl:otherwise>
                                                           <td
bgcolor="FFCCFF"><xsl:value-of select="@Result"/></td>
                                           </xsl:otherwise>
                                   </xsl:choose>
                             </tr>
                             </xsl:for-each>
                       </table>

<p>***************************************************</p>
                       </xsl:if>
                 </xsl:for-each>
             </xsl:otherwise>
         </xsl:choose>
      <applet
code="com/rational/test/ft/bootstrap/HtmlLogComparatorApplet.class"
name="ComparatorApplet" width="0" height="0"></applet>
      </body>
      </html>
</xsl:template>
</xsl:stylesheet>
```

Using Xalan-Java or msxsl.exe, you can pass this XSL transform (as a file), along with the XML log, displayed in Figure A.4, to create a clean-looking HTML file. The command-line strings would look like the following:

For the msxsl.exe command-line string:

```
msxsl.exe rational_ft_log.xml XSLTransform.xsl -o HTMLLog.html
```

For the Xalan-Java command-line string:

```
java -classpath serializer.jar;xalan.jar;xercesImpl.jar;xml-apis.jar
org.apache.xalan.xslt.Process -IN rational_ft_log.xml -XSL XSLTransform.xsl
-OUT HTMLLog.html
```

Figure A.5 shows what the resulting HTML log file looks like using the XSL transform.

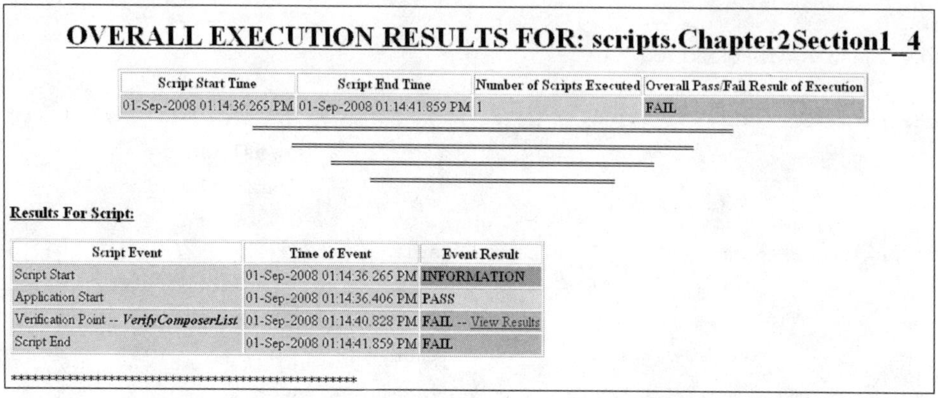

Figure A.5   HTML log using XSL transform

You now have a basic understanding of how to apply XSL transforms to your Rational Functional Tester XML logs. You are not limited to running command-line tools to perform the transformation. You can actually build your own utility that does this for you, transforming multiple logs at once.

Creating Your Own RSS Log Type

Rational Functional Tester provides you with the ability to create your own log type. This capability can be implemented only with the Eclipse version of Rational Functional Tester because you need to access the Plug-in Development perspective. You can, however, use the new log type with the .NET version. Rational Functional Tester's Help files provide the necessary documentation to get you started. If you search on the phrase "log extension," the section on creating your own log type should be at the top of the list (see Figure A.6).

The Extending a log topic discusses how to build the Eclipse plug-in project necessary for creating your own log type. Following these steps detailed in this topic, you are taken through the New Plug-In Project wizard. On the first page of the New Project wizard, you can simply provide the name for your project and click the **Next** button. You should deselect the **This plug-in will make contributions to the UI** checkbox on the second page. You can leave the default values for

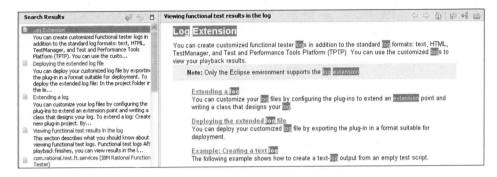

Figure A.6   Log extension topic in Help files

the Plug-in Properties. Clicking on the **Finish** button completes the wizard, creating the plug-in project for you.

After the project is created, the help instructions continue to discuss the specification of a dependency and definition of an extension. When you get to the point of extending an extension point (steps 6 and 7 in the Help topic), you need to provide a LogID in the Extension Element Details section. This is displayed as a selection in Rational Functional Tester's log type combo box. You also need to provide a class name, specifying any package that you place the class in. This maps to the plugin.xml file (found on the last tab of the MANIFEST.MF GUI). See Figure A.7.

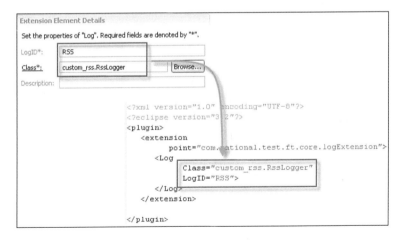

Figure A.7   Extension element details

You now have a new plug-in project, ready for coding. The Example: Creating a text log section in the Help files provides sample code to show you what's needed to create a new log type—in this case, a new text log. To begin, you need to enter in the .src folder of your project and expand the package that it contains. You then need to create a new class, supplying the same name that you placed in the Extension Element Details section of your MANIFEST.MF file (for example, Figure A.7 shows RSSLogger). An example of this is shown in Figure A.8.

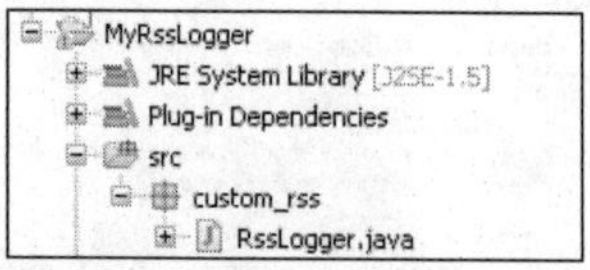

Figure A.8   Package and class structure for new log type

You need your new class to extend the `LogExtensionAdapter` class. Lastly, your class needs to provide the proper code to implement the necessary constructors and methods for initializing, writing to, and closing the log. Using the code supplied in the Example: Creating a text log help section provides you with an excellent example to prepare you for developing your own custom text log type.

To implement a log type that builds out an RSS feed, replace the code you used following the "text log" example with the code shown in Listing A.7.

Listing A.7   Java code for creating an RSS log

```java
import java.io.BufferedReader;
import java.io.File;
import java.io.FileInputStream;
import java.io.FileOutputStream;
import java.io.IOException;
import java.io.InputStreamReader;
import java.io.PrintWriter;

import com.rational.test.ft.services.ILogMessage;
import com.rational.test.ft.services.LogException;
import com.rational.test.ft.services.LogExtensionAdapter;

public class RSSLog extends LogExtensionAdapter {

    private String logName=null;
    private String logDirectory=null;
    private PrintWriter out=null;

    public RSSLog(String logName) {
        super(logName);
        this.logName=logName;
        this.logDirectory=null;
    }
```

```
public RSSLog() {
        super();
        this.logName=null;
        this.logDirectory=null;
}

public void closeLog() {
        try{
                out.println("</table></center>");

out.println("<center><p>*****************************************************</p></
center>");
                out.close();
                writeRSSFile();
        }catch(Exception e) {
                e.printStackTrace();
        }
}

public void initLog() throws LogException {
        try{
                this.logName=getLogName();
                this.logDirectory=getLogDirectory();
                File logFile=new File(logDirectory,logName+".html");
                FileOutputStream fos=new FileOutputStream(logFile);
                out=new PrintWriter(fos);
                out.println("<center><table border=\"1\">");
                out.println("<tr>");
                out.println("<th>Script Event</th>");
                out.println("<th>Headline</th>");
                out.println("<th>Event Result</th>");
                out.println("</tr>");
                out.println();
        }catch(IOException e){
                e.printStackTrace();
        }
}

public void writeLog(ILogMessage message) {
        String result=getResult(message);
```

```
        String event_type=getEventType(message);
        String headline=getHeadline(message);

        out.println("<tr>");

        out.println("<td>" + event_type + "</td>");

        if(event_type.contains("CALL_SCRIPT"))
                out.println("<td><b>" + headline + "</b></td>");
        else
                out.println("<td>" + headline + "</td>");

        if(result.equalsIgnoreCase("pass")){
                out.println("<td bgcolor=\"#CCFF99\"><b>" + result +
"</b></td>");
            } else if (result.equalsIgnoreCase("failure")){
                out.println("<td bgcolor=\"#FF9999\"><b>" + result +
"</b></td>");
            } else if (result.equalsIgnoreCase("warning")){
                out.println("<td bgcolor=\"#FFFF99\"><b>" + result +
"</b></td>");
            } else {
                out.println("<td bgcolor=\"#3399CC\"><b>" + result +
"</b></td>");
            }

        out.println("</tr>");
        out.println();
    }

    /**
     * Return the result from the log message.
     */
    private String getResult(ILogMessage message) {
        String result=null;
        switch (message.getResult())
        {
                case LOG_FAILURE : result="FAILURE";break;
                case LOG_PASS : result="PASS";break;
                case LOG_WARNING : result="WARNING";break;
                default: result= "INFO";
```

```
        }
        return result;
    }


    /**
     * Return string representation of event from the ILogMessage.
     */
    private String getEventType(ILogMessage message) {
        String eventType=null;
        switch(message.getEvent())
        {
            case EVENT_SCRIPT_START : eventType="SCRIPT START";break;
            case EVENT_SCRIPT_END : eventType="SCRIPT END";break;
            case EVENT_VP : eventType="VERIFCATION POINT";break;
            case EVENT_CALL_SCRIPT : eventType = "CALL_SCRIPT"; break;
            case EVENT_APPLICATION_START : eventType="APPLICATION
            START";break;
            case EVENT_APPLICATION_END : eventType="APPLICATION
            END";break;
            case EVENT_TIMER_START : eventType="TIMER START";break;
            case EVENT_TIMER_END : eventType= "TIMER END" ;break;
            case EVENT_CONFIGURATION : eventType="CONFIGURATION"; break;
            default : eventType="GENERAL";
        }
        return eventType;
    }


    /**
     * Returns the headline from the ILogMessage.
     */
    private String getHeadline(ILogMessage message) {
        return message.getHeadline();
    }


    private void writeRSSFile() throws IOException{
        // ACQUIRE NEWLY WRITTEN HTML LOG
        File logFile=new File(logDirectory,logName+".html");

        // DYNAMICALLY ACQUIRE RFTLog.rss, USING CURRENT LOG DIRECTORY
        String newLogDirectory = getLogDirectory().replace(getLogName(),
"rsslogs");
```

```
        File rssFile = new File(newLogDirectory, "\\RFTLog.rss");

        // DYNAMICALLY CREATE NEW TMP FILE, USING CURRENT LOG DIRECTORY
        File tmpFile = new File(newLogDirectory, "\\RFTLog.tmp");

        // SET UP TO READ CURRENT RSS LOG FILE
        FileInputStream fis_rss = new FileInputStream(rssFile);
        BufferedReader in_rss = new BufferedReader(new
InputStreamReader(fis_rss));

        // SET UP TO READ NEWLY WRITTEN TXT LOG
        FileInputStream fis_txt = new FileInputStream(logFile);
        BufferedReader in_txt = new BufferedReader(new
InputStreamReader(fis_txt));

        // SET UP FOR CATCHING OUTPUT
        FileOutputStream fos = new FileOutputStream(tmpFile);
        PrintWriter out = new PrintWriter(fos);

        String thisRSSLine = "";      // STRING TO READ LINES FROM FILE
        String thisTXTLine = "";      // STRING TO READ LINES FROM FILE

        // READ FILE, WRITING OUT TO NEW ONE
        while((thisRSSLine = in_rss.readLine()) != null){
            if(thisRSSLine.contains("</channel>")){
                out.println("\t\t<item>");
                out.println("\t\t\t<title>Test Execution Log for: " +
logName + "</title>");
                out.println("\t\t\t<link>http://localhost</link>");
                out.println("\t\t\t<description>");
                out.println();
                while((thisTXTLine = in_txt.readLine()) != null){
                    out.println("\t\t\t" + thisTXTLine);
                }
                out.println("\t\t\t</description>");
                out.println("\t\t</item>");
                out.println("\t</channel>");
                out.println("</rss>");
                break;

            } else{
                out.println(thisRSSLine);
            }
```

```
        }

        out.flush();
        out.close();
        in_rss.close();
        in_txt.close();

        rssFile.delete();
        tmpFile.renameTo(rssFile);
        tmpFile.delete();
    }
}
```

After you create the necessary pieces for your plug-in, you need to export it to the plug-ins folder. This is covered in the last section of the Extending a log Help topic, Deploying the extended log file. Keep in mind that depending on the version of Rational Functional Tester you use, your plug-ins folder path might vary. If you use version 7.x of Rational Functional Tester, your path is C:\Program Files\ibm\SDP70. The path for version 8.x is C:\Program Files\IBM\SDP. You might need to restart Rational Functional Tester for the new log type to show up as an option in your logging preferences. When completed, you see something similar to Figure A.9.

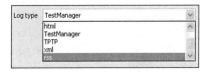

Figure A.9   Rational Functional Tester logging preferences for RSS

You need to do a few things before you try out your new RSS log type. You need to set up an RSS file template. You can find this on the Web, or just use the one shown in Listing A.8.

Listing A.8   RSS file template

```
<?xml version="1.0" encoding="ISO-8859-1" ?>
<rss version="0.91">

    <channel>
        <title>IBM Rational Functional Test Log</title>
        <link>http://localhost</link>
        <description>Test Execution Results</description>
    <language>en-us</language>
```

```
    <image>
        <title>IBM Rational Functional Tester</title>
        <url>http://localhost/images/RFT_v7.jpg</url>
        <link>http://localhost</link>
        <width>90</width>
        <height>36</height>
    </image>
    </channel>
</rss>
```

This template uses RSS version 0.91. You can also use version 1.0 or 2.0. The template is basically structured so that it provides some default Rational Functional Tester information (for example, log and description). It then is ready to accept the `<item>` and `</item>` tags provided by your custom log code. These tags are used to parse out new execution logs, displaying as new items to your feed reader. One thing to note is that the `writeRSSFile()` method in the XSL code looks in a rsslogs directory for the `.rss` file. This was manually created in the Rational Functional Tester project's log directory. The Java code is dynamic and based off of the executing script's information. You might want to change this, depending upon your web server's access.

You need to set up a web server to deliver the feed. It doesn't matter which web server you use. You need to set it up so it can access the RSS directory you have set up. This enables it to serve up the actual RSS file.

You also have to set up your favorite feed reader to access the feeds from your RSS file. For the most part, you simply specify the URL, including the .rss file. For instance, http://localhost:8080/ rftlogs/RFTLog.rss (see Figure A.10). Some feed readers enable you to set up how often it looks for new feeds. This can be useful for acquiring script execution information soon after playback has completed.

Figure A.10   Setting up the Feed Reader to grab the Rational Functional Tester log feed

After execution completes, you can review your log in the feed reader. Ideally, you want to have your reader set up so it notifies you when a new log has been added (for example, a new feed item has been inserted into the Rational Functional Tester RSS file). This informs you, not only of your completed scripts, but of your coworker's completed scripts you were unaware of (see Figure A.11).

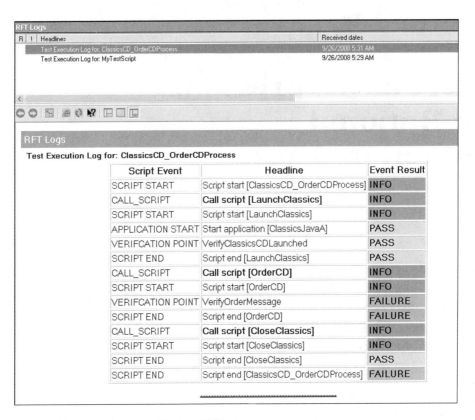

Figure A.11   Rational Functional Tester RSS log

Moving ahead, you might want to change the log format. Perhaps you want to add a link to the baseline and actual verification point files (shown in the XSL code). In any case, the Java code and RSS formats provided in this section give you an idea of how to create your custom log types in Rational Functional Tester.

Summary

You now have the knowledge necessary for extending Functional Tester's out-of-the-box logging and notification capabilities. These topics provide the basis for creating your own logs using either XML or an Eclipse plug-in and having Rational Functional Tester notify people when it is done executing. Not only can you acquire the information you displayed in the format that you want, but you can also get the information when it is ready. You no longer need to wait for an email from a team member. This is especially useful when your team members are dispersed across different time zones.

Regular Expressions in Rational Functional Tester

Jeffrey R. Bocarsly

Regular expression pattern matching provides a powerful way to match and parse strings. This power is brought to bear in Rational Functional Tester in the areas of object recognition (pattern matching recognition property values in the Object Map) or in Verification Points (pattern matching to captured data values). The history between Rational Functional Tester and regular expressions is a bit complicated, because the original (Java-only) version of the tool was released before Java had a standard regular expressions package. Because of this, IBM Rational included its own regular expression class based on the Apache package `org.apache.regexp`. *Through multiple releases of the tool (including two re-brandings), the regular expressions feature remains based on the Apache implementation, as it is with Rational Functional Tester currently* (`com.rational.test.util.regex.Regex`). *For this reason, the Apache-based Rational Functional Tester package is discussed in this appendix, and not the Java package. If you are interested, you can find the underlying Apache regular expression package documentation at http://jakarta.apache.org/regexp.*

When Rational released the VB.NET flavor of Rational Functional Tester, it included regular expression classes that maintain parallel syntax with the Java flavor (`Rational.Test.Util.Regex`), *so the discussion here applies to both the Java and the VB.NET flavors of Rational Functional Tester.*

In addition to using regular expressions for object recognition and in Verification Points, the Rational Functional Tester regular expressions package can be used in your scripts for matching test data (as can the Java and .Net regular expressions packages). Because there is a large amount of information about the Java and VB.NET packages available in print and on the Internet, this appendix covers only the Rational Functional Tester package.

Using Regular Expressions in Rational Functional Tester Scripts

You may have noticed that Rational Functional Tester actually has two classes to deal with regular expressions, `Regex` and `RegularExpression`. The `RegularExpression` class simply wraps a regular-expression pattern, and is used for interactions with Rational Functional Tester methods, such as Verification Point methods and `TestObject`'s `find()` method, which use the second class, `Regex`, to evaluate matches. The `Regex` class is a lightweight regular expression engine that actually performs matches and parses text. Because `Regex` is the actual engine, our discussion here is limited to it.

`Regex` can be used for string processing in a script. To access the Rational Functional Tester regular expression class in a script, you need to create a regular expression object. In Java, this looks like:

```
Regex re = new Regex("pattern");
```

In VB.NET, the analogous code is

```
Dim re As Regex = New Regex("pattern")
```

The pattern argument to the `Regex` constructor is a `String` containing a regular expression that describes a text pattern that you want to match. When you create your regular expression object, you "compile" a regular expression pattern. The pattern string may be any valid regular expression pattern.

The `Regex` class has two main methods that enable you to test for a pattern match and extract out the matched pattern: `matches()` and `getMatch()`. The `matches()` method takes a `String` as its argument, and returns a `boolean` evaluating whether the `String` matches the compiled regular expression pattern. A simple Java example is:

```
Regex re = new Regex("def");
boolean b = re.matches("abcdefg");
```

In this case, `matches()` returns `true` because the superset `String` argument "`abcdef`" matches the subset pattern "`def`". The same example in VB.NET is:

```
Dim re As Regex = New Regex("def")
Dim b As Boolean = re.Matches("abcdef")
```

The method `getMatch()` returns the portion of the argument `String` that matches the pattern. Because `getMatch()` returns a `String` based on a previous match, the `matches()` method must be called before `getMatch()`. A Java example of how this works is:

```
Regex re = new Regex("def");
boolean b = re.matches("abcdefg");
if (b) {
```

```
        String match = re.getMatch();
        System.out.println(match);
    }
```

In this example, the variable `match` is set to the value "def". If `matches()` has not been called before `getMatch()`, a `null` reference is returned (no exception is thrown). A `null` value is also returned if there is no match. The example in VB.NET is:

```
    Dim re As Regex = New Regex("def")
    Dim b As Boolean = re.matches("abcdefg")
    If (b) Then
        Dim match As String = re.getMatch()
        Console.WriteLine(match)
    End If
```

As noted earlier, in the Java flavor of Rational Functional Tester, the power of regular expressions was offered before they were a standard part of the Java libraries. Therefore, Rational Functional Tester uses the `Regex` class, a customized version of the Apache Regular Expression implementation instead of the standard Java regular expressions library. You are still free to use the Java Regular Expressions engine `java.util.regex` (released in Java 1.4) in any Java code you write in your scripts. Likewise, you are free to use `System.Text.RegularExpressions` in VB.NET to parse your string data. The Rational Functional Tester API also contains two other regular expressions wrapper classes, `ApacheRegExp` and `JavaRegExp`, each of which provides an interface similar to that of the `Regex` class.

You can access the full Apache package within Rational Functional Tester (`org.apache.regexp`) simply by importing `com.rational.test.util.regex.internal.*` into your Java scripts; however, this does not appear to be exposed in VB.NET.

Writing Regular Expressions

Regular expression patterns are built from a rich library of *operators* (also called *metacharacters*) that can be used to construct elegant patterns. The key to successfully writing the pattern that you actually want is *following the pattern matching rules precisely*. It is quite a simple matter to write a pattern that gives unexpected results, because it can be a challenge to see the implications of your operator syntax on a match, especially when you use multiple operators. Paying rigorous attention to each operator's rules will help you avoid writing a pattern that results in unintended consequences. Key regular expression rules include:

- Each regular expression operator represents a single rule

- A pattern consists of a single character, unless it is explicitly declared to have multiple characters.

- Operators can be combined by placing one operator to the immediate right of another.

- Operators are processed from left-to-right, subject to normal constraints imposed by parentheses.

- A superset string matches a subset pattern.

NOTE Although the broad outlines of how regular expression operators work are fairly standardized, there are differences between different implementations. If you are familiar with regular expressions from outside the Java context, or simply from a different implementation of regular expressions in Java, there might be some differences here that you will have to adjust to.

As noted previously, Regular Expression patterns are built out of common pieces of text along with operators that specify a text pattern to match. Operators are typically indicated by punctuation characters. The operators considered in this discussion are:

- * (asterisk)—Matches 0 or more of the previous pattern

- + (plus)—Matches 1 or more of the previous pattern

- ( ) (parentheses)—Defines pattern groups

- . (period)—Matches any individual character

- ? (question mark)—Matches 0 or 1 of the previous pattern

- | (pipe)—A logical Or

- [ ] (square brackets)—Defines a "character class"

- { } (curly braces)—Matches a pattern a defined number of times

This appendix looks at each of these operators in the context of specific examples that illustrate how the operators work, and in addition, how they can interact with each other (with apologies to Lewis Carroll).

Non-Operator Characters

Match themselves

As noted in Chapter 9, "Advanced Rational Functional Tester Object Map Topics," many regular expressions don't need any operators to be useful. If you need to match the beginning of a piece of text, but not its end, you can simply use the leading characters in the text for your pattern:

```
re = new Regex("www.alice-in-wonderland.com");
b = re.matches("www.alice-in-wonderland.com/id=342AF0B432ADF");
// returns true
```

The period in the preceding examples is actually an operator but ignore that for now. (See the following for a discussion of the period.)

The Asterisk Operator: *

Matches 0 or more of the previous pattern

In the pattern "`So*p!`", the asterisk (`*`) operator modifies the previous pattern, which is the character 'o'. Any string that has zero or more 'o's that trail an 'S' and lead a 'p' matches:

```
re = new Regex("So*p!");
b = re.matches("Beau--ootiful Soooooop!"); // returns true
b = re.matches("Beau--ootiful Soooooup!"); // returns false
```

Note that the second example does not qualify—it does not have 'zero or more 'o's trailing an 'S' and leading a 'p', because there is a 'u' in the position before the 'p'. As you'll appreciate from the following examples, a literal application of the rules is demanded:

```
re = new Regex("So*p!");
b = re.matches("Sop!");
// true; 'Sop!' is 0 or more 'o's between an 'S' and a 'p'
b = re.matches("Sp!");
// true; 'Sp!' is 0 or more 'o's between an 'S' and a 'p'
b = re.matches("Sip!");
// false; 'Sip!' is not 0 or more 'o's between an 'S' and a 'p'
```

The Plus Operator: +

Matches 1 or more of the previous pattern

The plus (+) operator is identical to the *, except that a minimum of one instance of the pattern is required for a match.

```
re = new Regex("So+p!");
b = re.matches("Sop!"); // true
b = re.matches("Sp!");
// false; 'Sp!' is not 1 or more o's between an 'S' and a 'p'
b = re.matches("Soup!");
// false; 'Soup!' is not 1 or more o's between an 'S' and a 'p'
```

The Parentheses Operator: ( )

Defines pattern groups

Thus far, you have seen how an operator can modify the previous pattern when the previous pattern is a single character (see the previous examples). You can start to create complex patterns by defining groups of characters as a single pattern. Enclosing multiple characters in parentheses causes the regular expression engine to treat them as a group. Any operator following the group applies to the entire group of characters. Note how the parentheses affect the regular expression processing in the following examples:

```
re = new Regex("(Beau--ootiful Soo--oop!)+");
b = re.matches("Beau--ootiful Soo--oop!Beau--ootiful Soo--oop!");
```

```
// true, since there is at least one occurrence of the pattern
b = re.matches("Soup of the evening, beautiful Soup!");
// false, since there is 0 of the pattern
```

The Period Operator: .

Matches any single character (except newline)

The period (.) operator matches one character of any sort, except a newline character (in Windows, a newline is actually indicated by two characters, a carriage-return followed by a line-feed). Zero characters do not match.

```
re = new Regex("Beau..ootiful Soo..oop!");
b = re.matches("Beau--ootiful Soo--oop!"); // true
b = re.matches("Beau.tiful Soo.oop!"); // false
b = re.matches("Beautiful Soo--oop!"); // false
```

As indicated, operators can be combined to operate on each other: for example, following a '.' with a '*' (meaning the pattern '.*') means 'zero or more repetitions of any character', or, in other words: match any number of any characters. If you have used wildcards (such as DOS wild-cards), the pattern '.*' is roughly equivalent to the wildcard '*'.

```
re = new Regex("'.*'");
b = re.matches("'Curiouser and curiouser!' cried Alice"); // true
```

Note that the '.*' operator combination is particularly potent—there is nothing it won't match. Use it with care.

The Question Mark Operator: ?

Matches 0 or 1 of the previous pattern

The question mark (?) operator limits the previous pattern to either 0 or 1 occurrences. In the examples that follow, you can see how the ? works with grouped and ungrouped patterns.

```
re = new Regex("Beau--?ootiful Soo(--)?oop!");
b = re.matches("Beau--ootiful Soo--oop!"); // true
b = re.matches("Beau-ootiful Soo--oop!"); // true
b = re.matches("Beau--ootiful Soo-oop!"); // false
b = re.matches("Beau-ootiful Soo-oop!"); // false
b = re.matches("Beau-ootiful Soooop!"); // true
```

The Pipe Operator: |

A logical Or

Sometimes, it is easiest to match to a set of discrete values rather than try to write a complex pattern that matches words that are logically related, but are not related in their spellings.

Common examples include colors, currencies, or city, state, province, and country names. The pipe (|) operator provides the ability match one of a set of possible values.

```
re = new Regex("Duck|Dodo|Lory|Eaglet");
b = re.matches("'Hand it over here,' said the Dodo.");
// true, since 'Dodo' matches one of the four choices.
b = re.matches("'Only a thimble,' said Alice sadly.");
// false, since the match phrase does not contain 'Duck', 'Dodo',
// 'Lory' or 'Eaglet'.
```

The Square Brackets Operator: [ ]

Defines character classes

A character class defines a set of characters, one of which matches to the specified position in a string. The specified position is the position of the square brackets in the pattern. So, if you place a character class at the beginning of a pattern, this class matches *only* to the first character in the match string. If you place it in the second position, it provides a set of characters that can match at the second position, and so on. In the following snippets, character matches to either 'M' or 'm' in the first position are accepted.

```
re = new Regex("[Mm]ad Hatter");
b = re.matches("Mad Hatter");
// true, since 'M' matches the class 'Mm'
b = re.matches("mad Hatter"); // true again
b = re.matches("Bad Hatter"); // false
b = re.matches("hmad Hatter"); // true, since the '[Mm]ad' is matched
```

Ranges of characters can be denoted in a character class by separating the beginning and ending characters of the range with a dash (-). Ranges include numeric range ([0-9]), and alpha ranges ([a-z], [A-Z]). Multiple ranges can be included in a single class. For example, [a-zA-Z] matches any alpha character regardless of case.

```
re = new Regex("[0-9]+");
b = re.matches("10038");
// true, since 10038 is one or more of the digits 0-9
re = new Regex("[0-1][0-9]-[0-3][0-9]-[0-5][0-5]");
b = re.matches("05-37-55"); // true
b = re.matches("05-37-65");
// false, since the second-to-last digit is restricted to 0-5
```

Character classes can exclude characters at a given position. This is done by placing the hat operator ^ at the beginning of the class. So, if you want to indicate which characters are *not* allowed to match at a position, you can write a pattern like the following pattern, which *excludes* the numbers 2 through 9 for the first position:

```
re = new Regex("[^2-9][0-9]-[0-3][0-9]-[0-5][0-5]");
b = re.matches("05-37-55"); // true
b = re.matches("25-37-65"); // false
```

The Curly Braces Operator: { }

Matches a pattern a defined number of times

The curly braces create complex patterns that follow these rules:

- x{n}—Match x exactly n times
- x{n,}—Match x at least n times
- x{n,m}—Match x at least n times and not more than m times

If you have repeated subpatterns (such as repeated words or symbols) in a pattern, you can use the curly braces to specify either the number of repeats of the subpattern, or the upper and lower limits for the number of repeats.

```
re = new Regex("(twinkle,){2}");
b = re.matches("twinkle,twinkle, little bat"); // true
b = re.matches("twinkle, little bat"); // false
re = new Regex("(twinkle,){1,2}");
b = re.matches("twinkle,twinkle, little bat"); // true
b = re.matches("twinkle, little bat"); // true
re = new Regex("(twinkle,){2,}");
b = re.matches("twinkle,twinkle, little bat"); // true
b = re.matches("twinkle,twinkle,twinkle, little bat"); // true
b = re.matches("twinkle, little bat"); // false
```

Note that the curly braces modify the pattern behavior, not the number of *matched groups*. If you check the value returned by getMatchCount() in the following example, Regex reports a value of 1:

```
re = new Regex("(twinkle,){2}");
b = re.matches("twinkle,twinkle, little bat");
System.out.println(b + "  :  " + re.getMatchCount());
for (int n = 0; n <= reg.getMatchCount(); n++){
    System.out.println("match " + n + ": " + reg.getMatch(n));
}
```

The code above returns the following matches. The zeroth match, which is retrieved by passing a 0 argument to getMatch(), always returns the complete match. Match 1 returns the contents that match the pattern in the first pair of parentheses:

```
true  :  1
match 0: twinkle,twinkle,
match 1: twinkle,
```

Now, if you need a pattern that returns two match groups, you can simply double your pattern instead of using the curly brace operator:

```
re = new Regex("(twinkle,)(twinkle,)");
b = re.matches("twinkle,twinkle, little bat");
```

This pattern with a match count of 2 returns two matches, one to each group, in addition to the zeroth match:

```
match 0: twinkle,twinkle,
match 1: twinkle,
match 2: twinkle,
```

However, you may want to use the curly brace syntax but also access to each match individually. To do this, you can use the underlying Apache implementation (as noted previously) based on the RE class. The following example shows how, with the Apache implementation, the curly braces produce three matches ("twinkle,twinkle,", "twinkle,", and "twinkle,"):

```
try {
    RE re = new RE("(twinkle,){2}");
    boolean b = re.match("twinkle,twinkle, little bat");
    int ct = re.getParenCount();
    System.out.println(b + "  :  " + ct);
    for (int n = 0; n < ct; n++){
        System.out.println("match " + n + ": " + re.getParen(n));
    }
} catch (RESyntaxException res){
    System.out.println(res.getMessage());
}
```

This code produces the output identical to the previous two-group pattern using the curly brace syntax.

Escaping Regular Expression Operators

Operators are escaped with square brackets (what you are actually doing is taking advantage of the fact that character classes treat the regular expression metacharacters as regular characters) or with a backslash. In the following example, the parentheses and the period are escaped:

```
re = new Regex("[(]If you don't know what a Gryphon is,"
    + " look at the picture[.][)]");
b = re.matches("(If you don't know what a Gryphon is,"
    + " look at the picture.)");
// true
b = re.matches("If you don't know what a Gryphon is,"
    + " look at the picture.");
// false, since the leading parenthesis is missing
```

You can escape operators with the backslash; an equivalent pattern to that in the previous example is:

```
\(If you don't know what a Gryphon is, look at the picture\.\)
```

In Java, backslashes in `Strings` must themselves be escaped, so the Java `String` for this pattern is:

```
"\\(If you don't know what a Gryphon is, look at the picture\\.\\)"
```

In the first example in this appendix, a pattern was shown that matches a URL. In that example, we left the periods in the URL unmodified and ignored the fact that the period is an operator. Because the period matches itself just like it matches any other single character, this pattern won't fail to match despite the fact that the period operator is not properly escaped. Properly escaping the pattern provides a more robust pattern that won't accidentally create an unintended match:

```
re = new Regex("www[.]alice-in-wonderland[.]com");
// alternate: re = new Regex("www\.alice-in-wonderland\.com");
b = re.matches("www.alice-in-wonderland.com/id=342AF0B432ADF");
// returns true
```

Mathematical formulas can be treated using this approach:

```
re = new Regex("a+b+c");
b = re.matches("a+b+c"); // false
re = new Regex("a[+]b[+]c");
b = re.matches("a+b+c"); // true
```

A common character that is useful to use in a character class is the dash (-). Normally, the dash is a regular character in a regular expression; however, the dash is an operator in a character class (it indicates a range; see the previous character class discussion). To use a dash in a character class as a normal character, it must be listed *first* in the class list (where it can't define a range). The regular expression engine will understand this and will treat the dash as a normal member of the character class:

```
re = new Regex("predicted temperature: [-1-9][0-9]?");
b = re.matches("predicted temperature: -10"); // true
b = re.matches("predicted temperature: 10"); // true
b = re.matches("predicted temperature: -4"); // true
b = re.matches("predicted temperature: 4"); // true
```

By using the character class `[-1-9]`, either a dash (used as a negative sign) or a number in the range 1–9 is accepted as the first character in the temperature field.

Escaped Characters

Regular expression patterns can use the regular "C-type" escaped characters, such as \r for carriage-return, \n for newline, and \t for the tab character. In addition, you can use the following escaped characters to define a pattern:

- \w—Matches any word character
- \W—Matches any nonword character
- \s—Matches any whitespace character
- \S—Matches any non-whitespace character
- \d—Matches any decimal digit
- \D—Matches any nondigit

These can be used as in the following, where any white space is accepted between the two phrases, including spaces and tabs:

```
re = new Regex("The Duchess!\\s+The Duchess!");
b = re.matches("The Duchess! The Duchess!"); // true
b = re.matches("The Duchess!     The Duchess!"); // true
b = re.matches("The Duchess!\tThe Duchess!"); // true
b = re.matches("The Duchess! \t The Duchess!"); // true
b = re.matches("The Duchess!The Duchess!"); // false - no white space
```

Greedy Versus Reluctant Closure

Regular expression packages have a feature known as closure, which refers to the manner in which the matching algorithm performs its task: Does the regular expressions engine look for the largest possible match, or the smallest possible match? A trivial example of this would be using the pattern j.*zz to match the string jazzjazzjazz. The maximal match would be to the whole string jazzjazzjazz. The minimal match would be only the first jazz sequence. If the algorithm looks for the maximal match, then it is termed *greedy closure*. When it looks for the minimal match, it is called *reluctant closure*.

Greedy or reluctant closure applies to a subset of operators called *closure operators*. These are +, *, ?, and {m,n}; however, reluctancy of {m,n} is not currently supported. The default closure behavior for all these is greedy closure. Reluctant closure is indicated by appending a trailing ? after the closure operator to which it applies. The greedy form of the pattern above, j.*zz, has the reluctant form j.*?zz. You can implement either greedy or reluctant closure as follows:

```
Regex re1 = new Regex("[Ww]ill you.*won't you"); // greedy closure
re1.matches(
"Will you, won't you, will you, won't you, will you join the"; + "dance?");
String greedy = re1.getMatch();
// returns greedy "Will you, won't you, will you, won't you"
Regex re2 = new Regex("[Ww]ill you.*?won't you"); // reluctant closure
re2.matches(
"Will you, won't you, will you, won't you, will you join the dance?");
String reluctant = re2.getMatch();
// returns reluctant "Will you, won't you"
```

Regex Games with the Queen of Hearts

To increase your comfort level with regular expressions, we show some additional examples in this section that illustrate some of the subtle ways the regular expressions engine interprets patterns. This first example sets the baseline by matching a lowercase alpha followed by a space and a name. The expected result 'f Hearts' is matched.

```
Regex re = new Regex("[a-z] Hearts");
re.matches("Queen of Hearts"); // matches 'f Hearts'
```

In the second example, you match an *uppercase* alpha followed by a space and Hearts. No match occurs because the character immediately before the space is lowercase.

```
Regex re = new Regex("[A-Z] Hearts");
re.matches("Queen of Hearts"); // false
```

Things get more interesting when you try to combine an uppercase and lowercase specification with the pipe operator (logical or). All that is matched is the single character 'u.' The reason for this is that the operators are processed left-to-right, so the regular expression engine reads this request as "find a lowercase character OR an uppercase character followed by a space and of Hearts." As the previous example shows, there is no uppercase character followed by a space and of Hearts. Therefore, the request is satisfied only by the first clause, the first lowercase character found, which is a 'u' in the word Queen:

```
Regex re = new Regex("[a-z]|[A-Z] Hearts");
re.matches("Queen of Hearts");
System.out.println(re.getMatch()); // returns 'u'
```

To satisfy yourself that this is the correct interpretation, group the second clause after the pipe in parentheses. When you do this, you get the same return value, 'u', confirming that Regex reads the operators left-to-right.

```
Regex re = new Regex("[a-z]|([A-Z] Hearts)");
re.matches("Queen of Hearts");
System.out.println(re.getMatch()); // returns 'u'
```

You can further verify this by switching the order of the character classes. In the two previous examples, the lowercase class appears first. In the following, the lowercase class is second, and the uppercase class is first. The return value is the expected uppercase 'Q', because 'the first uppercase character' satisfies the request, processing from left to right.

```
Regex re = new Regex("[A-Z]|[a-z] Hearts");
re.matches("Queen of Hearts");
System.out.println(re.getMatch()); // returns 'Q'
```

You can confirm this again by grouping the second clause with parentheses:

```
Regex re = new Regex("[A-Z]|([a-z] Hearts)");
re.matches("Queen of Hearts");
System.out.println(re.getMatch()); // returns 'Q'
```

If you group the `'or'` clause in parentheses, the order of the character classes becomes irrelevant because the request is for the first lowercase *or* uppercase character followed by a space and of Hearts. This is satisfied either way by `'f Heart'`.

```
Regex re1 = new Regex("([a-z]|[A-Z]) Hearts");
re1.matches("Queen of Hearts");
System.out.println(re1.getMatch()); // returns 'f Hearts'
Regex re2 = new Regex("([A-Z]|[a-z]) Hearts");
re2.matches("Queen of Hearts");
System.out.println(re2.getMatch()); // returns 'f Hearts'
```

Putting It All Together

Now, you are in a position to examine some robust examples. Although the typical regular expression that you might need is quite simple, periodically there are cases where a more elaborate pattern can solve a problem elegantly without forcing you to write a great deal of code. We look at a couple of examples here: handling common URLs with regular expressions, parsing HTML with regular expressions, and parsing data from strings with regular expressions.

Handling URLs with Regular Expressions

Let's say you have a web application development project, and instances of the application are deployed on multiple environments (for example, QA, staging, and production environments). You want a single suite of Rational Functional Tester regression scripts to run against all three environments, instead of having to maintain three sets of scripts (one for each environment). Assume that your URLs look like the following:

- http://www1.alice-in-wonderland.com/hatters?mad=true
- http://www2.alice-in-wonderland.com/hatters?mad=false
- http://www3.alice-in-wonderland.com/hatters?mad=true

These URLs have three possible hosts (denoted by www1, www2, and www3), and a parameter is passed in the URL ("mad") with different possible values.

As with the previous URL examples (see the previous examples in this appendix and those in Chapter 9), character classes are useful for pattern matching to URLs. For a first attempt, you can use the approach of the previous example in this appendix and simply match the host portion of the URL:

```
re = new Regex("http://www[1-3]\\.alice-in-wonderland\\.com");
b = re.matches("http://www2.alice-in-wonderland.com/" +
    "hatters?mad=true"); // true
```

If you want to write an even more specific pattern, you can include matches to the parameter and the allowed values that can be passed for the parameter:

```
re = new Regex("http://www[1-3]\\.alice-in-wonderland\\.com/" +
    "hatters?mad=(true|false)");
```

```
b = re.matches("http://www1.alice-in-wonderland.com/" +
    "hatters?mad=true");  //false
```

When you execute this match, the `matches()` method returns false, so something must be wrong. On reviewing the regular expression, note that standard URL syntax uses a question mark to indicate that parameters follow, but the question mark has its own meaning in regular expressions syntax—it matches 0 or 1 of the previous pattern (an 's', in this case). Therefore, the match fails not because the target string lacks 0 or 1 's' characters (it has an 's' in the proper position), but because it has the question mark as an element to be matched, and this is not represented in the pattern. To make this pattern work, the question mark has to be escaped:

```
re = new Regex("http://www[1-3]\\.alice-in-wonderland\\.com/" +
    "hatters[?]mad=(true|false)");
b = re.matches("http://www2.alice-in-wonderland.com/" +
    "hatters?mad=true");  //true
b = re.matches("http://www3.alice-in-wonderland.com/" +
    "hatters?mad=false");  //true
```

This pattern correctly matches not only to the different hosts in your URL, but also to the true/false parameter that is passed in the URL.

Parsing HTML with Regular Expressions

Almost any data found in HTML can be handled in Rational Functional Tester by the usual routes. However, you might have to parse HTML in your Rational Functional Tester code in a couple of situations to complete a test. One of these situations is where the HTML contains hidden tags that hold data that needs to be captured. Because these tags are not rendered, they often cannot be captured by the standard approaches. In this case, you can capture the HTML containing the hidden tags (often with a call to `getProperty()`), and then you can parse the tags and the data they contain with regular expressions. Consider the following HTML:

```
<input id="q" maxlength="100" name="q" type="text" />
<input name="v" type="hidden" value="16" />
<input type="hidden" name="en" value="utf" />
<input name="lang" type="hidden" value="en" />
<input name="Search" value="Search" class="ibm-btn-search"
    id="ibm-search" type="submit" />
```

If you want to pull the hidden tags out, you could write a pattern to match just those tags that contain the attribute `type="hidden"`. You would need to specify other characters that are permitted inside a tag to match the rest of the tag contents. In this case, it is easier to write a pattern to match what is *not* allowed in a tag because far fewer characters are not allowed inside a tag than are allowed. This can be done with a negated character class:

```
(<input[^<>]+type="hidden"[^<>]+/>)
```

With this pattern, the tag's angle brackets are required for a match, along with the tag name
(`<input>`), and the hidden `type` attribute. The pattern allows any characters that are not angle
brackets, which are the main characters not allowed inside a tag. This pattern matches any of the
individual hidden tags in the HTML; in order to pull all the tags out, you need access to the full
curly brace operator, which also means using the RE class, not the Regex class as Regex only
matches the first `<input>` tags as a group, while RE will give access to each tag as a separate
match. In Java, this looks like:

```
try {
        RE re = new RE("(<input[^<>]+type=\"hidden\"[^<>]+/>){3}");
        boolean b = re.match(html);
        int ct = re.getParenCount();
        System.out.println(b + "  :  " + ct);
        for (int n = 0; n < ct; n++){
                System.out.println(n + ") " + re.getParen(n));
        }
} catch (RESyntaxException res){
        System.out.println(res.getMessage());
}
```

Note that you have to modify the pattern slightly by appending the `{3}` to the end of the pattern to
match the three hidden tags in the HTML. The double quotes also need to be escaped with a backslash, as is required by Java. The output from this match is:

```
0) <input name="v" type="hidden" value="16" /><input type="hidden"
   name="en" value="utf" /><input name="lang" type="hidden"
   value="en" />
1) <input name="v" type="hidden" value="16" />
2) <input type="hidden" name="en" value="utf" />
3) <input name="lang" type="hidden" value="en" />
```

If you wanted to attack the problem at an even deeper level, you can modify the pattern so that the
individual tag attributes are themselves grouped as matches. To build an HTML attribute-based
pattern, consider the characteristics of the target HTML. First, all the syntactic entities in each tag
are separated by spaces. Second, each `<input>` tag has the same set of attributes (name, type,
and value) but they are not in a constant order. So, to write a more elaborated pattern, you have to
account for spaces and handle the attribute order.

The space problem is simply solved—you can place a leading or trailing space in the pattern for each attribute (while accounting for the space after the tag name and before the end of the
tag). The attribute order problem is also fairly easily solved—you can use the pipe operator to
match any of the three attributes. The resulting pattern is:

```
(<input ((name="[\\w]+" )|(type="hidden" )|(value="[\\w]+" ))+/>){3}
```

In this pattern, you match the attribute *values* with \w (any word character), and you use a trailing
space in each of your attribute patterns. You nest the attribute patterns in a pair of parentheses, so

that you can apply the + operator to the group. This enables RE to find all three attributes. Finally, the pattern needs a trailing space after the tag name. The output for this looks like:

```
0) <input name="v" type="hidden" value="16" /><input type="hidden"
   name="en" value="utf" /><input name="lang" type="hidden"
   value="en" />
1) <input name="v" type="hidden" value="16" />
2) value="16"
3) name="v"
4) type="hidden"
5) value="16"
6) <input type="hidden" name="en" value="utf" />
7) value="utf"
8) name="en"
9) type="hidden"
10) value="utf"
11) <input name="lang" type="hidden" value="en" />
12) value="en"
13) name="lang"
14) type="hidden"
15) value="en"
```

The full output has 16 lines, counting match 0, which always shows the full match. Note also that the value attribute is repeated in each group; this happens because submatches are defined by parentheses, and the pattern uses nested attribute subpatterns in order to apply the + operator to the group of attribute subpatterns.

Parsing Data with Regular Expressions

Imagine you have a series of strings that are captured from a target application of the form "Employee birthday: mm-dd-yyyy." However, because some of the data is quite old, the dates have been input in varying formats. The formatting rules that the date data must follow and that you must validate are the month and day fields can have either one or two digits, but the years should all be corrected to four digits. In addition, the years must be later than 1950. Sample data looks like:

```
Employee Birthday: 09-09-1991
Employee Birthday: 5-18-1993
Employee Birthday: 05-28-1995
Employee Birthday: 10-16-2000
Employee Birthday: 10-9-1950
Employee Birthday: 2-3-1875
Employee Birthday: 2-3-1975
Employee Birthday: 06-20-63
```

Your task is to validate all the rules and to capture the actual date from each valid string, or the whole string if it is invalid. You can use a regular expression to test compliance with the rules, and then write a bunch of string-handling code to pull out the dates. Or, you can take advantage of the `getMatch()` method and simplify your approach. In Java, this looks like:

```
String[] data = {
    "Employee Birthday: 09-09-1991",
    "Employee Birthday: 5-18-1993",
    "Employee Birthday: 05-28-1995",
    "Employee Birthday: 10-16-2000",
    "Employee Birthday: 10-9-1950",
    "Employee Birthday: 2-3-1875",
    "Employee Birthday: 2-3-1975",
    "Employee Birthday: 06-20-63" };
/* compile the pattern to match dates */
Regex re =
new Regex("[0-1]?[0-9]-[0-3]?[0-9]-[1-2][09][0,5-9][0-9]");
/* capture the date and the status */
for (int n = 0; n < data.length; n++) {
    b = re.matches(data[n]);
    capture = b ? re.getMatch() : data[n];
    System.out.println(b + ": " + capture);
}
```

The output from this example is:

```
true, 09-09-1991
true, 5-18-1993
true, 05-28-1995
true, 10-16-2000
true, 10-9-1950
false, Employee Birthday: 2-3-1875
true, 2-3-1975
false, Employee Birthday: 06-20-63
```

Regular Expression Control Flags

The final aspect to `Regex` that you examine is the class control flags. In Rational Functional Tester, three flags can be passed to the `Regex` constructor:

- `Regex.MATCH_NORMAL`—Case-sensitive match, the default
- `Regex.MATCH_CASEINDEPENDENT`—Case-insensitive match
- `Regex.MATCH_MULTILINE`—Match newlines

The following Java example shows a case-insensitive match to the street type designation (Street, Avenue, Drive, or Place). Note that the pattern is written with capitals, but the flag allows lower-case matches to be made.

```
String salesContact= "We are located at 123 Elm St.";
Regex reFlags = new Regex("[0-9]{3} [A-Z]+ (St|Av|Dr|Pl)[.]",
    Regex.MATCH_CASEINDEPENDENT);
boolean b = reFlags.matches(salesContact);
System.out.println(b + ": " + reFlags.getMatch());
```

Finally, in the VB.NET version, `System.Text.RegularExpressions.RegexOptions` constants are used, not `Regex` constants.

```
Dim salesContact As String = "We are located at 123 Elm St."
Dim reFlags As Regex = New Regex("[0-9]{3} [A-Z]+ (ST|AV|DR|PL)[.]", _
    System.Text.RegularExpressions.RegexOptions.IgnoreCase)
Dim bb As Boolean = reFlags.matches(salesContact)
Console.WriteLine(bb & ": " & reFlags.GetMatch())
```

Further Reading

Friedl, J. *Mastering Regular Expressions*, Third Edition. Sebastopol, CA: O'Reilly Media, Inc., 2006.

For a tutorial on Java's regular expressions package `java.util.regex`, see http://java.sun.com/docs/books/tutorial/essential/regex/.

Index